Rob,
To an AP
colleague and
friend, John Crum

E Pluribus Unum
A History of the United States

Combined, Volumes I & II

JOHN W. CRUM

© 2017 John W. Crum
All rights reserved.

ISBN: 1979180202
ISBN 13: 9781979180207

CONTENTS

INTRODUCTION

I was fortunate to teach for decades at Mount Pleasant High School, Wilmington, Delaware, and, even longer, as an adjunct for the University of Delaware, where I still teach. I have also been deeply involved with the U.S. History AP® program for over forty years. Because I taught at both levels, secondary and university, the survey course became my field of expertise. Several questions constantly confronted me as a teacher and professor. What do historians want their students to take from the survey course? What knowledge, understanding, and questions should they acquire in a history survey course to equipment them for future casual and political discussions? What do historians want students to understand about the discipline of history? Historians use various concepts to guide their research – comparison, change over time, (and continuity), causation, and periodization, all while occasionally placing American History in a global context. The most significant tool historians use is interpretation. After all the reading and research ends (it is never fully completed!), a historian weaves a story according to his or her emphasis, giving meaning to a portion of the past. Ultimately, history is what historians say it is. Thus, different historians can come to different conclusions about the same topic. It happens – a lot. In recognition of the fact that many students will often take only one history course during their academic career, I have not used the latest, but the clearest, and, sometimes, the most thought-provoking interpretations offered by historians.

Most intriguing to historians is a question repeatedly asked by Americans and foreigners. What is an American? An Australian reporter once chastised his own editor for using the phrase, "typical American." "You cannot pick an American out of a crowd, they come in all races and nationalities, until you begin a discussion of liberty, freedom, religion, equality, democracy, and capitalism." Those six words, which we constantly struggle to define and to apply to our everyday life, define Americans. That is the **Unum** of our **E Pluribus Unum**, our American Identity.

When I located the source for a quote or interpretation, I dutifully noted it in the text. Otherwise I fell back on the old phrase, "a historian once wrote." I purposefully kept the text informal, this is a one-on-one discussion, not a scholarly treatise. In order to keep the price down, this textbook contains neither pictures nor maps, both of which are readily available on the Internet. This gives teachers and professors the opportunity to alter their course to reflect new issues stirred up by current events or to respond to class questions. Unless attribution is given, I am responsible for the remaining interpretations, and, of course, the errors.

A Note To U.S. History AP® Teachers

U.S. History Advanced Placement® teachers will find this survey text especially useful in teaching and testing conceptual understanding. Each chapter topic is a potential essay question. By adding primary and secondary documents, students should be well prepared for the U.S. History AP® Exam. If additional resources are desired, the ninth edition of my review book, *Excel in AP® U.S. History*, will soon be published. It emphasizes writing, especially preparation for the DBQ and essay parts of the exam. In addition, a small handbook assisting U.S. History students interested in improving their writing is also being published, *Writing U.S. History Right: A Guide to Confused Words.*

Some Things Will Never Change – Why Should We Study History?

> "Laymen and educators are generally agreed that knowledge of our own history is essential in the making of Americans. The reasons for this belief may be summed up under four main heads. History makes loyal citizens because memories of common experiences and common aspirations are essential ingredients in patriotism. History makes intelligent voters because sound decisions about present problems must be based on knowledge of the past. History makes good neighbors because it teaches tolerance of individual differences and appreciation of varied abilities and interests. History makes stable, well-rounded individuals because it gives them a start toward understanding the pattern of society and toward enjoying the artistic and intellectual productions of the past. It gives long views a perspective, a measure of what is permanent in a nation's life. To a people it is what memory is to the individual; and memory, expressed or unconscious, guides the acts of every sentient being."

Committee on American History in Schools and Colleges, 1944

Another statement is the most important quotation to remember for students of history.

"Nothing capable of being memorized is history."

R. G. Collingwood

PREFACE

As a teacher I owe a great debt of gratitude to several sources. I have worked with thousands of fellow AP® teachers from all over the United States at numerous institutes and at the annual AP® grading. Over the years I have encountered a deep devotion to scholarship and teaching. One AP colleague, Joseph Villano, graciously volunteered to read my manuscript and offer advice and corrections. A second colleague, David Morgan, a retired professor from the University of Montevallo, Alabama, minutely proofread my manuscript. I am deeply indebted to my good friend of almost fifty years for his advice, encouragement, editing, and insight. His extensive knowledge of history saved me from numerous errors. Friendships forged at the AP Reading continue long afterwards. I will forever be indebted to three cherished friends – Bob Hodge, Karen Claborn DeVore, and David Morgan. Their friendship means the world to me. I have been fortunate to teach for decades as an adjunct at the University of Delaware. I am deeply grateful for the advice, support, and congeniality I have experienced in the History Department. It is hard to imagine more stimulating and supportive colleagues. I also owe a deep debt to the thousands of students who have challenged and stimulated me in the classroom. Most of all I want to thank my wife and our two daughters for their encouragement. My debt to them is beyond mere words. They sacrificed much to support my academic pursuits. I have won both recognition and awards as a teacher and professor, but no joy compares to that which has come from being a husband, a father, a father-in-law, and, now, a grandfather. For all these reasons I want to thank the most wonderful people in my life – my wife, Karen, and Laurette, Leslie, Rurik, Alexis, and Holden.

John W. Crum

ACKNOWLEDGEMENTS

Thanks are due to the following for permission to reprint copyrighted material:

Carson, Claybourne. "Two Cheers for Brown v. Board of Education." The Journal of American History, 91, No. 1(2004) 26-31 doi:10.2307/3659610.

Excerpt from *History Lessons* - Copyright © 2004 by Dana Lindaman and Kyle Ward. Reprinted by permission of The New Press. www.thenewpress.com

Excerpts from LINCOLN'S VIRTUES; AN ETHICAL BIOGRAPHY by William Lee Miller, copyright © 2002 by William Lee Miller. Used by permission of Alfred A. Knopf, an imprint of Knopf Doubleday Publishing Group, a division of Penguin Random House LLC. All rights reserved.

Excerpts from THE MONROE DOCTRINE AND AMERICAN EXPANSION, 1843-1849 by Frederick Merk, copyright © 1966 by Frederick Merk. Used by permission of Alfred A. Knopf, an imprint of Knopf Doubleday Publishing Group, a division of Penguin Random House LLC. All rights reserved.

From DR. SPOCK'S BABY AND CHILD CARE 9/e by Benjamin Spock, MD. Updated and Revised by Robert Needlman, MD., Illustrations by Grace Needlman. Copyright © 1945, 1946, (c) 1957, 1968, 1976, 1985, 1992 by Benjamin Spock, MD.: copyright renewed (c) 1973, 1974, 1985, 1996, by Benjamin Spock, MD. Revised and updated material copyright (c) 1998, 2004, 2011 by The Benjamin Spock Trust. Reprinted with permission of Gallery Books, a division of Simon & Schuster, Inc. All rights reserved.

Henry Holt and Company, for a quote from *I Saw Them Die: Diary and Recollections of Shirley Millard*, edited by Adele Comandini. Copyright © 1936. Reprinted by permission of Henry Holt and Company.

Houghton Mifflin Harcourt, for a quote from *Snow Falling on Cedars*, by David Guterson. Copyright © 1994. Reprinted by permission of Houghton Mifflin Harcourt.

New York University Press, for quotes from *American Constitutionalism Heard Round the World, 1776-1989*, by George Athan Billias. Copyright © 2009. Reprinted by permission of New York University Press.

North Point Press, Macmillan, for quotes from *We Talk, You Listen: New Tribes, New Turf*, by Vine Deloria, Jr. Copyright © 1970. Reprinted by permission of Macmillan.

State University of New York Press, Albany, for quotes from *Love Canal: My Story*, by Lois Marie Gibbs. Copyright © 1982. Reprinted by permission of State University of New York Press.

The North American Review, for quotes from "The Klan's Fight for Americanism," March, 1926, pp. 33-63

UNFREE LABOR; AMERICAN SLAVERY AND RUSSIAN SERFDOM by Peter Kolchin, Cambridge, Mass.: The Belknap Press of Harvard University Press, Copyright © 1987 by the President and Fellows of Harvard College.

W. W. Norton & Company, Inc., for a quote from *Our America: A Hispanic History of the United States*, by Felipe Fernández-Armesto. Copyrighted © 2014. Reprinted by permission of W. W. Norton & Company, Inc.

W. W. Norton & Company, Inc., for quotes from *The Social Conquest of Earth*, by Edward O. Wilson. Copyrighted © 2012. Reprinted by permission of W. W. Norton & Company, Inc.

1

THE WORLD FROM 1500 TO THE EARLY 1600S

Relative Balance

Around 1500 a relative balance existed among the major regions of the known world – Europe, Africa, India, and China. Then Europe began to dominate the globe politically, economically, technologically, and culturally. It still does. No matter where a person travels, there is overwhelming evidence of American-European influence. For example, the war against Iraq in the early twenty-first century resulted in Iraq adopting a new constitution, implemented with a coalition government. The country of Iraq was created by Europeans in 1923, out of the European induced breakup of the Ottoman Empire's domination of the Middle East. The terms "Middle East," constitution, and coalition government are all Western political ideas. The Middle East is the Middle East only from the European perspective, the "middle" between Europe and India and the East Asian trade centers. Western influence also shows in the fact that the two most widely recognized phrases in the world today are OK and Coca-Cola. Some competition between regions still exists, as in religion, but American and European values and institutions dominate the world.

Before 1500 buffer zones prevented much interaction between the regions. The major cultural regions existed in relative isolation. The word "Ukraine" can be traced back to Polish and Russian words for "the edge of the world." There were no gaping disparities between regions in terms of their economic and technological development, their political organization, or their cultural institutions. If ranked in terms of power and standard of living, China, India, and Songhai and Kongo in Africa were all higher than any European nation. The largest library in Western Europe in the early Middle

Ages had less than 50 books; by 950 it was up to 600. The library at Alexandria, Egypt, had over 500,000.

Around 1500 all this changed. Europe won. Today we all live in a Europeanized world, and, more specifically, the English language won. Anyone desiring personal economic gain and fortune today must master one or more European languages, preferably English. Over 60% of all the world's new books published now are written in English. Around the globe, airline pilots must use English to land and to take off. In China today, the number of people learning English equals the population of the United States.

An emphasis on science and technology is uniquely European, not invention nor discovery, but the profitable use of science and technology. The emphasis on human rights is also uniquely European and would have brought incredulous blank stares from many people throughout most of history. They would not have understood the concept.

Why was Europe able to win? How did it happen? How did five relatively small nations, and they were all hardly unified in the modern sense – England, France, the Netherlands, Portugal, and Spain – with a total of only 25-30 million people, come to dominate so much of the world?

The reasons for Europe's rise to dominance are complex. Europe's rise in the fifteenth and sixteenth centuries followed the disastrous fourteenth century, one of the low points in European history. Europe suffered through the Black Death, which killed one-third of the population, other plagues, wars, invasions, and economic depressions. Stalemate characterized the internal political situation in all countries, which were hardly countries in the modern sense of the word. Kings often had their power limited by lesser nobles and the Catholic Church. The day of the absolute monarch had not yet arrived.

Towns and Merchants

This division among the nobility permitted the rise of new players, in particular the merchants and the towns, which did not fit well into the feudal system. Feudalism, as it evolved during the Middle Ages, had as its prime characteristic a set of reciprocal obligations. Nobles protected those under them, lesser nobles and knights, in return for service. At the economic and social bottom were serfs, bound to the soil, unable to leave the land. But, some did, fleeing into the growing towns, becoming workers and craftsmen. The towns afforded their inhabitants too much personal freedom and gave the authorities few opportunities to control the population. It is still true that the larger the population in a city, the easier it is to avoid conventional social behavior or the police.

Merchants then and now desire stability above all else, thus the merchants and the towns allied with the king, creating the so-called nation-state. The king provided the peace necessary to make money; the merchants provided the taxes necessary for keeping the peace. Over time the other nobles and the church faded in power and influence. Merchants rose in status. In contrast to Europe's experience, merchants and business-men in Japanese society ranked below even artisans and peasants.

Renaissance and Reformation

At the same time, around 1500, two other factors appeared. The first was the Renaissance, chiefly remembered for its art, but at that time primarily a reorienta-tion of human attention from Heaven to Earth, and, therefore, focusing more on affairs of this life than on the afterlife, weakening the influence of the church. The second was the Reformation, which shattered the religious uniformity of Europe, but without undermining Christianity itself. While the Reformation established the dog-matic positions of various churches, it also laid the basis for challenging all authority. The English king, James I, summed it up with one remark, "No bishop, no king." Once there is criticism of the church's authority, challenges to political authority soon follow.

Much of subsequent European history is simply the story of the rise of each of the lower classes, or, the fall of the elite classes. First the nobles asserted their rights against the king, as happened with the Magna Carta in England in 1215. Then the middle class rose up, as shown by the French Revolution, which eventually brought the rise of democracy. Next came the political assertions of everyone else – the lower class, only males at first, followed, in varying order in different countries – by child labor, women's labor, women's political rights, minority rights, black rights, Indian rights, disabled rights, gay rights, etc., etc., etc. Now everyone is equal, and we have added the equality of personal dignity. Today one hears "I'm as good as you are." The concept of "rights" is embedded in our society's whole value system. Moreover, it has been transferred to every facet of our society and to the rest of the world. Notice how many causes today couch their arguments in the language of rights: the rights of the unborn child, the right to school choice, the right to home school. The next "rights" to come will probably be the lowering of the voting age and animal rights. When will it stop? Probably never.

Some people have not been pleased at the rise of the lower classes. Read *The Revolt of the Masses* by the Spanish philosopher, Ortega y Gassett, written in 1931. He bemoaned the way the lower class imposed their standards in all things cultural. He would under-stand our television shows. Television ratings are based solely on the number of view-ers, in order to determine the charge for advertisers. Mass viewing means more than quality programming, and it shows.

The two movements in the air around 1500, the Renaissance and the Reformation, combined to raise the self-image of the rising middle class. Now all occupations, hon-estly pursued, received God's blessing, at least according to Protestants.

Rise of Science and Technology

By focusing attention on the affairs of this life the Renaissance and Reformation stimulated the kind of thinking that lowered barriers to innovation, which greatly aided the rise of science and technology. Far too much is made of the medieval church's opposition to science, as with Galileo and Copernicus. In Christianity nature is God's creation; therefore, science is the unfolding of God's world, the discovery of God's creation. Science and invention follow God rather than challenge Him. James Crick and Francis Watson did not invent DNA; it was always there. $E=mc^2$ and $a^2+b^2=c^2$ were invented by God, only discovered by humans. Think of two other major religions, Hinduism and Buddhism, which regard this world as something to escape from ultimately. After many lifetimes of struggle to remove one's soul from the distractions of earthly life, escape is the reward. Not so for Christians. Science and technology, applied science, are activities that are not prohibited by God and do not challenge God's authority.

European scientific discoveries greatly aided the rise of Europe. This attitude also encouraged Europeans to take any other culture's scientific discoveries and immediately start searching for a practical use for it. The Chinese invented gunpowder and used it to make firecrackers. When Europeans acquired gunpowder, they used it to kill people! Overlook the morality involved; consider the adoption in its potential to make one region more powerful. Additional advances in military technology gave the Europeans even more advantages.

Sea Navigation

Europe's mastery of sea-borne navigation gave them control of the seas. Portugal's Prince Henry the Navigator, his nickname came from a nineteenth century scholar, led the burst of exploration into the South Atlantic. It tells us a great deal that their nickname for the Atlantic Ocean was "the sea of darkness." The most significant discovery around 1500 was not the existence of the New World, but of the usefulness of the oceans as avenues for trade. (Ninety percent of the world's trade today travels by ships.) The oceans were no longer seen as barriers. Two significant discoveries in regard to ocean travel were the circular nature of the trade winds in both the Northern and the Southern hemispheres and the existence of the Gulf Stream. Now Europeans knew how to more quickly get somewhere and then safely return home. Technological improvements also helped. Europeans developed the swift, stable caravel ship, were introduced to the astrolabe by Arabs, and learned about the compass and sternpost rudder from the Chinese. Since sea commerce was and is much cheaper than land based commerce, Europeans were able to sweep all the competition out of the way, such as competing trade routes across the Sahara from West Africa or land routes across Asia to China.

Oceans became places where military power ensured national wealth, hence the building of huge navies to control and to protect sea trade. The losses on the seas were high. The Dutch lost 50% of their ships involved in the East Indies trade, but still earned a massive profit. The annual rate of return for the Dutch East India Company, established in 1602, was 18% to 35%. Europeans established trading posts or outposts along the coasts of Africa and Asia. They entered into the existing local trade networks. In Africa and Asia Europeans did not yet establish what would later be termed empires or colonies.

Self-confidence, Weltanschauung

Another factor was the incredibly arrogant self-confidence Europeans (and Americans) possessed, and still do. Ask anyone from a former European colony. When Europeans encountered clearly superior societies and cultures, they responded by saying, "We can take these guys." Superior societies should have intimidated the Europeans. They did not. In almost all such encounters in history, inferior peoples have imitated their superior opponents. Europeans did not. Europeans absorbed new ideas without feeling the need to reassess their worldview, what Germans call *Weltanschauung*, a worldview or interpretation held by a particular group. Was the basis of this belief system cultural or religious? Whatever the source, their Weltanschauung gave Europeans a self-confidence that far exceeded reality. It probably came from religion.

Europeans justified taking land from American Indians because of two Bible verses: Psalm 2:8, "Ask of me, and I will make the nations your heritage, and the ends of the earth your possession." This verse was seen as a reference to North America, South America, and Central America. And, Romans 13:2, "Therefore he who resists the authorities resists what God has appointed, and those who resist will incur judgment." This verse clearly gave European Christians the right to kill Indians in the Americas and aborigines in Australia. In a court case in Australia in the 1920s the white defendant claimed innocence because he did not know it was a crime to kill an aborigine. Europeans considered Indian occupied lands to be hactenus inculta, meaning "hitherto uncultivated," and, therefore, free for the taking, or vacuum domicilium, meaning civil states are entitled to the uncultivated lands of those in a "natural" state. An Englishman, Robert Cushman, explained the rationale in a 1622 essay, "Reasons and Considerations touching the lawfulness of removing out of England into parts of America." Referring to the Indians, "Now it seemeth unto me that we ought also to endeavour and use the means to convert them or they come to us; to us they cannot come, our land is full, to them we may go, their land is empty." Overall, the population density of North America before the English arrived was approximately one percent of what it was in England. No wonder it looked empty and unoccupied.

Disunity

Unlike some other regions, Europe was not unified politically, although the nations of Europe enjoyed a cultural homogeneity in terms of how they viewed the functions and goals of their separate religious and governmental systems. Yet, they were hardly "nations" in our sense of the word, and all of them had only recently emerged from the feudalism of the Middle Ages. France was really only created with the victory over England by Charles VII in 1453, ending the Hundred Years War. Modern England begins with the reign of Henry VII, 1485-1509, after the Tudors won the dynastic struggle called the War of the Roses. Later both France and England endured nasty civil wars during the early American colonial period. John I (João I), 1385-1453, established independent Portugal, which was often threatened by its neighbor Spain. The marriage of two cousins, Isabella of Castile and Ferdinand of Aragon, artificially created Spain in 1479. Their marriage did not unite Spain, but their son inherited both Castile and Aragon, thus creating the nation of Spain. Any Spaniard living in 1493 would have said Spain's two most important events the previous year were expelling the Moors and the Jews rather than the discovery of the New World. Now creating the religious and culturally unified nation of Spain was possible.

Europe's rising nation-states competed with one another, causing kings and queens to finance exploration out of a fear that other nations would get ahead of them. No overarching political authority existed to stop exploration, such as declaring sea exploration contrary to God's will or too expensive. In 1405 the first Chinese expedition left China with a fleet of 62 ships carrying 28,000 men under the leadership of Chang Ho (Zheng He in pinyin), who sailed to India and westward into the Red Sea and down the coast of East Africa. It was the first of seven long voyages into the Indian Ocean by Chang Ho in the next eighteen years. The Chinese had nine huge "treasure ships," the largest in the world, over 400 feet long and 160 feet wide, larger than a modern football field, with four decks, capable of carrying enough grain for a year and containing tubs to grow vegetables. By comparison, Columbus's *Santa Maria* was only 85 feet long. The Chinese navy had over 400 armed ships, 2,700 coast guard vessels, and at least 400 long-distance ships for trade. However, in 1433 the emperor ended the sea trade and exploration. Cost was the crucial reason. Funds were needed to fight the Mongols, and, in addition, Confucian scholars increasingly grew suspicious of mercantile activity. Besides, when the authorities considered the potential benefits from trade, the Chinese questioned what other countries had that China needed. Nothing.

Diseases

Luckily, Europeans encountered three "empty" continents – North America, South America, and Australia – that gave Europeans four of the inhabitable six continents. They may not have been empty upon initial discovery, but diseases soon decimated the native populations. Why were Indians so susceptible to European diseases? One theory is that as the first peoples moved from Siberia across the Bering Straits to Alaska before turning south, the cold regions acted as a decontamination chamber. Some germs could not survive the trip.

On the island of Hispaniola in 1492 there were by the lowest estimate 100,000 Indians, by the highest, 8,000,000. In 1514 there were only 32,000; by 1542, 200; by 1555, none. One historian identified ninety-three devastating epidemics between 1520 and 1918 that hit Indian communities in the New World. Genocide, as this phenomenon has been called, is too strong a term to use to describe the impact of European diseases on the native population. It was unintended and incidental to discovery and conquest. Not until the 1880s did medical authorities clearly recognize that germs cause diseases. (As any person can probably guess, Native American historians get annoyed at the term "New World." "New" to whom?)

Mass migration into these three continents – North America, South America, and Australia – won them for Europeans, giving Europeans cultural control of four continents. Economic imperialism, followed by political and military imperialism in the nineteenth and twentieth centuries, completed the Europeanization of the world, creating a single global culture. This process in Asia and Africa was finally completed in the second half of the twentieth century as they converted to European standards in politics and economics. One can understand this process by differentiating between the concepts of westernization and modernization. Westernization is the spread of Western cultural ideas – music, equality for women, etc. Modernization is the adoption of Western technology, business, and administration models. The second is embraced more readily than the first. For example, Islamic terrorists used modern weapons and communications to fight against schools for young girls.

This Europeanization set in motion processes that are still with us. Diseases travel swiftly around the world. The book *And the Band Played On* described how AIDS traveled to the United States initially and spread in the early 1980s. There will be other diseases in the future. One million people a day travel in airplanes. In 1900 one million a day rode trains. We travel more swiftly than ever, we are more interconnected than ever, and we more effectively spread germs than ever before. Some germs have a life cycle of twenty minutes, which means in one year there are over 1.3 million life spans for that germ, which makes generational mutations more likely. The germ "improves," which means it could become stronger or deadlier. For example, modern tuberculosis germs are much stronger and more resistant to our modern drugs.

The Columbian Exchange

The European encounter with the New World is called the Columbian Exchange, the exchange of plants, animals, and diseases that accompanied European exploration.

Who got the better end of the deal, the New World or the Old World? Anthropologists claim that as a general principle both cultures gain when two different cultures initially collide. This exchange, however, was very one-sided. From America to Europe came corn, tomatoes, potatoes, sweet potatoes, peanuts, some beans (soy, butter, kidney, navy, string), pumpkins, squash, pineapples, avocados, tobacco, vanilla beans, peppers, and cacao, which was made into chocolate, nicknamed, appropriately, by the French "the feast of the gods."

Two crops were especially important to Europeans, corn and potatoes. They are two of the eleven crops that currently make up 93% of all the food humans eat – corn, potatoes, rice, wheat, beans, cassava, millet, sorghum, barley, rye, and oats. Approximately 60% of all the crops grown in the world came originally from the Americas. Corn is especially important because it provides a large amount of carbohydrates, sugars, and fats. Potatoes yield more food per acre than any grain, four times that of rye, a major European crop at the time. One and one-half acres of potatoes and a cow could feed an Irish family for one year. (A football field is about 1.3 acres, including the end zones.) Initially many Europeans avoided potatoes out of a fear they caused tuberculosis, fevers, or leprosy. They were not consumed in large quantities until the late 1700s, except by the Irish. Within a few decades after 1492 corn and sweet potatoes were grown in China and corn and peanuts in Africa.

From Europe to the New World came animals for food and work and nuisance – horses, cows, oxen, pigs, chickens, sheep, goats, honeybees, and rats. Escaped pigs quickly turned wild, ruining Indian fields of corn. Their reproduction rate rivals that of rabbits, 12 to 24 piglets each year. Modern farmers contend that a wild pig is the most destructive animal on earth; there is a reason why we use the word "hog" to refer to someone eating more than his or her share. The Europeans brought wheat, rice, olives, citrus fruits, coffee (from Yemen to Europe originally), sugar cane (from Syria to Europe originally), bananas, melons, and dandelions and crabgrass. We could have done without the last two.

Did any major disease come from the New World to the Old? Probably not. For years a scholarly debate has raged over syphilis, supposedly a gift to Europeans from American Indians. Recent scholarship casts doubt on this. Syphilis existed in Africa and Europe before 1492. In the mid-1490s a stronger strain of syphilis appeared in Italy. A similar experience happened with the outbreak of AIDS. Any disease a person gets leaves telltale marks on their bones. Medical researchers have found evidence of AIDS prior to the world outbreak in the 1980s, and of syphilis in European graves from the half century before 1492. Just as AIDS did, syphilis seems to have mutated into a stronger strain in the 1490s. Overall, the European diseases were far superior to any from the New World. Smallpox, measles, chicken pox, and mumps wiped out as much as 90% of the Indian population. In the Columbian Exchange Europe gained and the New World lost.

Consequences of the Columbian Exchange

The loss of the Indian population created a labor void filled by Africans through slavery. Unfortunately for Africans, they shared a germ pool with Europeans, a dubious honor, thanks to trade routes across the Sahara. Up to 1820 forced African migrants outnumbered Europeans 5-1, constituting 83% of all people who came to the New World. The average survival rate for slaves on Brazilian plantations was seven years, thus the labor force had to be constantly replenished. The subsequent mixing of races and peoples was unlike anything the world had ever seen before, and, it is still going on. This was a dramatic change in World History. Everywhere today nations around the world are struggling with the impact of diversity within their populations; nations in the Americas are far ahead of them. The United States is not an ethnic and racial paradise of equality, but compared to many other societies around the world, we are incredibly tolerant.

The second half of the twentieth century finished the Europeanization of the world. The modern technological revolution, the communications revolution, and the globalization of the world's economy homogenized the world. Change now comes so quickly that it unnerves some. One consequence has been an emphasis on fundamentalism in all religions. Throughout all history the two biggest forces causing change have been technology and changes in a society's population profile. Fundamentalists, be they Islamic terrorists or Christian defenders of the Ten Commandments in Alabama, can counter-attack against modernization, but they cannot stop either technology or population changes. Nothing can stop either technology or changes in a nation's population profile.

The rise of Europe after 1500 followed the decline and retrenchment of China, which centuries earlier looked like the likely candidate for world domination. The center of world power economically and then politically shifted to Western Europe and two extensions of Europe, the United States and Japan. Europeans and their descendants still rule the world. Over half of the world's economy is controlled from the straight line between Washington, D.C., and New York City. Some feel world power is now beginning to shift back to East Asia, that China will be the great superpower of the twenty-first century. China may be, but it is European values, economic systems, and political systems that now characterize the societies of East Asia. Europeans won, even if they no longer dominate in the future.

2

THE ATLANTIC WORLD

The Concept

The concept of **The Atlantic World** refers to how the conditions, experiences, and events in all the places bordering the Atlantic Ocean shaped, and were shaped by, the conditions, experiences, and events in other places and parts of the Atlantic Ocean. It sees the Atlantic Ocean as a bridge rather than a barrier. It is the continuous interaction between the European countries on the Atlantic, the west coast of Africa, and the entire continents of North and South America. It is literally a "history without borders," meaning that colonial or national boundaries are meaningless. There are three different ways to look at the Atlantic World. One is comparative, comparing regions washed by the waters of the Atlantic Ocean. A second is to focus on a single area or country within the region and its relationship with the rest of the Atlantic World. The third is to try to see the big picture by looking at the entire Atlantic World and the international forces influencing it.

People presently living in the Western Hemisphere think Europeans must have been thrilled with the discovery of the New World and that it occupied much of their attention. Not true. The Turkish military threat to Vienna at that time was really a threat to all Europe. There were twice as many books written in France in the 1500s about the Turkish threat as there were about discoveries in the Americas. The complete works of the religious reformer, Martin Luther, number over fifty volumes. He lived from 1483 to 1546, during the initial discovery and exploration of the New World. Not once in any writing does he make a reference to the Americas.

Expansion of Europe

Europe's mastery of sea-borne navigation gave Europeans control of the seas. The most significant discovery for ocean travel was the circular nature of the trade winds in both the Northern and the Southern hemispheres and of the existence of the Gulf Stream. Since sea commerce was, and still is, much cheaper than land-based commerce, Europeans were able to sweep all the competition out of the way, such as competing land trade routes across the Sahara from West Africa or across Asia to China. Oceans became places where military power ensured national wealth, hence the building of huge navies to control and to protect sea trade, and laws like the English Navigation Acts to control trade with their colonies.

The losses on the seas were high. The ships were small. John Cabot's ship that explored Newfoundland in 1497 for the British had a crew of only eighteen. The Dutch lost 50% of their ships in the East Indies trade, but still earned a massive profit from the spice trade. Before the Europeans found a direct sea route to the "Spice Islands," the present-day Moluccas in Indonesia, the price Europeans paid for nutmeg and mace was sixty thousand times the original price. The annual rate of return for the Dutch East India Company, established in 1602, was 18% to 35%. The first Portuguese captain to reach India, Vasco da Gama in 1498, earned a 700% profit for the king and his investors. Not surprisingly, he took twenty ships on his next trip. The Europeans established trading posts or outposts along the coasts of Africa and Asia. They entered into the existing local trade networks. They did not yet establish in Asia or Africa what would later be termed empires or colonies.

Initial Contact, Africa

Africans identified with their extended family, their village, and their common descendant groups. Most Africans held a worldview that a single supreme being had created heaven and earth, with many lesser deities or helpers aiding or impeding daily activities. Few kingdoms or empires existed across Africa in 1500, but some had previously. Fortunately for Europeans, these powerful kingdoms had declined. No European nation could have matched the armies of Songhai or Mali, or the wealth of Benin, or the political organization of the Kongo.

Models of European Settlement

Historians identify five different models as characteristic of European contact in Africa and settlement in the New World – Urban Center, Missionary Village, Trading Post, Plantation, and Family-centered Unit.

The Spanish experience combined three models, Urban Center, including mining towns in Peru and Mexico; Missionary Village, as shown by St. Augustine in Florida and the Pueblos region of Northern Mexico; and the Plantation model on the islands of the Caribbean. By 1650, 38 Spanish missions, radiating out from St. Augustine, Florida, served 25,000 Indians throughout our Southeast. Similar activity took place in California, where about 88,000 Indians were baptized. The religious nature of the Spanish Missionary

Villages in California and New Mexico made them vulnerable. Indians were not tied into a Spanish-Indian economy that mutually benefited both. Instead, Indians were converts under the leadership of virtually unarmed priests. The Pueblo Indians had little to gain from the Spanish, except a new God with strange practices. Popé's Rebellion, 1680-1682, called the most successful Indian rebellion in American history, was one result. It took almost sixty years, until 1740, for Spain to reestablish its authority in Northern Mexico. In Mexico and Peru, Spain took over existing Indian political, economic, and social networks, replacing the ruling class, but also integrating themselves into the previous hierarchy through intermarriage. Economically they established encomiendas, huge farms or ranches that were essentially a form of legalized slavery over the Indians. Religion became a secondary consideration where New World slavery was concerned. Pope Paul III tried to prohibit Indian slavery in a Papal Bull issued in 1537, *Sublimis Dei*, but it was annulled a year later, apparently after Spanish authorities objected. The king of Spain added his concern in the *Requerimiento* in 1513 (means the Requirement). Each conquistador had to read it to every group of Indians he encountered. It informed them that if they did not accept Christianity, war and enslavement would follow. It was to be read in Spanish. Spain governed her New World colonies tightly by establishing four viceroyalties, each with a capital – New Spain, capital at Mexico City; Peru, Lima; New Granada, Bogotá; and La Plata, Buenos Aires. Spain sent *intendants* to keep an eye on what was happening in the colonies. The *intendants* were officials with broad authority who were responsible to the king, not the *viceroys*, the Spanish rulers of each of the four viceroyalties.

Portugal used two models, the Trading Post model in Africa, and the Plantation model in northeastern Brazil for growing sugar cane. The Portuguese showed everyone the profitable benefits of growing sugar cane on the island of Madeira, off the northwest coast of Africa. By the 1470s they were exporting 200 tons per year from Madeira. All classes of Europeans acquired a taste for sugar. David S. Landes, *The Wealth and Poverty of Nations*, p. 93, differentiates between the Portuguese and Spanish empires. "As for objectives, the Spanish aimed at treasure; the Portuguese, at profits from trade. Two views of empire."

The French used the Trading Post model, with their fur trade that flowed out through the St. Lawrence River. By 1643 the population of French Canada was only 400, with very little agriculture. The colony never attracted many settlers. This small colonial population forced the French to interact with Indians in many ways; the English much less so. The English demanded Indians abandon all their religious beliefs and adopt their version of God. In contrast, the French Christian God proved less threatening to Indian customs. Jesuit priests modified Christianity to accommodate Indian beliefs. But, all was not perfectly peaceful. For example, the Huron Indians were deeply insulted when French Jesuits insisted that the Christian French dead not be buried beside pagan Indians.

The Dutch used the Trading Post model, with the fur trade nucleus at Fort Orange, present day Albany, linked by the Hudson River to New Amsterdam, New York City. The Dutch West India Company returned an annual profit of 18% to 35% for most of the seventeenth century, although the Dutch East India Company was much larger, therefore more profitable, and more important. Competition for Indian trade often aligned Indians with one European colony, such as the Pequots aligning with the Dutch against the English settlers.

The English used Plantations, centered on an agricultural export that relied on un-free labor, first indentured servants, then slaves, both Indian and African. The English used this model in the Caribbean for sugar cane, in the Chesapeake for tobacco, and in the Carolinas for rice. John Rolfe introduced tobacco to Virginia, providing the crop that saved the colony. Europeans acquired a taste for tobacco, in spite of the opposition of James I to the "noxious weed." In New England, and increasingly throughout the colonial era, the North American English colonies used the Family-centered Unit model to produce both subsistence and commercial agricultural crops. The Missionary Village model was not used by the English, except in New England, and there only on a very small scale. Dartmouth College grew out of an early school for Indians, which was established by Rev. Eleazar Wheelock in the early eighteenth century.

Interaction in the Atlantic World – Languages

In Europe the elite could communicate with one another in Latin, often the governmental language down to the village level. The diversity of languages did not hamper communication.

Anthropologists divide Indians in the New World into twelve linguistic stocks with about 2,000 different languages, differing as much as English and Russian do now. The diversity of Indian languages mystified Europeans; it was greater than that found in any other region in the world. Europeans looked at Indians without perceiving differences between them. If they were all the same, how did they come to speak so many different languages?

Population Migration and Its Consequences for Indians

In North America the arrival of diseases and fighting over control of the fur trade led to constant warfare between groups of Indians. The remnants of some tribes joined other tribes to survive. They also constantly moved to seek security. It is a mistake to assume tribes remained in one area during the entire colonial period. The Quaker policy of not fighting Indians led many to resettle into western Pennsylvania. The success of the Iroquois in resisting encroachment into their area in western New York also attracted newcomers. In the 1720s the Tuscarora migrated from the western Carolinas to New York to join the Iroquois Confederation.

The Columbian Exchange – Biological Consequences

Within the first one hundred years of European arrival, 90% of the native Indian popu-lation perished from European diseases such as smallpox, mumps, measles, whooping cough, and typhus. Historians have identified 14 epidemics that swept Mexico between 1520 and 1600, and 17 that hit Peru. The greatest killer was smallpox. Diseases traveled ahead of Europeans. As Indian runners arrived to spread the news, they unwittingly car-ried diseases in their early, infectious stage. By the time European soldiers or settlers ar-rived, many areas were cleared of Indians. New England Pilgrims and Puritans thought God had guided them to open agricultural areas previously occupied by Indians. Not so. Europeans fishing off the coast and landing to trade for food supplies decimated the Indian population before the first settlers arrived. For another example, in what became the Southeast, from the Carolinas and Georgia to the Mississippi River, three epidemics hit twenty years apart – 1698, 1718, and 1738. They devastated three generations, killing as much as 60%, weakening the Yamasee, Westo, Cherokee, Choctaw, Creek, Catawba, and Tuscarora. One must wonder what might have been the outcome of the Yamasee War, 1715-1717, if disease had not been a significant English ally.

Cultural Misunderstandings

For Europeans land was the most valuable form of property. Land ownership was not part of African law or custom; land was communally owned and parceled out based on need, and need was based upon the number of laborers one owned. Slaves were more valued than land because slaves were the only revenue-producing property. For Africans, owning other individuals, rather than land, was the mark of prestige, wealth, and power. They traded for European goods, particularly apparel and items to adorn themselves, such as cloth, beads, and glass, estimated to have been half of all Africa's imports during the slave exporting years. Metals and items made from metal were another portion, one-third, including guns, copper, iron, brass, and metal pots; next came liquor, particularly rum. African society was less stationary, hence the desire for portable items.

The word "property" did not exist in Indian languages. Be careful with words. They must be defined only within a legal and cultural sense. Other words missing from Indian languages were government, pollution, boundary, taxes, majority, writ-ten agreement, mine, and my. Particular territories were "owned" by a tribe only in terms of the right to use them for hunting, fishing, fuel, growing crops, and trap-ping, all functions of consumption. They were not possessions, neither personally nor for the village. It was just tradition. Often these territories, or hunting grounds, were not close. However, warfare pushed some groups of Indians into finding newer areas. Colonists mistakenly assigned areas to Indian tribes, assuming both the existence of a concept of "property" and a permanency in their semi-sedentary lives, neither of which existed. There was frequent warfare and shifting boundaries between Indian groups.

The idea of private possession was completely foreign to Indians. Nature was something to be used; they were part of it, indeed, their survival depended upon it. Nature and all things in it, both living and not, were part of the reciprocity of life. Respect it. Europeans saw nature as something to be conquered and dominated by their superiority. One's property became one's sole possession. When Indians signed treaties with Europeans, they thought they were granting the shared use of their hunting grounds or territory. Exclusive use was beyond their comprehension.

Here is a later Ohio Indian's response to a white farmer complaining about the Indian's horses eating grass overnight in the farmer's field. Note the assumptions behind the Indian's reply.

> "It seems you lay claim to the grass my horses have eaten because you enclosed it with a fence: now tell me, who caused the grass to grow? Can *you* make the grass grow? The grass that grows out of the earth is common to all; the game in the woods is common to all. You eat venison and bear meat. Did you ever hear an Indian complain about that? Be not disturbed at my horses having eaten only once of what you call *your* grass, though the grass my horses did eat, in the like manner as the meat you eat, was given to the Indians by the Great Spirit. Besides, if you will consider, you will find that my horses did not eat all your grass."

Europeans brought, or thought they brought, religion as the greatest gift to the New World savages, the message of Christianity. Indians were not impressed. Most converts "found" Christianity only after a war or an epidemic ravaged their tribe, leaving them desperate and hungry, ready to move into a Praying Town. Perceptive Indians soon realized "conversion" to Christianity brought them advantages in the fur trade and protection by whites against other Indians. "Sure we accept your God, what was his name again? But first let's get down to trading before worshiping." Normally the Christian message was ignored. Look at these three examples:

> "The Wise Ones said we might have their religion, but when we tried to understand it we found that there were too many kinds of religion among white men for us to understand, and that scarcely any two white men agreed which was the right one to learn. This bothered us a great deal until we saw that the white man did not take his religion any more seriously than he did his laws, and that he kept both of them just

behind him, like Helpers, to use when they might do him good in his dealings with strangers. These were not our ways. We kept the laws we made and lived our religion. We have never been able to understand the white man, who fools nobody but himself."

Plenty-Coups, Crow

"You say that you are sent to instruct us how to worship the Great Spirit agreeably to his mind; and if we do not take hold of the religion which you white people teach, we shall be unhappy hereafter. You say that you are right and we are lost. How do we know this to be true? We understand that your religion is written in a book. If it was intended for us as well as for you, why has not the Great Spirit given it to us; and not only to us, but why did he not give to our forefathers the knowledge of that book, with the means of understanding it rightly? We only know what you tell us about it. How shall we know when to believe, being so often deceived by the white people? Brother! You say there is but one way to worship and serve the Great Spirit. If there is but one religion, why do you white people differ so much about it? Why do not all agree, as you can all read the book? Brother! We do not understand these things. We are told that your religion was given to your forefathers, and has been handed down from father to son. We also have a religion which was given to our forefathers, and has been handed down to us their children. We worship that way. It teacheth us to be thankful for all the favors we receive, to love each other, and to be united. We never quarrel about religion."

Red Jacket, Iroquois

"Once there was an Indian who became a Christian. He became a very good Christian; . . . . Then he died. First he went to the Indian hereafter, but they wouldn't take him because he was a Christian. Then he went to Heaven, but they wouldn't let him in—because he was an Indian. Then he went to Hell, but they wouldn't admit him there either, because he was so good. So he came alive again, and he went to the Buffalo Dance and the other dances and taught his children to do the same thing."

Mersquakie Indian folk tale

The best example of cultural misunderstanding between Indians and Europeans was a 1740 humorous letter from the Iroquois Six Nations to the Virginia colonial legislature. (After the Five Nations added the Tuscarora, some referred to them as the Six Nations, although they continued to call themselves the Five Nations.) The Virginians had invited the Six Nations to send twelve young Indian men to attend William and Mary College to be "properly" educated. The Indians' reply:

> "our Ideas of this kind of Education happen not to be the same as yours. We have some Experience of it. Several of our Young People were formerly brought up at the Colleges of the Northern Provinces; they were instructed in all your Sciences; but, when they came back to us, they were bad Runners, ignorant of every means of living in the Woods, unable to bear either Cold or Hunger, knew neither how to build a Cabin, take a Deer, or kill an Enemy, spoke our language imperfectly, were therefore neither fit for Hunters, Warriors, nor Counsellors; they were totally good for nothing. We are, however, not the less oblig'd by your kind Offer, tho' we decline accepting it; and, to show our grateful Sense of it, if the Gentlemen of Virginia will send us a Dozen of their Sons, we will take care of their Education; instruct them in all we know, and make Men of them."

Europeans thought in terms of the individual. Society was a group of economically competing individuals held together by legal restrictions, loyalty to their government, and shared religious beliefs – sometimes, for all three. Indians rejected individualism, thinking of the group not the individual. Two examples illustrate this attitude. Among the Indians in the Pacific Northwest, the "potlatch" tradition called for the communal redistribution of wealth. A Bill Gates did not live in those tribes. The strangest, to Americans, were the Osage. They divided their villages or towns into two equal groups, an east and a west. They slept facing towards the other side and put their shoes on mimicking the other. The eastern group faced westward to sleep and put their left shoe on first when awakening. The western group faced eastward and put their right shoe on first when awakening. That is real group consciousness. The closest we come to that today is the school uniform or wearing the school colors the day before the big football game with the school's rival. However, it is estimated that forty percent of today's high school students never take part in any extracurricular activities, even as just spectators. The group never comes close to being as important as the individual in American society. Indians did not understand that thinking. Be leery of glib statements about Indians. As one historian wrote, they were "hosts, guides, converts, laborers, subjects, adversaries, and diplomats."

Gold, Silver, and the Price Revolution

The first explorers arrived in the New World with one thought in mind – becoming rich. They were soon rewarded. The Incas called gold the "sweat of the sun" and silver the "tears of the moon." Spanish greed soon redefined "tears." In just a few months in Peru, Pizarro, with only 168 men, acquired 13,420 pounds of gold and 26,000 pounds of silver. The big find came in 1545 when an Indian discovered the huge seams of silver at Potosí, the Cerro Rico, the "rich hill." By 1783 it had yielded 45,000 tons of silver, dug out under grueling working conditions by forced Indian laborers. Two silver mines in Mexico added immensely to the total, Zacatecas and Guanajuato. Add in the other gold and silver from Mexico and the total is staggering. It was staggering to the European economy also. The influx of gold and silver set off a Price Revolution. For the previous three hundred years European prices had been stable. Now there was, to put it simply, too much money. Try to picture the situation when two individuals are trying to purchase the last loaf of bread at a store, and, they each have buckets of money. The bidding would be lively. That is what happened to prices in Europe because of the influx of so much gold and silver. Between 1500 and 1800 New World mines poured 70% of the world's gold and 85% of the world's silver into Europe. From the 1540s to the 1640s the cost of living rose by a factor of seven. People on relatively fixed incomes, such as nobles who mainly derived their income from land and crops, suffered from the inflation, declining economically, socially, and politically. The Chinese demanded silver in payment for the goods they sold to Europeans. Thus, much of the New World's wealth eventually ended up in China.

Transatlantic Trade Patterns: Commodities and Consumption

For 150 years after Columbus, the main attractions of the New World were trade and plunder; more Europeans were involved in trade and fishing than in settling. In 1578 an Englishman counted 350 ships fishing for cod in the Grand Banks off Newfoundland – 150 French, 100 Spanish, 50 English, and 50 Portuguese. By 1600 it was up to 500 per year. The Dutch dominated European trade until the late seventeenth century. At one time they had more ships engaged in trade than all the other European countries combined.

The arrival of the Dutch in New York and the Delaware River Valley led to a demand for fur, especially beaver furs. Why? Europeans had no great supply of the kind of soft leather that came from American animal skins. Demand was high. This became part of the long "Beaver Wars," which lasted for about a century, incredibly disrupting Indian life, for the various tribes were already frequently at war with one another. The Beaver Wars led to constant wars. Add in diseases, and the impact of liquor, which Indians loved, and could not handle because they used it in almost a ceremonial or religious sense to purposefully become intoxicated, and one can see why Indian society fell apart. Raids, wars, and diseases decimated populations, leading to remnants joining to survive, complicating tribal genealogical charts. The tribal names used now for modern Indian groups bear little relationship to their actual historical experiences.

The European trade goods enriched Indian life, raising them out of the Stone Age, but it also made them dependent upon whites for new goods. For example, if Indians acquired guns, they needed to trade for bullets and gunpowder. What did they want or find useful? Items like woven cloth, glass beads, mirrors, combs, iron and copper kettles, pots, metal hoes, clay smoking pipes, hatchets, fishhooks, metal traps, guns, and knives. Women prized items for sewing: scissors, needles, and thimbles. The interaction was lopsided. In many respects Indians absorbed more of European culture than Europeans absorbed of Indian culture.

By 1650 Europeans wanted the New World's coffee, tea, chocolate, sugar, and tobacco. And, they were willing to pay. If only there was a labor supply.

Labor Need, the Slave Trade and Its Impact

Commercial plantation agriculture needed labor. Indians succumbed to European diseases so Europeans looked elsewhere and found a ready market. Africans already practiced slavery and willingly sold slaves to Europeans along the African coastal trading posts, because Europeans were unable to penetrate beyond the coast due to malaria. Quinine finally solved that problem in the nineteenth century. The ratio of Africans to Europeans migrating to the New World was 5-1. Up to 1820 five Africans came for every one European. Such was the depth of the need for labor. The ratio in the Caribbean was 289,900 Europeans to 2,045,550 Africans. However, the ratio was reversed for North America, approximately three Europeans came to North America for every African, 752,200 to 287,600. (Allison Games, "The Atlantic Ocean," *Europe 1450-1789: Encyclopedia of the Early Modern World*, Dewald, ed.) Only about five percent of all slaves imported into the New World came to the colonies of British North America.

England gained a valuable trading privilege in the 1713 Treaty of Utrecht that ended the War of Spanish Succession, called Queen Anne's War by the American colonists. England was granted the *asiento*, the exclusive right to sell African slaves in the Spanish ports of Buenos Aires, Veracruz, Cartagena, and Havana. Throughout the eighteenth century English ships transported an average of twenty thousand slaves per year. Many Englishmen invested in the slave trade, including the Duke of York and John Locke. Profits were high, slaves sold in America for twenty to thirty times their cost along the African coast.

Black slavery troubled the French. Louis XIV promulgated the *Code Noir* in 1685 to establish some rights and protections for slaves, but it was rarely followed in the French Caribbean Islands. Indian slavery in the Spanish colonies troubled some Spaniards. One critic, Father Bartolomé de Las Casas, who was given the title "Protector of the Indians," published his views in *A Short Account of the Devastation of the Indies*, in 1552. It was subsequently reprinted in other countries, fueling "The Black Legend," the idea that Spanish colonization was filled with atrocities, unlike the enlightened (?) policies of the more advanced Protestant anti-Catholic countries, the Dutch and the English. William I, the Prince of Orange, who led a rebellion in 1580 against the Spanish (and was therefore unbiased) declared Spain had "committed such horrible excesses that all the barbarities, cruelties and tyrannies ever perpetuated before are only games in comparison to what happened to the poor Indians."

Centuries before Thomas Jefferson's Declaration of Independence and the ideas of the Enlightenment, Las Casas declared in 1519 that "our Christian religion is suitable for and may be adapted to all nations of the world, and all alike may receive it; and no one may be deprived of his liberty, nor may he be enslaved on the excuse that he is a natural slave." Las Casas had owned slaves and a plantation on Hispaniola until 1514. He advocated African slavery as a substitute for Indian slavery, a position he later recanted.

Las Casas was not alone among the Spanish. In 1550 the advisory body to the king, the royal Council of the Indies, urged him to "consider the manner in which these conquests should be carried on . . . justly and with security of conscience." Charles I, the Spanish king, suspended New World conquest for sixteen years to discuss its morality. In the words of the preeminent historian of Latin America, Lewis Hanke, "Probably never before had such a mighty sovereign ordered his conquests to cease until it should be decided if they were just." The English certainly never did. Spain's "New Laws" of 1573 limited the use of force, prohibited slavery, and the taking of Indian homes. Obviously, these laws were poorly enforced in the Americas; those living here concluding that Old World good intentions misunderstood New World realities. Over time, by the end of the eighteenth century, the Spanish did become less restrictive, even granting slaves the right to sue for their freedom for cruel and unusual punishment.

Long before encountering the New World, Spain had enacted a series of laws concerning slaves, *Las Siete Partidas*, which granted slaves certain rights. Unlike the Spanish or the Portuguese, the English had no experience with slave laws nor Africans nor African slaves prior to the era of colonization. They therefore had no body of laws to govern chattel slavery. The Spanish and Portuguese law codes evolved out of Roman law, which permitted slavery, but placed some obligations upon the owner and provided the slave with some legal rights. Catholicism, aided by the high number and percentage of priests in the Spanish and Portuguese colonies, also softened slavery. Catholic priests saw slaves as potential converts. In contrast, early in the British colonial experience, Protestant ministers rarely looked at Indians or Africans as possible converts. Not until the First and Second Great Awakenings (1740s and after) did some Protestant ministers even begin to view slaves in this light.

The British colonists inherited their legal tradition from Anglo-Saxon law, which was silent on slavery, affording the colonists the freedom to develop their own rules and policies. Two plays by Shakespeare around the years 1600 to1625, *Othello* and *The Tempest*, illustrate the confusion the English had concerning race and stereotypes about Africans. England's lack of experience with slavery would, in 1772, lead to the *Somerset* decision, in which a judge freed all the slaves in England, who had been taken there by their American or Caribbean masters. Judge Lord Mansfield, The Lord Chief Justice of England, pronounced the air of England as "too free to be breathed by a slave."

Competition – The Borderlands

"Borderlands," sometimes referred to as the "middle ground," is a recently reemphasized concept in the study of American history. It refers to those places where colonial empires met one another, regions contested, not only between European powers, but also between their Indian allies. They were areas of constant intrigue, cultural clashes, trade wars, and diplomatic maneuvering, which drew Indians into an increasing dependency upon their European suppliers. In the colonial western South, the present states of Mississippi and Alabama, the French from their base in New Orleans in Louisiana wrestled with the English operating from Charleston and Virginia. Both powers used regional or local proxy wars involving one set of Indians against another, in this case the Choctaws versus the Chickasaws. The British offered high prices for Indian slaves to be exported to the West Indies, thus introducing a new disruptive element into the area. The French offered bounties for scalps of the Indian allies of the British. Both policies devastated the Indian population in the lower South.

Picture the other areas where European powers butted up against another's claim in North America. French and British claims overlapped in northern New England and Nova Scotia, northern and western New York, Pennsylvania, Virginia and the Ohio River Valley, and Virginia and North Carolina and modern Kentucky and Tennessee. Spain and England shared a border along northern Florida. In addition, of course, there were clashes in the Caribbean.

Competition – Wars

The European powers fought a series of wars throughout the colonial period. Initially they were European–centered wars, with the causes, prizes, and consequences located in Europe. However, increasingly colonial competition and colonial matters pushed to the forefront. Overall, these wars lasted over one hundred years. First were the Anglo-Dutch wars of 1652-1654, 1665-1667, and 1672-1674.

The War of the League of Augsburg, King William's War in the colonies, 1689-1697, was characterized by French and Iroquois raids along the Canadian frontier.

The War of Spanish Succession was called Queen Anne's War in the colonies, 1702-1713. This war was similar to King William's War in New England, with Indian raids, most notably Deerfield, Massachusetts. England acquired Newfoundland, Acadia, which is modern New Brunswick, areas around the Hudson Bay, and the valuable *asiento*, the exclusive right to sell African slaves in the Spanish ports of Buenos Aires, Veracruz, Cartagena, and Havana. The treaty ending the war, the Treaty of Utrecht, allowed the thrones of France and Spain to remain in the same royal family, known now as the Family Compact. Spain and France would be on the same side up to the Napoleonic Wars. England was always the enemy.

The War of Jenkins' Ear, 1739-1742, between Spain and England, was fought mostly in Florida and the Caribbean. It merged with the next war. The War of Austrian Succession, King George's War in the colonies, 1740-1748, did not involve much activity in the New World. New England colonists did aid in capturing Louisbourg at the mouth of the St. Lawrence River and New England suffered Indian raids along the northern border.

The Seven Years' War was also called The Great War, and in the colonies the French and Indian War, 1754-1763, where it began two years before fighting broke out in Europe. The French and Indian War proved to be a turning point in the relationship between the colonies and Great Britain. Significant factors in the war were George Washington, Fort Necessity, Fort Pitt, the Albany Conference, Benjamin Franklin's Plan of Union, William Pitt, the Plains of Abraham, Montcalm and Wolfe, the Treaty of Fontainebleau and Louisiana, the Treaty of Paris, 1763, and the huge British debt from the war.

The American Revolutionary War, or the War for Independence, also had a significant European component. The French, Spanish, and Dutch all declared war on Great Britain. That is the primary reason why the British decided to end it. In addition, the French Revolution and Napoleonic Wars, 1789-1815, were also part of this series of wars. Finally, in 1815 it all ended. The next war involving many European nations came 99 years later, in 1914, the First World War.

(This text uses England, Britain, and Great Britain interchangeably. Strictly speaking, Britain is the geographic island upon which England, Scotland, and Wales are located. Great Britain, in 1707, officially became the name of both the island and the political union of the three countries. You may also see the United Kingdom; it is Great Britain plus Northern Ireland.)

An excellent book on the concept of the Atlantic World, and the source of much of the insight and information in this chapter, is *The Atlantic World*, by Douglas R. Egerton, Alison Games, Jane G. Landers, Kris Lane, and Donald R. Wright.

3

PURITANISM AND QUAKERS: THE REFORMATION CONTINUED

The Reformation Begins, Luther, 1483-1546

On October 31, 1517, Martin Luther challenged his fellow Catholic Church theologians over the issue of indulgences. When he tacked his 95 theses to the door of the chapel at Wittenberg University, he was following a traditional means to invite debate. By the late Middle Ages the Roman Catholic Church was less of a church and more of a moneymaking institution and an international political power. Two different popes, Pope Pius V in 1570 and Pope Gregory XIII in 1580, absolved any assassin from bearing the burden of sin who would remove that horrible Protestant queen, Elizabeth I, from the English throne. Even murder was acceptable and forgiven, ahead of time.

By the late Middle Ages simony, the buying and selling of church offices and positions, was common. The Church had created a means for people to move deceased family members out of Purgatory, for a fee. The best way to quickly understand Purgatory is to think of it as a giant waiting room, where those who were mostly good waited and waited before getting into Heaven. Heaven was for pure Christians, and the nature of sin meant no one, except Jesus Christ, had immediately ascended into Heaven. Good people, who were not perfect, could not go directly to Heaven. Thus, the Church came up with Purgatory, a waiting station on the way to Heaven, and a means (i.e., indulgences) to move sinners more quickly into Heaven, for a fee.

The theological rationale for indulgences came from the Doctrine of the Keys, the phrase in the Bible, Matthew 16:19, that states that whatever a minister says on earth is binding in Heaven. This concept became very useful for raising money for the Church, especially for funds needed to build the Vatican. Pope Leo X authorized a new round of indulgences in 1515 to finish St. Peter's Cathedral. Spain, France, and

England prohibited such fundraising in their countries. A divided Germany could not fend off the powerful Roman Catholic Church. Many Germans were irate over the flow of German money to Rome. Thus, Luther struck a responsive chord; many endorsed his arguments, but not for his religious reasons. The Pope originally called the German ruckus over indulgences "a silly monk's squabble," but it broke apart the Catholic Church. The word catholic, lower-cased, means universal. After Luther the Catholic Church was no longer universal within Western Christianity.

Luther was offered a higher position in the Catholic Church if he would just shut up. That instead drove him on. In debates with other theologians Luther argued against the then dominant theological position that good works were more important than faith, and that what a person did showed one's faith, such as giving money, money, and more money. Luther argued faith was more important than good works. No agreed-upon body of Catholic Doctrine, no official church position, existed before this time. None was needed, because everyone was a Catholic. As an example, the question then of "What does it mean to be a Catholic?" was about as hazy as asking today, "What does it mean to be an American?" What must one believe to be an American? If asked to list the requirements, no two lists would be the same, in order or inclusion.

Luther did not intend to break away from the Catholic Church; he wanted to correct it. For him this was a dispute within the Catholic Church. Luther died in 1546 believing he was a good Catholic and the Pope was a bad Catholic. However, his initial theological opposition to indulgences became intertwined with many other issues. Many of these issues were not new; John Hus, a Bohemian church reformer, had raised similar ones earlier, and was silenced when Church authorities burned him at the stake in 1415.

Why the Dispute Became a Larger Issue

1. The printing press – Gutenberg's Bible first appeared in 1455, by 1500 there were 35,000 books published in Europe. Many pamphlets were also published during this time. Now news spread swiftly. Luther's translation of the New Testament into German appeared in 1522; in 12 years, 200,000 copies were printed. His translation of the Old Testament appeared in 1534. Prior to this people had to depend on the Church to tell them what the Bible said. Now one could read it for himself, in your own language, and form your own opinion.

2. Others also jumped on these theological issues – the most significant were John Calvin, 1509-1564, and Ulrich Zwingli, 1484-1531, both in Switzerland, and John Knox, 1505-1572, in Scotland.

3. There was genuine concern over corruption in the church, which is why many were attracted to Luther's cause. Many church positions were for sale, which, of course, is not biblically based. Expectancy, as an example, meant buying a

position before it became vacant. The Dutch scholar Erasmus wrote a play in which the Pope dies and goes to Heaven. There he confronts the Keeper of the Pearly Gates, Saint Peter, who according to Catholic tradition was the first Pope. Therefore, in essence, the first Pope meets the latest Pope at the gates to Heaven. The latest Pope yells, "Open the gate and let me in." St. Peter replies, "Open the gate with the key of faith." The latest Pope responds, "What is this faith stuff? Open the gate or I will excommunicate you." To which St. Peter replies, "What is excommunication?" Whatever the original church was; it was not that now. The two Popes could not understand one another.

Luther organized a survey of priests in his local area. Out of 205 priests, 195 could not repeat the Lord's Prayer or the Ten Commandments. Some had never heard of either. Why were they priests? They had purchased the position to live off the Sunday collection plate. If all this corruption is disheartening, please remember that there were many at that time quietly doing God's work, thousands of nuns, monks, and priests. However, in 1500, they were not in positions of authority within the church hierarchy.

4. German nationalism – There was no such thing as the country of Germany, not until 1871. It was at this time over 3,000 little countries. Imagine each county, town, and city in a state being a separate country, many completely within other countries. That was the geographical area called Germany. The kings of Spain, France, and England prohibited the sale of indulgences in their countries. Without a central government or king, Germany could not prevent the sale of indulgences. This made many Germans angry with the "Italian" Catholic Church, as they labeled it.

5. Religion was a factor in international diplomatic politics and a factor in international intrigue. The most prestigious throne in Europe was the position of Holy Roman Emperor, theoretically the continuation of the Roman Empire. As one historian later noted, it was really neither holy nor Roman nor an empire. It was not an inherited position; seven electors voted to select the next emperor. Since three were Catholic archbishops, the Pope was always involved behind the scenes in selecting the new emperor. A new emperor was named in 1519, Charles V of Spain. Both Henry VIII of England and the King of France wanted the title. Henry's anger surfaced shortly afterwards, when he broke with the Roman Catholic Church.

6. Questions had repeatedly been raised in the past about the Pope's authority. According to Church doctrine, it rests on several passages, primarily on Matthew 16:18, "thou art Peter and upon this rock I will build my church," which, according to Catholic tradition, means Peter was appointed as the first

Pope. Some theologians, then and now, argue this phrase refers to the idea that Christ was the Son of God, referring to the question preceding this verse in which Christ asks Peter, "Who do people say that I am?" Peter responds by declaring that Christ is the Son of the God. So, pick one, the idea or St. Peter; both Catholic and Protestant theologians did. According to the Catholic Church, the authority to lead the church given in Matthew 16:18 by Jesus to Peter and consequently to all the following Popes, (and, also to the whole body of the bishops, acting together, not as individuals) is the source of the dogma teaching that when the Pope issues a statement on matters of faith or morals, he is infallible. Thus, a challenge against Papal Infallibility was an attack on the foundation of the Pope's authority.

In the oldest manuscripts scholars have found, dating from around 400 to 800 A.D., the Greek word for "rock" is feminine, which means it probably refers to the idea of Christ being the Son of God rather than to Peter. In the Greek language ideas are feminine. To really complicate matters, Aramaic was the language of everyday Palestine during the time of Christ, not Greek. Aramaic scholars claim one cannot make an idiomatic reference such as "upon this rock" in Aramaic. However the passage is interpreted, there is no denying the Papacy exists and that it has had a considerable influence on Christianity and history.

Over the centuries the popes gradually assumed the power to name subordinate church officials. The rise of powerful monarchs threatened this right. One question swirling around at this time was who installs the bishops? Which would win, secular control of church officials or church control?

All these attacks on the church's doctrines and powers carried political implications. The English king, James I, 1603-1625, clearly saw the implications of attacking the church's power structure in his phrase, "No bishop, no king." If religious authority was attacked from the bottom up, political authority could be next. He ordered a new translation of the Bible, the King James Version, in order to emphasize obedience to authority. That version is widely regarded as the only inspired translation by modern Christian Fundamentalists; however, it was more politically motivated than religiously motivated. Fundamentalists see God's guiding hand behind this translation; historians see James I. In a 1610 speech to Parliament James I asserted that as king he had the power of "life and death" over his subjects, the power to treat his subjects "like men at the chess, a pawn to take a bishop or knight...."

Conflicting Ideas

The religious turmoil let loose a collection of ideas and caused debates, many of which continue today in more subdued form. Bear in mind that these ideas were, and are, considered very important; they determined whether one goes to Heaven or Hell. This era was more than just "a silly monk's squabble." These were issues everyone had to get correct. Eternity is a long punishment for believing the incorrect idea.

1. What is the nature of God? Is He a loving God or one who punishes and disciplines? God can be very useful to those who wield him as a weapon.

2. Which baptism is correct – infant or adult?

3. What is the role of the clergy? Who hires and fires them? How should they dress? What powers do they have? Should they be celibate? What education, if any, do they need?

4. Should there be set prayers or spontaneous prayers? How structured should the church service be?

5. What should be the layout of the church building? Until the nineteenth century almost all churches were built in the shape of a cross, with the altar pointing towards Jerusalem. This was hard to do in a city where the layout of the streets restricted building options.

6. What are the sacraments? The Catholic Church had not adopted the seven sacraments until 1439. During communion what happens? Does a priest, a minister, a layperson, or someone sitting beside you give communion to you? Do you take it individually or as a group? What happens during communion? Is it a remembrance, a memorial service, or does transubstantiation (i.e., the bread and wine actually become the body and blood of Christ) take place?

7. How is a church to be organized – a hierarchy or a community of believers? To what extent are people observers and to what extent are they participants? Who or what has to be present in order to have a worship service?

8. Who or what has authority over an individual church? Is it a hierarchy of officials, as in the Roman Catholic Church; or a synod, which is an assembly that votes on changes in policy and doctrine, as in the Lutheran Church; or a hierarchy of councils, in which the churches remain independent, as in the Presbyterian Church; or a federation of independent churches, as in Congregational churches?

9. Should a church own property? Owning land the church building is on should be a given, but what about a pension stock fund for ministers, or apartment buildings to earn rental income to be spent on charity?

Four Responses – The Reformation in England

In England there were four responses to the Reformation impulses, which became a factor in English national politics and international politics and in settling the American colonies.

The Anglican Church, the Church of England

The Anglican Church, or Church of England, grew out of events in British history. The English king during Luther's ruckus, Henry VIII, 1509-1547, wanted to annul his marriage. However, his wife was the daughter of the King of Spain. Because of this international complication, the Pope denied Henry's request. Henry responded by breaking away from the Catholic Church and establishing the Church of England, with himself as the head. One humorous part of this episode is that earlier the Pope had honored Henry VIII by awarding him a title, Defender of the Faith, for a pamphlet Henry wrote attacking Luther. The kings and queens of England still keep this title, in spite of the fact the reference alluded to is the Roman Catholic faith.

The Anglican Church, called the Episcopal Church in America, is what is called a high church, meaning it has a structured service, set prayers, and a hierarchy of officials, led by the Archbishop of Canterbury, who appoints bishops, priests, and deacons. Henry VIII tolerated no opposition; he jailed those opposing the Church of England. The question of religion continued to be a factor in British politics for the next two hundred years. Look at the following list of monarchs, church affiliation, and events in British history.

Henry VIII, 1509-1547
Edward VI, 1547-1553   Church of England, died at 16
Mary I, 1553-1558   Catholic, wife of Philip II, King of Spain
Elizabeth I, 1558-1603   Church of England
James I, 1603-1625   Church of England, but too close to
                         Catholicism in personal practice
Charles I, 1625-1649   Church of England, but too close to
                         Catholicism in personal practice
civil war, 1642-1649   King versus Parliament, won by
                         Puritans in Parliament
Protectorate, 1649-1660 Cromwell, Puritans rule, Long Parliament
1660   Restoration, monarchy returns
Charles II, 1660-1685   Church of England, but many
                         believed him to be a closet Catholic
James II, 1685-1688   Catholic, James converted to

Catholicism after marrying an Italian princess, a Catholic. James had two Protestant daughters, Mary and Anne, by his previous wife. His new Catholic wife became pregnant and had a son, who she took to France to raise, meaning he was certain to be a Catholic. Did this mean an endless string of Catholic kings on the throne of England? Never! Thus, the Glorious

Revolution of 1688, when Parliament kicked out James II and put James' Protestant daughters next in line for the throne. Parliament passed a law that the kings and queens of England must belong to the Church of England. Mary would not accept the throne unless her husband, William of Orange, shared the title.

William and Mary
    Mary II, 1689-1694
    William III, 1689-1702
Anne, 1702-1714

Puritans

Puritans wanted to de-Catholicize the Church of England, to purify it. To the Puritans it seemed too much like the Catholic Church without the Pope. This was essentially a fight within the Church of England. Puritans were concerned about set prayers and they wanted no bishops. In the decade after 1620, 75,000 Puritans left England, 17,800 going to New England. The New Englanders saw their colony as "A City Upon a Hill" in the phrase of their pious leader, John Winthrop. The quote was a paraphrasing from Matthew 5:14, "You are the light of the world. A city set on a hill cannot be hid." They would be a model to England, showing the mother country the proper way to establish God's community on earth. For this reason, they could tolerate no mistakes, no errors. People like Anne Hutchinson and Roger Williams had to go. The Puritans were single-minded, which could be seen by outsiders as narrow-minded. They formed a close-knit community. However, because they no longer faced persecution in America, it was difficult to maintain a sense of community, a sense of "us versus them."

For Puritans every event was related to God's plan; there was no such thing as an accident or happenstance. The battle on earth between Good and Evil was real. The leaders kicked Anne Hutchinson out for asking too many questions, and for favoring Antinomianism, which holds that Christ's grace brings salvation, not the adhering to moral laws. This implies that leading an outwardly moral life is not necessarily a sign a person is one of the elect. Puritan leaders were aghast. How then could the community recognize those who are God's elect? Also, to what extent does man have either predestination or free will? This really is the old question raised by Luther. Which is more important – good works or faith? How can everyone tell if someone is one of the elect, one of God's chosen, by your faith or by your good works? What does it mean to be "blessed"? Is someone obviously "blessed" if they become wealthy? Such strictness limited the number of "pure" Puritans; they were later forced to lighten up to avoid losing members. In the 1660s the Puritans adopted the Half-Way Covenant, which said one could be a member of the church if he or she were a baptized but unconverted child of a church member; but you were not a full member with the privilege of voting on church matters. That was for God's elect. Puritans believed one had to have a "conversion" experience. And don't try to fake it. We Puritan clergy and leaders can tell and you will burn in Hell.

Was colonial New England with its town meeting a birthplace of democracy? Many have argued so. However, historians have found that a sense of consensus really ran the town, with major questions decided by the local elite. Americans would not recognize it as our version of democracy, but it had more elements of democracy than anywhere else in the world at that time. As a mostly agricultural small community of true believers, it was already a democracy of equals in many ways.

However, to outsiders it was an intolerant society. Puritans in New England imprisoned Quakers, hanged several, lashed over 100, and branded one with an "H" for heretic. Four were stripped naked in January and locked in an unheated shed for a month. New England's Puritans were upset about the growth of religious toleration in England under the Puritan Commonwealth after their victory in the English Civil War. Cromwell even allowed Jews, who had been kicked out of England in 1290, back into England.

Puritans stressed the importance of education. Harvard was founded to provide a supply of orthodox ministers; schools were established in each village to ensure all could read the Bible. And, they did read it. The Reverend Cotton Mather's second wife read the entire Bible six times a year. When a question came up on any topic, New England Puritans knew which biblical verse addressed that question. One historian labeled them "moral athletes," who practiced for the BIG test, which came at death. They forsook the tradition of exchanging wedding rings, they were "married to the church." Puritans banned Christmas celebrating as a time of "amorous, mixed, unchristian dancing." In England the Puritan leader, Oliver Cromwell, suspended Christmas in 1647. It was not revived until the middle of the nineteenth century, by Prince Albert, Queen Victoria's husband, who introduced his native German customs, which included decorating a pine tree. In the late 1640s some unknown wag toasted the former holiday in this verse:

"Gone are the golden days of yore,
When Christmas was a high day,
Whose sports we now shall see no more,
Tis turned into Good Friday."

One must be careful when viewing and evaluating the Puritans. The journalistic wit, H. L. Mencken, said Puritanism was "the haunting fear that someone, somewhere, might be happy." *The Scarlet Letter* is Nathaniel Hawthorne's nineteenth century view of them. But, they were not a sour, gloomy people. Historian Daniel Boorstin saw them as primarily a pragmatic people, giving Americans a legacy as practical non-theorists. Americans do not think or philosophize, we do. In *From Puritan to Yankee* Richard Bushman argued that while religion was the goal of the first generation, New Englanders quickly, in succeeding generations, faded in religious zeal and pursued making money, becoming more like the stereotypical image of the Yankee businessman.

The Reformation elevated the idea of a "calling," which previously referred chiefly to those who entered a monastery, convent, or the priesthood, into a broader definition, one in which working hard in this life at your chosen occupation was answering God's call, for you. The Puritan minister, Cotton Mather, explained it as "a certain *Particular Employment* by which (a person's) *Usefulness*, in his Neighborhood, is distinguished." This easily translated into making money, to please God and to show how blessed you were. But individualism was not of primary importance to Puritans. The community was. The community "must oversway all private respects." However, by the third generation pretensions of being "God's elect" had disappeared, except among the complaining and lamenting Puritan ministers.

By the twentieth century the Puritan church evolved into three different churches – Reformed, Evangelical, and Congregational – which joined together in 1957 to form the United Church of Christ.

Pilgrims – Separatists

Before the Puritans left for America, the Pilgrims preceded them in 1620. Their experience comes close to being labeled a disaster. Of the 102 Pilgrims who sailed on the 66-day trip, 4 died in route. During the first winter, of the 26 men with families, 14 died; of the 18 married women, 15 died. John Carver was the first governor; but the best remembered one is William Bradford, 1590-1657, governor for 31 years.

The Pilgrims were Separatists, who believed the Church of England was so far beyond reform and fixing that they were better off leaving it. Unlike the Puritans, who worked to reform the Church of England from the inside, the Pilgrims had simply given up. Overall, the Pilgrim experience was a failure. It bequeathed to later generations two legacies. The Mayflower Compact, November 11, 1620, with 41 signers, included every adult bachelor and every head of a family, and most of the hired menservants. It was not referred to as a "compact" until an ancestor of signer John Alden, Alden Bradford, referred to it as the Mayflower Compact in 1793. It became famous because it was the earliest document in which Americans established a government by mutual consent. The second legacy is, of course, Thanksgiving, which was primarily a New England regional holiday until it became national after the Civil War. During the Great Depression President Franklin Roosevelt set the date as the fourth Thursday in November rather than the last Thursday, in order to lengthen the Christmas shopping season. The date of the original Thanksgiving is unknown.

Quakers

Into this turmoil over religion William Penn was born in 1644 (1644-1718) in the middle of the English Civil War, the Puritans versus Charles I. Penn later stated he felt the strong "Puritan" pull from the age of 11. After the Long Parliament and Cromwell faded in power, the Restoration arrived in 1660 with the return of Charles II from France. Quakerism was too close to the hated Puritans to suit the king's supporters. From 1661 to 1685, approximately 15,000 Quakers were jailed, and 450 of them died while incarcerated.

In 1667 William Penn became a Quaker. His father, Admiral Willian Penn, captured Jamaica for England in 1655. The king's brother, the Duke of York, the future James II, was a neighbor and a good friend of the Penn family. Young William shocked his upper class family and friends by embracing what we would today refer to as a cult, a dangerous cult. Quakerism can be very simply described as the extreme left wing of the Reformation. It had no ministers, no structure, and no set prayers. Communion is an important part of Christianity, but Quakers rejected the Lord's Supper. George Fox founded Quakerism around 1650 at the end of the English Civil War. He called his followers the Society of Friends, and also Quakers. Critics used unprintable names. Some Quakers interrupted Anglican Church services by breaking bottles, using the broken bottles to reveal the emptiness of the Anglican Church's "hollow" doctrines. And, sometimes they were not fully dressed, naked to emphasize the "nakedness" of Church practices. Try to picture that.

In 1667 Penn published *The Sandy Foundation Shaken*, a small pamphlet blasting the loose morals of English society. The Church of England and public officials called it blasphemy against the Trinity, and jailed Penn, putting him in the Tower of London. The Bishop of London (remember Penn's upper class connections) visited Penn to try to convince him of the error of his ways. Penn's response was, "My prison shall be my grave before I will budge a jot, for I owe my conscience to no mortal man." He promptly returned to writing his next pamphlet, *No Cross, No Crown*. In this he railed against the theater, foppish dress, and false pride. He called for a return to the unadorned simplicity of the early Christians and the observance of the basic precepts of Christianity. He opposed women's use of "curl, powder, patch, paint," and "false locks of strange hair." What makes this comment funny is that he, from a childhood illness, had patches of hair missing, and so he wore a wig, but it was not a painted, "false lock." The Duke of York intervened to get Penn out of prison. It pays to have good family friends in high positions. The duke's reward was another pamphlet, a scathing attack on religious persecution in England, *The Great Case of Liberty of Conscience*.

William Penn's father had loaned a large amount of money to the king. When the father died the son inherited the debt, which the king paid off by a grant of land in America, Pennsylvania. Pennsylvania had an advantage over the other colonies. It was the next to last one settled (Georgia being the last) and so Penn was aware of the mistakes previously made. He carefully planned his colony. It was to be a "holy experiment," one that valued both religious liberty and trust in humanity. Any settler could receive free land, 50 acres; 200 additional acres cost one cent. These easy terms and Pennsylvania's good soil attracted German Pietists, who were later called the Pennsylvania Dutch, because they spoke "Deutsch." Penn revised his government four times, creating a colonial government that contained many democratic features. In his charter, the Frame of Government, Penn came close to our definition of democracy, a remarkable statement for its time – "any government is free to the people under it where the laws rule, and the people are a party to those laws, and more than this is tyranny, oligarchy, or confusion." In celebration of Penn's Fourth Charter of government issued in 1701, the Pennsylvania assembly commissioned a huge bell in 1751 with the inscription "Proclaim Liberty throughout the land," Leviticus 25:10. It later became a famous cherished icon of American liberty, the Liberty Bell.

Penn carefully laid out Philadelphia's streets in a checkerboard square pattern. He wanted "A greene, country towne, which will never be burnt," as London had been several years earlier. The London fire of 1666 had destroyed 13,000 houses. Philadelphia had wide streets and open spaces between the houses. It grew to be the second largest city in the British Empire by 1775, something that would have disappointed William Penn. He disliked cities. In cities one sees "but the Works of Men" which are, "for the most part, his Pride, Folly, and Excess." The country "makes a better Subject for our Contemplation" because God's works are "for use," whereas man's works are "chiefly, for Ostentation and Lust." Philadelphia was intended to serve only as an export center for Pennsylvania's agricultural output.

Penn put his Quaker faith into practice in dealing with the Indians. He bought Pennsylvania from the Indians, and never put any money into the colony's budget for defense against Indians. He intended to live in peace with them. Over the long colonial era thousands of Indians migrated into Western Pennsylvania, seeking security from too frequent clashes with other tribes and white settlers pushing westward.

The French philosopher, Voltaire, was impressed with Penn's colony. He called it proof that neither absolute monarchy, feudalism, religious intolerance, nor national or racial intolerance was necessary. He called it the future of America. In many ways it was.

4

SLAVERY IN THE COLONIES

The question of the origins and early development of slavery frustrates historians. There are very few sources of any kind. Historians have an old saying – "no documents, no proof, no history." Scholars demand a footnote, giving the source for assertions. What would be nice would be a letter from a Virginian written in 1657 to his cousin in England with a paragraph explaining why they enslaved Africans. Historians do not have such a letter, or any other source. Here are the suggested reasons historians have presented.

Historiography of the Origins of Colonial Slavery

Oscar and Mary Handlin, *Race and Nationality in American Life*, argue that it was economic need. The labor shortage was the primary factor that led to a legal process to increase the labor supply. The laws that established slavery convinced whites that they had a higher status than slaves did.

Carl Degler, *Out of Our Past: The Forces That Shaped Modern America*, claims that prejudice preceded enslavement and was the primary reason for the establishment of slavery.

Winthrop Jordan, in a chapter entitled "Unthinking Decision, Enslavement of Africans in America to 1700," in *The White Man's Burden: Historical Origins of Racism in the United States*, or, *White Over Black: American Attitudes Toward the Negro, 1550-1812*. (The text is the same for both books, the second book, three times longer, has footnotes, but the first does not.) Slavery resulted from an "unthinking decision," it just happened. He researched the attitudes of both Americans and the English toward blacks in the years from 1550 to 1812. Racism arose as a result of slavery, not because of it.

Edmund S. Morgan, *American Slavery, American Freedom*, contends that slavery developed out of the creation of a society in which the need for white equality emerged, especially after Bacon's Rebellion, a brief uprising in Virginia in 1676 pitting disgruntled frontier whites against tidewater aristocrats. What cemented white equality was their common differentiation from the black slave. In essence, Americans created a Herrenvolk democracy, German for a democracy of the master race. John C. Calhoun told John Quincy Adams in the 1820s that slavery "was the best guarantee to equality among the whites."

Peter Kolchin, in *American Slavery, 1619-1877*, reasserts the economic argument, pointing out that everywhere there was the beginning of commercial agriculture, where crops were grown for export, slavery took root, both North and South. In addition, in the 1680s the supply of indentured servants shrank as conditions in Ireland and Great Britain improved. Fewer poor people left for the colonies as indentured servants, leading to an increased dependence on slaves to fill the labor void. The Great Fire of London, which broke out on September 9, 1666, and burned 80% of the city, created jobs rebuilding the city for many of the poor who would have had no option but to sell themselves as indentured servants. For the previous 150 years wages in England had steadily declined. Finally wages began a long upswing around 1670-1680 and provided the English poor with an alternative to becoming indentured servants in the colonies. Now one could stay and struggle rather than leave and struggle.

An intriguing question is why the English, or any other European people, did not enslave their own people. One historian, David Eltis, has argued that Europeans in this time had a collective view of the world, one that divided it into a status of insider and outsider, an "us versus them," a Weltanschauung (worldview) probably based on religion more than any other concept. Other peoples, Africans and American Indians, had a more limited version of outsider and insider status, making it easier to enslave nearby neighbors – something Europeans would not do to other Europeans by this time.

What difference does it make why slavery started? A lot. It affects current public policy. History is not just a dead subject about dead people. If racial prejudice was the primary cause of slavery, and slavery was primarily a racial institution, then that is the reason for the subsequent low statistical position of blacks in America today. Civil rights laws that prohibit or limit public acts of prejudice best attack this situation. If the need for labor was the primary cause of slavery and slavery had as its principal characteristic the lack of economic opportunity for blacks, then the primary reason for the subsequent low statistical position of blacks in America today is best attacked by economic means – affirmative action, preferential scholarships, job creation aimed at black neighborhoods, etc.

Which have we done the most? I vote for civil rights laws. Which should we do? I vote for economic laws. However, in our society it is difficult politically to give preferential treatment to one group over others. That legislator will likely be voted out of office. History is not a story from a long time ago that has no relevance to today's world. It is how we got here and provides guidance to where we should go.

By 1775 blacks made up 25% of the American population. Now it is 12-13%, lower due to the large number of European immigrants in the nineteenth century. The percentage will probably decrease even more in the future due to the patterns and nature of our current immigration.

Thinking of the English People at this Time (Zeitgeist)

What do historians know about the era of the beginning of slavery? What was in the air? What attitudes and ideas floated around in peoples' heads? The Great Chain of Being was a frequent discussion topic among scholars and even common people on the question of where everything and anything ranked in God's scheme of things. Which is more important and more valued by God, a pen or a pencil, a desk or a chair? Yes, they debated such things, especially after a few drinks. Guess who ended up at the bottom in English eyes when they debated ranking ethnic groups?

The English language is full of connotations over the colors white and black – black cats, white angels, blackballed, blacklisted, and behind the eight ball. The Oxford English Dictionary says black in the colonial era meant "deeply stained with dirt; soiled, dirty, foul . . . having dark or deadly purposes, malignant; pertaining to or involving death, deadly; baneful, disastrous, sinister . . . foul, iniquitous, atrocious, horrible, wicked." A 1790 Philadelphia-published encyclopedia included many disparaging terms associated with the word "Negro" – "idleness, treachery, revenge, debauchery, nastiness, and intemperance." (quoted in Shane White, *Somewhat More Independent: The End of Slavery in New York City, 1770-1810.*) Those connotations were part of the cultural baggage the English carried when they encountered Africans. Color carries connotations in other languages also. The phrase "born to purple" referred to one born into the Byzantine Empire's royal family. In Chinese culture, especially opera, black or red masks or faces represent the good people and those with white faces are the bad people. Imagine a Chinese person's reaction when they encountered a white person for the first time.

For the English another consideration was the suddenness of contact with Africans. Unlike the Mediterranean and Iberian experiences, Englishmen were unaccustomed to contact with Africans. Trade routes across the Sahara brought Africans into the Mediterranean world for hundreds of years before 1607. Africans, both slave and free, were 3% of Portugal's population in the early 1500s.

The biblical curse on Cain for killing his brother, Abel, in Genesis 4:9-15, offered another justification. God put a mark on Cain and his descendants, which many saw as meaning that God made Cain's descendants black as a punishment, offering a convenient religious explanation for skin color. In a later biblical story Noah cursed his son, Ham, in Genesis 9:20-27, making him a slave to his brothers. Obviously, or rather to those to whom it was obvious, blackness and slavery were divinely sanctioned as

God's punishment. The historian Winthrop Jordan saw the major factor to have been the Africans' heathen status. Jordan found an English law that used four words interchangeably – white, English, free, and Christian. Africans qualified on none of these. They were a people apart. Also, the Bible is very clear – "I will reveal myself to my people." Since God had not been to Africa, the only conclusion one could come to was that Africans were not His people. There is also the Tenth Commandment, a long list of what a person should not covet, including your neighbor's "man-servant, nor his maid servant." Finally, Jesus never condemned slavery.

Before 1492 Europeans divided their known world into Christian and infidel. In many respects, the initial contact with American Indians and a closer contact with Africans by Northern Europeans led to the invention of what we today would call amateur anthropology, leading to a continuous discussion of the characteristics of different peoples and the reasons for those differences. This usually ended with why "we" are superior. A new system of classifying living forms, devised by the Swedish biologist, Carolus Linnaeus, in the 1730s, lent a scientific aurora to the tavern debates.

Selective Borrowing of Racial Terms

Europeans already had a long experience with Indians and Africans before 1607 – the Spanish and Portuguese experience. Many terms existed to describe the groups and the various racial mixtures. In the French Caribbean colonies there were 64 gradations of color and class; colonial Mexico had 56 categories of race and class, called castas, such as peninsulares (Spaniards born in Spain), creoles (Spaniards born in the New World), Indian, Negro, mulatto (white and black offspring), mestizo (white and Indian offspring), mustee, sambo or zambo (black and Indian offspring), castizos (a child of a Spaniard and a mestizo; a child of a castizo and a Spaniard was a crillo), loba, bozales, quadroon, and octoroon. The French equivalent for mestizo was métis or metis. In the early 1700s in French Louisiana the black and Indian children were grifs. The English selectively borrowed only some of these racial terms. According to the Oxford English dictionary, the first use of "Negro" appeared in English in 1555. It says a lot that today many of these earlier racial terms are not found in the computer program for Microsoft Word's English language Spell Check. Unlike what happened in the English colonies, the half-white, half-black offspring of the Portuguese and Spanish were much more likely to be free, to enjoy more legal protections, and to be trained for skilled artisan jobs.

Prior to 1492 the major divisions within any European society were religious. In British North America race became the major division, rather than religion or class. What developed in the American Southern colonies, unlike the rest of the New World, was a social definition of race. Appearance labeled a person. The degree of mixture was not significant; any mixture was wrong, as long as it was apparent. Thomas

Jefferson, in response to a question from a letter writer, replied in 1815 that an octoroon, one-eighth black, if emancipated, becomes white and therefore eligible for citizenship. Some of Sally Hemings' children would have been octoroons. Perhaps that changed, to Jefferson, the nature of his relationship to her children, apparently fathered by one of his family members or by Jefferson himself. Historians do not know and cannot know for certain. The only currently available scientific test requires comparisons of a cell passed on through male descendants; Jefferson had none. Today there is no legal definition of the racial term "black." At one time the state of Louisiana had one, one thirty-second. That is your great-great-great-grandfather or grandmother. Who has any idea who those people were? There is a federal law defining a Native-American as one who is at least one-fourth Indian.

The Twin Characteristics of Slavery – Inherited Status and Lifetime Service

What do historians know about the early history of the origins of slavery? What evidence exists? When do historians see the arrival of the two characteristics of slavery as a system – inherited status and lifetime service – that were not previously present in the English experience, or in their histories of ancient Greece or Rome? Roman slaves were usually freed around the age of forty. The English practiced a harsh form of servitude, especially for those Irish and Scots who lost rebellions against English rule. They were shipped overseas as indentured servants. However, their service was for a limited time, unlike what New World slavery developed into. In the Roman-Greek legal tradition, the right of required servitude belonged to the victors in a war. The children of Roman slaves were considered citizens of Rome, far different from the status conferred on American slave children. The Latin term *servi* meant spared. "Spared" was certainly not what developed in the British colonies.

Before 1640

In 1619 a Dutch privateer, the *White Lion*, attacked a Spanish slave ship bound for Vera Cruz, Mexico, and seized some slaves. The *White Lion*, under Captain John Jobe, sold a few slaves in the West Indies and then, running low on food, proceeded to Virginia to sell 20 blacks at Jamestown. Note that this took place, as the title of a history of blacks in America would phrase it, *Before the Mayflower.* They were slaves, but historians think they were not slaves in the sense that slavery would later exist. However, the Virginians had one nearby example. In 1616, three years before, Bermuda became the first English colony to import black laborers.

In the 1620s the situation is very confused, because a free black man, Anthony Johnson, even owned slaves or indentured servants. In a 1624 court case a black man was permitted to testify in court because he was a baptized Christian. Whatever the initial labor system was, it was not strictly racial, at least not yet. In 1630 the population of Virginia was 30,000, but it included only 300 blacks, one percent.

1640 to 1660

In these years some evidence of slavery begins to appear, some indications of perpetual service. Some indentures for blacks were extended to twenty years or more. Given the life span back then, this approached lifetime servitude. A Maryland court in 1640 sentenced three runaways as follows: two white males were to serve their master for an additional year and the colony for three years, indicating that they were probably indentured servants. The third, John Punch, received a sentence to serve his master for "the time of his natural life." Was he a slave already? Or, was this a punishment given to an indentured servant? Why? Was he a habitual troublemaker? A frequent runaway? A ring leader? Someone who had to be made an example of? Or, was he black? All that historians know for certain is that no Englishman had ever been given a similar sentence by an English court. Inventories of estates gave the prices paid for servants and their value based on the number of years yet to serve. Why were some older servants more valuable than younger ones? Why were apparently black female servants valued more than white female servants?

Could custom have preceded the laws? Was slavery practiced before it was institutionalized as a system? Whatever was happening, it is clear that the Chesapeake society evolving in colonial Virginia and Maryland differentiated between whites and blacks in many ways. By the late seventeenth century, for example, all white males, black males, and black females had to work in the fields at harvest time. Who is missing? Why? Were white women privileged or incompetent? In 1640 Virginia prohibited blacks from carrying arms. There was also an unfavorable reaction to interracial sexual unions, miscegenation, a word apparently invented by racist New York City journalists in 1864 to attack what they considered that horrible abolitionist in the White House, Abraham Lincoln. According to a 1630 law, a white man could be whipped for having sex with a black female. In 1662 Virginia doubled the fine, and declared that "all children borne in this country shall be held bond or free only according to the condition of the mother," in other words, a child inherited his or her status as slave or free from the mother. This was a major change from traditional English common law, which said that a child was the child of the father. Now a slave child was the child of the mother, even if the father was free, or white.

After 1660: From a Society with Slaves to a Slave Society

After 1660 the colonial South slowly turned from a society with slaves into a slave society, complete with slave codes regulating the institution of slavery and slavery affecting every other institution, the church, the political system, the family, etc. In 1664 Maryland passed a law establishing slavery for life for blacks, Virginia at that stage was still unclear. However, increasingly slavery and considerations about slavery influenced every other aspect of society. In 1723 all the previous laws concerning slaves in Virginia were placed in a comprehensive slave code of twenty-four sections, nine pages long.

The number of blacks in the population had leaped, from under 1,000 blacks in 1660 to 16,000 by 1700. By 1720 slaves were 25% of the Chesapeake society's population; by 1740, 30%; by 1760, 40%.

The differentiation between blacks and whites continued, for example:

1667 – Virginia – baptism does not change one's status as a slave

1669 – Virginia – the killing of slaves while disciplining them is not a felony

1670 – Virginia – it becomes illegal for a black landowner to keep white Christian servants

1681 – Maryland – similar laws on the children of slave mothers being slaves

1691 – Virginia – prohibits black-white marriage; Massachusetts followed in 1705 and Maryland in 1715. Such laws were not just a Southern phenomenon. Other colonies soon followed suit, Delaware and Pennsylvania in the Mid-Atlantic colonies and Georgia and South Carolina in the deep South. Much later, in 1967, the Supreme Court declared such antiquated laws unconstitutional in *Loving v. Virginia*.

1732 – Virginia – revokes the vote for property-owning blacks

In 1672 and 1673 two court cases set free black indentured servants whose masters had tried to keep them in bondage. Confusion! What does all this mean? How much do laws tell us? Do laws reflect what is done, a fear of what is done, or a fear of what could be done?

Peter Kolchin, in two books, *American Slavery, 1619-1877* and *Unfree Labor American Slavery and Russian Serfdom*, updates the economic argument for the origin of slavery. In the late seventeenth century the labor supply dried up just as the Virginia farmers (not yet planters) increased their tobacco production. They even attempted to extend the term for indentured servants to twenty years or more. In a 1672 court case a black indentured servant obtained his freedom after twenty-eight years, long after the term stipulated in his contract. To solve the labor shortage, Virginia established the headright system, which awarded fifty acres of land to anyone who paid a migrant's transportation cost to Virginia. Many indentured servants arrived under the headright system, auctioned off at the dock to a Virginian. However, as Kolchin points out, the number of headrights declined just as the need for more labor appeared. Between 1650 and 1674, that number never fell below 7,900 each year. From 1675 to 1699, in a rapidly growing economy, it never rose above 6,000. A previously dependable labor supply of indentured servants began to dry up. Look at these figures from Kolchin's *Unfree Labor American Slavery and Russian Serfdom*.

E Pluribus Unum:
A History of the United States

ISBN: 9781979180207
available on Amazon, use full title

John W. Crum, PhD
University of Delaware

jcrum@udel.edu
Published, April, 2018

,0,910
7,926
7,979
10,390
9,876
3,991
5,927
4,474
5,128
4,251

roved difficult to buy for another reason. In one study of New
wspaper ads listed 13 times as many white runaway indentured
ways. Sharon V. Salinger, *To Serve Well and Faithfully: Labor and
Pennsylvania, 1682-1800*, found that white fugitives outnumbered
the last forty-five years of the colonial period. White indentured
easily blend into society, although Celtic accents often gave them
away.

Historians estimate that by 1775 only 5% of the world's workers were independent, in other words, debt-free. Historian Jack Greene points out that English indentured servants realized that true independence, "freedom from the will of others," was at least potentially possible in early America. Hence, "the most powerful drive in the early American experience was the desire for personal independence." By 1680 not enough Europeans were willing to sell themselves into indentured servitude to continue filling the labor needs of the colonies. Since one-fourth of all slaves imported into the Chesapeake Bay region died the first year, usually from respiratory ailments, a constant resupplying was necessary. By 1697 the Chesapeake society was annually producing 353,290,000 pounds of tobacco for export, using a system of slaves working in gangs. Meanwhile South Carolina specialized in another crop that demanded intense labor, rice, using a system of slaves working in a task system. By 1770 rice was 24% of America's exports to England. After 1672 England became a leading slave-trading country, creating a ready supply.

Be careful about Georgia's banning of slavery when the colony started in 1732. It did not grow out of a moral concern over slavery. Instead, the founders were primarily concerned that slavery would promote economic inequality and discourage industrious habits among the white settlers.

Also, be careful about the African end of the slave trade. Europeans did not penetrate into the interior; they purchased war captives or people sold for debts. Africans eagerly sought what Europeans had to offer — clothing, jewelry, and beads all served as indications of status. A fact about Africa that one must remember is that Europeans came to Africa twice, first during the age of exploration and the slave trade. They did not get beyond the coast in this early encounter; it was too dangerous. Europeans came back again later as explorers and colonizers around the 1850s, after the discovery of sulfur and quinine to treat malaria.

Why Not Indians?

There were two other possible peoples to enslave, Irish and Indians. The experiments with Irish slaves in the Caribbean proved unsuccessful. Indians in Virginia proved difficult to enslave, unlike the Spanish experience in Mexico and Peru. By the time the English arrived at Jamestown in 1607, Indians living along the Atlantic coast had a long history dealing with vessels that stopped to trade and to acquire food supplies. Thirty-six years before 1607 the Spanish had tried to plant a settlement in Virginia. It failed. Europeans also had a practice of kidnapping Indians to take to Europe. Some of them, especially those who were deemed Christianized and therefore ready to proselytize for the faith, were returned to their villages, where they served as interpreters, but also as wily assessors of European motives. Other tribes nearer the interior were less fortunate. In 1708 33% of South Carolina's slaves were Indians, captured by other Indians, and the colony sold thousands of Indians into slavery in the Caribbean. But ultimately Indian slavery did not work for a number of reasons.

1. North American Indians were less accustomed to settled agriculture, unlike Indians in Mexico and Peru.
2. The English intention, right from the beginning, was to get rid of the Indians, not to incorporate them into their society in any way.
3. Blacks were dealt with as individuals; Indians were dealt with as tribes or nations. Complications, such as communication, existed within African society, preventing newly imported slaves from banding together; almost five hundred different languages are spoken today in just Nigeria, over one thousand for the continent.
4. Indians represented a challenge to the English, a common testing experience symbolizing the conquest of the wilderness, proving the worth of God's plan in putting the English here. The challenge was to conquer the uncivilized savages or else they would drag whites down to an uncivilized state. African blacks presented no similar challenge.
5. To English settlers the Indians were savages, a word frequently used to describe them. An Englishman in 1625 said, "so bad a people, having little of humani-tie but shape, ignorant of Civilitie, of Arts, of Religion; more brutish than the beasts they hunt, more wild and unmanly than that unmanned wild countrey,

which they range rather than inhabit; captivated also to satans tyranny in foolish pieties, mad impieties, wicked idlenesse, busie and bloudy wickednesse." Certainly not the kind of people with whom any Englishman would wish to associate.

The Long View, Slavery's Impact on the New World

Historians argue over the long term effects of the enslavement of Africans. The mixing of the world's population was one. But what was the economic impact? By 1775 one-half of all the people who worked for someone else in colonial America were slaves, an essential component of the labor force. One historian, Kenneth Pomeranz, in *The Great Divergence: Europe, China, and the Making of the World Economy*, argues that slavery provided the wealth that fueled the modernization of Europe, what is termed the Industrial Revolution, giving Europe an advantage in the race with China and India for economic development. An earlier historian, Eric Williams, made a similar point in 1944. Was the wealth of Europe built on the productivity of slave labor? Was the wealth of colonial America built on the productivity of slave labor? The answer matters. Judgments in history and about history matter. History is not a subject about dead people who no longer matter. It affects current assessments of today's society.

5

THE COLONIAL ECONOMY

Mercantilism

In theory the colonial economy was governed under the rules and concepts of mercantilism, just as Americans today are, in theory, under capitalism. Laissez faire, or capitalism, as it is called today, was far into the future as an economic philosophy endorsed by merchants and governments. The first use of the word capitalism to describe an economic system even approaching our modern understanding of the word did not happen until 1793.

In this period mercantilism never had the coherence pictured in most textbooks. The chief feature of the system was the belief that the national government should regulate the nation's economic life to strengthen the government for competition against other nation-states. Everyone assumed that the total amount of economic wealth in the world was fixed, a static amount, what historian Richard Dunn termed "the psychology of limited wealth." Thus, the only way a country could become wealthier was to seize the wealth of another nation. We now operate under the philosophy that when we increase the total supply of wealth in the world we improve everyone. We bake a larger pie rather than argue over who gets what piece of a static pie. Under mercantilism there was no price competition set in the marketplace by supply and demand, unlike today's capitalism. The medieval concept of a "just price" set by the authorities for some commodities, like bread, remained part of the marketplace.

Different countries emphasized different features of mercantilism. For the British there were four:

1. Build up the merchant marine to control a country's own trade, called the carrying trade, aimed at the Dutch initially. The Dutch commercial fleet by 1670

was larger than that of England, France, Spain, Portugal, and Austria combined. (Austria was larger then, owning much of northern Italy, giving it access to the Mediterranean Sea.)

2. Protect your manufacturers from foreign and colonial competition. The Dutch also emphasized this, for example, in the Dutch colony of New Amsterdam manufacturers could not produce cloth. It had to be imported from the Netherlands.

3. Protect England's grain producers from foreign competition. This later appears in British history as the Corn Laws. The British called any grain "corn."

4. Accumulate hard currency, meaning gold and silver.

The Ideal Laborer

All these policies would make the country of England rich and strong, but not necessarily produce self-sufficient, wealthy English citizens. Indeed, the worker was described as follows: "It was the fate of the workers to be poor that the nation might be rich." "And to be ceaselessly diligent that the nation might be powerful." "The ideal laborer shunned idleness, raised a large family, lived in poverty, and received his pittance with a smile." The real laborer, as Daniel Defoe described him, was "saucy, mutinous, and beggarly."

The Ideal Colonies

The purpose of colonies under mercantilism was to supply England with markets and raw materials and to conduct trade to benefit Great Britain. The perfect colony under mercantilism was one in which "the inhabitants . . . wear not a rag of their own manufacturing; drive not a nail of their own forging; eat not out of a plate or cup of their own making; nay . . . produce not even bread to eat." The perfect colony never existed.

Protecting Manufacturers

One feature of mercantilism was to protect English manufacturers from competition. Three specific acts were passed.

1699 – The **Woolens Act** prohibited the shipment of wool outside the boundaries of a colony, to prevent competition with English producers. It was only partially obeyed.

1732 – The **Hat Act**, the result of a lobby effort by London hatters, prohibited the exporting of hats outside a colony, and added a long seven-year apprenticeship to become a hat maker. It was only partially obeyed.

1750 – The **Iron Act** prohibited the manufacturing of finished iron, but gave preferential treatment to the production of pig iron. Colonial assemblies and manufacturers ignored it. It was widely disobeyed. By 1775 the colonies produced one-seventh of the world's iron.

Life consists of more than wool, hats, and iron. Three laws in 51 years hardly oppressed the colonists. Moreover, they were poorly enforced and generally ignored. The colonists did receive some preferences in shipbuilding, particularly small ships.

Navigation Acts

Any attempt to control shipping in this era suffered from the lack of a good method to enforce laws and regulations. Historians estimate that smuggling accounted for as much as 50% of the economic activity in the Caribbean during the sixteenth and seventeenth centuries. The British Navigation Acts tried to channel colonial commerce to benefit England.

Navigation Act, 1651, tried to eliminate Dutch competition in overseas trade, especially the sugar trade; required most goods to be carried in English or colonial ships; and that the crews be at least one-half English or colonial on ships traveling between points within the empire. It was mostly ignored. Note that this was passed during Cromwell's years, the last stage of the English Civil War, after the king had been executed. Mercantilism was not just a royal policy or idea; it was embraced by the merchant class and the political leaders.

Enumerated Commodities Act, 1660, required all colonial trade to be carried in English ships; it created a list of goods that had to be shipped to England or to another colony: tobacco, sugar, indigo, and rice, for example. From 1660 to 1685 the king's heavy tax on tobacco exceeded the Virginians' profits. The British reshipped these products and goods to the European continent, making money as the middlemen. England consumed only 4% of the tobacco and 20% of the rice exported from the colonies, the rest was reshipped. Over the years more crops and goods were added, and eventually one-half of all exports shipped out of the colonies appeared on the enumerated commodities list. A provision in this act also raised the percentage for the crew on ships engaged in trade to be at least 75% English, which included colonial Americans. This act's provisions were only partially obeyed.

Staple Act, 1663, required most European, Asian, and African goods (not slaves) to be shipped to England before being shipped to the colonies. Again, the English middleman profited. It was partially obeyed.

Plantation Duty Act of 1673 attempted to reduce smuggling, it required captains of colonial ships to post bond that they would deliver enumerated goods to England or pay the "plantation duty" that would be owed in England. It was mostly obeyed. (Plantation was a common word at that time for a colony.)

Navigation Act of 1696 created vice-admiralty courts in the colonies to enforce trade regulations and plugged loopholes in previous navigation laws. It was mostly obeyed.

Molasses Act, 1733, enacted a prohibitory high duty (tax) on sugar, molasses, rum, and spirits (liquor) imported by colonists from non-British colonies in the West Indies. This law tried to force the colonists to buy British goods, rather than French, Spanish, or Dutch goods. It was poorly enforced and widely disobeyed. Most of the molasses imported into the colonies came from the French or Dutch islands in the West Indies. The Dutch island of Saint Eustatius was a notorious "international bazaar where the produce of all nations was bought and sold." One visitor described it thusly, "There is here a swarm of men from all parts of the world only occupied in settling their affairs quickly to get away as soon as possible . . . ." (quoted in Thomas M. Doerflinger, *A Vigorous Spirit of Enterprise: Merchants and Economic Development in Revolutionary Philadelphia*, pp. 217-218.)

Total Exports, by value, from the colonies, in 1770

tobacco – 33%
bread and flour – 18.7%
fish – 13.8%
rice – 12.6%
furs and deerskins – 5.5%
wheat – 4.8%
indigo – 4.8%
naval stores – 3.5%
iron – 2.5%

The Economy of the Three Sections
New England

New England was a mixed economy, in part because of its rocky soil and small farms, which limited its agricultural production. Fishing was a major part of the economy, with the best sent to England, next quality to the Mediterranean countries, and the worst to the West Indies for slaves. The second leading export in the early years was timber. Rum become important, for example, in 1774 there were 60 distilleries in Massachusetts, which made 2,700,000 gallons of rum from West Indian molasses, a byproduct from refining sugar. Colonial shipbuilding, mostly done in New England, produced 1/3 of the 7,000 ships engaged in English commerce. New England provided 4,500 masts for ships, most of which came from white pine trees. New England also built most of the ships involved in the colonial trade, the trade from one colony to another. Americans controlled this trade; 75% of all inter-colonial trade was in American ships.

As an example of the importance of the various trade destinations, look at these statistics for the tonnage of goods leaving Boston in one year. Note the importance of the coastal trade:

1. coastal trade – 213,000 tons
2. to the West Indies (British colonies and foreign colonies) – 191,000 tons. For New England as a whole, 63% of their trade went to the West Indies.
3. to Great Britain and Ireland – 189,000 tons

Here is a list of the ships entering the port of Philadelphia in 1773:

From the West Indies – 252
From the coastal trade – 250
From the British Isles – 79
From Southern Europe – 73

Middle Colonies

The Middle colonies revolved around the two major shipping ports, New York City and Philadelphia. These colonies were nicknamed the "bread colonies." In the ten years from 1760 to 1770, wheat was 1/2 of all the exports from New York and Pennsylvania. Pennsylvania in 1765 exported 350,000 bushels of wheat and 18,000 tons of flour. This is 7.2 million modern 5 lb. bags of flour, or 19,726 5 lb. bags per week. That is a lot of flour. Grain shipments made up 72% of the exports, by value, from the Middle colonies, most of it shipped to the West Indies, providing food for slaves. In 1770 Pennsylvania, New York, and Connecticut shipped the following animals to the West Indies, to be consumed as meat: 6,000 horses; 3,000 oxen; 18,000 hogs and sheep. Philadelphia was the outlet for goods and produce from the Carolina and Virginia backcountry, which traveled up the Great Wagon Road through the Shenandoah Valley. The Middle colonies' shipbuilding industry produced 25-55 ships annually in the fifty years before the Revolution.

South

From the viewpoint of England, these were the most ideal colonies in the mercantile system, other than those in the West Indies. Jamaica's wealth per white person, for example, was nine times that of the wealthiest North American colony. The Southern colonies supplied products England could not produce for itself; 2/3 of all colonial exports were from Virginia, Maryland, South Carolina, and North Carolina. There were two "Souths" – the Chesapeake Bay South and the Lower South centered around Charleston. Be careful with terminology. While some large farms did exist, they were not yet really "plantations." They came later.

In the Chesapeake the chief crop was tobacco, introduced by John Rolfe, the first shipment arriving in England in 1617. But as production grew, prices declined, and declined even more as individual farmers grew more in response to falling prices. Tobacco proved to be so politically important that the U.S. government later subsidized it, not finally ending the subsidies until 2004. The second most valuable export was grain, corn and wheat. Surprisingly, pig iron was also a large export, by the 1730s, 2,200 tons per year to England.

About half of the early white settlers and black slaves along the coast from southern North Carolina to Georgia came from the West Indian island of Barbados. In South Carolina and Georgia the chief crop was rice, introduced in the 1690s. By 1770 rice ranked behind only sugar, tobacco, and wheat in value of New World colonial exports to Britain. Rice exports reached 165,000 barrels per year. By the 1740s 1,000,000 pounds of indigo, a dark blue dye, were being shipped to England each year. The British paid a bounty to indigo producers. Bounties also went to those who produced naval stores and products used in building ships, such as pitch, tar, turpentine, hemp, and masts. North Carolina's pine trees proved to be a great source of tar, pitch, and turpentine. Referred to as naval stores, tar and pitch sealed the planks in ships to stop leaks. For 150 years North Carolina led the world in the production of naval stores. It was greatly prized by British and colonial shipbuilders.

How Well Did the System Work in Actual Practice?

The greatest impact on the colonial economy was not the presence of British rules and regulations governing economic life; it was the presence of LAND, lots of land. As a Philadelphia gentleman wrote in 1768 – "Every great fortune made here within these 50 years has been by land." Almost every one of the Founding Fathers engaged in land speculation and promotion. For example, George Washington owned land in almost all thirteen colonies and also across the Appalachians.

In his old age Roger Williams observed to John Winthrop, Jr., the son of the Puritan governor who had exiled him to Rhode Island, "Sir, when we . . . are rotting, a generation will act, I fear, far unlike the first Winthrops and their Models of Love: I fear that the common Trinity of the world, (Profit, Preferment, Pleasure) will here be the Tria omnia, . . . that God Land will be as great a God with us English as God Gold was with the Spaniards . . . ." His prophecy was accurate. The long run trend of the economy was "that God Land" and expansion – in population, productivity, capital accumulation, opportunity, land acquisition, social mobility, and open-mindedness of economic thought. Economic historians estimate that between 1650 and 1770 the economy of the British North American colonies grew at an annual rate twice that of the mother country.

The availability of land caused wages to be 30-100% higher than in Europe. Some colonies had to pass maximum wage and minimum hour laws to get artisans (craftsmen) to work. A few days a week often provided an adequate income. William Penn called Pennsylvania "a good poor man's country," but it was not so in the cities. Historian Jackson Turner Main observed that throughout the colonial period in Connecticut, in "contrast with most pre-industrial societies virtually all of the married men and their families . . . did not simply escape poverty but enjoyed real plenty." (By our standards life may have been "Spoonbash." I created this word to remember the following quote). The English philosopher Thomas Hobbes, who lived through the English Civil War, wrote that life was "solitary, poor, nasty, brutish, and short." However, by the standards of seventeenth or eighteenth century England or Germany, a colonist's life was free and productive. One historian estimated that one-third of London's "almost Pennyless" population went to bed hungry each night. For many living in the British Isles, their choices were limited. Some British leaders thought the island nation was already over-populated, overrun with the poor. If something was not done, anarchy lurked on the horizon. The population had risen 40% between just 1580 and 1640; however, prosperity did not seem to accompany the population increase.

The Navigation Acts were to be enforced by the colonial governors, who proved to be uninterested, and by informers, who were encouraged to "rat" on their friends and acquaintances. Few did. Smuggling circumvented British regulations. The Caribbean Dutch island of St. Eustatius was a virtual international bazaar, with everything available. Shippers arrived and departed, quickly. In 1769 Massachusetts imported 500 hogsheads (a 63-gallon barrel) of molasses legally from the British West Indies and 14,500 barrels, 96.6% of all the molasses imported, illegally from the French West Indies. It was the main ingredient in making rum. Everywhere the Navigation Acts were inadequately and ineffectively enforced. In some respects Americans today live in a similar world. For example, today the unofficial number one cash crop in California and Virginia, and in many other states, is marijuana.

Over the long colonial period, countless changes took place. On the eve of the American Revolution, colonial trade became even more important to the British. By then America was importing 50% of England's glass exports, 80% of its linen exports, 76% of its nails, and 60% of its wrought iron. Great Britain had the *right* to control the trade of the colonies and trade went increasingly to Great Britain. Look at the following trade statistics:

1700-1710 colonial exports = £265,000
              colonial imports = £267,000
1760-1770 colonial exports = £1,000,000
              colonial imports = £1,760,000
1700 – 1/6 of all colonial trade went to Great Britain
1770 – 1/3 of all colonial trade went to Great Britain

The jump in imports from 1700 to 1770 was part of a trend in the colonial economy that historians label a "consumer revolution." The standard of living rose; British goods were in demand. However, the resulting imbalanced trade pushed the colonists toward an unfavorable view of their economic relationship with the mother country. The British regulations were increasingly seen as unfair. As a Swedish traveler observed in 1748, the long-term trend of Great Britain's economic policies was to cause the colonies "to grow less tender for their mother country."

Statistics

Observations aside, was the economic system unfair? Here are the 1798 statistics one historian gives to compare the **percentage of wealth** owned by the top proportion of adult males for several countries or areas:

	Top 1%	Top 10%
United States	13%	45%
Scotland	24%	64%
Denmark	43%	80%
Sweden	31%	65%
Norway	33%	65%
Finland	19%	46%

Here are the 1798 statistics giving the **percentage of adult males owing land** for these countries or areas:

United States	49%
Scotland	22%
Denmark	24%
Sweden	29%
Norway	38%
Finland	23%

Land ownership was much more widespread in colonial America and in the new nation, which made wealth less concentrated at the top. One historian estimated that British regulation of the colonial economy cost the colonies between two and seven million dollars per year. But, crop bounties, such as indigo, and protection given to colonial ships by the British navy must also be part of calculating the burden or benefit. In the end, he concluded that the actual cost was about 54 cents per year per person, at a time when the average person probably made $100 or less a year. Now one can render a judgment – oppressive or not? I vote for not. Another historian called the trade system "the cement of empire."

If one argues that equality was not the main characteristic of the colonial American economy, one must state that, comparatively speaking, opportunity certainly was, at least to the American people of that time. And, many contemporaries argued that equality was a primary characteristic of American society. The clearest early statement answering the question, "What is an American?" was provided by Hector St. Jean de Crèvecoeur in his *Letters from an American Farmer*. Crèvecoeur, a French aristocrat, emigrated to New York in 1759, settling down as a successful farmer. Published in 1782 in London, *Letters from an American Farmer* was the first attempt by a European to explain the new **American Identity**. He wrote that "The rich and the poor are not so far removed from each other as they are in Europe." "Here man is free as he ought to be; nor is this pleasing equality so transitory as many others are." He added that a yet to be written American dictionary would be "short in words of dignity and names of honor." Colonial America was a great place; America still is. There are good reasons why many called, and still call, America the "land of opportunity."

6

COLONIAL POLITICS

Americans were British citizens, very British, with deep roots in British history, British traditions, and British institutions. A visitor today to reconstructed colonial Williamsburg will find children's games about British royalty. Kids memorized lists of kings, etc., just as American kids today memorize state capitals and presidents.

During the years from 1607 to 1776, British history evolved politically. Events in British history had a major impact on the colonists and on their thinking. They were keenly aware of the mother country and its past glory.

Events in British History
The reign of Henry VIII left a confusing legacy. His rule from 1509-1547 united the claims to the throne of the House of Lancaster and the House of York, ending a division dating from the civil strife and dynastic disputes of the War of the Roses, 1455-1485. Henry VIII had numerous wives and three children, greatly complicating succession to the throne. Here are his wives. Do not memorize them, just look at the confusion. The years given are when they were married to Henry VIII.

1. Catherine of Aragon, 1509-1533 (second marriage for her, widow of Henry's brother, Arthur, mother of Mary I, this marriage was annulled)
2. Anne Boleyn, 1533-1536 (mother of Elizabeth I, beheaded)
3. Jane Seymour, 1536-1537 (died after giving birth to Edward VI)
4. Anne of Cleves, 1540-1540 (married six months, marriage annulled)
5. Catherine Howard, 1540-1542 (beheaded)
6. Catherine Parr, 1543-1547 (died in 1548, outlived Henry)

Henry VIII's offspring ruled as follows:

> Edward VI, 1547-1553, sickly, died at 16
> Mary I, 1553-1558, died at 42
> Elizabeth I, 1558-1603, the Virgin Queen, she never married

Virginia was named in honor of Elizabeth I, the Virgin Queen, the illegitimate daughter, as some considered her, of Henry VIII. Fears of Catholic plots, both from Catholics in England and from Catholic countries, dominated her reign. An example of the first was the machinations of the supporters of her half-sister, Mary I, a Catholic, responsible for executing approximately 280 prominent Protestants during her brief reign. The best example of the second was the attempted invasion of England by the Spanish Armada in 1588. Fears of Catholic Spain attacking their little settlement caused the English to locate Jamestown up river, in an unhealthy area. Because Elizabeth never married and bore no children, succession was a major issue throughout her reign. Who would follow? The answer was the King of Scotland, James VI, who was a great-great grandson of Henry VII.

When he became king, James took the title James I, and ruled from 1603-1625. He called himself James I of Great Britain, but it would not officially become Great Britain until 1707. Britain is the geographic name of the island upon which England, Wales, and Scotland are located. Great Britain is the political name of the union of the three kingdoms, England, Wales, and Scotland. James was the son of Mary, Queen of Scots, and was Elizabeth's first cousin, twice removed. His wife was a Protestant, Anne of Denmark, indicating that the chance of a Catholic once again on the English throne was slim. The reign of James I is famous in English literature. Shakespeare wrote during these years, inserting many favorable comments in his plays about the kings of Scotland. *Macbeth*, for example, opens with praise for the kings of Scotland.

The other great lasting literary achievement was a new translation of the Bible, the richly worded King James Version. James ordered a new translation because previous translations did not sufficiently emphasize the need to obey those in authority, meaning him. He did not have religious motives. He wanted to impress his subjects with the idea of the "divine right of kings," a king's authority comes from God. Members of Parliament read the new Bible, but they did not absorb his new emphasis. During James' reign festering issues troubled the king, Parliament, and everyone else in a position of influence. Puritans felt the Church of England still had too many Catholic-like practices. The major foreign policy questions concerned Spain and France – ally or foe? Tax issues vexed the country. Who is more in charge – the legislature or the executive? What was the role of the king and Parliament in determining taxes? Was Parliament's approval necessary for new taxes? If this sounds familiar, it should. Our ancestors heard similar arguments before the American Revolution.

When James died his son, Charles I, ruled from 1625 to 1649. He was married to Henriette Marie of France, a Catholic. The same issues that troubled his father's reign continued. Charles was much feistier than James and more stubborn. In 1629 he dismissed Parliament and used old feudalistic-based taxes to run a barebones government. In other words, he did almost nothing, because of limited funds. Moreover, the head of the Church of England, Archbishop Laud, tightened up on the Puritans, causing many of them to leave for America during the 1630s. For instance, Anne Hutchinson's family came to Massachusetts during this time, along with many others.

The Puritans left England with a "City Upon a Hill" concept as their sense of mission. The Church of England was incapable of correction, thus Massachusetts had to be an example to Britain. This explains the seriousness of the Puritan leaders in dealing with Anne Hutchinson, Roger Williams, and Quakers; they were not just establishing a colony, they were setting an example to reform and save Great Britain – thus, no room for mistakes. It is one thing to save one's soul, it is quite another to save a whole nation.

Charles' peace and quiet fell apart when the Scots invaded northern England in 1642. He reconvened Parliament to obtain money to fight the Scots. However, Parliament's leaders raised other issues, especially taxation and the persecution of Puritans. All this pent-up anger and frustration led to a civil war. The Puritan army captured Charles in 1649 and beheaded him. Parliament took over.

The period of Parliament's rule is called The Commonwealth; it lasted from 1649-1660. Within a short time the Puritan government became unrepresentative and dictatorial under the Long Parliament (no new elections, therefore, a rump Parliament). Oliver Cromwell, the head of the Puritan army, took over as Lord Protector, a military dictator. This usually happens in history. The head of the winning army in a civil war assumes power. This is why George Washington is so incredible. He went home to Mount Vernon. When Oliver Cromwell died in 1658, his son Richard took over, and did what everyone agreed was a lousy job, paving the way for the return of the monarchy.

All throughout the Puritan Commonwealth years there was a great deal of plotting to re-establish the monarchy. One mastermind behind it was Admiral William Penn, who seized Jamaica from Spain in 1655, and was the father of Pennsylvania's founder, William Penn. Without the father's role in returning Charles II to the throne, the Quakers would never have gotten Pennsylvania. History works sometimes in strange ways.

Charles II returned from France in 1660, invited by Parliament. Imagine taking a position that got your father's head chopped off. He ruled from 1660-1685 and married Catherine of Portugal, a Catholic. Charles was an Anglican, a member of the Church of England, but for many Puritan-leaning Englishmen there was still too much pro-Catholic presence in the monarchy and in the Church of England. On his deathbed

Charles II received the last rites from a Catholic priest. A closet Catholic! Puritans were horrified. His brother took over as king.

James II, 1685-1688, had been married to Anne Hyde, a Protestant, who was the mother of his two daughters, Mary and Anne. His second wife, Maria of Modena, a small country in Italy, convinced James to convert to Catholicism. Then Maria had a son, who immediately became, as a male, the next in line for the throne. Maria whisked the baby off to France to raise him, where, surrounded by Catholics, he would surely be raised as a Catholic. In subsequent British history he became James, the Old Pretender.

The Glorious Revolution

Parliament would not tolerate an endless succession of Catholic monarchs on the throne of Protestant England. Therefore, Parliament kicked James II out in the Glorious Revolution in 1688. It was called "glorious" because there was virtually no bloodshed. Then Parliament invited James' older daughter, Mary, to become the queen. She wanted to bring along her husband, William of Orange, a province in modern Netherlands. They became joint rulers in 1689. William & Mary ruled jointly until Mary died in 1694. William was the king until 1702. His motto was *Non rapui sed recepi*, which means, "I didn't steal; I received." William had an English heritage. He was a grandson of Charles I. His father, William II of Orange, married one of the children of Charles I, thus William and Mary were first cousins.

Meanwhile the Glorious Revolution continued. Parliament quickly proceeded to pass laws to ensure the future power of Parliament. It resolved many festering issues.

1. The 1689 Mutiny Act provided for annual military budgets, which gave control of the military budget to Parliament. Control of the funds meant control of the military.
2. The 1689 Act of Settlement made it clear who would be next in line for the British throne. No Catholics! Ever! Even today only a member of the Church of England may be king or queen. Other Protestants are also out.
3. Judges hold office for life, which means that kings could not pack the courts with their appointees.
4. A Bill of Rights.
5. The Act of Toleration meant that all religions were to be tolerated. During the English Civil War there was much discussion and debate within the Puritan army about religion. Ultimately, the idea grew that toleration was a good thing, shocking the Puritans in America.

The right to bear arms in the Bill of Rights grew out of England's religious squabbles. During his brief reign, James II made it clear he intended use his army of professional soldiers to bully the Protestants. Thus, one consequence of the Glorious Revolution was the English Bill of Rights, which banned standing armies and guaranteed the right to bear arms. It was intended to protect the right to worship, not to protect property, as many today assume about our Bill of Rights. It was not intended as a blanket right to carry a concealed weapon or to own guns.

The Glorious Revolution sent shock waves throughout the colonies. What did the future hold? Up to the early 1670s the colonies had, in essence, governed themselves, with little oversight from England, often openly defying British authorities. Charles II established the Lords of Trade in 1675 to oversee colonial affairs and to gain control. A few years later James II formed the Dominion of New England, which included New Jersey, New York, and New England, ruled by Sir Edmund Andros. His harsh rule in unruly Puritan New England alienated and antagonized the colonists, who rose up to depose him when news of the Glorious Revolution arrived. All enemies of freedom must go! But Parliament did not see the New England colonists' actions in the same light. Similar anti-government uprisings in Maryland and in New York, known there as Leisler's Rebellion, led the British to increase their presence and control over the colonies.

Parliament's ouster of James II brought new thinking in both England and in the colonies. The idea grew that the legislature, Parliament, was the highest body politically, above the king, the executive. Changes continued. After 1707 the king could no longer veto legislation passed by Parliament; however, in the colonies governors still could.

Since William & Mary were childless, Mary's sister Anne became the queen upon the death of William, ruling from 1702-1714. She married George of Denmark. Anne had fourteen children, but not one of them survived to the age of six. If there are no heirs, the royal family ends. Now Parliament searched the family genealogy charts to find the next king. The selection was a great-grandson of James I, a grandson of Elizabeth, the sister of Charles I. He ruled as George I from 1714-1727. Parliament ran England because George I, a German from Hanover, never learned to speak English. His son, George II, 1727-1760, preferred to spend his time at the royal zoo teasing the bears with a long stick. Meanwhile, Parliament continued to run England. The Prime Minister during the years 1721-1742, Robert Walpole, followed a policy of leaving the colonies alone, "a wise and salutary neglect."

George II's wife urged her grandson, George III, 1760-1820, to "be a king." Thus, he began asserting his powers in the 1760s. Many in Parliament saw George III as going beyond his role. He spent the last years of his long reign in a padded room; he was mentally unbalanced. And, therefore, not able to "be a king." So, guess who ran England – Parliament.

Consequences

What were the consequences of these events in British history for the colonists? And, also, for England? Attacks on the king became a model for the colonists. The Declaration of Independence repeatedly used the language, "He has." It was an attack on the royal prerogative, which Parliament had been undermining for years. Initially the legislature was not seen as the source of the colonists' problems. It was the king. It was difficult for the colonists to attack a legislative body as not having the power to legislate.

Over time there developed an acceptance of the idea of legitimate opposition to the government. In Great Britain the cliques gathering around various politicians led to the development of nascent political parties, the Whigs and the Tories. Legitimate opposition meant that government policies could be criticized because such criticism was directed at people, programs, policies, and ideas, not at the nation itself, AND, therefore, was neither disloyalty nor treason.

It is easy to see the rise to power of the legislature, Parliament. Colonists saw their colonial legislatures as miniature Parliaments. Americans adopted the ideas and arguments involved in the debates in Parliament over the relative powers of the legislature and the executive, and, in the justifications given for the primacy of the legislature and of Parliament's actions. John Locke's *Second Treatise on Government* justified the Glorious Revolution. This great political theorist's ideas reappeared in the Declaration of Independence. However, in the colonies there was no king, no opposition for the colonists to confront. It is easy to win arguments when one's opponent is not present. The colonists were emotionally and philosophically involved in political arguments they did not participate in – yet they felt they did. In addition, they felt the outcomes applied to them also.

An Empire?

The British Empire was not a tightly organized empire. The responsibilities of the various departments of the British government overlapped. There was too much organization for detail, too little for consistency. It was easy for issues to slip through the non-system. Each of the following had some responsibility for some part of the Empire: King, Parliament, Board of Trade, Secretary of State, Privy Council, and Navy. Historians have described the British Empire as "India, Navy, Colonies," in that order. The needs of India were paramount, the navy second, and the other colonies last. The tea tax issue is a good example. The Tea Tax was done for the benefit of the East India Company; but it became a major issue in colonial America. Many British politicians seemed to care little about any of the colonies. One historian researching votes in Parliament on an important bill about India noticed that few even attended to vote. Looking at the next vote, immediately following, was a shock. Parliament was filled; every member was there. What was the issue? They were voting to select a dogcatcher for the city of London. In defense of their interest, understand that a dogcatcher needs assistants, plums for jobs for a politician's supporters.

The colonies and the empire were just not that important. We today have several different legal statuses for our territories – Puerto Rico, Guam, Midway Island, Wake Island, American Samoa, and the Virgin Islands. How important do their needs seem to be to our Congress? Over the long colonial period the ignored colonists grew to believe the near absence of government was a fundamental right. A Lutheran minister, Gottlieb Mittelberger, who lived in Pennsylvania from 1750-1754 before returning to Europe, declared America to be a "hell for officials and preachers."

Rise of the Lower House

The years from 1607 to 1776 represent a long period. Over these years colonial institutions changed slowly, evolving in ways that even the colonists did not readily perceive. By 1763 it became obvious how wide the gap had become. The primary political change was the rise of the colonial lower house. In a two-house colonial legislature the upper house was usually called the council. The example of the lower house of Parliament, the House of Commons, leading the fight against the English kings and the House of Lords, inspired or caused or guided, pick a word, the colonial lower houses to claim many of the same rights against the colonial governors and councils. The upper house, or council, was frequently composed of the governor's cronies and aligned with the governor.

Unlike the British kings, some of whom had ability, most colonial governors were Americans or fourth-rate British politicians. A British politician sought a position first in the beehive center of political activity, London. Next was anywhere in the British Isles; third was India, the jewel of the empire and the chance to become rich; fourth, the Caribbean, also offering a chance at wealth, but more hazardous to one's health. Last of all was a position in America, with few opportunities to line one's pockets with money and a wife constantly complaining that your career is going nowhere.

Colonial governors received little attention or support from London. The term "salutary neglect" could be shortened to just "neglect." Over time the governors lost more and more power. One governor complained that "Arguing with Assemblys is like philophising with a mule" The lower house asserted control over the governor's salary, threatening to reduce it to the rock-bottom, yet legal, amount of $1 per year. Appreciation for the effectiveness of this tactic led the Founding Fathers to put a clause in the Constitution that Congress cannot lower a president's salary during his term. Any change applies to after the next election. The lower houses also asserted control over taxation, claiming the governor's approval was unnecessary. They asserted their right to select their own speakers and to set their own rules, thus removing agenda-setting from the executive. Over time the lower houses of the colonial legislatures simply assumed the power to govern, with little supervision from Great Britain. New Hampshire passed 8,500 laws between 1702 and the 1750s. Every colonial law was supposed to be reviewed by the British authorities. About 5½% of New Hampshire's laws were disallowed. New Hampshire continued to enforce them. There was little British oversight over the colonies.

By the 1760s the lower house in each colony was a political force, serving as a forum for political statements and a training ground for those who would lead the protests against British policies. That training enabled them both to write constitutions and to assume positions of power in the future state and national governments.

Mixed Government

Colonial governments developed from the British concept of "mixed government," what the British considered the ideal government. The British "mixed government" consisted of three parts:

> democracy – the part ruled by the people, the House of Commons
> aristocracy – the part ruled by the titled nobility, the House of Lords
> monarchy – the part ruled by the monarch, the king

As the colonists applied this thinking while they created and shaped the colonial governments, they saw their colonial legislatures playing the same role as the House of Commons. In essence, the other two parts were missing. There were only a few nobles in America, and no king. The governors were just representatives of the king, who could be opposed, subverted, or hindered without any member of the colonial assemblies believing they were undermining the "mixed government" concept. However, they were.

From the first settlements the British "mixed government" tradition was changing, being changed by American practices. This change shows in the debates over representation in Parliament that took place during the 1760s over "no taxation without representation." The British practiced virtual representation, meaning that every member of the legislature represented every British citizen everywhere. This is why the British could not understand American cries of "no representation." However, over the long colonial period the colonists developed a tradition of direct representation, meaning that a member of the colonial legislature was supposed to vote the way his constituents wanted him to vote. In actuality, if the colonists had been represented in Parliament, they would have been outvoted on every law they protested against prior to the Revolution, by huge majorities.

Local Government – South

In the South colonial local government was based on the county. The same few people performed the executive, legislative, judicial, and administrative functions, all the time. The local elite constituted an oligarchy, rule by the few. The same elite ran the local militia, served on the vestry, the governing board of the local Anglican Church, and held positions as justices of the peace. If the governor, who theoretically held appointive power, did not endorse their suggested replacements for any local office, the whole colonial legislature simply refused to approve the governor's appointees, thus granting the local elite a veto over appointments.

This is similar to today's "senatorial courtesy" in the Senate. Appointments to federal positions within a state must have the approval of the senior senator from that state, otherwise, the entire Senate votes against the appointee, robbing the president of his power to appoint. This has the effect of increasing the influence of senators within their party in their state.

The colonial local elite in the South ran the county government, controlled the elections, served in the colonial assembly, and was virtually self-perpetuating. A person was either born into this elite or married into it. Those who rose in status or wealth could be accepted, but neither attribute guaranteed acceptance. Acceptance could take several generations, stretching over a long period.

Local Government – New England

In New England the town meeting was the local government. It is praised in history books and by modern locals. However, it does not deserve the amount of praise heaped on it. In truth, there was a great deal of polite oligarchic control and much apathy, especially in the smaller towns. In many respects the town meetings were about as exciting as a modern Parent Teacher Association or Parent Teacher Student Association, PTA or PTSA meeting. The town meeting could even be independent of some colonial control. Connecticut, for example, imposed no colony-wide taxes on a town unless that town sent a representative to the colonial assembly. Other laws applied. The early development of the concept of "no taxation without representation" was a unique American idea.

The town meeting appointed many unpaid minor officials, leading to a high degree of participation compared to other types of local government. Many New Englanders felt they were part of the local government and that their voice counted. For example, in 1720 in Ipswich, Massachusetts, there were 97 town officials, including fence-viewer and hog-catcher, in Boston, 141. The first kept an eye on everyone's fences to make certain they were secure; the second chased troublesome hogs. Not exciting jobs, but necessary in an agricultural community. If an animal broke into a farmer's field, the fence-viewer was called to testify in a subsequent lawsuit. A fence in good repair placed the blame on the owner of the animal. Otherwise, the farmer who owned the field was at fault for negligence.

How Democratic was Colonial America?

This topic has been endlessly debated by historians. Does the historian mean politically, economically, socially, or religiously? The word "democracy" itself is a problem. To us democracy implies the following: political equality, universal suffrage, majority rule, protection of minority rights, consent of the governed, and the opportunity to rise in social rank or to better yourself economically. Most of these characteristics were missing in colonial America. The glue that held the colonial political system together was **deference**, the idea that a voter selected one of his betters to represent him in public offices. The voter was expected to trust and to obey his leaders; there was no sense of direct responsibility to the electorate. After casting a vote, the voter was obligated to obey, quietly.

In a 1645 speech John Winthrop (1588-1649) explained the relationship between elected officials and the voters. He was the first governor of Puritan Massachusetts, serving for 12 years as the governor (one-year terms), and was the deputy governor all the other years until his death. He explained to the people that "we have our authority from God." When voters select leaders, they "take them (the elected leaders) from among yourselves, men subject to passions as you are." "The covenant between you and us is the oath you have taken of us, which is to this purpose, that we shall govern you and judge your causes by the rules of God's laws and our own, according to our best skill. When you agree with a workman to build you a ship or house, etc., he undertakes as well for his skill as for his faithfulness, for it is his profession, and you pay him for both. But when you call one to be a magistrate, he doth not profess nor undertake to have sufficient skill for that office, nor can you furnish him with gifts, etc., therefore you must run the hazard of his skill and ability." "If he fails in faithfulness, he violates his oath, and he must answer for it. But if he fails in ability, you have no alternative but to obey." In short, it must be clear that the elected leader has violated his oath to faithfully carry out his duties; if his shortcomings are due to a lack of ability in carrying out his duties, the voters must remain quiet until the next election.

Mechanics of the Political System

The mechanics of the political system, how people cast their votes, would not today be considered democratic. Voting was done orally, in front of the election officers. Anyone nearby could hear how a person voted. There was usually one polling place per county, necessitating a long trip to vote. Candidates were expected to treat the voters. During one of George Washington's campaigns for the Virginia House of Burgesses he treated voters to drinks, serving 28 gallons of rum, 50 gallons of rum punch, 38 gallons of wine, 46 gallons of beer, and 2 gallons of hard cider, for a total of 164 gallons of alcohol. There were 396 voters. Washington won. And, those who voted for him were likely inebriated.

The town meetings appear to historians to have functioned more as a mechanism to enforce consensus, a means to maintain social harmony in the community rather than as a forum for debate. New England town meetings could, and did, "warn out" troublemakers. Behave, or leave! Major decisions seem to have been made before the actual town meeting, which then ratified the decision. Lyndon Johnson once said, in his role as Senate Majority Leader, that one should never bring anything up for a vote unless you know the outcome ahead of time. Town meetings seem to have operated the same way. The records rarely record a contentious vote on any issue. The town meeting ratified a previously forged consensus. So, was the town meeting democratic? One historian claimed that consensus was a natural characteristic of the towns. "The schools, the church, and custom conditioned the town to think, to frown, to vote, and to reelect as its leaders directed." "Voting was connected to the concept of community, not the concept of democracy." Remember, 95% of the population farmed. Thus, there were few divisive issues in this agricultural-based society. The two dominating topics for any conversation were probably the weather and prices of crops, just as they are today in farming communities.

In defense of the New England local political system, a study of Kent, Connecticut, over a long period found two characteristics: the ability to raise one's voice as a voter and the right to participate in local government. If these two traits are considered the key features of democracy, then colonial Connecticut was democratic. Historian Robert Zemsky called Connecticut "a society of near equals." In England at this time only 200,000 property owners could vote, out of the population of five million. Widespread land ownership in colonial America accidentally created a large number of people who fulfilled the suffrage requirement. Historians argue over the percentage of adult white males allowed to vote, placing it somewhere between 50% and 80%. Exactness does not matter. It was the highest percentage anywhere in the world. Even by the late nineteenth century only France and Switzerland had universal male suffrage, long after the United States. English laws and traditions proved to be permissive rather than restrictive, which was their purpose in England. And, before we declare the colonial political system undemocratic, look at the quality of the leaders the colonial political system brought to the surface – Thomas Jefferson, George Washington, Patrick Henry, James Madison, Sam Adams, John Adams, Ben Franklin, John Dickinson – all of whom received their political training in colonial assemblies.

As another example, historians look at the 1735 trial of John Peter Zenger for seditious libel and smile. Of course one can criticize government officials. However, at that time freedom of speech was a right for only members of Parliament, not ordinary citizens. As the American Revolution neared, freedom of speech became a de facto right for the ordinary American, much to the astonishment of British officials. Unlike the Spanish colonies, the British never restricted printing. Thus, information, including criticism of British officials, flowed freely throughout the thirteen colonies. If the political system was undemocratic in many features we hold dear today, it functioned very democratically for the Americans who lived in the colonial years.

7

RELIGION IN THE COLONIAL ERA

Variety

Both historians and students of history should be careful making general statements about the colonial era. There are 169 years from 1607 to 1776. Adding 169 years to 1776 equals 1945. Certainly one would be cautious about making a general statement for this later era such as, "In these years cars, airplanes, and atomic bombs were invented." True, but not true for the whole period. While things changed more slowly between 1607 and 1776, one should still be careful about general statements designed to cover the whole period. Nevertheless, some generalities can be made, just be careful.

The colonial era was characterized by the slow evolution away from British traditions and control and the slow creation of an **American Identity** and nationalism, so subtle that it was virtually unnoticed. Remember, the American colonies were the world's first colonies in modern history to rebel and break away. Before 1775 such an act was beyond comprehension, on both sides of the Atlantic. (I am not considering the earlier Dutch revolt against Spanish control as a colonial rebellion.)

Historians cannot know how many people attended church services during the colonial period. However, we do know how many church buildings existed. A historian counted them using old maps. There were 3142 church buildings in 1775. Another historian, Clinton Rossiter, included the list in his book, *The First American Revolution*.

668 Congregational (Puritans)	21% (7 in the Middle colonies, 4 in the South, 98% in New England)
588 Presbyterian	(two thirds in the Middle colonies)
495 Anglican	(over half in the South, Virginia the leader)

494 Baptist

310 Quaker meeting houses   9.8% (Pennsylvania mostly)

159 German Reformed

150 Lutheran   (none in New England, 16 in the
                                 South, over half in Pennsylvania)

120 Dutch Reformed   (none in New England or the South)

65 Methodist

56 Catholic   1.78% (none in New England, none
                                 in the South, except for Maryland)

31 Moravian

27 Congregational Separatist

24 Dunker

16 Mennonite

7 Huguenot   (French Protestants)

6 Sandemanian   (A sect that split off from the
                                 Presbyterian Church of Scotland,
                                 many of whom moved to America.
                                 It gradually declined.)

5 Jewish Synagogues   (1/6 of 1%)

3 Rogerene   (A sect in Connecticut, influenced in
                                 doctrine and practices by Quakers,
                                 Puritans, and Baptists. What a
                                 mixture!)

Overwhelmingly Protestant, 98%

Catholic historians refer to the colonial period as the "Penal Period," because at one time or another every colony except Rhode Island had anti-Catholic legislation restricting voting, office holding, or land ownership. In all colonial America there were only 56 Catholic churches and 5 Jewish synagogues out of 3142 houses of worship.

The one colony established by and for Catholics was Maryland, named for the Catholic wife of Charles I, Henriette Maria. Modern Marylanders should be pleased it was not called Henrietteland. The proprietors were incredibly tolerant for that time. Even Indians had equal rights under the law. In 1642 and in 1647 the first black and the first woman, respectively, cast a vote in the Maryland colonial legislature, Mathias de Sousa and Margaret Brent, a single woman who was a large landowner. The governor, Leonard Calvert, appointed both to handle his private affairs in his absence and to vote on behalf of the proprietary family.

There is the possibility that Maryland's toleration was more than a pragmatic policy. Sir Thomas More's *Utopia*, 1516, gave as one characteristic of a perfect society a place where "every man might be of what religion he pleased." Note that this predated the beginning of the Reformation. One of the chief advisors to the Calvert family that founded Maryland was Father Henry More, a Jesuit priest and the great-grandson of Sir Thomas More. The devastation of the European Thirty Years' War, 1618-1648, also made toleration much more attractive. Religion was both a major cause and factor in that destructive war. American colonists hoped to avoid such a catastrophe.

Maryland's crowning religious achievement was the Maryland Toleration Act of 1649. It fined anyone who uttered any reproachful words concerning the Virgin Mary, the Holy Apostles, the Evangelists, and anyone who made offensive remarks about any other Christian religion. It specifically stated that no person would be in any way troubled in the free exercise of his religion as long as he believed in the Trinity. Jews and atheists were not tolerated. The Calvert family wanted to attract Protestant settlers as well as Catholics. The purpose of the Toleration Act was to reassure Protestants. However, reflecting the turmoil of the English Civil War, Protestants gained control of the colonial assembly in 1654 and repealed the Act of Toleration. Later, in 1702, the Maryland colonial assembly made the Church of England the official church. Included in this packet of legislation was a law extending religious freedom to all except Catholics and Jews. Two years later the sheriff, directed to do so by the governor, padlocked the door of the Catholic Church building in St. Mary's City, which had been the colony's capital up to 1694. Today Catholics make up almost 25% of America's population, which will probably increase in the future due to immigration from Mexico and Central and South America. The United States has the fourth largest population of Catholics in the world. The leaders ahead of us are Brazil, Mexico, and the Philippines.

Up until the 1890s the chief justice of the New Jersey Supreme Court was not only a Protestant, but he was always a Presbyterian. Religious toleration grew slowly in America. By the late twentieth century it was secure. In the early 1990s a momentous event took place. Supreme Court Justice Clarence Thomas returned to his former religion, Catholicism, leaving the Episcopal Church, and for the first time in American history the U.S. Supreme Court was not Protestant dominated. No one seemed to notice, or care. Most colonial period Americans would have been shocked.

Look carefully at the list of church buildings for 1775. The largest denomination had only 21% of them. No particular religion dominated. In addition, even within denominations there were doctrinal controversies, caused by the Great Awakening that began in the 1730s and 1740s. The Presbyterians had the New Sides versus the Old Sides, and the Congregationalists had the New Lights versus the Old Lights. All denominations experienced many internal disputes, in addition to fighting against one another. There was no real unity among the Protestant churches. Their only common characteristic, what defined them as Protestants, was their common rejection of the Catholic Church and its doctrines.

Catholics were not only rejected, they were a source of concern and even fear. This fear or suspicion of Catholicism reappears throughout the colonial period, in the wars against Spain or France and the French colony of Canada, and the fear of the SPG, the Society for the Propagation of the Gospel, the missionary arm of the Church of England, which to all American Protestants, except Anglicans, was virtually the same as the Catholic Church.

Some colonial founders tried toleration. The founders of the Carolinas were incredibly tolerant. The Fundamental Constitutions of the Carolinas in 1663 offered freedom of worship to all who believed in the deity, including Jews, heathens, and other dissenters from the purity of Christian religion as well as the "natives of that place . . . whose idolatry, ignorance, or mistake gives us no right to expel them." Still, the Church of England was the official church in the Carolinas because it was "the only true and orthodox and national religion of all the king's dominions."

Union of Church and State

Nine of the thirteen colonies had established, or state-controlled, churches — churches a person paid taxes to, unless he could prove he attended another church at least 26 times a year. In many European countries today, such as 24 of Switzerland's 26 cantons (like our state governments), the government still collects taxes for the official national church. In Germany the government deducts 9% of your paycheck for the Lutheran Church, if you officially belong to it. Think about it, many ministers here are completely dependent on their congregations for their income. Therefore, how often would they challenge their congregation on a touchy subject, even if their congregation needed to be challenged?

The Anglican Church, the Church of England, was the official church in Virginia, Maryland, North Carolina, South Carolina, Georgia, and New York. (During the Revolutionary War era Americans changed the name of their branch to Protestant Episcopal, now known as the Episcopal Church. It would have been awkward to continue the name, Church of England.) Virginia passed a law in 1611 that required colonists to "prepare themselves at home with private prayer, that they may be better fitted for the publique, according to the commandments of God, and the Order of our Church." In the New England colonies of Massachusetts, Connecticut, and New Hampshire, the Congregational Church was the official church and the town meeting taxed everyone to pay its ministers.

Pennsylvania, Delaware, New Jersey, and Rhode Island did not have an official church. In reality the Quakers ran everything in Pennsylvania. Historian Gary Nash's research on colonial Pennsylvania found that Quakers filled virtually every political office. In many respects, Delaware existed in the colonial era as an addendum to Pennsylvania. A historian doing modern research in the colonial archives in London will discover separate files for all the British colonies, except Delaware. The British government unofficially considered Delaware part of Pennsylvania. New Jersey suffered from one characteristic throughout the entire colonial era; it was unorganized. The two halves, northern and southern, called East Jersey and West Jersey, were really dominated by New York City and Philadelphia, just as they still are. For example, there are no commercial television stations in modern New Jersey. Everyone watches either New York City or Philadelphia stations.

The authorities in Massachusetts kicked out two critics to maintain their unified religion-based community, Anne Hutchinson and Roger Williams. Anne Hutchinson questioned a central tenet of Puritanism by arguing that grace could not be earned. Luther raised this question early in the Reformation, the question of good works versus faith. It was the central point of dispute in Luther's attack on indulgences. Are Christians identifiable by their good works? Consider the biblical story of Job and place that beside a comment sometimes heard today, "I have been blessed." Does that mean that those who suffer have not? Have they been cursed? Does God give someone cancer because he is displeased with them? Does God give someone wealth because he is pleased with them? Can good works earn entrance into heaven? Are good works evidence of God's approval? Luther said no; the Puritans said yes. How else could saints and sinners be identified?

Puritanism was a community of saints, a "City upon a Hill," as John Winthrop phrased it, a community of people visibly living the Christian life communally. God's church on earth, the visible church, should approximate God's church in Heaven, the invisible church. God required his people to live by a covenant, a legal-like agreement. If a Puritan followed God's laws, if he lived the visible Christian life, it was proof that he was one of the saints, a sincere Christian. Therefore, Puritanism demanded that the community keep watch and enforce the community's moral laws. Appointed "tithingmen" watched over 10 to 12 families to resolve points of family contention before they festered. Your soul and community harmony were more important than your privacy. Living alone was prohibited.

Then along came Anne Hutchinson – claiming that God's grace was granted by Christ's sacrifice, that grace could not be earned. It flowed from God's bountiful love, a love so complete that it was beyond human comprehension. Grace came to all who would open their hearts and receive it. If grace came to everyone, if all are saved by God's love, where in this theology is a role to be played by the community's leaders, those busybodies who watch for sins to surface? Anne Hutchinson challenged both church doctrine and the community's definition of a woman's role. She was both excommunicated from the church and politically expelled from the community. She was a dangerous Antinomian, or one who opposed legal requirements to be saved. Governor John Winthrop called her "a naughty lady."

Roger Williams wanted to establish the separation of church and state in order to maintain the purity of the church. Normally today such disputes are the reverse, to maintain the purity of the state, such as the dispute in Alabama over the judge displaying the Ten Commandments in his courtroom. Roger Williams' other weird ideas also offended many Puritans. He stated that the Puritan Church in Massachusetts was impure, that it had defrauded the Indians of their rightful title to the land, and that its laws were cruel and in contradiction to its communicants' stated purpose for coming to the New World. The Puritan fathers kicked Williams out. He threatened the cohesiveness of the community. As the Puritan minister, Cotton Mather, later wrote, Williams reminded him of an old Dutch folk tale about how a violent wind had overheated a windmill, first setting the millstone on fire, then the windmill, then the whole village. "There was a whole country in America like to be set on fire by the rapid motion of a windmill in the head of one particular man." Roger Williams was that windmill. He left for Rhode Island, where he separated church and state and practiced toleration.

Eventually Americans developed the theory of the separation of church and state, primarily because they could never agree on which church or which doctrine should be the official one. It was not theories of personal liberty that led to religious freedom, but the impossibility of naming an official church. Americans are seen around the world today as a religious people, yet our country lacks an official church or religion closely identified with our government or people. Over fifty percent of Americans claim they attend church regularly, defined as at least once a month. Only South Africa is higher. Some of the numbers elsewhere: Spain, 28%; Great Britain, 15%; France, 9%; and Denmark, 5%.

Among the Founding Fathers, Thomas Jefferson led the way in separating church and state. The Virginia Statute for Religious Freedom in 1786, proposed by Jefferson earlier, ended official support for the Anglican Church in Virginia. A similar clause was in the Northwest Ordinance of 1787, taken from Jefferson's proposed Land Ordinance of 1784, which the Confederation Congress never passed. The First Amendment, which became a part of the Constitution in 1791, permanently established separation, although many today still argue over the phrase "wall of separation," which was Jefferson's phrase rather than one in the Constitution. In 1790 only New Hampshire, Massachusetts, and Connecticut retained established churches. Puritans had a hard time letting go. It took the First Amendment to force them, eventually.

The Unchurched

In most communities there was an incredible amount of social disorder. Very few people went to church. Ministers were scarce. By 1700 only 10 Anglican ministers served Virginia's 50 Anglican parishes. In comparison, New England had about eight times that number of ministers. In Europe all Catholic, Lutheran, and Anglican churches had communion every Sunday. In America that tradition disappeared (it is now being re-vived) because often no priest or minister was available to offer communion. In 1775 in Philadelphia there were 18 small church buildings for a population of 40,000. Either al-most 2,000 people squeezed into each service or very few went to church. Obviously, it was the latter. The ratio of people to church buildings was 467-1 in the Middle colonies, 606-1 in New England, and 1,046-1 in the South. Ministers everywhere wailed that few went to church, and they complained bitterly about the "unchurched." In *America At 1750* historian Richard Hofstadter called the colonies one of "the most unchurched regions in all of Christendom."

Evangelical Calvinism
The weakness of church organization led to the growth of an Evangelical Calvinism, which stressed the individual's direct, personal relationship with God. One consequence of this growth of individualism was an increasing disdain for religious AND political authority, which surfaced during the years leading up to independence. The emotions stirred up by the Great Awakening, which began in the 1730s and 1740s, led to an attack on the established churches for not being sufficiently emotional. Emotionally based worship and institutionally weak church organizations led people to see many societal problems as moral problems, an approach that still characterizes evangelical religion.

Deism
The general acceptance of a deistic theory of inalienable natural rights and contractual self-government prevailed, especially among the intelligentsia. Sometimes called the Clock-Maker or Master Clockmaker theory, deism is the philosophical belief that God creates the rules, winds up the clock, and then just sits back and watches the world op-erate in conjunction with his natural laws. In other words, God does not intervene in human affairs. Why? He has a lot of other things to do; He is disinterested in individu-als; people have free will, etc. God's natural laws rule the world. In a contest between a truck and a small child, we know which wins. Why? Why did God let this happen? To a deist it is easy to explain by using one of the scientific laws of physics – force times mass equals force times mass, which, of course, came from God. If one force or mass is greatly unequal, the result is . . . . It is not a God-controllable situation because it is not a God-interested situation. In the whole history of the universe and in God's larger scheme of things, it simply does not matter. Many of the Founding Fathers were philosophical deists rather than doctrinaire adherents to the specific doctrines of any particular denomination.

Deistic thinking also had a strong impact on political thought. Politically it means that all rights and laws are natural rights and laws that come from God. God is the source, not the king, and, therefore, people answer to God, not the king. Despite what the king keeps saying, the king is not God's representative on earth. There is no divine right of kings. This also shows up in the beginning of the Declaration of Independence, "We hold these truths to be self-evident." In other words, a person cannot dispute natural rights, you cannot argue against them, they are "self-evident."

A Fear of Decline, Why the Great Awakening?

Throughout the entire colonial period religious leaders thought they saw a decay of godliness. (It is amazing how many times in history people think things are getting worse.) To the Puritans it was Anne Hutchinson and people not living up to the standards of the "city upon a hill." These fears partially explain the reception of the fire and brimstone preaching during the Great Awakening by George Whitefield and Jonathan Edwards, which was based upon emotion rather than doctrine. The perceived need for correct ministers led to numerous new colleges for producing ministers. In addition, there was always the specter of the Anglican Church's SPG (Society for the Propagation of the Gospel) missionaries or even Jesuit priests. Jesuits were especially seen as a threat because the Jesuit order was established specifically to reconvert Protestants to Catholicism.

Ben Franklin developed a deep friendship with the evangelist George Whitefield, building an outdoor, covered, open building for Whitefield's Philadelphia revivals. Despite his efforts, Whitefield was unable to convert Franklin. A deist, Franklin believed that one should live with restraint, good temper, reason, rationality, a sense of community, and the spreading of wisdom. These were the real goals in life; and the purpose of money was to serve these ends.

There were many reasons for fearing a societal decline. In 1679 the Puritan church fathers met in Boston to identify the failings among the "saints." Thank goodness none of these characterize modern America.

1. manifestations of pride – contention in the churches, insubordination of inferiors toward superiors, particularly those inferiors who had, unaccountably, acquired more wealth than their betters
2. a shocking extravagance in attire, especially on the part of those who persisted in dressing beyond their means (note the class basis for number one and two)
3. a notable increase in swearing and a spreading disposition to sleep at sermons
4. family government had decayed, fathers no longer kept their sons and daughters from prowling at night
5. lawsuits were on the increase and lawyers were thriving
6. the sins of sex and alcohol – militia days had become orgies, women threw temptation in the way of befuddled men by wearing false locks and displaying naked necks and arms, mixed dancing, and the bastardy rate was rising (Do

men seduce women or do women seduce men? Read the biblical story of Adam and Eve. Or, ask any Puritan man.)

7. New Englanders were betraying a marked disposition to tell lies, especially when selling anything
8. business morality of even the most righteous left much to be desired
9. the people showed no disposition to reform
10. they seemed utterly destitute of civic spirit

Richard Bushman's *From Puritan to Yankee* best described what was really happening. The original zealots' children evolved into becoming "Yankees," more interested in making money than practicing religion. Persecution makes religious faith stronger; the absence of persecution permits faith to fade.

8

COLONIAL SOCIAL STRUCTURE

American Identity

The social structure that evolved over the colonial period was contrary to the plans and expectations of the colonial founders. They expected a tight social structure with clear functionaries and peasants. The New World was an opportunity for the Old World to start over again, to create new societies, even utopias, that would avoid all the worst features of European society. Europeans spent many hours preparing elaborate plans for their American colonies. They did not work out as planned. Historian Daniel Boorstin called America a burial ground for European utopias. What developed here was far different from the European experience in other parts of the world at that time, such as the large estates in Spanish South America, and far different from the European social structure. Historian Gary Nash defines social development for the colonial and early preindustrial American periods as the "changing social relationships between different groups in society," especially the changes within "a triracial society" of whites, blacks, and Indians. Those changes led to a unique **American Identity**. The interaction of these three cultural groups in a new environmental setting, far different from Europe society, is what set American society apart. America was not simply Europe replicated. What developed was a society of small farmers, yeoman farmers, and craftsmen or artisans, who owned their own shops. Two features characterized colonial society – deference and mobility.

Deference

You were expected to defer to your betters. In a deferential society everyone knew his place and stayed in it and voters elected one of their betters to political office; that competition took place entirely within the upper class, what one historian has called "jousting at the top." Deference was the glue that held colonial society together, although the "better sort" constantly complained that there was little deference.

Mobility

Colonial society had a much higher degree of mobility compared to European society, in both geographic and economic mobility. Not much has changed; today the average American moves once every seven years. In the town of Kent, Connecticut, between 1740 and 1777, 77% of the people acquired some land. In western Virginia, 75% of 150 landless people acquired some land between 1764 and 1782. In eastern Virginia only 38% of the landless acquired some land, showing that economic opportunity was associated more with the frontier regions.

Why Was Colonial Society So Different?

The main reason was the existence of an extensive quantity of quality farmland. Even today, the United States has one of the highest percentages of arable land, good farmland, of any country in the world, 21%. In European society a person's social standing depended on land ownership, which was not readily available for purchase. Here there was plenty of it, for easy and cheap purchase.

Unlike the European experience in Latin America or in Africa or in India, the English encountered no large native societies in America with fixed social institutions. North American Indians were not as advanced as those in Mexico or Peru. No strongly structured societies existed for the English to just chop off the top and take over an ongoing system, as happened for the Spanish in Mexico and Peru. English colonial society had neither a place nor a purpose for Indians.

Disorder characterized the entire colonial era. Waves and waves of new immigrants continuously flooded communities. In addition, many who came had lives that were in personal disorder. Think about it. If life was good in England, why would a person leave? Many who came to America were leaving a bad life behind rather than traveling to a better life in a better place. It took courage to sail to the British colonies. Historians always prominently mention the horror and death rate of the "Middle Passage," the transporting of slaves across the Atlantic. The death rates for those leaving England were close to those of the Middle Passage. The best source of reliable historical data on the voyage comes from records of British troops shipped to fight during the Revolutionary War. One-eighth of the ships that left England never arrived in the colonies. The trip was dangerous, and everyone knew it. When John Adams served in Europe as an ambassador, he and his wife Abigail numbered their letters, because they knew not all of them would survive the Atlantic trip. That helped them understand gaps in the other's understanding of an event later referenced.

The conditions of life in the colonies were harsh. The North American weather extremes are unlike those in Europe. One Englishman in the 1790s described it as, "All is burning or freezing." It was literally a daily life and death struggle. One summer activity was cutting wood for the winter. The typical colonial house needed a minimum of fifteen to twenty cords of firewood to survive the winter. A cord is four feet wide, four feet high, and eight feet long. Imagine fifteen cords of wood piled around a house by October. Do not romanticize the restored colonial town of Williamsburg. It is a nice place to visit today, but Virginia death rates were horrendous. One historian has argued that it "is unlikely that a civilized society, anywhere in the world, has ever survived losses in proportion to those Virginia experienced in its first half century." Only 60 of the first 900 people to arrive in Jamestown were alive in 1610. From 1607 to 1623, 5,000 people arrived, but in 1623 the population was only 1,000. Orphans were shipped to Virginia as apprentices, 300 from 1619 to 1622. By 1624 only 12 were alive, a survival rate of 4%. Approximately one out of every twenty New Englanders died in King Philip's War, 1675-1676, a proportion not experienced for almost three hundred years, until what some countries suffered during the Second World War. One-half of the Plymouth Pilgrims did not survive the first winter. Fires were a constant problem in wooden warehouses and houses, which in the early years had wooden chimneys coated with mud. In Boston in 1711, 100 houses burned; in 1679, 80 dwellings and 70 warehouses burned. In 1760 there was yet another major fire. Homes were small, with little privacy for family, servants, or children.

On a bitterly cold windy winter day, reflect on what it must have been like in their drafty houses. Europeans had no prior experiences with hurricanes or tornadoes. America was, and is, much colder and much hotter than the British Isles and Western Europe. One evening Thomas Jefferson had to stop writing because the ink froze in his inkwell. Until the 1890s the British ambassador received extra compensation because he served in a dangerous sub-tropical zone, Washington, D.C. Many European visitors today are very uncomfortable in our summers. Colonial America was a place of frightening, forbidding forests. Historian Richard Hofstadter wrote that in 1750 approaching ships could smell America hundreds of miles out to sea. What was the smell? Pine.

Social Classes
In many respects, it is more correct to use only two categories to differentiate among the colonial population. *Independents* were those holding sufficient property to be free of control by others. *Dependents* were those who depended upon others – propertyless free laborers, those in debt, indentured servants, or slaves.

Eventually America developed a class-based social structure that differed from that in Europe. Class is a difficult word, everybody uses it, yet different definitions exist. Since Karl Marx's nineteenth century writings we have looked at societies through a prism of dialectic materialism, theories of crass economic class-consciousness and class struggle. However, class is too elusive for a purely economic definition. Every person has been, or will be, in social situations when he or she felt out of place, either too high or too low, overdressed or underdressed. Class is best thought of as a series of relationships recognized by others. The major divisions in colonial society were not primarily based on economics; social divisions tended to be ethnic and religious.

Originally the colonists tried to maintain European class standards. In 1651 the Massachusetts General Court passed a law that only gentlemen could wear gold or silver lace or buttons. In 1674 a tailor in Virginia was punished for racing a horse, a sport reserved for gentlemen. Class rank at Harvard and Yale was based not on GPA, grade point average, but on family standing. The Puritans continued the European tradition of assigning pews in the church. Church committees diligently labored over the community list to rank everyone in terms of social status to assign pews accordingly.

There was a colonial **Upper Class**, but not one based solely on birth and titles. Instead, it was a working aristocracy, one that lacked the sanction of time and custom. In many respects it was a plutocracy, rule by the wealthy, more than an aristocracy, into which one was born.

The size and characteristics of the colonial **Middle Class** are debated topics among historians. The phrase itself, middle class, was not even coined until 1745. Historian Richard Brown argues that if middle class is defined as some property, some social standing, and some participation in the government, then 80% of the population of Massachusetts was middle class. Another scholar, Jackson Turner Main, has pointed out that less than 30% of the people held no property. It was a "middling society" with widespread ownership of land, which enabled the development of a middle class.

There was a **Lower Class**, made up of the poor and the indentured servants, who served for 4-7 years before gaining a small piece of property, if they survived. The concept of indentured servitude apparently developed in the early seventeenth century to solve the colonial labor supply problem. Indentured servants have been celebrated in America history as ambitious, upwardly mobile opportunists. However, in actuality few rose out of their lower class poverty. Historians estimate that only 10% acquired some property, becoming farmers, and perhaps another 5-10% became artisans. Some of the colonial era nicknames tell a lot. Among the first Scottish immigrants a redneck was a Presbyterian and a cracker was a loud braggart or talker. Later, both nicknames would primarily carry lower class connotations.

Indentured servitude was a solution to the labor shortage; the servants received an opportunity, theoretically, and the owners obtained a certain labor supply. By 1683 one-sixth of the population of Virginia was descended from indentured servants. It was estimated that by 1700 two-thirds of Pennsylvania's population had descended from indentured servants. Historians can glean some idea of the number of indentured servants from the statistics for Scottish immigrants. Between 1717 and 1776, 250,000 Scots came to America, 100,000 as indentured servants, including some 50,000 convicts. Send out the undesirables. In *Red, White, & Black: The Peoples of Early North America*, historian Gary Nash quotes an article that sheds light on those shipped out of Scotland. In 1669 Scottish officials were searching for "strong and idle beggars, vagabonds, egyptians [probably meaning gypsies], common and notorious whoores, theeves and other dissolute and lousy persons banished or stigmatized for gross crymes." Anyone who traces his or her family tree back to the colonial period may be shocked. The total number of indentured servants for the colonial period is probably between 300,000 and 400,000. When their time was up the men usually received "freedom dues," such as tools, land, and seeds to begin farming. After Bacon's Rebellion, 1676, "freedom dues" in Virginia included fifty acres of land. Women got pots, pans, a bushel of corn, and a mattress. To both of these lists add a big "maybe." It is a myth that indentured servants rose to wealth by hard work. In actual practice, there was no incentive for owners NOT to work their indentured servants to death. In the mid-1600s one-half of all indentured servants in Maryland and Virginia died before the end of their term.

Indentured servants helped alleviate the severe labor shortage. Very few people were willing to work as laborers for others. Land was cheap. Because of the severe labor shortage, wages made it difficult to be able to afford hiring someone. When hired, workers understood that scarcity elevated their status. Hector St. Jean de Crèvecoeur, a French aristocrat who emigrated to New York in 1759, left an observation on the nature of the colonial work force. "When we hire any of these people we rather pray and entreat them. You must give them what they ask. They must be at your table and feed on the best you have."

Slavery

At the bottom of the social pyramid was the slave. All the others were potentially able to rise or fall in social ranking. Only the slave was cemented in place, a necessary answer to a severe labor shortage. The need was so pervasive that in 1775 one-half of all people who worked for someone else were slaves. Slavery lessened the differences between whites in different classes. No white person thought of himself as being on the bottom of society. That position was for slaves. Slaves were far more concentrated in the South, but they existed in all colonies. The ratio of whites to slaves was 1.3-1 for the Lower South, 1.7-1 for the Chesapeake South, 14-1 for the Middle colonies, and 35-1 for New England.

Women

Out of approximately 100,000 indentured servants who left Bristol, England, between 1654 and 1686, the ratio of males to females was 338 to 100. In a South Carolina census taken in 1708 there were 148 males to every 100 females. A census in Maryland in 1755 found 113 males to 100 females. Throughout the seventeenth century, women were only 20% of the Chesapeake Bay area's population. This imbalance led some to call colonial America "a paradise for women." One colonial in 1698 wrote that "old Maids" did not exist, and that there was "seldom any young Married Women but hath a Child in her Belly, or one upon her Lap." A German visitor, Gottlieb Mittelberger, related the story of a servant girl who became pregnant by her master. The court forced him to marry her or face a heavy fine. This would not have happened in England. It is estimated that in the 1700s one out of five female indentured servants had an illegitimate child.

Laws tend to adapt to the realities of their society. By the end of the colonial period the male-female imbalance led to some legal changes. Colonial society was a patriarchy; the father or husband was in charge. The legal concept of "coverture" meant that a woman's legal identity was absorbed into her husband's; her person, her property, and her decisions were his. In essence, she ceased to exist because two became one in marriage, and that one, for legal purposes, was the husband. This is why many widows who inherited property refused to remarry. "I do" meant "I no longer own." A wife was her husband's helpmate, not his equal.

However, women gained more power over their affairs by the end of the colonial era. By the late colonial period courts began to move towards a position that her husband could only dispose of a woman's property with her consent. In 1714 New Hampshire passed a law that if a husband's will proved to be inadequate in providing for the care of the widow, her traditional portion, her "dower rights," one-third, was assigned as if he left no will. Normally fathers preferred to leave their farm entirely to the oldest son, both younger sons and daughters lost out. However, some farms were subdivided repeatedly over generations, benefiting some daughters. That rarely happened in Europe. In town meetings in New England each household had one vote. Because it was assumed that the household spoke with a single voice, sometimes the wife was permitted to cast the family's vote if the husband could not be present. Overall, the position of women was far from living in what we would call a paradise, but compared to Europe, it was also far from a hell.

The Colonial Family

America proved to be a much healthier place than Europe. The average life expectancy in New England was 65, fifteen to twenty years longer than in England. In Virginia it was only 45. Seventeenth century New England was the first society in history in which grandparents were common. In early New England infant mortality rates were much lower than in Europe. In healthy areas it was 100/1000, meaning that only 10% of the infants died at birth, in unhealthy areas it was 333/1000, 33% died. Marriage was a property arrangement more than an emotional bond based on romantic love. Contrary to today's use of the word "Puritanical," for example, Puritans believed that sex was a natural urge, one of the purposes of marriage. The Puritan minister, Cotton Mather, had two wives die. He married his second wife one month after the death of his first. At the funeral for the second wife the town ministers were discussing who should be number three. Two weeks later there was a third wife. Romance? That was nice, if it happened. However, it was not necessary. What was more important was that single men and women were not threats to other peoples' marriages.

In New England Puritan communities there was a lot of interrelatedness by marriage and birth. Kinship ties were very important to the social, political, economic, and religious life of the community. Marriages cemented political and economic alliances. For example, in Connecticut seven intermarried families controlled the colony. Since many of them lived along the Connecticut River, they were nicknamed "the River Gods."

The family was the main unit of production in the economic system. It was also the primary educational and religious unit. A 1642 Massachusetts law required the head of a family to lead his household in prayers and scripture readings. In addition, the family functioned as the agency for vocational training. The larger community had a compelling interest in seeing that families functioned properly. Therefore, in the 1670s a Massachusetts law directed towns to appoint "tithingmen" to oversee 10 to 12 households to ensure harmonious marital relationships and proper discipline for children.

Children

The parents' role was to repress manifestations of original sin (everyone is predisposed to be bad) through harsh physical and psychological measures. The contrast with Indians is striking. For the Iroquois early sexual curiosity among kids brought chuckles. It was natural. Not for Puritans – sin, sin, sin! Among the Puritans, the belief in infant depravity and original sin led parents to internalize authority in children through catechisms, physical beatings, and intense psychological pressure. Parents intervened in their children's lives, even in the selection of a spouse. It sounds as if children were mistreated; but Europeans thought Americans spoiled their kids. American children were not swaddled, as they were in Europe. Their own mothers, not wet nurses, nursed American children. In addition, parents named their newborn child within a week. The prevailing idea in Europe was to not name children until they were around five or six, so the name would not be wasted at the death of the child. One-half of all European children died by the age of six. In colonial America the mortality rates were lower, except in the early Carolinas. In New England a child at 14 was often sent to live with another family, to receive proper discipline. It was assumed that the parents were unlikely to administer proper discipline. Love got in the way of the need for discipline. Even the names selected differed from those in England, showing the gradual evolution of American culture away from European traditions. Another change was the slow shift from fathers naming the child to the mothers naming the child, a shift of symbolic importance meaning that both marriage and the family were becoming less patriarchal and more egalitarian.

Colonial society underwent several changes by the time of the Revolutionary War. Parents had less control over their children's marriages due to a lack of land to give to them, which removed an important control mechanism. Farms, divided over several generations, shrank in acreage. By 1775 Americans saw America as a crowded society with declining opportunities, characterized by a lack of land and the inability to start one's own farm and family. Ministers complained bitterly about the increase in pregnancy at marriage. It had jumped up to around 40%, the result of the delayed age of marriage, now 25 plus for men and 20 plus for women.

A new concept of childhood had developed, which saw children as innocent and malleable creatures whose character could be molded. Earlier, in the seventeenth century, children stood while their parents ate their meal first. By the Revolutionary era European visitors reported that now American children sat at the table and got first choice at deserts and even interrupted conversations among adults. The old adage that children should be seen and not heard had been the prevailing dictum.

Fewer children were named for a dead sister or brother. Psychohistorians, historians who use psychology in their research and writing, claim this practice shows that the newer child was prized rather than the dead one missed. Each child, not just the first male, was important and loved. In many ways, by the American Revolution, the home and the family had become a place of peace and a haven in a heartless world.

The Long Range Impact on American Society?
What was the long-range impact on American society? Out of the colonial era came some distinctly American characteristics, an **American Identity**, and an American interpretation of our experience. What was God's purpose in putting Americans through all this turmoil? By the Revolutionary era many felt that Americans were God's chosen people and that Americans had a special mission and role to play in the world, nicknamed in modern politics, "American Exceptionalism." This idea took many forms in later American history. It was behind Thomas Jefferson's idea of a secularized liberal republic of farmers; a motive behind American imperialism, against both Indians and Mexico; and a factor in the overseas expansion that began in the late nineteenth century with Hawaii and the Philippines. In the twentieth century the United States became the moral policeman of the world with our Fourteen Points and Atlantic Charter, both idealistic, moralistic statements explaining what goals the United States sought for the world by participating in the First and Second World Wars. America fought wars to suppress totalitarianism and to spread democracy and capitalism. What justified this approach? America's belief that the world would be better off if it were more like the United States, democratic and capitalist.

American society, by the eve of the Revolution, had acquired a wide range of concepts and thinking from the colonial experience.

1. The acceptance of social disorder as normal; many foreign visitors today criticize our society as allowing too much freedom.
2. The acceptance of personal risk and the precariousness that goes with it.
3. The glorification of youth and vitality over age and wisdom. Why do words like nerd, curve-buster, and geek have bad connotations in modern America? They do not elsewhere. In addition, guess who makes a lot of money in our society? Usually nerds, curve-busters, and geeks.
4. The existence of a broad-based property owning class, the middle class.
5. The openness of opportunity and social mobility. Over the years they formed a solid basis for both capitalism and democracy.

Cadwallader Colden, who was later a colonial governor of New York, wrote in 1748, "The only principle of life propagated among the young people is to get money and men are only esteemed according to the money they are possessed of." What counted was not breeding nor ancestry nor occupation nor learning. It was the possession of money. Money was, and is, more important than an individual's background. An English aristocrat once referred to the lower classes as "the dirty people of no name," meaning that they lacked a distinguished family genealogy. But in colonial America everyone did. It is difficult to tell from the colonial records, but it appears that only two or three titled English nobles moved to one of the thirteen colonies to live permanently.

In America, everyone has the ability to rise. Americans glorify upward mobility, and if an individual does not rise, it is his or her fault. What holds anyone back is not the system nor the class structure nor one's background nor the times in which a person lives. Americans live in a society that has an incredibly strong belief in upward social mobility, for ourselves and for our family offspring. The roots for these attitudes come from the evolution of society during the long colonial period.

A Philadelphia newspaper in 1776 contained the following observation. "Is not one half of the property in the city owned by men who wear leather aprons?" (Meaning men who labored for their money through hard work.) "Does not the other half belong to men whose fathers or grandfathers wore leather aprons?" In other words, wealth came to those who worked hard and got ahead. One historian found that 60% of New York City's and 70% of Boston's colonial merchants began life as poor men. No American today or in the future needs to ever worry that capitalism is declining. Our widespread property ownership and presumed mobility provide the ultimate shield for capitalism. This legacy is a gift from our colonial forefathers.

9

THE COMING OF THE AMERICAN REVOLUTION

Perception

Looking backwards in retrospect, from 1776 to 1760, illustrates how significant perception is to understanding the coming of the American Revolution. How did Americans perceive British acts and actions? How did the British perceive American acts and actions?

The Whig Theory of History

All the Founding Fathers were greatly influenced by the Whig interpretation of history, also known as the Anglo-Saxon myth. Briefly, it goes like this. Long ago the Anglo-Saxons established an agrarian paradise in England. Their society of landowners, large and small, enjoyed security in their liberty and property through the operation of a perfect constitutional system (not a written document; constitution in this usage, the British usage, means all their political and governmental traditions). The elected English monarch shared power with elected representatives. Juries and elected judges dispensed justice through the common law. Men looked after their families and their lands, respected one another, and worshiped God freely. When the nation was threatened, they defended it with their militias, to which all men owed service. Their society was untainted by artificial privileges in any form, and priestly castes and standing armies were unknown among them.

Then came William the Conqueror and the 1066 Norman Conquest, achieved not by superior force, but by treachery, which taught that the price of freedom is eternal vigilance. For well over the next hundred years the nobles spoke French, not English, magnifying their image as "foreigners." The English began winning back their liberties through the Magna Carta in 1215. Ever since then, English history had been a seesaw struggle between the defenders of the ancient constitution with its liberties and conspirators who would impose despotism.

The climax of this struggle came in the English Civil War, 1642-1651, which cost Charles I his head, and the Glorious Revolution of 1688, which led to major changes in the balance of power between the king and Parliament. Now freedom of the press was ensured; freedom of religion, meaning no Catholic would sit on the throne, was achieved; and freedom of speech permitted elected representatives to say anything on the floor of Parliament (or in a colonial assembly, as Americans believed). These liberties preserved the ancient liberties. However, were these liberties now being subverted? Were traditional English liberties under attack? Worse yet, was it a coordinated, systematic subversion? Many Founding Fathers so believed.

John Adams: "There seems to be a direct and formal design to enslave America."

Sam Adams: "Is it not High Time for the People of this Country explicitly to declare, whether they will be Freemen or Slaves?"

John Dickinson, the author of *Letters From a Farmer in Pennsylvania*: "Those who are taxed without their own consent, expressed by themselves or by their representatives, are slaves. We are therefore – SLAVES."

John Jay: We are "determined to live free rather than live slaves and entail bondage on our children."

Thomas Jefferson in 1774: "(though) single acts of tyranny may be ascribed to the accidental opinion of a day . . . a series of oppressions begun at a distinguished period and pursued unalterably through every change of ministers too plainly prove a deliberate and systematical plan of reducing us to slavery."

In his famous "Give me liberty or give me death" speech, one month before fighting broke out in April, 1775, Patrick Henry called the confrontation with the British authorities "nothing less than a question of freedom or slavery." (As students of history, you need to be aware that extensive research by historians like Merrill Jensen, and many others, failed to find any evidence that Patrick Henry ever gave this speech. No primary historical document exists. The first mention of the speech is in a biography written by William Wirt in 1817, decades after it supposedly happened. Thomas Jefferson filed his copy of Wirt's book in the fiction section of his library.)

In 1776, Thomas Paine wrote in *The Crisis*, "Britain, with an army to enforce her tyranny, has declared that she has a right (not only to TAX) but 'to BIND us in ALL CASES WHATSOEVER;' and if being bound in that manner, is not slavery, then is there not such a thing as slavery upon earth."

Alan Taylor's *The Internal Enemy: Slavery and War in Virginia, 1772-1832*, provides the most hypocritical example of the disconnect between the institution of slavery and protests over Parliamentary taxation. "In Virginia, a leading Patriot, Richard Henry Lee, staged a protest by parading his slaves around a courthouse while carrying banners that denounced Parliament's taxes as 'chains of slavery.'" The slaves must have been amused by it all.

What was happening was that the strains, deficiencies, and inefficiencies that surfaced during the French and Indian War, or Seven Years' War as it was called in Europe, led all three New World colonial powers – Spain, France, and Great Britain – to tighten control over their colonial empires, to raise revenue from their colonies, and to restructure their home governments. The war dramatically increased each country's debt. England's rose from £75 million to £137 million after the French and Indian War. Just the interest on the debt consumed over 60% of the government's peacetime budget. It was time for the colonists to assume a fair burden. For every one dollar in taxes a colonist paid, the average British citizen paid twenty-five dollars. It was time to tighten up. No one in the New World appreciated it, in any one of the empires – Spanish, French, or British. Both England and Spain paid a heavy price for their new policies; they both lost large chunks of their empires.

In *Our America: A Hispanic History of the United States,* historian Felipe Fernández-Armesto described the policies, events, and consequences for both Spain and Great Britain. The brackets, which I added to the quotation, indicate the ease with which it is possible to substitute British for Spanish and Spain for Britain. After describing some British policies, he continues:

> "A period of increasing interventionism from Europe and increasing friction with colonial elites was broadly paralleled in the Spanish [British] monarchy, where "reformist" governments in the same period took increasingly burdensome measures in a similar spirit: reasserting bureaucratic controls, reorganizing imperial defense, eliminating traditional colonial customs, maximizing the power and fiscal reach of the crown. Spanish [British] administrators were as intrusive and troublesome in Spanish [British] colonies as governors were in those of Britain [Spain]. In both empires, the home governments tried to ease local bigwigs out of influential offices and replace them with creatures of the home government. In both empires the results included growing, and potentially revolutionary resentments. For both empires the Americas housed some of the remotest, most difficult-to-govern provinces, with the most marked peculiarities of interest. In both empires home governments encouraged militarization – mobilization and training for defense. These measures were in rational response to the problems of security in vast territories with ill-defined frontiers, but the effect was to create potential reservoirs of armed revolutionaries."

Both empires faced threats. The British felt threatened by the French still in Canada and by Indians organizing in the Ohio River valley. The Spanish in Mexico felt threatened by Russian expansion moving down from the Alaskan coast, placing Russians in a position to potentially interfere with Spanish shipping. Wind and ocean currents in the Northern Hemisphere flow clockwise, thus Spanish ships in the Pacific Ocean returning to Mexico from the Philippines, also owned by Spain, took a route towards Japan, the Aleutian Islands, and Northern California, past Russian territory. What future mischief might the Russians contemplate against Spanish shipping?

What Were the British Acts of Tyranny?

What was it that men like John Adams, John Jay, and Thomas Jefferson saw as part of the long "series of oppressions" and the "direct and formal design to enslave America"? Clearly the colonists exaggerated the threat posed by British actions. So why the alarm? Historian Gordon Wood has described what was happening by the eve of the revolution. "The Americans revolted out of *anticipated* tyranny, rather than *actual* tyranny. (Italics added.) They were frightened about the use of power. If the British Parliament could do what it had done in the previous decade, with the Stamp Act and so on, what would it do in the future?"

A **Writ of Assistance** was a tactic used by the British to control smuggling. They were widely believed to be illegal. A writ of assistance was a general search warrant, not specifying what the authorities were searching for. They were illegal in England. The Massachusetts colonial high court asked British authorities if they were legal here, because the court was uncertain. Almost all colonial lawyers thought them to be unconstitutional. The Fourth Amendment to our later Constitution, part of the 1791 Bill of Rights, limits search warrants; they must specify what the police are looking for and they are issued by a judge only after the judge is convinced there is probable cause to justify one. Neither of these restrictions applied to a writ of assistance.

The **Proclamation of 1763** was a logical British answer to Pontiac's Rebellion. As a solution to Indian troubles, it was cheap, involving only drawing a line on a map rather than positioning, paying, and supplying soldiers there to solve the Indian problem. However, it had an adverse impact on land speculators and colonial land claims in a society that increasingly thought of itself as crowded, and therefore in need of western land for expansion. Frontier settlers, many of whom were unaware of it, continued to push west.

Before 1763 **revenue laws** followed neither principle nor consistent policy. The British collection of customs revenues was so incompetent that in the years before 1767 the British spend £9,000 annually to collect only £2,000. After tightening up the system, from 1768 to 1774, they spent £13,000 to collect £30,000. A 40% increase in collection effort led to a fifteen-fold increase in the taxes collected. That hurt, especially those who were accustomed to smuggling and avoiding paying taxes. But it was not just the amount of the taxes, as Massachusetts Governor Francis Bernard explained, "The taxability and not the tax is what pinches." The colonists had assumed freedom from almost all Parliamentary taxation. The first use of the phrase "no taxation without representation" appeared in Massachusetts on May 24, 1764. It is still on Washington, D.C., license plates.

The **Sugar Act, 1764**, cut the tax rate on molasses, an important ingredient in making rum. The **Molasses Act of 1733** had set the tax at six pence, now it was reduced to three pence. Enforcement had been lax. The new tax was to be strictly enforced, taxing sugar and coffee, and also wine from Madeira. This was the first British law specifically designed to raise money in the colonies, to be used primarily for the defense of the colonies. However, Americans wondered, with the French Canadian threat gone after France lost Canada at the end of the French and Indian War, what was the need?

The **Currency Act, 1764**, prohibited the issuing of paper money by the colonies, hindering trade. The earlier 1751 Currency Act had applied only to Massachusetts and New England. The 1764 act was passed because the colonial assemblies printed paper money, which depreciated in value (inflation) and hurt creditors, especially British creditors in England.

The **Stamp Act, 1765** – Stamps were to be affixed to 54 different types of documents, from 1¢ to $10. Was the purpose to set a precedent for internal taxes? The amounts to be raised were small. Why did the British push for it? It even taxed tax receipts. Violators were not tried in colonial courts, but in vice-admiralty courts, traditionally used only for cases involving maritime law. The British had been paying a stamp tax for decades, beginning in 1705. From their viewpoint, what was the big deal? Americans argued that it was the principle of it. Really? We pay a stamp tax today on playing cards, cigarettes, and liquor bottle caps. The unity exhibited by the **Stamp Act Congress** and the accompanying decline in the purchasing of British goods forced England to back down. Parliament passed the Declaratory Act the same day they repealed the Stamp Act, but the colonists ignored it.

The **Declaratory Act** asserted that the king and Parliament have "and of right ought to have, full power and authority to make laws and statutes of sufficient force and validity to bind the colonies and people of America, subjects of the crown of Great Britain, in all cases whatsoever." In addition, any resolution or proceedings that deny "the authority of the parliament of Great Britain to make laws and statutes are hereby declared to be, utterly null and void...." This was how Great Britain dealt with rebellious colonies. Parliament had passed a similar act about Ireland in 1719. Declarations are easy to make; forcing their acceptance is not.

The **Quartering Act** ordered the colonial assemblies to provide places to quarter British troops. Because the headquarters of the British army for the colonies was located in New York City, New York would bear a heavy financial burden. The New York legislature refused, and was suspended. The colonists saw this as an attack on the principle of representative government. It also involved the issue of an unfunded mandate, ordering a subordinate legislature to do something while not providing the appropriations to carry it out. It is still frequently an issue today between Congress and the state legislatures.

The **Townshend Acts** were a dismal failure. Designed to raise revenue by taxing glass, tea, lead, paint, and paper, they instead led to colonial nonimportation. The new taxes raised £21,000 in new revenue, but cost British merchants £700,000 in sales. In addition, colonists felt threatened because the Townshend duties were designated to pay the salaries of colonial officials, which had been paid by the colonial assemblies. Was this an attack on representative government, on the right of representatives to control their officials by controlling their salaries?

Corruption in Great Britain

Many colonists believed in the Whig political philosophy, which grew out of the Whig theory of history, that liberty itself was under attack. They also believed that only America could save it. Americans were the "last, best hope of mankind." Americans thought of themselves as having a "republican society," one that valued personal independence and public virtue, and was suspicious of concentrated power. It carried connotations of equality, in a sense that personal background and ancestry mattered very little. Add to this overtones of equality of opportunity. However, liberty was fragile and a republican people must be eternally vigilant against those in power, who naturally try to expand their powers through corruption, vaguely defined as using money to influence political decisions. To philosophical Whigs, political decisions should always be devoid of self-interest or self-aggrandizement.

John Wilkes was a lower-class radical who was denied his elected seat in Parliament. Ironically, his district was where the Parliament building is located. After his election he was imprisoned for seditious libel against the king, and reelected three more times and denied his seat every time. Every legislative body has the power and the right to judge the qualifications of members elected to it and to toss them out as unqualified. However, to the colonists and to many in England's lower classes, this was another attack on the principle of representative government.

Wilkes's supporters gathered at St. George's Fields, an open field beside King's Bench Prison, to protest and to enable him to view their protest. The British army dispersed the mob, killing 11. This was clearly an unwarranted attack by a standing army. At least many perceived it that way. Wilkes's radical friend in Parliament, Colonel Isaac Barre (Barre apparently first used the term, "Sons of Liberty"), condemned the government's actions. Wilkes-Barre, Pennsylvania, is named for them and Wilkesboro, North

Carolina, for Wilkes. They were heroes on this side of the Atlantic. In the minds of the colonists, the Boston Massacre in 1770 and the St. George's Fields massacre of Wilkes's supporters were similar. Note the terminology; a few deaths became a massacre when fighting tyranny.

Around the same time **Pasquale Paoli**, who was leading a revolution in Corsica against the French, England's ancient enemy, came to England to seek aid. Instead, the British hesitated. (They later did help, it was the lack of an immediate British response that troubled Americans.) Why would the British do this? What were they afraid of? Apparently, the spread of liberty. Paoli, Pennsylvania, was named for him. The colonists saw a deep significance in these isolated events. The British government was now opposed to representative government and to republican ideals; it was reverting to the older monarchical principles.

One stark example of how far the British would go was their treatment of Ireland, virtually a colony, similar in status of the American colonies, in a legal sense. By 1700 Irish Catholics could not bear arms, establish Catholic schools, send their children abroad to be educated, sit in Parliament, marry Protestants, or vote, unless they took an oath renouncing Catholic doctrine. Was that the future for Americans?

The Boston Massacre

There was a long colonial history of mob actions defending the community. Three times – 1734, 1737, and 1771 – Boston mobs cleaned up the city by destroying all the houses of prostitution. The mansion of the hated Massachusetts Governor Thomas Hutchinson got the "Hillsborough treatment" from a Boston mob. It rendered his house unlivable. The Hillsborough treatment came from a practice by low-class farm tenants in Ireland of attacking the lord's manor house by spreading excrement all over the walls, inside and outside. In 1747 a Boston protest turned into a riot when a mob objected to the British practice of impressing, or coercing, recruits into the British navy. Similar events happened in other colonies. Keep this in mind while looking at the Boston Massacre and the Boston Tea Party. They were not one-of-a-kind events.

British troops had been sent to Boston in 1768. To do what? For what purpose? To keep order? To enslave the colonists? To protect them from what? To enforce the Townshend Acts, the British trade laws? Why were four thousand troops necessary in a city of only fifteen thousand inhabitants? The British soldiers had been called into Boston after the governor tried to get the Massachusetts Lower House to retract its endorsement of the Circular Letter, which condemned the Townshend Acts. The Lower House voted 92-17 to refuse; the governor asked for troops. Why were the British troops stationed across from the Boston Town House, with cannons pointing directly at the colonial legislative chamber?

The Boston Massacre took place on March 5, 1770. A scuffle between low-class Bostonians and off-duty soldiers had broken out at a factory, the Rope Works, days before the Massacre. Among the mob on March 5 was Samuel Gray, who had been one of the instigators in the previous scuffle. A mob surrounded eight British soldiers. John Adams later described the mob as "a motley rabble of saucy boys, Negroes, mulattoes (among those killed was a mulatto, Crispus Attacks), Irish teagues, and outlandish jack tars (sailors)." During the confrontation church bells began to ring, not only in Boston but, also, at the same time, in several adjoining towns. Was this a spontaneous event or the result of advanced planning? The British evaluation was the latter.

Two outstanding colonial lawyers, John Adams and Josiah Quincy, Jr., defended the British soldiers, who had already been assured of a king's pardon if convicted. Two were found guilty and branded on their thumbs, the rest were acquitted. Every year thereafter, there was a parade on March 5 in Boston to keep alive the story of the Boston Massacre. But, which story? The five Americans killed? The low-class scuffle, the mob, or the heroic fight for liberty? After March 5, 1770, the British troops left town; they returned only after the Tea Party in 1774.

Confirmation of Prior Suspicions
The years from 1770 to 1773 were a period of calm, with isolated events that kept alive some of the tension. A leader of the New York City Sons of Liberty, Alexander McDougall, was imprisoned. A British revenue ship, the *Gaspee*, ran aground off Rhode Island while chasing smugglers. One night it mysteriously burned to the waterline while a crowd cheered. The Committees of Correspondence in each colony remained active, keeping concern high.

What was happening in these years was the slow development of **dvoevlastie**, a Russian word that means dual power and describes a pre-revolutionary situation when there exists, side-by-side, two governments, both powerful, both claiming to be legitimate, and creating dual sovereignty, all of which should be impossible. The old authority, England and British colonial authorities, had their authority undermined by a shadow government, the new revolutionary authorities – the Sons of Liberty, the Committees of Correspondence, and later, the Continental Congress. By 1775 about 7,000 Americans were involved in local committees, an awakening of citizen participation.

Slowly people transferred their allegiance to the new government. Why, because it seemed to be more devoted to the ideals the people cherished. Boycotts were enforced by illegal means, but it was for a higher cause, justified by a higher purpose than obeying the law. All this perplexed the average citizen, but not the radicals nor the revolutionaries. They had already transferred their allegiance to higher ideals, to abstractions, such as liberty and freedom. It is a situation you will see again in your lifetime, the problem of ends and means. When do the ends justify the means, any means, or, are there only means? Is how something is accomplished more important than what is accomplished?

Boston Tea Party (first labeled as such in 1834)
During the early 1770s the British backed off of most attempts to tax and repealed the Townshend Duties, except the tax on tea. Taxes on tea were not new; they dated back to 1696. Look at these statistics on tea imports; they reflect the swings in British policy and colonial reaction. Remember, the French and Indian War lasted until 1763.

Tea Imports into the Colonies, in pounds:

1761	56,000	1769	229,000
1762	162,000	1770	110,000
1763	189,000	1771	362,000
1764	489,000	1772	265,000
1765	518,000	1773	739,000 (note, rising)
1766	361,000	1774	73,000
1767	480,000	1775	22,000
1768	874,000		

By the early 1770s the British East India Tea Company was in financial trouble, facing bankruptcy, with eighteen million pounds of unsold tea. The British government was a major stockholder, along with many members of Parliament. The government tried to solve several problems at once in a single piece of legislation, the Tea Act of 1773. It placed a three penny tax on tea while lowering the price by permitting tea to be imported directly from India, avoiding the London middleman. Now it was no longer possible for smuggled tea to be sold profitably below the price of East India Company tea. In addition, the authorized sellers of tea in the colonies were limited to only designated merchants favorable to British policies. For example, the two sons and the son-in-law of Governor Thomas Hutchinson of Massachusetts were commissioned as tea merchants. All this enraged the colonists.

On December 16, 1773, after an extralegal town meeting attended by one-third of Boston's population, a silent mob of 116 Indians (!) threw 342 large chests of tea, one year's supply for the city, weighing approximately 90,000 pounds, overboard from the *HMS Dartmouth* and two other ships, the *Eleanor* and the *Beaver*. The Davison Newman Tea Company owned the tea; the company still carries the debt on its books as an unpaid loss, worth millions of dollars in today's money. One so-called Indian, believing that some tea should be saved for his personal use, was found stuffing tea into his pockets. Late that night he was marched around Boston at the head of a torchlight parade, nude, with nowhere to hide any tea. A lesson from the mob. Similar incidents occurred elsewhere. At Annapolis a ship carrying tea was burned. At Chester, Pennsylvania, the *HMS Polly*, a ship bound for Philadelphia, was convinced to turn back. A wise ship captain in New York City decided not to test the mob. In Charles Town the tea was unloaded and stored, without paying the tax.

Why did the mob dress as Indians? In the colonial era Indians were still seen as a free people, answering to no authority for their liberty. Idealized, the Indian represented free, natural man. This is the reason why a profile of an Indian once graced one side of a nickel. One historian has pointed out a curious feature of American cultural history. During times of societal stress and tension, Americans tend to return to glorification of the natural Indian as a symbol of freedom. This certainly happened with the television and film industry during the early Cold War, when the struggle was presented symbolically as one between authoritarianism and freedom.

British Response – Coercive Acts
Governments follow a principle in responding to a pre-revolutionary situation. It is this – the response should be effective and adequate, either mild enough that it makes the anger evaporate or harsh enough to crush the rebels. The British response was neither, it straddled the middle, which led to further actions on both sides. The **Coercive Acts**, the British name for them, were a series of acts passed between March and May, 1774. This side of the Atlantic called them the **Intolerable Acts** or **Repressive Acts**. The various acts

1. closed the port of Boston until the tea was paid for
2. ordered that British troops could be quartered anywhere at colonial expense (but, not in homes)
3. restricted Massachusetts town meetings to one per year (One-third of Boston's population had attended the impromptu town meeting called by Samuel Adams prior to the Boston Tea Party.)
4. tried British officials in English rather than American courts

The Intolerable Acts led directly to the **First Continental Congress**, which asked, in essence, that Great Britain repeal every law affecting the colonies passed since 1763. The Massachusetts royal governor, Thomas Hutchinson, asked for a leave of absence and departed for England. Lieutenant General Thomas Gage, the commander of the British troops in North America, replaced him as the governor of Massachusetts. One bad Massachusetts governor was being replaced by the head of the British troops in America. Surely trouble is coming.

Quebec Act

This British law, enacted in May, 1774, was passed to appease Canadian French Catholics and to retain their loyalty. Remember, French Canada had become British only recently, in 1763, as a result of the French and Indian War. The British faced a real problem. How can the British gain the loyalty, or at least the neutrality, of the large number of French living in Canada, especially should another war break out with France? They asked the French Canadians what would be sufficient. Their answer – guarantee our religion and our language. The Quebec Act did that. It proved to be one of the most farsighted acts ever passed by a colonial government. French Canadians never were disloyal to the British; they were a pain in the side perhaps, but never disloyal. The Quebec Act angered Americans because it extended Canada's border to the Ohio River, which the colonists saw as jeopardizing colonial land claims. It also, therefore, was viewed as extending the area of Catholicism, encircling the Protestants. From the British point of view, the Quebec Act was similar to rearranging furniture in one's own house, after all, all the colonies involved were British colonies. The American colonists unfairly linked the Quebec Act to the Intolerable Acts. Quebec was to have no representative government. It had no tradition, history, or experience with representative government, but the colonists saw an ominous trend, possibly soon to be introduced into the other British colonies.

Remember two points in defense of British policy makers. First, both the Proclamation of 1763 and the Quebec Act were part of a broad-based policy to inexpensively pacify the Indian and French Canadian menace. Second, Britain's military expenses, in large part incurred to defend the empire, tripled between 1680 and 1780. The people of the British Isles were among the most heavily taxed in the world. Surely, Americans, who paid much less, could, should, and would bear their fair share. However, Americans just did not see it that way.

Reflections on Events After 1763

The First Continental Congress asked for a redress of their grievances, yet they denounced every British action taken since 1763.

After 1763 there had been a dramatic increase in the number of British officials in the colonies. Why?

England started a new policy of lifetime tenure for judges in the colonies. New York and Pennsylvania had tried it earlier in the 1750s and 1760s. It ended because of widespread opposition; it reduced the opportunity for popular pressure on judges. Is popular pressure not the voice of democracy? Not to the British. Judges in England had lifetime tenure since 1701. Americans saw it differently. In many states today, such as Pennsylvania, judges are elected.

The new vice-admiralty courts created to try violators of the Navigation Acts, including smugglers, seemed to violate the ancient guarantee of trial by a jury of ones' peers. However, the British saw American juries as filled with the accuser's fellow smugglers or anti-Britishers. The British began to shift the trial location for Americans accused of smuggling from Massachusetts to Nova Scotia, which placed a heavy burden on the colonists and made a favorable verdict for them impossible.

The Revolution in American Thinking

The years from 1763 to 1776 saw great changes in our self-perception and in our image of Great Britain. Do not underestimate the role of ideas in these years. The French author, Victor Hugo, once wrote that an invasion by "armies can be resisted, but not an idea whose time has come." America was seen as the citadel of natural rights, more purely expressed in America than anywhere else in the world, including Great Britain. The Americans thought of themselves as more English, in terms of upholding traditional English liberties, than the English. They had a long identification with, and sympathy for, the Whig opposition to the British king's ministry, known as the Whig interpretation of history.

The Whig interpretation of history saw the march of history as one of progress – material, moral, and intellectual – with an emphasis on politics and personalities. Americans had come to view history as the constant struggle between power and liberty, with America being the last defense of traditional English liberties and rights. Note that early appeals were to Parliament, until the colonists realized that Parliament sided with the stupid, corrupt, and evil ministers of the king. Then the appeals were to the king, until the colonists realized the king, the ministers, and Parliament were all of a single mind. This is why the Declaration of Independence refers to "self-evident" truths. And, why "He has" appears eighteen times, indicting the king. Americans were reluctant to attack the validity of a legislative body, since that was their primary government.

The entire British government and society was increasingly seen as corrupt. Before voting in England, a person had to swear that he had not accepted a bribe. John Dickinson wrote home to his father in the 1760s that many laughed as they took that oath. Corruption! America and Americans were viewed as crude, but morally superior. Slowly came the realization that American inferiority was really our superiority. As one historian, Bernard Bailyn, explained it, is the glass half-full or half-empty? It is how a person looks at it. Which is superior, book knowledge or practical experience? How well does a college diploma or aristocratic pedigree protect one from an Indian attack? Americans were less cultured and less sophisticated in many ways, but our practical traits added up to superiority in America.

The revolution erupted at the end of a long period culminating in the development of uniquely American political, social, and intellectual ideas. The colonists had begun, unknowingly, to establish a separate identity, an **American Identity**, which would become the basis for nationalism. The intense political debates from 1763 to

1776 convinced Americans that American society and institutions were not only different from, but also superior to, their British counterparts. Americans became convinced
that traditional English liberties could only survive on the pure American republican
continent. Thus, the revolution became a commitment to a moralistic, regenerative republic in which "public virtue" would be important. All that remained after this realization was for the Second Continental Congress to assume the power to govern, which it
did. Notice that the fighting had gone on for a year before independence was declared.

The fighting, the War for Independence, began on April 18, 1775, when Robert
Newman displayed the two lanterns in the steeple of "Old North," Boston's oldest
church, signaling Paul Revere on the opposite shore that the British troops were coming
"by sea," by boat up the Charles River to march, as they would later learn, to Lexington
and Concord. At the battles of Lexington and Concord and during the retreat back to
Boston, the Americans lost 95 and the British 273. The previous February the British
Parliament had declared Massachusetts to be in a state of rebellion, which permitted British soldiers to shoot suspected rebels. However, in many ways the American
Revolution was already over. The real American "revolution," as Thomas Jefferson observed in a letter to John Adams in 1815, was over before the fighting began. "What is
meant by the Revolution? The war? That was no part of the Revolution. It was only an
Effect and Consequence of it. The revolution was in the minds of the People," in their
thinking, in their perception of themselves, and their vision of the future of America.
We had acquired our **American Identity**.

10

THE AMERICAN REVOLUTION

The Revolution as a Military Event
Be careful which is meant. Was it the War for Independence or the American Revolution? It matters. They are two different events in American history. The first was the fighting. The second was the ideas that were part of that era. The Philadelphia patriot, Dr. Benjamin Rush, understood this in 1787. "The American war is over; but this is far from being the case with the American Revolution. On the contrary, nothing but the first act of the drama is closed."

The War for Independence, Fighting the War
Up to 1776 the sheer size of the opposition confused British strategy. In 1776 General George Washington switched to European style tactics. For the rest of the war, he never won a battle again with just American soldiers. When possible, he avoided a direct clash with the British army. He fought only nine battles the entire war. By 1776-1777 popular enthusiasm faded, it was gone by 1778. The American army had 18,000 men in 1776 and fell to only 5,000 in 1777.

Even Thomas Paine's call for patriotism could not reverse the trend. His *Common Sense*, published in January, 1776, was easily the most popular book in American history, going through twenty-five printings. Historians estimate that one out of every four households owned a copy. Paine called attention to the meaning of the revolution. "We have it in our power to begin the world over again."

By December he was trying to revive patriotic fervor for the cause of liberty. His words in *The Crisis*, penned as he accompanied the army in December, 1776, had little effect, but Americans today well remember them. (*The Crisis* was actually a series of sixteen pamphlets written over seven years, 1776-1783.)

"These are the times that try men's souls. The summer soldier and the sun-shine patriot will, in this crisis, shrink from the service of his country; but, he that stands it *now*, deserves the thanks of man and woman. Tyranny, like hell, is not easily conquered; yet we have this consolation with us, that the harder the conflict, the more glorious the triumph. What we obtain too cheap, we esteem too lightly: 'tis dearness only that gives everything its value."

"Let it be told to the future world, that in the depth of winter, when nothing but hope and virtue could survive, that the city and the country, alarmed at one common danger, came forth to meet and to repulse it."

"I love the man that can smile in trouble – that can gather strength from distress, and grow brave by reflection. It is the business of little minds to shrink; but he, whose heart is firm, and whose conscience approves his conduct, will pursue his principles unto death."

Great words – stirring, but what about actions? The army filled their quotas with a draft, and only financial incentives in the form of enlistment bonuses raised sufficient troops. By the end of the first year, desertion rates began to rise. In addition, do not forget General Benedict Arnold's treason, which shocked everyone. After a stellar career early in the war, Benedict Arnold conspired with an English officer, Major André, to surrender West Point to the British. Why? Arnold had many reasons: he had been accused of corruption, investigated by the Continental Congress, the target of petty jealousy from fellow officers, felt unappreciated, and had a wife who constantly nagged him that nobody respected his accomplishments in this nascent republic, which was going to lose the war. He and his wife, Peggy, daughter of a prominent Philadelphia family, lived the rest of their lives in England, shunned by British high society. Nobody respects traitors, even countries that benefit from their treason.

Valley Forge is an American icon, but starvation in the army was due more to the Americans' unwillingness to tax themselves or to maintain a stable currency rather than to a lack of supplies. Indeed, local farmers sold their crops to the British troops in Philadelphia at much higher prices.

British Strategy

Initially the British thought they saw a European society in America, in affluence and structure; thus, they applied European methods of warfare, the same strategy that had been effective in subduing frequent rebellions in Ireland. The first move was to capture the leaders. The premise was that since societies were hierarchical, capturing the leaders would end the rebellion, because those under the leaders were unable to think for themselves. British military and political leaders had great contempt for the average Irishman or American. This explains the British attempt to capture John Hancock and Sam Adams, one of the goals of the British soldiers who marched to Lexington and

Concord in April, 1775. The previous February the Crown had declared the colonies to be in rebellion. From the British point of view, Lexington and Concord did not begin the rebellion; it started the fighting.

The next strategy was to capture the cities, which would paralyze the revolt, because cities were the nerve centers of any society. The British captured every American city; but the strategy did not work. The British misunderstood the dispersed, subsistence agricultural basis of American society. In 1812 Napoleon made a similar misjudgment. He captured Moscow and waited for the Russians to surrender. They waited for the arrival of cold weather, knowing that the French army had summer uniforms. Neither the Russians nor the Americans seemed to have read the war strategy manuals.

The British misread the degree to which the rebellion had broad-based support. Historians estimate that about one-third of the population supported the rebellion; one-third opposed it; and the remaining one-third was uninterested. While many of those who supported the revolution did not feel a need to tax themselves nor to volunteer, they still supported it.

By 1778 the British Reversed Their Strategy

The British tried to encourage social conflict within American society, especially in the South where Virginia's royal governor, Lord Dunmore, offered freedom to slaves who fled their masters and joined the British troops. Thousands of slaves ran away to the British during the war, one third of Georgia's slaves fled. Later General Sir Henry Clinton simplified the appeal in the Phillipsburg Declaration by promising all slaves freedom if they just ran away. Ironically, among the Virginians was one of Patrick Henry's slaves, Ralph Henry. "Give me liberty or give me death" meant different things to different people. Instead of freedom, many died in a smallpox epidemic that broke out within the British army. Many Americans, such as Thomas Jefferson, accused the British of selling slave refugees back into slavery in the West Indies. That was a myth; it did not happen. The British tried to turn the rebellion into a civil war by using more loyalists in their army. The loyalists created a problem for the British. They were primarily interested in vengeance. The new policy and strategy still failed, mainly due to disillusionment at home in England over the lack of success.

The entry of the French into the war, covertly prior to but openly after the victory at Saratoga in 1777, led to the Treaty of 1778, which changed the war from a rebellion in America to a European conflict, with America as a sideshow. Later, in 1779, Spain, hoping to get back Florida and Gibraltar, declared war on England. The Dutch joined in 1780. Now the 94 warships in the British fleet faced an allied fleet of 137. The American conflict now became part of what is known in British and French history textbooks as the "Great War," the wars stretching from 1689 to 1815. The situation in Europe was now much more significant. By 1779-1780 neither side could win. The war became self-perpetuating. The question now was, who would quit? It had become, as one historian characterized it, "England's Vietnam." The use of Hessian mercenaries shows how little enthusiasm the English public had for the war. French aid was essential to victory, since ninety percent of the American army's gunpowder came from Europe.

At Yorktown, Virginia, the French-American coalition won a major battle in 1781. A large number of the troops were French; the French fleet had scared off the British fleet, the only time in 400 years that a British army found its back to the water, and, the British navy was not there to rescue them. Even with the surrender of Cornwallis's army, the British still had 50,000 troops in the thirteen colonies. The war could have continued. Instead, the British quit. It was not worth it. The war had nearly doubled their national debt. The important colonies were secure. The value of all the exports from the British West Indies – Antigua, Barbados, Montserrat, and Jamaica – was fourteen times the value of all the exports from the Middle and New England colonies.

The Intellectual Ideas of the Revolutionary Era

Beginning with the Declaration of Independence and the new state constitutions, there was a continuous discussion of the principles of government and of the philosophies of mankind. To an extent never encountered again in America, the air was filled with political pamphlets, commentaries, discussions, and debates. In addition to our national Declaration of Independence, there were approximately ninety similar state and local declarations. The issues, concerns, and concepts Americans debated were:

Human nature – Is mankind naturally good or naturally evil? It makes a difference when creating a new government. How much freedom is permitted? How much control is necessary?

A concern over the degree of the **lower class involvement in local, state, and national government and politics** – The need for mass support always brings the masses into the decision-making process. Are they welcomed? Is government to do things for the masses, to the masses, or in spite of the masses? Remember, in many respects this is a pre-democracy era. The Founding Fathers held an elitist theory of government. The better classes should run the government. However, war is hard on traditional concepts of deference. As deference eroded, the elite grew increasingly concerned for their place and power. What is to be the role and responsibility of representatives in legislatures – should they follow the will of the people or do what they know in their superior wisdom is truly in the people's best interests; do what is popular or what they see as necessary? For the first time, many state legislatures added visitors' galleries to open up their procedures to the public.

Liberty versus order – How much liberty does society allow before it degenerates into disorder? The author F. Scott Fitzgerald said that an artist is someone who can hold two inconsistent ideas at once. However, another author, Sir Walter Scott, had already said that all modern men hold two inconsistent ideas at once. The modern world generates opposing tensions which cannot be resolved without destroying the whole if one emerges supreme. Society must have both liberty AND order. Liberty preserves the individual and order preserves society. What is the proper balance between them, how does a government achieve it, and how does a government maintain it?

A leeriness of democracy – Note, according to the original Constitution senators were elected by state legislatures, the president by the Electoral College, and voting was restricted to the same group of voters as those allowed to vote for the state's lower house. Too much democracy equaled mob rule to that generation. Ben Franklin once observed that "Democracy is two wolves and a lamb voting on what to have for lunch." John Adams wrote in 1814 (note the date), "Democracy never lasts long. It soon wastes, exhausts, and murders itself. There never was a democracy that did not commit suicide." The fatal flaw in democracies, at least in all those in history up to that point, was that eventually demagogues appear, false leaders who are swept into power by the people (the mob). Once ensconced, they subvert the government from within and emerge as virtual dictators, such as Julius Caesar or Napoleon.

The relative *newness of "nation-making"* – The Founding Fathers were aware that they were creating an artificial entity, a "new nation." This goes a long way to explain why so much of their political debating was humorless. It is one thing to revise an existing government. It is another thing to create a model government that is worthy of the world's imitation. Saving a nation is one thing; saving humanity is a weightier responsibility.

A concern over the sheer size of the United States – Successful republics in history had all been small. Could a large republic work? It took about 30 days for news of the Declaration of Independence to go from Philadelphia to Charleston, to Pittsburgh, and to Paris. The Declaration of Independence was read first publicly in Boston on July 18. Early in the Revolution John Adams explained the major challenge facing the Continental Congress – trying to get thirteen clocks to all strike at once.

How Should We Look at the Entire Revolutionary Era?

Two models have found wide acceptance among historians. Crane Brinton's *The Anatomy of Revolution* compared four revolutions – the French, the American, the British, and the Russian – and found similarities in all four, regarding the American Revolution as more of a civil war. His model sees a long period of rising grievances (the 1763-1775 period), followed by an incident that sets off the fighting (pick one – the Boston Tea Party, the British decision to tighten up, or Lexington and Concord), accompanied by a heightened discussion of political ideas (writs of assistance, internal or trade taxation, virtual or actual representation, the writing of the new state constitutions, the two national governments, the Articles of Confederation and the Constitution, the political debates of the

1790s and the rise of political parties) and, finally, ending with the establishment of a society and government somewhat similar to that that predated the revolution (as some historians have described it, the British political system without the British).

R. R. Palmer's *The Age of the Democratic Revolution: A Political History of Europe and America, 1760-1800*, sees the era from 1760 stretching to 1830 as one characterized by many revolutions all over the world, in America, France, Haiti, the Latin American countries, and Greece, all inspired by ideas such as "the people as constituent power," "constitutional rights," "the sovereignty of the people," and "the consent of the governed." American sympathy for other revolutions is especially clear in our embracing of the Greek Revolution against the Ottoman Empire. That interest became the basis for the furniture style known as the Greek Revival and for the popularity of Edgar Allan Poe's poem, "To Helen," with that stirring line, "To the glory that was Greece and the grandeur that was Rome." This generation of Americans was the first in history to set up state and national governments by means of special or constitutional conventions, a mechanism that legitimized revolution by deriving its powers from the "consent of the governed."

The Formation of the New State Governments

As early as May 10, 1776, Congress passed a resolution urging the states to form new governments. New Hampshire and South Carolina already had. Note that this resolution happened before the Declaration of Independence was adopted. Within a year all but Massachusetts, Connecticut, and Rhode Island followed. Connecticut and Rhode Island were so pleased with their colonial charters that they just replaced the word "king" with "the people." Only Massachusetts in 1780 and New Hampshire in 1784 held popular referendums after constitutional conventions. In the other states the state legislatures or conventions framed and promulgated the constitutions. In these eleven states the mechanism used to create and to implement the new state constitutions was not what Americans today would consider a democratic procedure; they did.

Features of the New State Constitutions

It was not government of the people, by the people, and for the people. It was more like government by the upper class for the people. More could vote, but it was not widespread universal manhood suffrage.

The new state constitutions generally presented no sharp break with the past. Colonial experiences, English practices, and minimal theory went into writing the new state constitutions. The French political theorist Montesquieu's great work, *The Spirit of the Laws*, published in 1748, endorsed the separation of powers and checks and balances. His example of these concepts was his description of British practices. He praised England for having separate branches for the executive, legislative, and judicial powers.

Thus, political theories had a minimal impact on American constitution-makers. In essence, they recreated features of the British government.

The ideas in the Declaration of Independence are NOT found in the new state constitutions. Constitutions are legal documents; the Declaration of Independence is a spiritual document. Massachusetts put some phrases, such as "all men are created equal," into the preamble to their constitution. This led to the Quock Walker court cases in 1781 and 1783, in which a judge ended slavery in Massachusetts based on that preamble statement.

Other concepts floating in the political air were such ideas as natural rights, equality, the principle that the purpose of government is protection of individual natural rights, that governments are created by the people and responsible to the people, and that the purpose of government is to secure "life, liberty, and property," which was the original wording in the Declaration of Independence. Jefferson's fellow committee members changed "property" to "pursuit of happiness," which George Mason had defined three weeks earlier in the Virginia Declaration of Rights as "the enjoyment of life and liberty, with the means of acquiring and possessing property, and pursuing and obtaining happiness and safety." The word "property" meant something different to that generation. We tend to think of it in economic terms as a means of producing income or profit. To the Founding Fathers, still living in a pre-capitalist world, "property" primarily carried connotations of reputation, authority, and independence.

Eight state constitutions had a Bill of Rights, predating the one in our national constitution. None contained the right to revolt when governments become oppressive, an idea from John Locke's *Second Treatise on Civil Government* that is in the Declaration of Independence. The Founding Fathers did subtly change the "rights of Englishmen" to the "rights of mankind;" in short, they universalized what Americans called rights. "The Declaration was responsible for the first important human rights proclamation in history. The notion of individual rights is usually grounded on three propositions: the equality of all humankind, the inherent rights of people, and the duty of government to protect such rights." George Athan Billias, *American Constitutionalism Heard Round the World, 1776-1989: A Global Perspective*, p. 385, footnote 23. Also, Lynn Hunt, *Inventing Human Rights*, p. 20, "Rights must be *natural* (inherent in human beings); *equal* (the same for everyone); and *universal* (applicable everywhere)." The encouragement of "rights" all around the world has remained a consistent feature of American foreign policy.

Everywhere, in all the new state constitutions, the executive was weak. Only the Massachusetts governor had a veto power and only New York had anything resembling a strong executive. Pennsylvania and Georgia eliminated the position of governor. A law passed by the Delaware legislature became official when the state seal was affixed to it. The governor's approval was unnecessary.

Some aspects of the new constitutions and the procedures to create them were astonishingly democratic. Five of the state constitutions lasted over fifty years, while the Massachusetts Constitution, much amended, is still the constitution for Massachusetts. The procedure Massachusetts followed to adopt a constitution was incredibly democratic for its time. Massachusetts took five years to establish a constitution. After a state convention wrote the proposed constitution, it was sent to the towns, where town meetings debated every article and recommended changes. The proposed changes were then considered by the reconvened state constitutional convention, and after debate, some were adopted. Then the revised constitution was again sent to the towns for their approval. This extraordinarily democratic process took five years. This process of a constitutional convention, a written constitution, and popular ratification legitimized the revolution; in historian R. R. Palmer's phrase, it was "the people acting as constituent power."

Pennsylvania's 1776 constitution was very democratic in terms of governmental machinery. It provided for an annually elected one-house legislature, a carryover from its colonial assembly. Georgia also created a one-house legislature. Any bill passed by a two-house legislature must pass both houses in the exact same wording. Thus, opportunities exist for legislators to vote for a bill, knowing that they will vote against the slight revisions that the other chamber might make. This permits legislators to run for reelection claiming they supported a particular bill. "I voted for that popular bill. Reelect me!" However, in reality they voted against it. The voting public often finds it very confusing to assess how a legislator feels and which vote in a legislature really counts. That is why modern lobby groups can educate voters as to what is really going on. A one-house legislature negates such political trickery. The Supreme Executive Council, composed of a body of elected officials, one per county, carried out the executive functions for Pennsylvania. Judges were controlled by the legislature setting their salaries. The Pennsylvania Constitution also established a Committee on Reapportionment to adjust legislative districts and a Committee of Public Virtue to root out corruption. Finally, a Council of Censors, elected every seven years, reviewed legislation to ascertain if it was within the "spirit of the Constitution." Too democratic for politicians, the 1776 Pennsylvania Constitution only lasted until 1790, replaced by a more "appropriate" constitution.

Unintended Consequences of the American Revolution – The Emerging American Identity

In an essay by historian David Hackett Fischer, he noted that the Swedish scholar, Gunnar Myrdal, brought over to the United States during the Second World War to analyze the dilemma of American race relations, observed that the American Creed contains a paradox. America is "conservative in fundamental principles . . . but the principles conserved are liberal and some, indeed, are radical." Our society is "remarkably stable." For "two centuries [it] has remained stubbornly democratic in its politics, capitalist in its economy, libertarian in its law, individualist in its society and pluralistic in its culture."

Revolutions always result in consequences beyond the dreams of those who started them. Historian Gordon Wood, in *The Radicalism of the American Revolution*, said that one of the unintended consequences of the revolution greatly changed the United States. As a summary of Wood's arguments — The revolution discredited the older forms of paternalistic authority, the old hierarchical order, that everywhere delayed the coming of modern capitalism, which would result in creating the first, and so far, most completely, commercial society the world has seen. American society increasingly came to regard the business of America as business, buying and selling, with exchange for monetary gain the basic adhesive of society. The revolution destroyed the older colonial society that practiced deference, which had been held together by ties of blood, patronage, and kinship among the better classes. The elite expected to continue to be in charge and to be elected to office by the lower classes. Many were not. Only one governor, Jonathan Trumbull of Connecticut, remained in office after the war.

The new commercial society undermined and swept away this elite of disinterested gentlemen and replaced them with the go-getter, the moneymaker, the doer. In essence, what became a major component of democracy in the new society was the emergence of ordinary people who, by definition, have an economic interest, an occupation, that ties them to others in our society. This explains why people are primarily identified by their occupation, why all Americans claim to be busy, and why work is good for you (as older people keep telling you). Your strongest personal identification outside your home and family will be your occupation, and many of your social friends will be people in that occupational field.

Do not make the mistake of thinking this is a bad thing. Certainly, a capitalist society has some unattractive features. All societies have had and still have qualities and characteristics that any of us would change if we were in charge. Nevertheless, we have here in the United States a truly universal society, people from everywhere are here. Every race, every nationality, every ethnic group has somebody in the United States living as a citizen. It is an extraordinary thing in the history of the world, and it is a product of a purely commercial society without any particular claims of ethnicity or race. This democratic inclusiveness of economic go-getters remains immensely impressive. We all accept it because we all endorse the rules, one of which is that wealth belongs to those who earn it.

The dean of all the foreign ambassadors to the United States (the "dean" is the one who has served in Washington, D.C., the longest, in this comment the Swedish ambassador) observed in the 1960s that "America is not a country, it is a container of individuals." Then he paused and finished, "until you attack them." We lack the ethnic cohesion that characterizes many nations. A journalist, who had returned to his newspaper in Australia after spending several decades in America, once strongly objected to his own editor's comments about "the average American." He wrote, "There is no such thing as the average American; they come in all ethnic backgrounds, races, and nationalities. You cannot pick an American out of a crowd, unless you open a discussion about liberty, freedom, democracy, and capitalism." We daily go our separate, individual ways, held together by a collection of vague ideas, with each of us emphasizing different features of "The American Creed," the **American Identity**." The United States is what political scientists call a "creedal nation," one held together by a core of shared, endorsed ideals, ideas, and beliefs. In *The Long Shadow: The Legacies of the Great War in the Twentieth Century*, historian David Reynolds drew a distinction between a "*civic* nation" and an "*ethnic* nation." An "ethnic nation" is "a community of shared descent, rooted in language, ethnicity, and culture." Not a description of the United States. A "civic nation" is "a community of laws, institutions, and citizenship." Us and the U.S. – the United States. Where did this collection of ideas begin? They started to emerge during the long colonial period, coming into sharp, defined focus during the long years of the "American Revolution," what John Adams meant in 1815 when he wrote that the "real American Revolution" was over before the fighting began. The "real American Revolution was in the hearts and minds of the American people." It continues. The author, Thornton Wilder, said, "Americans are still engaged in inventing what it is to be an American." The key word in the previous sentence is "inventing."

The upper class did try to preserve itself. The purpose of the machinery of government espoused by James Madison at the Constitutional Convention was to accept the idea of binding like-minded economic interests together and devising a system of government that kept the ordinary people out of leadership positions by elevating and extending the national government. It is a principle of political science that the larger the geographical election area, the higher the social class of the winner. Read Madison's *The Federalist #10*. Television and the internet may negate this feature in the future and lead to celebrities winning elections. We shall see.

Women came to embrace the concept of republican motherhood, that their primary role and responsibility as mothers was to raise sons filled with "public virtue," who could lead this great nation. Public virtue, or republican virtue, meant that one always considered the impact of their actions on society as a whole rather than following self-interest. Read a biography of Abigail Adams, wife of John Adams and mother of John Quincy Adams. Early in 1769, women, termed the Daughters of Liberty, began organizing spinning bees to promote self-sufficiency. Once stirred, women continued to argue for more opportunities. Abigail is famous for her "remember the ladies" admonition to her husband, but the steady voice for women's rights came from Judith Sargent Murray.

In 1790 she argued in *On the Equality of the Sexes* that the similarities between men and women, especially in imagination, reason, memory, and judgment, far exceeded any differences. In England, Mary Wollstonecraft used similar arguments for educating women in *A Vindication of the Rights of Woman*. If "men contend for their freedom," is it "not inconsistent and unjust to subjugate women...?" "Who made man the exclusive judge, if woman partake with him of the gift of reason?"

The Revolutionary War resulted in the redistribution of some land, especially in New York, land seized from loyalist estates. However, many loyalists successfully sued in state courts after the Revolutionary War to regain their property. Protection of property rights proved to be more important as a legal concept than artificially rewarding patriots at the bottom of society by redistributing land. The precedent was set, or rather enshrined, that property, the chief means to make money in the emerging society of go-getters, was sacred.

There were some advances in religious freedom, such as the Virginia Statute of Religious Freedom, which Thomas Jefferson proposed. James Madison argued for an official national religion to teach morals to the young, which is still an assumption believed by many people. Often people assume that exposure to moral principles translates into the personal adoption of moral standards. But, does it? This was why many leaders pushed, unsuccessfully, for an officially endorsed religion. It could not happen. By the end of the colonial period there was too much diversity, and the largest church had only about one-fifth of the church-goers. America is a curious society, we are seen abroad as a deeply religious people, but without an official church.

The Revolutionary era led to changes in the institution of slavery. Southern planters lost between 60,000 and 80,000 slaves – runaways and those who fled to the British. Some states restricted the slave trade and others abolished slavery, such as Vermont. Pennsylvania enacted a gradual emancipation law in 1780. Among their reasons was this statement – "in grateful commemoration of our own happy deliverance from that state of unconditional submission to which we were doomed by the tyranny of Britain." Ideas are contagious. The first antislavery society was created in Philadelphia in 1775. Court cases also played a role. Several cases involving a slave, Quock Walker, in 1781 and 1783, abolished slavery in Massachusetts, *Massachusetts v. Jennison*. Earlier, in the *Somerset v. Stewart* court decision in 1772, British Judge Lord Mansfield declared "the air of England too pure to be breathed by a slave," and abolished slavery in England for colonists who had taken their slaves there, 15,000 of them. Before the invention of the cotton gin in 1793, slaves were considered economically crucial only in Georgia and South Carolina. The Founding Fathers, as a group, seemed to believe that slavery was on the road to extinction. The cotton gin changed that thinking among Southerners. The rapid expansion of cotton fields demanded a stable labor supply of slaves. The period from 1790 to 1810 saw major changes in the percentage of slaves within some states: New York, -29%; Pennsylvania, -79%; Delaware, -53%; Maryland, +8%; Virginia, +34%; North Carolina, +67%; and South Carolina, +83%. (figures from William H. Williams, *Slavery and Freedom in Delaware, 1639-1865*, p. 178.)

One of the mistakes students of history make is to read history backwards, to put today's ideas, values, and understandings into our criticism of yesterday's society. The phrase "all men are created equal" has been continuously debated. What did Jefferson and the Founding Fathers mean by it? Where should the emphasis be – on "all," "men," "created," or "equal?" In many respects, this is an unfair question. In a later remark on the Constitution, James Madison observed that, "No language is so copious as to supply words and phrases for every complex idea, or so correct as not to include many equivocally denoting different ideas." Jefferson's original phrase in his draft of the Declaration was that "all men are created equal and independent, that from that equal creation they derive rights inherent and inalienable." His original draft also condemned slavery. South Carolina and Georgia strenuously objected and it was deleted.

Abraham Lincoln best expressed the attitude of the majority of the Founding Fathers when he pointed out in 1857 that they had created a "free society which should be familiar to all, and revered by all; constantly looked to, constantly labored for, and even though never perfectly attained, constantly approximated, and thereby constantly spreading and deepening its influence and augmenting the happiness and value of life to all people of all colors everywhere." In other words, equality is a journey. We are not there yet; we never will be. The journey is more significant than the goal. Your grandchildren will chastise you for not believing that equality meant that (fill in the blank as you lie in bed at the nursing home).

It is also necessary to differentiate between democracy and constitutionalism. Today's political campaigns still ring with charges and counter-charges on these two concepts. Here is one scholar's differentiation in two observations. George Athan Billias, *American Constitutionalism Heard Round the World, 1776-1989: A Global Perspective*, p. 11, 474.

> "Democracy, in fact, is theoretically the antithesis of mixed government and has no particular solicitude for property rights or the rule of law. Constitutionalism, in contrast, supports property rights, the rights of minorities, and the rule of law. Democracy and constitutionalism are blended in American constitutional democracy, though often with great instability because of the tension between the two."
>
> "While it is true that historically, the principles of American constitutionalism gave rise to democracy, one must recognize the distinction between the two. Democracy emphasizes individualism and political rights, whereas constitutionalism emphasizes political order and the

need for societal control. Democracy, in theory, is the antithesis of constitutional government and has little sympathy for the rule of law or property rights as such. Constitutionalism, in contrast, supports property rights, rights of minorities, and the rule of law. When they blend in American constitutional democracy, the tension between them creates an unstable, ongoing compromise...."

The "blend" in American history is between the Declaration of Independence and the Constitution. It is perpetually ongoing, the chief legacy from the American Revolution, broadly defined.

11

CONFEDERATION AND CONSTITUTION

The Articles of Confederation

On June 7, 1776, Richard Henry Lee of Virginia proposed a motion at the Second Continental Congress to establish a committee to draw up articles for a national government. Note that this was before the Declaration of Independence. On July 12, John Dickinson, from Delaware and Pennsylvania, presented his committee's plan, which was greatly altered and never finally approved by all the states until March, 1781. Ben Franklin had suggested a similar plan in July, 1775.

It was our first attempt to reconcile unity and localism, but do not read history backwards; the Articles of Confederation was not a "loser" government just because it was later replaced by the Constitution. The Founding Fathers had only two choices in terms of governmental structure in 1776, a unitary government, in which the national government is superior to all local governments, or, a confederation, in which most government responsibilities and powers rest with the local governments. The Articles did not result from extensive debates over political philosophy or theory. In essence, the Articles of Confederation was simply a reflection of how the First and Second Continental Congresses had actually operated.

A Critical Period

Historian John Fiske gave the Articles of Confederation a failure image in a book written in 1888, *The Critical Period of American History, 1783-1789*. He argued that the just completed Civil War was not, as many were arguing, the most critical era in American history. The real critical era was the period of the Articles of Confederation, when our nation almost fell apart. A later historian, Merrill Jensen, disagreed. He is the greatest defender of the Articles of Confederation. He called it "the constitutional expression of the philosophy of the Declaration of Independence," the attempt to put into concrete political form the abstract principles of the Declaration of Independence.

Problems of the Articles of Confederation

Yes, the Constitution replaced the Articles of Confederation, but it is incorrect to present the Articles as a failure. The central government had some powers; it could create post offices, coin money, fight Indians, declare war, and conduct foreign affairs. However, there were problems with it.

The national government could not tax people directly; it had to ask the states for appropriations. This did not work. For example, in 1786 Congress sent requests to the states. Only New York, Pennsylvania, and South Carolina sent their full amount. North Carolina and Georgia sent nothing. Eight states sent partial payments. Imagine the situation today if the IRS only requested that income taxes be paid.

The national government could not regulate international commerce or commerce between the states. New Jersey taxed a New York lighthouse (for New York City harbor) on New Jersey soil at Sandy Hook, after New York initiated the battle by taxing New Jersey vegetables brought into the city. New York even taxed firewood from Connecticut. Virginia and Maryland fought over control of trade on the Potomac River. And, remember who lived on the Potomac River – George Washington. Virginia tried to tax all ships coming into the Chesapeake Bay. Look at the mouth of the bay at Norfolk. Virginia owns both sides. Maryland strongly objected.

American foreign policy was an embarrassment. It was the most obvious area exposing the government's lack of power. All European countries followed a similar foreign policy toward the infant United States – to prevent American expansion beyond the Mississippi River. The next natural barrier after the Mississippi River was the Rockies, and American expansion to the Rockies would create a huge country, one that could potentially be stronger than any nation in Europe, hence, the effort to stop the expansion of the United States.

One example of this approach concerned New Orleans and the "right of deposit," the right to switch goods and crops from river transportation vessels to ocean going ships. New Orleans was an outlet for American crops shipped down the Mississippi River and out into the Gulf of Mexico. It is a principle of international law that when two countries share a river as a border, both may use it for commerce. However, a quick look at a map shows that in Louisiana the Mississippi River was entirely within Spanish territory, just as it is within the modern state of Louisiana. The whole Southwest, meaning Mississippi, Alabama, and Tennessee, was an area of intrigue. General James Wilkinson was a general in the U.S. Army, a chief of the Creek Indians, and a spy for the Spanish, "agent 13" on their secret payroll. He later turned Vice President Aaron Burr in for treason!

Spain's unwillingness to permit Americans to use the Mississippi at New Orleans irritated Southerners and Westerners. Negotiations between Spain and the United States reached such an impasse that John Jay, who was handling foreign affairs, agreed to a treaty with Spain that gave up the "right of deposit" for 25 years in return for increased trade, which would immediately benefit the Middle states and New England. Congress never ratified the proposed Jay-Gardoqui Treaty because of the hostile response it drew from the South and West.

At the end of the Revolutionary War in 1783, the British adopted a policy of "strangling in the birth" America's infant shipping by closing all the trade benefits Americans previously enjoyed in the West Indies. The British also prohibited the importation of fish from American waters. Not until 1789 did trade levels again reach those of 1772, and British ships carried most of that trade. Moreover, with the increase in population, it was actually 1792 before trade per capita reached the level of 1772. In other words, America's international trade suffered twenty years of decline or stagnation.

British troops occupied the "Northwest posts," military forts on American soil along the Canadian border. They refused to vacate until the United States followed the provisions in the Treaty of Paris, 1783, that ended the Revolutionary War. The treaty guaranteed that British creditors could sue in American courts to recover their seized property. However, local courts (there were no national courts) refused to comply, especially in New York, which passed a Trespass Act permitting a person to sue for damages if a loyalist even tried to recover his abandoned property. Eventually, in 1802, the U.S. government paid the loyalists' claims, £600,000. The fact that little property actually changed hands during and after the Revolution, and that many loyalists regained their property, says more about American respect for property than it does hatred against the loyalists. It is also the reason why ex-slaves did NOT receive land after the Civil War, land that had been confiscated from Southern planters. Congress returned it to the planters. Never underestimate the pull of private property for Americans.

Many states had conflicting and overlapping western land claims. All states had to agree to the Articles of Confederation before it officially became the government of the United States. Three states without western land claims – Delaware, New Jersey, and Maryland, with Maryland leading the opposition – were the last states to accept the Articles of Confederation. As one of the states without western claims, Maryland faced the threat of permanently being a small state in a huge Virginia forest. Virginia's original charter granted it two-thirds of the North American continent. This is the main reason why the Articles of Confederation remained unratified until Maryland finally agreed in 1781. Historian Jack N. Rakove labeled the western lands dispute "the single greatest obstacle not only to the completion of the Articles of Confederation, but arguably to the survival of the nation." Many expected great revenues from the sale of western lands. Who would benefit, some states or the national government?

No machinery existed to achieve or to enforce cooperation for military defense or for confronting Indians. With the exception of military expenses for the War for Independence and the War of 1812, fighting Indians was the largest expense for the national government during the early decades.

The national government had neither an executive nor a judiciary; the states executed the national laws and enforced the national laws. Congress could not force a state to obey a national law.

Unanimous consent of all the states was necessary to add amendments to the Articles. At least one state objected to every attempt to strengthen the Articles. Rhode Island was frequently the culprit. Rhode Island's obstinate stands led many politicians to threaten to build a fence around it. Rhode Island was one of two states, North Carolina the other, that voted to NOT ratify the Constitution in 1787-1788. They joined after a second vote.

In short, the national government lacked power. Each state retained sovereignty, the power to rule. Article 3 referred to the Articles of Confederation as "a firm league of friendship." Some in Congress argued that the Articles lacked any firmness, only a "rope of sand" held the nation together.

When the Revolutionary War ended in 1783, many army officers wanted George Washington to take over the government. He refused. In a speech to his army at Newburgh, New York, he told them that republics are often inefficient and everyone should just go home. This caused George III to say that if Washington really said that he was one of the greatest men who ever lived. Think of the actions taken by Caesar, Cromwell, and Napoleon. The leaders of victorious armies in revolutions usually take over the government. There is no one to oppose them.

New York claimed Vermont, which was not one of the original thirteen states. In an effort to prevent becoming part of New York, Governor Thomas Chittenden and Revolutionary War hero Ethan Allen opened negotiations with the British for Vermont to possibly rejoin the British Empire as part of Canada.

Many of the defects the Confederation government faced resulted more from the situation than from the machinery of government. Having just revolted against a strong executive, the king, the states did not intend to create another strong executive to rule over them. The American people were simply unready to create a strong, effective government.

Inflation skyrocketed. At one point, 1779, the inflation rate hit 17% per month. The national government issued a grand total of $451,500,000 in paper currency during the war. There are three ways to finance a war – taxes, loans (bonds), or printing paper money. Americans chose the last for the Revolutionary War. Without the ability to tax, Congress had no other option.

After the war the economy was in trouble. For example, the Massachusetts ship-building industry built 125 ships the year before the American Revolution broke out; it built only 25 the year after it ended. Debtors asked for the postponement of debt collection. Instead, seven states issued new paper currency. Debtors then pursued creditors to pay their debts with worthless inflated paper currency. Creditors ran away from them. Conservatives and creditors were shocked; a policy of inflated currency may have been acceptable during a war, but not in peacetime.

One of the states that refused to help debtors was Massachusetts. There creditors controlled the upper house of the state legislature and refused to print new paper currency or to pass stay laws, a suspension of or stoppage of judicial proceedings, in this case mortgage foreclosures. Between 1783 and 1786, land taxes in Massachusetts rose more than 60%, making taxes four times higher than those in neighboring states. Widespread economic discontent led directly to Shays's Rebellion in 1787, when farmers in western Massachusetts took over the courts to stop foreclosures of farms. A citizens' army from Boston broke up the "rebellion." Remember the 1776 minutemen? Who were their spiritual heirs in this situation? George Washington spoke for conservatives everywhere when he said, "There are combustibles in every state that a spark might set afire."

Accomplishments of the Articles of Confederation

Problems, problems, problems. Yet, there were accomplishments, the biggest being that the Articles of Confederation won the Revolutionary War and secured a treaty of alliance with France, the Treaty of 1778. Most revolutions are not successful on their first attempt. Ours was. The Articles of Confederation deserve a lot of credit for holding the rebellion together and for defeating Great Britain.

A pent-up surge of settlers crossed the Appalachians after the end of the War for Independence. Kentucky's population, estimated at 150 in 1775, exploded to 73,000 by 1790. North of the Ohio River, the Land Ordinance of 1785 provided for surveying all land owned by the national government in the Northwest Territory, before it was sold. The western land was divided into townships with 36 sections per square mile. The revenue from the sale of the 16th section went to support public education, an incredible commitment in 1785. The minimum purchase was 640 acres, an entire section, for $1 per acre. This led speculators to form land companies, selling smaller parcels to eager settlers. Surveying before selling set a precedent for further orderly (too often it was not) westward settlement and minimized property disputes. Today, in any one of the thirteen original colonies, property line disputes are common. When a person purchases any property, it requires a "deed search." Did the person who sold that property actually own what they thought they owned? Are there conflicting deeds, dating back to colonial times? The Land Ordinance of 1785 also made the property boundaries and roads straight. Look down while flying over the states of the Old Northwest.

The Northwest Ordinance, 1787, established the procedure for admitting new states to the union. New states would enter the union with all the privileges of the original thirteen, equal to them in every way, an incredible end to traditional imperialism. James Monroe had characterized the relationship between the national government and the western territories as having "colonial principles." Not quite. Colonialism was dead; the Americans would not administer their territories as colonies in perpetual subservience and dependency to the original thirteen states. Think of the situation. If the U.S. government treated the western territories as perpetual colonies, dependent on the original thirteen, it would have been analogous to the relationship between the colonies and the mother country in 1774. That dependency fell apart, as virtually all colonial relationships have since. The thirteen colonies were simply the first set of colonies to become independent. The new nation would not repeat Britain's mistake. The Articles of Confederation resolved to welcome our colonies, or territories, into the union as equal partners. The Northwest Ordinance also contained the first national version of a Bill of Rights, borrowing heavily from the 1689 English Bill of Rights and the Massachusetts state constitution.

The Northwest Ordinance also prohibited slavery in the Northwest Territory. This provision accurately reveals much about the status of slavery before the invention of the cotton gin in 1793. Many political leaders expected it to die out slowly. This was the only *national* statement of an antislavery policy before the Civil War. However, local acceptance among the many Southerners who migrated into southern Indiana and Illinois led to "apprentices," slaves by another name, existing until the 1840s. The Southwest Territory permitted slavery.

So – Success or Failure?

Many thought the Articles of Confederation to be a failure, or, at least inadequate. Concern over impediments to interstate commerce led to a convention in Annapolis in 1785 to resolve difficulties on the Potomac River, and elsewhere. This Annapolis Convention sent out a call for a convention to meet in Philadelphia in 1787 to revise the Articles of Confederation. Congress reluctantly agreed. The convention met and quickly decided to scrap the Articles and write a new constitution.

Some historians characterize the supporters of the call for revision as those who thought nationally, the nationalists or cosmopolitans, as opposed to the defenders of the Articles as those who thought locally, the localists. Madison, for example, wrote to Jefferson in France that the vices of the state legislatures "contributed more to that uneasiness which produced the Convention, and prepared the public mind for a general reform, than those which accrued . . . from the inadequacy of the confederation." The state governments were too democratic. As Madison said, "Liberty may be endangered by the abuses of liberty as well as the abuses of power." Other historians have argued that the supporters of the new constitution held an elitist approach to democracy, while the constitution's opponents argued for a government more amenable to the people. Many opponents doubted that a central government could govern such a vast country. In terms of travel times, this was a huge country in 1787.

Major Features of the New Constitution

The new constitution invented a new form of government, a federal government, with power (sovereignty) divided between two levels of government, the national government and the state governments. One scholar aptly called it "self-rule plus shared rule." It was a brand new idea for a governmental structure, America's greatest gift to the science of government, a concept copied all around the world. In a federal government some powers are reserved to the strong central government and some are reserved to the strong state governments. Which government has the primary responsibility for education, police, mail, defense, or voting? Some powers are shared, such as the power to build roads. An American citizen is under two executives, two legislatures, and two judiciaries. In a confederate government power is shared between strong state governments and a weak central government, which usually possesses only those sovereign powers essential to survival, foreign policy and defense. The Confederate States of America and the Articles of Confederation are examples. In the first there was no judiciary, in the second, no executive nor judiciary. Never refer to the Articles of Confederation as a federal government; it was a national government or a central government but not a federal government. The only other possible governmental structure at that time was a unitary government, in which the central government exercises almost all the powers. Great Britain was and is a unitary government, where local governmental bodies executed policies decided at the central (national) level.

America's other political innovation was the Electoral College, which has not been copied anywhere. The idea, suggested by representatives from South Carolina, apparently came from the method Maryland used to elect state senators under the Maryland Constitution of 1776. A committee created the Electoral College, the committee on "unfinished parts." It was one of the last decisions made on the Constitution. Many scholars say it shows.

In previous governmental bodies, the First and Second Continental Congresses and the Congress under the Articles, each state had one vote, clear equality. The big states would not stand for that in the new constitution. Hence the Great Compromise, a Senate based on states and a House of Representatives based on population, which necessitated that the United States become the first nation to commit itself to conducting a periodic census, every ten years.

Voting qualifications were left to the states. The later national constitutional amendments on voting are chiefly negative, for example, a state may not prohibit the right to vote based on race, age, or sex in voting for a national office – in other words, only the president and vice-president. However, a state may raise or lower the voting age for local offices, which all are, except for the president and the tag-along vice-president. When the constitutional amendment passed allowing 18 year-olds to vote for the president, some states still required 21 for all other offices. Later they dropped it as too cumbersome; it required two separate lists of voters. And, they discovered that so few 18 year-olds voted that it did not affect the outcome.

Questions Not Debated at the Constitutional Convention

It is interesting to see what the Founding Fathers did not extensively discuss. Historians rarely mention the areas of agreement. Yet, nowhere else in the world would a group of government-makers have accepted the following without serious argument and disagreement.

1. The principle of representative government, an idea that did not take hold in Europe for almost fifty years.
2. A single executive; plural executives are common in revolutions. Within a short time after the establishment of our Constitution, the French Revolution produced a multiple executive, the five man Directory.
3. A bicameral legislature. Many national legislatures are unicameral, and almost all products of revolutions are unicameral, such as the French Revolution of 1789 or the Russian Revolution of 1917. Benjamin Franklin wanted a unicameral legislature, since colonial Pennsylvania had one.
4. A means to amend the Constitution in the future. This was an admission of imperfection and the belief that principles of government evolve out of that society at that time. This shows that the modern assertion of the sanctity of "original intent" ascribes to the Founding Fathers an eternal wisdom they did not themselves assume.
5. A fixed time for elections, which limited terms of office.
6. Two governments, a federal and a state, with overlapping powers and each having a legislature, an executive, and a judiciary.
7. The supremacy of the national government over state governments. Perhaps the Articles of Confederation could have been strengthened instead of discarded.
8. Slavery – Historians disagree on this subject. Some historians argue that slavery was behind most of the North-South issues, the ending of the slave trade and the 3/5 compromise the most obvious. Many of the Founding Fathers believed slavery would die out naturally after inserting into the Constitution a provision to outlaw the slave trade in twenty years. In all previous history, in every society studied by the Founding Fathers, slaves did not reproduce sufficiently either to maintain or to increase their numbers. This was one of the

"lessons" of history. In the antebellum South, however, that "lesson" proved to be false. The Southern slave population increased from 1790 to 1860, mainly through natural reproduction, although some slaves were smuggled in through the illegal slave trade.

Many of these ideas would not have been taken for granted or assumed anywhere else in the world, or even seriously discussed. This shows the shared underlying assumptions among the politically powerful. This general consensus resulted from thirty years of personal reading, discussion, private and public debate, and actual practices in the lower houses of the colonial assemblies before the Revolution, in the First and Second Continental Congresses, under the government of the Articles of Confederation, and in the states during the Revolutionary War and afterward. Think of the ideas and changes from 1763 to 1789, an incredibly high level of political thinking virtually unmatched in any other period of American history. Out of this swirl of ideas emerged the phrase, "We the People of the United States, in order to form a more perfect union." (Gouverneur Morris's phrase.) The preeminent historian of this period, Gordon Wood, stated that writing the Constitution "was probably one of the most creative moments in the history of American politics."

Just for fun, in case you are ever a contestant on a quiz show, many men held the title "President of the Continental Congress." After all the states accepted the Articles of Confederation, the title of the presiding officer became "President of the United States under the Articles of Confederation." Therefore, one could call them the first presidents of the United States. Listen carefully for what the quiz show is asking; this could make you rich. The first "presidents" of the United States were:

> First, Samuel Huntington, Connecticut
> Thomas McKean, Pennsylvania and Delaware
> John Hanson, Maryland
> Elias Boudinot, Pennsylvania
> Thomas Mifflin, Pennsylvania
> Richard Henry Lee, Virginia
> John Hancock, Massachusetts
> Nathaniel Gorham, Massachusetts
> Arthur St. Clair, Pennsylvania
> Cyris Griffin, Virginia

The word president just meant the presiding officer.

12

RELIGIOUS BELIEFS OF THE FOUNDING FATHERS

Far too often the public tends to read history backwards. They take issues that are important to them and research history to see what "relevance" and "lessons" it has for the present. The faith of the Founding Fathers and questions about the Constitution and religion are examples of this. It is essential to put their beliefs within the context of their times. The German language has a word for this, Zeitgeist, an untranslatable word that can perhaps best be understood by the German roots, time-ghost, what was in the air at that time.

Religious Freedom

Two ideas need clarification. **First**, people came to America to improve their economic standard of living more than for religious freedom, in spite of what many school text-books claim. The Pilgrims and the Puritans came for their own religious freedom; they did not grant it for others. The Pilgrims failed as a colony and as a church, leaving only the legacy of Thanksgiving and the Mayflower Compact. The Puritans lost their zeal within one generation. By 1679 a Puritan synod identified many failings among the "saints," such as

1. a spreading disposition to sleep at sermons
2. fathers no longer kept their sons and daughters from prowling at night
3. lawsuits were on the increase and lawyers were thriving
4. the sins of sex and alcohol – militia days had become orgies
5. New Englanders were betraying a marked disposition to tell lies, especially when selling anything

Historian Richard Bushman's explanation in *From Puritan to Yankee* is that the second and third generations were more interested in making money. Nothing reduces religious zeal quite as much as the absence of persecution, which is what happened to the Puritans.

Freedom From Religion

Second, over the long colonial period – 169 years from 1607 to 1776 – there were many changes, one of which was the slow growth of both **religious freedom** and **freedom from religion**. In their experiences and in the histories that the Founding Fathers read, church and state were often parallel, intertwined organizations, both equally oppressive, both contradictory to "natural rights."

Colonial Established Churches

Many of the thirteen colonies had established churches, churches one had to pay taxes to, unless you could prove you attended another church at least 26 times a year. Nine colonies had official churches. There were none in Pennsylvania or Delaware, but, the Quakers ran Pennsylvania and Delaware really had no separate existence from Pennsylvania. They had the same governor, but two different legislatures. New Jersey had no official church, but in many respects the colony was really completely disorganized. Rhode Island had no official church as a conscious decision; their founders, including Roger Williams, had been kicked out of Puritan Massachusetts. Therefore, only Pennsylvania and Rhode Island had anything approaching a modern definition of religious freedom.

While there may have been official churches, there were many different religions present, unlike the situation within every European country. In short, what developed here was without precedent, it was a uniquely new experience. Historians have counted the number of church buildings that existed in 1775; there were 3142 church buildings. Review the list of the churches in 1775 in Chapter 7 to understand the great diversity of religions and sects.

Eventually, out of the reality of so many different churches, the Founding Fathers developed the theory that church and state should be separated, but that came about primarily because they could never agree on which church or which doctrine should be the official one. It was not theories of personal liberty that led to religious freedom; it was instead the impossibility of naming an official church. Other countries see Americans as a religious people; but we still lack an official church or a religion closely identified with our government or people. Almost fifty percent of Americans claim they attend church regularly, defined as once per month. Only South Africa is higher. The numbers for several other representative countries are lower: Spain, 28%, Great Britain, 15%, France, 9%, and Denmark, 5%.

Debates Over Religious Freedom

In 1785 the Virginia state legislature was in the process of renewing a tax to provide for "teachers of the Christian religion." The taxpayer designated the Christian sect they wished to support. James Madison vehemently objected, arguing that it was wrong to force taxpayers to support religion. Instead, the next year the Virginia legislature passed a law Jefferson had proposed in 1777 while governor of Virginia. The Virginia Statute for Religious Freedom ended official state support for the Anglican Church. It marked the beginning of the struggle for religious liberty, not the end; the details needed to be worked out. Still do. Always will. Americans renamed the Anglican Church following the Revolutionary War, changing it to the Protestant Episcopal Church, today called the Episcopal Church.

The Founding Fathers did not instantly adopt religious freedom. Some attempted to establish Christianity as the official religion, as did Patrick Henry in Virginia. Remember the 98% Protestant percentage for the population. Why did they want an official church? They had, just as many people do today, a widely held belief that religion plays a role in maintaining and transmitting moral values to the next generation. Look at the McGuffey readers for schoolchildren in the nineteenth century and the writings of Horace Mann, the nineteenth century education reformer, who believed a school should use daily readings from the King James Version of the Bible. John Adams once said, "The Christian religion is good – indeed, as I understand it, the very best as the ally of morality." Religion, in short, was and is useful and necessary to a people and nation. "It is religion that teaches duty, that makes us responsible and honorable." Benjamin Rush said religion in schools would make children into "republican machines." This is still one of the most frequently argued reasons for Bible reading and prayer in public schools. However, it has no research basis. There is no scientific or scholarly proof that it is effective in transferring moral values to the next generation.

The Declaration of Independence emerged out of the Second Continental Congress. At the First Continental Congress, which met in 1774, the opening on the very first day raised the issue of religion. Thomas Cushing, from Boston, moved that the delegates begin with a prayer. John Jay from New York and John Rutledge from South Carolina objected, because, as John Adams recorded in his diary, "we were so divided in religious sentiment." Samuel Adams stood and declared that "he was no bigot, and could hear a prayer from a gentleman of piety and virtue who was at the same time a friend to his country." Note that on the very first day religion and patriotism united, as they have been ever since in the minds of many Americans. Samuel Adams then moved to have an Episcopal clergyman read prayers to Congress the next day. The next morning Reverend Jacob Duche arrived. He read from the 35th Psalm, the psalm assigned for that day in the daily lectionary, which begins, "Plead my cause, O Lord, with them that strive with me: fight against them that fight against me." The delegates were stunned.

Clearly, Providence moves in strange ways. From that day forth, wherever Americans gathered to govern, they felt assured that God was with them, and yet, they would be tolerant.

The Constitution Itself

During the debates over the Constitution a proposed resolution to have a minister begin the meeting with a prayer on July 4 mustered only four votes in favor. As originally written, the Constitution has no reference to God and only a few references to religion. They are:

> In Article Six – no religious test for office.
> One may affirm rather than swear their allegiance (for Quakers).
> Sundays do not count in the ten day window the president has to veto a bill.
> Finally, it refers to the year as "in the Year of our Lord one thousand seven hundred and Eighty-seven."

One must be careful at this point to correctly assess the attitude of the Founding Fathers; the Constitution is not anti-religious, it is not threatening to any religion's doctrines.

First Amendment

It was the First Amendment that spoke to religion. The lack of a Bill of Rights was one of the major arguments against approving the new Constitution in 1787-1788. This is why supporters promised that consideration of a Bill of Rights would be one of the first items addressed, which it was. The Bill of Rights restricted only the federal government. In the twentieth century the courts applied the Bill of Rights to the states, slowly, case by case, decision by decision. Originally some believed that one of the chief purposes of the Bill of Rights was to prevent the national government from interfering with the state government's establishment of an official religion.

The first part (sixteen words) of the First Amendment reads:

> "Congress shall make no law respecting an establishment of religion,
> or prohibiting the free exercise thereof."

This is a double guarantee. The "establishment clause," states that the government would do nothing to give official endorsement to a religion or to set one faith above another. Supreme Court cases decided under the establishment clause apply what is called the "lemon test," from the 1971 case, *Lemon v. Kurtzman*. It states that to satisfy the establishment clause a governmental practice must (a.) reflect a clearly secular purpose;

(b.) have a primary effect that neither advances nor inhibits religion; and, (c.) avoids excessive entanglement with religion by endorsing or coercing people into religious activities. The "free exercise clause," states that government would do nothing to inhibit the freedom of religion.

In 1791 the guarantees in the First Amendment were so novel in human history that the Founding Fathers themselves were unsure what it meant. Did it apply to Jews, Catholics, Muslims, Indians, and atheists? Did it prohibit government declarations of days of prayer or fasting, which had often been done, or, did it prohibit military chaplains?

Jefferson clarified his understanding in 1802 with his response to the Baptist Church of Danbury, Connecticut, which had asked for a national day of prayer to heal the wounds from the contentious election of 1800 and the resulting vote in the House of Representatives to select a president. He replied, "The legitimate powers of government reach actions only, and not opinions." In his reply is also the famous comment that the First Amendment erected "a wall of separation." However, that phrase appears in a private letter. A Supreme Court justice quoted this phrase for the first time in a dissenting opinion in *Evanson v. Board of Education, Ewing Township*, 1947, a 5-4 decision, which found that the use of taxpayer money to transport parochial school students was not a violation of the First Amendment. Shortly afterwards, in *Zorach v. Clauson*, 1952, the court upheld the practice of releasing students during the school day to attend religious instruction, ruling that the First Amendment "does not say that, in every and all respects there shall be a separation of Church and State." There was no "wall of separation," and there really cannot be – not if we are a religious people, which we are. The "wall" was not a very high wall.

Many of the early state constitutions, which are too often overlooked, said there was no "wall of separation." Delaware, in the 1776 constitution, required all public officials to swear their belief "in God the Father of Jesus Christ His only Son, and in the Holy Ghost." Maryland extended religious freedom to only Christians. Pennsylvania, in their 1790 constitution, denied state offices to any who did not believe "in a future state of rewards and punishments" meaning Heaven and Hell, thus neither Jews nor atheists could serve in public office. Only Protestants could be elected in New Hampshire, Massachusetts, New Jersey, South Carolina, and Georgia. The New Hampshire constitution required all state employees, until 1868, to not deny the existence of God or the validity of the Bible. The Massachusetts constitution required local governments to continue to support ministers from taxes. This provision did not end until 1818. The North Carolina constitution guaranteed freedom of religion, but also required all public officials to believe in the Trinity and both the Old and New Testaments. In 1806 a Jewish member of the state legislature had his right to sit in the legislature challenged as unconstitutional. He had just been reelected. His speech defending religious freedom so inspired the legislature that they immediately voted to take the "belief in the Trinity" clause out of their state constitution.

President George Washington reassured a Catholic congregation and a Jewish congregation, both of whom wrote to him questioning what the First Amendment meant for them. He replied to the Catholics that America would be "among the foremost nations in examples of justice and liberality." To the Jews of Newport, Rhode Island, he replied that the government of the United States "gives to bigotry no sanction, to persecution no assistance." Those two statements certainly clear it up. In a treaty with the Muslim nation of Tripoli in 1797, begun under the Washington administration, President John Adams and the Senate approved this wording, "the Government of the United States is not, in any sense, founded on the Christian religion . . . ." However, to confuse matters even more, each time George Washington took the oath of office as president, he added at the end of the oath written in the Constitution, "So help me, God," and then kissed the Bible.

Where Did These Ideas Come From?–The Enlightenment

Many of the Founding Fathers did not think much of established, privileged religion. The preeminent historian of this period, Gordon Wood, argues that "most of the Revolutionary leaders were the least emotionally religious of any generation of leaders in our history." The seventeenth and eighteenth century intellectual ferment known as the Enlightenment was full of ideas that humankind could, and should, achieve progress by advancing the cause of justice, freedom, equality, and material welfare, all of which were interwoven with one another. The original wording in the Declaration of Independence was "life, liberty, and property." The other four members of the draft committee changed Jefferson's original wording to "Life, Liberty, and the Pursuit of Happiness," by which they meant the pursuit of material wealth and status. In Washington's writings and speeches his religious ideas come neither from the Bible nor from Christian traditions, but from Nature and Reason. He always capitalized both Nature and Reason. He usually referred to God not as God but as "the great disposer of events." He rarely mentioned Christ. He also rarely attended church services and never took communion.

Jefferson's beliefs must be placed alongside what he believed from his study of history. Evil governments and oppressive religions had always existed side-by-side. From the fourth century to the eighteenth century, the clergy preserved their power by preferring mystery over clarity. An official state church creates lazy and corrupt clergy. He sought to protect all religions, including "the Jew and the Gentile, the Christian and Mahometan, the Hindoo, and infidel of every denomination." Jefferson condemned those who buried the "genuine precepts of Jesus under a pile of priestly jargon and philosophical subtleties." He personally did not believe that Jesus was divine or that he performed miracles. However, he considered Jesus' gospel of love to be "perfect and sublime." He once said, "I am a Christian, in the only sense in which he (Jesus) wished anyone to be: sincerely attached to his doctrines, in preference to all others." He summed up the best of religion as "fear God and love your neighbor." That position is hardly anti-religious nor strongly anti-Christian.

It was how governments used religion that concerned Jefferson. "The legitimate powers of government extend only to such acts as are injurious to others. But it does me no injury for my neighbor to say there are twenty gods or no god. It neither picks my pocket nor breaks my leg." In many respects, his attitude towards public religion was similar to Gandhi's later observation after living with Christians in England and India. "I like your Christianity; I don't like your Christians." James Madison saw the fruits of 1,500 years of privilege for Christianity as "pride and indolence in the Clergy, ignorance and servility in the laity, in both, superstition, bigotry and persecution." Religion was more often a source of oppression rather than a restraint upon those responsible for the oppression.

Jefferson, Washington, Madison, Franklin, and almost all of the Founding Fathers, were, to a great extent, philosophically, deists. The God of the Declaration of Independence is largely the God of Deism, referred to as "Nature's God," and the "Supreme Judge of the world." Deism is sometimes called the Master Clockmaker theory. It is the philosophical belief that God created the rules, wound up the clock, and then just sits back and watches. God does not intervene in human affairs.

This does not mean that religion had no impact on the Founding Fathers. Politically, Deistic thinking meant that all rights are natural rights. Those rights come from God. God is the source, not the king, and therefore, people answer to God, not to the king. In a contest between natural laws and the king, the king loses. This is illustrated by the beginning of the Declaration of Independence, "We hold these truths to be self-evident." In other words, a person cannot dispute them, one cannot argue against them. Another person could not convince one of the Founding Fathers that a particular denomination was the only one that was correct. They knew better, and they just smiled, securely knowing that you were wrong.

The Legacy of the Founding Fathers

Were they religious men? Yes, very much so. However, religion must be divorced from government. Our nation must have freedom of religion AND freedom from religion. Both government and religion flourish better that way. It is the minutia of deciding where and how to separate the two that drives us crazy.

Here are several examples of this. In many public schools today, teachers are not permitted to have Bibles on top of their desks. Yet at the beginning of the school day, in most states, a state law requires reciting the Pledge of Allegiance, which contains the phrase, "one nation, under God." "Under God," was added to the original Pledge of

Allegiance during the Cold War, in 1954. It is interesting that Francis Bellamy, who wrote the Pledge of Allegiance in 1892, was a Baptist minister, and he did not put any reference to God in the pledge. Yet, paradoxically, that same year the Supreme Court declared the United States to be a "Christian Nation" in *Church of the Holy Trinity v. United States*.

The confusion over the legacy of the Founding Fathers has continued throughout America's history. During the Civil War a bill was proposed in Congress to amend the Constitution's preamble to begin, instead of "We the People," as, "Acknowledging the Lord Jesus Christ as the Governor among nations, His revealed will as supreme law of the land, in order to constitute a Christian government," then what follows is "we the people of the United States . . . ." This bill has been introduced in every session of Congress since 1863.

No case reached the Supreme Court regarding religious issues until after the Civil War, when cases involving Mormons and polygamy arose. They have since. The courts have said that the "moment of silence" to begin the school day is acceptable, but it must be neutral and not encourage silent prayer. The teacher cannot say bow your heads for a moment of silence.

The Equal Access Act, passed in 1984, permits non-curriculum groups to meet on school grounds during non-instructional time, if they do not disrupt the educational process. Thus, Bible study groups can meet in a public school before or after required hours.

As another example, a court case in Arizona involved school tuition organizations. Arizona law permits deductions from state taxes for money given to organizations that award scholarships to private schools, including religious schools. The U.S. Supreme Court did not find this a violation of separation of church and state, in spite of the fact that it is a rerouting of money that otherwise would have gone to the state as taxes. Neither is it a violation of the Constitution to use state public funds to buy textbooks or to provide transportation to students attending parochial schools.

Remember something about the Supreme Court and the Constitution. The Constitution is what the judges say it is, and the membership and political ideologies of the Supreme Court change. Finally, the Supreme Court, which has decided many cases restricting prayer and Bible reading and public displays of religion, opens each session with the cry, "God save the United States and this honorable Court." The minute details about what is and what is not separation between church and state drive Americans crazy, and they would also drive the Founding Fathers crazy if they were alive today. Nevertheless, they would accept them, grudgingly, just as happens today.

13

POLITICAL PARTIES IN THE 1790S

The Essentials of a Political Party

At any time, a political party has certain characteristics and functions, such as:

1. the elaboration of an ideology, at least one that exists in the minds of voters and supporters, in their campaign political platforms, and in this era in newspapers: Jefferson and Madison created the *National Gazette*, edited by Philip Freneau, and Hamilton the *Gazette of the United States*, edited by John Fenno.
2. the development and nurturing of a party structure, with local organizations within the individual states
3. the recruitment of party leadership at different levels
4. the establishment of a faithful cadre of party workers
5. the development of party loyalty among the electorate

These functions and characteristics provided an institutional complexity and stability that earlier political groups lacked. In the contest between the Federalists and the Anti-Federalists over the adoption of the Constitution, both groups lacked the essential characteristics of a political party. The opposition of the Anti-Federalists ended with their defeat. Do not use the term Anti-Federalists after the adoption of the Constitution. What evolved in the 1790s were two new political groupings that became political parties, the Federalists and the Republicans. The Republicans were also called Democrats (as a smear, which they proudly accepted), or Democratic-Republicans, or Jeffersonians.

After the ratification of the Constitution, a consensus developed on the basic tenets of America's republican ideology. In the late eighteenth century "republican" referred to those principles and practices appropriate in a government in which ultimate authority rested in the people. Elected officials were responsible to the people and governed according to laws. A democracy, as described by Lincoln, is government of the people, by the people, and for the people. In a pure democracy every citizen votes on every decision affecting the entire political group, as in ancient Greece, although only a small percentage of the males could vote. Modern representative democracies function indirectly through elected representatives. A republic is a government in which sovereign power resides in a restricted, limited portion of the voting population, and where representatives responsible to only that part of the population exercise governmental power. The United States government established in 1789 was a republic. Not everyone could vote for senators or the president. It evolved into a democracy later. Thanks in large part to those who supported Andrew Jackson and others like him, Abraham Lincoln grew up in a democratic America.

No one argued any longer over the fundamental ideas in the Constitution. In the 1790s it was men and their policies that were at fault, not the Constitution itself, not the fundamental ideas in the Constitution. Most of the disputes of this decade centered around the dramatic personalities of Alexander Hamilton and Thomas Jefferson. Both served in Washington's cabinet, Hamilton as Secretary of the Treasury and Jefferson as Secretary of State.

Jefferson was an intellectual who spoke six languages. President John F. Kennedy once hosted a White House dinner for all of America's Nobel Prize winners. In his introductory remarks he stated that this gathering was probably the greatest collection of intellectual talent to ever sit down for dinner in the White House, except for the times when Thomas Jefferson dined here alone. Hamilton was equally brilliant. The wily French politician, Talleyrand, said that he had met the three greatest men of his generation: British Prime Minister William Pitt the Younger, Napoleon, and Hamilton. And, he said, the greatest of these was Hamilton.

Jefferson and Hamilton personally disliked and distrusted one another. Jefferson's diary contains a story about a dinner he hosted for the cabinet. During the dinner Hamilton asked Jefferson who the three portraits were on the wall. Jefferson replied that they were the three greatest men who ever lived: Isaac Newton, John Locke, and Francis Bacon, all scientists and philosophers. Hamilton replied that Jefferson was wrong. The greatest man who ever lived was Julius Caesar, who seized power in ancient Rome. The story may be apocryphal, the source is Jefferson's secret diary; but it accurately describes Jefferson's fears of Hamilton's ambition. Nowhere in Hamilton's writings does he praise Julius Caesar. Instead, he uses him as a shorthand reference for "an evil tyrant." Hamilton's primary personal trait was that he tended to look down on all those who did not match his intellectual talent, in other words, everyone else.

In our first decade under the Constitution disputes and disagreements arose over basic constitutional, economic, and diplomatic policies and the relative powers of the states and the federal government. Each political party believed the other party threatened its vision of the future of the United States, which, of course, was what was best for the new nation. In both parties those in office regarded themselves as the embodiment of the national will, with the Federalists taking an approach that has been called plebiscitarian. This is what we did, **what the people need**. Do the voters agree, after the fact? The Republicans, or Jeffersonians, saw themselves as doing **what the people wanted**, without, of course, asking them.

Hamilton's Program
Added together, the arguments for and against Hamilton's economic programs and proposals form the first ingredients in the **platforms** of the two parties.

The Public Debt
As Secretary of the Treasury Hamilton advocated policies to put the nation on a sound financial footing, as he understood that footing. The first issue concerned the nation's debt, which included the $12 million foreign debt, mostly held by Dutch banks; the $40 million national debt, owed to American bondholders; and the $25 million total for all the state debts. Hamilton's proposals for the debt contributed to the development of two differing ideological stands by the parties. Hamilton proposed to refinance the debt at par, face value, to the present bondholders. James Madison, Jefferson's trusted tactician in the House of Representatives, opposed paying the current bondholders, calling it an injustice to the original bondholders. He urged Hamilton to pay the original bondholders, many of whom had received only 15% to 25% of the face value from speculators. Our foreign bonds in Europe sold for only 25% to 33% of their face value. In short, U.S. government bonds were not considered to be worth much; the chance of them being paid off was slim. However, Congress accepted Hamilton's plan. The debt was paid in full to the current bondholders. Speculators reaped a rich reward. Jefferson and Madison and their followers felt it was unjust, unfair to the original bondholders. But, consider the difficulties in identifying the original bondholders. Hamilton's solution was practical.

Hamilton proposed refinancing the state debt, the responsibility of the various states, to strengthen the union and to increase centralization. A state's position on the national government absorbing their debt depended on the size of their debt and if they had already paid it. Overall, the division in Congress tended to be North-South, the North for, and the South opposed. Hamilton negotiated a trade, Southern support for the assumption of all the state debts in return for Northern support for a national capital located in the South, on the Potomac River, after ten years in Philadelphia, called the Residence Act. Why put the capital in Philadelphia for ten years? First, it would take time to build the rudimentary structure for the federal government in Washington.

Second, this gained the votes of Philadelphia and Pennsylvania, who believed that after ten years in the luxury of our largest city no one would really move the capital to a swamp on the Potomac. Yet, it happened. What a blow to Philadelphia's pride.

The debt – national, foreign, and for all the states – was paid off with a new debt, in essence refinanced. Why? What was gained? You will understand when you first apply for a credit card or loan. The first question asked will be, "What debts have you paid in the past?" If you had none, the creditor cannot assess your reliability. You must create some record of having faithfully and responsibly paid off a debt. That reassures future creditors that you will pay your debts, making them willing to lend new money. Improving a credit rating is the main reason to refinance, for a person or a nation. Hamilton understood the need to create a good image for the fledgling nation. By 1795 U.S. bonds sold at 110% of their face value, a good investment.

When Washington took the oath of office in 1789 the United States government consisted of only 75 post offices, an army of 46 officers and 672 soldiers, and a large debt. There was no navy, no federal court system, nor any means to collect taxes. Considering how huge the "To Do List" was, it is no wonder that Europeans were betting the new government and country would not last.

Hamilton sincerely believed that it was necessary to tie the wealthy to the government. He reasoned that if the wealthy supported the government, stability was possible. He once wrote that "A national debt if it is not excessive will be to us a national blessing; it will be powerful cement to our union." Some modern day commentators are concerned that every country's wealthy elite will lessen their loyalty to their country in the future, due to multiple homes abroad, foreign stocks owned, international corporations, ease of travel, etc. In essence, they become citizens of the world, not of their country. However, this is similar to the European upper class situation prior to the First World War. The outbreak of the First World War reasserted national loyalty. Let us hope it does not require such an event in the future.

The Bank Proposal

The vote in Congress on creating a national bank to serve the economy and the government was sectional, North 33-1, South 6-19, overall, 39-20. On this issue, at the president's request, Hamilton and Jefferson wrote explanations of their opinions on the constitutionality of a Bank of the United States. In essence, the dispute was over the question of "ends and means." Which is more important – how something is done or the result? The dispute centered on the meaning and purpose of the Constitution's Article I, Section 8, Clause 18, the "necessary and proper" clause or "implied powers" clause. Hamilton argued for using the implied powers clause to say, if the Constitution does not specifically prohibit it, then it can be done. Jefferson argued that unless the Constitution specifically permits it, then it was prohibited. In a similar statement,

Madison called the Bank "condemned by the silence of the Constitution." These statements of loose (Hamilton) and strict (Jefferson) construction became the ideological positions of the two parties.

In 1789 the nation had no national banking system. There were three banks in the whole country, each serving a limited, local area, in Philadelphia, New York City, and Boston. The stability provided by the Bank of the U.S. led to fifty-five banks by 1800, eighty by 1805, including the Bank of the U.S.'s branches. The growing economy now had places where entrepreneurs could borrow money to start a business.

An Excise Tax on Whiskey

Hamilton urged an excise tax on whiskey, 25% of the net price, to raise revenue and to impress on Westerners that the federal government existed. The tariff, a tax on imports, was the chief tax, paid only at the port of entry, thus most of the population never saw any evidence of the federal government nor of any federal tax. Not now; look at your pay stub. The voting on the whiskey excise tax was sectional, North 28-6, South 7-15, overall, 35-21. The tax eventually led to the Whiskey Rebellion in western Pennsylvania, put down by a 12,600 man army, an army larger than any that could be mustered at most times during the Revolutionary War. Republicans raised their voices in protest. Adding a cynical view, Jefferson said that "An insurrection was announced and proclaimed and armed against, but could never be found." Twenty prisoners were captured, two were found guilty of treason, and both were immediately pardoned. Since the exercise tax raised only a small amount of revenue, Jefferson's followers questioned the "real" purpose of Hamilton in trying to impose such a burden on western farmers. Is this similar to the Stamp Act crisis before the Revolution? Today, what would be the purpose of a huge new tax on gasoline, $10 per gallon, to raise revenue or to reduce use? Are cigarettes taxed to raise revenue or to reduce use? Taxes can have multiple purposes. Excise taxes are still with us, check your next concert tickets.

The Whiskey Rebellion was not an isolated event in American history. Throughout the colonial period and the early national era, tensions simmered over what westerners felt were economic advantages and unequal power held by elite Easterners, who ran the colonial and state governments. The most significant armed confrontations were Bacon's Rebellion in 1676, the Carolina Regulator movement in 1771, Shays's Rebellion in Massachusetts in 1786-1787, the riot against the ratification of the Constitution in 1788 centered in Carlisle, Pennsylvania, and the Whiskey Rebellion, 1791-1794. This West versus East theme continued in American history; almost always due to unequal representation in legislatures and an unfair distribution of economic influence. Reducing those tensions was a factor behind the movement of state capitals inland after the Revolution, for example, Richmond, Virginia, Harrisburg, Pennsylvania, and Columbia, South Carolina.

A Protective High Tariff

Hamilton proposed a high tariff to protect American producers from foreign competition. A tariff is a tax on imports. The primary impact of a high or protective tariff would be a boon to "infant American industries" struggling against the competition of foreign goods. The primary impact of a low or revenue tariff would be to provide tax income for the government. A revenue tariff passed. Hamilton lost on this issue. The main source of revenue for the federal government in this period was the tariff, followed by land sales. Almost all modern economists assert that low tariffs, or even no tariffs, are better for all nations. Each nation should concentrate on what it does best, trading its surplus to other countries. If all countries followed this idea, which is the economic concept labeled "comparative advantage," then the prices of all commodities and goods fall to a lower level, benefiting all consumers everywhere.

Report on Manufacturers

Hamilton argued that the government should pursue pro-manufacturing policies to achieve national self-sufficiency, which was also part of his argument for a protective tariff. In his **Report on Manufacturers**, he urged other financial incentives to encourage manufacturing. Congress never acted on his proposals. In a society of 95% farmers there was little political support for this idea. It did not matter. Entrepreneurs sensed a new atmosphere of government support. By the end of the 1790s, states were issuing charters for an average of thirty new businesses each year, ten times the rate in the previous decade.

Finally, Hamilton introduced a major economic change in 1791, when Congress adopted the dollar as our currency, thus officially separating it from the British Pound.

Election of 1796

Washington announced that he would not run again in 1796. Elected in 1789 and 1792, he declared two terms enough. Both parties used a caucus, a meeting of their members in Congress, to select their presidential and vice-presidential candidates. Note that the initial organization of both parties was from the top down. Meanwhile, Washington's Farewell Address in September, 1796, warned against BOTH foreign alliances and political parties. Due to the mechanics of the Electoral College in 1796, John Adams won the presidency, 71-68, but Jefferson won the vice-presidency. The Federalist Electors split their votes among several vice-presidential candidates, creating a situation in which the president and the vice president were from two different political parties.

XYZ Affair

Early in his term President Adams sent negotiators – Charles Pinckney, Elbridge Gerry, and John Marshall – to France to try to resolve our differences. He had asked Jefferson and Madison, but they declined to serve. The French foreign minister demanded bribes before he would even speak to the Americans. The negotiators returned home and submitted a report on the failed negotiations to the president and the Senate, because of the Senate's responsibility to approve treaties. Jeffersonian Republicans in the House of Representatives criticized the president and the Federalists, charging that the negotiators had not tried to negotiate. President Adams defended his conduct in a speech before the Senate, substituting X, Y, and Z for the names of the three French agents who delivered the demand for bribes. The country exploded in an anti-French war fever. An undeclared naval war with France developed and the Federalists gained twenty seats in the House in the 1798 midterm elections. The British tried to take advantage of the anti-French uproar by urging Americans to begin taking over their trade between the British West Indies and Great Britain, freeing up British ships and making it impossible for the French to interfere with that trade, which would cause a diplomatic incident with the United States. The British ambassador discussed with Hamilton the possibility of a joint U.S.-British strike against the French and Spanish colonies in the New World. Spain was included because it was now France's ally. Meanwhile French refugees here were trying to counter the anti-French feeling. The Federalists argued that all this foreign meddling into our domestic politics had to end.

Alien and Sedition Acts
Many immigrants flooded into Philadelphia, the nation's capital in the 1790s, especially Irish fleeing a failed rebellion in that decade and French fleeing the nuances of the French Revolution. Most became Republicans and voted immediately. Remember, the states controlled voting. Still do. The most famous immigrant was Albert Gallatin, a Swiss who became a leader in Jefferson's party and a thorn in the side of the Federalists. He had a stellar career as a Pennsylvania politician. Although elected to the U.S. Senate in 1793, the senate disallowed his election because he had not been a citizen for the constitutionally required number of years, nine. Instead, he won election to the House of Representatives. Denounced as a French agent, he was a target of the Sedition Act of 1798. He served as Secretary of the Treasury for 13 years under Jefferson and Madison. He was largely responsible for the peace treaty that ended the War of 1812. Later he served as minister to France and then to England. Greatly interested in American Indian tribes, he found time to write extensively on ethnology.

The Federalists were concerned about the immigrant problem. (Sounds familiar?) To protect the new nation they passed four acts.

1. The Naturalization Act extended the years required for residence for citizenship from 5 to 14.
2. The Alien Friends Act gave the president the power to remove aliens in wartime.

3. The Alien Act said the president could order out of the country all aliens suspected of "treasonable activities," which were not clearly defined.
4. The Sedition Act specifically made it illegal to falsely criticize the government or government officials.

As an example, two Republican newspaper editors were convicted under the Sedition Act; one received a sentence of 6 hours in jail and a $5 fine, the other, 18 months and a $400 fine. What they wrote was the following:

> "No Stamp Act, no Sedition, No Alien Bills, No Land Tax; downfall to the tyrants of America, peace and retirement to the President (Adams), long live the Vice-President (Jefferson) and the Minority; may moral virtue be the basis of civil government."

Hardly rough commentary. Twenty-five Republicans, mostly editors or printers, were indicted, ten convicted. One was a drunk, Luther Baldwin, who, upon hearing cannons fired by Federalist supporters celebrating that President John Adams was traveling through their New Jersey town, remarked, "that he did not care if they fired through the president's arse." He got two months and a fine.

The Virginia and Kentucky Resolutions protested against the Alien and Sedition Acts and declared the doctrine of state nullification of federal laws. Written by Madison (Virginia) and Jefferson (Kentucky), the resolutions passed by these state legislatures were an overreaction to the Alien and Sedition Acts, not a party doctrine in favor of nullification and states' rights; the issue was liberty, not constitutional doctrine. States' rights would never be a particular party's doctrinaire ideological position in any period of American history. It was always raised, by Southern or Northern states, over something concrete, such as the Alien and Sedition Acts, the tariff, or the Fugitive Slave Law.

The Federalist Party was weakened before the next election because President Adams opted for peace with France in the undeclared naval war. He thought peace advocates in both parties would support his reelection in 1800. Adams had also pushed Hamilton's supporters out of his cabinet in a personal split with Hamilton. John Adams referred to Hamilton as "the bastard brat of a Scotch peddler." It may have been true, but such statements do not build party unity. The Federalist Party divided into supporters of Adams and supporters of Hamilton. Adams lost the election.

The Election of 1800
This election represented the crystallization of the political parties, with clear platforms and established party organizations. It ended, technically, in a "tie," with Thomas Jefferson and his vice-presidential candidate, Aaron Burr, each receiving 73 Electoral

College votes. Adams got 65. The Electors did not, nor could not, specify who they intended to be the president and who they intended to be the vice-president. Some of the Democratic-Republican Electors, who were supposed to not vote for Aaron Burr, failed to do so, out of a fear that Adams would come in second, reversing and repeating the scenario from 1796. Since Electors voted for any two men for president, theoretically Burr and Jefferson were tied for president, in spite of the fact that everyone knew that Jefferson was to be the president and Burr the vice-president.

Under the procedure established by the Constitution the election for president now went to the House of Representatives, which was controlled by the opposition party, the Federalists. The Senate selected the vice-president. Thus the opposing political party would select the next president, maybe. Many Federalists were sincerely frightened by Jefferson, who had on occasions made some extreme remarks. Think about it, if voters concentrated on the most extreme things any candidate for public office ever uttered, anyone can look extreme.

Between the November election in 1800 and the voting in the House of Representatives in February, (the inauguration date back then was March 4) many saw a possible civil war breaking out or the country going without a president. Outgoing President John Adams wrote that "civil war was expected." Pennsylvania Governor Thomas McKean stated his intention to call out twenty thousand troops to put Jefferson in the White House. Governor James Monroe of Virginia ordered four thousand state militia troops to guard a federal arsenal against a threatening Federalist army, which was really the nation's army.

The Twelfth Amendment, adopted in 1804, made certain this situation did not happen again. It provided for separate votes by Electors for president and vice-president. Under the procedure established by the Constitution, the 1800 election voting for a president was by states in the House of Representatives, each state having one vote.

It took 35 ballots to pick the winner. The final vote was 10 states for Jefferson, 4 for Burr, 2 blank. The Federalists finally selected Jefferson without casting a single vote for him. Delaware's only representative, Federalist James A. Bayard, broke the deadlock by announcing at a Federalist Party caucus that he was switching his vote, giving Jefferson the victory. Instead, the whole caucus accepted Bayard's real plan, that within each state delegation Federalists cast blank ballots; therefore, if there was at least one Republican Representative, that state voted for Jefferson. This way no Federalist would have to live with the awful shame of having voted to make Jefferson the president. For example, Delaware's Federalist Representative, James A. Bayard, voted blank; thus, Delaware cast a blank vote. Hamilton had been working behind the scenes to elect Jefferson rather than Burr. He considered Burr treacherous. Remember the later dual between Hamilton and Burr in 1804. Ill will from this election was a factor in causing it. In a letter to Federalist leader Harrison Gray Otis, Hamilton wrote: "Mr. Jefferson, though too revolutionary in his notions, is yet a lover of liberty and will be desirous of something like orderly Government – Mr. Burr loves nothing but himself – Thinks of nothing but his own aggrandizement – and will be content with nothing short of permanent power in his own hands . . . . In a choice of Evils, let them take the least – Jefferson is in my view less dangerous than Burr."

The election of 1800 introduced two new features into American politics: acceptance of the decision of the electorate and toleration of opposition to the party in office. It was the first time in history that a political party that lost an election peacefully handed over the reins of government to the winning opposition. In truth, both parties pursued an approach to become the only party in the nation, because they each believed they were the embodiment of the national will, or what was best for the future of the country. Both had a vision for the future and the policies needed to get there. However, even toleration had its limits. When Jefferson took the oath of office John Adams had already left Washington, the new capital.

Political Parties in the 1790s

Each party feared tyranny, but each expected tyranny to come from a different source. What were their differences? Historians have identified the following:

The Federalists were pro-merchant and pro-manufacturing, pushing for a diversified economy in which trade, finance, and manufacturing supplemented agriculture. They were New Englanders and others who lived in seaport cities and towns along the Atlantic coast and saw connections to Europe as crucial to our future; farmers producing for markets; shipping and banking interests; and urban artisans. They favored a loose construction of the Constitution, meaning that it could be done unless the Constitution prohibited it. Pro-British in foreign policy, meaning they did not see Great Britain as a threat. They admired the stability of the British structure of government; feared the mobs in the cities and the unruly, popularly elected House of Representatives. They favored having a standing regular army. Congregational and Episcopalian clergy and leaders supported them. The Federalist approach was plebiscitarian – this is for your own good. A plebiscite takes place after some policy has already been implemented. Do the voters approve? It is too late to oppose or reverse it. The Federalists believed strongly in a tradition of civic humanism. "The essence of civic humanism was disinterestedness – public service engaged in by a leisured gentry for the common good." "Federalists believed in a hierarchy of ranks, a social order of uneven and unequal parts made up of gentlemen and everyone else." (George Levesque, "Slavery in the Ideology and Politics of the Revolutionary Generation.") Yet, in spite of their identification with the old order, many of their policies characterized subsequent American history.

The Republicans were pro-farmer, especially backcountry and subsistence farmers, who saw Western land as crucial to our future, and also Southerners, small merchants, tradesmen and artisans. They favored a strict construction of the Constitution; if the Constitution does not specifically allow it, then it is prohibited. They were pro-French in foreign policy, meaning they did not see the French as a greater threat than the British. They feared the rich, political corruption, and the concentration of power in the president and the Senate. They favored a reliance on state militias rather than a regular standing army. They appealed more to Baptists, Methodists, and Catholic clergy and leaders. The Republican approach was "we understand the general will," what voters want and need. They preferred the future to be like the past.

Neither party was democratic, asking the people what they wanted. In both parties, the elite ran things, although the Republicans saw the Federalists as an elite based more on hereditary. It was said that the Federalists did things **to** the people and the Republicans did things **for** the people. Neither advocated government **by** the people. That would come later. In *The Federalist #71*, Hamilton argued that the people do not always understand what is truly in their best interests. Only by entrusting power to those capable of rendering correct judgments can the people be saved from "the very fatal consequences of their own mistakes."

We tend to give to the word "democratic" some connotations and meanings that they did not yet give. Our emphasis on universal suffrage lay in the future. But as historian R. R. Palmer pointed out in *The Age of the Democratic Revolution: A Political History of Europe and America, 1760-1800*, in this era, throughout the period of democratic revolutions in America, in Mexico, in South America, in France, in Haiti, in Greece, and elsewhere, there was a "new feeling for a kind of equality, or at least a discomfort with older forms of social stratification," which challenged the justice, the reasonableness, and the basic common sense of the old order. The Federalists represented the disappearing old order; the Jeffersonian Republicans were introducing the new society, a more equal society. As Jefferson explained once, "the mass of mankind has not been born with saddles on their backs, nor a favored few booted and spurred, ready to ride them legitimately, by the Grace of God."

The debates between the two parties clarified thinking and sharpened policies, leading to well thought-out policies and institutions in the 1790s. The politicians of the 1790s deserve our thanks and praise for establishing our governments, state and national, on firm foundations.

14

THE 1790S – THE SPLIT OVER FOREIGN POLICY

The First New Nation

As European colonial empires evaporated in the 1950s and 1960s, historians realized that the experiences of the new nations of Africa and Asia were somewhat similar to those of the infant United States. They compared those experiences. Here are some of their assertions.

A new nation wants no part of what it calls "the great power struggles." New nations do not see such struggles as "moral" struggles. After the Second World War, both superpowers, the United States and the Soviet Union, and most of their allies, saw the Cold War as a moral struggle. The emerging new nations of Africa and Asia did not. They opted for neutrality. Returning to the 1790s, war between Great Britain and France began in 1792 and continued intermittently until the end of the Napoleonic wars in 1815. Both countries saw the struggle as one involving different moral visions of what the world should be. The emerging new nation, the United States, constantly faced being drawn into a war during those years. The United States tried to remain neutral, to stay out of the European powers' struggle, and yet, somehow, to benefit.

The new nation wanted to be left alone to develop its economy and to unify its people. America eagerly sought and accepted aid from the French, Dutch, and Spanish governments to win the Revolutionary War. Afterwards the new country wanted to trade with everyone and anyone, getting rich selling goods to both sides during any war. The U.S. was open to loans, trade, and investment from anyone, but, no strings attached. As Jefferson said, the "new world would fatten on the follies of the old." This is similar to Egypt's strategy during the Cold War while seeking funds for building the Aswan Dam. Egypt played one superpower off against the other one, and they got the funding, from the Soviet Union.

The former colonies opposed foreign military presence in their part of the world, while seeking to avoid military commitments or alliances. After the Revolutionary War ended, the United States faced the humiliation of the presence of 6,000 British soldiers on American soil in a string of forts along its border with Canada. The British refused to leave until American merchants paid their prewar debts to British merchants. Our government finally assumed that debt and paid it in 1802, £600,000. America's desire to avoid military commitments or alliances would lead in 1823 to the Monroe Doctrine, which declared the Western Hemisphere off limits to European meddling. This was quite an ambitious statement from a new nation that had not beaten the British by themselves in the Revolutionary War. Approximately 90% of the gunpowder used by the rebellious colonies during the Revolutionary War came from France. In addition, the fledging United States could gain only a stalemate against Britain's second-string army and navy in the War of 1812.

The new nation believed it had a unique ideological message for mankind. Americans saw in Europe monarchy, a privileged aristocracy, and monopoly economic institutions benefiting the favored few. Americans KNEW republicanism was the wave of the future and that eventually all these old European institutions would be replaced. Both the government and the American people enthusiastically applauded all revolutions or rebellions against decadent European powers, such as the Greek Revolt against the Ottoman Empire in 1821.

The new nation governed its own affairs without donning the moral restraints that it urged upon the great powers. The United States seized territory; something it condemned in the past when other nations did it. Our minister to Russia, John Quincy Adams, tried to justify to the czar the American seizure of West Florida in 1810. The czar stopped the attempted explanation with a simple statement. "Everyone is getting a little bigger these days." John Quincy Adams had no response, because his justifications were woefully inadequate given American principles and our criticism of typical European diplomacy.

The new nation oppressed minority groups and sharply limited domestic opposition. "Correct ideas" justified some unusual actions. Examples are the Alien and Sedition Acts, forcing Indians further west, and slavery. The United States continued the slave trade decades after the major powers had begun to stop it. Keep these characteristics of the United States between 1789 and 1823 in mind when studying the emergence of the "new Nations" of Africa and Asia in the 1950s and 1960s. There are similarities.

The French Revolution

The French Revolution began in 1789 with the storming of the Bastille prison on July 14. It was the dominating event of the 1790s, especially as radical impulses began to play a larger role. The word "ideology" was coined during the French Revolution, which says a great deal about the importance of ideas associated with it and reactions to it. The historian R. R. Palmer, in *The Age of the Democratic Revolution: A Political History of Europe and America, 1760-1800*, called the French Revolution and other similar revolutions the birth of the idea of "the people as constituent power." The initial reaction for most Americans was enthusiastic support. Lafayette gave Thomas Paine (who was overjoyed at another revolution to play a role in) the key to the Bastille, instructing him to give it to President George Washington. However, early enthusiasm waned by 1793 as excesses appeared, such as the Reign of Terror and the guillotine execution of Louis XVI on January 21, 1793, and his wife, Marie Antoinette, in October of the same year. Among Americans, disagreements emerged over what the French Revolution symbolized and whether it differed from ours.

John Adams explained the conservative Federalist view, "Ours was resistance to innovation; theirs was innovation itself." Our Revolution was conservative; the French Revolution was radical. The radicalism that disturbed conservatives included widespread anti-religious actions against the Catholic Church. The French revolutionaries saw the church and king as closely linked, parallel engines of oppression. They converted the Cathedral of Notre Dame into the Temple of Reason. They invented the metric system, based upon nature, to replace the foot and yard, which had monarchical origins. Originally, a yard was defined as the distance from the king's nose to his outstretched thumb.

The new French calendar was freed from the contamination of religion, both Christian and Roman, and also Roman gods and emperors, for example, Sunday, Easter, Christmas, March, July, and August (Mars, Julius Caesar, Augustus Caesar). The birth of the new revolutionary French Republic replaced the birth of Christ as Year One, the beginning of the calendar. A.D. and B.C. were gone. The calendar coincided with nature, at least nature as found in France. It had ten-day weeks, 30-day months, and 5 "revolution days" of celebrating the new order. Each day was named for something in "nature," such as field turnip, hog, cauliflower, honey, cricket, cork, olive, shovel, eggplant, plow, spinach, tuna fish, and even manure. Imagine having a birthday on manure, our December 28. A month stretched from around our calendar's 20th to the next month's 19th. The new months, starting with late September, were vintage, fog, frost, snow, rain, wind, budding, flower, meadow, harvest, heat, and fruit; in French, Vendémaire, Brumaire, Frimaire, Nivôse, Pluviôse, Ventôse, Germinal, Floréal, Prairial, Messidor, Thermidor, and Fructidor. Try to image the average French peasant trying to keep track of all these changes. Not doing so could get one branded as a traitor to the revolution, imprisonment or death could follow. The only part of all this turmoil that has remained is the phrase "Thermidorian reaction," used by historians to identify the end of the most radical phase of the French Revolution, when Robespierre lost power and the Reign of Terror ended, during the month of Thermidor, July. Historians use it to designate the point in any revolution when a conservative reaction, conservative to the revolutionaries, stops the most extreme phase of the revolution. For the American Revolution, some historians see the Constitutional Convention, 1787, as a Thermidorian reaction.

There is a saying among revolutionaries that a revolution has "no enemies to the left," meaning that revolutionaries fully embrace the revolution's abstractions, such as "life, liberty, and the pursuit of happiness," or, in the French Revolution, "liberty, equality, and fraternity." There is no place for a half-hearted revolutionary. Be super exuberant or face the consequences from those who are "truly" committed. A revolution at this stage minimizes the "means" of accomplishing its objectives because the "ends" are so pure. In normal civil society, the means are important. How an objective is achieved matters. Not so during a fanatical revolution. This was a time when ideas became important politically, similar to Red state – Blue state divisions in the early twenty-first century. Today it appears mandatory to shoehorn every subject into a brief slogan, making it either conservative or liberal, Red or Blue.

Jefferson summarized the pro-French Revolution position with a statement. "The liberty of the whole earth was depending on the issue of the contest, and . . . rather than it should have failed, I would have seen half the earth devastated." Jefferson had been the U.S. minister to France when the revolution broke out on July 14, 1789. He witnessed three months of the revolution, including the fall of the Bastille. However, this is an example of how carefully one should use quotations. Jefferson wrote this in a private, personal letter. He did not intend it as a statement of public policy towards the French Revolution or as a statement of desired American policy. Too often juicy quotes show up in history books because they are so juicy.

Treaty of 1778

The treaty of alliance with France from the Revolutionary War, according to one of its provisions, was a "perpetual alliance." Now, that caused complications. France was involved in a war against virtually everyone in Europe. Was the United States obligated under the treaty to help the new French revolutionary government? Hamilton said no, the treaty lapsed with the end of the French monarchy, the death of Louis XVI. Jefferson said yes, treaties are between nations, not governments. The nineteenth century German statesman, Bismarck, said it best, a treaty is a "scrap of paper," a promise, which does not always obligate a nation to honor it.

The French government tried to influence our indecision by sending a special envoy, Citizen Edmond Charles Genet. (His name does not have an accent, contrary to what appears in some textbooks.) Note the non-title, which is typical of revolutions. The later Russian Revolution used "comrade" to equalize everyone and to get rid of titles. Our Constitution prohibits Congress from granting titles. Genet arrived in America on April 8, 1793, coming to Charleston, South Carolina. He left ten days later, taking 28 days to get to the capital, Philadelphia. The entire trip was a succession of dinners sponsored by Jefferson's supporters. Along the way, Genet commissioned 14 privateers, legalized pirates, who captured 80 British merchant ships. He also tried to interest Americans to form volunteer military expeditions to invade Canada.

President Washington responded to Genet's actions by issuing a Neutrality Proclamation on April 22. Read it. It is an example of diplomatic double-talk. It never mentions the word neutrality, but it is clear the United States is going to be neutral. Washington worded it this way because his Secretary of State, Jefferson, raised a question. If only Congress had the authority to declare war, was not a declaration of neutrality a declaration to not go to war, and, therefore, a statement that only Congress could make? Washington ordered Genet out of the country. Just then, a message from France arrived ordering Genet to return home. Questions were being raised about his loyalty to the revolution. Wisely, Genet did not return to France, and was allowed to remain in America. He married the daughter of the governor of New York and settled down to a quiet, non-revolutionary life as a gentleman farmer on Long Island. Another saying about revolutions is that "they devour their own children." One runs the risk of not being on the side of those currently in charge or those poised to take change. Questions may be raised about one's "commitment to the revolution." It is safer to leave before these accusations appear. Lafayette did. Unfortunately, when he fled to Austria for safety the Austrians still saw him as a "dangerous revolutionary." He spent five years in an Austrian prison.

Just as America's relationship with France went downhill, our relationship with England did also. The war between the two powers, France and England, had become labeled as one between the tiger and the shark, or, the elephant and the whale, each supreme in one area, either on the European continent or on the seas. Because of the war, trade between the United States and England had more than tripled. In 1792, a brief year of peace, it was $20,750,000. By 1796 it was $67,060,000. In order to interfere with American trade with France, the British issued secret orders-in-council, admiralty decrees concerning trade policies, creating a long list of contraband goods that could be seized. It also justified seizing ships carrying contraband. According to international law, it was an accepted practice that belligerents could restrict neutral trade during a war. If American ships were caught trying to sneak contraband through a blockade, a shipper had nothing to complain about and the ship's government had no right to protest or to take action. In 1793 the British seized 250 American ships.

There were other festering issues with the British. The British occupied the Northwest forts on our soil, practiced impressment of American sailors, and protested the inability to satisfy the property claims of English loyalists. The Treaty of 1783 guaranteed the right of loyalists to sue in American courts to recover damages for losses suffered during the Revolutionary War. It did not happen. Courts and juries ruled against them. A clause in the Treaty of Paris, 1783, permitted the British to remain on western soil until the United States resolved land issues with Britain's Indian allies. The defeat of the Indians at the battle of Fallen Timbers in Ohio in 1794 resolved those issues with the 1795 Treaty of Greenville.

The British navy needed 20,000 sailors. Approximately one-half, 10,000, needed to be replaced each year due to refusals to reenlist or desertion. One historian has estimated that approximately 250,000 British sailors were impressed during the eighteenth century. Not only Americans were caught in the dragnet. The British navy practiced harsh discipline, too harsh for many sailors. Impressment, forcing deserters from a weak nation's navy or merchant marine back into your navy, even if they had never been in your navy, helped to fill the void. The United States was the weak nation. From the British point of view, why risk a war over impressment? The answer, given by historian Denver Brunsman in *The Evil Necessity: British Naval Impressment in the Eighteenth-Century Atlantic World*, is that the very existence of Great Britain and the empire, as seen by British leaders, required a strong merchant marine, the primary source of tax revenues, and a superior navy to protect and maintain it. He summarizes British policy as "no sailors, no navy; no navy, no empire." Impress to the fullest, to survive as a nation.

Jay's Treaty

President Washington sent John Jay to England to work out our differences. The result was Jay's Treaty, submitted to the Senate for two-thirds approval. During the negotiations Hamilton told the British ambassador what the United States would and would not accept, undermining our bargaining position. Hamilton wanted to protect American trade with Great Britain. Over 90% of our imports and 50% of our exports were with Great Britain. As a practical matter, does a nation stand up for a principle of international law and assert its rights, or, shallow its pride, knowing the United States is powerless, and, therefore, become in essence a junior partner of the British, accepting their dictated terms? Weak nations have few options.

The provisions in Jay's Treaty clearly favored the British.

1. The Northwest forts were to be surrendered by June 1, 1796.
2. Some ports in British India were to be opened to Americans on a limited basis.
3. U.S. trade with the British West Indies was made virtually impossible.
4. The United States had to accept paper blockades, which were unenforced, and therefore supposed to be illegal under international law. A paper blockade meant that no ships were actually blockading that port. An American ship was guilty of running the blockade if a British ship later stopped it elsewhere, anywhere.
5. Free ships no longer equaled free goods. The British could seize French property on American ships. Technically the deck of an American ship (and today also the inside of an American airplane) is the same as American soil. Therefore, when the British boarded an American ship to seize non-contraband goods, it was theoretically an invasion of the United States, an act of war. No longer.
6. The issue of impressment was not addressed, and therefore would continue. This satisfied the severe shortage of sailors in the British navy. About 10,000 per year were needed.

Hamilton tried to give a public speech in New York City to drum up support for the treaty. Five thousand people showed up, one-tenth of the city's population. The mob pelted him with stones. Someone wrote graffiti on a wall in Boston, "Damn John Jay! Damn everyone who won't damn John Jay!! Damn everyone that won't put lights in his windows and sit up all night damning John Jay!!!" Putting lighted candles in your window was a message that you supported the cause endorsed by the mob roaming the streets. Otherwise, your windows might be broken. And, glass was expensive.

The Federalist Party controlled the Senate, which ratified the treaty, barely, by two-thirds, 20-10. A great deal of intrigue and many rumors followed ratification. Part of the intrigue involved charges that Federalist cabinet members, to make the French sound as if they were interfering in our internal politics, deliberately mistranslated statements by the French government. According to the Constitution, all money bills must originate in the House of Representatives. The Jeffersonians, in control of the House, tried to block the treaty by not appropriating the money to carry it out, $90,000. The appropriation barely passed, 51-48. The party meeting to determine strategy on this issue was the first congressional caucus in our history. Even more than Hamilton's financial policies, Jay's Treaty led to the division into two political parties. Jay's Treaty was THE significant step in the development of party ideology, loyalty, and policy. Historians estimate that about 42% of the voting in Congress before the ruckus over Jay's Treaty was not clearly linked to a party line. Afterwards, it was just 7%.

One unexpected benefit was Spain's fear that a secret clause in Jay's Treaty made the U.S. and Great Britain allies. It did not. Spain agreed to Pinckney's Treaty with the U.S., granting westerners the "right of deposit" at New Orleans and recognizing America's claim to the Southwest, modern Mississippi and Alabama.

French anger at this treaty, and the suspected secret alliance with Britain it contained (again, it did not), contributed to France's decision to begin an undeclared naval war with the United States, 1797-1800. The Convention of 1800 with France, also called the Treaty of Mortefontaine, ended both the undeclared naval war and the Treaty of 1778, freeing the United States from the complications of its "perpetual alliance."

Election of 1796

Washington announced that he would not run again. He had been elected in 1789 and 1792. Both parties used a Congressional caucus to select their presidential and vice-presidential candidates. Note that the initial organization of the political parties began at the top. Meanwhile, Washington's Farewell Address in September warned against BOTH foreign alliances and political parties. Not everyone took his advice.

Due to the mechanics of the Electoral College, as stipulated by the Constitution, John Adams won over Thomas Jefferson, 71-68. Several candidates split the voting to be the Federalist vice-president. Thus, the president and the vice-president were from two different political parties. John Adams' gruff personality during his two terms as vice-president under Washington, and Jefferson serving as Adams' vice-president, explain why the vice-presidency became an office strictly limited to its constitutional duties. One old story frequently told about the vice-presidency was about the old woman who had two sons. One ran away to sea and the other one grew up to be vice-president. Neither one was ever heard from again. Everyone usually ignored vice-presidents. A quipster once joked that the only real job of the vice-president was to inquire daily as to the health of the president.

The Alien and Sedition Acts, and the Virginia and Kentucky Resolutions as responses, described previously, were an additional aggravation to both parties. Foreign and domestic problems overlapped in their lives. This text splits them to concentrate on each perspective. Add them together and it becomes easier to understand why historians label the 1790s as a crucial decade for students to grasp. So many issues in the next 30-40 years grew out of this decade.

Election of 1800

President John Adams, opting for peace with France to end the undeclared naval war, hurt the Federalist Party's chances in the election of 1800. He hoped that peace advocates in both parties would support his reelection. Adams also pushed Hamilton's supporters out of his cabinet following a split with Hamilton. This divided the Federalist Party into supporters of Adams and supporters of Hamilton, and made victory for Jefferson's party easier.

15

JEFFERSON AS PRESIDENT

The Dying Federalist Administration

On December 14, 1799, George Washington died. Henry Lee, the father of Robert E. Lee, praised him as "first in war, first in peace, first in the hearts of his countrymen." Now there was a huge void on the political scene; the country no longer had someone who was seen as above partisan politics. A unifying force had died. What would become of the United States? Now either politics or time would produce national unity. A combination of both would eventually forge unity, but not right away.

Jefferson's First Term as President

Jefferson first labeled his 1800 election "the revolution of 1800" in an 1819 letter. In some respects it was. Jefferson's first term is very significant when viewed as his contemporaries did. Evaluate Jefferson's first term against the background of the harsh politics of the 1790s. Many Federalists honestly feared Jefferson. They believed the hard-earned gains of the Washington and Adams administrations would be lost. We know the United States would last; they did not. In truth, Jefferson understood that repealing Hamilton's system was impossible. He wrote in 1802, "We can pay off his debt in 15 years; but we can never get rid of his financial system."

Federalists believed that under Jefferson's administration:

> All governmental power would shift to the states.
> All commerce would suffer.
> Hamilton's financial system would be dismantled and destroyed.
> Jefferson would destroy all churches, because he was an atheist.

Our foreign policy would suffer.   As a Francophile revolutionary
Jefferson would ruin the army and navy under the guise of economy and then involve the nation in a war against Great Britain.

Thomas Paine, considered Jefferson's good friend by Federalists (which he was not), denounced churches in his book, *The Age of Reason*, published in 1794.   Paine called churches "human inventions set up to terrify and enslave mankind, and monopolize power and profit."   Jefferson was a deist, not an atheist, and he was far from an opponent of churches.   He once said, "I am a Christian, in the only sense in which he (Jesus) wished anyone to be: sincerely attached to his doctrines, in preference to all others." He sincerely believed in religious freedom and that government should erect, as he later stated, a "wall of separation" between churches and the government.   *The Age of Reason* must be viewed as part of Paine's participation in the radical phase of the French Revolution.   For both Jefferson and Paine, you must understand that their criticism of the church as an institution was based upon their study of history, of the many times when the church primarily functioned as an oppressive arm of the government rather than as a religious institution doing good works and saving souls.   Once a particular religion becomes any nation's official church, its outlook turns conservative, in order to preserve its favored position within that nation's power structure.   While some church leaders may become agents advocating change, the church as an institution does not. The Lutheran theologian, Dietrich Bonhoeffer, criticized Hitler's policies in the early 1930s; the officially sanctioned German Lutheran Church did not.

As president, Jefferson proved to be more of a political realist than an ideological theorist.   Jon Meacham's book, *Jefferson and the Art of Power*, explains that Jefferson is highly rated by historians as an effective president because he understood how and when to use power as a practical politician.   He had an ideological vision, but he was realistic in pursuing his goals.   Many of his famous quotes are from his private letters, known to us because he kept a copy of all of them.   However, as an officeholder he proved to be very cautious and practical.   He decried Hamilton's strong central government; however, Jefferson asked his Secretary of the Treasury, Albert Gallatin, to draw up a plan for roads and canals built at federal government expense to aid commerce.   His plan anticipated every future canal built along the east coast and a road almost paralleling what is currently Interstate 95, from Florida to Maine.   Jefferson also pushed for the building of the National Road westward.   He was more opposed to Hamilton personally than to the idea that one should not use governmental powers to aid commerce.   As president, Jefferson simply ignored the Alien and Sedition Acts, and allowed them to lapse rather than stirring up a fight in Congress by trying to repeal them.

What really characterized the political scene during Jefferson's presidency was a series of battles *within* each party more than battles *between* the Federalists and the Jeffersonians. Each party had wings. Within the Jeffersonians, some radicals wanted to rewrite the Constitution to make the language more precise; somehow make the Senate, elected by the state legislatures, and the federal judiciary, more amenable to popular control; make the states more powerful than the federal government; and abolish the Bank of the U.S. The moderates within the Jeffersonians joined with moderate Federalists to push economical government to reduce the debt and to make the United States economy more self-sufficient. In essence, the harsh political rhetoric of the 1790s gave way to moderate policies.

Jefferson was not an ideologue, but a moderate and a nationalist who believed strongly:

> In education.
> In policies that promoted a virtuous populace.
> In freedom from the past. He said that each generation should write its
> own constitution. And, he defined a generation as only seventeen
> years.
> In reducing the national debt, and
> In the equality of all men before God.

He asked that only three accomplishments be placed on his tombstone: the author of the Virginia Statute for Religious Freedom, and of the Declaration of Independence, and the founder of the University of Virginia. Those three summarized his values. He donated his personal library, 6,487 volumes, to form the nucleus of the Library of Congress.

His inaugural address in 1801 contained the phrase, "We are all republicans; we are all federalists," suggesting that very little separated Americans. In Jefferson's draft of his speech, he wrote "republicans" and "federalists" in the lower case. Some editors and historians later mistakenly capitalized them. Jefferson may have been referring to ideas more than to the two opposing political parties. Historians do not know.

As president he pushed for social simplicity, for personal liberty, and for governmental economy; he reduced the debt from $83 to $57 million. He deplored what he saw as the aristocratic customs associated with the regal Washington and Adams administrations. Now visitors were invited to shake hands rather than expected to bow. He once met an ambassador for a scheduled appointment by answering the White House door himself, while wearing a bathrobe, pajamas, and slippers. The ambassador was dressed according to proper diplomatic etiquette. He ordered his cabinet heads to have an oval table for meetings, so no one sat at the head or foot. Jefferson ended the practice of the president going before Congress to give speeches. His reason may have been personal as well as a desire for simplicity. Jefferson stuttered. He simply sent his speeches over to Congress to be read by a clerk. Woodrow Wilson revived speaking before Congress in 1913. (This infuriated Theodore Roosevelt, a previous president. He wished he had thought of it!) Jefferson kept many of the 600 people Adams appointed to office, replacing only the last minute "midnight appointees." He even kept Hamilton's hated bank. His administration was much more moderate than Federalists feared it would be. Feared by Federalists to be a pacifist, Jefferson founded West Point and sent the navy to fight against the Barbary pirates.

The Courts

The Jeffersonians did move against Federalist judges to teach them to stay out of politics. Congress impeached and removed Judge John Pickering of New Hampshire and impeached Associate Supreme Court Justice Samuel Chase, who was not removed. To impeach means to bring charges. The trial for removal takes place in the Senate. Chase was impeached for bias in the Fries trial. The modest, insignificant Fries Rebellion took place in Northampton, Bucks, and Montgomery counties in Pennsylvania. Opposition arose there to a short-lived direct property tax on window glass by the federal government. Opponents urged people to throw buckets of whatever (use your imagination!) out their upstairs windows as the tax agents counted their downstairs windows. The leaders were captured and convicted of treason by Justice Samuel Chase, but pardoned by President Adams.

Among the last acts of the outgoing Adams administration (the presidential term ended March 4 back then) was the February 27 Judiciary Act, which created 16 circuit courts packed with Federalist appointees, the so-called "midnight appointees," and reduced the number of Supreme Court justices to five in order to avoid having the incoming president, Jefferson, appoint a new Supreme Court justice. Congress repealed the Judiciary Act in 1802. The additional courts were needed, but only Federalists had been appointed as judges, marshals, attorneys, and clerks. On January 20, 1801, Adams appointed John Marshall, his Secretary of State, as Chief Justice of the Supreme Court. Marshall played a crucial role in both ends of what legal scholars call the most important Supreme Court case in American history.

Marbury v. Madison, 1803

In March, 1801, the new Secretary of State, James Madison, refused to give William Marbury a commission as a justice of the peace for Washington, D.C., after the previous Adams administration had authorized the commission, and Congress, the government for the District of Columbia, had approved it. Any commission, after approval by Congress, is sent to the Secretary of State to have the official seal of the United States affixed to it. The Secretary of State is the office that keeps the official seal of the United States. Four of the twenty-five individuals who were denied commissions decided to sue. William Marbury sued under a writ of mandamus to obtain his commission. The Supreme Court's decision, written by Chief Justice John Marshall, dismissed Marbury's suit because he had sued under a writ of mandamus, and, the Constitution did not originally include such writs within its listing of the powers of the Supreme Court.

Almost any court can issue a writ of mandamus. It is an order to do something that is clearly justified but for which there is no law. If something is wrong, it is wrong. A writ of mandamus resolves the problem. The Judiciary Act of 1789, which created the federal court system, contained a provision that authorized the Supreme Court to issue a writ of mandamus, a power that was NOT listed in the Constitution as originally written. Nevertheless, claimed Marshall, Congress could not enlarge the powers of the Supreme Court. His logic included the implied idea that if Congress could enlarge the powers of the Supreme Court, it could also reduce the powers of the Supreme Court, altering the Constitution by legislation rather than by amendment. Therefore, Section 13 of the Judiciary Act of 1789 was unconstitutional. This case is significant because it is the first time the Supreme Court declared an act of Congress unconstitutional. This is known as judicial review, and it simply means that the Supreme Court can decide the constitutionality of enacted laws. Marshall in essence contended that without judicial review and oversight the theoretical establishment of limited government by the Constitution was meaningless in practice.

The second case declaring an act of Congress unconstitutional did not occur until the Dred Scott decision in 1857. The Supreme Court would not declare a state law unconstitutional until 1810, in *Fletcher v. Peck*. The Supreme Court had earlier ruled an act of Congress constitutional in *Hylton v. Dallas* in 1796. That case involved the question of whether a federal tax on carriages passed in 1794 could be levied without direct apportionment among the population, as required by the Constitution.

The Founding Fathers probably intended or assumed that the Supreme Court had the power to decide constitutionality. In *The Federalist*, written to explain the Constitution during the state debates on ratification, there is an essay, *Number 78*, written by Hamilton, in which he states clearly that the Supreme Court would decide constitutionality. During the Constitutional Convention Madison wrote to Jefferson, our minister to France, explaining the features of the Constitution under consideration. In his reply Jefferson responded favorably to the president's veto power, and added, "though I should have liked it better had the judiciary been associated for that purpose, or invested separately with a similar power." The Founding Fathers were aware of three state court cases during the 1780s in which constitutionality was determined, and they never voiced objections to those decisions regarding a state court's authority. Those cases are extensively discussed in Gordon Wood's *The Creation of the American Republic, 1776-1787*. The quotes and paraphrasing that follow are from Wood's book, pp. 457-461.

Rutgers v. Waddington, 1784

This case involved a clash between a legislative law and common law, which includes the law of nations, the prevailing international law. The New York Trespass Act of 1783 prohibited military use of abandoned property. Accepted international law permitted using abandoned property during wartime. The New York judges in this case avoided this issue by not ruling the New York Trespass Act illegal or unconstitutional. When the legislature passes a law that is unreasonable, the duty of the court is "to give their *intention* its proper effect." After all, the judges concluded, the legislators did not really mean to contradict the law of nations, the common law, because they never said they intended to do so.

Trevett v. Weeden, 1786-1787

The Rhode Island legislature passed legislation to force merchants to accept paper money. The merchants closed their shops in protest. In his argument for Weeden, a merchant, his attorney asserted that the judge's responsibility was to "reject all acts of the legislature that are contrary to the trust reposed in them by the people." Since the people created the legislature, the responsibility of the judiciary, also a creation of the people, is to prevent the legislature from exceeding their original responsibilities. The people may constitutionally change the legislature's responsibilities; the legislature may not constitutionally change the legislature's responsibilities. Weeden won the case.

Bayard v. Singleton, 1787

This court case preceded the Philadelphia Constitutional Convention. In this case the North Carolina Supreme Court declared a state law void. It is the clearest application of judicial review in this period.

Jefferson and Madison's Virginia and Kentucky Resolutions of 1798 claimed the Alien and Sedition Acts were unconstitutional. Both resolutions invited the other state legislatures to pass similar resolutions. Instead, seven northern state legislatures passed resolutions declaring that it was up to the Supreme Court to decide the constitutionality of an act of Congress, not the state legislatures. For example, the Rhode Island legislature responded that Article III, Section 2 of the Constitution vested judicial power in the courts, which gave the Supreme Court "ultimately the authority of deciding on the constitutionality of any act or law of the Congress of the United States."

Northern Confederacy Scheme, 1803-1804

This curious affair grew out of New England's fear that the growth of the West would dilute its power and influence in the federal government. New Englanders expected the agrarian interests of the South and West to ally in Congress against the commercial and industrial interests of New England. Conspirators tried to enlist others in a scheme to create a new country composed of New England, New York, and New Jersey, and maybe Canada. Senator Thomas Pickering of Massachusetts was the leader and tried to enlist the aid of the British ambassador and others. Hamilton vehemently refused when asked. One of those involved was Burr, Jefferson's vice president. While serving as vice president, Burr ran for governor of New York, supposedly to deliver New York to the Northern Confederation. He lost that contest. During the campaign Hamilton publicly criticized Burr. Hamilton wrote on February 16, 1804, that Burr was "a dangerous man, and one who ought not be trusted with the reins of government." Burr wrote Hamilton asking for a public apology. Hamilton replied, "I trust on more reflection you will see the matter in the same light as me. If not, I can only regret the circumstances, and must abide the consequences." Burr challenged Hamilton to a duel. They held the duel in Weehawken, New Jersey, because New York outlawed dueling. (So did New Jersey.) Hamilton had a wife and seven kids. Burr was a widower with a married child. Hamilton was fatally wounded and died the next day.

Later, after a strange series of events out West, Burr and 400 armed men gathered on an island in the Ohio River and floated slowly to New Orleans. To do what? Even historians are unsure. Burr was arrested for treason. Supreme Court Chief Justice John Marshall, sitting as a circuit judge, ruled that treason had not been proven in the trial. The Constitution strictly defines treason as an overt act with at least two witnesses. These events ended Burr's political career.

Louisiana Purchase

From the colonial exploration era, both the French and the Spanish claimed Louisiana. During the Seven Years' War (French and Indian War) France was forced to cede Louisiana to Spain, an ally of Great Britain, in the Treaty of Fontainebleau, 1762. However, when Napoleon successfully invaded Spain he forced Spain to give Louisiana back, in the secret Treaty of San Ildefonso, October 1, 1800. It remained nominally under Spanish control at New Orleans until actually transferred to the French in October, 1802. Since 1792 French foreign policy had a goal of establishing a political and commercial base in North America to reawaken the old colonial empire lost in the Seven Years' War. In preparation, Napoleon sent an expeditionary force to Haiti to put down a slave rebellion. Diseases and the former slaves defeated the French troops. Napoleon concluded that France could not defend Louisiana from the British; hence, he decided to sell it to the Americans for cash needed for war supplies.

All this thinking was unknown to Americans. They feared the French would close the port of New Orleans, as the Spanish had repeatedly done, in an effort to wean the Western states away from the United States, creating a new country and preventing the growth of the United States westward. Jefferson, supported by Congress, called on the state governors to raise a militia force of 80,000 men for a potential war with France. From October 16, 1802 to April 19, 1803, in one of the last acts by the lingering Spanish authorities, New Orleans was closed to American shipping, mostly corn, pork, and whiskey, which had grown in value to over one million dollars. When the port re-opened in 1803, the West breathed a sigh of relief, but the new treaty keeping the port open was for only three years.

Jefferson wanted the West securely tied to the new nation. He believed that what best preserved a republican government was a nation of small farmers, the solid proper-ty-owning, politically involved, virtuous backbone of the population. He envisioned an "empire of liberty" stretching across the continent.

Jefferson decided to buy New Orleans. Congress appropriated two million dol-lars for "expenses in relation to the intercourse (trade) between the United States and foreign nations." James Monroe and Robert Livingston traveled to Paris to purchase New Orleans. Their secret orders, if the negotiations failed, were to "open a confi-dential communication with ministers of the British government" with a view to "a candid understanding, and a closer connection with Great Britain." Jefferson, con-sidered by the Federalists to be an anti-British Francophile, said privately, if France would not sell, "We must marry ourselves to the British fleet and nation." While negotiating, the French ministers casually asked what the United States would pay for all of Louisiana. The stunned Americans realized they had no authority to buy it all, but it was too good to pass up. At $15 million, the cost amounted to 3¢ per acre. The purchase treaty guaranteed all the inhabitants citizenship and eventual admission to the union, neither of which were in the Constitution. The Constitution also nowhere clearly gives any part of the government the right to purchase new territory. Hamilton was delighted; Jefferson was following a loose interpretation of the Constitution. In a court case in 1828, *American Insurance Co. v. Canter*, Chief Justice John Marshall settled the constitutional question: "The Constitution confers absolutely on the Government of the Union the powers of making war, and of making treaties; consequently, that Government possesses the power of acquiring territory, either by conquest or by treaty."

Were Jefferson and Secretary of State Madison new converts to loose interpretation? Did they change their position from their earlier stand on the Bank of the U.S. issue? In *Ratifying the Republic: Antifederalists and Federalists in Constitutional Time*, historian David J. Siemers sees a range of opinions on interpreting the Constitution in the early 1790s, with Hamilton and Jefferson toward opposing ends with Madison in the middle. Garry Wills, in *Explaining America*, always puts Madison in the loose construction category. Two historians, Stanley Elkins and Eric McKitrick, in *The Age of Federalism: The Early American Republic, 1788-1800*, put the loose versus strict quarrel in a different context. They concluded that the use of strict constructionism was "the resort of persons under ideological strain. It represents a willingness to renounce a range of positive opportuni-ties for action in return for a principle which will inhibit government from undertaking a range of things one does not approve of. It marks the point at which one prefers to see the Constitution not as a sanction for achieving one's own ends but as a protection against those designs of others which have come to be seen as usurping and corrupting." In short, I do not trust you; but, once in power, I trust me. The Constitution as an ideological foundation has nothing to do with how I view your actions and mine. But it is a convenient source for my arguments against you. A political scientist once noted that all the presidents who have been ranked as great presidents functioned as if they had told their Constitution-minded advisors, "This is what I am going to do, you figure out how to use the Constitution to justify it."

After purchasing Louisiana, Jefferson sent Meriwether Lewis and William Clark to explore to the Pacific Ocean. Both were former military officers. Lewis, who led the expedition, had been Jefferson's personal secretary since1801. Clark was the brother of George Rogers Clark, the Revolutionary War militia commander who secured the Northwest Territory by his victories at Kaskaskia and Vincennes. Their expedition lasted from May 14, 1804 to September 23, 1806, greatly helped by a Shoshoni woman, Sacagawea, who served as an interpreter. Then Lt. Zebulon Pike explored the purchase by two expeditions, one to the headwaters of the Mississippi River and a second to the Colorado mountain named for him, Pike's Peak. In 1819 Major Stephen Long explored the Great Plains, and labeled it the "Great American Desert," "almost wholly unfit for cultivation, and of course uninhabitable by a people depending upon agriculture for their subsistence." Why did all these early explorers come to the same conclusion? Because the rainfall limited what types of crops could grow there. Later farmers would successfully adapt crops to the limited rainfall.

Spanish authorities in Mexico sent troops after Lewis and Clark, but failed to capture them. The Spanish did arrest Zebulon Pike when he reached Santa Fe, but he was later released. The roots of the Mexican War extend backwards. The expansion of the United States clearly threatened Spain's, and later Mexico's, claims to much of what is now the American West.

Jefferson's two terms as president allayed Federalist fears for the infant country. Thomas Jefferson richly deserves being one of the faces on Mt. Rushmore. Historians consistently rank Jefferson as one of our greatest presidents. In many respects the combined sixteen years of the Jefferson and Madison administrations sidelined the extremists in both parties, the Federalists and the Democratic-Republicans. Politically the early Democratic-Republicans seem to be best characterized as radical left-wingers and centralists. The Federalists seem to be conservative right-wingers and centralists. Within both parties, the common-sense centralists grew to control the party, isolating those who held more radical views. The blinders imposed on political debate by ideological straitjackets faded. The bitterness of the Electoral College voting in 1801 became a distant memory. The practical feasibility and functioning of proposed laws replaced knee-jerk reactions. The nation was going to survive, which was clearly apparent after the end of the War of 1812.

16

FOREIGN POLICY, 1800-1815

Goals – Jefferson and Madison

In their two administrations, stretching from 1800 to 1816, Jefferson and Madison pursued similar goals.

1. Protect American interests on the high seas.
2. Secure our Western territories against foreign threats. The Louisiana Purchase achieved this, opening the West to settlement. In 1790 almost all of the nation's four million Americans lived within fifty miles of the Atlantic coast. The largest inland town in 1775 was Lancaster, Pennsylvania, population, 3,300. By 1830, 30 percent of the population lived west of the Appalachian Mountains.
3. Break free from our historic economic dependence upon Europe.
4. Secure markets for American agricultural products in both Europe and for feeding slaves in the West Indies.
5. Protect our fragile republican liberty from the threats that would come from
    a. inflamed politics
    b. stifled free speech – the Alien and Sedition Acts
    c. increased public debt – Hamilton's program
    d. expanded governmental power
    e. the influences that accompanied a war
6. However, all this was to be done cheaply, to avoid raising taxes or increasing the public debt. For example, Jefferson wanted small gunboats to protect our coastline, not large ships. He ordered 75 gunboats built, the largest one 75 feet long, each having only one or two cannons. The idea was that maneuverability and numbers would be able to defeat a large warship. Hardly. One of the

gunboats ended up in a cornfield after a hurricane hit Georgia. A Federalist in Congress quipped, "If our gunboats are of no use on the water, may they at least be the best on land."

7. Jefferson called for being alert when opportunities arose. He wrote that while European nations were busy fighting one another, the "new world will fatten on the follies of the old" by gaining territory and increasing trade.

Jefferson as President

One of his first acts as president was to cut the army from 4,000 to 2,500 and to reduce the size of the navy as far as the laws allowed. However, paradoxically, his greatest achievements as president during his first term were in the area of diplomacy.

With everyone in Europe preoccupied by the wars against France and Napoleon from 1792 to 1815, the Barbary pirates in the Mediterranean Sea – Algiers, Morocco, Tunis, and Tripoli – had a ball. Presidents Washington and Adams paid tribute to the pirates to protect American shipping, on the grounds that it was cheaper than waging war against them. In 1795 that sum amounted to twenty percent of the federal budget. In ten years the United States lost thirteen ships and had over 100 sailors captured as slaves. Jefferson thought it would be cheaper to fight the pirates, which he did. The United States won, eventually. Think of the line from the Marine Corps hymn, "from the halls of Montezuma to the shores of Tripoli." The marines are the army of the navy. The bashaw of Tripoli, Yussuf Karamanli, was the first foreign ruler to declare war on the United States, 1801.

Louisiana Purchase

From the colonial exploration era, both the French and the Spanish claimed parts of Louisiana. During the Seven Years' War (French and Indian War) France was forced to give Louisiana to Spain in the Treaty of Fontainebleau, 1762. However, when Napoleon successfully invaded Spain, he forced Spain to give Louisiana back, in the secret Treaty of San Ildefonso, October 1, 1800.

After 1792, French foreign policy had a goal of establishing a political and commercial base in North America to reawaken the old colonial empire lost in the Seven Years' War. First Napoleon had to regain control of sugar-rich Haiti, formerly the source of 40% of France's trade. In order to do so, he sent an expeditionary force to Haiti to put down a slave rebellion. The French army was defeated. European armies suffered miserably in the Caribbean due to yellow fever and malaria. (See J. R. McNeill's chilling *Mosquito Empires: Ecology and War in the Greater Caribbean, 1620-1898.*) Yet, Haitians also paid a high, bitter price to secure their independence. By 1804 two-thirds of their population was dead. Napoleon concluded that without a supply base in Haiti, France could not defend Louisiana from the British; hence, he decided to sell it to the Americans for cash for badly needed war supplies.

Impressment

Why did the British have to use impressment to find enough sailors? The British navy followed a policy of harsh discipline and punishment for infractions aboard its ships by sailors. Among the punishments was keelhauling, where a sailor had his hands tied to a rope that went around the hull and connected to his feet. He was pulled under the ship and up the other side. Many sailors walked away during visits to a port, any port. There were 20,000 sailors in the British navy, half of whom deserted each year. Thus, the British needed 10,000 new recruits each year. By 1811 nearly 10,000 Americans had been impressed into the British navy. Those who refused to serve languished in British prisons.

Americans had long hated the practice of impressment. As early as 1747 a mob attacked impressment gangs in Boston. It was not an isolated event. The U.S. merchant marine employed 40,000, obviously a nice potential source of sailors for Great Britain's navy. (Merchant marine refers to non-combat ships, cargo ships.) It was not unusual for many different nationalities to serve in any country's navy. The *U.S.S. Constitution*, a warship, had a crew of 419 in 1807, only 241 of whom were American citizens; 149 were British citizens. The British practiced "indelible citizenship." A person could not renounce British citizenship, once a British citizen always a British citizen. Impressment resumed in earnest in 1803 when fighting resumed against Napoleon's France.

Chesapeake Affair

On June 22, 1807, the British warship *Leopard* hailed the U.S. frigate *Chesapeake*. This action was common, usually to exchange mail bags. Instead, the *Leopard* hit the *Chesapeake* with a cannon broadside. The *Chesapeake* could not respond. Firing a cannon at this time required a hot coal. When preparing for battle each cannon had a bucket of hot coals beside it. Not expecting a broadside, the ship was virtually helpless. British officers boarded the *Chesapeake* looking for deserters, especially a ringleader, Jenkin Ratford. They took him and three others. British authorities paid no attention to protests that a sailor was an American or that he had citizenship papers to prove it. The British officers knew that British deserters were able to obtain false U.S. citizenship papers easily in any American port. One Norfolk, Virginia, justice of the peace even had an adult-sized baby cradle for a deserter to climb into. This permitted him to issue a citizenship certificate and swear that he had known this man since he lay in the cradle, "known since birth to be an American." Close to the truth.

Congress was out of session in June, not scheduled to return until December. Jefferson refused to call its members back into session early. Declaring war would have been very popular. Instead, Jefferson asked British authorities for an end to impressment, reparations, and an apology. The apology, ONLY, finally arrived in 1811, nearly four years after the incident. Meanwhile, the president ordered 188 new gunboats built and ordered all British ships out of U.S. waters, which our navy could not enforce. On October 17, 1807, Great Britain responded with a new order-in-council directing the British navy to impress neutrals to the fullest.

Continuous Voyage versus Broken Voyage

Prevailing international law and British policy followed the "Rule of 1756." It stated that a port closed to other nations in peacetime remained closed in wartime. The French could not open their colonial ports previously closed to American ships and claim that it involved neutral shipping. To get around the "Rule of 1756" the United States claimed the doctrine of "broken voyage." French goods brought into the United States became American goods, as soon as they were unloaded. They were immediately reloaded for export. Since American ships coming from America were neutral, they sailed under the doctrine of "free ships, free goods," meaning that anything carried on a neutral ship could not be seized as contraband. Between 1803 and 1805, U.S. exports averaged $42 million, but re-exports rose from $13 million in 1803 to $36 million in 1804 to $53 million in 1805, almost all of it from French colonies previously closed to American ships. An American ship, the *Essex*, sailed from Barcelona, Spain, to Salem, Massachusetts, and then, after reloading, left on its way to Havana. (Havana was a colony of Spain, which France had defeated and forced to become an ally.) The British seized the *Essex* after it left Salem. The British argued "continuous voyage," a ship was going to wherever it ended up. The United States appealed the seizure to the British. A British order-in-council issued a decision on the *Essex* case on July 23, 1805. A ship was going wherever it intended to end up, therefore it could be seized anywhere along the way, according to the British.

Non-Importation Act

So, how does the United States react? What policy could work? In April, 1806, Congress passed a Non-Importation Act, under which the United States refused to buy from Great Britain and France because they violated our neutral rights. Remember, this tactic worked well for Americans prior to the outbreak of the Revolution. Therefore, we tried it again. We would sell American goods; the United States would not buy British or French goods. The British responded by placing a blockade on all of Europe controlled by Napoleon. Great Britain asserted the right to search every ship that approached Europe to determine its destination. Meanwhile, Napoleon, in the Berlin Decree, later expanded by the Milan Decree, declared that any neutral ship that had been searched by the British, or had visited a British port, or paid British duties, was "denationalized" and susceptible to seizure as a British ship. Nicknamed the "continental system," it also applied to any British ship caught entering any port on the European continent controlled by Napoleon's army. The U.S., the largest neutral trading country not at war, was making huge profits off trading with everyone. Now that commercial windfall was jeopardized.

Embargo

Jefferson was not a doctrinaire pacifist. But, he had a deep faith in the power of commercial exclusion as an alternative to war. Boycotts had been successful in the years before the American Revolution. In addition, realistically, the United States did not have an army or navy strong enough to attack Great Britain. On December 22, 1807, Congress passed the Embargo Act, which restricted trade to only coastal trade, up and down the Atlantic coast. An embargo is a refusal to sell. To ensure compliance, shippers had to post bond for double the value of their cargo to assure delivery to an American port. Shippers were outraged; they had been making lots of money in spite of the dangers of being seized by France or Great Britain. Exports dropped 80%, imports dropped over 50%. Farm prices fell sharply. Nearly thirty thousand sailors were thrown out of work. Meanwhile, on April 17, 1808, France issued the Bayonne Decree, stating that searched American ships were British ships with false papers, justifying seizing every American ship. The British were doing the same thing.

As a weapon, an embargo only works when other sources are unavailable. In the December 1807 to March 1809 period, other sources were available to the British. South American ports threw themselves open to British trade when Napoleon conquered Spain and placed his brother on the throne as Spain's new king. The Spanish colonists refused to recognize him. Great Britain also benefited from good harvests at home. Thus, Great Britain did not suffer from our embargo. That policy did not work.

Non-Intercourse Act

Next Jefferson tried, as his administration approached its last days, the Non-Intercourse Act. The primary definition of intercourse at that time was commerce, trade. The U.S. refused to sell to or buy from Great Britain or France. It also did not work.

The Embargo Act was repealed March 1, 1809, just as James Madison's administration was about to begin on March 4. The Non-Intercourse Act replaced the embargo, reopening trade with everyone but Great Britain and France. The United States refused to sell or to buy from Great Britain or France. The United States would reopen trade with either Great Britain or France if the other one ceased violating our neutral rights. Subsequently, David Erskine, the British ambassador to the United States, negotiated an agreement with the U.S. Hence, trade with Great Britain reopened on April 19, 1809. Six hundred American ships sailed for Great Britain the day the Erskine Agreement was signed. On May 30 the British Foreign Minister, George Canning, disavowed the agreement. Madison revived Non-Intercourse again. The Erskine Agreement was formally ended August 9, 1809. Meanwhile, Congress had no idea what to do. Neither did the president have any leadership to offer.

Macon's Bill Number 2

On May 1, 1810, Congress passed Macon's Bill Number 2, which ended the Non-Intercourse policy. Macon's Bill Number 2 said that if either Great Britain or France, before March 3, 1811, would modify or revoke its edicts, the president could prohibit trade with the other country. If three months later that country failed to modify or revoke its edicts, non-intercourse would be revived against them. Shipping immediately reached levels not seen again for twenty years.

Napoleon took the American bait, and tricked the U.S. In July, 1810, he ordered the sale of all American ships and cargoes seized by France, at that point over 300 ships. Then he told the U.S. minister that he had revoked his Berlin and Milan decrees, provided the British revoked their orders-in-council, which he knew Great Britain would not do. Madison took Napoleon at his word, hearing only the first half of the statement. On February 11, 1811, Madison prohibited trade with Great Britain.

This was our fourth major effort in four years to try to gain respect for our neutral trading rights. Luckily for the U.S., Great Britain suffered a harsh winter during 1811-1812, leading to food shortages. Crop failures added to the high food prices. In addition, the British warehouses were filled with merchandise for export. Public pressure led Great Britain to suspend its orders-in-council on June 16, 1812. However, Congress declared war on Great Britain just two days later, on June 18, 1812. Communication did not travel across the ocean very fast.

Official War Message

The official war message President Madison sent to Congress gave four reasons for declaring war:

1. impressment (which the United States had not officially protested against since 1806)
2. violations of our three mile limit, according to international law armed ships could not come within three miles of a nation's coast, unless permitted (at one time this was the distance a cannonball traveled; thus it was adopted by international law)
3. paper blockades (a declared blockade without the blocking ships present, illegal according to international law)
4. orders-in-council (interfering with our trade as a neutral)

Historian Bradford Perkins called the violations of our neutral rights the most important reason. Since 1803 the United States had suffered from a steady diet of diplomatic humiliation. The vote for war in the Senate was 19-13, 79-49 in the House. A 9% switch, 4 Senators, and a 12½% switch, 16 Representatives, would have changed the result. Representatives from New England, New York, and New Jersey voted 34-14 against war;

those from Southern, Western, and frontier states, 65-15 in favor of war. Congress adjourned July 6, after having voted no new war taxes; neither did it provide for an increase in the navy. Apparently, Congress thought it would be a cheap, short war.

From 1803-1812 Great Britain had seized 917 American ships, France 558. However, in the what-have-you-done-lately mode, France had seized only 34 in 1811-1812, and so Great Britain was regarded as the worst enemy. Congress should have declared war against both. But that would have been insane. Given the size of our army, seven thousand soldiers, and the American navy, fewer than twenty ships, declaring war against anyone was risky.

The "**War Hawks**" clamored for war – led by Henry Clay from Kentucky, John Calhoun from South Carolina, Felix Grundy from Tennessee, and Peter Porter from western New York. These new members of Congress entered when the election of 1810 swept 63 of 142 Representatives out of Congress. The War Hawks' primary goals were to fight Indians and expand to the west. Warfare with Indians had constituted a major expense for the federal government. In the 1790s a majority of the federal government's budget often went to fighting Indians. As for expansion, the U.S. had taken West Florida in 1810 from Spain. The rest of Florida and Canada were the next goals for the War Hawks.

The War Itself

Our invasion of Canada was a failure. Our defense of Washington, D.C., was another failure. There were 72,000 militiamen in the Washington area; 6,000 showed up to defend our capital, and they quickly fled. British troops finished President Madison's meal, still warm. British soldiers held a mock session of Congress in the Senate. Afterwards they burned the Executive Mansion. It was later painted white to cover up the burn marks, hence, the White House. (Theodore Roosevelt was apparently the first president to officially call it the White House; prior to that it was often called the Executive Mansion.) Dolley Madison barely escaped being captured by the British, fleeing with several portraits, including one of George Washington. The burning of our capital was in retaliation for our earlier burning of Canadian government buildings in Toronto.

Our two biggest victories were the Battle of Lake Erie and the Battle of New Orleans, which was fought after the peace treaty was signed in Ghent, modern Belgium. The country did gain our national anthem, the *Star Spangled Banner*, from words by Francis Scott Key and music from a British drinking song. It is meant to be sung by a group, which is why it is so difficult for one person's range. It was officially adopted in 1931.

Hartford Convention

Federalists in the shipping-dominated New England economy opposed the war. In spite of all the British and French violations of our neutral rights, shippers still made money. In December, 1814, some Federalists gathered at Hartford, Connecticut, to recommend new laws or constitutional changes:

1. exclude slaves in counting for representation in the House of Representatives and for taxes (This would reduce the South's bloated presence in the House of Representatives and the Electoral College.)
2. 2/3 vote for new states to enter (To delay the entry of new states; New England was losing power and influence in the national government.)
3. 2/3 vote for war (The War of 1812 would not have happened. A declaration of war requires only a majority vote.)
4. no naturalized citizen is eligible for the House, Senate, or other civil offices (No more Secretary of the Treasury Albert Gallatin.)
5. one term limit for presidents (Too many Virginians!)
6. no consecutive presidents from the same state (Darn Virginians!)

Its report with these recommendations reached Washington almost the same day as news of the Treaty of Ghent, signed on Christmas Eve, and news of the Battle of New Orleans, January 8, 1815, a great American victory. The Americans lost 8, the British over 2000. The United States won the war! Or, so it now seemed. The Hartford Convention branded the Federalist Party as wimpy and disloyal. It never was a factor in national politics again. The Federalist Party did run a presidential candidate in 1816, but never after that. New England's economy actually gained from the war. Shipping was hurt but the textile industry boomed.

Treaty of Ghent
The peace treaty did not mention impressment. Both sides agreed to status quo ante bellum, going back to the status before the war. What the United States conquered will be returned; what Great Britain conquered will be returned. The Duke of Wellington, who had defeated Napoleon, had been offered the command of the British forces in North America before the war ended. He asked one question, who controlled the Great Lakes? They were significant as supply routes. When he found out the United States did, he said Great Britain could not win the war. Indeed, neither side could win.

After the War of 1812
The war resolved one cause, the Indian menace. During the war Andrew Jackson's militia crushed the Creek Indians at the Battle of Horseshoe Bend, March 27, 1814, ending effective resistance in the Southwest. Over the previous decade Tecumseh and his younger brother, Tenskwatawa, both born of a Shawnee father and a Creek mother, had tried to forge a pan-Indian confederacy to resist American expansion across the

Appalachians. Tenskwatawa, the Prophet, urged a return to ancestral ways and a rejection of all things American. His followers gathered at Prophetstown, where General William Henry Harrison defeated them at the Battle of Tippecanoe in November, 1811. Tecumseh rallied his remaining followers and joined the British fighting against the Americans. The defeat of the British and their Indian allies in the War of 1812 ended organized Indian resistance to American expansion. Tecumseh's death during the Battle of the Thames in Canada in 1813 symbolized the futility of continued resistance. Now without influence or power in the Northwest, the British no longer aided and encouraged Indian attacks against Americans pushing westward.

In many respects the War of 1812 was our "Second War for Independence." It functioned as a war to recover self-respect. Two presidents had achieved NO important diplomatic objective since 1803. However, America survived the war; our future seemed more secure. Probably the most significant result of the War of 1812 was that it led the British in Canada to abandon their practice of encouraging Indian resistance to westward-marching Americans.

A glance at the following list shows the significance of foreign affairs in the nascent United States. The almost continuous wars in Europe from 1789 to 1815 gave us fits, but also opportunities to gain territory, such as West Florida and the Louisiana Purchase. The absence of a major European war for the next 99 years would prove to be the most important diplomatic factor in our history during the entire nineteenth century. In the infant U.S., for 26 of our first 36 years, the most capable cabinet member served as the Secretary of State, and often became the next president. Not after 1825. No former Secretary of State since John Quincy Adams has become president.

Presidents	Secretary of State
George Washington	**Thomas Jefferson**, 1789-1793
	Edmund Randolph, 1794-1795
	Timothy Pickering, 1795-1797
John Adams	Timothy Pickering, 1795-1800
	John Marshall, 1800-1801
Thomas Jefferson	**James Madison**, 1801-1809
James Madison	Robert Smith, 1809-1811
	James Monroe, 1811-1817
James Monroe	**John Quincy Adams**, 1817-1825
John Quincy Adams	Henry Clay, 1825-1829

17

FORCES FOR NATIONALISM

Three Great Nationalistic Events

Following the end of the War of 1812, three unrelated events fed the growth of nationalism.

The First was our overwhelming victory in the War of 1812. This is, of course, questionable, but many Americans viewed it that way at the time. Why? Because the greatest American victory – the Battle of New Orleans – arrived with the peace treaty news which left everyone with a good image of the war. Pictures of American naval victories and statues of military heroes and famous Americans became a minor industry after the war. Many families had small mementos of the war on their walls or mantels. After the War of 1812 the country had a unity of purpose. Now the constant meddling of European powers in our affairs became a thing of the past. Up to 1815 the word "Americans" was often applied more to Indians. Now it began to achieve its modern meaning.

Out of the War of 1812 came what would eventually be adopted in 1931 as our National Anthem, "The Star-Spangled Banner." Shortly after the war, Samuel Woodward wrote the most popular song linked to the war, "The Hunters of Kentucky," which took some liberties with facts while celebrating Jackson's overwhelming victory over the British at the Battle of New Orleans. Look up the lyrics on the internet. In addition, in 1831, on the fifty-fifth anniversary celebration of the Declaration of Independence, a Boston Sunday School choir sang, for the first time, "My country, 'tis of Thee."

The Second was an event. On July 4, 1826, the fiftieth anniversary of the Declaration of Independence, two of the Founding Fathers died, Thomas Jefferson and John Adams, a clear message that the United States was a special nation blessed by God. John Adams' last words were, "Jefferson still lives," but he had died 13 hours earlier.

Five years later James Monroe also died on July 4. Surely, Americans were a people chosen by God for greatness. As one commentator wrote, "These are *really* wonderful things."

The Third was a visit by the beloved French general, the Marquis de Lafayette, who joined the American cause during the Revolutionary War. Americans elevated him to a status of genuine hero, and held him in high esteem. He also played a role in the beginning of the French Revolution in 1789, earning the nickname, "Hero of Two Worlds." In 1824 President Monroe invited him to visit the United States. Congress gave him a gift of $200,000. For more than a year, thirteen months, he toured the country in triumph and honor, a continuously moving celebration of banquets, parades, displays, and nationalism that visited every state, covering almost 6,000 miles. Lafayette's speeches stressed that out of their revolution Americans had created better government institutions than other nations. As proof he offered the growth of the nation and the economy from the 1780s to the 1820s. It was a wildly popular message. Lafayette, forever linked to America, returned to France with soil from Bunker Hill, which graces his grave in Paris.

American, Not British

One man, Noah Webster, set out to counter American reliance upon British English. The British had great contempt for American culture, best expressed by the famous quote of the British author and literary critic, Sydney Smith, in 1820. "Who reads an American book? Or goes to an American play? Or looks at an American picture or statue?" After touring the United States in the 1830s, an English author, Frances Trollope, wrote a scathing book on *The Domestic Manners of the Americans*. She wrote about Americans with great disdain. "I do not like them. I do not like their principles, I do not like their manners, I do not like their opinions."

Noah Webster cautioned Americans against mimicking British educational practices and completely following British spelling and grammar rules. We needed to protect our collective **American Identity**. "America must be as independent in literature as she is in politics — as famous for arts as for arms." His "blue-backed speller," first published in the 1780s, sold almost 100 million copies in the nineteenth century, unifying American spelling. He removed the British "u" in words like harbour and favour and dropped the "k" in words like musick. His greatest scholarly achievement was his 1828 *American Dictionary of the English Language,* a monumental achievement celebrated on both sides of the Atlantic for its precise definitions, something lacking in previous dictionaries. He also wrote guides for grammar, boosting democracy by insisting that popular usage should establish the rules. In all his works Webster used American towns and cities, American leaders and heroes, and American laws, accomplishments, and politics as examples, teaching patriotism along with grammar and spelling. In addition to

Webster's effort, a distinctly American school of art grew, celebrating America's natural beauty, the Hudson River School.

What is Nationalism?

Nationalism is a difficult word to define for Americans. In other countries what ties people together is a common ethnic, linguistic, religious, or political heritage. The only one of these four that Americans have is a somewhat common political heritage. However, the freedom of opinion Americans tolerate means that a wide range of political ideas is always present. That leaves "a common adjustment to conditions of a new land, a common commitment to shared values, a common esteem for certain qualities of character, or a common set of adaptive traits and attitudes." (See Chapter One, "The Cultural Meaning of Nationalism," in Lloyd Kramer, *Nationalism in Europe & America: Politics, Cultures, and Identities Since 1775.*)

Two themes have been identified as shared or "common" for Americans – Jefferson's image of the American as an idealistic individual, the independent yeoman farmer, and French visitor Alexis de Tocqueville's image of the American as a grasping, conformist, materialistic person. De Tocqueville claimed that "Liberty is not the chief object of their desires; equality is their idol." He also asserted that conformity of opinion was stronger in America than anywhere else; there is "enormous pressure of the mind of all upon the individual intelligence." Majority opinion pressed with great force upon the nonconformist. "Freedom of opinion does not exist in America." The American was "a majoritarian democrat," "a mass-dominated conformist." We all know what happens to a television show that is not number one in its time slot. Majority rules! Ruthlessly.

The historian Frederick Jackson Turner added another perspective. The frontier experience shaped and molded his American.

> "The American intellect owes its striking characteristics to the frontier. That coarseness and strength, combined with acuteness and acquisitiveness; that practical inventive turn of mind, quick to find expedients; that masterful grasp of material things, lacking in the artistic but powerful to effect great ends; that restless, nervous energy; that dominant individualism, working for good and for evil; and withal, that buoyancy and exuberance which comes with freedom – these are the traits of the frontier, or traits called out elsewhere because of the existence of the frontier."

Where does all this leave us? It means that a student of American history must search for what he or she would identify as the fundamental characteristics of a typical American in American society. Those shared traits, attitudes, beliefs, and characteristics are what hold us together as a nation. Certainly, equality of opportunity is high on the list.

(Quotes in the above two paragraphs are from David M. Potter, "The Quest for the National Character," *The Reconstruction of American History*, John Higham, ed.)

Clay's American System

One of the most prominent political figures of this era was Henry Clay. Outside the United States Senate are statutes of the five greatest senators of all time, as voted by the Senate. Three are in this period – Henry Clay, John Calhoun, and Daniel Webster. All aspired to the presidency, but none made it. The other two are Robert La Follette and Robert A. Taft.

Clay devised a plan for building a nation, a nationalistic plan to tie together the interests of the different sections; he called it "The American System."

1.   Maintain a high tariff to protect infant American industries from foreign competition. The British had purposefully "dumped" cheap goods on the United States in the years immediately following the end of the Napoleonic Wars in 1815 in order to drive U.S. industries out of business, securing the American market for British industry and trade.

The Tariff of 1816 was our first high, protective tariff. One strange anomaly about it was that its supporters and opponents reversed their positions ten years later. South Carolina's John Calhoun sponsored the Tariff of 1816 because he expected the South to industrialize and to manufacture textiles, which was logical since the South was the source of the cotton. Massachusetts' Daniel Webster opposed the high tariff because in New England the major economic interest was shipping, not manufacturing, as it would become later. A high tariff reduces trade and therefore hurts the shipping industry.

2.   Recharter the Bank of the U.S. The original Bank of the U.S., chartered in 1791 for twenty years, expired in 1811. The Republicans, led by Jefferson and Madison, let the evil Bank expire. However, they soon discovered that the Bank had benefited the economy by restraining the state banks from issuing too much currency. In 1811 there were 88 state banks in operation; by 1816 there were 256, all of them issuing paper money, which led to inflation. Obviously, the nation needed a central bank.

The Second Bank of the U.S. was chartered in 1816, again for twenty years. Within a short time Nicholas Biddle, a member of a prominent Philadelphia family, became the bank's president and brought inflation under control, after the previous bank president's policies aggravated the Panic of 1819. John Calhoun proposed that the money raised from the initial sale of the bank's stock be used to build roads and canals at federal government expense. Congress passed this as the Bonus Bill, $1.5 million from the sale of stock in the Bank, but President Madison, who doubted its constitutionality, vetoed it.

3. This idea was also part of Clay's American System, called internal improvements. (Do not confuse this with the "American system of manufactures," the European nickname for the American concept of interchangeable parts, a revolutionary advance in manufacturing, thanks to Eli Whitney's firearm production innovations.) Clay's American System idea was to tie the sections together economically by a federally financed system of roads and canals, similar to the way the Interstate Highway System functions today. Clay said we could get around the constitutionality issue by claiming that it was built for the primary benefit of the military, which was the rationale behind the creation of the Interstate Highway System in 1956.

Hamilton had proposed such an idea earlier and Jefferson had asked his Secretary of the Treasury, Albert Gallatin, to draw up a national plan for roads and canals. Gallatin presented his plan in 1808. It included a highway up the East Coast, almost perfectly paralleling our present-day I-95, a series of national roads going west, and also canals across all the peninsulas on the East Coast, including today's Chesapeake and Delaware Canal, one across northern New Jersey to the Delaware River, and one across Cape Cod. All these highways and canals were needed, to lower costs. The cost of shipping something by water from Louisville to New Orleans was one-half the cost of shipping the same thing from Philadelphia to Baltimore by wagon. The two greatest symbolic events showing the significance of internal improvements took place on July 4, 1828. The last living signer of the Declaration of Independence, Charles Carroll of Maryland, ninety-one years old, participated in the groundbreaking ceremony for the building of the Baltimore and Ohio Railroad. Nearby, President John Quincy Adams did the same for the Chesapeake and Ohio Canal.

Clay saw internal improvements as the way to create a huge internal market for American goods. Even today Americans consume about 97% of what we produce. This is why the economic indicator called "consumer confidence" is so significant in forecasting the economy. For example, retail businesses always want to know how much Americans plan to spend this year for Christmas.

4. The national government should sell federally owned land in the West at cheap prices. Clay was from Kentucky, still considered a frontier state, and he wanted low land prices to encourage the settlement of the West. Proceeds from the

sale of federal land would be distributed to all the states. This policy provided an answer to a question that continually came up for the new nation. Is the publicly owned unsold land primarily a source of opportunity for people or is it primarily a source of income for the federal government? Our land policy originally was designed to produce revenue for the federal government. Westerners held the view that western land had no value until settled and improved by the expenditure of public funds to build roads and railroads. It should be primarily a source of opportunity for settlers rather than a source of income for the government.

Marshall Court

The decisions of the Supreme Court under Chief Justice John Marshall, 1801-1835, were another stimulus to nationalism. For 34 years he exercised strong influence over the Supreme Court. His ability to convince the other judges by his reasoning was legendary. Long after the Federalist Party evaporated, Marshall continued to write Federalist ideas into American constitutional law. He participated in over 1,000 decisions and was on the minority side in only a few, about a dozen. Before Marshall's arrival the Supreme Court was clearly the least important of the three branches of government. He ended the practice of each judge writing a separate opinion for every case. Now only one official opinion was generally written, often by Marshall; he wrote 519, after he had used his considerable persuasive powers to convince the other Supreme Court judges that he was correct. His second cousin, Thomas Jefferson, said once that he hated to say even "good morning" to Marshall, because Marshall could convince him it was not.

Marbury v. Madison, 1803

This court case was explained earlier, in Chapter 15. Review the details there. It is included again to illustrate the extent to which it was a factor in nationalism. The Supreme Court's decision, written by Chief Justice John Marshall, declared unconstitutional Section 13 of the Judiciary Act of 1789. Section 13 had added the power to issue a writ of mandamus to the powers of the Supreme Court. Marshall reasoned that if Congress was permitted to enlarge the powers of the Supreme Court, it could also reduce the powers of the Supreme Court, altering the Constitution by legislation rather than by amendment. Enlarging or reducing the powers of the Supreme Court was unacceptable. This case is the first time the Supreme Court declared an act of Congress unconstitutional, thus establishing judicial review, meaning that the Supreme Court decides the constitutionality of enacted laws. The second employment of judicial review did not occur until the Dred Scott case in 1857. The Supreme Court did not declare a state law unconstitutional until 1810, in *Fletcher v. Peck*.

By establishing the concept of judicial review, the Supreme Court gave a degree of permanence to its decisions. There are only two ways to reverse Supreme Court decisions. One is to amend the Constitution. The second is for the Court itself to reverse a previous decision. Both happen very infrequently.

McCulloch v. Maryland, 1819

The state of Maryland levied a stamp tax on all banknotes, paper money issued by banks not chartered by Maryland. Congress had chartered the Second Bank of the U.S. James W. McCulloch, an officer of the Baltimore branch of the Bank of the U.S., refused to pay the tax. Maryland sued him for $110, the penalty for circulating unstamped banknotes in violation of Maryland's law. The case raised the question of the constitutionality of the 1791 act of Congress that created the Bank and the question of whether a state could tax the federal government. Three lawyers represented each side; Daniel Webster was the primary lawyer for the Bank. The other side included Luther Martin, the attorney general for Maryland, who had been a delegate to the Constitutional Convention in 1787, 32 years earlier. As one of the Founding Fathers, he should have known what the Founding Fathers intended when they wrote the Constitution. Martin argued for a strict interpretation of the Constitution, and argued that the Tenth Amendment clearly stated that, "the powers not delegated to the United States by the Constitution, nor prohibited by it to the States, are reserved to the States respectively, or to the people."

In essence, *McCulloch v. Maryland* forced the Supreme Court to decide the issue debated by Jefferson and Hamilton over the creation of the First Bank of the U.S. in 1791. Does the Constitution, specifically Article I, section 8, clause 18, also known as the implied powers clause, or the necessary and proper clause, permit a loose interpretation of the Constitution?

It states that Congress shall have the power "To make all Laws which shall be necessary and proper for carrying into Execution the foregoing powers, and all other Powers vested by this Constitution in the Government of the United States, or in any Department or Officer thereof." And, it means?

Marshall wrote the opinion for the court, which was unanimous, in support of the loose construction theory of the Constitution. "Let the end be legitimate, let it be within the scope of the Constitution, and all means which are appropriate, which are plainly adapted to that end, which are not prohibited, but consist with the letter and spirit of the Constitution, are constitutional." The act of Congress creating the Bank was constitutional. Thus the implied powers clause, also known as the necessary and proper clause, Article I, Section 8, clause 18, could be used to greatly expand the powers of the Constitution, endorsing the loose interpretation position originally proposed by Hamilton. Marshall wrote, "The Constitution is intended to endure for ages to come, and consequently, to be adapted to the various crises of human affairs." Some people today argue that the Constitution should only be interpreted according to the *original intent* of the Founding Fathers. Marshall, our greatest Chief Justice, would disagree.

In answering the second question, the Court ruled that "the power to tax involves the power to destroy." The phrase was Daniel Webster's, who argued the case for the Bank of the U.S. Think of the logic of taxation. The annual tax on the Baltimore branch was $15,000. Once the Bank and the federal government accepted the principle that a state could tax the federal government, what is to keep the state from enacting a tax so high as to put the Bank of the U.S. into bankruptcy? Marshall said, "the states have no power, by taxation or otherwise, to retard, burden, or in any manner control the operations of the constitutional laws enacted by Congress." One government may not tax another government. This case has been called "second in importance to the Constitution itself" because it clearly established the loose interpretation of the Constitution and the justification for Congressional or national power at the expense of the states.

Dartmouth College v. Woodward, 1819

In 1816 the New Hampshire state legislature took over Dartmouth College, a private college. The old board of trustees sued the newly appointed board of trustees to regain control. Who was Dartmouth College? Was the original charter granted in 1769 a contract within the meaning of the contract clause of the Constitution? Can a state legislature change a contract? The Supreme Court ruled that the Constitution protected the charter of a private corporation and the people could not alter it through their legislature. The voice of the people as expressed through their legislature is NOT the voice of God. Daniel Webster had argued the case for the original board of trustees, with the well-remembered statement, "It is a small college, but there are those who love it." (The exact quote is unknown.) Both parties in a contract must agree to break the contract.

In a later case, *Charles River Bridge v. Warren Bridge*, 1837, the Supreme Court ruled against a state created monopoly on other grounds. The community has rights that a contract cannot override. Contractual rights are not absolute and perpetual. The Charles River Bridge Company sued to prevent the state of Massachusetts from authorizing the construction of a rival second bridge across the Charles River at Boston. The company had prospered; its stock rose from $444 per share in 1805 to $2,080 in 1814. Was the original charter to build the first bridge a contract, an implied perpetual agreement? Chief Justice Roger B. Taney, in his first significant decision, ruled that no charter granted to a private corporation permanently vested rights that might harm the public interest. Taney wrote, "the continued existence of a government would be of no great value, if by implications and presumptions, it was disarmed of the powers necessary to accomplish the ends of its creation; and the functions it was designed to perform, transferred to the hands of privileged corporations." Try to imagine the situation if the Charles River Bridge Company still owned the only permitted bridge across the Charles River. The rights of the community supersede a broad interpretation of the private rights of a corporation. "While the rights of property are sacredly guarded, we must not forget that the community also have rights . . . ." It is not the duty of the legislature to specify what the corporation charter does not say.

Gibbons v. Ogden, 1824

This is the first case decided under the Constitution's commerce clause. Two steamboat operators clashed over their respective monopoly charters to control steamboats in New York City harbor. This decision affirmed the exclusive federal control of interstate commerce, even in the absence of federal legislation or action.

Nationalism in Foreign Policy

In contrast to the first 15 years of the century, the United States was quite successful in achieving its foreign policy objectives after 1815. The Treaty of Ghent that ended the War of 1812 contained a clause committing both Great Britain and the United States to resolving outstanding issues.

Rush-Bagot Agreement, 1817

The 1817 Rush-Bagot Agreement began the disarming of the Great Lakes, although not really. The *USS Michigan*, a four-gun ship, patrolled the Great Lakes from 1844 to 1926. Try to picture how effective it must have been against prohibition era rumrunners in the 1920s zipping across the Great Lakes, outracing an eighty-year-old ship! Border fortifications did not begin to fall into decay until the Treaty of Washington in 1871. The U.S.-Canadian border is still the world's longest undefended border. Visit the International Peace Garden and Monument on the North Dakota-Canada border celebrating this. Over 150,000 visitors do so annually.

Convention of 1818

The Louisiana Purchase defined the territory's northern border as the Mississippi-Missouri watershed line. The Convention of 1818 reset the northern border as the 49th parallel, from the Lake of the Woods westward to the Continental Divide. Because no agreement dividing the Oregon Territory was acceptable to either side, they agreed to "joint occupation," meaning the Oregon Territory was "free and open" to both sides, not that it was jointly governed. The Convention of 1818 also resolved the leftover issue of American fishing rights granted by the Treaty of 1783 by designating specific Canadian coastlines in the Newfoundland area where Americans could fish or go on land to cure fish.

Adams-Onis Treaty, Florida Treaty, Transcontinental Treaty, Step Treaty, 1819
(ratified in 1821)

Earlier, the United States had simply grabbed parts of West Florida in 1810 and 1812-1813. John Quincy Adams, then the U.S. minister to Russia, tried to explain to the czar of Russia our moral justification for doing so. The Russian monarch interrupted Adams by saying, "Everyone is getting a little bigger these days." Adams could offer no better explanation. From our viewpoint Florida was not really under Spanish authority; pirates, runaway slaves, and Indians controlled it.

In 1818 Andrew Jackson, the hero of the Battle of New Orleans, pursued Indians into Florida. In a few weeks he captured every important Spanish fort except St. Augustine, deposed the Spanish governor, executed two British citizens, Robert Ambrister (name given as Richard Armbrister in some official sources) and Alexander Arbuthnot for supplying guns to the Indians, and declared in force "the revenue laws of the United States." Originally the Monroe administration and cabinet, with one exception, agreed that Jackson had committed an unauthorized and unwarranted act. The exception, Secretary of State John Quincy Adams, convinced the others that perhaps the United States could somehow use the incident to pressure Spain to relinquish Florida. Spain was upset about the independence revolts by her Latin American colonies, which many Americans openly supported and aided, in violation of international law. Further complicating the situation from Spain's viewpoint was the simple fact that Spain could no longer prevent the United States from taking Florida anytime it wanted to, as shown by Jackson's maneuvers. Spain sold Florida to the United States for nothing, really. The United States assumed the "claims" Americans had lodged against Spain for runaway slaves or losses to pirates based in Florida. The United States also gave up its vague claim to Texas and Spain gave up its solid claim to Oregon. The treaty set the boundary between the Louisiana territory and Northern Mexico, hence the name Step Treaty, because on the map it looks like steps. It has also been called the Transcontinental Treaty, because some historians argue that setting the western boundary of the Louisiana Purchase was the most significant part of this treaty.

Monroe Doctrine, December 2, 1823

This resulted from two events. The first was Russia's 1821 ukase (i.e., imperial decree) forbidding any foreign ship from coming within one hundred miles of their claim on the Pacific coast, which reached from Alaska down close to present-day San Francisco. The second was that the powers in Europe, anxious to stifle the revolutionary ideas that had been carried by Napoleon's army, discussed a joint expedition to reconquer Spain's Latin American colonies for her. The British, who had benefited from South American ports opening up for trade, approached the United States with an offer of a joint alliance to prevent a reconquest of Spain's colonies. Secretary of State John Quincy Adams convinced President Monroe to instead issue our declaration, knowing that Great Britain would support the United States, alliance or no alliance. Up until the 1850s Americans and others often thought of the Americas as one continent, hence the sense of unity that underlay the idea of protecting "our" continent. The term "Latin America" was first used in the 1860s by the French in their ill-fated attempt to plant a puppet emperor in Mexico.

The basic ideas in the Monroe Doctrine were not new. For example, Thomas Paine wrote in *Common Sense*, "It is the true interest of America to steer clear of European contentions." In *The Federalist, # 11*, Alexander Hamilton had written, "Let Americans disdain to be instruments of European greatness. Let the thirteen states, bound together in a strict and indissoluble Union, concur in erecting one great American system, superior to the control of all transatlantic force or influence, and able to dictate the terms of the connection between the old and the new world." (Hamilton could not say anything simply.) Implicit in the Monroe Doctrine was the idea of American innocence and European corruption. It persists as part of our **American Identity**, our American Exceptionalism.

The December 2, 1823, message contained three principles.

1. no colonization – No new European colonies in the New World. "The American continents, by the free and independent condition which they have assumed and maintain, are henceforth not to be considered as subjects for future colonization by any European powers."
2. nonintervention – That European nations should not intervene in the affairs of independent nations in the Western Hemisphere.
3. two hemispheres and nonentanglement – That the United States would not interfere in the affairs of European nations and the two hemispheres endorsed two different ideologies. In 1815 only the United States and Haiti were independent; by 1822 most countries in the Western Hemisphere were.

In the early years, republican disdain for the pomposity of European diplomacy led the United States to inaugurate unusual diplomatic practices. We did not appoint "ambassadors," only "ministers," considered beneath ambassadors in the diplomatic pecking order. Our first ambassador was not appointed until 1893. Jefferson refused to seat foreign ambassadors at White House dinners according to customary European protocol. European foreign ministers and diplomats returned the disdain. But, by the 1820s it was clear that the United States was here to stay, a force to be reckoned with in the Western Hemisphere. While American military might was minimal, its potential existed. Nationalism and potential combined to demand respect. Europeans could think of American diplomacy as immature and petty, but they could not ignore the United States. However, into this heady atmosphere of nationalism intruded the specter of sectionalism, illustrated by the Missouri crisis and the election of 1824.

18

FORCES FOR SECTIONALISM

Nationalism and sectionalism coexisted in this era. While nationalism drew the country together, sectionalism threatened to split it apart. They were parallel forces, vying for the public's heart and soul. Two political crises in the 1820s brought sectionalism to the forefront.

Missouri Crisis, 1819-1821
In 1790 the North and the South had been relatively equal in population and therefore equal in the House of Representatives. By 1820 the North's population was 5,152,000 and the South's 4,485,000, giving the North 105 Representatives and the South 81. The North was not satisfied with its advantage. Northern politicians objected to the "federal ratio," as it was called, the impact of the 3/5 clause, which counted five slaves as three for representation in the House of Representatives. In the years since the adoption of the Constitution many Northerners reached the conclusion that slaves should not be counted for representation. The concept, 3/5, had arisen during intense debates over taxes during the Articles of Confederation. Not adopted at that time, it became part of the Constitution. Northern politicians estimated in 1820 that the 3/5 clause gave the South 20 more seats in the House of Representatives and, therefore, 20 additional votes for president in the Electoral College. From the Northern point of view, the South's extra Electoral College votes in 1800 put Thomas Jefferson in the presidency over John Adams. The issue simmered.

Expansion westward advanced rapidly after the War of 1812 ended, because it was now safer to move west and transportation improvements made it easier. Four states joined the union in four years – Indiana in 1816, Mississippi in 1817, Illinois in 1818, and Alabama in 1819. Note that slave states and free states entered the union in pairs.

Politicians realized that because of the imbalance in the House they had to maintain a balance in the Senate between the slave states and the free states. Missouri applied for admission as a slave state in 1819. The lack of a free state to pair up with Missouri brought the issue of balance in Congress to the surface. During the debate in the House of Representatives in February, 1819, James Tallmadge from New York introduced an amendment to the admission bill prohibiting any further introduction of slaves into Missouri and freeing all children born of slaves upon reaching the age of 25. Rather than granting immediate freedom, this was the method used by many Northern states to abolish slavery, usually at age 35. This protected property rights, and the owner received some return for his or her investment. The primary issue about Missouri was the expansion of slavery and the continued impact of the 3/5 clause, not the existence of slavery in Missouri. This was not primarily an antislavery amendment, although Tallmadge had helped end slavery in New York in 1817. His amendment set off a fierce debate. The first provision, no new slaves taken into Missouri, passed the House, 87-76. The second, children freed after twenty-five years, passed the House 82-78. Both provisions failed in the Senate, 22-16 and 31-7.

In these years Congress was frequently in session only from early December to early spring, and when it convened after a fall election, it did not include the newly elected senators and representatives. They began to serve 13 months later. When Congress adjourned in March, 1819, the debate exploded in the national press, partially because it now included some new members of Congress who had been elected in the 1818 elections. The Congressional debate resumed in December, with the crisis lasting until March, 1820, 13 months after it began.

The so-called Missouri Compromise ended with both the North and the South gaining, or so everyone thought. The South got Missouri as a slave state, the North gained Maine, created out of Massachusetts. The future issue of slavery in the territories was resolved with the provision that the southern boundary of Missouri, the 36° 30' latitude line, would divide the remainder of the Louisiana Purchase into free territory and slave territory. Slavery was prohibited north of the 36° 30' line, except in Missouri. And, as Section 8 of the act stated, slavery "shall be and is hereby *forever* prohibited." (Italics added.) The issue was settled. This is why the Kansas-Nebraska Act in the 1850s rankled so many Northerners. "Forever" is supposed to mean forever. The bitter debate left many ill feelings in both the North and the South. Thomas Jefferson called the crisis a "firebell in the night, it wakened and filled me with terror." John Quincy Adams wrote in his diary, "I take it for granted that the present question is a mere preamble – a title page to a great, tragic volume." No new perspectives or issues were introduced in future debates over expansion and slavery, all the way up to the Civil War. The positions just hardened.

Election of 1824

Earlier, because of the slow decline of the Federalist Party, James Monroe faced virtually no opposition in 1816. He defeated Rufus King, 183-34. Only Connecticut, Massachusetts, and Delaware voted Federalist. In 1820 Monroe received 231 of 235 possible Electoral College votes. Three abstained, supposedly to deny him the honor of being elected unanimously, as had George Washington, and one voted for John Quincy Adams. By 1824 the First Party System had evaporated. One of the roles of a political party is to recruit candidates. Now mainly state legislatures performed that function, but the old method also continued, a party caucus in Congress. Ten candidates ran for president.

It is not good that political party loyalty seems to be declining today. Parties select, groom, and rally behind candidates. Now many millionaires or celebrities run for office, partly because they can afford the expense and also cash in on their name recognition.

The Democratic Party congressional caucus, with only 66 of the 216 Democratic members of Congress even attending, selected Secretary of the Treasury William Crawford of Georgia as a candidate. Northern state legislatures, especially in New England, picked the Secretary of State, John Quincy Adams. Western states selected the Speaker of the House, Henry Clay of Kentucky, and the Southern and some Western states chose General and former Senator Andrew Jackson of Tennessee. Jackson's views were largely unformed and therefore unknown. He was the hero of the Battle of New Orleans, and to many Americans that was enough.

It was a nasty campaign. Jackson was labeled a gambler, duelist, military tyrant, and adulterer. Before marrying Andrew Jackson, his wife Rachel divorced her first husband. At least both of them believed the divorce had been made final. It was not. After learning of their real circumstances, they quickly made the divorce legally final and remarried. However, the political fodder was there for Jackson's opponents. And they used it, but not to his face. Jackson had a temper! Clay was called a drunkard and a gambler. He did enjoy both drinking and playing cards. Crawford, the Secretary of the Treasury, was branded a dishonest man who mismanaged the budget. Not true. He suffered a stroke in 1823 that left him partially paralyzed, but, during the campaign, news of his condition was kept secret. John Quincy Adams was ridiculed for his sloppy dress, high education, and intelligence. He was very bright. When his father was a diplomat in Europe, John Quincy Adams served as his father's secretary, beginning at the age of 14. It is very interesting that only in America are political candidates ridiculed for being intelligent. John Quincy Adams read the Bible three times a day – once in English, once in French, and once in German. John Calhoun smartly ran for vice president on both Jackson's ticket and on Adams' ticket. He got 182 electoral votes for vice president, and won.

The Election Results

Here are the election results. Please be aware that often historians doing research encounter different numbers when something is counted. It drives them almost crazy trying to get the exact, correct numbers. It cannot be done; you may see different numbers for this election or any other counted totals in history.

> Jackson, 152,901 popular votes, 42%, 99 electoral votes from 11 states, mostly from the South, and Pennsylvania, New Jersey, most of Maryland and Indiana, and some scattered.
>
> Adams, 114,023 popular votes, 32%, 84 electoral votes from 7 states, New England and most of New York.
>
> Crawford, 46,979 popular votes, 13%, 41 electoral votes from Virginia and Georgia.
>
> Clay, 47,217 popular votes, 13%, 37 electoral votes, from Missouri, Ohio, Kentucky, and 4 from New York.

While Clay was third in the total popular vote, he was out because the Constitution specified that if no person received a majority then the House of Representatives selected a president from the top three in Electoral College votes. However, Clay was the Speaker of the House of Representatives and his influence would greatly affect the outcome. By the time the choice reached the House, Crawford's physical condition was known and most considered him unfit for the presidency. Thus, the voting was really between Jackson and Adams.

The Twelfth Amendment, adopted after the election of 1800, states that if the presidential election fails to produce a clear winner, the House of Representatives selects from the top three candidates, with each state having one vote. With 24 states in the Union, 13 were needed to win. Clay personally preferred Adams over Jackson. Clay won over a number of western representatives for Adams. Several of their states had voted for Jackson. Clay even delivered Kentucky's vote for Adams, in spite of the fact that Adams had not been on the ballot and had not won a single popular vote in Kentucky. In addition, the Kentucky state legislature had instructed its state's representatives in Congress to vote for Jackson, a resolution that, however, was not binding. The House met on February 9, and on the first ballot declared John Quincy Adams the winner with 13 states. He had gained six states. Jackson, who originally had seven, had lost four states. Crawford got four.

Shortly afterwards Adams appointed Clay as his Secretary of State, a traditional stepping-stone to the presidency in this period. Jackson's supporters charged there was a "corrupt bargain," a political deal. After all, Clay and Adams shared a mutual, personal disdain for one another. However, their disdain did not match the animosity between Clay and Jackson. Clay stated during the campaign that Jackson's only qualification for the presidency was killing Englishmen in New Orleans. In 1819 Clay had asked the House of Representatives to censure Jackson for his unauthorized exploits in Florida. Jackson invaded the territory of a country with which the United States was not at war, executed two unsavory British citizens for supplying guns to the Indians, and declared the laws of the United States in force. Spain should have declared war against us, and Britain also. Neither did, cooler heads prevailed in Europe. Instead of a censure, the House voted its "public thanks!" Jackson ever after hated Clay, and Clay returned the hated. Was there a deal between Adams and Clay? It is likely. However, the appointment of Clay as Secretary of State was not an obvious indication of a "deal." Clay and Adams both advocated many similar policies. Of the two possibilities, Clay preferred Adams to Jackson, and, Adams respected Clay's political ability, but not his personal behavior.

From Three Sections to Two: the Civil War is Coming

The South, blessed with many navigable rivers, saw little need for investing in canals or railroads for her agricultural-centered economy. Many railroads in the South were short, intended for answering some local need to ship a particular resource, such as coal. The South did not have connected railroad systems. In 1860 only three railroads connected the North and the South, while numerous railroads connected the Northeast to the Northwest. The Transportation Revolution changed the country from three sections to two. It linked the Northwest and the Northeast together. Logically, the two agricultural sections, the Northwest and the South, should have united to oppose the political agenda of the manufacturing Northeast. As late as 1850 Western farmers shipped most of their agricultural produce to market via the Mississippi River. Not by 1860. Now it was the railroads heading east that carried it.

The South fell behind economically, believing that cotton was "King" and represented the future. Southerners had good reasons to believe cotton was essential to the world's economy. By the late 1850s the American South was the world's leading supplier of raw cotton; it supplied 77% of England's, 90% for France, 60% for Germany, and 92% for Russia. How could the world get by without the South?

Meanwhile the Transportation Revolution was boosting the Northern economy. Within months of the opening of the Erie Canal in 1825, the governor of Georgia was complaining that wheat shipped from upstate New York was lower in price in Savannah than wheat shipped from the Atlanta region. The Erie Canal catapulted New York City into the nation's number one economic center. By 1860 New York City was the leading port for all but seven American items exported and for 976 of the nation's top 1000 different items imported. With that lead it did not matter which city was in second place.

Debates Over Federal Government Policy

The need to obtain federal legislation to benefit one's own section led to a new brand of national and congressional politics. What developed was a constantly shifting set of alliances and combinations between individual politicians and sections before sectional positions solidified by the late 1840s and early 1850s. Four areas of federal governmental policy dominated congressional and presidential politics in the sixty years preceding the outbreak of the Civil War. Think of the nation as comprised of four sections with different interests and outlooks – the Northeast, the Northwest, the Southwest, and the Southeast. Here are the issues and the positions generally taken by each of the four sections in debates over control of public policy. Each section sought to control federal policy to benefit its section, just as today what is behind many debates in Congress is a battle between the Rust or Frost Belt and the Sun Belt, the Blue States versus the Red States.

Land Policy

	Northeast	Northwest	Southwest	Southeast
size	large	small	small	large
price	high	low	low	high

The questions over land policy were the price and the size of the initial sale of the land. Remember, all land never sold is the property of the federal government. Should the price be high or low? Is the purpose of government land to raise revenue? This can be accomplished by either a high price to discourage buying or stipulating that a person must buy a large number of acres. Is the purpose of government land to encourage people to move west? This can be accomplished with a low price or by stipulating a small number of acres. The trend in the almost 400 land laws passed by Congress up to the Civil War was toward lower prices and a smaller initial size, eventually reaching the Homestead Act of 1862, which gave land away. The ever-expanding western population, which welcomed new people as a source of increased business, fed this trend. Note that on this issue the division is East-West. Population losses threatened both the Northeast and the Southeast, because it reduced the number of their representatives in the House of Representatives and, thus, their influence.

Internal Improvements at Federal Government Expense

Northeast	Northwest	Southwest	Southeast
yes	yes	no	no

Here the issue was whether the federal government should pay for new roads, canals, or railroads. The South opposed internal improvements at federal expense because they had many useable rivers. Constitutional qualms and a lack of funds also hampered and limited support. Arguments over the intended routes complicated funding.

The beginning and ending cities would gain, while rival cities would lose. Think of the economic benefits and damage done today by new highway construction on local shops, stores, and gas stations. States or local governments funded most early internal improvements. After the Depression of 1837 many states added a provision to their constitutions prohibiting state funding. This led the railroads to rely more on corporate funding. The overall effect of the expansion of the transportation network was to tie the Northwest and Northeast closer together.

Protective Tariff

Northeast	Northwest	Southwest	Southeast
high	high	low	low

Did the United States want a high protective tariff or a low revenue tariff? The tariffs were initially high, in reaction to the British dumping goods cheaply on the American market after the War of 1812. The British intended to drive Americans out of business and then corner the market. This led to high tariffs. The first protective tariff, passed in 1816, set a 25% rate on imported goods, raised in 1824 to 33%, in 1828 to 50%. The 1828 and 1832 tariffs created a political crisis resulting in the lower tariff of 1833, which began the trend towards gradually lowering the tariff rates up to the Civil War. For example, the Tariff of 1857 was 17%.

Expansion of Slavery to the West

Northeast	Northwest	Southwest	Southeast
against	against	for	for

The issue was neither abolition nor antislavery. It was the expansion of slavery into the western territories. Northern family-centered settlers believed slave labor gave an unfair advantage to Southern plantation owners in the race to develop western land.

Other factors played a role complicating sectionalism. Immigrants saw no reason to go into the South to compete against free black labor or slave labor. Waves of German and Irish immigration helped shift the population imbalance even more to the North's favor, increasing the North's numbers in the House of Representatives and foreshadowing the day when a president could be elected with only Northern support, as happened with Abraham Lincoln in 1860. This gradual population shift put the South into a loser's role. The South increasingly sensed it was losing its ability to influence or to control or to guide national policies to the benefit of the South. In addition, the eastern states of the South lost population to the southwestern South of Mississippi, Alabama, and Louisiana, creating a dismal local economic outlook in the east. South Carolina, for example, lost 56,000 whites and 30,000 slaves in the decade of the 1820s. Hundreds of thousands of slaves were sold out of Virginia in the four decades prior to 1860.

Note that for three of the four issues – internal improvements, tariff, and expansion of slavery – the primary division is the North versus the South. Is the Civil War coming? Yes, clearly, but do not read history backwards. No politician knows for certain where a policy or decision is ultimately going to lead a nation – into prosperity or into tragedy. The assertion that the Civil War could have been avoided by more intelligent political decisions is premised on knowledge that later generations have. That perspective, understanding, and knowledge was not there for those political leaders who lived during the antebellum years. Should it have been? *The Fate of Their Country: Politicians, Slavery Extension, and the Coming of the Civil War,* by Michael F. Holt, addresses this question for the 1850s. Politicians looked to the next election, searching for short-term political advantages that would bring political victories. Partisan politicians USED issues more than they sought solutions. They thought and acted short-term for political advantage.

19

THE TRANSPORTATION AND MARKET REVOLUTIONS

The World That Was Lost

An English historian once used a similar title, *The World We Have Lost*, to describe the momentous changes taking place for the average person during a period in British history. This title would be appropriate to use to describe the early nineteenth century. As traditional colonial culture gave way to a spreading market culture, new beliefs, values, behaviors, emotions, and interpersonal relations spurred work and consumption. By 1815 a market revolution was well underway, establishing a distinct legal, social, financial, and transportation infrastructure.

Previously, subsistence agriculture had been typical. It was too costly to ship farm products more than 30-40 miles. Family obligation and communal cooperation characterized the economy. This society was later idealized as a world of family, trust, cooperation, love, equality, patriarchy, and inexpensive property. One prized value was independence, of anyone or anything, especially debt. The family supplied all the necessary labor. Wives were work partners. An old Ohio Valley folk saying captured that society's marital relationships.

> *First month, honey month,*
> *Next month like pie,*
> *Third month, you dirty* (rhymes with witch!),
> *Get out and work like I.*

Money was a commodity in this world, necessary only for purchasing a few store goods or paying taxes. Because money was difficult to obtain, many people intensely hated taxes, which had to be paid in cash. This partially explains the widespread sympathy for Shays's Rebellion and the Whiskey Rebellion. Debt and taxes were the poor's two great enemies, because through these two means a farmer could have his farm seized by the market world.

The urban poor also suffered. In 1809 over 1,000 men were jailed for debt in New York City, one-half for less than ten dollars. Freedom came when they paid. How?

The older urban working class consisted of artisans or mechanics, with dozens of different crafts – such as bakers, butchers, tailors, sailmakers, shoemakers, cabinet-makers, and chandlers. This part of the population existed in a world of shared values of quality products, independence, and serving neighborhood and local customers. Immigrants were one of the factors that undermined the pre-market world.

Immigration

Immigrants gravitated to the North partly because of the cheaper travel to the interior. Thousands of immigrants used the Erie Canal on their way west, passing through Buffalo. As a young boy in the early 1840s, Andrew Carnegie and his family traveled from New York City via the Erie Canal to Cleveland, then by railroad to Pittsburgh to join relatives. Immigrants, both Irish and German, found work in building the transportation systems and in the rapidly expanding factories. If they could find employment. NINA appeared on many job notices – "No Irish Need Apply." Landing in Northern cities, immigrants changed the nature of the city's population, just like today. The immigrants also fed the increasing antislavery feelings in the North. Immigrants saw no reason to go into the South to compete against free black labor and slave labor. They assumed that both free blacks and slaves threatened an immigrant's ability to find suitable work, hence their decision to locate in the North, swelling the labor pool. As a theory, economic competition results in what is best for society's consumers, but do not try to tell that to someone just fired because the boss found a cheaper immigrant worker.

The Transportation Revolution

Innovations in transportation led to the nation growing into a single commercial market. The country was, in effect, shrinking in terms of the time necessary to transport goods and information. Look at the following examples.

In 1776 there were 37 newspapers in the country; by 1810, 359; by 1828, 861; by 1840, 1,403. Unlike today's newspapers, advertisements from wholesalers and merchants advertising goods dominated the first pages. Merchants' ads, indicating an expanding range for their products, fueled the great increase in newspapers. After the invention of the telegraph in 1844, 50,000 miles of wires strung by 1860 further linked the nation together.

Travel times shrank. In 1800 it took four days to travel from New York City to Washington, D.C., and over five weeks to St. Louis. By 1830 the journey from New York City to Washington, D.C., was only a little over one day, to St. Louis, 16 days. When the Panic of 1837 collapsed the economy, the news from New York City hit St. Louis in 11 days. Steamships contributed, especially by reducing upstream travel time. In Abraham Lincoln's youth one floated a raft loaded with goods from Kentucky or Illinois down the Mississippi River to New Orleans. After busting up the raft to sell for firewood, you walked back. Even downstream travel was slow. In 1815 the record from Louisville to New Orleans was over 25 days; by 1828, a little over 8 days; by 1853, a little over 4 days.

The cost to ship goods dropped dramatically throughout the early nineteenth century. In 1800 it cost eight to ten cents a mile to ship a ton of goods downstream. By 1840 the upstream rates were less than one-half cent per mile, almost the same as downstream. Canal rates were below one cent per mile. Wagon rates remained high throughout the era, declining from 40 to 15 cents per mile. Road building was costly and roads seemed to add less value to the economy than canals. The eighty-three locks on the 363-mile long Erie Canal dropped rates from Buffalo to New York City from $100 per ton to $7. Mother Nature holds boats up, and, a horse or mule can pull fifty times its weight through still water. Canal boats zipped along at 4-5 miles per hour. Railroads would further shrink distances, especially between areas not well served by rivers or canals. This "transportation revolution" of building highways, canals, and railroads had a dramatic impact on the economy and on political alignment, linking together the Northwest and Northeast.

The Rise of the Factory

As the economic market widened due to improved transportation, it intensified competition and lowered prices. Merchant-capitalists began to use a new system to reduce costs, the putting-out system, initially in making clothes and shoes, by simplifying the steps in the production process. Under the putting-out system a factor, hence the later term "factory," delivered materials to a house and returned later to pick up the finished products. Another advance came in 1791 when Samuel Slater, an Englishman with knowledge of British machinery, emigrated to Rhode Island. There Moses Brown, a wealthy merchant, financially backed Slater's plans to build a cotton-spinning mill. Next entrepreneurs centralized the manufacturing process, bringing the workers together with all the processes under one roof to convert raw cotton into finished fabrics. Lowell, Massachusetts, is the best example, and could be called America's first factory town. It had been built by a group of investors, the Boston Associates, led by Francis Cabot Lowell, who opened the first integrated cotton factory in Lowell in 1814.

Cheap clothing, furniture, gloves, stockings, and hats were soon mass-produced, much to the delight of consumers. This situation is similar to making your own bread or ice cream today. Yes, it is possible, but is it worth your time? Would your time not be better spent specializing in another product, which your particular skills permit you to make quickly?

Consequences

This process, unfortunately, was accompanied by some consequences. Economic changes and advances always are. As more goods were factory produced, the previous high status of a craftsman degenerated as artisans and apprentices became increasingly dependent on wages. The easy-going pace and friendly camaraderie of the workshop evaporated under the pressure to reduce costs or to produce more.

Farm families soon found that with a little more crop production for the market they could avoid all the complicated labor involved in raising and processing fiber, spinning thread, and weaving and dyeing cloth. Try to imagine what it would be like if your family could get food and clothes from ONLY what they raised or made at home. Textbooks emphasize the impact of the Erie Canal, but smaller, local canals significantly altered daily life. For example, the 325,000 people who lived near Philadelphia within fifteen miles of the Schuylkill (River) in 1830 used the 62 miles of new canals along the river built by the Schuylkill Navigation Company. As historian Andrew Schocket explained in *Founding Corporate Power in Early National Philadelphia*, "If the Schuylkill navigation allowed residents to wet their feet in the market, a good many of them dove in headfirst." Products flowed both ways. Farm produce and various building materials – stone, coal, iron ore, marble – floated to Philadelphia. Upriver came not only bolts of cloth, but also foreign imports such as "sugar and Madeira (wine), and even the oceanic delicacy of fresh sea bass." Life got better, much better.

However, there were ramifications for society. Rev. Horace Bushnell, a New England Congregational Church minister and prominent theologian, observed, "This transition from mother-and-daughter power to water-and-steam power carries with it a complete revolution of domestic life." Bushnell was correct. What was beginning was a *Kulturkampf,* German for a cultural war, a struggle over an unknown future that would bring a repositioning and reestablishing of all human relationships, both in the workplace making products and elsewhere – the home, the church, the family, the marriage, and the community – due to the new methods employed in the workplace and a greater reliance upon cash transactions. It was during these years that the author, Washington Irving, created the phrase, "the Almighty dollar," calling it "that great object of universal devotion throughout the land."

The entrepreneurial elites in the booming cities, members of merchant families, saw new enterprises as places to invest their money. However, they needed the state governments to guarantee their property rights, to enforce contracts, and to provide financial and transportation infrastructures, such as the Erie Canal.

In opposition, the rural majority idealized the disappearing republican society. Democracy promised farmers protection from intrusive government. Dreading taxes and meeting most of their social needs through their own institutions of family and church, they jealously resisted any enlargement of public functions or expense. As the primary base of support for Jefferson's Republican, also called Democratic, political party, they would have endorsed a statement credited to him, "That government is best which governs least." To preserve the independence and equality of a self-sufficient, self-governing citizenry, they wanted their government weak, cheap, and close to home. The market's forces were a corrupting threat to farm families. Thomas Jefferson's political program of low taxes, rigid economy, and retirement of Hamilton's public debt suited them perfectly. Throw in an ostentatious simplicity of style surrounding official duties, no grandiose projects, and small farmers and urban artisans were happy.

Most of the significant political and economic action was at the state and local level. The entire federal government, from doorkeepers to president, numbered 153 people in 1800 and 352 in 1829. More senators resigned to enter state government offices than failed at their effort to gain reelection. A former governor of New York, De Witt Clinton, resigned from the Senate to become mayor of New York City.

By threatening this yeoman republic, investors, large manufacturers, and those supporting the market economy stirred up a powerful democratic counterforce. The clashes between the two groups played out in three areas:

1. How democratic, how responsive to democratic majorities, would government be?
2. Would government power be extensive, concentrated at the federal level or limited, and diffused among the states?
3. To what extent and in what ways would government promote economic growth?

Commercialism threatened public virtue by engendering luxury and self-indulgence among the rich. Thomas Jefferson understood that political equality required economic equality. He hoped cheap land would preserve a just and humane society. He referred to his Louisiana Purchase as "an empire for liberty," and reduced the price and the number of acres for an individual's purchase of western land from the federal government.

From Three Sections to Two

The economic changes brought about by the Market Revolution and the Transportation Revolution profoundly changed the nation. The Transportation Revolution changed the country from three sections to two. It linked the Midwest and the Northeast together, boosting the Northern economy. For example, by 1860 the Erie Canal had catapulted New York City into the nation's number one economic center. In Congress politicians sought policy adjustments in response to the economic changes sweeping the nation. However, by the late 1840s and early 1850s, sectional attitudes hardened. Four areas of federal governmental economic policy dominated congressional politics in the decades preceding the outbreak of the Civil War – land policy, internal improvements, tariffs, and the expansion of slavery. Each section took strong positions on these issues, making compromise difficult. By the decade of the 1850s slavery in the territories emerged as the most contentious issue, incapable of compromise.

20

ANDREW JACKSON AND THE AGE OF JACKSON

Andrew Jackson – Symbol for an Age
Andrew Jackson dominated the years from 1820 to 1850, so much so that some historians refer to these years as the Age of Jackson. No American has as many places named for him as does Andrew Jackson, over 130. He is always in the top ten in any list of great presidents.

The Second Party System
Some historians and political scientists use the concept of party systems or realignment theory to study American political history. Simply stated, it means grouping the presidential elections into six different systems, and seeing similarities between the politics and elections within the years of that party system. The dates for the party systems vary slightly from historian to historian, but generally, they are as follows:

> First Party System – 1790 to 1824
> Second Party System – 1828 to 1860
> Third Party System – 1860 to 1896
> Fourth Party System – 1896 to 1932
> Fifth Party System – 1932 to 1968
> Sixth Party System – 1968 to ?

The debate goes on. Has the nation begun the Seventh Party System?

The previous party system dissolves due to some crisis, usually economic, or what a political scientist once termed a "societal trauma," such as the outbreak of the Civil War or the turmoil of the 1960s. In addition, a weakness in party loyalty allows major shifts in popular political support among the major parties and the arrival of new issues. The elections that usher in a new system are termed "defining elections." The First Party System ended with the death of the Federalist Party on the national scene, the ending of many foreign policy issues, and the expansion of suffrage to almost all white males. Universal suffrage was a dangerous idea to the European elite, "utterly incompatible with civilization," in the words of a member of the British Parliament. The Second Party System ended with the outbreak of the Civil War. The depression of 1893 and the resulting economic chaos ended the Third. The Fourth ended because of another depression, the Great Depression. The Fifth was a casualty of the turbulent decade of the 1960s. If one wants to win the presidency, be ready with the right issues when the Sixth Party System ends, unless it has already and historians are not yet aware of it. Remember, historians designate and assign names and arbitrary dates to eras, what is called "periodization."

Each party system has unique characteristics that differ from those that precede or follow. As an example, look at the first two. There is a dramatic change in the presidents of the First and Second Party Systems. All of the first six presidents would have been remembered in American history books if they had not served as president. George Washington, John Adams, Thomas Jefferson, James Madison, James Monroe, and John Quincy Adams are giants among the Founding Fathers and early leaders. Some historians argue that the times make the man, or, the woman. This means that if Jefferson had not written the Declaration of Independence then someone else would have, and equally as well as Jefferson did. The times created the need and the man. Personally, I doubt it. I think great men and great women do appear at times in history and they do make a difference in that period's history. The times may create conditions that aid in the rise of an individual, such as Hitler in Germany between the two world wars. However, Hitler certainly placed his own twisted, personal, evil stamp on that era.

Comparing the First and Second Party Systems

In contrast to the First Party System, almost no president during the Second Party System would have been remembered at the national level, with the exception of Andrew Jackson and his escapades against the British and the Indians and in taking Florida. James K. Polk would also be an exception. When one thinks of great or even above average presidents, the names Martin Van Buren, John Tyler, Zachary Taylor, Millard Fillmore, Franklin Pierce, and James Buchanan do not roll off one's tongue. They were military heroes or professional politicians who headed state political machines. Van Buren, the son of a tavern owner, ran a political machine nicknamed the Albany Regency. The machine was based on unswerving loyalty, getting out the vote, and providing jobs for its faithful workers and supporters.

Those in lower positions of political power were also seen as a step down compared to their counterparts in the First Party System. Walter Bagehot, the editor of the influential British journal, *The Economist*, observed,

> "The men of thoughtful minds and lofty purpose, the men of noble sentiments and stainless honour, have retired from public life; and, naturally enough, as the work of politics became dirtier and rougher, have left it to dirtier and rougher men. The consequence, as everyone is too well aware, and as even Americans themselves have repeated *usque ad nauseam*, has been that the rulers and legislators of the United States are, almost without exception, either the vulgarer and shallower men of the nation who share the popular faults and passions, or cleverer minds who flatter and obey them without sharing them – unworthy in the one case intellectually, unworthier still, in the other, from voluntary moral degradation."

The national party convention selected the national candidates, unlike the First Party System's dependence upon a caucus of Congressional party leaders. In the First, qualified bureaucrats doing a good job served for life. The Second promoted the idea that any man could perform any government job and depended on the spoils system to reward the faithful and to build up the political machine. After his victory in 1860 Lincoln removed 1,195 of the federal government's 1,520 officeholders to fill patronage positions for his fellow Republicans. Politics was a business, a way for the ambitious to rise. For the First, politics was a call to serve the nation, one often reluctantly answered.

The leaders of the First came from the wealthy elite; the Second from anywhere, even humble origins. Try to imagine the shock on the face of Washington or Jefferson if their opponent proudly ran glorifying his early career as an uneducated rail-splitter, as Lincoln did. The disorderly mob scene at Jackson's inauguration would have made all the Founding Fathers roll over in their graves. Some of the early presidents spoke several languages. John Quincy Adams read from the Bible three times a day, once in English, once in French, and once in German; he was fluent in seven languages, including Greek and Latin. With the exception of Van Buren, who was fluent in Dutch and traveled in Europe, the rest of the Second were much less rooted in the classics, foreign languages, or even travel. John Quincy Adams spent twenty-one years living abroad. His father, John Adams, and Jefferson, Madison, and Monroe all were ambassadors or treaty negotiators in Europe. By tradition, many of the First Party System presidents received an honorary degree from Harvard, to which they responded with a speech in Latin. The tradition ended when Jackson accepted his degree and then sat down with a nod to the audience. In disgust, many Harvard alumni mailed their diplomas back to the college.

In the First, the leaders ruled FOR the people, who were not fully capable of understanding what was in their best interest. In the Second, the leaders governed in the

NAME of the people. It was not yet government of the people, by the people, and for the people, Lincoln's phrase, but it was a lot closer to it than in the First Party System. Historians consistently rank only two presidents in the Second Party System, Andrew Jackson and James K. Polk, as strong presidents. The rest are closer to the bottom. Two were defeated for reelection, John Quincy Adams and Martin Van Buren. Two died in office, the first to do so, William Henry Harrison and Zachary Taylor. Three – John Tyler, Millard Fillmore, and Franklin Pierce – were passed over by their own party as candidates for reelection, practically an admission of failure.

Property requirements restricted suffrage in the First. Candidates for office usually had to meet a higher property qualification than did the voters. In the years from 1812 to 1821, six of the new western states adopted universal white male suffrage – Louisiana, Indiana, Illinois, Alabama, Mississippi, and Missouri. Four older states modified their suffrage requirements to increase the number who could vote. By 1828 only six states still had property requirements, by 1860 only two, Rhode Island and South Carolina. However, five states – Delaware, Georgia, Massachusetts, North Carolina, and Pennsylvania – still restricted the vote to male taxpayers.

The basis for determining the right to vote changed greatly from the First to the Second. Do not focus on those who could not vote – blacks, slaves, and women. Almost nobody supported that. (Blacks could vote in some states, chiefly in New England.) The American spirit of democracy with its promise of both equality and freedom impressed the insightful French visitor, Alexis de Tocqueville, who wrote about his observations in *Democracy in America*. Reserved campaigns characterized the First Party System. Presidential candidates did not campaign. Voters already knew enough about them to make up their minds. In the Second, campaigns were mass hoopla with slogans, parades, and bonfire rallies. By 1840 over 80% of the potential voters voted. The quintessential Second Party election took place in 1840 when the Whigs ran on slogans and no platform. The Whig nominee, William Henry Harrison, was the first presidential candidate to give speeches. One wonders what he said without a platform.

The issues that dominated the politics of the First Party System were missing in the Second. After the Monroe Doctrine in 1823 foreign affairs took a back seat in national politics. Europe entered a long period of relative tranquility, permitting the United States to turn to domestic issues and expansion. The First Party System argued over the Bank of the U.S. Jackson did not argue over it; he killed it. The politics of the 1790s revolved around the two colorful personalities of Hamilton and Jefferson, leaders of their respective parties, Federalists and Democratic-Republicans. In the Second, the Whigs had a split personality – Henry Clay, Daniel Webster, and John Calhoun. But, of the three, it was Clay who was nicknamed "the Embodiment of Whig Principles." The Republican Party of Jefferson became the Democratic Party of Jackson, giving the entire era a nickname, Jacksonian Democracy, or, the Rise of the Common Man. Democrats disliked "nonproducers"

– bankers, merchants, lawyers, and speculators. Their bedrock of support came from the "producers" – farmers, laborers, and urban artisans.

Jackson's personality dominated the period. So did the Democratic Party. Six of the nine presidents were Democrats and Democrats controlled the Senate and the House of Representatives for most of this era, the Senate for 28 years and the House for 24. The new issues in the Jacksonian era were the tariff, Indian removal, internal improvements, land policy, and the abolition or expansion of slavery. Unlike the earlier period, most politicians began to make the United States a singular noun. The implications, connotations, and assumptions behind the singular noun in "The United States is" are quite different from those behind the plural noun, "These United States are." Now Americans and their politicians were sure the United States would endure. By the end of the Second Party System the question became whether or not the United States would endure half slave and half free. The Civil War and Reconstruction ended the Second Party System. The Republican victory in 1860 was clearly sectional. The elections of Jackson, Van Buren, Harrison, Polk, Taylor, and Pierce had all been by bisectional majorities, winning a majority of the free states and a majority of the slave states.

Know the characteristics of each party system and be able to differentiate between the system that precedes it and the one that follows. Especially know the defining elections that usher in the change. Use similar criteria – characteristics of the leaders, the nominating procedures and the conventions, changes in the suffrage base, which group of voters lean toward which party, the role of money in campaigns, the role of the media, and the foreign and domestic issues of that period.

A good summary of the differences between the Jacksonians and the Whigs is the following excerpt from William Lee Miller's *Lincoln's Virtues: An Ethical Biography*, pp. 112-113.

> "The Whigs had different cultural emphases than the Democrats. When you read Daniel Walker Howe's *The Political Culture of the American Whigs* you find yourself picking up from page after page two words: 'improvement' and 'industry,' both used in more than one application. Economic improvement, certainly, but not superior to, or divorced from, a broader cultural improvement, or even—it was an age and place not embarrassed to say it—moral improvement. Also self-improvement. But not 'self-improvement' in formulas and in isolation, and not as narrow and shallow as some of the vast later American cult of 'self-improvement' would be. Social improvement—the self and society joined. Intellectual improvement, educational improvement, even—perhaps especially—moral improvement."

> "The Whigs in general were less expansionist than the Jackson Democrats, and some Whigs put the point this way: Rather than *quantitative* development by the spreading of the American population over ever

more territory, let us continue the *qualitative* development of the young society where it is. The Whig Party was a combination of elements unlike that of either of the later parties. It was the party of commerce, industry, and the economic elite; businessmen and bankers were usually Whigs. But it was also the party, as we have said, of positive government (the Jacksonians would say, because government action aided business and commerce—to the detriment of the farmer and the poor man). And it was also, somewhat more than the Democrats, the party of *reform*: The Whig Party included Horace Mann, the great originator of public schools; Joshua Giddings, the leading opponent of slavery in Congress (and almost all other opponents of slavery in Congress, who were few); Lyman Beecher, the leading clergyman, from whose influence (and family) would come a host of reforms. It would also be, somewhat more than the Democrats, the party of artists and intellectuals, of leading lawyers and judges. Lincoln had in him, the extravagant endings to his early speeches reveal, and as his later life would certainly reveal, a powerful moral idealism: a yearning, a purpose, to move toward something more worthy—in and for himself, certainly, but by no means only that. Something more worthy generally—morally better, as we might say. But he was not the sort of moral idealist who regards the material base of life as beneath the dignity of a moralist's attention."

"The Whig Party had been born in conflict with one whom they regarded as an overbearing president, a 'tyrant,' 'King Andrew' Jackson, with his 'usurpations.' And there was doctrine in the English Whig past and the classical sources upon which they drew that centered 'republicanism' in legislatures, with the menace found in tyrants, Caesars, kings, and courts. The American Whigs inherited some of that, so that even though they were, as compared to the least-government Jacksonian Democrats, the party of positive government, they were *not* the party of positive *executive* government. (The parties in this different time put together the elements of politics and morals in different ways from later days; one cannot make one-to-one analogies between their parties and ours.) When in 1837 this Illinois Whig (Lincoln) would give that first major public address, the much-examined Lyceum speech, a central theme would be a very Whiggish warning against a Caesar."

Today's Americans live in the Sixth Party System. The primaries of the Sixth Party System have negated the role of the national convention. All the national party convention does now is ratify the result from long campaigns in the primaries. By the time the convention meets, it is clear who will be the party's candidate. Hubert Humphrey in 1968 was the last candidate selected by the Democratic Party's national convention without entering a single primary. Ideology is much more important in the Sixth Party System, substituting for thoughtful discourse and compromise. Little is accomplished, according to each voter's list of what is important. Worse yet, the lists vary widely from one person to another and from one time to another. Thus, all seem frustrated with politics, politicians, and the political system. We hear cries for term limits all over the country. Maybe term limits are not such a good idea. In 1860 no member of the Senate had served more than twelve years. Previously, Congress compromised over slavery many times. Perhaps, if more senators had more experience in 1860, they could have avoided . . . . We will never know.

Jackson's Personal Background

Andrew Jackson was born on the North Carolina-South Carolina border, both states claim him, North Carolina is more likely. His father died the same month he was born; his mother's death left him orphaned at 13. His mother died of a fever while serving as a nurse to American wounded soldiers. Everyone in his family was either killed in the Revolutionary War or died during the war. At one point British troops took over Jackson's house. Jackson, about 13, was cut on the face by a British officer's sword. Why? Because after being ordered to clean and shine the officer's boots, Jackson told the officer where to stick his boots! For the rest of his life Jackson remained very proud of his scar. He had little formal education, but he inherited money, apparently from a distant Irish relative, and proceeded to waste it in wild living. After he squandered it, he moved to Tennessee, became a lawyer, and allied himself with the wealthy landowning class, often suing poor settlers for foreclosure on mortgages.

He married Rachel Robards in 1791, believing that her divorce was final. It was not. The Virginia legislature in 1790 had only granted her the right to apply for a divorce; she mistakenly thought she had been granted a divorce. At that time the only way to obtain a divorce was to have the state legislature pass a law granting a divorce. In 1793 her first husband, Lewis Robards, divorced her for desertion and adultery. Jackson and Rachel quietly remarried on January 17, 1794. It became a source of gossip and innuendo smearing throughout the rest of his life. Rachel died shortly after Jackson won the 1828 election, disgraced by the comments made about her during the campaign. When Jackson lived in the White House for the next eight years, he placed her picture on the nightstand table beside his bed in such a way that it was the last thing he saw before falling asleep and the first thing he saw when he woke up. It was a marriage filled with deep love, and, public snickering.

Well connected to the political elite in Tennessee, Jackson briefly served in the U.S. House of Representatives, 1796-1798; he was elected to the U.S. Senate in 1797, but resigned a year later due to financial reverses; he was appointed to the Tennessee state supreme court, serving until 1804, when financial losses again forced him to resign. From 1804-1812 he was a major general in the state militia, his only public office at that time. During the War of 1812 he won the Battle of Horseshoe Bend, defeating the Creek Indians, allies of the British. On January 8, 1815, came his greatest triumph, the Battle of New Orleans. By then he was nicknamed "Old Hickory," and considered a potential presidential candidate. President Monroe in 1818 sent Jackson to put down the Seminoles. Without authorization, Jackson pursued them into Spanish Florida, invading Spanish territory. As noted earlier, while there, he executed two British citizens, Ambrister and Arbuthnot, for selling weapons to the Seminoles, creating political turmoil with two governments, Spain and Great Britain. Both Spain and Great Britain would have been justified in declaring war on the United States. All this made everyone in Washington nervous, but the Secretary of State, John Quincy Adams, wisely realized that all this unauthorized and illegal action might lead to the United States acquiring Florida, which it did. While many in Washington criticized Jackson, officially no one did. His exploits added to his reputation among hardnosed Westerners. Curiously, he became the hero of the West and South and a symbol of the democratic spirit of the western frontiersman, which he was NOT.

A Symbol of the Age

Why was Jackson so loved and so hated? One historian, John William Ward, in *Andrew Jackson: Symbol for an Age,* used three ideas — Nature, Providence, and Will — to study the years from 1810 to 1850 to describe how Jackson came to symbolize these concepts in myth and in fact. (More in myth than fact.)

Providence

Clearly, Jackson was an instrument through which God worked out His plans for God's chosen people, Americans. How else could one explain Jackson's incredible victory at the Battle of New Orleans, where the U.S. lost 13 killed and wounded, and the British lost 2,036 killed and wounded.

The Embodiment of Nature

Jackson was the leader of the citizen-farmers, those who drop their plows, grab their rifles, and rush to the defense of their country. His militia defeated Britain's crack troops at New Orleans, aided by the Kentucky riflemen. Out of the myths of the Battle of New Orleans arose the song, *"The Hunters of Kentucky."* Check out the lyrics on the internet.

Jackson became a symbol of our previously virtuous society, one that America and Americans were moving away from. The country was entering an era of moral decline that needed to be reversed. America had strayed from our former state of virtue;

Americans needed to return to it. Who better to lead us there than God's own appointee? Jackson stood for anti-privilege, anti-monopoly, and anti-aristocracy. He was our first president born in a log cabin. Politically he favored the spoils system, believing that any person could do any government job because the work required was simple.

Jackson was pragmatism glorified, a man of action, not thought. It was said in the elections of 1824 and 1828 that "Jackson made law, Adams quoted it." It was the doer versus the thinker; common sense wisdom was more important than book learning. His opponents pictured Jackson as grossly uneducated. However, when Lincoln wrote his first inaugural address, one of the four documents he used to prepare it was one written by Jackson.

As previously noted, many of the early presidents received an honorary degree from Harvard, LL.D., a doctorate of laws. They then made a speech in Latin. Jackson just nodded his head and sat down. Critics said the degree should have been an A.S.S. degree, (remove the periods!). His supporters cheered. The donkey (an ass) was an animal of humble origins, hard-working, and it was good enough for Mary and Joseph. Many Harvard graduates mailed their diplomas back to Harvard in protest. Former president John Quincy Adams declined to attend Jackson's ceremony, writing to the president of Harvard, "As myself an affectionate child of our alma mater, I would not be present to witness her disgrace in conferring her highest literary honors upon a barbarian who could not write a sentence of grammar and hardly could spell his own name." However, George Washington and many others of that time were also bad spellers. Poor spelling never embarrassed Jackson. In the spirit of individualism, Jackson stated that he distrusted any person who had such a poor sense of imagination that they could only think of one way to spell a word.

A Man of Iron Will

Jackson was self-determination personified. He lifted himself up from poverty. On May 30, 1806, he fought a duel against the best shot in Tennessee, Charles Dickinson. He was hit by his opponent's first bullet and did not flinch or react, causing Dickinson to believe he had completely missed. As Charles Dickinson honorably stood still, because dueling etiquette gave each one shot, Jackson raised his pistol and drilled Dickinson, killing him. Then Jackson turned, took two steps, and collapsed. Dickinson's bullet had lodged in his chest, inches from his heart, and Jackson had not even blinked. When his aide asked how he did it, Jackson replied that he would have taken a bullet in the brain and still killed him. For the rest of his life Jackson periodically suffered through bloody coughing spells. Iron will indeed!

On January 30, 1835, during Jackson's presidency, Richard Lawrence, a mentally unbalanced house painter, aimed his two pistols at Jackson, who was coming out of a viewing for Warren Ransom Davis, a South Carolina congressman. Both pistols misfired.

Mathematicians calculated the odds of this happening as 125,000 to 1. Clearly, God protected Jackson, just as Jackson protected the nation. Lawrence was punished. Jackson jumped on his would-be assassin and beat him with a cane!

Peggy Eaton Affair

Peggy Eaton (Margaret O'Neale Timberlake Eaton) was a sharp-witted, rough-tongued beauty who worked in her father's boarding house-tavern in Washington, D.C. At this time, since Congress was usually in session only from December to early March, Congressmen generally lived in boarding houses without their families. John Timberlake, her first husband, was an alcoholic navy purser who was, strangely, always at sea. He committed suicide. Gossipers claimed it was over the rumors about her conduct. Several men immediately expressed an interest in her, the Adjunct General, Major Belton, and Captain Root. Duels were announced to fight for her. Then she announced she had fallen out of love with all of them.

She had always been linked to Senator John Eaton, a widower from Tennessee, who was Andrew Jackson's best friend. When he was elected president, Jackson appointed John Eaton as his Secretary of War. Jackson was very sensitive to the attacks swirling around Washington about Peggy Eaton's virtue, or lack of it. He felt that they were also indirect attacks on his wife, Rachel. All of his life Jackson strongly believed in conspiracies, and he viewed the attacks on the Eatons as devious attempts to discredit him. John Eaton married Peggy eight months after she became a widow. The critics had a ball describing the newly wed Mrs. Eaton. The governor of Virginia described her as "a woman destitute of virtue and of morals." Senator Louis McLane of Delaware said, "Eaton has just married his mistress, and the mistress of eleven dozen others." Jackson's nemesis, Henry Clay, commented in response to Jackson's public pronouncement that Peggy was "as chaste as a virgin." Clay said, "Nothing is as infinite as Peggy Eaton's virginity, it goes on and on forever." Dinners at the White House became a location for social maneuvering and snubbing. With a table set for as many as 30-40, often only six came – Jackson, Martin Van Buren, a widower, John Eaton and Peggy, and two ambassadors, one a widower and one a bachelor, the British and the Prussian ambassadors. Vice President John Calhoun's wife, Floride, led the social snubs.

During Jackson's 1818 campaign in Florida against the Seminoles, Calhoun had been the Secretary of War, Jackson's boss. Calhoun argued in cabinet meetings that the president had to take action against Jackson for an unauthorized invasion of Spanish territory and for executing Robert Ambrister and Alexander Arbuthnot, two British citizens who were selling guns to the Indians. The Secretary of State, John Quincy Adams, convinced President James Monroe that the United States could use this to scare Spain into selling Florida, which is what happened. Now, with the Eaton affair boiling, Martin Van Buren, Calhoun's rival to follow Jackson as president, told Jackson about Calhoun's criticism during the Florida campaign. Jackson had been unaware of Calhoun's criticism. Jackson confronted Calhoun. Calhoun wrote a fifty-page defense of his actions. Jackson never read it, claiming that an honest man does not need fifty pages to prove his innocence! After several months, Jackson forced Vice President Calhoun and the whole cabinet to resign. John Eaton later became the ambassador to Spain. The Spanish loved his wife. The last we hear about her she married, at 59, a 19-year-old Italian dance instructor, who later ran off with Peggy's money and granddaughter.

The Political Issues of the Era
The Tariff

A tariff is a tax on imports, collected at the port of entry by federal government officials. A high tariff is primarily intended to reduce foreign competition by raising the price on imported goods. A low tariff is primarily intended to raise revenue for the federal government. In today's world economists argue for low tariffs, if any at all. Free trade, no tariffs, keeps the price of imported goods low, and by other countries reciprocating, provides markets abroad for American products. In short, all consumers everywhere win. However, foreign competition may drive some American companies out of business, causing unemployment. Therefore, it is a politically volatile topic. President Lyndon Johnson once said, "Be a free trader, but don't tell anyone." In these years the tariff was an important issue, both as a symbol and as a reality, for three reasons.

1. It was the major source of federal government income up to 1913.
2. Therefore, it determined the limits of potential federal government spending.
3. It indicated the federal government's policy toward industrialization.

Our first tariff, passed in Washington's administration, was a low tariff, but the 1816 tariff was a protective tariff, and was a reaction against the British dumping cheap goods on the American market to drive American factories out of business. In 1824 another high tariff passed, and in 1828 a very high tariff was passed, raising rates to nearly 50%. Nicknamed the Tariff of Abominations, it was part of a campaign trick played on President John Quincy Adams. His opponents assumed that either way – veto or signing – Adams would lose support. He signed it. The South was furious. Most politicians expected him to veto it.

The Tariff as an Economic Issue

The South depended on exporting goods, chiefly cotton. In many respects the South was really still an economic colony of Great Britain. In 1829 the U.S. had $44 million in agricultural exports, and $34 million of it came from the South. The total value of our manufacturing exports was only $6 million. Thus, it seemed as if the interests of the South, $34 million, were sacrificed to the interests of the North's $6 million. Since the

South imported more than the North, it disproportionately bore the cost to build up the "infant industries" of New England. In 1835 the treasury had a surplus of $440,000, seen by Southerners as gained at their expense. The South also suffered when the price of cotton plummeted. In 1815 it was 27¢ a pound; by the mid-1820s it was down to 9¢ a pound. Southerners blamed the tariff, unfairly. Overproduction was the problem. South Carolina, Calhoun's home state, was particularly hard hit.

The Tariff as a Constitutional Issue

Then there was the constitutional question, the theory of the federal union. A Senate debate that originally began over land policy degenerated into a long debate over the nature of the union. The debate dragged on and on. If published as a book today it would run over 500 pages. The two chief combatants were Daniel Webster from Massachusetts and Robert Hayne from South Carolina, thus it is often referred to as the Webster-Hayne Debate. As the vice president, John Calhoun could only watch as the presiding officer of the Senate. The vice president does not participate in Senate debates. Hayne argued Calhoun's position that the federal government was a compact, an alliance of sovereign states. Webster argued that the federal government was a new and distinct government, equipped with self-sustaining powers, not a mere creation of the states. In short, the argument was whether the United States was the United STATES or the UNITED States. In a strict legal and constitutional sense, Calhoun and Hayne had a good argument about the 1787 mindset. The preamble to the Constitution originally read, "We the people of the states of" . . . and listed all thirteen states. It was shortened as a stylistic improvement to "We the people of the United States."

By the 1830s much had changed. What about the states created after the original thirteen? Were they ever "sovereign"? The tariff clearly threw a burden more on those states that imported the most goods. The Constitution required federal taxes to be apportioned among the states based on population, so that the percentage of the taxes paid by the people of a state equaled the percentage of that state's population. Later, the Sixteenth Amendment authorizing the income tax would wipe this out. The Constitution also gave the federal government the power to regulate national and foreign commerce in the national interest. All these issues raised two questions:

1. What constitutes the national interest?
2. Is the tariff a disproportionate tax?

In addition, behind the tariff as a political and constitutional issue lurked another one. If the national government had the authority to use the tariff to the disadvantage of the South, did it also have the power to interfere with a state's domestic institution of slavery?

Exposition and Protest

In response to the Tariff of 1828, or "Tariff of Abominations," the South Carolina state legislature endorsed a theory contained in Vice President Calhoun's anonymously written *Exposition and Protest*. Everyone knew who wrote it; Calhoun was one of the most original political and constitutional thinkers in American history. In it Calhoun advocated the political theory of nullification. Because the states were supreme, the basic premise was that a state has the power to declare acts of the federal government null and void within its state, to protect their people from the oppression of the federal government. A convention of all the other states could overturn an individual state's action. Southerners claimed that their position was merely a reassertion of the theory found in the 1798 Virginia and Kentucky Resolutions against the Alien and Sedition Acts. However, one of the authors, James Madison, was still alive. He strongly objected. He pointed out that in every instance he and Jefferson had used the plural form, *states*, "the term *State*, as a single party, being invariably avoided." "[Laws] cannot be altered or annulled at the will of the States individually."

The election of 1828 brought a friend of the South into the White House, a Southern slave owner, Andrew Jackson. Jackson had said nothing publicly about the *Exposition and Protest*, about the Webster-Hayne debate, or about the tariff. Southerners assumed Jackson agreed with their position on the tariff and other issues. He did not.

Each year April 13 is a major fundraising and celebrating day for the Democratic Party. It is Jefferson's birthday. On April 13, 1830, during the Jefferson Day dinner toasts, President Jackson looked Calhoun right in the eye and offered a toast, "Our Federal Union – It Must be Preserved." Vice President Calhoun jumped to his feet to offer the next toast, "The Union – Next to Our Liberty Most Dear." A wide breach opened between the two. Adding to the gap between Calhoun and Jackson at this time was the Peggy Eaton affair. Calhoun's wife, Floride, orchestrated the widespread social snubs against Peggy Eaton. Soon afterwards, Jackson said to a visiting South Carolina Congressman, "if a single drop of blood shall be shed there, in South Carolina, in opposition to the laws of the United States, I will hang the first man (everyone assumed he meant Calhoun) I can lay my hands on engaged in such treasonable conduct upon the first tree I can reach." Calhoun resigned as vice president in December, 1832, shifting to the Senate to become the voice of the embattled South. Now no longer a presidential possibility, he was a sectional politician, only looking out for the South.

In the middle of all this tension, exacerbated by fears generated by Nat Turner's slave revolt in Virginia during 1831 and Britain's movement to emancipate all their slaves in the Caribbean, Henry Clay and others feverishly worked to lower the tariff. A lower tariff had passed in 1832, but the South said it was not low enough. It was due to go into effect March 3, 1833, the day before Jackson's second inauguration. In November, 1832, a South Carolina convention nullified both the Tariff of 1828 and the Tariff of 1832, as of February 1, 1833. In December Jackson declared his intention to enforce the federal laws. In January he asked Congress for special powers to enforce the nation's revenue laws, which he already had. He wanted a clear statement of opposition to South Carolina by Congress.

Meanwhile Clay hammered out the Compromise Tariff of 1833. It was lower than the Tariff of 1832 and gradually lowered tariff rates over the next ten years. A Force Bill also passed, giving the president the power to enforce the tariff laws. The two together, the Force Bill and the Tariff of 1833, are sometimes referred to as the Compromise of 1833. The Compromise Tariff of 1833 was due to go into effect on March 1, 1833. That meant that the tariff of 1832 was never repealed; the tariff of 1833 went into effect prior to it. This raised a question in everyone's mind. Did the federal government back down because of South Carolina's threat? South Carolina, after repealing its nullification of the Tariff of 1832, nullified the Force Bill. South Carolina had not enforced its February 1 deadline in the nullification ordinance for the tariffs of 1828 and 1832. Since the Force Bill was unnecessary, South Carolina nullified a law that had no reason to be enforced. This meant that there was no real test of Calhoun's theory of nullification.

Nullification now went from a political theory to a political practice, according to some in the South. Trouble. Political scientists argue that the genius of American politics is the practicality of our political system. Americans rarely appeal to political theory, any political theory, as the basis for a political act. Americans are not an ideological people. As historian Daniel Boorstin once wrote, Americans "don't think, we do."

Bank Recharter

The charter for Hamilton's Bank of the U.S. had expired in 1811. Madison and Jefferson waved goodbye, good riddance. However, it turned out that Hamilton understood the functions of a national bank better than the Jeffersonians. The number of state banks exploded, from 88 to 256, causing inflation because each printed its own currency. Congress rechartered the Bank of the U.S. in 1816, again for twenty years. Within a short time, Nicholas Biddle became the head of the Second Bank of the U.S. He did an excellent job managing the economy, but he did so arrogantly.

In 1832 Henry Clay was searching for a campaign issue to rally support against Jackson. Clay convinced his political ally, Nicholas Biddle, to apply for a bank recharter early. It was due to expire in 1836. If Jackson signed it, many opposed to the bank would be upset. If Jackson vetoed it, those in favor of the bank would be upset, and so either way, Clay wins the presidency. The recharter bill passed the Senate on June 11, 28-20, and the House 107-86 on July 3. Note the considerable opposition. Jackson vetoed it on July 10, only the tenth veto ever cast by a president. A two-thirds vote to override his veto would be 32 in the Senate and 129 in the House. It was a safe veto. Jackson was the first president to veto a bill simply because he politically objected to it. Previously presidents had vetoed only because they doubted a bill's constitutionality. Jackson vetoed more bills, twelve, than all his predecessors added together, nine. Critics called him King Andrew. His Whig opponents made it a principle of their party that no president should ever veto a bill unless it was unconstitutional.

Jackson's opponents, chiefly Clay, Calhoun, and Webster, had little in common, except their extreme dislike of King Andrew; hence their coalescing as the Whig Party, named after the eighteenth century opponents of the British king's powers. During the winter of 1833-1834 the Democrats first used the term "Whigs" for their opponents. Jackson wrote a vicious bank veto message evoking class warfare, unlike any previous public statement by a president. He called the bank a monopoly, a special and artificial privilege. He declared, in commenting on the Supreme Court's decision in *McCulloch v. Maryland* in 1819, which declared the creation of a central bank to be within the powers of the Constitution, that, "The opinion of the judges has no more authority over Congress than the opinion of Congress has over the judges, and on that point the president is independent of both."

He charged that the bank was controlled by the wealthy for the wealthy. The majority of the bank's stockholders lived in the East, especially in New England. A few lived in Europe. The government should not promote the wealthy over the people. It was true also that the Bank loaned money to Congressmen. Out of 261 Congressmen, 52 borrowed from the Bank in 1830, 59 in 1831. Such practices influenced legislation for the Bank. Farmers, wage earners, and small businessmen could not obtain loans from the Bank, only big manufacturers and the wealthy. The Bank controlled the state banks' policies on loans by requiring them to have gold and silver backing their currency, stifling expansion and economic growth in the West.

The President of the Bank, Nicholas Biddle, counterattacked Jackson's veto by tightening credit, but it did not work. Jackson loved a good fight. He also loved only hard money, gold and silver, not paper currency. On several occasions he had been driven into bankruptcy, or close to it, mostly because of accepting worthless paper currency. In response to Biddle he removed the federal government's deposits from the Bank of the U.S. Two secretaries of the treasury, Louis McLane and William Duane, were removed from office before Jackson found a replacement to do his bidding, Roger B. Taney. By the end of 1833 all the federal government's funds had been moved to 23 state banks, nicknamed "pet banks," almost all controlled by prominent Democrats. The impact on the economy was disastrous. The amount of currency in circulation issued by state banks increased by a factor of fifteen. Some historians see the Bank War as a contest for control over the economy between Chestnut Street, where the Second Bank of the U.S. was located in Philadelphia, and Wall Street in New York City. Wall Street won. Still today, one-half of the world's wealth is controlled along the line between Washington, D.C., and New York City. Clay lost the election, while Jackson got four more years. In 1836 the Second Bank of the U.S. died.

Indian Removal

History books unfairly portray Jackson for his part in the Cherokee Removal. Every administration from George Washington's favored removal as a policy, referred to as "concentration," restricting Indians to certain areas west of the Mississippi River, where they could continue their traditional way of life or at least be out of our way. Washington put both wolves and Indians in the same category, "both being beasts of prey tho' they differ in shape." As president, Jefferson had made specific promises to the Southern states to remove the Indians. Jefferson said the ultimate solution was removal beyond the Mississippi or the Great Lakes. Even many missionaries who worked among the Indians favored removal, as a means to preserve Indian culture and identity. Jackson was not alone in his stand. It was the nation's stand. In 1830 the House Committee on Indian Affairs asserted its belief "in the natural superiority" of civilized peoples "over those of savage tribes." There had long been widespread prejudice against Indians. Massachusetts, which hardly had any Indians in 1789, made it punishable by death for a white person to teach an Indian to read and write. The governor of Georgia said in 1830, "Treaties are expedients by which ignorant, intractable, and savage people were induced without bloodshed to yield up what civilized people had the right to possess." Actually, the Cherokee Indians, who called themselves the Ani-Yun-Wiya or Yunwiya, meaning "real people," became too civilized. They adopted white farming methods, created an alphabet, wrote a constitution, published a newspaper, and adopted many modern customs and practices. Clearly, they had to go. The Indian Removal Act passed Congress in 1830, 28-19 in the Senate and 103-97 in the House. The Cherokee removal was not unique. The Jackson administration forced seventy removal treaties on Indians.

Chief Justice of the Supreme Court John Marshall may have sympathized with the plight of the Indians, but be careful about attributing later attitudes to him. He referred to the Indians as being in a "state of pupilage." In an earlier case, in 1823, *Johnson v. McIntosh*, Marshall ruled that Indians did not own their land; they just had a "right of occupancy." In *Cherokee Nation v. Georgia* in 1831, he referred to the Indians as being in a relationship to the federal government that resembled "that of a ward to his guardian." However, the next year, 1832, in *Worchester v. Georgia*, Marshall declared that the supremacy clause of the Constitution put Indian treaties above federal or state laws. He defined Indians as "distinct political communities, having territorial boundaries, within which their authority is exclusive, and having a right to all the lands within those boundaries, which is not only acknowledged, but guaranteed by the United States." The state of Georgia, a party in both court cases, defiantly refused to take part in either case before the court. In defiance of the Supreme Court ruling, Jackson ordered the removal. The idea of a nation inside a nation seems legally foolish; yet it remains one factor behind the legal basis for the rights and privileges that modern tribal governments possess.

Historians and the Historiography of Jacksonianism

Historians have ranged all over the map about Jackson and Jacksonianism. Early nineteenth century aristocratic New England historians emphasized the barbaric, low class, democratic riot at the White House on the day of the inauguration. Around 1900

Western and Mid-Western historians, who sprang from the democratic West, called Jackson the hero of the people against the money interests, symbolized by the Second Bank of the U.S. Arthur M. Schlesinger, Jr., in 1945, characterized Jacksonianism as a class war, not a sectional contest of North versus South or West versus East, but rather one of poor farmers, laborers, and noncapitalists against the business community. Schlesinger said that in American history "reform" is always anti-business; it is the periodic attempt to correct the worst practices in the business community. Richard Hofstadter called Jacksonianism a fight between two sets of capitalists, the entrenched capitalists of the Second Bank of the U.S., Chestnut Street, versus the emerging capitalists of Wall Street. Lee Benson saw not economic issues, but religious and ethnic splits among the voters, just as today, with religious fundamentalists voting Republican and blacks voting Democratic. Sean Wilentz highlighted anger toward the emerging and changing economy, the impersonal capitalist economy that threatened the old, virtuous republic. Jackson's followers were seeking a return to the fading Republic of Virtue. Charles Sellers characterized these years as a market revolution that paralleled an emerging mass democracy that tried to check capitalist expansion.

Today, Americans live in a society that is changing with the emerging global economy. If that is a concern, to whom does one direct anger or questions? The emerging super-rich? International villains? Other countries? International companies? Voters who foolishly support policies you dislike? The stupidity of another section of the country? All of this assumes that you fully understand all the changes going on around you. In this respect the Age of Jackson was similar to our own, a period of fundamental changes in the economy.

21

INDIANS, UP TO 1848

Terminology

I am not trying to make a statement for or against "political correctness." I usually use "Indian" rather than Native-American, Original Peoples, First Peoples, First Nations, Natives, or Amerindians. Why? Because modern Indian people overwhelming use that term to describe themselves, often after first using their tribal name. I believe people have a right to self-description. In many respects the original Indians encountered by Europeans had the correct approach. They had no name for all Indians as a distinct group. Europeans gave them one, mistakenly believing they had reached Asia and encountered the people of India. The commonly used word "tribe" also presents difficulties. As one historian pointed out, the modern Navajo Tribe Reservation is larger than Switzerland. So do the Swiss people live in a nation while the Navajo live in a tribe? Let's try the reverse, that the Swiss live in a tribe and the Navajo live in a nation. See how silly labels can be? In some respects words like clan, grouping, or band may be, at times, more accurate at a specific moment in history when describing a particular group of Indians. Warfare, diseases, and movement complicate any attempt to create clear genealogical charts that cover a long period of time.

French and Indian War and the American Revolution

Historians usually do not link these two wars together, since after all, the American Revolution is usually regarded as the important one, because it gave us the 4th of July. From the Indian perspective, however, the two constituted one continuous disaster. When the French first arrived in Canada they linked up with the Huron tribe in an extensive fur trading network, alienating the Iroquois, who had established a competing link with the Dutch in New Amsterdam, which became New York when the English Duke of York and Albany took it from the Dutch in 1664. The endless competition between tribes was labeled the Beaver Wars. The French fur trade radiated out from Quebec; the Dutch emanated from Ft. Orange (Albany). All the European powers armed their Indian allies. The Iroquois emerged as the superior Indian power, virtually wiping out the Hurons and their allies, the Algonquins. Throughout the entire colonial period, the militarily powerful and diplomatically astute Iroquois controlled upper New York and the northern Ohio Valley region.

However, the end of the French and Indian War removed the French from the complex diplomacy of the "Middle Ground," the Ohio Valley area of contention between the European powers and the Indians. The Iroquois had been experts at playing the French and British off against one another to preserve Indian control of the Middle Ground. This ended by 1760, when the French surrendered Canada to the British. The Treaty of Paris, 1763, officially transferred Canada to British control. The legacy of the French and Indian War for the British colonies was a whole series of new laws, new policies, and colonial reactions, beginning with the Proclamation of 1763 attempting to prevent westward movement across the Appalachians and with Pontiac's Rebellion in response to colonial noncompliance. Ultimately, the American Revolution led to the Indians' loss of the Ohio Valley. From the initial English contact through the Beaver Wars through four colonial wars involving France, Spain, and England, Indians craftily used diplomacy and shifting alliances between different tribes to achieve their goals. Understanding that the American colonists offered nothing to their liking, almost every tribe allied with the British during the American Revolution. The Iroquois split, the Mohawks and the Cayugas supported the British, while the Oneidas, Tuscaroras, and most Senecas the American cause. The British surrender effectively ended the influence and power of the Indians. Once again they were on the losing side, as most were with the 1763 Treaty of Paris. And, the 1783 Treaty of Paris removed yet another power, the British, from the diplomatic mix. From Canada the British tried to continue to play a role in influencing what happened in the Middle Ground. Although supplying some weapons, the British lacked a willingness to become too deeply involved. Remember that within a short time, starting in 1789, the French Revolutionary wars and the Napoleonic wars would occupy Britain's primary attention, for the next 25 years. Even the War of 1812 was a military sideshow, with the British using their second-string forces against the United States.

1780s, 1790s, the Ohio Country, and To the War of 1812

The floodgates opened up after the Revolutionary War and settlers flowed into Ohio. The Indians fought the onslaught, and, at the Wabash River, achieved the greatest Indian victory ever over an American army. In 1791 Ohio Territorial Governor Arthur St. Clair led his forces into the Battle of the Wabash, losing over 600 killed and 300 wounded to Indians led by Little Turtle, Blue Jacket, and Buckongahelas. The news stunned the nation's capital, Philadelphia. Washington ordered General "Mad Anthony" Wayne to retaliate. At the Battle of Fallen Timbers in 1794 (the site was so-named because an earlier tornado had knocked over the trees) Wayne decisively defeated the Indians, leading to the Treaty of Greenville, opening up almost all of Ohio to settlers. Curiously, this treaty was the first to use a new terminology, one ripe with connotations. Previously the language in treaties generally referred to Indians as "brothers." Now it was "children of the White Father." One negotiates with a brother; one chastises a child to make him or her behave.

One Indian leader, Tecumseh, realized that only through unity did his people stand a chance. He carried some credibility. He had participated in both battles, Wabash and Fallen Timbers, a victory and a defeat. Now he moved from tribe to tribe, urging unity against whites. His father was Shawnee; apparently (historians do not know for certain) his mother was Creek. Thus, in the Middle Ground and in the South he found many listeners, but few converts to his Pan-Indianism. Concerned, William Henry Harrison, governor of the Indiana Territory, attacked Prophetstown in 1811, also called Tippecanoe, the large village where Tecumseh's followers had gathered, and there he decisively defeated the Indians. Tecumseh now turned to the British in Canada, seeking their help, and shortly became entangled in the War of 1812. He was killed in the Battle of the Thames, fought in southern Ontario. The death of Tecumseh and Andrew Jackson's victory over the Red Sticks, a band of Creeks who followed Tecumseh, at the Battle of Horseshoe Bend in Alabama ended Indian resistance. Some conflicts continued in the upper Northwest in Minnesota, but elsewhere resistance ended east of the Mississippi River.

The Debate: Gradualists Versus Removalists

What to do about the Indians was a major consideration in the new United States. Cost and the ultimate goal were the two chief factors involved in determining policies. Fighting Indians was the largest single expenditure in the national budget during the decade of the 1790s. Behind financial costs lurked the larger question of where Indians would fit in the nascent nation. It came down to two choices – remove them or absorb them, nicknamed the debate between the Removalists, get them out of here, and the Gradualists, teach them to be just like us and absorb them into our society. The assumption behind the first was that there could be no place for Indians in civilized society; the assumption behind the second was that Indians really wanted to be like Anglos, their nickname for both whites and blacks. Evidence for both assumptions was faulty. However, when one's mind is made up the last thing you want is to have it confused by facts.

After the 1790s, generally speaking, for the next two decades the Gradualists held sway over the Removalists. The Ohio Valley opened up to settlement after the War of 1812. The British carried less influence among the Indians and focused their foreign policy goals and attention elsewhere. Gradualists believed that a hunting lifestyle presented the biggest impediment to absorption. Indians must be taught to farm, which had the added benefit of freeing up land for white settlers. As Thomas Jefferson explained it, "While they are learning to do better on less land, our increasing numbers will be calling for more land, and thus a coincidence of interests will be produced between those who have land to spare, and those . . . who want land." Perfect! Add in missionary work and education to learn superior white ways, and both peace and reduced expenses followed, leading to assimilation. Removalists also sought peace, but firmly believed that Indians were neither desirous of nor capable of becoming "white." Scientists, or rather pseudo-scientists and what might be called very amateur anthropologists, added their learned opinion that Indians were incapable of being elevated all the long way up to white culture. Similar arguments were used in assessing blacks.

Jefferson disagreed about Indians. In the 1790s, as settlers moved across the Appalachians, they slowly began to encounter remnants of the old Mound Culture in the Ohio Valley and the South. The Serpent Mound in Ohio, which may pre-date the Mound Culture, and the city of Cahokia opposite St. Louis are the best-known today. Three feet high, the sinuous Serpent Mound stretches for 1348 feet, the length of four and one-half football fields. Cahokia was a city of 30,000 to 40,000 people, larger than London around 1200, and the largest city north of Mexico. There are 120 mounds in the area, the highest the largest man-made structure in North America at that time. Nearby is a circle reminiscent of Stonehenge in England, both of which were built to track the seasonal changes of the sun. Reports of the mounds intrigued Jefferson. Who were these people? They must have been intelligent to accomplish these feats. This thinking led Jefferson to conclude that Indians had once achieved a high culture, and with education they could return to that former high status – hence his conviction that Gradualism was the better approach. As a sidelight observation, since he knew nothing of ancient African cultural achievements, he reasoned that blacks were incapable of high culture. When a friend asked him to explain Benjamin Banneker, the black mathematician and surveyor who, from memory, redrew the plans for laying out Washington, D.C., Jefferson, always intellectually honest, replied, "I can't explain Banneker." In addition to his rationalization about the Indians, the cost of the Indian wars pushed the budget-conscious Jefferson towards Gradualism.

By the 1820s, except for some Cherokees, Gradualists began to realize that their approach, if it worked, would take too long. Indians did not want to become farmers. It clashed with their cultural beliefs that farming was women's work and that men must be free to roam. In a curious way the two approaches now merged. Removal, to Gradualists, became a means to preserve the best of Indian culture. Moving them farther West would save the Indians. Absorbing Indians into the white culture would take longer than previously thought; but, there was time. Jefferson once observed that settlers would not reach the Pacific Coast until around the year 2000. If this sounds bizarre, reflect for a moment upon the experience since 1607. It took white settlers 200 years to reach the Mississippi River. Logically, it would take 200 more years to see settlers in California and Oregon. Trust me, your grandchildren will laugh at some of the common sense logical things believed now.

Both Jefferson and President Monroe endorsed removal in 1824 to accomplish a more gradual assimilation. Most northern tribes accepted their fate and left. Within two years three Southern tribes also forfeited their land, the Creeks, Chickasaws, Choctaws, and some Cherokees. Two fought removal – the remaining Cherokees and Seminoles. The Seminoles fled into the Florida Everglades, where their guerrilla tactics held off the U.S. Army from 1835 to 1842. One chief, Osceola, was captured treacherously under a flag of truce. Rules of honorable warfare apparently only applied to civilized enemies. Several hundred of the Indians hid when most Seminoles were taken to the Indian Country, modern Oklahoma. That Everglades' remnant remained in Florida, with the name Seminoles becoming the nickname for the Florida State University athletic teams. Along with the NFL Washington Redskins, they are part of the current controversy over disrespectful nicknames for athletic teams.

The remaining Cherokees, led by Chief John Ross, contemptuously referred to by whites as a half-breed, had accepted the challenge from the Gradualists and had begun to modernize. The Cherokee, who called themselves the Ani-Yun-Wiya or Yunwiya, meaning "real people," became too civilized. They adopted white farming methods, created an alphabet, published a newspaper, wrote a constitution, and adopted many modern customs and practices. Some even owned black slaves. After gold was discovered in the Cherokee land that Georgia claimed, whites poured into the Cherokee territory, law or no law, right or wrong. After all, gold! This population pressure added to the persistent Georgia agitation for its "rightful" land. It was just a matter of time. Clearly, the Cherokee had to go.

The Separation Policy Wins

History books tend to unfairly portray Andrew Jackson as solely responsible for the Cherokee Removal. Every administration from Washington's favored removal as a policy, referred to as the "Separation Policy," removing them from contact with settlers and restricting them to certain areas west of the Mississippi River where they could continue their traditional way of life. As president, Jefferson made specific promises to the Southern states to remove the Indians. In 1802 the Georgia legislature received the following from Congress in exchange for Georgia's cession of claims to land on her western border. "The United States shall, at their own Expense, [obtain for] the use of Georgia, as early as the same can be peaceably obtained on reasonable terms, the Indian Title . . . to all the other Lands within the State of Georgia." Jefferson, and almost everyone else, believed that since Indians hunted and fished, it did not matter where they lived. Thus, a reasonable solution was removal beyond the Mississippi River or the Great Lakes. Whites simply did not understand that a place could be sacred to Indians.

To paraphrase one historian's explanation: To Indians Place was sacred and Time was unimportant; to Europeans Time was sacred and Place was unimportant. Europeans had, as Americans still do, little attachment to a place; we think nothing of moving frequently, even away from "home." The average American family moves once every seven years. Also, our lives are controlled by clocks. No one catches the bus that comes around 8 o'clock or so. We get the 8:03 bus, and complain when a cell phone says 8:04. Indians did not understand or appreciate such punctuality.

Jackson was not alone in his stand regarding Indian removal. Even missionaries who worked among the Indians favored removal, as a means to preserve Indian culture and identity. There was also widespread prejudice against Indians. In 1830 the House Committee on Indian Affairs asserted its belief "in the natural superiority" of civilized peoples "over those of savage tribes." Even treaties signed with Indians lacked honor. The governor of Georgia said in 1830, "Treaties are expedients by which ignorant, intractable, and savage people were induced without bloodshed to yield up what civilized people had the right to possess." The Indian Removal Act passed Congress in 1830, 28-19 in the Senate and 103-97 in the House. The Cherokee removal was not unique. The Jackson administration forced seventy removal treaties on Indians. The subsequent Van Buren administration actually enforced the Cherokee removal, the infamous "Trail of Tears." It became necessary when a large number of Cherokees refused to leave – hence a forced, military removal. Seventeen thousand left; eight thousand arrived in Oklahoma, although historians differ on the second number. Soldiers accompanying the march who later served in the Civil War said that the Trail of Tears march exceeded any wartime misery they ever witnessed.

As noted earlier, Chief Justice of the Supreme Court John Marshall may have sympathized with the plight of the Indians, but be careful about attributing later attitudes to him, because his legacy is mixed. He referred to the Indians as being in a "state of pupilage." In an earlier case in 1823, involving the question of whether a white individual could purchase land from an Indian tribe, *Johnson v. McIntosh*, Marshall ruled that neither the tribe nor individual Indians owned their land; they just had a "right of occupancy." Because individual Indians did not own land, Marshall ruled that only the tribe could sell land, and that only the federal government could purchase land from Indians. A white individual could not buy Indian land. In *Cherokee Nation v. Georgia* in 1831, he referred to Indians as being in a relationship to the federal government that resembled "that of a ward to his guardian" and that the Cherokee constituted "a domestic dependent nation" within our federal system. Indians were not subject to state laws; Georgia had no legal power in Cherokee land. However, in the next year, 1832, in *Worchester v. Georgia*, Marshall declared that the supremacy clause of the Constitution put Indian treaties above both federal and state laws. He defined Indians as "distinct political communities, having territorial boundaries, within which their authority is exclusive, and having a right to all the lands within those boundaries, which is not only acknowledged, but guaranteed by the United States." The idea of a nation inside a nation seems legally foolish; yet it remains the constitutional and legal basis for the extensive rights and privileges that modern tribal governments possess.

The state of Georgia, a party in both court cases, defiantly refused to take part in either case before the court. In defiance of the Supreme Court ruling, Jackson ordered the Cherokee removal. He is the only president to openly defy a Supreme Court ruling. The story may be apocryphal, but Jackson is often quoted as having said something such as, "Marshall has made his decision; now let him enforce it!" Our courts, of course, must rely on the executive branch to carry out court rulings. Jackson refused. In 1835, seeing no alternative, one faction of the Cherokee led by Major Ridge signed a treaty agreeing to move. The majority, following Chief John Ross, refused to budge, until forced to do so in the Trail of Tears three years later. Jackson, from his retirement in Tennessee, still exhibited his split Gradualist/Removalist thinking. "The States which had so long been retarded in their improvement by the Indian tribes residing in the midst of them are at length relieved from the evil, and this happy race – the original dwellers in our land – are now placed in a situation where we may well hope that they will share in the blessings of civilization and be saved from degradation and destruction." He was sincere. He leaves students of history with the need to assess which policy he really favored.

So, is this a simple situation in which Georgia won and the Cherokee lost? It seems so. However, the debate in Congress over the Indian Removal Act and subsequent military actions, including the Trail of Tears, aroused vigorous opposition in the North. Northern senators and congressmen condemned it. Newspaper editorials vehemently railed against it. The vote on the Indian Removal Act was clearly sectional. We must look at the Cherokee removal within the context of the other issues of that period. Consider how many Southerners might have felt after reflecting on the following:

1. The dispute over the Tariff of Abominations in the late 1820s, Calhoun's *Exposition and Protest*, and South Carolina's threat to nullify the tariff.
2. The first issue of the abolitionist newspaper *The Liberator* in 1831, William Lloyd Garrison's anti-slavery harangue.
3. The fears resulting from Nat Turner's slave rebellion in 1831.
4. Add to this list Northern opposition, centered in New England, to Indian Removal.

Life is not lived in isolation. Multiple issues might confront anyone at any time in history. Studying one issue at a time in a history class is artificial. Life was, is, and will be more chaotic. Southerners wondered if there was an anti-South pattern emerging. If the South celebrated the Cherokee Indian Removal as a victory, it was bittersweet.

The Mexican War Brings A Vast Land Cession

Within a short time the presumably settled "Indian Problem" reared its ugly head again. Victory in the Mexican War brought the Mexican Cession in 1848, a huge addition to the territory of the United States. Thank goodness it was empty, ready for white settlers to exploit nature's bounty. Empty? Only if we did not consider Indians or Mexicans to be people. Most Americans did not regard either as such. It says a great deal that following the war, in 1849, the federal government finally created the cabinet position of the Department of the Interior. America now had a very large interior. The Bureau of Indian Affairs, established in 1836 in the War Department (not renamed as the Department of Defense until after the Second World War) was transferred to the new Department of the Interior. This set off a decades' long debate over where it belonged. Overtones of Removalism versus Gradualism underlay the positions taken. Were Indians a problem best solved by the military or a problem best solved by acculturation?

Complicating potential land use was the belief that the Great Plains were a barrier to the rich West coast and the mines of the Rocky Mountains. Remember the 1849 gold rush, the 49ers. Earlier, in 1819, Major Stephen Long had explored the Great Plains and labeled it the "Great American Desert," "almost wholly unfit for cultivation, and of course uninhabitable by a people depending upon agriculture for their subsistence." Why? Because the rainfall limited what types of crops could grow there. Not until later would farmers successfully adapt crops to the limited rainfall. At this point in our history the Great Plains were a barrier, a long distance to cross. If you drive across it today, you may become homesick for the sight of large trees. Before the introduction of the horse by the Spanish around 1700, virtually no one lived on the empty Great Plains. Later, after adopting the horse and inventing a new lifestyle, the Plains were inhabited by about 100,000 Indians, living mostly in small groups, brandishing a warrior ethos and displaying incredible feats of horsemanship. This "Indian problem," this challenge to progress, differed from that encountered in the East.

Periodization and Indian History

The history of Indians continues in a later chapter, Chapter 48. But, why pause this story here, in 1848? Most history books divide U.S. History at the Civil War and Reconstruction, 1865 to 1877. Periodization is a tool used by historians to break a particular topic into recognizable parts, with significant dates used as turning points delineating a change or the arrival of new issues, events, laws, etc. As one example, if we define the twentieth century as a century of hot and cold wars, it makes sense to label it as extending from 1914 to 1991, from the outbreak of the First World War to the end of the Cold War. If a historian defines it as a century of great technological inventions, one could make the automobile, transistor, and computer as the major turning points.

The year 1848 ended the Separation Policy. It became obvious that there was no longer a place to send the "red man." In addition, the Plains Indians presented a different challenge. Nomads, they roamed widely over the prairies. As long as settlers only wished to pass through the Plains, Indians were just a nuisance rather than an impediment to progress, demanding fees for passing over their land. However, with the introduction of the Homestead Act in 1862 providing free land, and the adoption of Russian wheat, the steel plow, and barbed wire, farming proved tentatively possible. From 1865 to 1900, around the world, the total acreage of new land brought under cultivation equaled that farmed up to 1865. In short, the world's farmland doubled in 35 years. Farmers needed a means to transport their crops, hence the long distance railroads crisscrossing the Great Plains. Many problems hampered this Agricultural Revolution. The Plains Indians were one, they had to be curtailed and contained. This demanded a switch in policy. The new policy was called the Concentration Policy. Round them up and put them on reservations, out of the way of progress. Foolishly for the government, some tribes were deposited on what later proved to be rich pools of oil. Among the fortunate Indians were the descendants of the Trail of Tears forced march. By the 1920s they were no longer marching; they were driving luxury automobiles. One lesson of history, depending on one's degree of religious faith, is that God or fortune sometimes works in strange ways.

22

ANTEBELLUM REFORM

A Period of Transition

The era from the end of the War of 1812 to the Civil War was a time of fundamental changes in the American economy, which means there were fundamental changes and adjustments in society's institutions, such as the role of the church, the nature of the family, the composition of the work force, and the characteristics of the workplace. When widespread changes occur there is always a concern over the impact of these changes, which leads to cries for reform to correct perceived problems, which may lead to new problems. Often these cries for reform have a backward-looking orientation, nostalgia for the good old days when society seemed more stable.

The globalization of the economy has set in motion a similar set of changes today. An example of the impact is the perceived decline in the family. What is really happening is that the family is changing, rather than declining. As one example, today we have the stay-at-home dad, something unheard of 50 years ago. Why? Because the rise of the women's movement, opening careers for them in the professions and especially in the business world, means that the wife's income AND potential income could far exceed the husband's. Logic leads to the stay-at-home dad. The so-called ideal family – dad works, mom and kids are home – is only 7% of all families. In the 1950s this was seen as the "normal" family in American history and memory, but in truth it was then only 60%, and hardly typical in our nation's history. The decade of the 1950s was a brief era in which incomes were high enough that many families could survive on one income and purchase a house. Colonial families were hardly like the 1950s families. Slave families were never like that. Define the word "family." Is a gay family possible? Can gay couples serve as foster or adoptive parents? Is a single parent a family? Can two divorced people create a family by merging their kids? The family functions as a unit, today primarily as a unit of socialization that interprets the outside world for its members. It is also an economic entity; a political unit; a nurturing unit for children and for one another; an educational unit; and a source for companionship. Each family arranges these functions in a different order of priorities.

During a period of institutional changes many critics assume an ideal and measure current institutions against their definition of that ideal. Many Americans in the future will work at home. What will then be the definition of "work"? Forty hours a week? What will be the definition of "home"? And, of "child-rearing"? Today there is a lot of confusion over truancy because of "home-schooling." In a 1995 essay, later expanded as a book in 2000, *Bowling Alone*, Robert Putnam, a Harvard political scientist, reported there was a 10% increase in bowlers and a 40% decline in membership in bowling leagues. Does that suggest that our society is becoming more solitary and less associational? We average only 2.55 people per residence. Today, in 35% of all residences, only one person lives there. Look at how many cities have created high-occupancy vehicle lanes (called HOV lanes) on highways leading into their cities, a lane reserved during rush hours for cars with more than one person. In many ways Americans are more solitary today, interacting less. What does it all mean?

The Fundamental Changes in the Antebellum Economy – The Composition of the Work Force

Two major changes in the antebellum economy were the composition of the work force and the nature of work, especially in the North and upper Midwest. Irish and German immigrants flooded into the country. By 1860 Germans were 60% of the population of St. Louis. Up to 1840 the United States usually received no more than 20,000 immigrants a year, mostly illegally smuggled slaves from Africa or immigrants from the British Isles. Now a flood began, thanks to limited economic opportunities in Europe and the Irish potato famine, known in Ireland as *an gorta mor*, "the great hunger," that began in 1845. In 1641 Catholics owned 59% of the land in Ireland. By 1776 British policies had reduced that to 5%. The famine plus limited future opportunities meant it was time to leave. The trip from Liverpool to New York City or Boston took only 10-12 days and the fare dropped as low as $17. However, the journey was hazardous. Twenty percent of those crossing the Atlantic to reach the United States perished at sea in 1847. Between 1850 and 1900 thirty million immigrants arrived. In addition to the Irish Catholics, 40% of the German immigrants were also Catholic, coming from Southern Germany. Concerned over this threat to Protestantism, the American Bible Society handed each arriving immigrant a King James Version of the Bible, not the one Catholics use. One wonders what Catholic immigrants did with it.

The Nature of Work

In this evolving society, work became separated from the home. Prior to this era people worked at home or under supervision in the master craftsman's home, living in that family, constantly supervised, guided, and watched, even when not working. Now workers went from their homes to the factory, and at the end of the day from the factory back to their own homes, away from the watchful eyes of the factory owners and their bosses. The separation of work and housing led to the creation of "working class neighborhoods," with their own characteristics and their own set of rules, many of which astounded and disturbed middle and upper class people. For example, public drinking, unsupervised dating, poor attendance at church, holidays out of control, bad habits, and bars became commonplace. Upscale bars today with pool tables and large television screens are an attempt to attract the middle class, who are more accustomed to drinking at home. In 1800 70% of the North's population worked in agriculture. In 1850 only 40% did. There was now a large urban work force, something new in society. Concerns arose over how to control the working class.

The Market Economy
The emergence of the Market Economy led to other changes. It brought a new set of values. America was now seen as a rising young society, a nation of "go-getters," with the primary purpose of life now being the improvement of the individual's well-being and the acquisition of money or wealth. The primary purpose of government, in the mind of the average person, became the facilitating of that pursuit by creating equality of opportunity, so that all had a chance to get ahead. One example was the demand for lower land prices for western land. This function of the government fostered an additional definition of equality, the equality of individual self-worth, which was seen as strengthening our democratic society. Note that there was no place in all of this for blacks or women, but please do not read history backwards. Just because Americans believe today that these two groups deserve to be included does not mean that everyone then felt the same way. To them it was a democratic society of overwhelming opportunity for energetic white males, AND, effecting that should be the purpose of government. Read John Greenleaf Whittier's poem on the internet, "The Poor Voter on Election Day," 1852, which describes the voter as king for that day, with no higher peer. Class distinctions, never strong in America, declined even more. Foreign visitors, raised in societies where distinctions of class and wealth mattered, found it "impossible to know who is who in this land of equality," and therefore, impossible to know how to greet someone. The new American custom of shaking hands with everyone unnerved them.

From Concern to Reform
Reform is difficult to define; it is multifaceted. In addition, it is difficult to achieve in the political arena. One old saying is that "politics is the art of the possible; reform the art of the desirable." Reform is change, but not necessarily change for the better.

Reformers may see it as an improvement or change for the better, but the objects of the reform impulse, the people that the reformers are trying to change, often do not see reform as an improvement in their lives. Talk to recent immigrants about efforts today to reform the immigration laws. Are those attempts pro-immigrant or anti-immigrant? Certainly current educational reform has a lot of "stick-it-to-em" in disguise. Many teachers and students see educational reform as punishment more than improvement. State testing, accountability, and 100% learning have been added to all the previous responsibilities schools had, such as preventing smoking, driver education, and fighting child obesity with lunch menus and physical education classes.

A Philosophy of Reform?

During periods of reform there is no consistency, no overarching philosophy of reform. Reform is always a patchwork approach. Each set of reformers tried to fix a different area of society. Reformers historically became identified with one reform. While many did embrace other reforms, they also often rejected some. Reform activity and enthusiasm usually takes place during periods of a belief in the power of the environment to overcome the forces of heredity. In the 1960s *Sesame Street* was created to teach kids in poor urban neighborhoods, to even the playing field before they got to school. Head Start, also begun in the 1960s, was also supposed to level the field. It has not worked; research indicates that the benefits are gone by third or fourth grade.

Reform Has Three Components

The **political-economic**, the politics of money, as shown by Jackson's Bank War against the Bank of the U.S.

A push for **social justice, for civil rights and civil liberties**, as shown by the women's movement and the antislavery movement.

An attempt to remake and remold society, driven by **utopian-perfectionism**, when planners and dreamers think up solutions to the problems of, for example, public schools, prisons, asylums, and temperance. "If we just adopt this reform of (fill in the blank) then society will improve and many problems will be solved." You will hear that repeated many times in your lifetime.

By 1820-1830 Americans consumed the highest per person amount of alcohol in our history, perhaps as much as seven gallons of alcohol per year, approximately three to four times today's rate. In 1827 in Rochester, New York, there was one tavern for every eighty people. Many Americans were greatly concerned about alcohol. Get a box of tissues and sit down to read *Ten Nights in a Barroom*, by T. S. Arthur, published in 1854. It is pure Victorian melodrama. The leading anti-alcohol reformer, Neal Dow, dreamed of completely prohibiting alcohol across the nation. However, since this responsibility fell under the states' constitutional powers to maintain the "health, safety, and morals" of their state's population, it required an effort in each state legislature. Dow's first accomplishment was only half a loaf. He was able to push a local option law through the Maine legislature in 1851. Local option meant that a local governmental unit such as a county, a township, a town, or a city *could* vote to prohibit alcohol. This shifted the effort to the local level. By 1855, while no state had enacted prohibition, thirteen states had passed laws permitting local option. However, even when enacted, the local option laws were rarely enforced.

A movement among the working class created the Washingtonian Temperance Society, founded in a Baltimore tavern in 1840. The working-class based Washingtonians signed the pledge, "T" for total abstinence, and became "teetotalers." It had nothing to do with drinking tea. Of all the era's reform movements, temperance attracted the most followers. Do not confuse temperance and prohibition, which means a person cannot obtain alcohol. Temperance means alcohol is available, but you personally pledge not to purchase or consume alcohol. By 1850 per capita consumption was down to two gallons per year.

Another reform sought two seemingly contradictory goals – improving conditions for the insane while isolating them in out-of-the-way asylums. After her visit with fellow Quakers in Great Britain pursuing similar goals, Dorothea Dix led the American drive to improve the care of the mentally ill. She began her efforts in her home state of Massachusetts, and subsequently led similar campaigns in other states. In many states she was the first female to address the state legislature. Carefully gathering factual proof of poor treatment, she successfully convinced many states to reform conditions for the insane. Any improvement would have been better. Visit the cages for the mentally ill in the hospital at Colonial Williamsburg. Try to imagine living naked in a horizontal six by three foot wire cage, one foot high, suspended off the floor (for easier sanitary cleanup). If a person was not mentally ill before being put into one, you quickly became so.

Prison reform was driven, as almost all reforms are, by a belief in the power of the environment to reform and reshape human character. One reform was the penitentiary, where one did penance, rather than merely serving time in a prison. Religious ideas, theoretically, sought to remind every prisoner that he or she had sinned, and must repent. For example, a visitor to Eastern Penitentiary in Philadelphia today sees Christian crosses in the iron gates throughout the prison, placed there to urge repentance. Other ideas tried to improve prisons. The state of New York adopted the Auburn system in 1821, characterized by individual confinement at night and group activities during the day. However, it was a "silent system," if one talked, that day did not count off your sentence. Pennsylvania opted for solitary confinement in 1829 when it built Eastern Penitentiary. It led to high suicide rates. From 1773-1827 Connecticut had used an old abandoned cooper mine as a prison, named Old Newgate Prison. Any alternative was better. Note that all these reforms were done both for the prisoners and to the prisoners.

The Means to Achieve Reform in this Era – Perfectibility

Perfectibility was a belief that individuals, groups, or entire nations could make themselves morally blameless through a sudden act of will, a conscious decision. Listen to the assumptions underlying perfectionism in a statement by a reformer, Adin Ballou. He was a pacifist, abolitionist, and Unitarian minister who founded the religiously based Hopewell Community.

> "Man as a religious being and moral agent acts more or less in three general areas. The individual, the social, and the civil or governmental spheres. It follows, therefore, that there are individual duties and virtues and sins; social duties and virtues and sins, and governmental duties and virtues and sins. In each sphere our religious and moral obligations are the same. Right and wrong confront human beings at every step. To be perfect, one must think, say, and do what is right in each and all the spheres of responsibility named."

The implication was that private and public morality were identical; nations were judged by the same standards that weighed on individuals. In all spheres right and wrong are total or absolute. There can be no mixing of the two. Anything that is not morally right is utterly wrong. Human beings could achieve not only salvation, but could overcome sin altogether for themselves and, collectively, for their whole society.

The secret to achieving perfectibility was self-reliance, self-denial, self-control, and self-discipline. As explained by historian Nathan Huggins, "Since the essential inner genius corresponded to the soul of every man, self-reliance would lead one to universal principles and ideals." One example of applied self-discipline was that shown by those who took the pledge in the Washingtonian Society to abstain from alcohol. In a society that was becoming weaker institutionally, an individual could no longer depend on the family, the church, and the community to control and to discipline. In our age many individuals practice moral relativism; right and wrong depend on the context. Antebellum reformers could not understand moral relativism. In their minds, right or wrong were clearly right or wrong.

The Voluntary Association

The chief organizational means to carry out reform was the voluntary association. Note that the government was not involved. Government was itself considered an institution in need of reform, hence the Bank War. Reformers created many associations to reshape society, such as the Antislavery Society, the Washingtonian Society, the American Peace Society, New Harmony, Brook Farm, etc. The problem with this approach was that within the group like-minded people reinforced faulty thinking.

New Institutions

New institutions needed to replace older institutions that no longer worked; new institutions would address the new concerns. The institutions seen as declining or weakening were the political party system, the church, the family, public morals, schools, and a sense of community. This is why they experimented with new institutions and new solutions to problems that older institutions no longer adequately addressed. The worn-out, ineffective old ways of doing things needed to be replaced by new institutions, such as asylums, prisons, public schools, and Indian removal, the last of which was justified by some as the only way to preserve Indian culture and existence.

We would not have liked all their "reforms." Probably the most unusual was phrenology, the "science" of discerning moral traits by studying bumps on the head. Nativism arose to protect the country against the awful immigrants. In 1790 there were approximately 30,000 Catholics, by 1830 500 priests and 500,000 Catholics, by 1850 1500 priests and 1,750,000 Catholics. Catholics were the second fastest growing congregations in the antebellum era, from 50 churches in 1780 to 2,500 in 1860, almost all the growth coming after 1840. A best-seller, selling over 300,000 copies by 1860, Maria Monk, *The Awful Disclosures of Maria Monk: the Hidden Secrets of a Nun's Life in a Convent Exposed*, told the story of young girls forced into being nuns, who then served as sex slaves to priests. Public excitement led a mob to burn down a convent in 1834 in Boston. It takes real courage to attack a heavily-armed convent. The mob found no evidence to support the book's claims. In truth, Maria Monk was a woman of ill-reputation (I am being kind) from Montreal. Even her mother did not endorse her book. Mom said Maria had a history of mental problems, including making things up. Lurid exposés caught the public's attention, then and now. The inventor of the telegraph, Samuel F. B. Morse, was a well-known professor of the fine arts at New York University and an outstanding artist. However, he was also one of the leading anti-Catholic bigots of his day, publishing *Foreign Conspiracy against the United States* in 1855. Curiously, it was published by the "American and Foreign Christian Union Press." Ralph Waldo Emerson, also extremely anti-Catholic, referred to immigrants as "guano," a widely used fertilizer from bird droppings gathered from islands off the west coast of South America.

Examples of Reform – Education

The public school movement resulted from giving up on the family as a teacher of "republican values." Remember "republican motherhood"? Now education was seen in a new light. Previously, kids needed education primarily for reading the Bible. Now school became a place for moral inculcation and the source of individual opportunity. Horace Mann, the Secretary of the Massachusetts State Board of Education and the leading education reformer of his day, said, "Education, then, beyond all other devices of human origin, is the great equalizer of the conditions of men – the balance wheel of the social machinery." "It gives each man the independence and the means by which he can resist the selfishness of other men. It does better than to disarm the poor of their hostility towards the rich: it prevents being poor."

Earlier, education consisted of colonial dame schools in a home, with little preparation for the world of work. Sunday Schools were the next innovation, an early version of public education, with a little religion mixed in. By the 1820s more children attended Sunday Schools than public schools. The purpose of the Sunday School, as noted by historian Paul Boyer in *Urban Masses and Moral Order in America, 1820-1920*, was to "promote deferential and disciplined patterns of behavior based on an image of society as stable, orderly, and securely hierarchical." Why? Because that ideal was disappearing due to the changes taking place with the arrival of the Market Revolution. However, with the rise of the public school, Sunday Schools changed their emphasis by 1840 from teaching the fundamentals of education to teaching religion, and from serving primarily the poor to serving everyone.

Behind the impulse for educational reform was a change in the conception of childhood, from seeing children as miniature adults to a new concept of childhood as a malleable stage of life. Education became the key to progress, to democracy, and to individual fulfillment. Schools socialized kids more effectively than their families could. The Industrial Revolution and the Market Revolution led to changes in the family and in the home, especially for the middle class, as work and home now became separated. In a similar fashion, kids went off to school, leaving the mother in charge of the home, the now idealized family refuge against the outside world of work. When mothers did leave the house, it was to go "shopping," a new phenomenon brought on as more consumer products became available.

Issues Facing Educational Reformers

The greatest education reformer of this era was Horace Mann. He served as the Secretary to the Massachusetts State Board of Education and wrote twelve annual reports on different aspects of education. He had little regard for theory and urged practical and useful schools. His faith in the public school was complete. "On schools and teachers I rely more than on any other earthly instrumentality, for the prosperity and honor of the state, and for the reformation and advancement of the race. All other reforms seek to abolish specific ills; education is preventive." The common school was "the greatest discovery ever made by man." He was, as many reformers were, very moralistic and believed most problems were moral. His favorite words were Man, Duty, and God. One of his last statements was, "Be ashamed to die until you have won some victory for humanity."

Educational reformers struggled with many different issues, some of which are still debated. Should public schools charge tuition? Since educators felt that education was the key to eradicating poverty, they feared that charging tuition would fail to break the cycle of poverty. Poor kids would work rather than come to school to receive the education and discipline they needed. Compulsory attendance laws would not become part of public education until the twentieth century. In a society plagued by widespread institutional breakdown, discipline was important, because the young received it nowhere else. One school in Boston averaged 65 floggings per day, and this in a school population of only 400. Principals needed a strong arm.

Two groups perplexed education reformers – blacks and Catholics. Most cities relegated blacks to inferior segregated schools. In St. Louis during the nineteenth century all the segregated black schools were numbered, such as school #12, while all the white schools were named for famous Americans. A major squabble developed between Catholics and the Protestants who controlled the schools, over the question of which Bible to use for daily Bible reading, the Catholic Bible, which has additional Old Testament books, the Apocrypha, or the Protestant King James Version. Eventually Catholics pulled out of the urban public school systems and created their own schools, at tremendous cost.

Staffing and organization questions had to be addressed. Should schools be staffed with male or female teachers? Horace Mann argued for female teachers because of "the greater intensity of the parental instinct in the female sex, their natural love of the society of children, and the superior gentleness and forbearance of their dispositions, all of which lead them to mildness rather than severity, to the use of hope rather than fear as a motive of action, and to the various arts of encouragement than to annoyances and compulsion, in their management of the young." Female teachers were also paid less, the real reason for many school boards. Education reformers studied school systems in Europe. Calvin Stowe, a professor of Biblical Literature at Lane Theological Seminary in Cincinnati, and the husband of Harriet Beecher Stowe, of *Uncle Tom's Cabin* fame, wrote a *Report on Elementary Education in Europe*. It led to the widespread adoption of the twelve-grade system by 1850, with schools divided into elementary, grammar, and high school. The junior high, grades 7-9, did not arrive until the 1920s; the concept of the middle school, grades 6-8, later replaced it.

Results of Educational Reform

Education reformers could not imagine a workable pluralistic society composed of different cultures, values, and traditions. They were often disappointed in their efforts. The gains for public education were not uniform. Out of the nation's 320 high schools in 1860, 167 were in just three states – New York, Ohio, and Massachusetts. The great expansion of public education came later. By 1860 reformers established three principles of public education that would last:

1. Secondary and primary education should be free and available to all.
2. Teachers should be given professional training.
3. All children should be required to attend, up to a certain age, but not necessarily the free public school.

Examples of Reform – The Women's Movement

The much celebrated first women's convention in 1848 in Seneca Falls, New York, was a local meeting, not a convention. It was locally advertised, only five days before it convened. It had been called by Lucretia Mott, Elizabeth Cady Stanton, Lucretia's sister, Martha C. Wright, Jane Hunt, and Mary Ann McClintock. About 300 women and 50 men attended. The meeting grew out of the experiences of Lucretia Mott and Elizabeth Cady Stanton at an antislavery convention in London in the early 1840s. Women, even those sent as official delegates, were not allowed to sit on the convention floor. Lucretia Mott was an official delegate. Elizabeth Cady Stanton was on her honeymoon; her husband was an official delegate. Infuriated, the two women vowed to do something about it. Years later, when Lucretia Mott visited Elizabeth Cady Stanton at Seneca Falls, they remembered their pledge.

The meeting produced *A Declaration of Sentiments*, a rewriting of the Declaration of Independence; 68 women and 32 men signed the declaration. When she completed the draft of the resolutions at her home, Elizabeth Cady Stanton added Resolution Number Nine, the vote for women, without the support of the other four planners. It was the only resolution not to receive unanimous support. Suffrage was not the chief demand. However, one woman in attendance, Charlotte Woodman Pierce, a 19 year-old who was incensed by her father's demand that she turn her glove factory paycheck over to him, lived to cast a vote in 1920.

No permanent women's rights movement emerged from the Seneca Falls meeting; that movement materialized in the early 1850s. Disconnected efforts by individuals had characterized the beginning of the women's movement. The various early reformers were primarily concerned with changing state laws for legal status, property after marriage, and guardian rights after separation or divorce. Susan B. Anthony, a prominent agent for the New York state chapter of the American Antislavery Society, was already well-known for petitioning the New York legislature. When Susan B. Anthony and Elizabeth Cady Stanton met in 1851, they began a lifelong collaboration for women's rights. With the blessing of Elizabeth's husband, Anthony frequently lived with the Stantons and their seven children. Anthony became the organizer of the women's movement. (And also the disciplinarian of the spoiled, rambunctious Stanton children.) Stanton was the writer and the intellectual leader. Their early achievements were minimal.

In 1854 Susan B. Anthony presented the New York state legislature with a petition for women's rights with 6,000 signatures. In 1855 she tried again with a huge petition. Both times the legislators just laughed. Finally, in 1860 some property and divorce rights were granted, along with the right to hold property separately after marriage. Women were a significant part of many reforms in this era, especially regarding the gathering of signatures on antislavery petitions, but they found their skills and influence diminished as reforms became more politically oriented. Because women could not vote, they were relegated more and more to the sidelines in the fight for reforms such as the abolition of slavery and laws restricting alcohol.

One historian, Barbara Welter, has argued, based on a study of women's magazines in this era, that what really characterized these years was not a rebellion by women, but the "Cult of Domesticity," or "The Cult of True Womanhood," which emphasized *piety, purity, submissiveness,* and *domesticity.* A woman's primary responsibility was to build her home into a haven of serenity for her husband, an antithesis to the competitive marketplace he labored in daily. In *The Young Wife,* 1838, William A. Alcott urged women to be supportive and passive while promoting moral improvement, in order to exert a civilizing influence upon the home and society. Catherine Beecher, the sister of Harriet Beecher Stowe, the author of *Uncle Tom's Cabin,* wrote *A Treatise on Domestic Economy, for the Use of Young Ladies at Home, and at School.* It contained practical advice on cleanliness, dressing, and even on washing the dishes.

Some gains hardly qualified as genuine advances. Elizabeth Blackwell applied to a male medical college, Geneva Medical College, in upstate New York. Twenty-nine other medical schools had already turned her down. The faculty, uncertain what to do, gave the student body the right to decide, feeling that they would reject her. Thinking it would be a great joke on the faculty, the students voted to accept her. In 1849 she became the first female to earn a medical degree. As an illustration of the interconnectedness among reformers, her brother, Henry, married Lucy Stone, the women's rights and abolition reformer.

Examples of Reform – Religion

By the 1790s fewer than 10% of Americans belonged to churches, although 40% attended intermittently. Change was in the air. The Second Great Awakening was beginning. In 1801 the Cane Ridge, Kentucky, camp meeting attracted some 25,000 participants that gathered to listen to preachers, mostly Methodists. The older established churches were losing out to the newer, emotional churches. (Just as they are today. Some historians are calling the present the Third Great Awakening or the Fourth Great Awakening, labeling the late nineteenth century as the Third.) The new message was different. Charles G. Finney, a Presbyterian minister who later became a Congregational minister, argued that any good Christian could attain eternal salvation by accepting Christ. Known as the "Father of Modern Revivalism," his emotional revivals featured the "anxious seat" (also called the "mourner's bench"), a designated area for potential converts. This was a democratic and optimistic message. Besides the "anxious seat," his preaching included an emphasis on emotion, a common-sense speaking style, and the inclusion of women in public prayer meetings.

Puritans had believed in the doctrine of predestination, the idea that salvation depended on God's predetermined decision to send a person to heaven or hell. Now a new idea spread, the Methodist concept of the Arminian doctrine that salvation depended on one's own choice to accept Jesus as Savior. Choice was in the air, society had shaken off colonial era ideas and restrictions. Now one chose marriage partners, occupations, where to live, political party affiliation, AND religion. The values that were part of the Second Great Awakening dovetailed with the emerging values of the market economy – industry, sobriety, self-control, and self-reliance. In many respects the Second Great Awakening was a "women's awakening," which gave women, especially young women, a sense of identity and purpose at a time when they were expected to prepare for a life of secluded domesticity.

The Shakers, officially the United Society of Believers in Christ's Second Appearing, also grew in these years. Mother Ann Lee founded the Shakers in England in 1774 when she received a revelation that told her she was Jesus Christ in female form. Eight Shakers left for America that year. They shook and danced at their services, shaking their bodies free of sin out through their fingertips. Believers in Millennialism, the immediate or soon return of Christ, they saw no need for children. They practiced celibacy, even for married couples, because sin was originally introduced into the world when Adam and Eve had sexual knowledge of one another. They grew by taking in orphans, 6,000 by the 1830s. They excelled at making simple, functional furniture, far different from the elaborate Empire and Victorian furniture styles then in vogue.

The Mormons originated during these years. In 1830 Joseph Smith discovered gold plates on his farm that he could read with the aid of two magic "seeing stones." He dictated the messages written on the plates, which became the Book of Mormon. Non-Mormon scholars see the Book of Mormon as a combination of Old Testament theology, popular history, and contemporary social beliefs. For example, Indians are identified as one of the original ten tribes of the Israelites, one which wandered off to North America. Smith appears to have been intrigued by the discovery of the Mound Culture in the Mississippi Valley. Two previously published books had also suggested that the Indians were lost Jews: James Adair, *History of the American Indians*, 1775; and Elias Boudinot, *A Star in the West: or, A Humble Attempt to Discover the Long Lost Ten Tribes of Israel Preparatory to Their Return to Their Beloved City, Jerusalem*, 1816. Adair's conclusions came from the similarities of two customs: a separate lodge for Sioux women before and after childbirth was similar to the Jewish purification rite, and the Sioux "virgin feast" was similar to one for Jews. Since childbirth takes place in all societies, it is not surprising that any two societies would have similar practices. Another Mormon belief, modified and then ended in 1978, said that there was no equality before God for blacks.

The Mormons grew rapidly for several reasons. In many respects, their theology and practices met the needs and energies of many of society's unsuccessful and neglected. All white males held a clerical status. The church stressed the sanctity of secular accomplishments and the need for a community of "saints," thus the proper full name,

The Church of Jesus Christ of Latter Day Saints. It also promised salvation to all. As a tightly knit community in an increasingly individualistic society, those around them continually harassed Mormons. Two characteristics, voting as a bloc in state elections and rumors of polygamy, led to a mob attack at Nauvoo, Illinois, killing the leader, Joseph Smith. Their solution to persecution was to move. Their new leader, Brigham Young, led the trek to Utah, an empty spot in Mexican territory. It shortly became American territory, a result of the Mexican War. The Mormons survived and flourished mainly because of their communal efforts, especially in regard to managing their scarce water resources. Because of their location across routes to the West, settlers trekking to California and Oregon purchased much-needed supplies in various Mormon towns, further enriching their communities. Congress insisted that they abandon polygamy before acquiring statehood, and the Church officially outlawed it by 1890.

Another new religion originated in these years, also in the so-called "burned-over district" of western New York, so nicknamed because it was a hotbed of revivals. The Millerites became the modern Seventh Day Adventists. William Miller was certain he knew the date of the Second Coming of Christ. By studying the Bible and various calendars, he arrived at the expected, or, hoped for date. In one year Miller gave 627 long lectures on the Second Coming. It was to arrive in 1843, but nothing happened. He announced that he had miscalculated, being off by one year. He gave a new date of October 22, 1844. By this time he had approximately one million followers. The night before the new date there was an earthquake in western New York. Some people committed suicide and one person jumped over Niagara Falls. However, there was no Second Coming. Miller died broke and disgraced.

In a curious mixture of nationalism, patriotism, and religion, the idea that the Second Coming of Christ will take place in America has had a long history. Two Puritan ministers, John Cotton and Increase Mather, predicted it as 1655 and 1680, respectively. Others joined in, including the Shakers under Mother Ann Lee, opting for 1770, Joseph Smith, the founder of Mormonism, and his successor, Brigham Young. Young declared that the American hemisphere was where "Jesus will make his appearance the second time."

Perhaps William Miller's biggest mistake was depending on our calendar. Any biblical scholar or historian realizes that our present calendar is way off. It was created hundreds of years after the birth of Christ. Christ was born somewhere between 4-11 B.C. Most scholars opt for 6 B.C. Remember the biblical story about Joseph, Mary, and Jesus fleeing to Egypt to escape the wrath of King Herod? According to our current calendar, King Herod died in 4 B.C. Why 11 B.C.? Halley's Comet appeared in 11 B.C., leading some scholars to suggest it would have been the star that guided the Three Wise Men. Thus, our calendar, theoretically based on the birth of Christ, is behind by 4-11 years.

Examples of Reform – Communal Groups

Two other new communal groups show the range of different thought in this era. The Amana Community, "the Community of True Light," migrated from Germany to Buffalo, New York, in the 1840s, led by Christian Metz. Members of this group settled in western New York and then moved to Iowa, buying 25,000 acres of farmland once they arrived. Eventually the community became a corporation and prospered in the appliance business. The other group, led by John Humphrey Noyes, founded the Oneida Community, also in upstate New York. It became famous for advocating free love. In 1881 they abandoned their unusual sexual practices and reorganized as a joint stock company, making silverware, now the world's largest manufacturer of silverware.

Anyone searching for a reform, any reform, to create a better world certainly had many to choose from in the antebellum years prior to the Civil War. Probably no other period in American history featured such a diverse range and mixture of movements to improve American society. All of them could point to some successes, however, none fulfilled all the goals their advocates sought. Why? Because as the years rolled on one particular reform absorbed more and more attention and came to dominate the political arena, pushing aside every other topic. That issue is the one reform not yet fully addressed. It deserves its own chapter, because it superseded every other reform. It was the effort to end slavery.

23

THE OLD SOUTH AND SLAVERY

The Image and Reality of The Old South

From movies, restored plantations, and especially from Southern nationalists, we get an image of antebellum slavery, with the slaves happily and slowly working and singing in the fields, while their owners sit on the porch of "the big house" and sip mint juleps. This image seems to have a fixed position in the collective American memory – but – it is not the complete picture and it is an incorrect image of reality.

First, only 25% of all Southern whites owned slaves. Second, 95% of all slaves lived in rural areas and worked on farms or plantations – note, *farms* or plantations. Many owners worked alongside their slaves on relatively small farms. Historians estimate that by the 1850s nearly 200,000 slaves labored in industrial sites such as textile mills, sugar refineries, or iron works. The best known was the Tredegar Iron Works in Richmond, Virginia.

This is the breakdown of the South's population according to the 1860 census:

> 986,895 whites were members of families owning 5 or more slaves
> 931,280 whites were members of families owning 1-4 slaves
> 6,120,825 non-slaveholding whites

This makes a total of 1,918,175 slave-owning whites out of a white population of approximately eight million.

> 251,000 free blacks
> 3,953,760 slaves

These numbers hold several surprises. The **First** must be the disproportionate influence of large slave owners. How else can one explain why 25% of the white population led the rest? **Second** is the small percentage of slave-owners.

Below are the statistics from the 1790 and 1860 census, providing a state by state numerical look at how slavery changed over 70 years:

1790 Census Statistics

Virginia	292,627	New Jersey	11,423
South Carolina	107,094	Pennsylvania	3,737
Maryland	103,036	New York	21,324
North Carolina	100,572	Connecticut	2,764
Georgia	29,264	Rhode Island	948
Delaware	8,887	New Hampshire	158
		Massachusetts	0

1860 Census Statistics

Virginia	472,494	Texas	182,566
Georgia	462,198	Missouri	114,931
Mississippi	436,631	Arkansas	111,115
Alabama	435,080	Maryland	90,374
South Carolina	402,406	Florida	61,745
Louisiana	331,726	West Virginia	18,371
North Carolina	331,059	Delaware	1,798
Tennessee	225,483		

The **Third** surprise is the presence of free blacks. As early as 1830 there were more free blacks in the United States than the population of fifteen different states. The number of free blacks in the South came from those who either purchased their freedom, were set free in wills, if state law permitted, or lived in urban areas and performed servile occupations for whites, such as blacksmith, barber, gardener, etc. They had to purchase a license in South Carolina to go into business; whites did not. Across the South free blacks could not own boats, except those who fished for a living. Other restrictions in South Carolina included an annual tax on free blacks and a cap on daily wages. Unlike the experience in other parts of the New World, the trend in the South was toward increasingly harsher treatment of free blacks. They encountered much prejudice in their daily activities, but as they were constantly reminded by slave owners, there was even more prejudice in the

North. Slave owners made it a practice to gather their slaves to hear a newspaper account of a race riot in a Northern city such as Cincinnati or Philadelphia.

There were black slaveholders, one in Louisiana owned 147. This helped Southerners argue that it was a labor system, not a racial system.

If 75% of all whites did not own slaves, why would they support a slave system and the existence of a slave society? A slave society differs from a society with slaves. In a slave society slavery dominates and influences all other institutions, everything in that society.

Almost all whites had a dream of rising in society. Everyone knew the rules – work hard, save money, purchase a slave, work hard, purchase more slaves, work hard, purchase more slaves and, finally, enter genteel society, first at a lower level, and gradually, through marriage and inheritance, elevate the family to higher social status. All this was possible. In addition, along the way one had the security and pride of knowing that you were already higher than the lowest rung on the social ladder, the slave. Shared racial pride made all whites equal in the South, even if their pocketbooks indicated that they were unequal. The German language has a perfect word for this, Herrenvolk democracy, democracy within the master race.

This solidarity of whites was a myth in many ways. One Southerner, Hinton Helper, wrote a book in 1857, *The Impending Crisis of the South: How to Meet It.* Helper attacked slavery as the cause of the South's economic weakness, arguing that the ruling oligarchy of slaveholders and their slave labor led to poverty and backwardness, degraded labor, inhibited urbanization, and stifled the progress of both non-slaveholding whites and of the South generally. A rabid racist, Helper was no friend of slaves; he wanted colonization to Africa. However, he soon had to leave the South for his own safety. A number of men were lynched for merely possessing a copy of this book. His attack on the institution of slavery expressed no sympathy for the slaves themselves, but the book was still widely quoted in the North. During the election of 1860 *The New York Tribune* distributed thousands of free copies.

Far From a Monolithic Culture

The South was far from a monolithic culture. Many poor whites, "poor white trash" and mountain whites outside the cotton belts, hated the political power and social smugness of the plantation elite. Look at the various nicknames given to poor whites: hillbillies, crackers, red necks, and clay eaters. Actually, what a lot of poor white Southerners suffered from was a disease, trichinosis, a parasitic roundworm consumed by eating undercooked meat, especially pork. It was not until the 1920s that the Rockefeller Foundation began a campaign to wipe out the various diseases that sapped Southern energy and helped create the image of the lazy poor white Southerner.

Southern elitists viewed poor whites with contempt. The most shocking example was George Fitzhugh's *Cannibals All or Slaves Without Masters*, published in 1857. Even his fellow slaveholders rejected his logic. Fitzhugh argued that slavery was the appropriate condition for most people, even poor whites. "Some were born with saddles on their backs, and others booted and spurred to ride them – and the riding does them good." He stated that most people cannot live with freedom; they needed someone to tell them what to do. Northern antislavery advocates loved quoting from his book.

In a book entitled *The Mind of the South*, twentieth century journalist Wilbur Cash identified several characteristics that distinguished the South from the North and West in the antebellum period. Not all of them were flattering. He called the South a self-contained and largely self-sufficient intellectual plantation mentality. The South had:

1. Ineffective state governments with few social services, because large landowners would not permit high taxes on their large plantations and farms.
2. A tendency toward violence. Between 1840 and 1860 mobs in the South burned or hanged over 300 people; fewer than 10% were blacks. Lynching was not yet primarily a means of racial control.
3. A glorification of military virtues. Southerners attended West Point and military schools in disproportionate numbers.
4. A tendency toward romanticism. The most widely read author in the South was the British author Sir Walter Scott, famous for *Ivanhoe*, 1819, and *The Talisman*, 1825. Historians have compared the reception across the nation of theatrical adaptions of his poem, *The Lady of the Lake,* to the popularity of some modern Broadway musicals, such as *Hamilton.*
5. A tendency toward hedonism, the pursuit of pleasure for the sake of pleasure, as a social value, but also a contradictory emphasis on chivalry.

Some historians have argued that social values were of primary importance in this pre-capitalist society. In many respects, the South was not congenial to capitalist values. Historian David Potter cited many differences that distinguished the South from the North and West – the hierarchical nature of society; the lack of machinery and industrialization; the dominance of "clan values rather than the commercial values," and the predominantly rural nature of life. Almost all the major Southern cities were on the rim of the South; it was a rural society.

Trends in the South Up to 1860

Good cotton land was becoming concentrated more and more in the hands of fewer and fewer owners. Opportunity declined along the Atlantic Coast and in the older tobacco areas as soil fertility declined. There was intense competition to expand into the new cotton lands of Tennessee, Louisiana, Alabama, and Mississippi. Later, Southerners dreamed of expanding slavery and cotton cultivation into the trans-Mississippi West and into the

Caribbean, through newly acquired territory. This explains the 1853 Ostend Manifesto urging the federal government to seize Cuba. Between eight hundred thousand and one million slaves moved inland from the Atlantic states between 1820 and 1860. According to historian Maurie McInnis, the total value of slaves sold "down the river" from Richmond, Virginia, auctions in just one year, 1857, equaled $440 million in today's dollars.

Slaves proved to be a very profitable investment. By 1860 a good healthy male farm-hand sold for $1500-$2000, females for less. However, investing in slaves was not a certain means to wealth. You could lose your investment through runaways, diseases, illnesses, or natural disasters. One owner in Alabama lost a lot of money when lightning killed twenty of his slaves, a financial loss of $30,000 to $40,000, equivalent to more than two million dollars today. Owners sometimes rented slaves to nearby farms and plantations. Female slaves rented for one-half of the male rental, a clear indication that females were not considered as productive as males. So, why was the price of female slaves so high? The answer is the reproduction value of a female slave. Newborn babies sold for $200.

Very few immigrants went into the South. Immigrants with no skills and no money, the Irish, in particular, would have to compete with the very low wage scales established for free blacks. So the Irish tended to stay in the Northern cities. In one very dangerous occupation, screwmen, Southerners used Irish immigrants rather than slaves. The task entailed squeezing cotton bales into the ship's cargo space, using long jacks. It was very dangerous. Just as a jack used to change an automobile's tire can snap if it is off center, imagine what a long jack could do. If the jacks snapped they flew all over the hold of the ship, placing everyone present in serious danger, since there was no place to hide. Irishmen could be replaced; slaves were too valuable.

The Problem of Sources – the Historiography of Slavery

Historiography is the study of the writing of history. Historians collect and analyze both primary and secondary sources in order to describe, compare, and interpret historical phenomena. Different historians may present the same phenomenon or event from a variety of perspectives because:

> Historians choose different questions to guide their inquiries.
> Historians may have varied access to historical materials.
> Historians analyze those sources differently.
> Historians are led by their own beliefs and points of view to weigh causes in distinct manners.
> Historians are creatures of their time and place, and in many ways prisoners of it. A colonial historian writing now would be remiss if he or she ignored the topic of women during the colonial era.

Any comparison or evaluation of competing historical interpretations must take these factors into account.

Slavery presents many challenges to historians. There is an old saying among historians, "no documents, no proof, no history." A researcher must have documents, something to base his or her opinions upon. Slaves left few documents. In addition, the question, "What was slavery like?" raises another significant question. To whom? To the slave, the master, the non-slaveholding Southerner, the Northern abolitionist, the prejudiced Northerner, or the ambitious politician?

The first historical accounts of slavery, written before the Civil War, were stark expressions of the author's political views. Southerners emphasized the benevolent features of slavery – the paternalism of the masters, the contrast with the plight of Northern "wage slaves," and the carefree, happy demeanor of the slaves themselves. Northerner writers, many of them abolitionists, pictured slavery as a brutal and cruel system that dehumanized everyone touched by it.

By the end of the nineteenth century, in popular literature, there emerged a romantic picture of the Old South as a graceful and serene civilization. Into this climate, or maybe because of it, appeared Ulrich B. Phillips's *American Negro Slavery*, in 1918. Phillips portrayed slavery as a "schoolhouse for civilization," an essentially benign institution in which kindly masters looked after childlike, submissive, contented blacks. Slavery was an inherited, unprofitable economic institution that masters accepted as a responsibility to elevate the inferior slaves entrusted to their kindly care. Slaves were "submissive rather than defiant, light-hearted instead of gloomy, amiable and ingratiating instead of sullen." Any harshness in the system such as whipping was a necessary part of supervising a backward labor force. This is almost like blaming the victim for the crime. For nearly thirty years this apology for the Southern slave owner was considered the authoritative work on the subject.

W.E.B. Du Bois wrote a history of Reconstruction in 1935 that attacked Phillips' assumptions, but it was not well received by the professional history community. Du Bois was dismissed. He was, after all, they said, a black political activist who was the editor of *The Crisis*, the NAACP's newsletter, and therefore biased.

By the 1940s other challenges to Ulrich B. Phillips began to appear. In 1943 Herbert Aptheker attacked the notion that slaves were submissive and contented. He claimed, "Discontent and rebelliousness were not only exceedingly common, but, indeed, characteristic of American Negro slaves." He defined a revolt as something involving a minimum of ten slaves with freedom as its object. He claimed to have found over 250 of these happenings, but he could document only 15-20. He stretched his own definition to include conspiracies and alleged conspiracies. In addition, he included events in the Spanish and Portuguese colonies. His creditability suffered because Aptheker was an important early leader of the American Communist Party. The history profession ignored his research and writings because, as everyone knows, a communist cannot write honest and objective history, even if he had it right.

By the 1950s two historians, Kenneth Stampp and Stanley Elkins, claimed the apparent happiness Phillips saw was a false front to adjust to the harshness of slavery. They attacked Phillips' picture of slavery as a system that lacked brutality. Kenneth Stampp's *The Peculiar Institution*, 1956, emphasized the physical and psychological impact on men and women kept in a virtual prison, with little room to develop their own social and cultural patterns. Even more devastating was Stanley Elkins' *Slavery*, 1959. Elkins argued that many slaves were childlike and submissive because they adopted what he termed a "Sambo personality." Elkins used the term "infantilization" to describe this personality type. He was influenced by looking at the Second World War Nazi concentration camps and the adjustments made by those prisoners who survived. He saw the development of defensive personality characteristics as an "adjustment to absolute power" leading to the adoption of the "Sambo personality," the happy go lucky, singing slave, hiding his true feelings, stuck in a "no exit" situation.

During his research in the South Carolina state archives, Stampp grew perplexed at the large number of runaway slave ads in newspapers and on posters that described a slave as one who "stutters" or "has a speech defect." He asked psychiatrists what could account for the disproportionate number of speech defects. Their answer – internalized role-playing, acting like the dumb, happy slave in order to reduce the amount of work expected and to appear unthreatening. If you are smarter than your boss, are you not a threat to your boss? In many respects these two books reflected a widespread attitude in white society in the 1950s and 1960s that slavery had inflicted gross injustices upon the slaves, and whites must undo the damage. Remember, the civil rights movement was in full swing during the 1950s and 1960s.

By the late 1960s much had changed. The emergence of "black power" as a slogan led to an emphasis on black pride and achievement, which produced a new view that emphasized the cultural and social accomplishments of blacks under slavery. Now the main thrust in historical writing shifted to the viewpoint of the slave rather than that of the slave owner or the abolitionist. Three books in the 1970s, John Blassingame, *The Slave Community*, 1973, Herbert Gutman, *The Black Family in Slavery and Freedom, 1750-1925*, 1976, and Lawrence Levine, *Black Culture and Black Consciousness*, 1977, were part of this approach. Blassingame used slave narratives, slave songs, and religion to argue that slaves were not submerged by slavery. Slavery was not a one-way street; it was a two-way relationship, a social system, not a prison camp experience as suggested by Elkins. The black author, Ralph Ellison, best remembered for *Invisible Man*, framed a similar question in another book. Do a people, like slaves, live "by simply reacting?" Was the black experience one of only reacting to whites? Obviously not.

There was ample room for carving out their own space and culture through noncooperation and slowdowns. Slaves fought back in their own way with any means they had. The system provided enough room for blacks to retain and to nourish their separate culture – religion, songs, stories, family, community, African traditions, and covert resistance. Frederick Douglass's autobiography talks about his keeping a "magic root" in his pocket, an African tradition.

Gutman studied the black family and found that far from being weakened and destroyed by slavery, the black family survived with remarkable strength. Moreover, this existed in spite of misgivings on the part of the owners. Bennet Barrow, a Louisiana planter who owned over 200 slaves, was among the many Southerners who urged caution concerning slave marriages. In his 1838 diary he was especially concerned about marriages between slaves living on different plantations.

> "First – in allowing the men to marry out of the plantation, you give them an uncontrollable right to be frequently absent – 2nd Wherever their wives live, there they consider their homes, consequently they are indifferent to the interest of the plantation to which they actually belong – 3rd It creates a feeling of independence, from being, of right, out of the control of the masters for a time – 4th They are repeatedly exposed to temptation from meeting and associating with negroes from different directions, and with various habits & vices –."

The family was a buffer, a survival mechanism. Gutman found complete records for one small area in a county in Tennessee. They showed that 67.6% of all slave marriages lasted until the death of one partner. Was the splitting up of families by selling either the husband or wife "down the river," as abolitionists charged, typical? Maybe, maybe not. Gutman's sample is small. The percentage of slave marriages that stayed together in his sample exceeded the percentage for whites. This question, the durability of slave marriages, was part of the debate during the 1960s on welfare and the single parent, the female-headed black family. What were its roots? Did it come out of slavery? What governmental policy should or could address this?

The 1960s emphasis on the ability of blacks to maintain their own culture and society under slavery formed the basis for two 1970s books that looked at slavery as a system. *Time on the Cross*, by Robert Fogel and Stanley Engerman, used quantitative methods to show that slaves were skilled and efficient workers, that the black family was strong and healthy, and that slaves were generally better off than Northern industrial workers. They were roundly criticized for dispassionately looking at a brutal system and expressing conclusions in terms of numbers. They were certainly not endorsing slavery. However, all comparative questions can ultimately come down to "compared to what?"

If one argues that slavery was not a very bad system, the assertion becomes attached to the question of – "Compared to what?"

Eugene Genovese's *Roll, Jordan Roll: The World the Slaves Made*, revived the old paradigm of paternalism, but Genovese now saw it as working in both directions, enabling slaves to make demands on white masters as well as the other way around. Genovese claimed that within the slave system slaves retained a large cultural space of their own, within which they developed their own family life, traditions, social patterns, and above all, religion. Theirs's was a distinct, separate society within white society. In *Black Culture and Black Consciousness*, Lawrence Levine looked at the symbolism of slave songs, jokes, old photographs, and lyrics in blues songs to uncover a previously unappreciated world of resistance to slavery, including playing the role of ignorant Sambos to confound their masters.

Peter Kolchin, an internationally recognized expert on the history of slavery, looked at the institution by comparing American slavery and Russian serfdom, gaining insights into both. He effectively put to rest the question of whether or not slavery began because of labor need, the economic argument, or, because of racial prejudice. Did racism precede or follow slavery? His research showed that slavery flourished anywhere commercial agriculture gained a foothold – for example, in colonial New York and in Rhode Island. Clearly labor need and labor supply problems played the crucial role in cementing race-based slavery onto the American scene.

Historian Thomas Doerflinger offered another economic perspective for the South in the conclusion of *A Vigorous Spirit of Enterprise: Merchants and Economic Development in Revolutionary Philadelphia*. He differentiated between *economic growth* and *economic development*. The South was economically and culturally chained to land, THE dominating factor in the plantation-based society. The economic and cultural prominence of LAND limited business entrepreneurship and enterprise in the South. Doerflinger asserted that the South's cultural mindset led it to focus on *economic growth*, merely spreading the plantation system. The South continued to grow, but only in one direction, a direction dooming it to a future agricultural, second-rate economic status in the emerging industrial, commercial society. It was not slavery that retarded the South; it was the region's lack of entrepreneurial spirit, which is associated with a city's opportunity-oriented economic thinking. The South's lack of cities cemented it into slowly becoming more and more backward economically. The only exception for any slave state was Maryland, where Baltimore led the way into *economic development*.

Finally, be careful using the idea of race as a category. It does not have an exact definition. Indeed, today, gene pool is more useful as a descriptive term. Anthropologists do not use the term race anymore. Race is a social construction that changed both its content and meaning over time. See Nell Painter's incredible book, *The History of White People*. She traces the history and misuse of history behind the evolution of race as a categorizing term. After reading *The History of White People*, it will be impossible to think of the word race in the same way again.

What was the Impact of Slavery upon the Slave?
Ownership

The following chart illustrates how difficult it is to describe the "typical" slave owner. Look at the number of owners towards the bottom of the ownership pyramid. The majority owned 4-5 or fewer.

> 1,733 white families owned 100 or more slaves
> 6,196 white families owned 50-99 slaves
> 29,733 white families owned 20-49 slaves
> 54,595 white families owned 10-19 slaves
> 80,765 white families owned 5-9 slaves
> 105,683 white families owned 2-4 slaves
> 68,820 white families white families owned 1 slave

Slave Songs as Sources

Oh, the image of the happy slaves singing as they leisurely labored in the cotton fields. Historians have learned to look carefully at the words in the slave songs. Some contained information, such as "follow the drinking gourd," the North Star, if you run away. The "Blue Tailed Fly" is the sad song of a slave who cannot understand the death of his master, thrown from his horse. It must have been the bite of the Blue Tailed Fly, or, could it have been the burr the slave put under the saddle? It is us against them; do not rat on anyone to the enemy, the white owner. That is the message in the short song about Judas, who betrayed Jesus and ended up hanged, as you might be, by us, if you become a traitor.

Workload

What about the workload? Was it heavy or not? On the rice plantations, and frequently in the tobacco fields, slaves worked under a "task system." They were assigned a task, and when finished with that task they were free to pursue their own personal agenda, such as tending to their small gardens. On the Louisiana sugar plantations and on cotton plantations a different organization prevailed, the "gang system." Slaves labored in gangs under the watchful eye of an overseer. Planters complained bitterly of their inability to get much work out of their slaves. The diaries of planters claim that they had to make constant compromises to get work done – small gifts, praise, smaller quotas, minimal demands, and beatings. When a planter wrote in his diary that he had to beat so-and-so again today, who is actually in charge? Think of your high school's experience. Do schools discipline the same kids over and over? Does discipline change that student's behavior?

The slave workday stretched from sunup to sundown; but it did for almost everyone in the antebellum years. Between 1825 and 1860 the average Mississippi slave picked 130-150 lbs. of cotton per day. But, on some plantations slaves averaged less than 100 lbs. per day. Was this a heavy burden? In 1836 two Mississippi planters, arguing over who had the better slaves, arranged a race. The fourteen slaves in the contest picked an average of 323 lbs. per day, twice the daily average. Were the other slaves lazy? Were these selected pickers outstanding? Probably. What should have been the "typical" daily average?

Living Conditions

There are very few historical records describing the living conditions for slaves. Few planters wrote anything about their slave quarters. Former slaves, however, did provide some details about their living conditions. In *Slavery in the United States: A Narrative of the Life and Adventures of Charles Ball*, published in 1836, Ball, an escaped slave, described one plantation on which he lived as having 260 slaves housed in 30 cabins, an average of 8.7 per cabin. Louis Hughes, in *Thirty Years a Slave*, described his former plantation as having 160 slaves in 18 cabins, an 8.8 average. Some other plantation records go as high as 10-12 and as low as 3.7. It was rare for one family to have their own cabin. Privacy was nonexistent.

Health

The life expectancy for slaves was 36; but it was only 40 for whites, and in Ireland in these years it was only 19, as it also was for the poor in England's industrial cities. It was not much better for anyone in any class in an English city, 30. Historians estimate that female slaves in the South experienced puberty 1-3 years earlier than slaves in the West Indies. American slaves were also reportedly, on average, approximately 3 inches taller. Both are conditions associated with nutrition. This means, perhaps, that American slaves enjoyed better overall health than did slaves in the Caribbean. However, this comparison involves two very different societies. For example, in Jamaica 80-90% of the slaves were African born. The slave population needed to be constantly replenished. Once a slave arrived in Jamaica, conditions were so harsh that the average slave survived only seven more years. Modern research in outhouse pits near slave quarters reveals the consumption of a surprising variety of food. Slaves supplemented their diets with food from their own garden, from trapping animals, and from fishing. Historians believe that the variety of food and the calories consumed by slaves probably was not much different from that of whites. Life back then was harsh, for everyone.

Sexual Exploitation

According to the census of 1860, 10% of all slaves had some white ancestry in 1860 and 5% of all children born that year to slave mothers were fathered by whites. Remember the phrase historian Stanley Elkins used to describe slavery, a "no exit" situation. Now, answer this question. Are these high numbers or low numbers? What a question. This is what historians do — interpret and assign significance. Wrestle with an answer.

Legal Position

Slaves lived in the South under strict slave codes, which varied from state to state. Delaware had one of the less oppressive slave codes. Delaware slaves could not be sold out of the state without the legislature's permission and could testify in court against a white person. By 1860 only 11% of Delaware's blacks were slaves. Louisiana was perhaps the most bluntly honest state about the institution of slavery. Louisiana's slave laws were in the statute books under the Real Estate section. Slaves were property.

Free blacks existed in the South, but in an ambiguous legal position. They were consistently viewed as potentially dangerous to the institution of slavery. Real freedom was minimal. For example, in 1822 South Carolina passed the Colored Seamen's Act, requiring the imprisonment of all free black seamen working on merchant ships that came into Charleston harbor, for the entire time their ships remained in port. On the eve of the Civil War, the South Carolina legislature seriously debated enslaving all the free blacks in the state.

Northern free blacks were not much better off. From 1820, when Maine joined the union, until the Civil War, every new state denied the right to vote to free blacks and many did not allow them to serve on juries or even to testify in court cases involving whites. Ohio, Illinois, Indiana, Oregon, and Michigan barred free blacks from entering the state, unless they posted bond prior to emigration. California's constitutional convention in 1850 came within just two more votes of completely barring blacks from the state. Before 1820 free black men in Massachusetts, Vermont, New Hampshire, Rhode Island, Connecticut, New York, New Jersey, and Pennsylvania voted on an equal basis with white men. Three states subsequently took the suffrage away — Pennsylvania, New Jersey, and Connecticut — and New York added property ownership qualifications for blacks, but not for whites. Only 4% of America's free black males could vote by 1860.

Summary

The best source for understanding slavery from the viewpoint of the slave is John W. Blassingame, *The Slave Community: Plantation Life in the Antebellum South*. The question of the impact of slavery upon the slave is complex and contradictory, as some slaves were rebels, and some were Uncle Toms. Frederick Douglass's superb autobiography said it best. "The man who gets a good master aspires to get a better master, the man who gets a better master aspires to get the best master, and the man who gets the best master aspires to be his own master." A black actor, employed to play the part of a slave on the auction block in a film made in Colonial Williamsburg in the 1990s, said the emotions he experienced overpowered him and almost made him break down. And, he was a professionally trained actor making a movie. Try to imagine the emotions involved in the real experience 150 years earlier.

Slave Revolts and Rebellions

About 89% of all runaways were males, aged 16-25. However, most did not head north. Most runaways went to a nearby plantation to visit a relative, returning quietly a few days later.

There were slave revolts, and they frightened the white South, especially after Haiti gained its independence. Fear was a constant factor in Southern society. For historians information about many of the revolts is limited and sketchy. On the night of April 6, 1712, a revolt in New York City killed between 8 and 16 whites. In response, 13 of the captured rebel slaves were hanged, others were burned alive or broken on a wheel, meaning they were pulled apart. In 1739, again in New York City, 20-30 whites were killed. Also in 1739, in South Carolina, in the Cato conspiracy at Stono, rebels attacked, sacked, and burned an armory with the intention of marching to freedom by going to Spanish Florida. They were captured. The whole affair caused the deaths of 30 whites and 44 blacks. The colony responded by passing a law that no one over 4 feet 2 inches could enter the colony as a slave – thus, no adults. In 1740 a plot was uncovered at Charleston, South Carolina, and 50 blacks hanged. The next year, 1741, in New York City rumors surfaced of a poor white-black alliance. The rumored revolt was crushed before it began – 101 blacks were convicted of rebellion, 22 blacks and whites were hanged, 70 banished, and 13 burned alive. In the colonial era New York City had a significant slave population. One reliable source in 1760 shows that one-seventh of New York City's population was black, much of it slave.

The Haitian Revolt

The most frightening revolt to Southern slave owners was the Haitian revolt. Haiti is the western half of the island of Hispaniola, which France gained from Spain in 1697. Southerners constantly labeled Haiti the ultimate absurdity, a country run by former slaves. Haitian Independence Day, January 1, 1804, was widely known among American slaves, and celebrated. South Carolina Senator Robert Hayne, of the famed Webster-Hayne debate, declared, "Our policy with regard to Haiti is plain. We can never acknowledge her independence." The United States did not; Lincoln finally extended diplomatic recognition to Haiti in 1862 during the Civil War.

Gabriel's Plot

In the new United States revolts continued. In 1801 the Gabriel Plot convulsed Henrico County in southern Virginia. Gabriel was a slave, but one well acquainted with liberty. His former owner was a good friend of Patrick Henry, of "Give me liberty or give me death" fame. The revolt was brutally suppressed by Governor James Monroe with somewhere between 16 and 35 executions. Virginia passed a law in 1806 that required all freed slaves to leave the state or be sold back into slavery.

In 1811, 500 slaves marched on New Orleans. The militia stopped them. The 16 leaders were executed and their heads placed on poles on roads leading into the city, remaining there for years as a warning. To whom – whites or slaves?

Denmark Vesey

Denmark Vesey became a free black man after he won the South Carolina lottery in 1799, but he was unable to purchase and free his children. The owner would not sell. He was arrested in 1822 in Charleston, South Carolina, when authorities caught wind of a planned massive uprising of free blacks and slaves. The leaders were so cool that the authorities dismissed the rumor, which had come from three mulatto house slaves. A few days later a house slave told them the date had been moved up. The leaders were arrested again, tried, and 35 executed; 35 more, including Vesey's son, Sandy, were sold into slavery in the Caribbean. Historians have argued whether or not there really was such a plot. Richard Wade's book, *Slavery in the Cities*, extensively studied the sources and concluded that there was no planned massive uprising. Some other historians claim there was a planned uprising. The people of Charleston were certain. Blacks in the area outnumbered whites about 8 or 9 to 1. By 1830 slaves were 55% of South Carolina's population, the largest proportion for any slave state. South Carolina was the only state in which a majority of the white families owned slaves.

Nat Turner's Revolt

Finally, the most significant of all was Nat Turner's revolt in 1831 in Southampton County, near Norfolk, Virginia. Southampton was a county where slaves outnumbered whites by one thousand. Nat Turner was an unusual slave. His mother was a house slave, and so he grew up as a houseboy, doing errands around the house. A recent novel related a cute story explaining how Nat could have become educated. One day his master sent him down to the cellar for sugar. He brought up the white stuff, and the master put it into his cup of coffee, and then spit out the salty coffee. After he beat Nat, the master took him downstairs to teach him the words salt and sugar on the boxes. After that Nat snuck into the library, looked through the books for the words salt or sugar, and tried to figure out what the words beside them were. He taught himself to read. When the owner found out he was not angry; he was proud, he had something rare, a smart slave. However it happened, Nat Turner grew to become a literate, privileged, honored slave. He was permitted to preach to the slaves on Sunday and even preached occasionally in the local white church.

One night the angel Gabriel came to him in a dream and said, "Nat, kill white people." He carefully organized a mass uprising with the intention to "carry terror and devastation." On the night of August 20-21 he began, killing his master and the family. The group worked their way to nearby plantations and farms, quietly killing whites, 57 in all, the vast majority children. When the killings were discovered, the militia squashed the rebellion. Over 100 blacks were killed and 20 executed after a trial. Nat Turner eluded capture for ten weeks. He was accidently discovered by a farmer in the forest. He was brought back and put on trial. During the trial, he said that his master, Joseph Travis, was "a kind master." "I had no cause to complain of his treatment of me." When hanged, he glared at the crowd, never asking forgiveness, an arrogant stare that seemed to say, "I will get you in the next life." Chilling, absolutely chilling.

A few weeks prior to Nat Turner's revolt, the state of Virginia had been in the process of writing a new constitution. The legislators came within a few votes of considering outlawing slavery in Virginia. The Virginia soil was so worn out that the farms were not profitable; hence the labor supply of slaves made less sense in monetary terms. Virginians annually sold thousands of slaves in this era, mostly to the booming cotton states of Mississippi and Alabama. Hence the phrase, "being sold down the river," the Mississippi River. During the constitutional debate the motion to end slavery had been tabled, and was still alive and under consideration. Not after Nat Turner. If a kind master could not trust a privileged, educated, never mistreated slave, what about the rest? Adding to the hysteria, Thomas Gray, a lawyer, interviewed Nat Turner and published *The Confessions of Nat Turner* a few weeks after the trial. It struck at the latent fears throughout the South. Gray wrote that Turner's revolt was "not instigated by motives of revenge or sudden anger, but the results of long deliberation, and a settled purpose of mind." Which slave would be next? Where? Ending slavery became unthinkable. If slavery ends, what will we do with all the ex-slaves, the dangerous ex-slaves? As Jefferson Davis, the future president of the Confederate States of America, put it, "If we kill slavery, what are we going to do with the corpse?"

The Abolitionist Impulse in the South

In the antebellum years the leading abolitionist was William Lloyd Garrison. He was a founder of the New England Antislavery Society and the American Antislavery Society. He argued for the immediate emancipation of slaves. While genuinely sympathetic to the plight of the slave, Garrison's major focus was the sinfulness of the slave owner. He even advocated that the North secede from the South to prevent the sin of slavery from tarnishing Northerners. That would, of course, leave the slave securely under the control of the South, doing nothing to improve the lot of the slave. Eight months before Nat Turner's revolt, Garrison began publishing his antislavery newspaper, *The Liberator*, on January 1, 1831. Southerners blamed Garrison for causing Turner's revolt. He did not. Nat Turner was unaware of *The Liberator*. But, Garrison defiantly responded to his Southern critics, "I do not justify the slaves in their rebellion: yet I do not condemn *them.*" And added, "If any people are ever justified in throwing off the yoke of tyrants, the slaves are that people."

After Nat Turner, hysteria gripped the South. By 1860 ten states had curbed or outlawed voluntary emancipation. In North Carolina a person could be executed for giving a book to a slave. Before 1831 abolition was a Southern phenomenon. That was where the slaves were; that was where the problem of slavery was debated. Still, it is true that the earliest abolitionist societies were in the North. The Quakers first outlawed slavery among themselves, as a way to reduce their sinfulness. The rhetoric of the American Revolution spread abolition. For example, slavery was outlawed by the following:

> Pennsylvania – 1780
> Connecticut and Rhode Island – 1784
> The Northwest Territories through the Northwest Ordinance – 1787
> New York – 1799 and 1817
> New Jersey – 1804

Usually slavery ended by gradual emancipation; children born of slaves were not slaves and when current slaves reached a certain age, such as 21 or 35, they were free. Thus, the owner was not deprived of his or her investment. The last New York slave was freed in 1827, in Connecticut, 1848.

From 1789 to 1831, prior to Nat Turner's revolt, the chief abolitionist impulse was in the South. In 1826 there were 143 abolitionist societies, 103 of them were in the South. There were four abolitionist newspapers in the South. Thomas Jefferson suggested African colonization in 1776. The state of Virginia passed resolutions in favor of colonization in 1800, 1802, 1805, and 1816. In 1817 the American Colonization Society was formed, headed by such notable leaders as James Madison, James Monroe, John Jay, Henry Clay, Daniel Webster, Francis Scott Key, and Supreme Court Justice Bushrod Washington, George's nephew, who became the first American Colonization Society president. He was also the executor of his uncle's estate and had inherited Mount Vernon. The men behind colonization were honored, respected, politically powerful men. It was considered a good idea. In 1821 the American Colonization Society purchased land in Liberia and established Monrovia, the capital city, named for James Monroe. The idea of colonization weakened considerably in the 1830s. When it finally folded in 1867, the American Colonization Society and similar organizations had shipped fifteen thousand blacks to Liberia, which equaled the number of slave births for several months. Obviously, shipping blacks back to Africa was not a viable means to rid the United States of their presence.

After Nat Turner's revolt, many realized that colonization was not a solution and that slave codes needed to be tightened. Abolitionism now shifted to the North, and

the South increasingly defended slavery as a positive good rather than a difficult inheritance. Elsewhere slavery was on the path to extinction. England ended it throughout
its empire in 1833, France in 1848. Among the larger countries only the United States
and Brazil retained slavery. Southerners were developing a siege mentality, feeling a
mounting pressure on their "peculiar institution," as they called it.

The Defense of Slavery – An Economic Necessity

Southerners claimed their slaves were better off than Northern "wage slaves," a term
they used to refer to the Northern factory workers precariously balanced between the
boom and bust cycles of the emerging capitalist system. Slaves suffered no layoffs, never
starved, and were always housed and fed. In reality, slavery had become an economic
necessity to the South and to the nation. Cotton and tobacco were labor-intensive crops.
Tobacco required year-round work. In February or March slaves planted seeds in flats
and covered them with straw or bushes, placed to catch the late winter sun. In April or
May the seedlings were transplanted to the fields. One seedling was carefully placed in
a tiny hill of scooped up dirt. Throughout the summer worms were hand picked off the
plants, then excess leaves pruned back, and plants topped to prevent the development
of too many seeds. Each hill had to be repeatedly hoed to prevent weeds. In August
the plants were carefully cut and taken to curing barns. Finally, the heat-cured tobacco
leaves were packed into four-foot-high hogsheads for shipment. Cotton also needed to
be constantly weeded and hoed.

A Schoolhouse for Civilization

Slavery was defended as a schoolhouse for civilization, a paternalistic system preparing blacks to stand on their own two feet, eventually. For now, they were not ready.
Thomas Jefferson once characterized slavery as a dilemma with no solution. "We have
the wolf by the ears, and we can neither hold him, nor safely let him go."

The Bible

The Bible sanctioned slavery in Leviticus 25:44-46. In the words of the widely used
King James Version of that time:

> "Both thy bondsmen, and thy bondmaids, which thou shalt have, shall
> be of the heathen that are round about you; of them shall ye buy bond-
> men and bondmaids. Moreover, of the children of the strangers that
> do sojourn among you, of them shall ye buy, and of their families that
> are with you, which they begat in your land; and they shall be your
> possession. And ye shall take them as an inheritance for your children

after you, to inherit them for a possession; they shall be your bondmen for ever; but over your brethren the children of Is'rael, ye shall not rule one over another with rigor."

Finally, the Cain and Abel story sanctioned slavery by branding blacks as the descendants of Cain, upon whom God had placed a "mark" as punishment for killing Abel, his brother. Clearly, said Southerners, the "mark" was making Cain and his descendants black. Thus, blacks inherited more than just the original sin of Adam and Eve. All these reasons justified extreme measures, such as restricting abolitionist literature flowing through the mail. After 1835 virtually no piece of abolitionist literature was delivered in the South. The local postal authorities impounded it.

Abolition – a Failure?

After Nat Turner the South rarely discussed emancipation. Abolitionism shifted entirely to the North, and it was not very successful there, at least not as a political movement. Some abolitionists tried third parties, such as the Liberty Party or Free Soil Party; some tried to work through the existing major parties; and some tried petitioning Congress to abolish slavery. Nothing worked. Abolition was by any measurement a failure. One of the great questions in American history is a simple one. How did a nation opposed to black equality come, in a relatively short period of time, to embrace that idea, first through ending slavery and then through adding black suffrage to the fundamental law of the land, the Constitution? The events of the Civil War and Reconstruction provide the answers, answers that few dreamed of even a few years before the outbreak of the Civil War.

24

MANIFEST DESTINY

Mexico – Revolution and Independence

In 1810 a revolution against Spanish control began in Mexico, with Mexico eventually winning independence eleven years later in 1821. During the turmoil accompanying the revolution some Mexicans in Texas, joined by a few Americans from Louisiana, attempted to create a Republic of Texas, and, apparently, add Texas to the United States. Suspicions ran high in Mexico that the U.S. government was behind this endeavor. It clearly had the encouragement, if not overt involvement, of President James Madison and Secretary of State James Monroe. However, this brief Republic of Texas collapsed in 1813 after lasting only four months, from April to August.

Texas and Mexico – Cultural Conflict

In spite of this incident, in 1821 the Mexican government granted a tract of land to an American, Stephen Austin, to bring 300 families to Texas as settlers. There are few hints in either Texan or Mexican archives to explain why Mexico encouraged this. Was it supposed to be a barrier to American expansion? Were bribes involved? Did Mexican authorities hope to populate and develop an underdeveloped region? Why did they not foresee potential problems? At that time Mexican officials laughed at the possibility of Texas breaking away. As they humorously stated, in their minds Texas was to Mexico what Siberia was to Russia, both unable to stand alone. The idea of an independent Texas was absurd. Texas needed to be attached to the rest of Mexico for Texas to survive.

Problems soon arose. Austin had agreed that all settlers would become Catholics; the Mexican government prohibited worship for any other church. Of course Americans failed this test. Since 90% of the Texas settlers came from the South, they confidently expected slavery to follow them to Texas as soon as conditions permitted. Three years after Austin arrived the Mexican government merged the provinces of Texas and Coahuila, which later provided for gradual emancipation of all bondservants, shocking Texans. In 1829, a presidential decree abolished slavery throughout all Mexico. Texas was later exempted from both rulings, but ill will and suspicion remained, on both sides. By 1834 there were 17,000 "immigrants" in Texas, and 2,000 slaves.

In reality, the root of the suspicion was fundamental cultural conflict between the American settlers and Mexicans. The two cultures clashed – over languages, customs, religions, laws, slavery, and institutions. For example, in the Mexican judicial system there were no jury trials. The trial transcript was sent to another judge, an assessor judge, who made the actual decision. There was no opportunity for courtroom theatrics or the kind of comments that would force an American judge to advise the jury to "disregard that remark." It was not in the transcript. Texans intensely disliked this system. Trial by your peers had a long tradition in Anglo-Saxon jurisprudence.

Mexico – Santa Anna

In 1832 Santa Anna, a proclaimed liberal, took over the government and half-heartedly began a reform program. The two major conservative forces in Mexican history – large landowners and the Catholic Church (neither the Church's income nor property was taxed) – soon convinced him to abandon reform and to declare himself the dictator. Minor revolts against Santa Anna broke out all over northern Mexico, and Santa Anna moved north to quell them. Hearing exaggerated reports about Texan hotheads harassing Mexican garrisons, he sent a small detachment north to investigate. Fighting took place; blood was shed.

The Texan Position at This Point

Ostensibly, Texans were not yet interested in independence. On November 3, 1835, twelve Texan communities sent representatives to meet at San Felipe where they drew up a protest that they were loyal Mexican citizens defending the principles of the Mexican Constitution against the evils of Santa Anna's dictatorship. Californians took the same approach. In early 1836 Santa Anna arrived in Texas, leading an army. On March 1, 1836, Texan wrote their declaration of independence. Independence proved to be easier to write than to win. Note – while the Alamo was under attack, Texans declared their independence.

The Alamo

The Alamo in San Antonio is a cherished icon in Texan and American history. Mexican troops killed 187 Texans; only three survived, Susana Dickinson, her 15-month-old baby, and Colonel William Travis's slave, Joe. There have been two different movies made about the battle of the Alamo, John Wayne's 1960 one, or more from the Mexican viewpoint, the 2004 movie, both titled *The Alamo*. Watch them one after the other. It will give you a new perspective on the role of films in giving a slanted opinion of reality. The truth is that historians have few documents upon which to base a description of the actual battle. The only historical document from a participant that has surfaced is a reference in a diary written by a Mexican officer, ten years after the battle. What historians do know is that a Mexican army of 4,000 overran the Alamo after 10 days of attacks. At dawn on the 11th day, March 6, 1836, the entire Mexican army attacked. The third assault won. Among the dead were folk heroes Davy Crockett, Col. William Travis, and Jim Bowie. The Mexicans lost 1,544 killed, an 8-1 ratio, hardly a "victory."

Shortly afterwards at Goliad, south of San Antonio, a Texan force of 350 was surprised and surrounded. They surrendered on March 19. On March 27 the Texans were lined up in three columns and shot. In revenge Texans later razed the town. From the Mexican viewpoint the Texans were guilty of treason and armed rebellion against their government. Do not get caught rebelling against your government. Do not be on the losing side in a failed rebellion. You are guilty of treason. If you win you will be a hero. If you lose . . . . The new government of Texas was temporarily entrusted to Sam Houston, the commander of the army.

Sam Houston

Sam Houston had recently arrived in Texas. While he clearly possessed leadership qualities, he brought no military background with him. Houston had resigned as the governor of Tennessee in 1829 after a very short failed marriage to go to live with Cherokee Indians in Arkansas. There he married the niece of a Cherokee chief. The Indians nicknamed him "Chief Big Drink," which was probably the reason the Tennessee marriage failed. Houston holds one political record; he is the only person to serve as the governor of two different states, Tennessee and Texas. In 1861, as the governor of Texas, he opposed secession and refused to take an oath of loyalty to the new Confederate States of America. This mixed legacy causes Texans to have mixed emotions about him. Houston, although he owned twelve slaves, was opposed to secession, to the extension of slavery, and to the reopening of the slave trade. Only his popularity associated with the Texan revolution enabled him to win and to keep political offices in Texas. He was twice elected president of the Republic of Texas and served as a U.S. senator and a governor after Texas joined the United States.

In 1836 Sam Houston proved to be the right man for the challenge facing Texas. At this point the Texans had two slogans, but no victories. "Remember the Alamo" and "Remember Goliad" sound heroic, but victories would have been nicer. He took sole responsibility for planning the campaign for independence. Houston never suffered from a lack of confidence. He said, "Had I consulted the wishes of all I should have been like an ass (donkey) between two stacks of hay. (perplexed over which one to eat) I consulted none – I held no council of war. If I err, the blame is mine." He led a motley army filled with many GTTs, men who had left troubled marriages or bill collectors in states like Tennessee or North Carolina by carving GTT on the wooden front door, "Gone To Texas," and now outside your legal jurisdiction. After the defeat at the Alamo the civilians retreated in panic towards Louisiana. Houston and the army did also, in less panic.

After retreating for a long time, Houston finally turned on the Mexicans. At the Battle of San Jacinto, near the modern city of Houston, a Texan force of 783 men faced a Mexican army of 1,360. The Texans attacked during siesta, killing 630 Mexicans, wounding 220, and taking 730 prisoners. Santa Anna was found hiding in tall grass, not fully dressed. He tried to disguise himself, a disguise so bad that his soldiers saluted him as he passed by. The Texans lost 9 killed and 34 wounded. Houston forced Santa Anna to sign a treaty, the Agreement of Velasco, granting Texas its independence. However, treaties signed under duress are not valid according to international law. Was Texas now independent? It depended whom one asked.

Annexation?

Texas immediately sent an agent to Washington; he was instructed to "make every exertion to effect annexation with the least possible delay." Shortly after the Battle of San Jacinto, Texans voted in favor of annexation, 3,277 to 93. President Andrew Jackson was cool to the idea. So were many others. Why? There were three reasons. First, Jackson did not want to risk a war with Mexico. Second, Northern Whigs opposed annexation, believing that Jackson and the Democrats engineered the Texan revolution to bring another Democratic state into the union. This argument will come up again in the future. The next two most likely candidates for statehood are Washington, D.C., and Puerto Rico, both of which vote heavily Democratic in local elections. Republicans will come up with many reasons to oppose statehood, which would add senators and representatives and Electoral College votes for their opponents.

Third, slavery cast a dark shadow over annexation. Emotional Southerners felt that Texas would be better off as an independent republic than under the domination of a high tariff, centralized, slavery-hating government in Washington. Remember the recent nullification crisis and the fighting over the tariffs of 1828, 1832, and 1833. Northern abolitionists opposed annexation because the Texan revolution was part of the "dark lanterned conspiracy of the slavocracy to secure more slave territory." Despite being viewed from two different sectional perspectives, many Southerners and Northerners curiously arrived at the same conclusion, no Texas.

The only accomplishment the Texan representative gained was diplomatic recognition by the United States, which made reconquest by Mexico unlikely. Meanwhile, thousands of Americans went to Texas. By 1846 the population was 142,000. From the Texan viewpoint, it was now an independent country. From the Mexican viewpoint, Texas was a province in rebellion, not an independent country. Santa Anna repudiated the treaty of independence as soon as he was freed. Skirmishes continued between Mexican troops and the Texan army.

The Election of 1844

In the spring of 1844 the Whig Party expected Henry Clay to run; the Democrats expected Martin Van Buren to be their candidate. Both promised to keep Texas out of the election and to not raise diplomatic or slavery issues. Both men personally believed that the annexation of Texas would involve us in an unjustified war with Mexico. On April 27 each expected candidate published letters to clearly state his position. Clay published his "Raleigh letter" in the *National Intelligencer.* In it he stated, "I certainly am not willing to involve this country in a foreign war for the object of acquiring Texas." The Whig Party's Convention, meeting in Harrisburg, Pennsylvania, nominated Clay, with Theodore Frelinghuysen of New Jersey as his vice-presidential running mate.

The Democratic Convention met next, in Baltimore, but the delegates did not nominate Van Buren. After Van Buren's "letter" stating his opposition to the annexation of Texas was published in the *Washington Globe,* former president Andrew Jackson dropped his endorsement of Van Buren. Jackson had changed his mind on Texas, now advocating annexation. He threw his considerable influence within the Democratic Party behind James K. Polk. Polk won on the ninth ballot, aided by the "two-thirds rule." The "two-thirds rule," adopted at the 1832 Democratic Convention, required the winning nominee to obtain two-thirds of the delegates, which effectively always gave the South a veto over the Democratic Party's candidate. The party's candidate had to be acceptable to the South. Polk's vice-presidential running mate was George M. Dallas, a former mayor of Philadelphia.

Polk was the nation's first "dark horse" candidate. An outspoken expansionist, his platform called for the "Re-annexation of Texas and the Reoccupation of Oregon." A "dark horse" was a nineteenth century nickname for an unknown horse that came from nowhere to win a race. It referred to a practice by gamblers of entering a horse in a race at the last minute, presumably his very first race ever, with a name like Molasses or Slow Poke. Obviously, the odds would be high against him, meaning that a small bet would yield a huge return. As the horse raced around the track, his painted dark coat dripped off from the perspiration, causing many in the crowd to remark how much he resembled a light-colored, well-known fast horse. As soon as the race ended, the gamblers picked up their winnings from their big last-minute bet, along with their horse, and quickly left town. Polk had come from nowhere to win the nomination, a "dark horse." The Whigs derisively taunted the Democrats with, "Who is James K. Polk?" They found out. Actually, Polk was not an unknown; he was more of an unexpected. He was the former Speaker of the House of Representatives and his nickname was "Young Hickory." As a Tennessee politician that implied he was a protégé following in the footsteps of Old Hickory, Andrew Jackson. In this era, that association paid dividends.

During the campaign Polk successfully lifted the Texas issue out of its irresolvable slavery context by joining it to other expansion issues – Oregon and California. (More on Oregon and California follows.) Polk won the election by a vote of 170 to

105 in the Electoral College. Polk and others believed the nation had spoken for expansion. A mandate! Polk won the state of New York by only 6,000 votes; a switch of a few thousand votes would have made Clay the president. Some abolitionists had decided to pursue abolitionist goals through political activity, creating the Liberty Party, which advocated abolishing slavery by Congressional action, by amendments to the Constitution, or by laws to keep slavery out of the territories. The majority of abolitionists rejected this political approach – too difficult to achieve with Southern opposition. The Liberty Party garnered few votes, however, the party played a significant role in determining the outcome of the election of 1844. The Liberty Party ticket ran James G. Birney, a fiery abolitionist. A former slaveholding Southerner who moved out of Kentucky to the North, Birney won 15,812 votes in New York. Most of those voters would have supported Clay in a Polk versus Clay choice. New York had 36 electoral votes; if Clay had won New York, he would have had 141 electoral votes to Polk's 134. Thus, the third party caused the election of a candidate most unfavorable to their position.

This election's result illustrates the adverse impact to their own cause that single-issue third parties often have in national elections. They hurt their cause by running a third party candidate. A moralistic, absolutist position in our political system does not win, but it does take votes away from the candidate those voters probably would have voted for, if they had only two choices. In the 2000 election Ralph Nader was a third party candidate. George Bush won and Al Gore lost in the Electoral College, barely. Which candidate was closer to Nader's ideas? Gore. By running and taking votes away from Gore, Nader helped elect someone who more strongly opposed his views.

Forces Behind Expansion

Just because Polk advocated expansion does not mean that expansion had to become our policy. There is no one as lonely as a leader who looks over his or her shoulder and sees that no one is following. Why was the nation ready for expansion?

First, the Persistence of the Westward Movement

Wherever American settlers went, they demanded that the United States government expand to include them. The mere presence of Americans justified adding these new areas to the United States. Loyalty to the government that owned that land was unthinkable. John L. O'Sullivan, the New York newspaper editor credited with popularizing the term "Manifest Destiny," explained this thinking:

> "There is in fact no such thing as title to the wild lands of the new world, except that which actual possession gives. They belong to whoever will redeem them from the Indian and the desert, and subjugate them to the use of man."

The key factor was that Americans would make better "use" of these areas, as compared to Indians or Mexicans. Lewis Cass, the Democratic Party's candidate for president in 1848, said, "The Indians are entitled to the enjoyment of all the rights which do not interfere with the obvious designs of Providence." It is so comforting to know God approves of one's policies.

Second, Rumors of French and British Intrigue
Many British citizens harbored a great deal of ill will and outright contempt toward Americans. One British newspaper labeled Americans as "less popular and esteemed among us than the base and bigotted Portugeze, (as spelled in the original) or the ferocious and ignorant Russians." The United States was hardly a military threat, "the weakest government in the world." One source of this ill will was the nine state governments who defaulted on their state debts, much of it borrowed from British investors, during the economic depression that began in 1837. The British also realized they were too dependent on American cotton; they hoped Texas could become an independent source of cotton for Britain. Moving towards the adoption of free trade, the British resented high American tariffs. The British were also increasingly active as a world antislavery force, having abolished slavery in 1833 in their colonies in the West Indies. Their ships patrolled the African coast, stopping American ships involved in the illegal slave trade. Americans held bitter memories of British destruction during the Revolutionary War and the War of 1812, especially the burning of our capital. In truth, it was retaliation for the Americans burning Toronto, the capital of Upper Canada.

British intellectuals and the public held very low opinions of Americans in general. One widely known remark by a British critic captured their disdain for American culture, "Who reads an American book?" The implication, of course, was that no American author was worth reading. After touring the United States, Frances Trollope wrote about the *Domestic Manners of the Americans*, a scathing portrayal of Americans as rude, crude, and uncultured. Charles Dickens complained bitterly about the lack of American laws to protect foreign copyrights. American publishers pirated his books and paid no royalties.

On both sides of the Atlantic Ocean, the public believed their country had gotten the worst of the Webster-Ashburton Treaty of 1842, which settled the Maine boundary and the northern border with Canada from the Lake of the Woods to the Rockies. However, each government knew it got a better deal than it deserved. The diplomats on both sides discovered in their own archives an old Maine map that supported the opposite of what they were asking for. It was hard to negotiate knowing you were wrong in asking for too much land for Maine's northern border.

Both France and Great Britain had as a pillar in their general foreign policy objectives a desire for a country, a new republic, to block American expansion westward to the Pacific coast or southward towards Mexico. This had been a cornerstone of their policy toward the United States since the American Revolution. Otherwise, the United States could grow to become a huge country and a rival power. Another independent country would also serve as a potential haven for runaway slaves. France recognized Texan independence in 1839, Great Britain followed in 1840. Both nations hoped to secure the California harbors to control trade to the Far East. There are only three good harbors on the West Coast of North America – San Diego, San Francisco, and Seattle. The Los Angeles harbor, man-made, came much later.

Third, An Ideological Emphasis

In this atmosphere all that was needed was a focus and a catchy phrase. John L. O'Sullivan, the editor of the New York *Morning News*, supplied it in December, 1845. It is

> "Our manifest destiny to overspread and to possess the whole of the continent which Providence has given us for the development of the great experiment of liberty and federated self-government entrusted to us."

This idea had been around from the first settlers. John Quincy Adams had earlier, in 1819, written in his diary, "The United States and North America are identical." Representative Lewis C. Levin of Pennsylvania said that the nation must repel "the contaminating proximity of the monarchies upon the soil that we have consecrated to the rights of man."

Andrew Jackson, who died on June 8, 1845, had changed his mind after leaving the presidency and wanted Texas in the Union. He spoke of taking positive steps to extend the "area of freedom" and to prevent the spread of the "area of absolutism." In a letter to Congressman Aaron V. Brown of Tennessee, February 12, 1843, Andrew Jackson wrote that "the annexation of Texas to the United States promises to enlarge the circle of free institutions, and is essential to the United States, particularly as lessening the probabilities of future collision with foreign powers, and giving them greater efficiency in spreading the blessings of peace."

Walt Whitman, remembered to later generations as a poet, was a newspaperman who wrote an editorial in the *Brooklyn Daily Eagle* on July 7, 1846.

> "We love to indulge in thoughts of the future extent and power of this Republic – because with its increase is the increase of human happiness and liberty . . . . What has miserable, inefficient Mexico – with her superstition, her burlesque upon freedom, her actual tyranny by the few over the many – what has she to do with the great mission of peopling the New World with a noble race? Be it ours, to achieve that mission! Be it ours to roll down all of the upstart leaven of old despotism, that comes our way!"

In a cruder statement, a prominent politician of that era, Caleb Cushing, widely mentioned as a possible vice-presidential or Supreme Court nominee, labeled Mexico as a land of failures, populated by Indians and half-breeds.

Frederick Merk, recognized as one of the finest historians of the westward movement for his book, *Manifest Destiny and Mission in American History, History of the Westward Movement,* succinctly summarized the ideological forces behind Manifest Destiny in another book, *The Monroe Doctrine and American Expansionism, 1843-1849*:

"Manifest Destiny was a popular theory that the continent of North America was intended by Providence to be possessed by the United States. North America was intended for a showroom to exhibit republicanism in its finest form to the oppressed of Europe. Republicanism in its finest form meant government by the United States. It meant a combination of principles – representation for the masses; confederation of states, all equal; and states' rights governing relations between Union and states and protecting differences in institutions of states. It meant government powered by democracy – political, economic, and social. It meant universal white adult male suffrage, frequent elections, a presidency limited in the future to a single term for each incumbent, a classless society, easy land acquisition, and unfettered trade. It meant for all citizens religious equality, freedom of speech, of the press, of assembly, indeed, the whole range of freedoms that were part of the national heritage. In all these respects republicanism was antithetical to monarchy. Monarchy was tyranny, aristocracy, hereditary privilege, legalized monopoly, restrictive land tenure, recurrent famine, religion imposed by a ruling prince, and servile obedience enforced by repressions.

Inasmuch as all the continent was to be republican some day, the land should be cleared as rapidly as possible of untidy remnants of monarchy, which certainly ought not to be allowed to get bigger by new colonizations."

God had apparently decreed that Americans should rule the continent. Such were the ingredients that shaped American public opinion by the middle of the 1840s.

Annexation of Texas

After the 1844 election, and before Polk took the oath of office in March, 1845, the incumbent president, John Tyler, seeking a feather for his cap, informed Texas that the United States was anxious to reopen negotiations for annexation. A joint resolution proposing annexation passed Congress. The vote in the House was 120-98, and in the Senate 27-25, on January 25, 1845. The Senate vote margin shows why a treaty could not have been used; it would never have passed the Senate by a two-thirds margin, which would have to have been 35-17. A resolution is much less significant than a treaty. A resolution simply expresses the sentiment of a legislature. It is not binding. It proved to be sufficient to Texas. On June 16, 1845, the Congress of the Republic of Texas unanimously voted to join the United States.

Oregon

The 1844 Democratic Party platform called for the "Reoccupation of Oregon," hardly an accurate reflection of the history of that area. Four nations – Spain, Russia, Great Britain, and the United States – originally claimed the Oregon Territory. Spain and

Russia bartered away their claims in treaties. In 1818 the United States and Great Britain agreed to a joint occupation of the Oregon Territory in a treaty, the Convention of 1818, that set the 49th parallel as the northern border of the Louisiana territory. Britain's major interest in the Oregon Territory was the fur trade; the Hudson Bay Company's interests and desires determined British policy in the area.

American settlers began to move in, fed by "Oregon fever" and stories of super-rich soil. By 1846, 5,000 Americans lived in Oregon, mostly in the Willamette Valley, south of the Columbia River. The Oregon Territory stretched from the 42nd parallel to 54° 40', but the crux of the dispute was the area located between the 49th parallel and the Columbia River. Great Britain had repeatedly offered to accept the Columbia River as the border, while the United States had on four occasions offered to extend the 49th parallel to the Pacific. This deadlock ended when the Hudson Bay Company moved its operations to Vancouver Island, because the influx of American settlers endangered the beaver trade. A treaty was quickly drawn up and signed, despite all the "54° 40' or fight!" cries. Note that in both cases, Texas and Oregon, American population pressure forced the issue. Thomas Jefferson foresaw this earlier, prior to the Louisiana Purchase, stating in regard to Louisiana that the movement westward of American population would be "the means of delivering to us peaceably what may otherwise cost us a war."

California

The third jewel in the crown of expansion was California, won the same way, the classic pattern of American settlers moving into California, which was Mexican territory. Charles Dickens quipped in this era that the typical America would hesitate over going to heaven unless assured that he could also go further West. It seemed as if the West was heaven. The U.S. government had repeatedly tried to purchase the harbor of San Francisco, and the American Pacific Squadron continuously patrolled off the coast of California. Americans were concerned that both France and Britain had designs on California's harbors, which both did. Mexico also believed that the United States had designs on California's harbors, which we did.

American actions soon confirmed Mexican suspicions. Commodore Thomas ap Catesby Jones (ap Catesby means "son of Catesby" in Welsh), commander of the American Pacific Squadron, heard rumors that war had broken out between the United States and Mexico. Fearing British action, he sailed into the small harbor of Monterey, the capital of Mexican California, on October 20, 1842, with his guns leveled. No British ships were there and the Mexican garrison was not protecting the town; they were working peacefully in the fields, helping to harvest crops. The Americans hurriedly took control, only to discover that they had captured the port of a friendly power. Trying to make the most of the embarrassing situation, Commodore Jones returned Monterey to its rightful rulers in an elaborate ceremony, staged a ball for the Mexican governor, and sent the fleet's band ashore to entertain the people. Mexico demanded he be punished. The U.S. government refused. His only misconduct or crime, apparently, was bad timing.

In 1845 President Polk sent John Slidell to Mexico to offer up to $40 million for as much of the Southwest as he could get from Mexico. Slidell was a Congressman from Louisiana who later played significant roles as a diplomat in the Confederacy. Remember, the United States had just annexed Texas, which Mexico refused to recognize diplomatically. Mexican authorities refused to receive Slidell, which was a diplomatic insult to the United States. Earlier President John Quincy Adams had sent Joel Poinsett, a well-travelled physician and South Carolina politician, on a diplomatic mission to Mexico. His instructions were to purchase the modern American Southwest, arguing to Mexican authorities that selling northern Mexico to the United States would benefit Mexico because it would have the effect of making the Mexican capital more centrally located. It was the best argument Americans could come up with. He was unsuccessful, but he brought a flowering plant back to his home in South Carolina, a plant named the poinsettia in his honor. Grammar purists insist that too many Americans mispronounce this word. They vouch for four syllables, poin-set-ti-a.

Polk had written to the American consul in Monterey that "the President will make no effort and use no influence to induce California to become one of the free and independent States of this Union, yet if the people should desire to unite their destiny with ours, they would be received as brethren, whenever this can be done, without affording Mexico just cause of complaint." In other words, if a situation in California resembled the Texan Revolution, the United States would annex California.

In April, 1845, John Charles Frémont, a famous explorer and the son-in-law of Senator Thomas Hart Benton of Missouri, a leading advocate of Manifest Destiny, set out from St. Louis with 60 men. He spent the next year roaming around California. Didn't Aaron Burr do something similar and be accused of treason? In June, 1846, Frémont captured the California town of Sonoma and proclaimed the "Bear Flag Republic." He then proceeded to Monterey, where he discovered that the U.S.-Mexican War had broken out and the U.S. Pacific Squadron had captured the harbor, using a maneuver rehearsed four years earlier. Did Mexico have good reasons to suspect the United States had designs on California?

From Mexico's Viewpoint – What Caused the War Between the U.S. and Mexico?

First, Mexico's cold-blooded anger at the American desire to beg, to buy, or to steal half of her country. How inconsiderate. Second, Mexican anger over the lack of U.S. neutrality during the Texan rebellion, when weapons and volunteers were provided by recruiters in the United States, both violations of international law. Third, the need to defend Mexican honor. Here is a quote from a Mexican newspaper.

"We have more than enough strength to make war. Let us make it, then, and victory will perch upon our banners. Were not Mexican soldiers man for man more than a match for the lily-livered Americans who had shown their impotence by failing to capture helpless Canada in the War of 1812."

Both armies, the Mexican and the American, each numbered about 7,000 men. European military observers were betting that Mexico would be victorious. All that was needed to start a war was "the incident." Polk supplied it. Polk ordered American troops into the area between the Nueces River and the Rio Grande, the Rio Bravo del Norte to Mexicans, territory claimed by both Texas and Mexico. On April 25, 1846, a clash occurred. Word reached Polk late on May 9. He had called a cabinet meeting earlier that day, Saturday, to discuss his intention to ask Congress for a declaration of war, citing claims against the Mexican government for damages to American property during Mexico's periodic revolutions and Mexico's slight to our national honor by refusing to receive John Slidell in his attempt to purchase Northern Mexico. The cabinet was generally opposed. Then news of the armed clash arrived. Now Polk revised his war message, throwing greater weight on the issue of "American blood shed on American soil." Congress voted for war, the House of Representatives 174-14, the Senate 40-2. However, 67 Whigs in the House of Representatives voted against an immediate bill calling for 50,000 volunteers and appropriating $10 million, foreshadowing the opposition that surfaced more strongly as the war progressed. The war was most popular in the South. All the opposition votes on the war declaration, the call for volunteers, and the appropriations bill came from Northern representatives.

Abraham Lincoln, elected in the election of 1846 to Congress as a Whig, took office December 1, 1847. He repeatedly introduced resolutions defying Polk to locate and to name the "spot on American soil where American blood had been shed." His efforts became known as the "spot resolutions." This was similar to the tactic used by opponents of the 2003 Iraq War against Saddam Hussein, over the issue of the "weapons of mass destruction" Saddam supposedly had. They were never found; they never existed. Neither did the "spot" on America soil; it was on disputed soil.

Opposition

There was a great deal of opposition to the war. One name forever linked to this war is Henry David Thoreau, a Transcendentalist author most remembered today for *Walden*, an early statement of environmental principles. Thoreau, who spent only one night in jail, refused to pay his taxes in an example of his idea of civil disobedience. (His embarrassed aunt paid his taxes to get him out of jail.) A friend visited him in jail and asked him, "Henry, what are you doing in there?" Thoreau replied, "What are you doing out there?" Gandhi and Martin Luther King, Jr., later picked up his concept of passive resistance to a bad law.

The different geographic rates of enlistment reveal the sectional opposition to the war. Of those eligible in the South, 1 in 33 enlisted; in the Midwest, 1 in 110; in the Mid-Atlantic, 1 in 1,000; and in New England, 1 in 2,500. There is an old saying among military people that Americans make bad soldiers and good fighters, meaning that Americans do not take well to discipline. Too much egalitarianism. Throughout American history many generals had suggestion boxes outside their office. Any soldier could make a suggestion. General Eisenhower used some of these suggestions in planning the Normandy invasion during the Second World War. Anti-egalitarianism assumes those beneath you are stupid. Maybe not. In the U.S.-Mexican War European military observers, a long way from egalitarian, were appalled at the disorder within the U.S. Army. Add Mexican incompetence and it appeared to them to be a contest between the world's two worst armies. The United States won.

The Treaty of Guadalupe Hidalgo and Nicholas Trist

Nicholas Trist, the chief clerk in the U.S. State Department (and the husband of Thomas Jefferson's granddaughter) was a "special secret commissioner" sent by Polk to negotiate a peace treaty. He accompanied the army that landed at Vera Cruz. His instructions were to secure California, New Mexico, and the Rio Grande as the border of Texas, everything Polk had originally given as his goals before the war. In November, 1848, after Mexico City was captured, Trist was ordered home for new instructions; Polk wanted more territory, nicknamed the All-Mexico movement. However, General Winfield Scott feared that the new moderate Mexican government would collapse, leading to a long guerrilla war. In addition, if the Mexican government resigned, there would be no one to surrender or to negotiate. Therefore Scott insisted that Trist first negotiate a treaty. Trist secured all that he was originally instructed to get. However, in the meantime, an "All-Mexico" movement swept the country, urging that the United States seize the entire country of Mexico. Among those in favor of taking all of Mexico were President Polk and Secretary of State James Buchanan, Trist's boss and a future president. But, Polk could hardly repudiate his agent for following his original instructions, so, he reluctantly submitted the treaty to the Senate. In the witty words of one Whig senator, "The treaty negotiated by an unauthorized agent, with an unacknowledged government, submitted by an accidental President to a dissatisfied Senate, has been confirmed."

Two Colors – Gold and Black

In the 1820 Missouri Compromise the two sections had agreed to keep a balance of slave and free states, to preserve equality in the Senate. The discovery of gold in California upset this cozy arrangement. In 1849 and 1850, 1450 ships arrived at San Francisco, part of the surge that quickly populated the territory, making California eligible for state-hood far sooner than anticipated. The population surge was a disaster for Indians. In the years following the gold rush 90% of California's Indians died. With no slave state ready to join the union, California's instant population growth threatened to upset the balance in the Senate. Many Southerners had hoped California would become a slave state. (Ironically, California, much later, became the nation's leading producer of cotton and rice, two "Southern" crops.)

Further aggravating the tension between the North and the South was the Wilmot Proviso. During the U.S.-Mexican War, David Wilmot, a member of the House of Representatives from upstate Pennsylvania, introduced a resolution in the House pro-hibiting slavery in any territory acquired from Mexico. Twice it passed the House and then disappeared in the Senate. Eventually 14 of the 15 Northern state legislatures passed resolutions favoring it. These actions carried no legal force, but they carried a political and emotional force. The South saw Wilmot's proposal as a threat to its politi-cal future. It was; but it was not an abolitionist effort. Instead, Wilmot's motive was to "preserve to free white labor a fair country, a rich inheritance, where the sons of toil, of my own race and color, can live without the disgrace which association with negro (sic) slavery brings upon free labor." He referred to it as the "White Man's Wilmot Proviso."

The Compromise of 1850 admitted California as a free state. Earlier, by 1820, the South had lost equality in the House of Representatives. Now it lost any opportunity to control the Senate. If the U.S.-Mexican War was a conspiracy to spread slavery, the slavocracy was a foolish architect.

Last Piece of the Puzzle: Gadsden Purchase
In 1853 the United States bought the Gadsden Purchase from Mexico, a section that is today the southern part of Arizona and New Mexico. It was needed for a railroad route through low terrain. Critics said that the high price we paid was conscience money. The United States now reached its full development in what is today called in Alaska, the "lower 48." Future expansion would not be contiguous to the "lower 48."

The Aftermath of the U.S.-Mexican War in the Southwest
The Treaty of Guadalupe Hidalgo guaranteed to all non-Indians living in the Mexican Cession their property rights and "land grants located and duly recorded in the archives in Mexico." Not so. Mexican land grants were vague compared to American deeds. They read like the boundaries in a pick-up football game in a city park – "over to near the big tree, down to the rock, across the stream, and up to near the top of the hill." The California Land Law of 1851 required detail and specificity. After legislation stripped many Mexican-Americans of their voting rights and left them underrepresented in the state legislature, crafty American lawyers repeatedly used laws and court suits to cheat

landowners out of their huge ranches. For example, one Mexican family, twenty years later, owned only 200 of its original 50,000 acres. Sometimes squatters simply moved onto land and stayed, with the courts later granting them that property through the "right of occupancy." The state's 1850 Foreign Miners Tax effectively limited mining to Anglos.

The transferring of vast amounts of land was slower in Arizona and New Mexico, but just as complete; Mexicans lost 80% of their land. Most American children know the story of Zorro, the masked Hispanic rider who fights for justice in Southern California. The targets in the original Zorro, written in the early twentieth century, were Anglo politicians and lawyers who stole property from the rightful owners. In late nineteenth century New Mexico the *Gorras Blancas*, the "white caps," were vigilantes who targeted railroads and ranchers who had seized land owned by Mexican-Americans through "usual knavery and unfair treatment" by lawyers and judges. As a contemporary comment – be aware that Mexicans today do not use the term "illegal immigrants" to describe Mexicans who sneak into the United States. They say that the immigrants are not illegal; instead, the Americans illegally moved the border in 1848.

Finally, two different statements illustrate the mixed feelings many Americans have, first, over the U.S.-Mexican War and, second, over its results. In 1962 Robert Kennedy, Attorney General of the United States and brother of President John F. Kennedy, said that "Some from Texas might disagree but I think we were unjustified. I do not think we can be proud of that episode [the U.S.-Mexican War]." Earlier, in 1936, Samuel Flagg Bemis, an eminent diplomatic historian, wrote that . . . "it would be well-nigh impossible today to find a citizen of the United States who would desire to undo President Polk's diplomacy."

25

THE 1850S

The Compromise of 1850

The Congress that met in December, 1849, was deeply divided. The Democrats had a majority of 10 in the Senate, but in the House of Representatives there were 112 Democrats, 109 Whigs, and 13 Free Soilers. The Free Soil political party had developed in the early 1840s as the result of two ideas merging. The economic depression that began in 1837 reinforced the old idea that economic independence for any individual could be found by moving to western land. The new caveat was that it should be free, to provide an equal economic opportunity for all white males. The second component was the increasing Northern desire to kept slavery out of the western territories, as Congress had done with the Northwest Ordinance in 1787 and the Missouri Compromise of 1820. Thus, Free Soil carried a double meaning – free farmland for poor whites and free from competition with slaves. The election of a Speaker of the House from the majority party was not possible – no party had a majority. There were 234 members of the House, thus, 118 votes were needed to elect a Speaker. That assumes that each party was united – which was not the case. The issue of the status of slavery in the territories divided both major parties.

The most likely coalition was for the Free Soilers to join the Whigs to elect a Whig as Speaker. However, Southern Whigs opposed Robert Winthrop from Massachusetts, the previous Speaker, because the Whig caucus refused to pledge its opposition to the Wilmot Proviso. Robert Winthrop was a descendant of John Winthrop, the first governor of Massachusetts. He was a moderate, more interested in reconciling the two sections than confronting the South over slavery. Eventually, after three weeks and 63 ballots, the Democrats were able to select a speaker, Howell Cobb from Georgia, a previous Speaker. The whole episode foreshadowed the divisions that would characterize the decade.

Cobb's career reflected the events and emotions of the 1850s. He was a pro-union Southerner from a mountainous district in northern Georgia. Because of his support for the Compromise of 1850, he was kicked out of the Georgia Democratic Party. His district sent him back to Congress. President James Buchanan appointed him Secretary of the Treasury in 1857. He resigned following Abraham Lincoln's election in 1860, urging Georgia to secede. He served as the president of the Montgomery Convention that organized the Confederacy. He was even widely mentioned as a possible president of the Confederacy.

Into this tumultuous atmosphere of the late 1840s and early 1850s came several divisive issues for Congress to consider. The president from the 1848 election, Zachary Taylor, who took the oath of office on March 4, 1849, caused a crisis by ignoring the advice of Congressional leaders and advising both California, which had been quickly populated because of the gold rush, and New Mexico, to draft constitutions and apply for statehood. California did so in September, 1849. Taylor, a slaveholder, believed the people in the territories had the right to determine the status of slavery in their territory, but that Congress should have the final say upon admission to the Union.

Issues Confronting Congress in 1849-1850

1. The possible admission of California created a crisis because there was no slave state ready for admission to continue the practice of balancing the Senate, currently 15 free states and 15 slave states. California would make it 16-15. The admission of New Mexico was postponed when New Mexico applied for territorial status instead of admission as a state.

2. What was to be the status of slavery in the nation's capital, Washington, D.C.? The capital was located between two slave states, Maryland and Virginia. Northerners had to travel through slave territory to reach the nation's capital to serve in the national government. While there, they lived with constant reminders of slavery – it was all around them. There had been numerous petitions introduced in Congress over the years either to abolish slavery or to end the slave trade in the District of Columbia.

3. The boundary dispute between New Mexico and Texas needed to be settled. This issue involved more than just drawing a line on a map. Any enlargement of Texas meant the expansion of slavery. Mexico had outlawed slavery. Texas Governor Peter Bell threatened to capture Santa Fe and incorporate much of New Mexico into the state of Texas. At one point it looked as if war would break out between the U.S. government and Texas.

4. The question of whether or not to absorb the Texas debt into the federal debt needed to be addressed.

5. What was to be the status of slavery in the territories acquired from Mexico? Often overlooked in history textbooks is the simple fact that slavery was already *outlawed* in the territory acquired from Mexico, by Mexican law. The real question Congress faced was whether or not slavery would be *reintroduced* into the newly acquired territory. Many Northerners were adamant. They knew that every previous territory that permitted slavery had ended up becoming a slave state.

6. How to placate Southern anger over the growing Northern refusal to return runaway slaves?

Henry Clay worked feverishly to enact a compromise addressing all these problems. He failed. Senator Stephen Douglas of Illinois then broke the proposed compromise into five separate bills and was able to shepherd all of them through Congress by appealing to distinct and different coalitions for each bill. Together they are known as the Compromise of 1850; but it really was no compromise. Instead, sectional positions hardened.

1. California was admitted as a free state, skipping the stage of being a territory. This permanently gave the Senate to Northern control, 16-15.

2. The rest of the Mexican cession was organized under popular sovereignty, a term meaning that the local population determined the status of slavery in the territories. This would later become a source of controversy because it was never defined when the territory decided conclusively for or against slavery. Was it upon organizing a territorial government, during their status as a territory, when drafting a proposed constitution, when applying for statehood, or upon becoming a state? It was an idea that was not well thought out, but it seemed good because it sounded democratic.

3. The federal government assumed the $10 million Texas debt in return for Texas giving up her claim to a Rio Grande border all the way to its source, which would have made half of modern day New Mexico part of Texas.

4. Abolishing the slave trade, but not slavery, in the District of Columbia.

5. Enacting a more stringent fugitive slave law. Note, a more stringent law; it was not a new idea to return runaway slaves. The first fugitive slave act was passed in 1793. Many Northern Congressmen abstained, willing to accept the overall compromise, but unwilling to vote for the Fugitive Slave Act.

The debate had been bitter. Senator John Calhoun from South Carolina and Senator Jefferson Davis from Mississippi opposed the compromise, arguing that the resulting minority position for the South jeopardized the South's ability to protect its institutions.

Calhoun was dying of throat cancer during the early stages of the debate. He sat listening as Senator James Mason of Virginia delivered Calhoun's written speech on March 4. Calhoun would die on March 31. He argued that because the Constitution protected slavery, it was a national institution, not a sectional institution, meaning that one section could neither restrict it nor abolish it. In his speech Calhoun also advocated the idea of a "concurrent majority," as opposed to the democratic idea of majority rule. This would restore to the South the equal power it enjoyed when the Union began in 1789. Any law passed by Congress would need a majority of each section, North and South. In his posthumously published unfinished writings, Calhoun even advocated a dual executive, two presidents, each having a veto power, thus protecting the South as a minority. The historian Richard Hofstadter claimed that Calhoun had been the only American political thinker who came up with new, original ideas. The North did not buy any of Calhoun's ideas.

During the debates Senator William Seward of New York introduced the idea of a "higher law" that made slavery illegal, a law higher than the Constitution, understood by all to mean God's law or natural law. That comment and his later famous "irrepressible conflict" observation in 1858 would cost him a shot at being the Republican presidential candidate in 1860. While attitudes during the 1850s were hardening over the issue of slavery in the territories, almost everyone believed this contentious issue could once again be politically compromised. It always had been. Americans – Southerners and Northerners – must come together to compromise. The nation did not need prophets of division. Thus, Seward's implication that an armed conflict was inevitable was seen as precluding any attempt to find a political solution to this vexing issue.

Among the moderates during the debates was the aging Daniel Webster. In his 7th of March speech he appealed for moderation and Union. Poor health and this speech equally ended his political career in the Senate. After briefly serving as Secretary of State, he retired and died in 1852. Clay also died in 1852. Now Clay, Calhoun, and Webster were gone. By 1860 the longest serving senators had been in the Senate for only 12 years. Term limits may not be a good idea. These three political giants had battled for decades, championing the interests of their sections. However, they always compromised, and the Union endured. One of the great "What if?" questions in American history is this one. What might have happened if Clay, Calhoun, and Webster were still alive in 1861? Would they, could they, have compromised once more and avoided a bloody Civil War?

What finally made the separate bills become the Compromise of 1850 was the death of President Zachary Taylor on July 9, elevating Vice President Millard Fillmore to the presidency. Fillmore had become the vice-presidential candidate in 1848 to geographically and politically balance the Whig Party ticket. General Zachary Taylor, a military hero from the Mexican War, had been born in Virginia. His family later moved to Louisville, Kentucky, where he, in 1848, owned slaves. Millard Fillmore was from

New York and a moderate on slavery and abolition. He and Zachary Taylor met for the first time after winning the election. They clashed over everything – personalities and issues. Taylor had vowed to veto parts of the proposed compromise. Remember, it was actually five separate bills. Prior to the death of President Taylor, Fillmore, a close friend of Democratic Senator Stephen Douglas, the architect of the compromise, had stated his willingness to sign all the bills if he were president. Taylor's sudden death from a stomach ailment made Fillmore the president. For years rumors persisted that Taylor had been poisoned. His body was dug up in 1991 to check. He had not been poisoned.

Who Won, North or South?

Who won the Compromise of 1850 – the North or the South? Northerners felt the South had won, mainly because of the Fugitive Slave Act. It extensively amended the first fugitive slave law of 1793, making enforcement an exclusive federal responsibility. An accused fugitive slave was now denied a jury trial. It also denied the accused fugitive the right to testify on his or her own behalf. The act appointed special federal commissioners to issue warrants for the arrest of runaways, placing fugitive slaves under exclusive federal jurisdiction. These special federal commissioners decided if an accused runaway was actually a runaway. For each case they received $5 if they decided he or she was not a runaway, $10 if he or she was a runaway. This was based on the claim that it involved more paperwork. Just a sworn affidavit was accepted as proof of ownership of a runaway slave. Anyone pursuing a runaway slave could call for help, *posse comitatus*, the legal principle that a citizen is obligated to aid a law officer in the pursuit of his or her responsibilities. (Still true.) There was a fine for not doing so, up to $1000, and imprisonment up to six months. If the neglect of duty by any public official led to the escape of a fugitive slave, that official could be sued for the value of the slave. The Fugitive Slave Act passed the Senate 27-12 and the House 109-76, only because many Northerners stayed in the hall outside the House or Senate chambers, refusing to vote.

Fugitive Slave Act

While the majority of Northerners accepted the Fugitive Slave Act, it aroused opponents of slavery. The law enabled the capture and return of any supposedly former slave, even one who had lived in the North for decades. Because accused runaways were not permitted to testify on their own behalf, virtually any black person in the North was threatened with a return to slavery, even those who had never been slaves. About fifteen thousand frightened free blacks fled to Canada, Africa, or the West Indies. However, in the decade of the 1850s, there were only about 300 cases involving the Fugitive Slave Act, and only half of those accused were found to be runaway slaves. That is only 15 a year. Is that a lot or a little? Decide. Everyone else did in this decade. The South focused on the runaway slave, and yet, historians generally estimate that from 1830 to

1860 only about fifty thousand slaves ran away to the North or Canada, out of a slave population of almost four million. (Although some estimates are higher.) Three events focused attention on the Fugitive Slave Act.

Uncle Tom's Cabin (original subtitle, "The Man Who Was a Thing")
The first event was the publication of *Uncle Tom's Cabin*, written by Harriet Beecher Stowe, the wife of the public education reformer, Calvin Stowe, a minister. She came from a large family with a strong religious and reform background. Her father and six of her brothers were ministers. Her other six siblings were deeply involved in various reform movements. *Uncle Tom's Cabin* was originally published in an antislavery newspaper, *The National Era*, in forty installments, June 5, 1851 to April 1, 1852. When published as a book, the first 5,000 copies sold out in two days. Within a year the number was three hundred thousand, by five years, five hundred thousand, and numerous overseas editions were published, especially in England. It was adapted as a play and performed all throughout the North, adding to its popularity. In the beginning of the modern musical *The King and I*, the king of Siam proudly shows his knowledge of Western culture by treating his British visitors to his play, "The Little Cabin of Uncle Tom."

The Southern reaction was immediate and vicious. In addition to editorials, speeches, and letters, Southerners published over thirty novels depicting slavery as a benign system, such as *Aunt Phyllis's Cabin, or Southern Life As It Is*, by Mary H. Eastman. In 1854 George Fitzhugh published *Sociology for the South*, which not only defended slavery but also the philosophical assumptions of inequality upon which it was based. This strong Southern reaction led Stowe to publish a second book, *A Key to Uncle Tom's Cabin*, showing the factual basis for her fictional characters and fictional events – each one based on a real person or event. Eventually, when Abraham Lincoln later greeted Harriet Beecher Stowe at the White House, he said something to the effect, "So you are the little woman who wrote the book that made this big war." A loyal Southerner, writer Thomas Nelson Page, later said about *Uncle Tom's Cabin*, "By arousing the general sentiment of the world against slavery, the novel contributed more than any other one thing to its abolition in that generation" and "did more than any one thing that ever occurred to precipitate the war." A black abolitionist, William Nell, added to the verbal ruckus with his book, *The Colored Patriots of the American Revolution*, 1855, detailing stories of black individuals who fought for freedom. It did not sell well in the South.

Anthony Burns
The second reaction was strong opposition to the law throughout the North, as exemplified by the return to Southern captivity of Anthony Burns, a self-educated escaped slave captured in Boston in May, 1854. A mob gathered outside the jail to prevent him from being sent to a ship in the harbor. A battalion of U.S. Army artillery soldiers, four platoons of marines, the sheriff's posse, and twenty-two companies of the state militia held back the

mob and spectators. It cost the federal government $100,000 to return Anthony Burns to slavery. For that they could have purchased his freedom many times. He was returned to Virginia and sold to a new master for $905. A group of Bostonians later bought Burns and sent him to Oberlin College, where he studied theology. He became the pastor of Zion Baptist Church in St. Catherine's, Ontario, and died there in 1862.

Personal Liberty Laws

Third, many Northern states passed Personal Liberty Laws, which penalized citizens who helped federal officials enforce the Fugitive Slave Act. Thus, a person could be arrested by a state official or a federal official, one for helping, the other for not helping. Earlier, in *Prigg v. Pennsylvania*, 1842, the United States Supreme Court decided that the Fugitive Slave Act of 1793 was constitutional and the Pennsylvania Personal Liberty Law of 1826 was unconstitutional, because it interfered with the right of the master under the federal Constitution and federal statutes. The master had the right to recapture his slave in a state other than his own. Since this case made it clear that enforcement of the Fugitive Slave Act of 1793 was a federal government responsibility, many Northern states began to pass laws forbidding state and local law enforcement officials from enforcing the law or housing runaways in local jails. By 1854 nine states had personal liberty laws, which infuriated Southerners.

That year, 1854, Sherman Booth, a Wisconsin abolitionist editor, was arrested by federal authorities for violating the Fugitive Slave Act by aiding a fugitive slave. The Wisconsin Supreme Court immediately freed him from the custody of the federal marshal by issuing a writ of habeas corpus (which is the right to be brought into a courtroom to be charged, and therefore eligible for bail or for a scheduled trial – the alternative is to remain in a cell, uncharged, for an indefinite period of time). The marshal appealed the case to the U.S. Supreme Court. Chief Justice Roger B. Taney denied the right of a state court to interfere in federal cases. In a brief *obiter dictum*, which means a judge goes into commentary not necessarily needed for arriving at his decision, Taney upheld the constitutionality of the Fugitive Slave Act. The Wisconsin legislature responded by adopting resolutions defending state sovereignty, in the spirit of the Virginia and Kentucky Resolutions, the Hartford Convention, and the South Carolina ordinances of nullification. Booth was rearrested.

The Breakdown of the Second Party System

What was happening politically was a reorientation of the national political party system. The Second Party System was dying over the issue of slavery. Both parties, the Whigs and the Democrats, had Northern and Southern wings; they were both truly national political parties. In the presidential election of 1848 the Whigs avoided the issue of slavery by nominating a popular general from the Mexican War, Zachary Taylor, a Southerner, with no party platform. The Democratic candidate, Lewis Cass, ran on a platform that did not mention slavery. Taylor won. In eleven states the vote for a third party, the Free Soil Party, exceeded the victory margin of the winning party. Clearly, Free Soilers held the balance between the two parties, enticing one party to move closer to their position of anti-slavery in the territories. Remember the numbers in the House of Representatives – 112-109-13 – Democrats, Whigs, Free Soilers.

In the 1852 presidential election the Democrats nominated Franklin Pierce, a "dark horse," on the 49th ballot. Pierce, a career politician from New Hampshire, had all the credentials – service in Congress as a representative and senator, and, briefly, as a general during the Mexican War. He wholeheartedly endorsed the Compromise of 1850, gaining the support of the South and some Northern states. The Whig candidate, General Winfield Scott, won only 42 electoral votes in four states – Kentucky, Tennessee, Massachusetts, and Vermont – to 254 electoral votes for Pierce. The Whig Party was disintegrating in the South as Southerners increasingly voted Democratic. However, one Southern planter labeled the Democratic Party a party "without policy, without discipline, without leadership." It was held together nationally by adopting Southern positions on slavery. The Free Soil Party's vote was cut in half in the election of 1852. Which indicated what? Maybe, the decline of slavery as an issue? Or, maybe not. Because the Compromise of 1850 had settled all the outstanding slavery issues, none could ever come up again. There was nothing left to argue about. Unless someone monkeyed with the existing compromises, which the proposed Kansas-Nebraska Act did.

Meanwhile a new political party was gathering steam, the American or Know-Nothing Party. This party was concerned not with slavery, but with the real problem – immigrants. It advocated a 21-year waiting period before an immigrant could gain citizenship and the exclusion of Catholics and foreigners from public office. The party reached its zenith in 1854-1855 when it elected seven governors and between 75 and 100 Congressmen, but it quickly evaporated over the larger issue of slavery, which it tried to ignore. Impossible.

The Kansas–Nebraska Act

Into this turbulent political situation entered ambition. Stephen Douglas, the Democratic senator from Illinois, introduced a bill in the Senate to organize the Kansas-Nebraska Territory. It was not needed. In 1853, exclusive of government employees, there were only three white men living in the whole territory. It was hardly ready for territorial status. While territorial organization was necessary to secure legal title to land claims, no wave of farmers was poised to move into Kansas or Nebraska. Included in the bill was a provision opening up the Kansas-Nebraska territory to popular sovereignty, therefore theoretically opening it up to slavery. Douglas had long championed popular sovereignty as a concept. He tried to allay Northern fears of the expansion of slavery by asserting that slavery was associated with cotton, and cotton agriculture could never expand into the Great Plains of Kansas and Nebraska; hence popular sovereignty guaranteed these areas would be non-slave. This proposed bill altered the 36° 30' line of the Missouri Compromise. The Missouri Compromise would not be repealed; it would be ignored. In return for theoretically opening up Kansas and Nebraska to slavery, Douglas would get Southern support for a transcontinental railroad that began in Chicago. He was from Illinois. A grateful North and a grateful South would surely respond by electing Douglas president in 1856. The bill passed, 35-13 in the Senate and 113-110 in the House, after a bitter debate, with two unanticipated political consequences.

The first was that it led immediately to the rise of an anti-Kansas-Nebraska Act political party, the Republicans. Douglas misjudged the depth of Northern opposition to the expansion of slavery into the territories. Not one Northern Whig still in Congress voted for the Kansas-Nebraska Act, which eased their absorption into the new Republican Party, which stood for no further extension of slavery, period. In the 1856 election only 7 of the 40 Northern Democrats who voted for the Kansas-Nebraska Act won reelection to the House of Representatives. The national political system was realigning into two distinctly sectional political parties, whether Washington politicians realized it or not.

Bleeding Kansas
Second, the Kansas-Nebraska Act led to a contest to win Kansas as a slave state or a free state, causing a virtual civil war in Kansas. The death of 200 people further fueled the national political realignment. In spite of the threat of violence, there was a race to flood Kansas with either Northerners or Southerners. Looking at a map shows that in all likelihood most people moving into Kansas would have come from Missouri, making Kansas a slave state. In actuality, while many Southerners arrived, few slaves were brought into Kansas. The census of 1860 listed two in Kansas and five in Nebraska. Southern slave owners suspected, rightfully so, that anti-slavery proponents would encourage slaves to run away. The New England Emigrant Aid Society moved both anti-slavery Northerners and rifles, in boxes labeled Beecher's Bibles, into Kansas. Southerners sacked the town of Lawrence and abolitionist John Brown led a raid on Pottawatomie.

Meanwhile pro-slavery politicians created the Lecompton Constitution and applied for statehood as a slave state. Another proposed constitution for Kansas was also sent to Washington. Both sides claimed they represented the wishes of the people of Kansas. The majority of settlers opposed slavery; most members of the territorial legislature supported slavery. Both sides boycotted an election ostensibly giving the territorial settlers the choice of which constitution to accept. Before becoming a state Kansas wrote two more constitutions. The Lecompton Constitution, seen as an affront to the concept of popular sovereignty, deeply divided the Democratic Party in Congress. In the Senate Senator Charles Sumner of Massachusetts gave a nasty speech in which he insulted Senator Andrew Butler of South Carolina. Butler's cousin in the House, Representative Preston Brooks, brutally beat Sumner with a cane. Censured by the House of Representatives, Brooks went home to South Carolina where he was the guest of honor at many banquets and got reelected. Merchants in Charleston gave him a gold-headed cane inscribed, "Hit him again." Brooksville, Florida, is named for this Southern hero. It took Sumner three years to recover and to return to his Senate seat. Ever after Senator Sumner suffered from what was called "fits of melancholy." However, he never suffered defeat; he won reelection by huge margins.

The Rise of the Republican Party

Simultaneously, in many places in the North, anger erupted over the Kansas-Nebraska Act and events in Kansas. The Republican Party's first election was the congressional elections of 1854, when they won 46 seats in the House of Representatives. During the presidential election year of 1856, at their Philadelphia convention the new party gathered those who had no other political home — temperance advocates, Know-Nothings, Free Soilers, high tariff advocates, Northern Democrats, former Whigs (nicknamed "conscience Whigs"), and abolitionists. The party's presidential candidate was the flamboyant John Charles Frémont. Abraham Lincoln came in second in the voting for the vice-presidential nomination. The chairman of the Republican Convention Committee on Resolutions was David Wilmot. Remember him from the Wilmot Proviso during the Mexican War? In many respects Wilmot's career is an example of the transition Northerners made from the Democratic Party into the new Republican Party. David Wilmot had been elected as a Democrat in 1844 to the House of Representatives, serving a Pennsylvania district from 1845 to 1851. Then he was a Pennsylvania judge, 1851-1861. He was appointed to finish Simon Cameron's Senate term, 1861-1863, after Cameron joined Lincoln's cabinet as the Secretary of War. In June, 1862, during the Civil War, Congress enacted Wilmot's Proviso idea by passing an act forbidding slavery in the territories.

Election of 1856

The Republicans did very well in 1856, immediately rising to the status of a major party. The winning Democratic candidate, James Buchanan, a doughface from Pennsylvania, got only 45% of the popular vote, but won the South, plus New Jersey, Illinois, Indiana, and Pennsylvania. A "doughface" was a nickname for a Northerner with Southern sympathies. Republican Party leaders realized that they would win the presidency in 1860 if they held the Northern states they had won and gained Pennsylvania and either Illinois or Indiana. Thus, the search was on for a viable candidate from one of these three states, such as Abraham Lincoln, a man who had served only one term in the U.S. House of Representatives and four terms in the Illinois State House of Representatives.

Dred Scott Case

Shortly after the election, a momentous court case shocked the nation, the Dred Scott case. Dred Scott had been born in Virginia and moved with his owner, Peter Blow, to a cotton plantation in Alabama, which did not prove profitable. Blow sold the plantation and bought a hotel in St. Louis, Missouri. In 1833 Blow sold Scott to an army physician, Dr. John Emerson. The doctor, while serving in the U.S. Army between 1833 and 1842, took Scott with him to Rock Island and Fort Armstrong in Illinois, a free state, and to Fort Snelling in the free Wisconsin Territory, near modern St. Paul, Minnesota. Illinois was a free state because of the 1787 Northwest Ordinance and the Wisconsin Territory was free because of the 1820 Missouri Compromise. (The Wisconsin Territory extended farther west than the present border of Wisconsin.) At Fort Snelling Emerson bought a female slave, Harriet, who eventually became Scott's wife. The doctor later died in 1843. Scott, encouraged by the Blow family, his former owner, sued in a Missouri state court in 1846 to gain his freedom.

Dozens of similar cases had been decided in Missouri in favor of slaves who had lived on free soil. The legal precedent in Missouri was "once free, always free." In many respects this was similar to the medieval principle that a serf who ran away and was free for "a year and a day" had earned his freedom. It took two trials to resolve the case. The first trial ended because of a technicality and the second was decided in 1850 when a jury of twelve white men sided with Scott, granting him his freedom in *Scott v. Emerson*. The doctor's widow had moved to Massachusetts. While technically retaining ownership, she had given Scott to her brother-in-law, John Sanford. Determined to keep her slave, she appealed the decision. On appeal, the Missouri Supreme Court overturned three decades of state precedent and reversed the lower court decision. The national debate over the Compromise of 1850 clearly influenced their decision. Chief Justice William Scott, a cute twist of fate, said,

> "Times are not now as they were when the former decisions on this subject were made. Since then, not only individuals but States have been possessed with a dark and fell spirit in relation to slavery, whose gratification is sought in the pursuit of measures, whose inevitable consequences must be the overthrow and destruction of our government. Under such circumstances it does not behoove the State of Missouri to show the least countenance to any measure which might gratify this spirit."

The decision could not be appealed to a federal court because a decision in *Strader v. Graham*, 1851, affirmed the right of a state to apply its own laws and policies to slaves domiciled outside its jurisdiction who returned to that state. However, John Sanford was now a resident of the state of New York, and under the diversity-of-citizenship clause in Article III of the Constitution, Scott could sue Sanford in a federal court. The term "citizen" was not clearly defined legally until after the Civil War in the Fourteenth Amendment. In *The Federalist #54*, James Madison had characterized slaves as being of a "mixed character," somewhere between property and full citizenship. Why? Because some laws applied to them, such as being punishable for individual crimes, thus making them members of society. When the case, *Scott v. Sandford* (Sanford was misspelled in the legal documents), reached the U.S. Supreme Court, Scott's chief counsels were Montgomery Blair, Lincoln's future Postmaster General, and George Ticknor Curtis of Massachusetts, a brother of one of the Supreme Court justices, Benjamin Curtis.

The decision was announced on March 6, 1857, two days after James Buchanan took the oath of office as president. Supreme Court decisions are usually written by one justice. Not the Dred Scott decision. Nine justices wrote different opinions, although on the two major issues there were clear majorities. The crux of the case was that it ended in a vote of 7-2 against Scott. Seven Democrats, five Southern Democrats plus two Northern Democrats, voted against Scott and two Northerners, Benjamin Curtis, a Whig, and John McLean, a Republican, supported Scott.

The composition of the Supreme Court for the Dred Scott Case shows that even though five Supreme Court judges were from the South, the Court was hardly a bastion of hard-core slave owners.

The two justices who voted to grant Scott his freedom:
John McLean, Ohio, 1830-1861, appointed by Andrew Jackson
Benjamin R. Curtis, Massachusetts, 1851-1857, appointed by Millard
Fillmore

The seven justices who voted to deny Scott his freedom:
James M. Wayne, Georgia, 1835-1867, appointed by Andrew Jackson,
once owned 30-40 slaves, in 1856 owned 9 slaves
John Catron, Tennessee, 1837-1865, appointed by Martin Van Buren,
owned several slaves, letting them live as if free, in violation of
Tennessee state law
Peter V. Daniel, Virginia, 1842-1860, appointed by Martin Van Buren,
had only 4 or 5 house servants
Samuel Nelson, New York, 1845-1872, appointed by John Tyler
Robert C. Grier, Pennsylvania, 1846-1870, appointed by James Polk, he
was a close friend of James Buchanan
John Archibald Campbell, Alabama, 1853-1861, appointed by Franklin
Pierce, had emancipated his slaves

> Chief Justice Roger B. Taney, Maryland, 1836-1864, appointed by
> Andrew Jackson, had emancipated his slaves, and, as a defense at-
> torney, once stated that "slavery was a blot on our national char-
> acter." However, reflecting the ambiguities many whites felt, he
> called blacks "people of an inferior race" who were "unfit to asso-
> ciate with the white race." Ironically, he died the same day in 1864
> that his home state of Maryland abolished slavery.

Chief Justice Roger B. Taney (pronounced Tawney) rejected Scott's citizenship claim. Racism clearly influenced his decision. Taney said that blacks were "so far inferior, that they had no rights which the white man was bound to respect." Scott was property, not a citizen; therefore, he could not sue. Neither slaves nor free blacks were citizens of the United States, although they could be citizens of a state. He made this statement in spite of the fact that the definition of citizenship was fuzzy and still evolving as a legal principle. The original Constitution did not define American citizenship. As a resident of Missouri, the laws of Illinois did not have any effect on him. This statement raised a question. Did this perhaps guarantee the right of a slave owner to take his "property" anywhere, including into the North? Were Northern antislavery laws now meaningless? The Missouri Compromise line of 36° 30' did not emancipate Scott because Congress had no right to deprive any citizen of his property without "due process of law," as guaranteed by the Fifth Amendment. Therefore, the Missouri Compromise was unconstitutional and void, and the concept of popular sovereignty, the right of the residents of a territory to decide the status of slavery in their territory, was also void. In essence, the Chief Justice said that the national Constitution protected slavery; it was not just a sectional or state institution. This decision marked the second time the Supreme Court declared an act of Congress unconstitutional, the Missouri Compromise of 1820. However, the Kansas-Nebraska Act had already obliterated the Missouri Compromise. Nevertheless, declaring the Missouri Compromise unconstitutional provoked an incredible outcry throughout the North. Why?

Taney's reasoning contradicted 65 years of Congressional actions. For example, the Northwest Ordinance, 1787, which outlawed slavery in the Northwest Territory during the Articles of Confederation, was reenacted almost immediately after the new government began in the first Congress. It was passed even before Congress got around to creating the Treasury Department or setting up the federal court system. That Congress was filled with men who knew, after months of debating, what was in the Constitution and what it intended. Obviously, it was a high priority. As additional examples, Congress ended the slave trade, passed the Missouri Compromise, and, often overlooked in history books, enacted the 1836 Wisconsin Enabling Act, which specifically prohibited slavery in Wisconsin, Iowa, and Minnesota. The assertion that Congress could make no law restricting slavery in any of the territories scared those opposed to the extension of slavery. Up to this point in American history, every territory that PERMITTED slavery BECAME a slave state. Thus, to permit slavery in all the territories, which seemed to be the consequence of the Dred Scot decision, in effect made ALL the territories future slave states, at least in the fears of many Northerners. See *James Buchanan and the Coming of the Civil War*, ed. by John W. Quist and Michael J. Birkner.

Dred Scott remained a slave; John Sanford won. However, at the time of the decision John Sanford, the winner, was in an insane asylum. Dred Scott, the loser, was soon purchased by his former owner's family, the Blow family, who had become abolitionists. They set Scott free. He died sixteen months later of tuberculosis.

As a lawyer, one would have expected Abraham Lincoln to support the Dred Scott decision. However, Lincoln made important distinctions. He asserted that a Supreme Court's decision was up in the air until "fully settled." Lincoln cited several criteria: the Court's lack of unanimity, the decision's disdain for precedence, the inaccuracy of the facts in the Court's opinion, and the obvious partisan political bias. (William Lee Miller, *Lincoln's Virtues: An Ethical Biography*, New York, Alfred A. Knopf, 2002, p. 369.)

Lincoln–Douglas Debates

In 1858 the Dred Scott case played an important role in the Illinois election for a U.S. senator. Stephen Douglas, a Democrat, ran for reelection; Lincoln, a Republican, opposed him. Remember, up until the Seventeenth Amendment in 1913, state legislatures elected senators, not the voters. Remember also the results of the presidential election of 1856 – the crucial states were Pennsylvania, Indiana, and Illinois, with their electoral votes, 27, 13, and 11. The Republicans needed 35 from these three states. James Buchanan had gotten 174 electoral votes, John C. Frémont 114. Pennsylvania, plus Illinois or Indiana brought victory for the Republicans, 174-27=147, 114+27=141. Adding Illinois's 11 or Indiana's 13 to 141, while subtracting 11 or 13 from 147, would result in a Republican victory. The real issue in the race for senator in 1858 was not the Illinois seat in the Senate; it was the nomination by their respective party in 1860. Lincoln's supporters running for the state legislature actually won a majority of the state's popular votes. However, it did not matter. The Illinois state legislature was already gerrymandered to benefit a Democratic candidate.

The two candidates agreed to seven debates all over Illinois over a four-month period. They were long debates, not those modern, contrived presidential things we get these days as short sound bites. By 1858 the North was becoming more anti-slavery, but it was far from pro-black, and even further from supporting abolition. The main issue was slavery in the territories. A secondary issue was the status of blacks in American society. Lincoln argued for establishing a floor below which free blacks would not sink, granting them minimum rights, while doing nothing against slavery where it existed. He was certain that slavery was a dying institution that would be gone by 1900; he, and many others, including Daniel Webster, believed that the Founding Fathers had purposefully placed slavery on a path toward eventual extinction.

As everyone knew who had studied the history of slavery in ancient times, in no society had the number of slaves increased by natural reproduction after capturing new slaves ended. Therefore, reasoned Lincoln, the Founding Fathers believed that the South's slave population would decrease in the future and ultimately evaporate, that it was on the path "of ultimate peaceful extinction." However, for the first time in the history of any slave system anywhere, the reverse happened. The South's slave population grew from natural reproduction. The confidence that Lincoln and others had that slavery had been placed on the road to extinction was badly shaken by events in the 1850s. The Compromise of 1850, the Kansas-Nebraska Act, and the Dred Scott decision led Lincoln to believe, as he argued in the debates with Douglas in 1858, that "a tendency, if not a conspiracy" was underway to expand the institution and to "make slavery perpetual and universal in this nation." Strong language; he believed it. Southern influence over national policy was growing.

Contrary to the dominant judicial and political thinking in America today, the idea that the Supreme Court possessed the ultimate *power* and *right* to decide the constitutionality of laws was not set in concrete. Remember, 54 years separated the second assertion of judicial review in the Dred Scot case from the first, *Marbury v. Madison*. Lincoln spoke out in opposition to the Court's assertion of power. "If the policy of the government upon vital questions affecting the whole people is to be irrevocably fixed by decisions of the Supreme Court, the instant they are made in ordinary litigation between parties in personal actions, the people will cease to be their own rulers, having to that extent practically resigned their government into the hands of that eminent tribunal." Either the people rule or the Supreme Court does; it cannot be both. In truth, it is usually the minority judges in Supreme Court decisions who assert that the Court should not possess such power. Think of several court decisions that went against your preferences – perhaps *Roe v. Wade* or *Citizens United v. Federal Election Commission*.

Newspapers all over the country reprinted the Lincoln-Douglas debates. For Stephen Douglas slavery was **AN** issue, "a question which the people of each State must decide for themselves," but for Abraham Lincoln slavery was **THE** issue. At Freeport, Illinois, Lincoln hit Douglas with an unanswerable question. Did he support the Dred Scott decision, which pleased Southerners, and popular sovereignty in the territories, a term Douglas helped invent and around which he based his appeal in the North? Douglas needed Southern support at the Democratic Party convention to win the nomination, because the Democrats had adopted a convention rule that the winning candidate must win two-thirds of the delegates. He also needed Northern support to win the election. Either way Douglas risked alienating half his potential support. Someone once said that such a question is like asking someone, "Have you stopped beating your wife?" Yes, meaning you used to, or, no, meaning you still do. A carefully crafted question leaves an impression and no wiggle room. Douglas was well aware that the first thing he had to do was win reelection as a senator from Illinois, then mend fences in the South. His answer, known as the Freeport Doctrine, said that as a practical matter the territorial legislature could effectively negate the Dred Scott decision through its police powers. The territorial legislature could fail to enact supporting legislation to maintain slavery in that territory. "Slavery cannot exist a day or an hour anywhere unless it is supported by local police regulations." (Suppose, for example, that a territory required slave catchers to obtain a license, which cost $2,500. The territorial government is not saying you cannot capture runaways; but, as a practical matter, it is not worth it.) His answer enraged Southerners. It won him reelection to the Senate in 1858, but cost him the presidency in 1860.

John Brown's Raid on Harpers Ferry

Tensions between the sections boiled over when an abolitionist, John Brown, led a raid on the federal arsenal at Harpers Ferry, Virginia, on October 16, 1859. Harpers Ferry is now part of West Virginia, created as a state during the Civil War. Historians disagree about what Brown intended to accomplish by his attack. Brown once stood up at an abolitionist meeting and chastised everyone, "All you people do is talk, talk, talk." He took action. To accomplish what? He talked vaguely about creating an abolitionist republic in the mountains as a haven for slaves to run to. There were 300 blacks living in Harpers Ferry – half of them free, half slave, and approximately 18,000 slaves in the surrounding area. After the Civil War ended former slaves in the area were asked why they did not join Brown. Many replied that they were there, in the hills watching to see what happened. Most normal people never join a movement until they are sure there is a chance of success. Was Brown normal? That has been debated ever since. The leader of the federal troops that captured him was Colonel Robert E. Lee. Lee believed slavery was regrettable, but that it was sanctioned by God and would only end when God ordained it. This was a public statement; his private letters indicate that he condoned slavery and regarded blacks as racially inferior. Governor Henry A. Wise ordered Brown put on trial for treason against Virginia; he was found guilty and hanged on December 2, 1859. He became a martyr to Northerners. Among those present to watch the hanging was John Wilkes Booth, who would assassinate Lincoln in 1865.

Election of 1860

The Democratic Party convention met in Charleston, South Carolina, and ended without nominating a candidate. It then split into two follow-up conventions, one in Richmond, Virginia, and one in Baltimore, Maryland. Each nominated a different Democrat. The last remaining national political party was splitting up. The Republican Party platform called for high tariffs, a federal central banking system, admitting Kansas as a free state, free farm homesteads carved out of Western public land, a transcontinental railroad, and no interference with slavery where it existed. Stephen Douglas, the candidate of the Baltimore Democrats, campaigned hard, everywhere. In October, as he realized what might happen, Douglas campaigned only in the South, hoping to stop disunion.

Lincoln won with less than 40% of the national popular vote; but he carried the entire North, getting 54% of the Northern vote, winning the crucial states of Pennsylvania, Indiana, and Illinois. He won 23% of the vote in Delaware and 10% in Missouri, both slave states. He was not on the ballot in ten states below Virginia, Kentucky, and Missouri. States controlled voting and Southerners refused to put a man they viewed as a crazy abolitionist on their ballot. Not all states held their elections in November. Maine and Vermont voted in September, with no surprises. Pennsylvania, Indiana, and Ohio voted in October, forecasting a national Lincoln victory in November. Lincoln got 1,800,000 votes. Of these only 26,000 came from slave states. In essence, 1,250,000 Southerners voted for someone other than Lincoln.

Southerners saw the election of 1860 as the triumph of a new pro-Northern government. In many respects the South had controlled the federal government from 1789 to 1861. In those 72 years slaveholders held the presidency for 50 years. Of the 36 Supreme Court justices, 20 had been from the South. Congress was similar – 23 of 36 Speakers of the House of Representatives and 24 of 36 presidents pro tempore of the Senate were Southerners.

Before 1856 no major party had ever expressed clear opposition to any aspect of slavery. The first party that did, the Republicans, won in 1860. The North won control of the House of Representatives by 1820, the Senate in 1850, and the presidency in 1860. The Supreme Court would quickly follow. Southerners felt as if they had been permanently pushed out of national power and influence. This election ended the bisectional Second Party political system. Andrew Jackson, Martin Van Buren, William Henry Harrison, James K. Polk, Zachery Taylor, and Franklin Pierce all won with bisectional majorities, winning a majority of the free states and a majority of the slave states.

In 1860 there were, in essence, two elections. One took place in the North between Lincoln and Douglas. Lincoln won 17 free states and no slave states. Douglas won Missouri with 35% and its 9 electoral votes plus 3 from New Jersey. In the South John C. Breckinridge, who had been James Buchanan's vice president, was the nominee of the Southern Democrats. His primary opponent in the South was the moderate candidate of the Constitutional Union Party, John Bell of Tennessee, who won only Virginia, Kentucky, and Tennessee. Breckinridge won 11 slave states and no free states. Since neither Lincoln's supporters nor Lincoln campaigned in the South, the South never had an opportunity to see Lincoln as a human being. He became an image, a pariah, a black Republican. It is hard to demonize someone you know, but, in truth, the South would not have listened to Lincoln. It was good Douglas did not win. He died of typhoid fever on June 3, 1861, long before he would have completed his first year.

Between the election in November, 1860, and the inauguration on March 4, 1861, the Deep South embraced secession. A faint-hearted attempt to stop it failed, the Crittenden Compromise, which included numerous constitutional amendments to essentially freeze the status of slavery and all laws in regard to it, and to permanently extend the 36° 30' line to include all the territories. Congress did pass a constitutional amendment that was sent to the states for ratification. It would have prohibited the federal government from *ever* interfering with slavery in the slave states. Forty percent of the Republicans in both houses of Congress voted for it. Ohio and Maryland actually ratified it. However, war broke out before any other states could ratify. Lincoln supported the permanent constitutional protection of slavery, but only where it existed. Southerners feared, realistically, that the president's power to appoint judges, postmasters, military officers, and other officials would surely bring antislavery advocates into positions of power. As James Buchanan handed over the reins of power to Abraham Lincoln on March 4, 1861, Buchanan said to Lincoln, "If you are as happy, my dear sir, on entering this house as I am in leaving it and returning home, you are the happiest man in this country." When the South fired on Fort Sumter in April, the tension evaporated and war fever swept the entire nation. Senator John Sherman of Ohio captured the emotions when he wrote home that the "Civil War is actually upon us, and strange to say, it brings a feeling of relief: the suspense is over." As the historian Arthur Schlesinger, Jr., once said, "All wars are popular for the first thirty days."

Politicians in the 1850s took positions on slavery that led to consequences they did not visualize. This is the eternal problem of ends and means in a democracy. How something is done may be more important than what is accomplished. When the issue is more important than the procedure, the democratic system can fall on its face. In our political system political parties play a role by reconciling diverse interests within the party. The party debates its position or platform and compromises divergent views. Then the two major parties present their views on issues in Congress, where they are forced to compromise. In the end what is passed and enacted into law has been compromised at least twice, and often more than that. But how does one compromise on a moral issue? Our system does not handle moral conflict very well; one cannot compromise moral positions. As a modern example: Is only some outlawing of abortion acceptable to those who oppose it? In only a few states? Yet, America did face the moral issue of slavery, the major cause of the Civil War. We did resolve it, and we did stay together as a nation. The vision and strength of one man, Abraham Lincoln, overcame our greatest weakness as a political system.

But, It Was States' Rights

What about the Southern claim, often heard, then and much more now, that it was not a conflict over slavery, but over constitutional principles, states' rights? Otherwise, why would the South have enacted the Negro Soldier Bill, which provided for one hundred thousand slaves enlisting in the Confederate Army. But, be careful, this law was passed in March, 1865. The war ended in April, 1865. Too late. It was a desperate measure by a sinking cause. Not one black slave actually served in the Confederate Army under the Negro Soldier Bill. In contrast, here is the opening paragraph for Mississippi's statement justifying secession, January 9, 1861. Clearly their action was primarily based on protecting slavery. Note their emphasis on "King Cotton."

"A Declaration of the Immediate Causes which Induce and Justify the Secession of the State of Mississippi from the Federal Union."

> "In the momentous step which our state has taken of dissolving its connection with the government of which we so long formed a part, it is but just that we should declare the prominent reasons which have induced our course. Our position is thoroughly identified with the institution of slavery – the greatest material interest of the world. Its labor supplies the product which constitutes by far the largest and most important portions of commerce of the earth. These products are peculiar to the climate verging on the tropical regions, and by an imperious law of nature, none but the black race can bear exposure to the tropical sun. These products have become necessities of the world, and a blow at slavery is a blow at commerce and civilization. That blow has been long aimed at the institution, and was at the point of reaching its consummation. There was no choice left to us but submission to the mandates of abolition, or a dissolution of the Union, whose principles had been subverted to work out our ruin."

Here is a paragraph from the Texas declaration, February 1, 1861.

> "In all the non-slave holding States, in violation of that good faith and comity which should exist between entirely distinct nations, the people have formed themselves into a great sectional party, now strong enough in numbers to control the affairs of each of those States, based upon an unnatural feeling of hostility to these Southern States and their beneficent and patriarchal system of African slavery, proclaiming the debasing doctrine of equality of all men, irrespective of race or color – a doctrine at war with nature, in opposition to the experience of mankind, and in violation of the plainest revelations of Divine Law. They demand the abolition of negro slavery throughout the confederacy, the recognition of political equality between the white and negro races, and avow their determination to press on their crusade against us, so long as a negro slave remains in these States."

The columns in the chart below give the percentage of slaves in a state's population and the percentage of white families owning slaves. High percentages foreshadowed when and if a state seceded – before February 1st, reflecting a concern over Lincoln's election, after the fighting began with the firing on Fort Sumter in April, or, not at all. Clearly, the percentage of a state's slave population dictated that state's decision to secede or not.

Slavery and Secession, 1861

	Percentage of Slaves In the State's Population	Percentage of White Families Owning Slaves
First Round of Secession - Seceded by February 1st		
South Carolina	57%	47%
Mississippi	55%	49%
Georgia	48%	38%
Louisiana	47%	29%
Alabama	45%	35%
Florida	44%	35%
Texas	30%	29%
Second Round of Secession – Seceded After Fort Sumter, April, 1861		
North Carolina	33%	29%
Virginia	31%	27%
Arkansas	28%	20%
Tennessee	25%	25%
Slave States That Did Not Secede		
Kentucky	20%	24%
Maryland	13%	15%
Missouri	10%	13%
Delaware	2%	3%

Look at any one of the many statements made by Southern leaders, such as this one by Alexander Stephens, the vice president of the Confederacy, in February, 1861.

> "Our [Confederate] government is founded upon . . . the great truth that the negro is not equal to the white man; that slavery, subordination to the superior race is his natural and normal condition."

Not until after the war ended, in books written to defend their "high" cause, did the Southern leaders push states' rights and constitutional principles to the forefront as the main cause of the war. Here again is Alexander Stephens, writing in 1868.

> "The contest, so commenced, which ended in the War, was, indeed, a contest between opposing principles; but not such as bore upon the policy or impolicy of African Subordination. They were principles deeply underlying all considerations of that sort. They involved the very nature and organic Structure of the Government itself. The conflict, on this question of Slavery, in the Federal Councils, from the beginning, was not a contest between the advocates or opponents of that peculiar institution, but a contest, . . . between the supporters of a strictly Federative Government, on the one side, and a thoroughly National one, on the other."

As a student of history, always differentiate between statements made at the time by participants and later observations. Statements by Southern leaders in 1860-1861 did NOT justify secession as a political or constitutional argument over the tariff or over states' rights. That appeared after the war. Which deserves more weight? The original statements. As historian Allan Nevins wrote in 1947, "It was a war over slavery *and* the future position of the Negro race in North America."

26

THE CIVIL WAR

The last widow of a Union Civil War veteran died January 17, 2003, Gertrude Janeway, 93 years old. This explains why pensions for veterans eventually cost more than the war itself. By 1893 pensions took 40% of the federal budget. Veterans are a politically powerful group that Congressional representatives and senators have difficultly opposing.

Military Reasons Why the North Won the Civil War

First, a look at the war itself as a military event. Then a look at the social, economic, and political issues that accompanied it. At the start of the war the United States Army numbered only 16,000 soldiers, spread around the country at 200 army posts from Maine to California.

Northern War Aims

The initial Northern war aims were to:

1. Blockade the Southern coastline, the "Anaconda Plan" of strangling the South.
2. Split the Confederacy in half along the Mississippi River.
3. Split the Confederacy in half again by marching through Georgia to the sea.
4. Capture the Confederate capital, Richmond.

The Union's Anaconda Plan proved to be easier to announce than to establish, but it became effective in the long run. The east coast of the United States has hundreds of harbors and small coves where ships can slip in and out. Today this is a numbing factor in trying to stop the illegal drug trade. The Confederate coastline added up to 3,500 miles. The Union Navy had only 90 ships, with just 3 immediately available for blockading.

But, by the end of the war over 600 patrolling ships cut access to Confederate ports to about one-third of the prewar traffic. The celebrated 1862 attempt to break the blockade, the battle between two ironclads – the *Monitor* and the *Merrimac*, renamed the *Virginia* by the South – ended in a draw. However, the *Virginia* was scuttled when the Union navy captured Norfolk a few weeks later, while almost 50 additional ironclads were built by the North by 1865.

The Mississippi River campaign sought to cut the Confederacy in half and end the South's ability to use three major rivers – the Mississippi, the Tennessee, and the Cumberland. General Ulysses S. Grant's advance in early 1862 captured Ft. Henry and Ft. Donelson on the Tennessee River, but he was driven back in southern Tennessee at Shiloh, also known as the Battle of Pittsburg Landing. Coming up from the south, Admiral David G. Farragut captured New Orleans.

Meanwhile the war in the east featured the Union army's attempts (?) to move (?) against General Robert E. Lee's Army of Northern Virginia. Why the question marks? After the initial battle of the war, the first Battle of Bull Run, the Union Army under Generals George B. McClellan and George G. Meade had "the slows," as Lincoln said, constantly crying for more men before they could advance. Finally, McClellan attacked in the unsuccessful Peninsular Campaign. Then Lee took the offensive and was stopped at Antietam in Maryland in September, 1862, by General McClellan, who failed to follow up by pursuing Lee's battered army. The total dead at Antietam set a record for American deaths in one battle. The east settled down to a seesaw exchange while action shifted to the west. Grant successfully secured the whole Mississippi River valley, capturing Vicksburg, Mississippi, on July 4, 1863. Several weeks previously Lee invaded the North again, where Union troops met him at an obscure little town in southern Pennsylvania – Gettysburg – soon to become world famous as the largest battle ever fought on the North American continent. The Northern victory at Gettysburg, July 1-3, and Vicksburg the next day, sealed the fate of the South. It could now not win. Would the South lose?

Lincoln answered that question by appointing the architect of the victorious Mississippi campaign, Grant, as the commander of the Union Army in Virginia. His relentless pursuit whittled down Lee's army. Grant's losses were high, but Lee had fewer resources. Meanwhile, General Sherman captured the remaining Confederate railroad centers at Chattanooga and Atlanta, and divided the Confederacy in half again by marching through Georgia to the sea. Grant's final push captured Richmond, the Confederate capital. Lee fled west. Grant followed. The end came at the small village of Appomattox Court House. In one of the great ironies of American history, Lee and Grant signed the formal surrender papers in the home of Wilmer McLean. Earlier McLean had lived near Bull Run, Virginia. His family witnessed the first battle of the Civil War. After that battle he moved his family to Appomattox for safety! Although some small skirmishes continued elsewhere, the end of the bloody Civil War took place in his house. One thinks of the first and last letters of the ancient Greek alphabet, Alpha and Omega, the beginning and the end.

Total War

The American Civil War was an unusual war, and also an unusual civil war. In 1861 the Confederacy already controlled all the land it claimed, politically and militarily. Most civil wars do not have such clear territorial separation, usually each side has pockets of supporters. It was in many ways the first modern war in history, the first war in which there would be no negotiated surrender nor compromise, only total victory. Political objectives were foremost in this war. War has been defined as only diplomacy carried on by other means. The military mind thinks in terms of victory. "There is no substitute for victory." However, victory is only a means to an end, a political end. There is life after the war. General Ulysses S. Grant understood that wars were fought for political objectives, much more clearly than any other Civil War general. The three most significant Northern generals – Ulysses S. Grant, Philip Sheridan, and William Tecumseh Sherman – understood total war as a concept; Confederate General Robert E. Lee did not. Sherman was blunt, "We are not fighting hostile armies, but a hostile people, and must make old and young, rich and poor, feel the hard hand of war." "War is cruelty and you cannot refine it." Sheridan ravaged the Shenandoah Valley, explaining, "The people must be left nothing but their eyes to weep with over the war." Despite a widely held modern popular belief, the North had better military leadership. Early in the war Confederate General Robert E. Lee excelled because he was the best commander, at the older methods of fighting.

After looking at six major wars in history in *Nothing Less than Victory*, historian John David Lewis argues that an aggressive military offense can win wars and establish lasting peace. The opposite, a defensive strategy, such as the South pursued, leads to prolonged bloodshed, indecision, and stalemate. To achieve a long-term peace the military must identify the basis of the enemy's ideological, political, and social support for the war, strike at this objective, and then demand that the enemy acknowledges defeat. War, in short, is a "clash of moral purposes." Wrestle with the question of how well this describes the military aspects of the Civil War and how well it describes what took place during the Civil War and Reconstruction.

Antoine-Henri, Baron de Jomini

In fifty-five of the sixty largest battles of the Civil War the commanding officers on both sides were West Point graduates, each trained in the same tactics and strategy. The Confederate Army had over 300 West Point graduates. This means that in confrontations the commanders on both sides were similar to two people playing chess, with both immediately recognizing his opponent's strategic approach. West Pointers learned the military tactics and strategy of Antoine-Henri, Baron de Jomini, a Swiss military tactician who fought in Napoleon's army. He, during the Napoleonic wars, wrote THE book on military strategy and tactics. His approach to war emphasized five principles. First, bring a major force to bear on the decisive areas; capture places, especially the enemy's capital and important cities. This explains the North's obsession early in the war with capturing Richmond. Napoleon captured Moscow in 1812 and the British captured Washington, D.C., during the War of 1812. However, in both cases the countries – Russia and the United States – were too stupid to know they should surrender. Apparently, they had not read THE "rule book." What it really meant was that neither capital, Moscow nor Washington, D.C., was the crucial political center in either society. Second, maneuver a mass force against the enemy's fractions, in short, out-maneuver the enemy. This was behind the "I need more men" constant cry by Northern generals early in the war. Lincoln, who had also not read the book, urged them to use what they had. Third, use a mass attack at the decisive moment in a battle, directed against the decisive area of the enemy lines. This explains the insanity of the infantry advances against well-fortified positions, such as Confederate General George E. Pickett's charge attacking the center of the Union lines at Gettysburg. Fourth, avoid unnecessary bloodshed. This seems like a contradiction of number three, but it is really behind number two. If you outnumber an opponent, victory will come quickly, and further bloodshed avoided. Finally, war is for professionals; it is something separate from politics.

These guidelines explain the North's efforts against Richmond, the Confederate capital, and against Lee's Army of Northern Virginia. Lee was by far the greatest Jominian tactician; he fought a superb defensive war. However, he was not the commander in chief of the Confederate Army until February 4, 1865. Until then he was the commander of only the Army of Northern Virginia. Thus, he was not responsible for the overall military strategy of the Confederacy, President Jefferson Davis was.

Grant

Grant, a poor student at West Point, graduated in the bottom of the class; apparently he did not absorb much during the classes on military strategy. Instead of using Baron Jomini's tactics, Grant used his own, original strategies, which included, first, attack on all fronts and coordinate the attacks by using railroads to move troops rapidly from one area to another. Second, chase armies, not points of geography. Exert continuous pressure on Lee. After the middle of 1864, Grant's army never permitted Lee to rest, not one day. When Lee fled from Richmond, Grant chased him instead of marching triumphantly into Richmond.

Third, war is total; it involves civilians. "War is hell." Depress the enemy's morale by economic and psychological warfare. When Sherman marched through Georgia, he burned everything on a path sometimes reaching sixty miles wide. He burned all the crops and barns and seized all the livestock. He burned Atlanta, a town of 10,000 people. But, Sherman was not totally heartless, he supposedly preserved Madison, Georgia, because it was "too pretty to burn." Fourth, since attrition wears down the enemy, use the mass frontal attack tactic. High battlefield losses were not a deterrent to keeping on the pressure. Grant lost 7,000 men in one-half hour at Cold Harbor. His response was, "next wave, attack." These tactics gave Grant an image in the public mind subsequently that unlike Lee, Grant did not value the lives of his soldiers. However, add up the total killed under Grant's command and under Lee's command for the entire war. Lee's losses were higher, in percentages and in absolute numbers. Grant was the superior general. Giving Lee's ability high marks was part of the "Myth of the Lost Cause," a complicated collection of stories concocted after the war by Southerners defending the Old South and their conduct during the Civil War. Fifth, Grant recognized the political realities of war; he accepted generals urged by politicians and released Republican soldiers to go home to vote in the 1864 election. Democratic soldiers could not get permission.

Losses in the Civil War were incredible; two percent of the population died. Today, two percent would be over seven million people. Grooved rifle barrels and cone-shaped bullets permitted a sharpshooter to hit his target from a quarter mile away, 440 yards. It saw the first use of land mines and shrapnel. Near the end of the war the Gatling gun arrived, an early version of the machine gun. Early in the war, at Shiloh, Tennessee, also called Pittsburg Landing, the North and South together lost over 5,400 killed and 16,500 wounded. This is more than the losses in the Revolutionary War, the War of 1812, and the Mexican War added together. On September 17, 1862, 23,000 were killed or wounded at Antietam. Only 4,300 (historians think, the records are unclear) were killed on D-Day, June 6, 1944, the invasion of Nazi-held France during the Second World War. At Gettysburg the South lost 28,000 killed, missing, and wounded, the North 23,000. A new record. Lee's wagon train of wounded leaving Gettysburg was 25 miles long. On the heels of the South's defeat at Gettysburg came the loss of Vicksburg on July 4, 1863, cutting the Confederacy in half. It would be almost one hundred years before the citizens of Vicksburg would resume celebrating Independence Day, July 4.

	North	South
Total Forces mobilized	1,556,678	1,082,119
	50% of potential men	75% of potential men
Died from wounds	110,070	94,000
Died from disease	249,458	164,000
Death rate	23%	24%
Wounded	275,175	100,000

The Confederate figures are less accurate but not overestimated. The killed, missing, and wounded totals are, for the North, 40.7%, for the South, 33.1%. Look at the total who died from disease and wounds – North, 359,528; South, 258,000. Out of the total dead for both sides, 617,000, two-thirds, 413,000, died from disease and dysentery. (Recent research using census data estimates the total deaths as closer to 750,000.) Contemporary journalist Walt Whitman described the war: "Future years will never know the seething hell and the black infernal background of countless minor scenes . . . the real war will never get in the books." In 1860 the medical department of the U.S. Army had 98 officers and a budget of $90,000. By 1865 the Union Army had 12,000 medical officers and the medical department had an appropriation of $20 million, larger than that for the entire army in 1860.

Political Reasons Why the North Won the Civil War – Too Much Democracy

The South died from too much democracy. In many ways the South was the more democratic of the two societies. Southern soldiers were more individualistic, less disciplined, and more liberty-loving. They frequently threw away blankets, provisions, and heavy backpacks. Many left after a victory, to go home. They avoided routine duties like standing guard or sentry duty. Some units elected their officers. In short, Southern soldiers were not cogs in a machine. Over half the Confederate soldiers facing General William Tecumseh Sherman's March through Georgia deserted.

The Southern government was far too libertarian. The South insisted on maintaining their democratic liberties during wartime. The Southern press constantly criticized Southern leaders. The South also preserved judicial due process and freedom from arbitrary arrest. The Confederate Congress prohibited martial law in Richmond without its explicit permission. Habeas corpus was suspended for only three brief periods in very limited areas during the war. Two Southern organizations, the Peace and Constitution Society and the Order of Heroes, operated openly; both opposed the war. Soldiers even had relatives use court ordered writs of habeas corpus to get them out of the army. Considering all the decades of complaints against the structure of the federal government created by the U.S. Constitution, the Confederate Constitution was not very different from the original. The major political change, other than explicitly approving of slavery, was that the Confederate president had a six-year term. Unlike Abraham Lincoln, Jefferson Davis lacked the tact and necessary skills to work with others. His presidency was marked by constant squabbles with the Confederate Congress, his vice president, Alexander Stephens, and many Southern governors. The six year term became a source of frustration for many Southerners very early in Jefferson Davis's presidency.

Blacks and Irish As Soldiers

In contrast, the North had two groups unaccustomed to individuality and inexperienced in democracy – blacks and Irish immigrants. (And also German immigrants, many of whom had supported liberal revolutions and movements in Germany, which had failed. They joined the Union army in large numbers.) By 1864 one out of every four or five soldiers was foreign born. By 1865, 178,895 blacks were in the army, 166 regiments, and over 10,000 in the navy. About 70,000 came from just three states – Tennessee, Kentucky, and Louisiana. Blacks were less than one percent of the North's population, but they were ten percent of the army by the end of the war. Initially paid less than white soldiers, Congress finally equalized their pay in June, 1864. Four black sailors and sixteen black soldiers won the Medal of Honor during the war. (It is not necessary to use the word "Congressional" before Medal of Honor, since all medals have to be authorized by Congress.) The North made good use of this source of manpower; sixty percent of the Union's black soldiers were former slaves. The South did not, or would not, or could not use their slaves. Yet, slaves were 40% of the South's potential manpower.

The draft left an ugly taste in the mouth of many Union soldiers. One could buy his way out of the draft. Of the 207,000 draftees, 87,000 paid the fee to avoid service, 42% of the Union's draftees. It was the major factor causing the New York City draft riots in July, 1863, shortly after the news of the bloody battle at Gettysburg. The list of those named in the first draft appeared in the newspapers, beside the long list of those killed at Gettysburg. The riots began the next day. About two-thirds of the rioters were poor Irishmen, who resented competing with blacks for low class jobs. Now they were supposed to fight and die to free more blacks? The South had a similar draft evasion policy, the "Twenty Negro Law," which exempted any white man on a plantation with twenty or more slaves. In the North and the South, many saw it as a "rich man's war, but a poor man's fight."

Lincoln and Davis Compared As Presidents

Compare Lincoln's actions in the North with Davis' in the South. Lincoln tried to arrest Clement Vallandigham, a Congressman from Ohio who openly opposed the war. He fled to Canada. Lincoln twice suspended habeas corpus throughout the North, and then told Congress, which was not in session at the time. He suspended habeas corpus seven more times during the war for limited areas. He seized as many as 38,000 people and put at least 15,000 allegedly disloyal people in jail, and suppressed 300 newspapers for varying periods. A Presbyterian minister spent 15 months in jail for commenting at a private dinner that our flag no longer represented its original "high and noble principles." Dangerous talk!

Confederate President Jefferson Davis refused to try to influence local elections or to confront obstinate state officials. The governor of North Carolina had shoes and uniforms that Lee desperately needed, which was partly the reason why he invaded the Gettysburg area, where many shoe factories were located. The North Carolina governor declared that he was saving his supplies for the defense of North Carolina.

In the North the governor of Indiana, a Republican, faced a hostile Democratic state legislature. He visited Washington and left with enough federal government money to run the state's government, $250,000, so that he did not have to call the Indiana legislature into session for two years. Illegal, unconstitutional, unfair, underhanded? All of the above! Lincoln asked Grant and Sherman to send Republican soldiers home to vote in 1864. They did.

While both presidents suffered a consistent and constant barrage of criticism throughout the war, Lincoln proved to be more politically skilled at handling his critics. No one could have foreseen this. Lincoln's lightweight political résumé consisted of four terms as a state legislator, one undistinguished term in the House of Representatives, and no public office since 1849. In contrast, Davis served one term in the House of Representatives, ten years in the Senate, and four years as the Secretary of War, the latter two positions since 1847. Lincoln's background pointed towards mediocrity; Davis's towards greatness. It turned out to be the opposite. Lincoln had a cabinet of his rivals, many of whom began the administration certain that they should have been the president. Lincoln skillfully handled them and won them over. Meanwhile, Davis recruited a mediocre cabinet, which he unskillfully irritated and alienated. His presidency led to early cries for getting rid of the six-year presidential term in the Confederate Constitution. Political parties did not exist in the Confederacy. Lincoln could blame all the unjustified sniping at his policies on the Democrats; it was politically motivated. Davis had no opposition party to blame.

Diplomatic Reasons Why the South Lost the Civil War –
Lack of Foreign Aid

The South really had no policy to use its greatest asset in foreign trade, its supply of cotton. By 1860 England was importing 2.6 million bales per year, 84% of the South's cotton exports. Southern officials tried, early in the war, to destroy 2,500,000 bales of cotton to try to create a shortage in England; but, Southerners smuggled out 1,000,000 bales through the Union naval blockade. So much for loyalty to the rebel cause. By 1862, as the Union naval blockade grew tighter, only 72,000 bales reached England. From their point of view both Great Britain and France had little to gain by becoming involved in the American Civil War. They would have enjoyed a weaker, smaller, divided United States, but they would not do anything to cause that to happen. It was not worth it.

Economic Reasons Why the South Lost the Civil War –
Economic Resources
There is an old saying among military historians that God seems to always jump on the side that has the most, the idea that economic resources are the determining factor in deciding who wins a war. If so, the North's overwhelming domination made the outcome a foregone conclusion. Look at this chart of economic statistics. Note how in so few categories the South led the North. Some figures are in ratios.

	North		South
Population	21.5 million		9 million
Free Males, 18-20	81%		19%
Combat age	4 million		1.2 million
18-60	4.4	to	1
Railroad mileage	21,700 miles		9,000 miles
Railroad equipment	96%		4%
Number of factories	110,100		20,600
Number of factory workers	1,170,000		111,000
Iron production	15	to	1
Coal production	38	to	1
Firearms production	32	to	1
Value of products	$1,620,000,000		$155,000,000
Bank deposits	$207,000,000		$47,000,000
Gold specie	$56,000,000		$27,000,000
Farm acreage	3	to	1
Corn, bushels	446 million		280 million
Wheat, bushels	132 million		31 million
Oats, bushels	150 million		20 million
Cotton, bales	4,000		5,000,000
Tobacco, pounds	229 million		199 million
Rice, pounds	50,000		187,000,000
Horses	4,200,000		1,700,000
Donkeys and Mules	300,000		800,000
Milk Cows	5,700,000		2,700,000
Beef Cattle	6,600,000		7,000,000
Sheep	16,000,000		5,000,000
Swine	16,300,000		15,500,000
Naval tonnage	25	to	1

In only four areas did the South out-produce the North – cotton, rice, donkeys and mules, and beef cattle. Not much of an economic base upon which to fight a war. Add to this list the overwhelming Northern advantage in ship tonnage, factory production, textile production, and overall wealth production. The South was a section of farmers, 80% of the South's population. The South's largest industrial center in the 1850s was Louisville, Kentucky, but it ranked as only the nation's twelfth largest industrial center. However, remember, a similar listing of economic statistics in 1775 would describe the situation between the thirteen colonies and Great Britain. Just like the thirteen colonies in 1775, the South had to fight only a defensive war; the South had to defend in order to not lose. Similar to the challenge faced by the British, the North had to conquer the South to force it to remain in the Union. Extensive Southern sacrifices could have brought victory; the South suffered, but it rarely would sacrifice.

Financing the War

If the South was committed to winning the war, it was not apparent in the way they financed the struggle. Wars cost money. Money has to be raised. There are three major ways to finance a war, or any other government program – taxes, bonds, inflation. Each has advantages and disadvantages. However, that order – taxes, bonds, inflation – is a gauge of the degree of commitment. The South financed the war with 5% taxes, 30% bonds, and 60% inflation, plus fees and licenses. The North used 21% taxes, 63% bonds, and 13% inflation, plus fees and licenses. The North was more committed to winning; by 1865 the federal budget was twenty times that of 1860. Prices rose in the South approximately 90-100 times above what they had been at the beginning of the war. By 1863 a chicken cost $15 and a barrel of flour $275. The South had a limited railway system, in many ways it was not a system but rather an unconnected collection of local railroads, incapable of being unified into a system. The Union's capture of the two most important rail centers, Chattanooga and Atlanta, ended their limited usefulness to the South. Many of the major Southern cities were located on the edge of the South – St. Louis, Baltimore, Charleston, Norfolk, New Orleans, Louisville, and Mobile. This made it easy for the North to conquer the South's economic and financial centers during the first half of the war, disrupting the South's economy. All these economic factors meant that long before the South crumbled militarily, it did economically.

Arrange the four reasons – military, political, diplomatic, economic – in any order. No matter which order they are placed in, it adds up to either a Northern victory or a Southern defeat. Now we turn to the political and social aspects of the Civil War.

Purposes of the Civil War: Preserve the Union

When the Civil War began, Abraham Lincoln's primary goal was to keep as many states in the union as possible, by not pursuing policies that would alienate the Border states, those slave states that did not secede – Delaware, Maryland, Kentucky, and Missouri. This explains his oft-repeated remark that his purpose in fighting the war was to preserve the Union.

However, as the war grew and changed, so did Lincoln grow and change as the president. At first he attempted to keep the war from degrading, as he put it, "into a violent and remorseless revolutionary struggle." Consequently, his initial war strategies were cautious and limited, but as the war ground on and on with no end in sight, Lincoln embraced one harsh measure after another to subdue the rebellion and to save popular government.

He eventually approved the confiscation of enemy property, embraced emancipation, the enlisting of black soldiers, conscription, and a scorched-earth policy of warfare, all considered radical policies at the beginning of the war. War does that; it redefines what is radical. Something unthinkable becomes acceptable. War speeds up change. As a later example, the first civilian population bombed from the air occurred during the Spanish Civil War in the middle of the 1930s. Less than ten years later two atomic bombs were dropped.

Purposes of the Civil War: End Slavery

Ending slavery became a goal after it became apparent that it was absurd to win the war and leave slavery intact, thus giving the South every reason to fight again in the future. At the beginning of the war, Lincoln adopted a hands-off policy concerning slavery in deference to the loyal slave states and to his bipartisan war effort. In a (too) much-quoted letter to an abolitionist newspaper editor, Horace Greeley, August 22, 1862, after the fighting had gone on for 16 months, Lincoln wrote, "If I could save the Union without freeing *any* slave I would do it. And if I could save it by freeing *all* the slaves, I would do it." Often overlooked by people using just these two sentences is the quote's ending. "I have here stated my purpose according to my view of *official* duty; and I intend no modification of my oft-expressed *personal* wish that all men, every-where, could be free." (Italics in Lincoln's original statement; note the distinction he makes between *official* and *personal*.) 1862 was an election year and the relatively new Republican Party feared losses in Congress in November. Also, steps had already been taken in the direction of ending slavery. Congress repealed the Fugitive Slave Act of 1850, which required the return of fugitive slaves, and passed a Confiscation Act in 1862, designed to free slaves able to reach Union lines. Months before his letter to Horace Greeley, Lincoln had already informed his cabinet of his plans for emancipation. Why did he change his public policy? There was no single reason, but the result of many pressures brought on by the war itself. Never underestimate war as an instrument of change.

The leading so-called Radical Republicans – Senators Charles Sumner from Massachusetts, Benjamin Wade from Ohio, and Zachariah Chandler from Michigan, and Representative Thaddeus Stevens from Pennsylvania – pressed Lincoln to destroy slavery as a war measure. If the rebel South returned to the Union with slavery intact, Southerners would start another war the next time they perceived a threat to their institution. In the end, the current sacrifice would mean nothing. If Lincoln really wanted to save the concept of popular government, he had to abolish slavery and smash the arrogant planter class, which these senators and Stevens believed had masterminded secession and started the war. Frederick Douglass, the black abolitionist, Senator Sumner, and members of Lincoln's cabinet raised another reason for emancipation. In 1862 volunteering was falling off sharply, and reinforcements were needed for the army. "You need the slaves." said Sumner. Eventually over 180,000 blacks served in the Union army and navy.

Meanwhile the war itself created a strange situation. As the Union Army captured territory in the South early in the war, slaves fled to the Union Army. Telegraph messages came from the generals – what should we do with them? This created a difficult legal problem, since slaves were legally property. If Lincoln was only fighting to preserve the Union, with slavery intact, what was to be done with the slaves streaming into the areas occupied by the Union troops? Initially he left the decision in the hands of the local commanders, some of whom returned the slaves to the Confederates. However, things became complicated in the absence of a clear policy. General John C. Frémont, the Republican presidential candidate in 1856, issued an order declaring martial law in Missouri and emancipating slaves who took up arms against the rebellion. Lincoln removed him. In 1862 abolitionist General David Hunter issued "General Order Number 11," which declared martial law in Georgia, South Carolina, and Florida and freed the slaves there. Lincoln quickly revoked the order.

At first Lincoln rejected the idea of a presidential move against slavery. Would it be constitutional? The reactions of the border states were also a primary concern. The southern portions of Ohio, Indiana, and Illinois were settled primarily by Southerners from Virginia and Kentucky. The Ohio River-Mississippi River economy linked these three states to the South. Nicknamed "Butternuts," due to the widespread practice of dyeing their clothes with walnut or butternut oil, the populations in these states generally opposed many Northern ideas.

However, Lincoln had good reasons to believe that many in the upper South states remained loyal to the Union. In Missouri, Kentucky, and Maryland the percentage of slaves in the population had dropped from 1830 to 1860, down 8%, 5%, and 10% respectively. Four Confederate states – Virginia, Tennessee, Arkansas, and North Carolina – had originally voted against secession. He did not want to antagonize Unionists in those states or to isolate them politically. Missouri and Kentucky, both border states, had representatives in both the Union and the Confederate Congresses.

Compensated Emancipation Fails

Lincoln attempted to persuade the border state of Delaware to accept compensated emancipation. The federal government would buy the slaves from their owners for $500 each. The average price of a slave in Delaware was only $400, because selling a slave to someone outside of the state required the approval of the state legislature. Only 3% of white families in Delaware owned slaves. Slaves were only 2% of the population. The proposal was never actually brought up for an official vote in the Delaware state legislature; those counting the votes realized that the measure would be rejected in the Delaware House of Representatives by one vote, thus the plan was shelved. In the election of 1860, 23% of Delawareans voted for Lincoln, clearly the highest vote total he achieved in any slave state. Out of Delaware's 11,000 blacks, only 1,798 were slaves. A slave in Delaware could testify in court against a white man. In short, Delaware was easily the most lenient slave state in existence. If Delaware rejected compensated emancipation, obviously, no other state would accept it. Ending slavery by compensated emancipation was impossible.

Emancipation Proclamation

How could Lincoln justify the radical step of announcing the Emancipation Proclamation by presidential proclamation? In one of his typically folksy examples, he explained his logic.

> "By general law life and limb must be protected, yet often a limb must be amputated to save a life; but a life is never wisely given to save a limb. I felt that measures, otherwise unconstitutional, might become lawful, by becoming indispensable to the preservation of the Constitution, through the preservation of the nation."

The nation is above the Constitution. Otherwise unconstitutional acts are acceptable in order to preserve the nation. The issue is *survival*. The Constitution would be meaningless if the nation dissolved.

Today we face similar questions. Is this logic of *survival* a justification of the modern practice of holding terrorists without charging them? Do you support a policy of permitting government authorities to have access to all phone conversations and emails, in order to ferret out terrorists? When do the needs of preserving the nation supersede the Constitution, or do they ever supersede the Constitution? These debates will arise again in the future.

The Emancipation Proclamation, announced after the Northern victory in the battle of Antietam in September, 1862, was officially proclaimed January 1, 1863. The Emancipation Proclamation was a powerful symbolic statement to the world that Union and Freedom, one and inseparable, were now Lincoln's war objectives. Lincoln had seized the moral high ground. As he had said earlier, "If slavery is not wrong, nothing is wrong." During the 1860 presidential election campaign Lincoln was asked what books had most influenced him – he named six: the *Bible* ("A house divided against itself cannot stand." is from Matthew 12:25), John Bunyan, *Pilgrim's Progress*, *Aesop's Fables*, Mason Weems' *Life of Washington* (Weems is usually referred to as Parson Weems), Benjamin Franklin's *Autobiography*, and James Riley's *Authentic Narrative of the Loss of the American Brig Commerce*. All these books reinforced ideas of self-reliance and hard work, justified by divine Providence, which might at any moment call upon an ordinary man to do extraordinary things. All of a man's life is preparation for that moment when Providence would call upon him. Each of these books delivered this message. Only in Riley's book did Providence call on men to end slavery, the issue that called Lincoln to action.

Too often history books present the Emancipation Proclamation primarily as a military measure designed to demoralize the South and to prevent British aid to the Confederacy. However, do not forget, there was an election coming in 1864. In addition, Lincoln had in 1860 won only 40% of the popular vote, and the Emancipation Proclamation was not popular in the North. It was easily the most explosive and unpopular act of Lincoln's presidency. He also understood that the Emancipation Proclamation changed the character of the war. It marked the transformation of a war to preserve the Union into a revolution to overthrow the old social order in the South. A Northern victory would destroy the Old South, permanently; thus, it stiffened Southern resistance. At this time Lincoln also demanded unconditional surrender as part of his terms for peace. There would be no negotiated ending of the war. The fighting would now go on to the bitter end.

As 1864 approached, these harsh war policies became the central issues in the presidential election of 1864. Lincoln thought he would be defeated, yet he refused to reverse any policy. The Democratic Party platform contained a "war failure" plank, which made peace the first priority and reunion a distant second, and which promised to leave slavery intact. Most Republican Party leaders thought the election was lost. Some even urged the president to cancel the election and seize temporary dictatorial powers. He refused. "The election is a necessity," he insisted. "We can not have a free government without elections; and if the rebellion could force us to forego, or postpone a national election, it might fairly claim to have already conquered us." Many historians and contemporaries said Lincoln won the election, 55% to George McClellan's 45%, because of dramatic Northern military victories right before the election – Sherman's capture of Atlanta and Sheridan's victories in the Shenandoah Valley. If one analyzes the popular vote within each state that Lincoln won, the election could have gone the opposite way if just about 30,000 voters switched to voting Democratic. It was closer than the numbers indicate, popular vote and electoral vote. Lincoln saw the election as a popular mandate for his policy of emancipation and reunion. It was the first national election during a civil war in the history of the world, and, to Lincoln, it proved the strength and endurance of the Union and its principles.

Purposes of the Civil War: Equal Rights for Blacks

Very few people advocated equal rights for blacks in 1860, even among abolitionists. Be careful, the issue in the 1850s was slavery in the territories, not race, not racial equality. Lincoln was always aware of what he referred to as the "race-consciousness of Northern whites who favored white supremacy." This third purpose for the war grew out of Lincoln's gradual realization that a constitutional amendment was necessary to guarantee the freedom of all slaves in America, including those in the border states of Delaware, Maryland, Kentucky, and Missouri. After West Virginia separated from Virginia, it can be included with the border states. Lincoln also worried that the Supreme Court, Congress, or a future administration could overturn the Emancipation Proclamation.

The Thirteenth Amendment

The Senate passed the Thirteenth Amendment in April, 1864, but the House of Representatives turned it down. The vote was 93-65 in favor, but short of the two-thirds needed to pass a proposed amendment. Twenty-three Representatives did not vote. Over the winter of 1864 to 1865, Lincoln put tremendous pressure on individual Representatives. Watch the movie, *Lincoln*. He used patronage, released Confederate prisoners of war related to Northern Democratic Congressmen, and granted a railroad in New Jersey a monopoly. In the words of Representative Thaddeus Stevens, "The greatest measure of the nineteenth century was passed by corruption, aided and abetted by the purest man in America." It finally passed January 31, 1865, by three votes more than the two-thirds required, 119-56. Two-thirds was 116; it squeaked through. If the decision had waited until the South rejoined the Union, it never would have passed.

The Fourteenth Amendment and the Fifteenth Amendment were reactions to the ways in which the South reacted to the Thirteenth Amendment. One purpose of section one of the Fourteenth Amendment was to establish a constitutional validity for the recently enacted 1866 Civil Rights law, passed over President Andrew Johnson's veto. An amendment would make it difficult for a future Congress to repeal. History books today focus more on the Fourteenth and Fifteenth amendments, but without the Thirteenth, the other two would never have happened. And, without Lincoln, the Thirteen Amendment would never have happened.

Was Lincoln a Racist?

In the era of the civil rights movement during the 1960s several black historians and journalists sharply criticized Lincoln, asserting that he was a racist. The leading critic was Lerone Bennett, Jr. In an article in *Ebony* magazine, "Was Abe Lincoln a White Supremacist?" he argued that events during the war forced emancipation, not Lincoln's desire to end slavery. Later Bennett wrote *Forced into Glory: Abraham Lincoln's White Dream*, published in 2000. He criticized Lincoln's frequent use of the "N" word. Lincoln was a great storyteller who loved "off-color" jokes, and what were then called "darky" stories about blacks. However, that was typical of that era. Bennett saw in Lincoln's actions and inactions a man who was the very embodiment of the American tradition of racism, as shown by Lincoln's reluctance to use black soldiers and his inaction concerning civil rights bills and black suffrage.

A more balanced view by two black historians exonerating Lincoln can be found in *Lincoln and Black Freedom*, 1981, by LaWanda Cox and Henry Lewis Gates's long introduction to his collection of all Lincoln's private and public comments on race, slavery, and emancipation, *Lincoln on Race and Slavery*, 2009. Also, see a white historian, Allen C. Guelzo, *Lincoln's Emancipation Proclamation*, 2004. He says the Emancipation Proclamation was the result of a "deeply moral commitment balanced by Lincoln's realistic assessment of what he could and could not achieve."

What Did Lincoln Believe?

Lincoln opposed granting free blacks full citizenship rights, but he did believe they had a right to life, liberty, and the fruits of their own individual labor. His position was far more liberal than that held by most Americans. Just as did many Republicans, Lincoln drew a distinction between social rights and economic and political rights. He did not support granting to blacks the right to associate with whites in public or private social interaction.

In an 1854 speech at the state capital of Illinois, Lincoln stated that Southerners themselves had admitted the essential humanity of blacks. As proof, he said that in 1820 Southerners had joined the North in declaring the international slave trade to be piracy and punishable by hanging; yet this was not true of people who caught and sold horses or hogs. So much for the argument that slaves were just property. Second, there was a universal disdain in the South for the slave trader; but not the trader in corn, cattle, or tobacco. Third, the existence of 433,643 free blacks in the United States, worth about $200 million if they were slaves, proved that SOMETHING operated on their owners to sacrifice pecuniary benefit to liberate them. Perhaps a sense of justice and human sympathy?

Lincoln made a distinction between "superiority of right" and "equality of condition." The fact that slaves and blacks were inferior in intelligence or wealth did not justify white superiority towards them; otherwise, a white man becomes inferior, and therefore also subject to being enslaved, to the first white man he encounters who is his superior in intelligence or wealth. Such thinking applies falsely to individuals, just as it applies falsely to whole groups or categories of individuals.

Perhaps the final assessment of Lincoln and racism should come from his contemporary, Frederick Douglass, the well-known black representative of that era. They both shifted their positions during the war. Lincoln moved from reluctantly defending slavery as a constitutionally protected institution to supporting its extinction. Douglass moved from criticism of Lincoln to understanding that a pragmatic white politician in mainstream politics could not cater to the abolitionist fringe, as the public called it. Lincoln was the first president to meet with a black man, Douglass, in the White House. He also welcomed Sojourner Truth into the Oval Office. After delivering his second inaugural address in 1865, Lincoln made it a point to immediately and publicly shake Douglass's hand. In addition, he publicly referred to Douglass as "my friend." Douglass came to believe that Lincoln was personally devoid of racism. Finally, it was during Lincoln's administration that the United States first established diplomatic relations with two black nations, Haiti and Liberia.

Lincoln's Position on Slavery and Blacks in American Society

When looking at Lincoln, one must differentiate between the personal and the political. Up to 1854, Lincoln believed that slavery was a dying institution that would not last to the end of the nineteenth century. It was dying a natural death, following the path the Founding Fathers had envisioned.

William Lee Miller succinctly summarized Lincoln's rationale on page 268 in *Lincoln's Virtues: An Ethical Biography*. (Grammar rules concerning quotations are skipped to emphasize that the quoted phrases and sentences are Lincoln's.)

> The earliest Congress "hedged and hemmed it in to the narrowest limits of necessity," prohibiting an outgoing slave trade in 1794; prohibiting the bringing of slaves from Africa into the Mississippi Territory in 1798, prohibiting American citizens from trading in slaves between foreign countries in 1800, restraining some state-to-state slave trade in 1803; and then in 1807, "in apparent hot haste," "nearly a year in advance," they passed the law to take effect on the first day of 1808 – "the first day the constitution would permit" – prohibiting the African slave trade. And then in 1820 "they declared the trade piracy, and annexed to it, the extreme penalty of death . . . . Thus we see that the plain unmistakable spirit of the age, towards slavery, was hostility to the PRINCIPLE, and toleration ONLY BY NECESSITY."

Then appeared the Kansas-Nebraska Act and the Dred Scott decision, which seemed to open up all the territories to slavery and to justify slave owners taking slaves into the free states, as property.

Illinois was an extremely anti-black state, one of the worst in the North. In 1853 Illinois voters put a clause into the state constitution, not well enforced, prohibiting free blacks from entering the state. The vote was 50,261 to 21,297. Did Lincoln make what we would today consider anti-black statements as a politician? Yes. However, in defense of Lincoln's seemingly racial remarks, consider the following:

1. The extreme Negrophobia in Illinois at that time.
2. He made defensive concessions to racial prejudice on all points except the crucial minimum – the black man's humanity and basic right to live his own life.
3. Lincoln was a man of his times, his place, and his role. Moreover, his role was that of a politician. As president he had to deal with Congress, which many presidents find difficult. Historian Paul Findley, in *A. Lincoln: Crucible of Congress*, credits Lincoln with learning "to temper his idealism with pragmatism, to reject unrealistic objectives and settle for steps that were within reach." (p. 261) Do not compare Lincoln's comments with those of the antislavery advocates, who were not politicians and who did not have to answer to any group of voters, anywhere.

Look at his logic in his famous "house divided speech," given in response to his nomination as the Republican candidate for the Senate at the Illinois Republican State Convention in June, 1858. Too often students of history focus on just the first half of the following quotation. Carefully read the rest of the paragraph and especially note the last sentence.

> "A house divided against itself cannot stand. I believe this government cannot endure permanently half slave and half free. I do not expect the Union to be dissolved. I do not expect the house to fall, but I do expect it will cease to be divided. It will become all one thing or all the other. Either the opponents of slavery will arrest the further spread of it, and place it where the public mind shall rest in the belief that it is in the course of ultimate extinction, – or its advocates will push it forward until it shall become alike lawful in all the States, old as well as new, North as well as South. Have we no tendency to the latter condition?"

Slavery was now growing, becoming national. The union would not remain "half slave and half free." It was on the road to becoming all slave, everywhere, North and South. He was not threatening the South. Lincoln was trying to alert the North that the South's institution of slavery was threatening the North and its free institutions.

He opposed the extension of slavery into the territories because that was a place for white free labor to thrive. It was not an anti-black position; it was an anti-slavery position. However, Lincoln was not motivated by concern for the slave; it was concern for the common white man. The West existed as a place of opportunity, and competition with slave owners was unfair to whites. Slavery was wrong primarily because it denied the laborer the fruits of his own labor and because it gave an unfair advantage to the slave owner in the competition between free white laborers and slave owners. In addition, slavery was an embarrassment to the American tradition of liberty and made us look like hypocrites to the rest of the world.

Lincoln opposed abolition, especially immediate abolition, because "it is not much in the nature of man to be driven to anything; still less to be driven about that which is exclusively his own business, and least of all, where such driving is to be submitted to, at the expense of pecuniary interest."

Yet, in a speech in Chicago in 1858, he departed from his text and said, "I have always hated slavery." His consistent public policy was composed of gradual emancipation for slaves, achieved by popular referendum, compensation for the owners, and removal of blacks from the country through colonization. Colonization was the only sensible policy because:

a. Lincoln had been heavily influenced by his political idol, Henry Clay, who advocated colonization to Liberia.
b. Obtaining civil rights equal to those of whites was impossible. Since there was no way for blacks to achieve civil rights from a white legislature, there was no way "up" for them in American society, hence, "out" was the only viable option.
c. British abolitionists also favored colonization.
d. At the end of *Uncle Tom's Cabin*, the former slave family goes back to Africa, a position supported by abolitionists who addressed the question of what happens after slavery ends. The most famous abolitionist, William Lloyd Garrison, never did address that question.
e. Full political participation was impossible to achieve. Of all the prominent pre-Civil War abolitionists, only Wendell Phillips had ever advocated giving the vote to blacks.
f. The astute French observer, Alexis de Tocqueville, had written in *Democracy in America* in 1835 that while slavery seemed to be receding, "the prejudice to which it has given birth is immovable . . . [and] appears to be stronger in the states that have abolished slavery than in those where it still exists; and nowhere is it so intolerant as in those states where servitude has never been known." Racism precluded integration.
g. Advocating colonization addressed the fears many whites harbored about a future society with whites and free blacks. How would it work?

Blacks and whites shared common universal rights as human beings, the rights found in the Declaration of Independence, although the Declaration of Independence never had the force of law. Please be aware that saying this did not win Lincoln any friends or political votes. Civil rights are different from universal rights. Civil rights are the result of legislative action. Americans today are accustomed to court-driven enforcement and spreading of civil rights. Lincoln and his generation saw this function as one exclusively controlled by legislative majorities in the states and in Congress. Those majorities would always be white. Majority rule was the fundamental basis of American governments, both state and national. White majorities would determine who got civil rights, and, they would never give them to free blacks.

Lincoln came to see the Declaration of Independence, rather than the Constitution, as the statement of what our country should be and what the Founding Fathers intended it to be. Lincoln's approach in 1858 and 1860 was to restore the original position on slavery set by the Founding fathers. Slavery was local, unnatural, and fading. Freedom was national, natural, and growing.

Lincoln's Changing Position as a Result of the War

Secession forced Lincoln to concentrate on restoring the Union. Slavery would have to wait. Over time, he shifted his thinking. It can be followed, although many of these actions were the result of Congress. It is more correct to say that in the early years of the war Lincoln acquiesced in them. He often did not lead the effort to pass Congressional laws in regard to slavery. Overall, it is unfair to select a statement by Lincoln and say this is his view of blacks or slavery or emancipation or equality. His views were constantly changing and moving forward, neither static nor moving backwards. The First Confiscation Act, August 6, 1861 – provided for the seizure of all property used for "insurrectionary purposes" and property used "in aid of the rebellion." The Second Confiscation Act, 1862 – the main provision defined the punishment for treason as death, fine, or imprisonment, and provided for the confiscation of property. Aimed at Confederate leaders, it provided for the confiscation of their slaves for those involved in "rebellion or insurrection." Think of it as primarily *against* Confederate leaders rather than *for* their slaves. Lincoln hesitated over this law. He actually wrote a veto message, thought better of it, but attached it to the bill, to become part of the record. Third, the abolition of slavery in the District of Columbia Act, 1862. Now Lincoln begins to lead – the Emancipation Proclamation – in July, 1862, he informed his cabinet; in September, he announced his intention to the public; on January 1, 1863, he proclaimed it. In terms of what it actually did, it really only restated what was in the Second Confiscation Act. But now the president joined Congress in clearly stating the Union's policy. Finally, the use of black soldiers, although Congress established pay rates below those for whites, $10 a month minus $3 for clothing for blacks versus $13 plus $3.50 for clothing for whites. In his last public speech, April 11, 1865, on the proposals for the reconstructed government for Louisiana, he advocated public education for freedmen and giving the vote to the "very intelligent" and to those who had served in the Union Army. He had come a long way from 1860.

Lincoln's Vision of America's Role in the World

To Lincoln the Constitution was the fulfillment of the Declaration of Independence, the attempt to put into practice the ideas of the Declaration of Independence. He found in the Declaration of Independence the idea that an equal start in life and an equal opportunity in life were the central ideas of the republic and the essence of the American dream, the foundation of our **American Identity**.

In his eyes the American experiment was the wave of the future for nations across the globe. It stood as a beacon of hope for the oppressed throughout the world. It must not fail. He believed the struggle against slavery was part of the larger worldwide movement from "absolutism to democracy, aristocracy to equality, backwardness to modernity." See Thomas Bender's excellent book, *A Nation Among Nations*, which places American history in a world context.

Lincoln once said to his personal secretary, John Hay, "The central idea of this struggle is the necessity that is upon us of proving that popular government is not an absurdity." In Europe the liberal revolutions of 1848 had failed; France's republic, the only one in Europe, lasted from 1848 to 1853. Monarchy and aristocracy seemed securely entrenched, neither republicanism nor democracy appeared to be the wave of the future. Not to Lincoln.

If the people govern themselves, then the minority does not have the right to break up the government whenever they choose to do so, such as losing an election. To Lincoln, the right to revolt mentioned in the Declaration of Independence had to be backed by a high moral cause. The South's cause was not moral; therefore, their claim that they were following the right to revolt in the Declaration of Independence misused that concept. The United States had to prove to the world that "those who can fairly carry an election, can also suppress a rebellion," and that popular government was a workable system, that the people could rule themselves through majority rule.

Slavery as the Antithesis of America

Lincoln detested slavery for two reasons. First, it deprived our republican example of its influence in the world. It enabled the enemies of free institutions, with plausibility, to taunt us as hypocrites. It caused the real friends of freedom to doubt our sincerity. In the New World only Brazil, Dutch Guiana, Cuba, and Puerto Rico still practiced slavery. Between 1833 and 1869 all the European powers abolished slavery in their colonies and ended serfdom at home, Russia being the last.

He also detested slavery because it denied black people the right to elevate themselves. There was much discrimination and segregation in the North during the Civil War itself. Lincoln saw equal opportunity as the key to America. "I want every man to have a chance and I believe a black man is entitled to it – in which he can better his condition – when he may look forward and hope to be a hired laborer this year and the next, work for himself afterward, and finally to hire men to work for him! That is the true system." He wished "to afford all, an unfettered start, and a fair chance, in the race of life." Lincoln was translating the abstract promises of political equality found in the Declaration of Independence into a real, every day, opportunity for economic improvement. The opportunity to improve one's self now became *the right* to be able to improve yourself. A central idea in Lincoln's mind was that both – popular government and the right to rise – could not survive if our society denied *some* the right to elevate themselves. In his mind, this idea is what made America "the last best hope of earth."

The Triumph of Nationalism: Economic Nationalism

During the Civil War the ideology and institutions of free-labor entrepreneurial capitalism replaced the institutions and outlook that characterized American society in 1861. The industrial North was now guaranteed that the government would be permanently friendly to business enterprise. The laws Congress put into effect reflected a desire for order over the divided, quarrelsome society of the 1850s. Opposition to these measures ended when 56 Congressmen and 21 Senators went home to the South in 1861. Now the industrially-oriented North had the opportunity to pass laws favorable to industrial development.

1. **National Banking system** – Before the Civil War more than fifteen hundred unregulated state and local banks printed thousands of different kinds of currency. Now the country had a central banking system.
2. **High tariff** – Since the 1833 tariff the trend of tariff rates had been downward; now it went up, to the pleasure of Northern industrialists.
3. **Morrill Land Grant College Act** – Professor Jonathan B. Turner of Illinois College began arguing early in the 1840s for a university in each state, nicknamed the "Turner Plan." The Morrill Land Grant College Act achieved this by allocating 30,000 aces for each senator and representative for their states to establish colleges, with the funds raised from the sale of the federal land. This legislation led to sixty-nine colleges, including those ending in A&I, A&T, and A&M, which stands for Agricultural and Industrial, Agricultural and Technical, and Agricultural and Mechanical. The Hatch Act in 1887 established agricultural experimental stations at land-grant colleges to give farmers scientifically based advice.
4. **Homestead Act** – Passed May 20, 1862, the Homestead Act opened up 250 million acres of land to individuals willing to live on it and to make improvements to it. The paper work and fees made the total cost only $18. It finally ended when Ken Deardorff filed the last claim in 1979 in Alaska. A previous 1842 homesteading law had applied to just Florida. All opposition to it in the

1850s had come from the South. In a vote in the House of Representatives before the Civil War on the proposed Homestead Act, the South provided 64 of the 65 votes opposed to it. The Northerners voted 114 for, 1 opposed. It failed in the Senate due to Southern opposition. The first claim was made by Daniel Freeman in Brownville, Nebraska. By 1890, 957,902 people had filed claims for homestead land, and even more filed after 1890.

5. **Transcontinental Railroad** – It ended disputes in Congress over which section would gain the eastern terminus, a Northern city or a Southern city. Both the North and the South believed, correctly as it turned out, that wealth would flow to the eastern terminus of the transcontinental railroad. Would it be New Orleans, St. Louis, or Chicago? Chicago clearly gained the most.

The Triumph of Nationalism: Political Nationalism

Now the states would be permanently put into a subordinate position, our political institutions would now be more nationally-based than state or sectionally-based. In the process of preserving the Union, the Civil War transformed it. Before 1860 the phrase *United States* was sometimes a plural noun, especially in the South; "these United States were." Ever since 1865 the *United States* has always been a singular noun. "The United States is." The North went to war to preserve the *Union*; it ended up creating a *Nation*. The United States was not the only country experiencing this transformation. Nation-building created modern Japan in 1867, Canada in 1867, Italy in 1871, and Germany in 1871. In all these countries, including the United States, the industrial areas or interests emerged from their internal political struggles to play a more powerful role in molding and shaping governmental policies to favor industrialization. Often overlooked in the Civil War statistics is the number of white Southerners who joined the Union Army, estimated by historian Richard Current in *Lincoln's Loyalists: Union Soldiers from the Confederacy* to be over 100,000. National loyalty trumped loyalty to their state or section. Many white Southerners did not make the same decision Robert E. Lee did.

From Union to Nation

Lincoln's major speeches during the war trace the transformation from a Union to a Nation. Lincoln's first inaugural address contained the word Union twenty times and the word Nation not once. In Lincoln's first message to Congress on July 4, 1861, he used Union forty-nine times and Nation only three times. In the Gettysburg Address in November, 1863, he did not refer to the Union at all, but used the word Nation five times. In his second inaugural address in 1865, looking back over the past four years, Lincoln spoke of one side seeking to dissolve the Union in 1861 and the other side accepting the challenge of war to preserve the Nation. In a Memorial Day address in 1915 at Arlington Cemetery, President Woodrow Wilson stated that the Civil War "created in this country what had never existed before – a national consciousness." (See Garry Wills' brilliant analysis of the Gettysburg Address, *Lincoln At Gettysburg: The Words That Remade America.*)

This transformation is also apparent in the Constitutional amendments. Eleven of the first twelve amendments to the Constitution limited the powers of the national government. Six of the next seven, starting with the Thirteenth Amendment in 1865, radically expanded the powers of the national government at the expense of the states.

Two final comments on Lincoln: first, he was such a symbol of the Union that his funeral train took twenty days to get his body to his burial site in Springfield, Illinois. Seven million Americans came out to reverently watch the train pass. In addition, in his Second Inaugural Address, delivered a little over a month before his assassination, Lincoln spoke of Southerners as "adversaries," not as "enemies." The long Civil War, the endless casualties, and the never-ending difficulties had not, after four years, transformed Lincoln into a vindictive, bitter man. Incredible!

27

THE MEANING OF RECONSTRUCTION, 1865-1877

Films About the Civil War and Reconstruction

Carl Becker, a famous American historian, once said: "Every man has some knowledge of past events, more or less accurate . . . . (History) as we commonly think of it . . . is only an extension of memory . . . . The kind of history that has the most influence . . . is the history that common men (and women) carry around in their heads."

However, that version of history may not be accurate. What the public most readily accepts is what the public already believes. Also, historians are products of their times. The prevailing ideas of their time, what the Germans call Zeitgeist (literally "time ghost" or "time spirit"), color their conclusions. Napoleon once quipped, "History is a lie agreed upon." Not really, but when historians write the historical context of the times influences their perspective, their emphasis, their point of view, and what is written. In addition, one should always ask three questions of anything a historian writes. To what audience is this directed? What is the historian's purpose? What was the context, the ideas floating in the air during that period?

Think of some major films produced about blacks, the Civil War, and Reconstruction. Begin with *"Birth of a Nation"* in 1915, the story of how the Ku Klux Klan saved the South from black rule and oppression. It was the first full-length feature film, a major box office hit. President Woodrow Wilson said, after he watched it in the White House, "It is like writing history with lightning, and my only regret is that it is all so true." If a president with a PhD in political science misread Reconstruction history, then certainly the public easily could. *"Gone With the Wind"* in 1939 was the story of the South enduring the Civil War and Reconstruction and successfully recreating much of the glorious antebellum South. *"Glory"* in 1989 was the story of the 54th Massachusetts Regiment, the all-black unit that fought bravely in an assault on Fort Wagner, near Charleston, South

Carolina, proving that black soldiers would and could fight, and do it well. Eventually over 180,000 blacks served in the Union Army.

None of these films could have been made in the other two years – 1915, 1939, 1989. The public would never have accepted them. It would have violated that generation's image of the history of the Civil War and Reconstruction. Forget the question of how accurately that image resembled what really happened. Over six hundred blacks served in Southern state legislatures during Reconstruction, but they were a majority for just a brief time in only one state, South Carolina. Characterizing Reconstruction as an oppressive period of black rule is a stretch. The glorious antebellum South existed for very few wealthy people, and after the Civil War, it existed more in memory and myth than it ever did in reality.

Historians' Views of Reconstruction

Reconstruction is often confusing to students. This period in American history can be organized around different themes. One theme of Reconstruction is the North versus the South, or, the Civil War continued. Among the salient points in this emphasis are the triumph of Northern economic interests; the North first aiding blacks in the South and then losing interest and commitment; and the question of which came first, Southern intransigence or Radical Republican laws and constitutional amendments.

A second theme looks at Reconstruction as either a success or a failure, with an emphasis on the differing viewpoints of the Dunning school of historians and the Revisionist historians. William Dunning was a Columbia University professor who did not believe in racial equality and painted Reconstruction as a failure, one long ex-slave and black oppression of defenseless whites. He was a leading historian around 1900 in the American Historical Association and an advisor for numerous students earning their doctorates, specializing in Southern history. His good friend, Political Science Professor John W. Burgess, bluntly stated that few nations possessed the high intellectual capacity needed to create and run a government, chiefly the Aryan nations. The Revisionist Reconstruction historians started to attack the Dunning thesis when the civil rights movement began in the 1950s.

A third view concentrates on the South, seeing the essence of Reconstruction in the political struggles between Democratic Southern whites and Republican former slaves, who were aided by Northern opportunists who went South, called Carpetbaggers. However, this oversimplifies Southern politics in this era. There were 113 white Republican Congressmen from the South during Reconstruction, 53 of them were native white Southerners. Nicknamed Scalawags, this term is a poor description. Many were from wealthy families that pragmatically accepted the end of slavery. They genuinely believed that the South's salvation lay in following the example of the North by building railroads, industrializing (nicknamed the "New South"), and creating a public school system, all of which the pre-Civil War South lacked.

A fourth method for viewing Reconstruction is through the political contest between the President and Congress over the issue of civil rights for blacks, ending with the so-called Compromise of 1877.

Notice what is in every view of Reconstruction – the ex-slave and what is to be his or her status in American society. Both Congress and Southerners struggled with this question during Reconstruction. The years from 1865 to 1877 set the Southern and national tone for race relations and politics for the next 35 years. The South suffered economically after losing the Civil War. Look at the subsequent redistribution of wealth. In 1860, five states that joined the Confederacy were among the top ten in per capita wealth – Texas, Louisiana, Mississippi, Georgia, and South Carolina. Four more were in the second ten – Alabama, Virginia, Florida, and Arkansas. By 1880 all the former Confederate states were in the bottom twenty. The South would not experience an economic revival until the impact of the Second World War.

Interconnected, Intertwined Questions

Three interconnected, intertwined questions faced policy makers in Washington, D.C., and in the Southern legislatures.

1. What was to be the relationship between Congress and the president? Congress demanded that the president recognize the prerogative of Congress. The Constitution lists the powers of Congress first because the legislative power is paramount. Ask any Senator or Representative. Much of the fighting between Congress and the president during Reconstruction explains why Congress became more important than the presidents in the late nineteenth century. The major issue behind the fight between Congress and the president during Reconstruction was the demand by Congress to guarantee, somehow, civil rights for blacks, legally and constitutionally.

2. Who would control local governments in the South?

3. What is to be the role and position of blacks in American society, and not just the ex-slave in the South? What would that position be in a social, economic, legal, political, and constitutional sense? Slavery had been a system of labor, a system of race relations, and a system of property. The property aspect of slavery disappeared with the Emancipation Proclamation and the Thirteenth Amendment. New institutions would have to be developed to replace the systems of labor and race relations. Those new institutions that eventually replaced the labor and race relations features of slavery were sharecropping, discrimination, and Jim Crow segregation.

The Relationship Between the President and Congress

During the Civil War the relationship between Lincoln and Congress created a residue of ill will. At the beginning of the Civil War Lincoln did not call a special session of

Congress until July, although the fighting began in April. In contrast, Jefferson Davis, the President of the Confederacy, called the Confederate Congress into session immediately after the attack on Fort Sumter. Remember, Congress declares war, according to our Constitution. Today the presidential use of armed forces for international police actions, UN actions, NATO actions, and other limited interventions infringes on this power of Congress. Lincoln interpreted his Commander-in-Chief power broadly, much more than any previous president. "I conceive that I may in an emergency do things on military grounds which cannot be done constitutionally by Congress." Congress was irritated at Lincoln for many additional reasons.

1. Lincoln suspended habeas corpus (which is the right to be brought into a courtroom to be charged, and therefore eligible for bail or for a scheduled trial – the alternative is to remain in a cell, uncharged), suppressed 300 newspapers, arrested 15,000 war critics, and even tried to arrest a Congressman who criticized the war, Clement Vallandigham of Ohio, who fled to Canada.

2. The president announced his intention to issue the Emancipation Proclamation without informing or consulting Congress.

3. Some in Congress raised serious questions about Lincoln's commitment to the ex-slaves. He once brought up the possibility of colonizing blacks outside the United States, in Central America; and, he occasionally discussed permitting the South to work out the details of their white-black relations after the war.

4. As the end of the war neared, Lincoln began to visualize and to articulate his thoughts on policies to follow during Reconstruction. His incomplete plans seem to have been aimed at placating the Border States. However, he died before the war ended. As tentatively presented, his Reconstruction policy was:

    a. That a number of ex-Confederates equal to 10% of that state's vote cast in the 1860 election had to take an oath of allegiance to the United States. That was incredibly lenient. Remember, Southerners were only guilty of treason. The traditional punishment for treason was, and remains, death. Instead, Robert E. Lee became a college president.

    b. That the seceded states had to agree to the Thirteenth Amendment.

    c. That after approving the Thirteenth Amendment the seceded states could set up a new state government. Tennessee, Arkansas, and Louisiana had already done so prior to Lincoln's death.

The reaction of Congress to Lincoln's moves was the Wade-Davis Bill, which asserted Congressional control of Reconstruction. It was pocket-vetoed by Lincoln, done by simply taking no action for or against a bill after Congress adjourned. The Constitution states that a president may sign a bill, veto a bill, or show his displeasure by doing nothing. If a president takes no action, a bill passed by Congress automatically becomes a law in ten days, if Congress remains in session. But, if Congress is no longer in session, the ignored bill does not become a law within ten days. Congress later responded by passing the Wade-Davis Manifesto, which asserted that a majority, not 10%, must take the loyalty oath; the states must repudiate the Confederate debt; high Confederate officials were disenfranchised; and, similar to Lincoln's plan, the states must accept the Thirteenth Amendment. Here is a quote from the Wade-Davis Manifesto. Note the strident tone.

> The President "must understand that our support is of a cause and not of a man; that the authority of Congress is paramount and must be respected; that the whole body of the Union men of Congress will not submit to be impeached by him of rash and unconstitutional legislation; and if he wishes our support, he must confine himself to his executive duties to obey and execute, not to make the laws — to suppress by arms armed rebellion, and leave political reorganization to Congress."

The Election of 1864 and Andrew Johnson

Elections come every four years whether anyone cares or not, whether we are at war or not. The Republican Party dissolved, in name, and the Union Party took its place, with a former Republican from the North, Lincoln, as the presidential candidate and a former Democratic senator from a state now in the Confederacy (Tennessee), Andrew Johnson, as the vice-presidential candidate. This was done to present a balanced ticket to win the election. No one intended Andrew Johnson to ever become president. Making him the vice-presidential candidate was not a wise decision.

Lincoln's Second Inaugural Address, March 4, 1865, was very conciliatory, "with malice toward none, with charity for all, with firmness in the right as God gives us to see the right, let us strive on to finish the work we are in, to bind up the nation's wounds...." This was not how Congress felt.

Lincoln was assassinated at Ford's Theater on Good Friday, April 14, 1865, while watching a performance of *"Our American Cousin."* Andrew Johnson assumed the presidency. He had been vice president for 41 days; he was the third vice president to take over as president, all in just 24 years.

Johnson came up with his own Reconstruction Plan. The Civil War ended in late April, 1865. Johnson's plan was that

a.   The South must abolish slavery.
b.   The South must accept the Thirteenth Amendment.
c.   The South must repudiate the Confederate debt.
d.   The South must disavow secession.

e. And, similar to Lincoln's plan, high Confederate officials lost the franchise; but they could apply for personal reinstatement of their franchise right, essentially a presidential pardon.

Congress was not in session from April to early December in 1865, which was typical back then. Congressional sessions normally ran from early December to early March. Many former Confederate leaders, after receiving pardons from President Johnson, won elections in November in the South. For example, Alexander Stephens, the Vice President of the Confederacy, won election as a senator from Georgia. Many of those elected to Congress arrogantly demanded their seniority positions back and some even asserted that their time spent in the Confederate Congress should count towards seniority for committee positions in Congress. By December all the Confederate states except Texas had accepted Johnson's requirements for readmission to the Union. In theory, things were back to the way they were prior to the Civil War. When Congress met in December, 1865, the clerk refused to call the names of Southerners during the initial roll call. Congress then voted 133-36 to kick the ex-Confederates out, as unqualified. Any legislative body has the authority to rule on the qualifications of its members; any elected legislator, anywhere, anytime, may be kicked out of that legislative body by a majority vote.

The Position of Blacks in the South: The Black Codes
One source of Northern anger was the first reaction by Southern state legislatures immediately after the Civil War ended. They passed "Black Codes," which clearly showed that the South was unrepentant in spirit. The war ended in April, and without Congress in session, the Southern states were free to adopt any policy they wished, short of re-enslaving blacks, as long as the Union Army or the president did not interfere. President Andrew Johnson did not interfere. The Black Codes were an attempt to replace slavery, which had been a system of race relations, a system of labor, and a system of property. Slavery as a system of property had ended. Eventually sharecropping would replace the system of labor and segregation the system of race relations, but for now, there was much confusion. Look at these examples of the Black Codes.

Marriage: South Carolina – Marriage between a white person and a person of color shall be illegal and void.

Mississippi – "It shall not be lawful for any freedman, free Negro, or mulatto to intermarry with any white person; nor for any white person to intermarry with any freedman, free Negro, or mulatto." The law defined a Negro as one descended from a Negro to the third generation, one-eighth.

Working Conditions: South Carolina – Labor contracts were to be signed between white "masters" and black "servants." Black servants had to reside on the employer's property, remain quiet and orderly, work from sunup to sunset, except on Sundays, and not leave the premises or receive visitors without the master's permission. Masters could "moderately" whip servants under 18 to discipline them. Servants who quit before the end date of their labor contract forfeited their wages and could be arrested and returned to their masters by a judge's order. Louisiana added, "that in the case of sickness wages for the time lost will be deducted, and if the sickness was faked, double the wages deducted; if he refused to work after three days the offender shall be forced to work on roads and other public works, without pay, until he consented to return to his labor. He shall obey all proper orders of his employer. Bad work shall not be allowed. Failure to obey a reasonable order, neglect of duty, or leaving home without permission will be deemed disobedience; swearing or indecent language to or in the presence of the employer, his family or his agent shall be deemed disobedience."

Mississippi – "All contracts for labor with freedmen, free Negroes, or mulattoes shall be in writing, and, if the laborer shall quit the service of an employer before the expiration of his term of service, without good cause, he shall forfeit his wages for that year up to the time of quitting. Any civil officer, and every person may arrest and carry back to his or her legal employer any who leave before the expiration of their term of service without good cause. The cost and penalty were to be deducted from the runaway's wages. Any person who attempts to persuade or entice any freedmen, free Negro or mulatto to desert from his legal service or who employs a deserted freedman, or gives him food or clothing could be fined $25-$200." Blacks could testify in court, but only in cases affecting "the person or property of a person of color."

Remember, slaves were illiterate, they could neither read nor understand contracts. If an ex-slave could "forfeit his wages for that year up to the time of quitting," when was payday? Apparently – slaves, excuse me, a Freudian slip – ex-slaves, were paid once, at the end of a contract or the year. At least, now slavery was abolished. Or, was it? You can understand Northern Congressmen asking one another, "Didn't we win the war?"

Vagrancy Laws: Mississippi carefully defined vagrants as the following: "all rogues, vagabonds, idle and dissipated persons, beggars, jugglers, or persons practicing unlawful games of play, runaways, common drunkards, common night-walkers, pilferers, lewd, wanton, or lascivious persons in speech or behavior, common rilers and brawlers, persons who neglect their calling or employment, misspend what they earn, do not provide for the support of themselves or their families or dependents, all other idle and disorderly persons, including all who neglect lawful business, habitually misspend their time by frequenting houses of ill-fame or gambling shops. And, all white people associating with freedmen, free Negroes or mulattoes on terms of equality shall be deemed vagrants – fine $50 for blacks, $200 for whites, imprisoned, blacks, not exceeding ten days, whites, not exceeding six months. Any freedman, free Negro or mulatto who fails to pay any tax shall be hired out for the shortest time to anyone who pays it for him." Alabama defined a stubborn or disobedient servant or laborer as a vagrant. Any justice of the peace had the power to sentence a vagrant to work on public works and highways.

Many Northern Union Army officers and U.S. government officials sympathized with the South's need to control the newly freed ex-slave. For example, army officers and officials in the occupied South generally approved of segregated public schools, which also characterized most of the North. This attitude had been reinforced by the 1849 Massachusetts court case, *Roberts v. Boston*, which upheld segregated schools. The only exception was in New Orleans, where schools were integrated until 1877. In most public places segregation, separation, and discrimination of an unofficial sort existed before the advent of Jim Crow segregation laws, but the degree of it differed from one place to another and from one situation to another.

Congress Seizes Control of Reconstruction Policy

In response to the South's ingenious creation of laws and policies that seemed to continue slavery, Congress established the Joint Committee on Reconstruction, the Committee of Fifteen, run by Representative Thaddeus Stevens, Senator Benjamin Wade, and Senator Charles Sumner, of the pre-Civil War Sumner-Brooks "caning" incident. First, Congress considered the theoretical question of what happened in 1861. Did the South secede and therefore revert to the status prior to statehood, becoming a territory, which Congress controls? Senator Charles Sumner argued that the seceded states committed state suicide and their state governments ceased to exist, and therefore that land reverted to being territories. Thaddeus Stevens argued that the Confederate states were conquered provinces, and under international law, they were under the control of the legislative body of the conqueror, i.e., Congress. Either justification – territories or conquered land – Congress was legally in control, not the president.

Lincoln claimed that his power as Commander-in-Chief gave the president the authority to control Reconstruction policy, because the Southern states were out of control, rather than out of the Union. The admission of West Virginia, carved out of Virginia during the war, undermined his argument. Article IV, Section 3, of the Constitution states that no state may have its borders changed without its permission. If Virginia was still in the Union, West Virginia could not have constitutionally broken off. As a further complication, Congress admits new states; the president plays no role whatsoever. What difference does all this bickering make? It determines who – Congress or the president – is constitutionally, legally, or politically in charge of Reconstruction policy.

What were the motives of the Republican Senators and Congressmen?

1. Protect the policies and programs passed during the war to ensure a future for the Republican Party. Southern congressmen and senators had opposed all these laws.
    a. The National Banking system now regulated over fifteen hundred state and local banks that had previously printed different kinds of currency.
    b. A high tariff now protected Northern industry from foreign competition.

    c.   The Morrill Land Grant College Act established colleges to promote agriculture and industry.

    d.   The Homestead Act opened up the western land to settlers. Now that slavery was ended, settlers no longer competed with plantation owners for western land.

    e.   A transcontinental railroad secured the West for Northern commerce and settlers.

  2.   Their belief that the federal government had a role to play in enforcing political equality for the ex-slave.

  3.   Their need to protect the vote for the ex-slave, which was necessary for the Republican Party to win at the national level.

Contemporaries and some later historians applied the term "Radical" to the Republican Senators and Congressmen, but, in many respects, it is a misnomer. All but a handful of Republicans in Congress opposed President Johnson. In addition, one should be leery of that word, radical. After all, Lincoln had confiscated four billion dollars' worth of property, without awarding compensation. That was easily the most radical act in all American history.

Congress wrestled with the question of seizing the rebels' land and redistributing it to the ex-slaves. Thaddeus Stevens, in a speech on September 6, 1865, advocated "40 acres and a mule." General William T. Sherman had already issued Order No. 15, giving old army mules and 40,000 land titles to freedmen, requiring the redistribution of 485,000 acres. President Johnson ordered the land returned to the former owners. Congress passed the Southern Homestead Act in July, 1866, which expired on January 1, 1867, to extend the principle of the 1862 Homestead Act to public land in Alabama, Mississippi, Arkansas, Louisiana, and Florida. It was open to all who did not support the Confederacy. It failed miserably because the available land was inferior and freedmen lacked the capital to purchase farm equipment.

The first clash over black civil rights concerned the Freedmen's Bureau, established by Congress to help the ex-slaves adjust to freedom and traditional American values. For example, no contract between a former planter and a former slave, almost all of whom were illiterate, would be legally valid without the approval of an agent of the Freedmen's Bureau. It originally passed in March, 1865. In February, 1866, Congress voted to extend it. Johnson vetoed it. Congress revised it in July, passed it, saw it vetoed again, and passed it over Johnson's second veto.

In March, 1866, Congress passed a Civil Rights Act, 111-38 in the House, 33-12 in the Senate. Virtually every Republican supported it. Johnson vetoed the bill. The bill granted citizenship to blacks, for the purpose of reversing the Dred Scott decision. Johnson said blacks needed time to prepare for citizenship. President Johnson repeatedly voiced his plain disdain for blacks. He once said to Frederick Douglass, "If blacks could not prosper with the vote in the South, let them emigrate." In May, 1866, race riots in Memphis and New Orleans killed 37 blacks and wounded over 100. Congress was alarmed. Congress passed the Civil Rights Act of 1866 over Johnson's veto. Moderate Republicans no longer defended Johnson. In essence, he undercut the "ground upon which to stand and defend him" as a successor to Lincoln. Democratic Party newspaper editors praised Johnson for saving the republic from blacks.

Congress proposed the Fourteenth Amendment. Remember that at this time the states defined citizenship and controlled voting. Therefore, the Fourteenth Amendment attempted to force the states to protect and to respect black voting. Note that in the amendment process the president has no role whatsoever. In essence, Congress used the amendment process to bypass the president. The Fourteenth Amendment was sent to all the states for ratification. All the Southern states except Tennessee refused to ratify. Radicals nicknamed these states the "sinful ten."

In the congressional elections of 1866, President Johnson campaigned all over the North against individual Radical Republicans. He charged abolitionists and secessionists with EQUAL guilt for starting the Civil War. However, Radicals won over 2/3 of the seats in the Congressional elections. Often voters really had no alternative, either a so-called Radical Republican or a tainted Democrat. Many voters found it impossible to vote for any Democrat. It was said that while not every Democrat was a traitor, every traitor was a Democrat, meaning Southerners or Northerners who sympathized with the South, nicknamed Copperheads during the Civil War.

Congress in Control
Endorsed by the voters, the newly formed Congress elected in 1866 took control. In January, 1867, Johnson vetoed a bill giving the vote to blacks in Washington, D.C. He claimed they had not asked for it. In March, 1867, Congress passed the First Reconstruction Act, dividing ten Southern states, the "sinful ten," into five military districts occupied by the army. The president vetoed it on the grounds that its premise, that the seceded states did not have lawful governments, was incorrect. However, Congress overrode his veto the same day, 138-51 in the House, and 38-10 in the Senate. This Reconstruction Act stipulated that to reenter the Union the Southern states must ratify the Fourteenth Amendment and write new state constitutions that guaranteed black suffrage. By the 1868 election, only three states had not accepted these terms – Virginia, Texas, and Mississippi.

In the 1868 election the Republican presidential candidate, Ulysses S. Grant, narrowly won. The Democrats won two Southern states, Louisiana and Georgia. Radicals claimed the Democrats won these two states only because blacks were not allowed to vote. Therefore, they proposed the Fifteenth Amendment to guarantee the right of blacks to vote. Note that in both cases, the Fourteenth and the Fifteenth Amendments, the proposed amendments grew out of what the Radicals saw as a solution to practical political problems. Before the Fifteenth Amendment, Kansas, Ohio, and Minnesota all defeated proposed state laws to give blacks the right to vote. In the popular vote in Ohio and Minnesota over 80% of the white voters opposed black suffrage.

Congress also handcuffed the Supreme Court. This Reconstruction Act stipulated that no appeals to a court were allowed under any of the Reconstruction Acts (there were four Reconstruction Acts). Congress claimed this right under the Constitution, Article III, Section 2, Clause 2, "the supreme Court shall have appellate Jurisdiction, both as to Law and Fact, with such Exceptions, and under such Regulations as Congress shall make." This clause has a curious history. In the debate over repeal of the Judiciary Act of 1801, the Federalists did not deny this right for Congress. Neither did any living participant from the Constitutional Convention deny Congress' right to do so. On March 27, 1868, Congress passed a law repealing an 1867 law that conferred upon the Supreme Court the right to hear certain appeals involving habeas corpus. In *Ex Parte McCardle*, 1869, (also spelled McArdle in the official records) the Supreme Court acknowledged Congress' right to define and to limit appellate jurisdiction by unanimously declaring that no appeal from a federal Circuit Court under the repealed act of 1867 was reviewable. Scholars still debate the "exceptions clause." Congress did not care whether or not this power existed constitutionally. It was running the federal government, all branches. Congress also reduced the number of Supreme Court judges, which it has the constitutional authority to do, in order to prevent President Johnson from appointing a new Supreme Court judge if a vacancy occurred.

What the Republican Congress was trying to do was to assure a future for the Republican Party. To understand what went on it is necessary to back up a little — to March, 1868, prior to the election, when Congress impeached President Andrew Johnson.

The impeachment of Andrew Johnson was part of the struggle between Congress and the president over civil rights. The House passed eleven articles of impeachment, nine of them dealing with issues involving the Tenure of Office Act. Congress had passed the Tenure of Office Act to trap Johnson and to control the executive branch. The idea behind it was simple. If the Constitution required a two-thirds vote by the Senate to approve presidential appointments, then it made sense that a two-thirds vote of the Senate was necessary for the president to fire a presidential appointee. Two later presidents, Ulysses S. Grant and James Garfield, strongly objected to it. In 1887 President Grover Cleveland, involved in a squabble with the Senate over civil service and the spoils system, insisted that the Senate repeal the Tenure of Office Act. They did. A 1925 court case added a nail to its coffin. The Chief Justice of the Supreme Court, William Howard Taft, a former president, declared that it had never been constitutional in the first place.

As always, Andrew Johnson had a chip on his shoulder. Once while campaigning in Tennessee he climbed down from a platform to beat up a heckler. He accepted all challenges. The Reconstruction Acts put the Secretary of War, Edwin Stanton, in charge of the five military districts; therefore, he was now in control of Reconstruction policy, not the president. Since the Secretary of War is under the authority of the president, this law was absurd. On February 21-22, Johnson tried to remove Stanton, replacing him with General Ulysses S. Grant. Grant gave the office back to Stanton; Stanton was then replaced by General Lorenzo Thomas, from Delaware. When he went to take over, Stanton and Thomas had a few drinks and Stanton convinced Thomas to leave. On Monday, February 24, the House voted to impeach Johnson, 128-47. Nine of the articles of impeachment concerned the events of February 21-22, Johnson's violation of the Tenure of Office Act. The other two articles of impeachment were trivial. One charged Johnson with bringing contempt, ridicule, and disgrace to the presidency. He had been unsteady at his inauguration as vice president. He was a nondrinker, but that morning he had taken a doctor's advice to drink whiskey to fight a bad cold. He drank too much! The second accusation stated that Johnson brought disgrace on Congress. In August, 1866, Johnson called Congress a body without constitutional authority to exercise legislative power, since the South was not represented, and, therefore, its enactments were not binding. Thank goodness no other president in American history had ever argued with Congress.

The Senate voted to remove Johnson from the presidency, 35-19; it failed by one vote, because a two-thirds majority was required, 36-18. The vote had many sidelights. Johnson's son-in-law, Senator David Patterson, a Democrat from Tennessee, voted not guilty, good for family harmony. Senator Benjamin Wade voted guilty. His position as president pro tempore of the Senate meant that under the presidential succession law then in effect, Wade would have been the next president. Therefore, he voted to make himself the president. Wade is the only person to ever vote for himself to be president. Every other presidential candidate casts a vote for an elector in the Electoral College who then votes for the candidate. Remember that for the quiz show. Seven Republican senators voted no. One, Edmund G. Ross of Kansas, did not announce his decision ahead of the vote. His dramatic "not guilty" vote was unexpected. The Senate chamber exploded in anger, denouncing Ross. All seven were never elected to another political office again. Their businesses were wrecked and some members of their families were attacked. Such were the passions of the era.

The Republican candidate, Ulysses S. Grant, won the presidency in November, 1868. The remaining "sinful ten" – Virginia, Texas, and Mississippi – accepted the Fifteenth Amendment and were readmitted. Georgia was readmitted after being again put under military rule for anti-black measures. After 1870, Southern conservatives gradually regained control of the individual Southern states. A General Amnesty Act in 1872 for all but about 500 top ex-Confederates restored the franchise. Republicans in Congress continued to work to protect blacks and their civil rights, as shown by the 1871 Ku Klux Klan Act and the Civil Rights Act, 1875. The Ku Klux Klan Act made it a federal crime to conspire to deprive others of their rights, specifically listing wearing disguises, forming conspiracies, intimidating officials, and resisting officers of the government, all typical Klan activities. The Civil Rights Act of 1875 was declared unconstitutional by the Supreme Court in 1883. This Civil Rights Act had guaranteed equal treatment for blacks in public transportation and public accommodations, and also prohibited exclusion from juries. Ultimately, both laws were not successful. Jim Crow won.

Putting the Commitment to Equal Rights in Perspective

The United States was the first major nation to commit itself to equal rights for all; but in truth, historians do not know exactly what the Founding Fathers meant by "All men are created equal." Did Jefferson mean all men are CREATED equal? Or, all men are created EQUAL. Or, ALL men are created equal. Or, did it mean, as one of the Founding Fathers, Nathaniel Ames, observed, "All men are created equal, but differ greatly in the sequel."

In the twentieth century quest for equality blacks appealed to the national government to obey the established fundamental national law – the Constitution – rather than to change the Constitution, unlike what had to happen in South Africa to end apartheid. It was easier to end segregation and discrimination than apartheid. What our nation needed were judges who enforced the Constitution, not legislators who would have to change the Constitution.

Why did the Civil War and Reconstruction era fail to secure civil rights for the freedman? The push for black equality required interference with local government on a massive scale. The major weakness of the Radical program was this dependence on national intervention. Local governments, those governments closest to the people, hold an almost sacred status in America. We have one nationally elected office, the presidency. We have over 87,000 elected officials, the vast majority at the local level. The right to vote for blacks was supported on principle and on the Republican Party's dependence on the black vote. As the second reason weakened, so did the first. In 1868 the majority of white voters did not support Grant, the Republican candidate. Only slowly did the Republican Party grow a national constituency.

It was difficult to ensure legal and constitutional racial equality in a society that did not popularly believe in the equality of the races in any sense. The popular belief in racial equality arrived in the middle of the twentieth century. Charles Darwin's 1859 book, *On the Origin of Species*, led others to apply the concept of natural selection to humans, thus showing conclusively and scientifically (they believed) that the races of humankind, then meaning nationalities, were unequal. In addition, the immigrants, obviously of inferior racial stock, who were flooding into the Northern cities in the late nineteenth century, gave the North a group seen as similar to blacks in the South. The "better people," North and South, increasingly opposed granting full citizenship rights and participation to both blacks and immigrants, leaving the South free to handle its race problem while the North handled its immigrant problem. Many, North and South, came to believe that the right of suffrage had been bestowed too quickly to both blacks and immigrants. Historians need to be less critical of the Radical Republicans. While it is possible to say they failed, they tried, very hard, to lay a foundation for legal racial equality. It would not really arrive until the "Second Reconstruction," the civil rights movement of the mid-twentieth century.

Equality is a very difficult concept to deal with politically. Any attempt to achieve equality tends to emphasize inequalities by magnifying them, leaving those who supposedly benefited from a new policy or law more keenly aware that true equality has NOT been achieved, while those who passed the law are congratulating themselves on a problem resolved. Equality is also a difficult word to define. There are really only three kinds of equality. There is equality in the eyes of God – which offers no definition of a person's place in human society, it becomes operable after death. The second is equality under the law – which assumes it is self-fulfilling and creates no political or social revolution, because it kicks in after an individual's arrest. The third is equality of opportunity – which often leads to inequality of achievement, which in the nineteenth, and much of the twentieth century, confirmed the basic assumptions of white supremacy. Lining everyone up on the starting line may seem to be an endorsement of equality and equal opportunity. However, what about the handicapped person, or the one who has just been released from the hospital after an operation, or the one with the badly sprained ankle, or the one who never finished elementary school? Equal opportunity leads naturally to an inequality of results. Any sports fan understands that, not every team finishes in first place. In the twentieth century Americans added a fourth definition – equality of social worth. "I'm as good as you are." However, this changes nothing. Equality is one of those words that sounds deceptively simple, until applying it.

Finally, as some historians have pointed out, any time Americans have faced a choice between equality and liberty, they tend to opt for liberty. Liberty seems to rank higher than equality in the **American Identity** scale of important qualities. Any political or judicial creation of a law or policy to ensure more equality for your group is likely to diminish another group's liberty, as they define it, thus they will oppose your advance, not because they desire inequality for you, but because they treasure liberty more. What is perceived as an *artificial* equality is often perceived as another's *artificial* limitation of liberty. When you look at the long history of an issue such as civil rights or freedom of speech, the swinging pendulum over the long term becomes obvious. What America needs is a balance between equality and liberty. But, where?

Now the story of America's history moves on to the significant changes that came to the nation following the Civil War and Reconstruction, changes such as the rapid growth of American industry, the expansion of cities, the influx of immigrants, and the emergence of the United States as a world power.

28

BLACKS IN THE LATE NINETEENTH CENTURY

The Legacy of Reconstruction

Reconstruction was not without accomplishments – the Thirteenth, Fourteenth, and Fifteenth Amendments and four civil rights bills. Reconstruction ended with the Rutherford B. Hayes – Samuel J. Tilden election of 1876 and the dispute over the winner. The outcome was resolved by the Compromise of 1877, which put Hayes into the White House and withdrew the last Union soldiers stationed in three Southern states. What followed, hesitantly, was the beginning of Jim Crow segregation.

Between 1870 and 1900, social relations between the races in the South were inconsistent. What existed is best characterized as self-separation. For example, look on the Internet at maps that show how blacks moved away from their former master's house on the Barrow plantation. While still dependent upon their landlord, who owned the land they farmed, ex-slaves clearly desired some degree of physical separation. Racism was more widespread than segregation, which often existed informally through choice and the threat of force. For example, in Virginia the trains were not segregated. Throughout the South some restaurants, bars, or waiting rooms were segregated, while some were not. It is simply not true that legal segregation immediately replaced slavery in the South following the Civil War. The end of Reconstruction, 1877, is not a dividing mark between two different "Souths." Instead, there was a period of uncertainty, of confusion, of a gradual working out of the public relationship between the races. The end of Reconstruction did not mark the beginning of political and legal segregation, although social segregation was widespread.

After Reconstruction ended, between 1876 and 1894, 52 blacks were elected to the Virginia state General Assembly and 47 elected to the South Carolina state legislature.

Ten blacks served in the U.S. House of Representatives from the South during Reconstruction and ten served afterwards. Every Congress from 1869 to 1901 had at least one black Congressman from the South. George Henry White served two terms in the House representing North Carolina's Second Congressional District. But after his term ended in 1901, the South did not elect a black Representative until Andrew Young of Georgia and Barbara Jordan of Texas in 1972. Blacks voted during Reconstruction and continued to vote after Reconstruction ended. In the 1880s both political parties in some parts of the South actually courted the black vote. Be careful, voting and holding an office are not necessarily the same as holding power or influence. "Sandwiching" was widely practiced, which referred to the practice of putting one black on a commission or committee and making certain he could be outvoted, and yet, his name was associated with all decisions and publications. Whites rarely voted for any black candidate.

Black Codes

The first reaction by Southern state legislatures immediately after the Civil War ended was to pass the "Black Codes," which clearly illustrated the Southern mind. The war ended in April, Congress did not come back into session until December. Thus, the Southern states were free to adopt any policy they wished, short of re-enslaving blacks, as long as neither the Union army nor the president interfered. President Andrew Johnson did not interfere. The Black Codes were an attempt to replace slavery, which had been a system of race relations, a system of labor, and a system of property. Eventually sharecropping would replace the system of labor and segregation the system of race relations, but at that time, there was much confusion.

Since it was widely believed that former slaves would never work without compulsion, it was necessary to force them to work. The working conditions were carefully laid out. "He shall obey all proper orders of his employer. Bad work shall not be allowed. Failure to obey a reasonable order, neglect of duty, or leaving home without permission will be deemed disobedience; swearing or indecent language to or in the presence of the employer, his family or his agent shall be deemed disobedience." Congress quickly ended the Black Codes early in Reconstruction, but what replaced the Black Codes was inconsistency.

Segregation, But Inconsistency

In most public places, an unofficial segregation and discrimination existed before the advent of segregation laws, but the amount of it differed from one place to another and from one time to another. Some Northern visitors were shocked at what they saw in the South after Reconstruction. Col. Thomas Wentworth Higginson had a long history fighting against slavery. He led the Boston mob that attempted to rescue the fugitive slave, Anthony Burns, in 1854. Col. Higginson was one of the "secret six," the six people who were aware, beforehand, of John Brown's plan to attack Harpers Ferry. He was an officer in a black regiment during the Civil War – the First South Carolina Volunteers, one of the first black regiments in the Union army. He visited Virginia, South Carolina, and Florida in 1878 and in 1884, by ship, and was surprised at what he saw. Higginson reported that "The Southern whites accept them precisely as Northern men in cities accept the ignorant Irish vote – not cheerfully, but with acquiescence in the inevitable; and when the strict color-line is once broken they are just as ready to consider the Negro as the Northern politician is to flatter the Irishman. Any powerful body of voters may be cajoled today and intimidated tomorrow and hated always, but it can never be ignored."

In 1885 T. McCants Stewart, the black editor of a Northern black newspaper, the *New York Freeman*, toured the South by train through Virginia, North Carolina, and South Carolina. During the entire trip he purposefully sat at tables or seats near whites, often right beside them, intentionally invading that person's "air space," the imaginary zone of privacy that all of us have around ourselves. He expected rejection and discrimination, but instead found conversation. He reported, "He failed to find what he was looking for!" Charles Dudley Warner, Mark Twain's neighbor and the co-author of *The Gilded Age* with Twain, went South in 1885 to visit the World's Fair at New Orleans. He was shocked, "The races mingled in the grounds in conscious equality of privileges."

Paternalism

Do not misunderstand this era. It was not a golden age of race relations; but it was also not yet widespread, vicious segregation. What dominated intellectually was a conservative philosophy of paternalism, an updating of Senator John Calhoun's antebellum "mud-sill" theory, that in every society that advances there must be a class of people that labor so that the upper, intellectual class can discover, discuss, invent, and rule. Otherwise civilization does not take positive steps forward. Paternalism is the concept that every society has superiors and subordinates. Each class has responsibilities and obligations, and each should be guaranteed its status and protected in its rights. "Blacks were inferior, but they did not need to be humiliated; they were subordinate, but they did not need to be ostracized." Believers in paternalism could not envision a pluralist society, a society in which different races and nationalities live in relative equality and relative harmony. That concept was not widely accepted by the common person until the middle of the twentieth century.

For paternalism, class distinctions were more important than racial differences. Here is an example of this thinking, from Governor Thomas G. Jones of Alabama: "The Negro race is under us. He is in our power. We are his custodians…we should extend to him, as far as possible, all the civil rights that will fit him to be a decent and self-respecting, law-abiding and intelligent citizen…. If we do not lift them up, they will drag us down." Upper class conservative whites dominated the Democratic Party in the South and their philosophy of paternalism endorsed black suffrage. Blacks voted, as Republicans, in thankfulness to Lincoln and the North. However, all the white Southerners voted Democratic, against the party of Lincoln and the North. In other words, blacks voted, but it did not matter much in the presidential national elections or in the state and local elections. This characterized Southern politics from the end of Reconstruction until the 1890s – when everything fell apart. (The chapter's quotes and perspectives to this point are from C. Vann Woodward, *The Strange Career of Jim Crow.*)

In the 1890s – Things Fall Apart
Why? First, Interest and Commitment Faded

Many things caused both Northern interest and commitment to fade away in the 1890s. Shortly before he died in 1895, the black leader Frederick Douglass explained what had happened by the 1890s in the following observation: ". . . the cause lost in the (Civil) War is the cause regained in the peace, and the cause gained in the war is the cause lost in the peace." In other words, the Northern commitment to civil rights for blacks weakened. The entry of new western states – North Dakota, South Dakota, Montana, Idaho, Wyoming, and Utah – brought Republicans into the Senate, the House, and the Electoral College. As the Republican Party grew in strength in the North and the West, the black Southern Republican vote became less important. In addition to the political reasons, Northerners grew tired of fighting for a cause, an ideal, as Americans habitually do.

For example, the Blair Bill, sponsored by Senator Henry W. Blair of New Hampshire, was an education bill to provide millions of dollars for Southern black and white schools. It passed the Senate three times and failed in the House each time. It was needed. In 1887 only two-thirds of eligible black children were enrolled in schools. As another example, Senator Henry Cabot Lodge of Massachusetts in 1890 made one last effort to pass the Federal Elections Bill, which would have permitted federal investigation of alleged election fraud. It failed. No other political measures to assist black voters were even proposed between 1891 and the First World War.

Why? Second, Court Decisions

The federal courts, for several decades, slowly weakened protection of black civil rights. An unprecedented increase in the size, power, and presence of the federal government accompanied the Civil War and Reconstruction. As two examples, think Emancipation Proclamation and Freedman's Bureau. Most politicians are local politicians and think locally. The potential for misuse of the federal government's powers concerned both Northern and Southern politicians. Thus, many favored cutting back the federal government's interference into those areas traditionally reserved for the states. Civil rights is such an area. At this time in American history, most civil rights were state rights, not national rights – voting, licensing, police and arrest, juries, courts, etc. These powers, collectively, granted to the state governments the responsibility for the health, safety, and morals of their population. Remember the range of reform activity by state governments during the antebellum period – prisons, alcohol, asylums, schools, women's property rights after marriage, etc. – all possible under the legal doctrine of the state's police powers, advancing the health, safety, and morals of their people. Not until the 1960s did the Supreme Court vigorously apply the Constitution's Bill of Rights to state and local police powers. For example, in the *Slaughterhouse Cases*, 1873, the Supreme Court ruled that the Fourteenth Amendment only protected citizens against federal government action, not state infringement. Since most civil rights were state, not federal, the Fourteenth Amendment's "equal protection" clause actually protected very few civil rights.

Many textbooks present the late nineteenth century as one in which the Supreme Court seemed to go in two contradictory directions. The Court applied a laissez faire approach towards big business, while at the same time limiting attempts to provide equality for blacks. For the economy, "governments, keep your hands off"; for blacks, "governments, you may keep your hands on," anything to prevent blacks from rising politically, socially, or economically. However, this paradigm is too simple. The Supreme Court was consistent. From the 1790s up to the New Deal, and even a little beyond, the Supreme Court consistently applied the legal doctrine that state governments retained their police powers, the right and the obligation to protect the health, safety, and *morals* of their state population. Thus, if a state legislature felt that social mixing of blacks and whites was *immoral*, that state had the legal power and right to create and to enforce segregation, as in *Plessy v. Ferguson*, which sanctioned "separate but equal" segregation in 1896 (more below); or to prohibit marriages between whites and blacks, which was not declared unconstitutional until the 1967 decision in *Loving v. Virginia*. Up until the 1960s, the LEGAL doctrine of state police powers overrode the PROMISE of equal treatment in the Bill of Rights and the Fourteenth Amendment. Then things changed. But not completely. In the 1970s a woman sued the state of Louisiana to change the race designation on her birth certificate. She believed she was white; her birth certificate said she was "colored." The Supreme Court ruled that the state of Louisiana had the legal right to designate their population in any way. From the 1700s to the repeal of the law in 1983, Louisiana defined a person who had one-thirty-second black ancestry as a black person. One-thirty-second is your great, great, great grandparents. How many people have any idea who those individuals were? The 1983 repeal was not retroactive. The lady, Susie Phipps, officially remained "colored." Try to imagine the puzzled expression on the face of the Paris customs agent looking at her passport.

After the *Slaughterhouse Cases*, the second important Supreme Court decision involved the 1883 *Civil Rights Cases*, which ruled the Civil Rights Act of 1875 unconstitutional because the Fourteenth Amendment did not apply to individual or business action. Corporations are legally individuals; therefore, a business could discriminate. As Frederick Douglass aptly put it, "All the parts can violate the Constitution, but the whole cannot. It is not the act itself, according to this decision, that is unconstitutional. The unconstitutionity of the case depends wholly upon the party committing the act. If the State commits it, it is wrong, if the citizen of the State commits it, it is right."

In a reaction against this trend, seventeen Northern states passed state civil rights laws by 1895, although most were weak and enforcement was lax. None of them offered any help to blacks in Southern states. In his majority opinion in the Supreme Court decision in the *Civil Rights Cases*, Justice Joseph P. Bradley of New Jersey wrote that after a man has been released from slavery "there must be a stage in the progress of his elevation when he takes the rank of mere citizen, and ceases to be the special favorite of the laws, and when his rights as a citizen or a man, are to be protected in the ordinary modes by which other men's rights are protected." In other words, blacks in the South were on their own now. In a stinging minority opinion, Justice John M. Harlan, of Kentucky, contended that blacks were not asking for special treatment, but equal treatment according to the laws.

In *U.S. v. Harris*, 1883, the Supreme Court ruled that the Fourteenth Amendment's equal protection clause applied only if an affirmative act by a state government took place. A mob had seized several blacks from a sheriff, killing one of them. Neither the mob's action nor the state government's failure to defend the prisoners against the mob violated the Fourteenth Amendment. This ruling invalidated part of the second Ku Klux Klan Act of 1871. Earlier, in *U.S. v. Cruikshank*, 1875, the Supreme Court invalidated the First Ku Klux Klan Act, limiting Fourteenth Amendment rights to protecting against state acts, not individual acts.

In a significant decision in 1896, *Plessy v. Ferguson*, the Supreme Court found "separate but equal" segregation legal. Justice Henry B. Brown, a native of Massachusetts, wrote the decision, citing the 1849 Massachusetts case, *Roberts v. Boston*, which had upheld segregated schools. He denied that the *Plessy* decision would lead to an expansion of segregation practices and statutes. Of course, it did. This case opened the gates to a flood of discriminatory state laws. Three years later, 1899, in *Cumming v. Richmond County Board of Education*, the Supreme Court sanctioned separate schools for blacks and whites, in spite of the complete absence of schools for blacks in Richmond County. So much for equal!

The concept of separate but equal was part of that era. The principle of "separate but equal" had been part of an 1890 law, the second Morrill Act, nicknamed Morrill II, that granted federal funds to land-grant colleges and universities, with a provision that funds to a state could go to separate black and white universities, if given equally. Two years after *Plessy*, in 1898, the case of *Williams v. Mississippi* opened the road to depriving blacks of the right to vote in Mississippi by approving the requirement for a literacy test to qualify for voting.

One can also see the progression of thinking in two transportation cases. In *Hall v. de Cuir*, 1877, the Supreme Court ruled that a state could not *prohibit* segregation on a common carrier, such as a train, because states had no authority over interstate commerce. Later, in 1890 in *Louisville, New Orleans, and Texas Railroad v. Mississippi*, the Supreme Court said a state could constitutionally *require* segregation on a common carrier, such as a train. Thus, either the train company or the state government could require segregated railroad cars. This left no basis to sue to end segregated trains.

Why? Third, The Political Rise of the Lower Class

When Southerners regained control of their state legislatures and state governments with the end of Reconstruction in 1877, the upper class conservatives were in charge. Southern conservatives worked out an alliance for black support in some local and state elections, called "fusion." Blacks voted for upper class conservatives for some local and state offices, and in return, blacks were rewarded with some offices and some influence.

Meanwhile, poor whites, nicknamed white trash, crackers, hillbillies, clay eaters, or rednecks, pushed by mounting difficulties affecting all farmers on relatively unproductive small farms, began to organize politically to solve their economic problems. Initially poor whites sought poor blacks as political allies. Tom Watson of Georgia, in a speech to a mixed audience of poor whites and poor blacks, said, "You are made to hate each other because upon that hatred is rested the keystone of the arch of financial despotism which enslaves you both." "We are all in the same ditch." A black minister who supported Watson made 63 speeches for Watson's campaign for governor. When a racist mob came after him, Watson put out a call for protection, and 2,000 armed, white Georgia crackers showed up to protect the black minister. The racist mob had threatened the black minister because Southern upper class conservatives had begun to use racism to drive a wedge between the poor whites and the poor blacks, to scare voters into recognizing their upper class, superior ability to "control" blacks. This is the old "divide and conquer" approach.

After failing to achieve victory in election after election, Southern radicals abandoned their black allies and adopted racism as a tactic to win, which they did, clawing their way to political power. "Pitchfork" Ben Tillman in South Carolina, and Tom Watson of Georgia were the most colorful populist segregationists. Tillman served for decades in the U.S. Senate and Watson became linked to the farmers' Populist Party (more below). "Pitchfork" Ben Tillman proudly defended disenfranchisement in 1920. "We have scratched our heads to find out how we could eliminate every last one of them. We stuffed ballot boxes. We shot them. We are not ashamed of it." Watson, earlier, in 1917 stated, "In the South, we have to lynch him occasionally, and flog him, now and then, to keep him from blaspheming the Almighty, by his conduct, on account of his smell and his color." One wonders if "the Almighty" was pleased?

The fight between conservative whites and lower class whites, with both using racism as a tactic, meant that victory by either side necessitated adopting racist segregation laws to respond to their voters' support. In short, in a political contest between upper class whites and lower class whites, blacks lost. All over the South black voters disappeared. For example, in Louisiana in 1896, 130,334 blacks voted, in 1904, 1,342. Mississippi removed 123,000 overnight in 1890 by rewriting their state constitution. In Alabama, out of 181,471 potential black voters, only 3,000 were registered.

Why? Fourth, Contributing Factors

Contributing to the times, the Zeitgeist of that era, were a number of other factors. A depression that began in 1893 ushered in a decade of high unemployment and frayed nerves. Guess who were the last hired and first fired? For the rest of your lives you will see an increase in racism and anti-immigrant feelings when the economy dips.

The Spanish-American War of 1898 carried with it, or brought to the surface, ideas of Anglo-Saxon superiority. The poem *"The White Man's Burden"* was written in England during the Senate fight over the ratification of the Treaty of Paris in 1898. Read it on the Internet. The Philippines, Hawaii, Guam, and Puerto Rico were the first territories acquired by the United States in which the inhabitants were NOT automatically granted American citizenship. That would come later. Americans daily read in their newspapers about the progress of imperialism at work in Africa and Asia, where attitudes of superiority were part of the "cargo" Westerners carried. See Jared Diamond's *Guns, Germs, and Steel* for a discussion of the imperialistic mood of the late nineteenth century. Imperialism was not considered a bad word, since whites had a duty to bring the world's inferior peoples up to European and American standards. It did not take much thinking to conclude that America's black population was similar to inferior peoples elsewhere.

The decade of the 1890s was a decade of reunions celebrating the Civil War with parades, encampments, monuments, etc., all of which excluded blacks from participation, despite the fact that 186,000 blacks had served in the Union Army during the Civil War. The animosity of the Civil War era and the issues associated with it faded away in the euphoria of these celebrations. Black contributions were minimized or ignored. One example was the controversy over the monument erected in front of the Massachusetts State House to honor the 54th Massachusetts Regiment, the black unit featured in the movie *Glory*. In the original design the black soldiers were large enough that they had individual features. Whites argued that the white officer, Col. Robert Shaw, should be more prominently featured than the black soldiers. He was. The small black soldiers lack individual features.

The Rise of Jim Crow Laws – Disenfranchising Blacks

First, a word about the origins of the phrase Jim Crow. In the 1820s and 1830s several vaudeville performers blackened their faces and performed parodies of ignorant blacks, much to the delight of the white audiences. One, Thomas D. "Daddy" Rice, called himself Jim Crow, another Zip Coon. By the end of those decades Jim Crow became part of the popular culture and an adjective applied to blacks.

The following methods disenfranchised blacks to prevent them from voting.

1. Literacy test – an applicant had to read and interpret a section of the state or national constitution, and the clerk judged the response. In 1890 Mississippi used the literacy test to wipe 123,000 blacks off the voting rolls. As late as the 1950s Mississippi still used questions such as "How many bubbles are in a bar of soap?" The clerk asked one black applicant to explain a passage of the state constitution in English. He did. Then in French. He did. Then in Spanish. He did. Then in Arabic. He could not. He failed the test, clearly unqualified to vote. Once the NAACP sent a black Howard University constitutional law professor down to Mississippi to take the test. His written answer went on for pages, sprinkled with references to court cases and citations. The clerk respectfully read it, and told him it was wrong! If a person failed the literacy test, you were not allowed to attempt to register for six months. This gave time, through your boss's stern advice about your future employment or KKK threats, to pressure you to not try to register again.

2. Paying a poll tax – the receipt was necessary for voting. The tax had to be paid in the spring, when farmers needed all their money for seeds and equipment.

3. The grandfather clause, introduced by Louisiana in 1898, said that an applicant was permanently registered to vote if his grandfather or father would have been qualified to vote on January 1, 1867. If not, an applicant had to satisfy property, educational, or literacy requirements. Since blacks had not been eligible to vote before the passage of the Fourteenth Amendment or the Fifteenth Amendment, the grandfather clause applied to them and only to them.

4. Intimidation by means of the Ku Klux Klan or lynching.

5. Stuffing ballot boxes – in Louisiana the officials did not count the vote; they just estimated the vote. It saved time.

6. Moving polling places on election day, forcing a voter to find it, or, blocking roads leading to the polling places.

7. Virginia had a time limit for casting a vote. There were no party affiliations on the paper ballot, which forced the voter to quickly match the candidate with the office that candidate was seeking.

8. South Carolina had separate ballot boxes for each office. Election officials were not allowed to help a voter. The voter had to find the correct box for each office.

9. White primary, only whites were allowed to vote in the Democratic Party primary, which was held just a few weeks before the general election. On election day every white person voted for the Democratic candidate. The real election was the primary.

10. Complex voter registration forms or procedures. A voter in Louisiana had to fill out the voter registration form "without assistance." The registering voter had to calculate his age in years, months, and days, which raised the question – does the applicant count today? No matter which a person picked, this left the clerk free to say you were incorrect. The applicant also had to know his precinct number and ward number, and his previous ward and precinct numbers. Ask any voter today, what is the number of your election district and state representative district? Few know. An applicant had to swear that he had not been convicted of a felony or more than one misdemeanor within the previous five years; that he had not lived with another in common law marriage; and that he had not fathered an illegitimate child within the previous five years. High fees for marriage licenses forced many lower class whites and blacks to skip the legal formalities of getting married. They just lived together, which negated any possibility of ever registering to vote.

The Switch in Lynching

Antebellum Southern society had as one of its characteristics, according to journalist Wilbur Cash in *The Mind of the South*, a tendency towards violence. Between 1840 and 1860 mobs in the South burned or hanged over 300 people, but fewer than 10% were blacks. Lynching was not yet primarily a means of racial control. Up until 1889 that trend continued. Then it savagely reversed itself and increased. In the 1890s and beyond almost all lynchings were only of blacks. Black leaders protested, referring to lynchings as "strange fruit" hanging from a tree. A black Memphis journalist, Ida Wells Bennett, led the investigative reporting into the many myths behind lynchings. Only rarely was a lynching a respond to a specific crime. Later historical scholars endorsed her findings – it was primarily a means of social control. Between 1900 and 1930, 345 of the South's 551 cotton-growing counties had at least one lynching. Thirty-one percent had 10 or more. Fear is an effective means of control.

The Black Response

Black leaders faced a dilemma. What should be the black response? How do you fight back? What do you fight for?

Do we integrate or separate?

Do we seek white support or go with self-support?

Do we use violence or nonviolence?

Do we enter the political system or stay out of it?

Adding to their dilemma was a disagreement within the black community between the *"internalists"* and the *"externalists."* Is black behavior the main problem or is white treatment of blacks the main problem? To what extent is our situation due to us (*internalists*) and to what extent is it due to them (*externalists*)?

Booker T. Washington

Booker T. Washington (April 5, 1856 - November 14, 1915) offered one approach. He was born a slave in Virginia. After the Civil War, his family moved to Charleston, West Virginia, where he worked in salt and coal mines. He taught himself to read and write, but only occasionally attended school. He also cleaned the house for Mrs. Ruffner, the wife of General Lewis Ruffner, the owner of the local coal mine. In 1872 he walked hundreds of miles to eastern Virginia to enroll in college at Hampton Institute, founded by General Samuel Armstrong. To save money along the way he slept under wooden sidewalks in Richmond. At Hampton Institute the officials tried to get rid of him by assigning him a specific task as an entrance exam – cleaning a room. Mrs. Ruffner had been a stern taskmaster; Washington knew how to clean a room. He cleaned it three times; it was spotless! They had to accept him. When he graduated, he first taught school in West Virginia and then spent a few months at Wayland Seminary. In 1881 General Armstrong recommended him to become the head of a new school for blacks, eventually called Tuskegee Institute, established by Southern philanthropists in Alabama. When he arrived he found forty students and two shacks. When he died in 1915 Tuskegee had over 100 buildings, 2000 acres of land, and an endowment of $2 million. He was one of the founding forces behind two organizations, the National Negro Business League, 1900, and the Urban League, 1911.

Cotton Exposition Speech

Washington is forever linked to his speech known as "The Atlanta Compromise" delivered at the Atlanta Cotton Exposition on September 18, 1895. There was an opening for someone to emerge as a national black leader. Frederick Douglass had died on February 2, 1895. Booker T. Washington's speech offered a clear statement of his beliefs. Bear in mind that he gave it to a white audience. They saw him as the new spokesman for black Americans.

Many statements in "The Atlanta Compromise" were not new. In all his public statements and writings, several themes constantly reappeared.

1. Personal hygiene – "In all my teaching I have watched carefully the influence of the toothbrush, and I am convinced that there are few agencies of civilization that are more far-reaching."

2. Education should be practical – He identified an ailment that plagued blacks, which he called "divine discontent," the discontent that grew out of too much of an academic education, without the ability to change conditions, which caused discontent. He was very critical of black ministers, politicians, and intellectuals, all of whom he labeled "unfit to lead."

3. Politics is NOT important – "Politics and the holding of office were too largely emphasized, almost to the exclusion of every other interest." While he said he favored giving up nothing guaranteed by the Constitution, he personally favored property requirements for voting for whites and blacks. After Alabama disenfranchised blacks in the 1890s, he was proud that the county authorities invited the Tuskegee faculty to register to vote.

4. Solid personal morals and middle class values, the Protestant work ethic – He advised blacks that their "pillar of fire by night and pillar of cloud by day shall be property, economy, education, and Christian character." The basis of racial advancement was moral. At the bottom of everything – economic foundation, economic prosperity, and economic independence – lay personal morals. Among the frequent themes for his chapel talks each Sunday night were "Brains, Property, and Character." Student attendance was mandatory. He believed in self-help, always stressing duties and responsibilities more than rights.

5. Little interest in social equality – Blacks, he asserted, must be willing to start at the bottom of society to earn a chance to achieve economic security. Part of "The Atlanta Compromise" speech was his famous "buckets story." The gist of it was that blacks will stay in the South and be willing workers for white folks. We will be the "most patient, faithful, law-abiding, and unresentful people that the world has seen." We "shall stand by you with a devotion that no foreigner can approach, ready to lay down our lives, if need be, in defense of yours, interlacing our industrial, commercial, civil, and religious life with yours in a way that shall make the interests of both races one."

6. Stressed agriculture – Booker T. Washington hired George Washington Carver to wean Southern black farmers away from cotton. The two worst crops any farmer can plant in terms of drawing nutrients out of the soil are cotton and tobacco, the two primary Southern crops. Carver's research centered around finding new uses for peanuts (such as peanut oil) and sweet potatoes. Washington urged blacks to stay in the South and to stay on their farms. He said that in the cities money jumps out of your pockets. (All of you have had the experience of going into a shopping area or mall and coming out with

something you had not intended to buy.) The question "should blacks stay in South?" was always a subject of great debate among black leaders. Frederick Douglass also said stay, but for a different reason. This obligates the national government to protect blacks; migration would lose the strength that comes from concentrated numbers. Booker T. Washington believed blacks could push their way upward more easily through the barriers of Southern prejudice than through Northern competition with immigrants. One example he cited was that in the decade of the 1880s there were more than fifty strikes led by the American Federation of Labor in which the primary purpose was to end black presence on that particular job site. In reality, most blacks in the South simply could not afford to leave. By 1910 ninety percent still lived in the South. In spite of great financial hurdles, by 1880 20% of Southern blacks did own farms.

Washington's philosophy came directly from General Armstrong, the founder of Hampton Institute. The son of Hawaiian missionaries, Armstrong said labor was a "spiritual force, that physical work not only increased wage-earning capacity but promoted fidelity, accuracy, honesty, persistence, and intelligence." He emphasized acquiring land and homes, vocations, and skills. In many respects, Booker T. Washington was the most eloquent advocate of Armstrong's ideas. He once advised a young black man to "Work! Work! Work! Be patient and win by superior service."

Booker T. Washington stressed that blacks should not antagonize the white South. They should develop habits and skills that would win places for them in their Southern communities. The intelligent management of their farms, ownership of land, habits of thrift, patience and perseverance, and the cultivation of high morals and good manners were the keys. Every race rose on an economic foundation of cultivation of and ownership of the soil. In essence, this is what is sometimes referred to as the "bootstraps" theory. You lift yourself up by individual and group effort, not by relying on others. Governmental help is neither expected nor necessary. We will do it ourselves.

Washington expressed many of the same ideas in an earlier speech to the NEA, the National Education Association, in 1884 in Madison, Wisconsin. He opposed identification with Africa and "back to Africa" ideas. Booker T. Washington was an American. He disapproved of the term African-American, commonly used in this era. He believed in Social Darwinism. The survival of the fittest required you to make yourself fit; progress would come, but there could be no artificial forcing to achieve progress.

One facet of the Atlanta Cotton Exposition Speech was new. Booker T. Washington specifically tossed out any quest for social equality, and attempted to set forth a practical program for black-white relationships. He also was willing to forgo political rights.

He aimed his speech at a white, upper class audience and told them what they already believed and wanted to hear. This is a tactic economist John Kenneth Galbraith in a later context called using "conventional wisdom." If you tell people what they already believe or want to hear, the audience will say it was a wonderful speech.

William Edward Burghardt Du Bois, always referred to as W.E.B. Du Bois
Booker T. Washington's greatest critic was W.E.B. Du Bois, born February 23, 1868. He died August 27, 1963, the day before Martin Luther King's March on Washington and his "I Have a Dream Speech." Du Bois grew up in western Massachusetts, proud of his ancestry – black, Dutch, French, Indian, and, as he often said, "Thank God, no Anglo-Saxon."

He graduated from Fiske University in Tennessee and then studied at the University of Berlin and Harvard University graduate schools. In 1895 he became Harvard's first black PhD. His dissertation was on "The Suppression of the African Slave-Trade to the United States of America, 1638-1870," published as a book in 1896. He published the first in-depth sociological study of a black community in 1899, *The Philadelphia Negro*, which is still well respected by historians. From 1896-1910 he was a professor of Economics and History at Atlanta University.

After 1903 Du Bois became a critic of Booker T. Washington, publishing his views in *Souls of Black Folk*. "In the history of nearly all other races and peoples the doctrine preached at such crises has been that manly self-respect is worth more than lands and houses, and that a people who voluntarily surrender such respect, or cease striving for it, are not worth civilizing." A young black man asked Frederick Douglass, shortly before he died, what advice Douglass had for him. Douglass replied, "Agitate! Agitate! Agitate!" Du Bois would have responded likewise.

His early opposition to Washington coalesced in the 1905 Niagara Movement, which consisted of a small group of educated black professionals. In 1909 he was one of the founders of the National Association for the Advancement of Colored People, the NAACP. Du Bois insisted on the term "colored people," rather than Negro, African, African-American, or Black, because he hoped the organization would address issues facing darker peoples all over the world. A group of concerned blacks and descendants of abolitionists created the NAACP after a race riot in Springfield, Illinois. They were shocked by a race riot within sight of Lincoln's tomb. For decades Du Bois edited *The Crisis*, the newsletter of the NAACP. He reflected on these years in *Dusk of Dawn*, his autobiographical essay published in 1940. In 1961, at age 93, he finally gave up on the United States and joined the Communist Party. He moved to Africa, became a citizen of Ghana, and died there in 1963 at the age of 95, the day before the massive march on Washington. His death was announced to the crowd minutes before Martin Luther King's "I Have a Dream Speech."

Du Bois called Booker T. Washington an "Uncle Tom" who accepted the inferiority of blacks. Du Bois wanted three goals:

1. The right to vote, without which no gains in property could be protected.
2. Civic equality.
3. The academic education of black youth according to their ability, especially the "talented tenth" who would then serve as leaders.

"The Negro race is going to be saved by its exceptional men." "If we make money the object of man-training, we shall develop money-makers but not necessarily men; if we make technical skill the object of education, we may possess artisans but not, in nature, men. Men we shall have only as we make manhood the object of the work of the schools – intelligence, broad sympathy, knowledge of the world that was and is, and of the relation of men to it – this is the curriculum of that Higher Education which must underlie true life." He considered Booker T. Washington's emphasis on industrial and vocational education menial and degrading.

In truth, there were weaknesses in Booker T. Washington's program. He sought to build through small businesses, the family farm, in a period when big business was sweeping all before it. Worse yet, it was in agriculture, the sickest industry in America at the time, and it was in the South, the sickest agricultural region. He also emphasized skills soon to be obsolescent trades, such as blacksmith. In 1900 blacks were 50% of the population in South, but they owned only 15% of the farms. A South Carolina farm worker in 1900 earned $10.79 a month, $129.48 a year. Laborers in New York City made $8.94 a week. Why stay in the South? (As late as 1947 Mississippi plantation workers received $22.50 per week, when there was work.)

As a summary of their differences, it may help to picture a triangle with a very wide base as representing the position of Southern blacks at this time. What is the best way to move the triangle? By pushing from the bottom, trying to help the average black man and woman, the approach of Booker T. Washington, or by pulling from the top, the approach of W.E.B. Du Bois?

Comparing the Two:

Booker T. Washington
a practical realist with tangible goals

W.E.B. Du Bois
a romantic, willing to fight for a principle even if it cost him everything

simple, direct in temperament,
liked to deal with men and things

emotional, liked to deal with ideas

genuine humility and ability to identify with the common person	imperious, aloof, egocentric, often wore gloves, did not like to be touched
faith in people and God	believed Washington's faith in people and God was somewhat naïve
the white man is part of the solution	the white man is the problem
blacks faced two enemies – white racism and black behavior, which, regrettably, confirmed racism	blacks faced one enemy – white racism
the South is the best home for blacks	blacks have no future in the South
vocational trades and crafts, especially the trades	education according to ability, talented tenth, academic education
social and economic equality will follow as a well-deserved reward for good behavior	social and economic equality will follow political victories
primary organizational approach Urban League – opportunistic, behind the scenes, economic his approach was called a "gradualist economic approach"	primary organizational approach NAACP – legalistic, political, constitutional, sue in court his approach was called a "gradualist political approach"
died November 14, 1915	died August 27, 1963

Washington called himself "first and last an American." Du Bois said he was "first and last a black man." Du Bois brilliantly identified the sticking point in the black quest to become part of the **American Identity**. Am I African or am I American? He called it "two unreconciled strivings; two warring ideals in one dark body" and "twoness, – American, a Negro, two souls, two thoughts, two unreconciled strivings."

Which approach works best is still a topic of debate within the black community. Does economic advancement follow political advancement or does the political follow the economic? On the other hand, do both have little to do with one another? The debate goes on. Which of the following would agree with Booker T. Washington or Du Bois?

Marcus Garvey
Martin Luther King, Jr.
Malcolm X
Farrakhan
Jesse Jackson
Barak Obama

A black poet, Dudley Randall, later summarized the differences between Booker T. Washington and W.E.B. Du Bois in a witty, insightful poem. Look up his poem on the Internet, "Booker T. and W.E.B."

PSHP – Another Factor

Using over fourteen million pieces of computerized information culled from manuscript census data and city directories for the late nineteenth and early twentieth centuries, the Philadelphia Social History Project offered another factor limiting black advancement in the late nineteenth century – job discrimination and the subsequent adjustment by blacks to the lack of jobs in the emerging industrial economy. See *Philadelphia: Work, Space, Family, and Group Experience in the Nineteenth Century*, edited by Theodore Hershberg.

A typical black male in late nineteenth century Philadelphia had within one mile of his house approximately 15,000 potential unskilled factory jobs. However, virtually no blacks found employment in factories. This presented a question. How do blacks adjust? They responded by turning to the only part of the urban economy open to them – prostitution, gambling, numbers, petty crime, and robbery, the first three more nuisances in the public mind than crimes. This presence of, and acceptance of, petty criminality led whites to justify further discrimination and segregation. This issue, petty crime, made it especially difficult for the black middle class to defend blacks as a group. This argument is fully developed in Roger Lane's Bancroft Prize winning account, *Roots of Violence in Black Philadelphia, 1860-1900*, and also, his *William Dorsey's Philadelphia & Ours: On the Past and Future of the Black City in America*. It was not primarily the residual effects of slavery that hampered the ex-slave in the late nineteenth century. Industrial employment presented the nation with an opportunity to include blacks in the unskilled labor pool. However, discrimination kept blacks from the types of jobs that immigrants used to earn a living, and, which, in some cases, presented their children with an opportunity to advance economically. Widespread employment discrimination made black survival difficult and advancement impossible. In short, as Du Bois would have said, "It was not us; it was them."

29

INDUSTRIALIZATION IN THE LATE NINETEENTH CENTURY

Incredible Growth

Between 1859 and 1914, the American economy increased its output of manufactured goods, in value, 18 times, and by 1919, boosted by the First World War, 33 times. In 1840 the United States ranked fifth in output among the world's manufacturing countries, by 1860, fourth, by 1894, first, when the United States produced twice what Great Britain produced and half of what all of Europe together produced.

There are three overlapping industrial revolutions in history. The first lasted from the 1760s to the 1840s, with Great Britain leading and the United States, Germany, and France close behind. The second, much more broadly based, stretched from the 1840s to the 1950s. Many historians cite the 1920s as a "second industrial revolution," as the internal combustion engine, electricity, electric motors, and appliances revolutionized factories and the domestic life of the typical household. However, the majority of rural and urban households did not have electricity until after the Second World War. The third industrial revolution, from the 1950s to the present, is based on scientific discoveries and innovations in communication and information technologies.

Why Such Growth?

The main reasons for this phenomenal American growth were: **First**, the United States had very liberal patent laws, which gave an incentive to human ingenuity. The greatest example of a holder of patents in the late nineteenth century was Thomas Edison, who registered 1,093 patents. In 1910 the Patent Office announced that it had just issued patent number one million. In the preceding forty years, it had registered 90% of our first one million patents. The American economy was incredibly innovative. It still is.

Second, another cause was the scarcity and high cost of labor, that gave employers the strongest possible motive to invent, to purchase, and to install labor-saving machinery, essential to mass production. High labor costs push employers toward the increased use of machines. One pays no benefits to machines. They neither go on strike nor get sick. In your lifetime you will be continually astounded at the different ways businesses seek to replace employees with machines. Two examples are grocery stores and self-scanning and ATM machines.

Third, the rapid increase in mechanization promoted the standardization of machinery and parts, as illustrated by the adoption of the standard width, 4' 9" for railroad tracks in the South in June, 1886. The North and West had done that earlier. This permits other trains to use a company's tracks, often for a fee. The standard gauge width avoids the expensive process of unloading and reloading to a different train. Today, if a person travels from China to Mongolia, the train stops at the border to spend the night. It seems like a nice feature from a thoughtful travel agent, the chance to spend the night in a hotel during the middle of a long trip. The real reason you stop is that during the night the railroad cars must be lifted from the Chinese train tracks and refitted with different wheels that fit the Mongolian train tracks, which are a different width. Try to imagine that procedure repeated all over America, if each railroad company followed a policy of maintaining different track widths to keep potential competitors off their tracks. Railroad transportation would be a nightmare. To coordinate travel the railroad companies got together to adopt time zones, which began on November 18, 1883. Congress would finally officially adopt time zones on March 19, 1918. Time zones are necessary because "time" is relative to the position of the sun. When the sun is directly overhead, by definition that is noon. However, noon in Detroit is 18 minutes before noon in Chicago. So, does the train heading for Chicago leave Detroit on Chicago time or Detroit time? After 1883, it left on Eastern Time and arrived on Central Time. Why does it matter? Different trains are using the same tracks. Standard time permits station engineers to determine the position of each train, alerting one to move over to a side track.

Fourth, the extraordinary success of American agriculture was another factor. For example, by 1860 the production of flour was the single biggest industry in the United States; later it was the meat-packing industry.

Fifth, there was the abundance and variety of energy sources, initially water-power, and then steam-power fueled by wood and coal, and then electricity. America produced and distributed energy more cheaply than any other country in the world. The United States still has enough coal to last 500 years.

Sixth, federal and state governmental policies played a role. Governmental assistance took many forms – protective tariffs, subsidies and land grants to railroads, and free access to public land for grazing and mining. One underappreciated factor is the sheer size of the United States. America's size and the freedom of interstate commerce made it, by the 1860s, the world's largest free-trading area. High tariffs caused the home market to buy 97% of all the goods produced by domestic manufacturers by 1900. Even today, once a company saturates its domestic market, it usually tries to increase sales by exporting. However, with America's huge domestic market, it is difficult to saturate the market and exhaust the pool of potential customers.

The policies of the federal government, the state governments, and the local governments greatly aided businesses. For example, railroad companies were legally granted eminent domain, meaning they had the power to take property (they had to pay a just price) to lay their tracks where they decided. Direct government aid to railroads in the nineteenth century amounted to over $350 million. Early railroads often obtained exclusive charters from state legislatures, securing monopoly protection against competitors. Free railroad passes rewarded the compliant state legislators. Sometimes the charters permitted railroads to use special banking privileges to raise money, to avoid paying taxes, and to raise capital by federal, state, county, or municipal bond subscriptions. The most valuable gift was the large amount of federal and state land given to railroads to entice laying their tracks: one-quarter of Minnesota and Washington; one-fifth of Wisconsin, Iowa, Kansas, North Dakota, and Montana; one-seventh of Nebraska; one-eighth of California; and one-ninth of Louisiana. The grand total was 242,000 square miles, larger than Germany or France. Why? In some areas transportation facilities had to precede settlement, such as on the Great Plains, where there was no alternative to the railroad. The rivers in that region are inadequate for transportation.

The speed with which the railroads grew was remarkable. Chicago got its first train in 1848; in 1853 regular service to the East began. By 1860 Chicago had eleven railroad companies with one hundred trains arriving or departing daily. The cost to ship goods by rail plummeted, from 20 cents per ton-mile in 1865 to 1.75 cents per ton-mile in 1900, which greatly expanded a business's potential sale territory. Freight carried rose from 10 billion ton-miles in 1865 to 366 billion ton-miles in 1916.

The Major Business Functions

One way to look at industrialization is by looking at the major business functions, what businesses do. All businesses perform four functions. **The first is innovation**. Think of companies in the news today. McDonald's is known for carefully researching locations. One of its sources of stability is the value of the real estate owned by McDonald's. And you thought it was the French fries! Like other franchises, they offer standardized products promoted by national advertising. McDonald's has grown so large that it is the world's largest customer for beef, chicken, and potatoes. Federal Express can guarantee overnight delivery because the company flies every package into its facility in Memphis, Tennessee, where it is resorted and put on a plane to its destination. When a student first broached the idea for Fed Ex, his business professor said it would never work. The originator thought otherwise. It was an innovative idea, and it did work.

The second is efficiency. How do you keep costs under control? How and where do you cut costs? Remember, one of the costs of doing business is the cost of labor. The best way to ensure a profit is to control costs.

The third is control of risks, both risks in the market place and in the political system. What federal, state, or local laws hinder your business and how do you get them changed? Most often it is done by lobbying and contributing to political campaigns.

The fourth is to raise capital by projecting future growth, "for capitalism depends on investment, and investment depends upon expectations of *future* income." (Harold Livesay, *American Made: Shapers of the American Economy*.)

The Entrepreneurial Firm

The major business organization around 1860 was the entrepreneurial firm, which had many weaknesses. Most significantly, it lacked access to capital. Structured as a single proprietor or partnership, entrepreneurial firms found capital difficult to obtain. Typically, bank loans in the mid-nineteenth century were for no more than 60-90 days, hardly enough time to launch a successful business. Therefore, one had to use personal or family savings and partners for start-up capital. This left a slim margin for error. Historians do not know for certain, but there were apparently fewer than twenty millionaires in the United States in 1860, an insufficient national pool of funds for capital investment. As an example, Frank Weyerhaeuser started a lumber company on the Mississippi River during the Civil War. He was so short of cash that he had to barter his goods for a while. His experience buying a sawmill for $4,616.51 illustrates the entrepreneur's dilemma. Even after he added his uncle's money to his meager savings to buy the sawmill at a sheriff's sale, he paid only $3,000 in cash. He paid the remainder in assets, including a buggy, seven hogs, and a brass collar.

The entrepreneurial firm lacked resources to achieve economies of scale in mass production and distribution. Small businesses are notoriously short on operating efficiency, what an economist labels per unit cost, the cost to produce one item. Many entrepreneurs simply could not grasp the concept of economies of scale, meaning the more you make, the lower the cost to make one of your products. Local businesses lacked the power to influence the market, and thereby to control risks. Their major strength was, and still is, innovation. In addition, a business liability was a personal liability, meaning that you were personally responsible for any business debts. However, be kind to small businesses; today small business is crucial to our society. Most new jobs come from small firms. At the middle of the nineteenth century, all businesses were either the entrepreneurial firm or a partnership. The arrival of the corporation greatly changed the business climate.

The Advantages of the Corporation

The rise of bureaucratic management permitted the corporation to allocate overall planning to the central office, while middle management, a new idea, ran the day-to-day operations in the various facilities and in sales. New accounting methods kept track of costs. Corporate managers became professionals, separating ownership from management.

The experiences of two early corporations – Western Union and Telegraph Co. and the Pennsylvania Railroad – illustrate the advantages of the corporation. A corporation excels at raising capital. It also has a greater control of risks – both risks in the market by monopoly practices and risks in the labor force due to size and political connections. Think of the many strikes in the late nineteenth century, especially the monumental Great Railroad Strike of 1877, which engulfed the nation for weeks. Labor won very few strikes. Corporations could achieve greater efficiency through economies of scale, lowering the per unit cost. One could also employ substantial technological and legal resources. Andrew Carnegie, the consummate steel magnate, employed a highly-paid chemist to analyze his steel to ensure quality and to look for potential ways to lower costs. Finally, a corporation is legally an individual before the law. The Supreme Court, led by Chief Justice Morrison Waite, first clearly stated this interpretation of the equal protection clause of the Fourteenth Amendment in the 1886 case of *Santa Clara v. Southern Pacific*. This is why a corporation can be taxed and why it has limited liability. If a person sues a corporation, as far as the court is concerned, it is one individual suing another individual. Guess which one can muster the greater legal resources?

The corporation's major weakness was, and is, poor ties to the local political system. Corporations are vulnerable to local labor problems and to local political opposition; communities generally support their neighbors when they go on strike. There are over 87,000 elected offices in the United States today, which means that businesses must deal with numerous local government officials. In spite of the image held by many, in truth it is difficult for even a large corporation to control the whole political system. There are too many forms to fill out, too many officials to deal with, too many overlapping legislative bodies, and too many governments – from city councils and departments to county councils and regulatory agencies to state legislatures and state regulatory agencies to Congress and federal regulatory agencies.

All corporations followed a similar pattern. Each company usually tried to expand vertically or horizontally, vertically to obtain control of the manufacturing processes from beginning to end, or horizontally to monopolize one aspect of a business. The best vertical integration example was Carnegie's Steel Company, which controlled its iron ore and coal mines, the railroad transportation system leading to all its factories, and the production of all of its fuel, coke. Because of Carnegie's ownership of all these resources and manufacturing facilities, transportation costs fell, enabling the national distribution of Carnegie Steel Company's products at prices below that of competitors. The horizontal organization of John D. Rockefeller's Standard Oil Company, created by joining forty-one companies together in 1882, only performed one function, controlling the refining of oil. Eventually it expanded vertically also, into drilling, transportation, and the wholesaling and retailing of oil products.

Major Driving Forces in the Economy

One way historians label periods in our economic history is by the major driving forces behind the economy. For example, from 1800 to 1840 it was the westward movement. From 1840 to 1870, it was building the railroads and the expansion of markets the railroads brought. One historian referred to this process as the "breakdown of the island communities," meaning the provincial small town mentality and markets of the isolated towns prior to the coming of the railroads.

From 1900 to 1920, it was the application of two new sources of energy, the internal combustion engine powering cars and trucks, which expanded the market range, and the arrival of electricity for the masses. The price of a model T Ford was $950 in 1910 and $290 by 1924. Automobile registrations hit one million in 1913, and ten million by 1923. The first "motel" appeared in 1926. The number of trucks grew from 158,000 to $3\frac{1}{2}$ million, 1915-1930; the proportion of trucks to private cars doubled. When college students were asked at the end of the 1920s to rank the greatest people of all time, many selected Jesus Christ, Napoleon, and Henry Ford, in that order.

From 1920 to 1970, research and development drove the economy through the application of the principles of chemistry and physics to create new products. Be careful criticizing modern business practices. The United States was a net importer of science and technology until after the Second World War. Our strong point was the making and selling of goods, not the innovations or the research that lay behind the product. It is not true that the United States must, today, lead the world in research, or fall behind economically.

Since 1970 world markets, globalization, information management, and services – fast food, cleaning houses, day care centers, lawn service, and franchising – are some of the forces driving the economy. Note that all the major forces driving the economy at any time in history are always functions of changing technology or changing demographic profiles. For example, the increase in mothers in the work force is a stimulus behind the first three – fast food, cleaning houses, and day care centers.

The Urban Markets – Infrastructure, Consumer Goods

In the years from 1870 to 1900, the major driving force in the American economy became the rise of the urban markets, mainly because 40% of the population lived in urban areas. By 1900 the United States was the world's largest economy. All businesses began to respond to the new emerging urban market.

The first response involved the building of the urban infrastructure. The demand for lighting, communication, heat, power, transportation, water, sewer systems, and other services directly and indirectly took more and more quantities of telephones, copper wire, newsprint, streetcars, coal, iron, steel, copper, lead piping, structures and fixtures, and power equipment. One symbol of this trend was Carnegie's decision in 1887 to switch his Homestead plant near Pittsburgh from producing railroad rails to making structural steel for skyscrapers.

The second impact involved the production or providing of consumer goods. The industries first dominated by large corporations were mainly those making goods for consumers concentrated in the urban market of the growing cities. If the product was new, first marketing was emphasized, and then the corporation expanded into vertical integration, building its own transportation systems, gaining control of raw materials, improving production, etc. Examples are fresh meat, cigarettes, high-grade flour, steel, sewing machines, typewriters, and bananas. If the item was not new, horizontal combination tended to precede vertical integration, as in the production of sugar, salt, whisky, kerosene, rubber, and oil.

Examples of Industrial Response to Urbanization

In 1885 James Duke, the owner of a North Carolina tobacco company, purchased a patent from James Bonsack. Bonsack had dropped out of school to devote all his energy to inventing a machine to make cigarettes. A Virginia tobacco company had offered a prize of $75,000, a large amount of money in these years. Duke bought the Virginia tobacco company and the patent. The new machines produced over 100,000 cigarettes per day. Supply soon outran demand. Duke decided to use innovative advertising to increase demand. Today the average person sees, often without realizing it, well over three thousand ads each day. Think about all the signs your mind sees as you travel on any business street. In 1884 Duke had moved his corporate headquarters from North Carolina to the nation's largest urban market, New York City. The company resolved to produce every tobacco product, what came to be called in the business world, "the full line." Then the company expanded both toward the customers and toward control of production, creating an extensive network of warehouses and buyers to purchase tobacco from farmers. Duke's American Tobacco Company dominated the industry. Only R.J. Reynolds and P. Lorillard were able to create comparable organizations and both eventually were absorbed into the American Tobacco Company. A Supreme Court decision in 1911 split them apart again. However, as was typical of industries responding to the urban market, the tobacco industry remained oligopolistic. An oligopoly means there are few sellers. If one looks at the wide range of cigarette cartons lining the shelves of a store, you get the impression there must be many different companies producing cigarettes. Not so. Pick up each carton and read the name of the company producing them.

The National Biscuit Company, now Nabisco, began in 1898 by merging 114 cracker and cookie bakeries. In the 1890s it gave us the first brand name, "Uneeda," to create brand loyalty. Note that a brand name tells the consumer nothing about the product; it just creates a memorable association. One of the most widely recognized ads in the twentieth century was a five-year-old boy, Gordon Stille, in a rain hat and raincoat clutching his Uneeda Biscuits. A biscuit is what today is called a cracker. Uneeda crackers remained on the shelves until 2009. Nabisco's best-seller hit the market in 1912, Oreo cookies. By 2007 the company had sold nearly 500 billion. Brand loyalty counts. Modern research indicates that consumers loyally buy based on brand names. Just before graduating from college, students receive numerous ads and discounts for new cars from car manufacturers. They know that after his or her first purchase, that individual will tend to stick with that automobile company.

Two brothers, Gustavus and Edwin Swift, started the Chicago-based Swift Meat Company in 1885. Born and raised in Massachusetts, the brothers appreciated the potential of the Eastern urban market. The refrigerated railroad car, invented in 1878, enabled the expansion of their market. The Swift brothers began to ship meat east from Chicago, encountering opposition from local butchers, who spread tales of reduced taste and quality. Because only 40% of a cow's weight is usable meat, the company began using "the full line" of meat products, such as the fat (margarine and soap), brains (soup), and bones (glue, buttons, and knife handles). Swift proudly claimed the company used "everything but the squeal" of the pigs. The company used telephones and telegraphs to constantly adjust for supply and demand. There is an 18-month turnaround in the meat business. If prices rise or fall, it is 18 months before more or less beef or pork can reach the markets, and by then, who knows what will happen to prices. The Swift brothers also built new meat plants nearer to the herds on the Great Plains, between 1888 and 1892 in Kansas City, Omaha, and St. Louis, and after the depression of the 1890s, in St. Joseph, St. Paul, and Ft. Worth. By the 1890s the meat industry was an oligopoly, dominated by five meat companies: Swift, Armour, Morris, Cudahy, and Schwarzschild & Sulzberger. In Chicago the meat packing industry was the largest industrial employer, producing one-third of the city's manufactured goods and accounting for 10% of the city's wages.

Carbonated drinks go back into the late eighteenth century and by the 1840s the soda-fountain store was a fixture in every American city. By the late 1880s America had 1,377 soft drink or soda bottling plants producing 17.4 million cases a year. The driving force behind the industry was the hot and humid South. Not surprisingly, Atlanta gave birth to the industry's masterpiece. A druggist, John Pemberton, experimented with the coca leaf and the cola nut to create Coca Cola, the second most widely recognized term in the world; the first is "OK." He wanted a drink to fight alcohol. By 1905 it was advertised as "The Great National Temperance Drink." However, the success of Coca

Cola was not anti-alcohol. It was in marketing, salesmanship, and organizing skills. Pemberton sold his patent to Asa Griggs Chandler in 1887 for $283.29, which has to be the biggest steal since the purchase of Manhattan Island. In the 1930s Coca Cola sold 322 million cases. In 2015 the company reported that the average household in the world consumed 1.4 bottles or cans each day.

Caleb Bradham, a North Carolina druggist, invented Pepsi as a cure or relief for dyspepsia (an upset stomach) and peptic ulcers, and, as an alternative to hard liquor. The success of both Pepsi and Coca Cola is still marketing. Either one often has the exclusive right in restaurants or fast food chains. In the late twentieth century both tried to obtain exclusive rights in China and India, and failed. Try to picture future sales if only one could sell in either China or India.

Elias Howe invented the first practical sewing machine in 1846. However, the Singer Sewing Machine Company was an unsuccessful, weak company, a business failure before the arrival decades later of William Clark as the new CEO. He created numerous marketing innovations. Before this time, sewing machines had been sold by commission sellers who were paid a percentage for each machine sold. Clark ended commissions; workers were put on salary, even if one produced no sales. His business friends were horrified. The salesmen would do nothing! Clark believed otherwise. A lazy salesman would soon be discovered and fired. Clark also opened up branch stores in towns with repair facilities that sold cloth, fabric, and patterns, and also offered sewing classes. The company prospered. All his successful innovations were in marketing. Cyrus McCormick followed Clark's ideas with his International Harvester Company, taking his salesmen off commissions for farm equipment.

Andrew Preston, a ship owner who traveled between Boston and the West Indies, sold a new fruit, bananas. His business was the nucleus for the United Fruit Company. James Bell took over the Washburn-Crosby Company, which is now Pillsbury, and introduced pre-sifted flour. His associates disputed his claim that a market existed for pre-sifted flour. Bell knew better. Try to imagine what a typical kitchen would have looked like after sifting your own flour to get out the lumps. Everything would have a thin layer of white. Pre-sifted was a great improvement.

Note that most of these innovations were in marketing in response to the urban population's needs or desires. Today, supermarkets are moving more and more into prepared foods to cater to singles and families where all adults work, meals for those with more money and less time. Some fast food companies, such as Boston Market, are fighting back by offering their products as frozen entrées in the supermarkets. The most bizarre marketing innovation in recent times is bottled water, in a nation with the purest water supply in the world! The profit margins are huge. In spite of labels that claim "spring water," some bottled water comes right out of the tap. There is no legal definition of "spring water."

One company was itself a marketing innovation, Sears. Sears, Roebuck & Company went into marketing only, with its own production brand, Kenmore. No Kenmore factory exists. Sears contracted with various manufacturers to make tires, washing machines, refrigerators, etc., all bearing the Kenmore name. Sears pushed prices down by guaranteeing a large market to the manufacturer. For example, Sears Kenmore sewing machines in 1897 cost $13.50, while other brands sold for 3-6 times that.

The United States was the first nation to introduce a voting democracy, but equally central to the ethos of the country was market democracy, in which ordinary people vote with their wallets. In essence, our political ethos, democracy, and our economic ethos, capitalism, became interwoven, each essential to the other. Salesmanship, market research, advertising, and the rapid response of production machinery to customer demand are not the failings of a materialistic society, but instead, the strength of its democracy, economically. Historian Lizabeth Cohen, writing about a later era, used a phrase that could also be applied earlier, a "consumers' republic," in which the country reaffirmed our "democratic values through promoting the expansion of mass consumption." Everyone's dollar is equal in the marketplace.

Oligopoly, a few sellers or producers, characterized almost every industry. By 1904 one-half of all the output in seventy-eight different industries was oligopolistic. By the 1890s it was estimated that the financial firm of J. P. Morgan controlled 40% of the nation's banks and industries. The two hundred largest corporations held 48% of all corporate assets in 1929.

Reduce Costs, Labor

All businesses try to reduce their costs. One concept inherited from England's early industrialization was the idea that cutting wages benefited workers because it stimulated them to work harder. In a book published in 1747, a wool manufacturer explained. "The poor in manufacturing countries will never work any more time in general than is necessary just to live and support their weekly debauches . . . . We can fairly aver that a reduction of wages in the woolen manufacture would be a national blessing and advantage, and no real injury to the poor." This outlook was still typical of industrialists and businessmen in the late nineteenth century and into the twentieth. Henry Ford is remembered for the introduction of his $5 per day wage in 1913, a huge change. However, he was not thinking of the needs of his workers. His grinding assembly-line methods led to an annual labor force turnover rate of 380%. Keeping trained workers at $5 was cheaper than constantly training new workers.

Andrew Carnegie

Andrew Carnegie reduced costs by internal competition. He pitted departments against one another as he perused detailed departmental reports, dashing off memos. Praise went to those parts of the company that found a new way to cut costs and criticism to those that did not. His philosophy was to reduce costs and to reinvest the profit back into the company to expand and to reduce costs even further. As one example of cutting costs, Andrew Carnegie noticed that one new building had a high fire insurance expenditure. Why? It was a wooden building. Carnegie ordered it torn down, rebuilt with brick, and the fire insurance canceled. This attention to detail drove down the cost of making a ton of steel from $100/ton to $12/ ton, and Carnegie still made money. His competitors could not keep up.

One of the costs of doing business is the cost of labor. Carnegie switched his iron and steel factories from three 8-hour shifts to two 12-hour shifts, with every other Sunday off, which meant that a worker put in a 24-hour day every other Sunday, when the shifts changed. The steel industry was dangerous work. Periodic wage cuts were also a means to reduce costs. In 1892 workers went on strike at Carnegie's Homestead Plant, southeast of Pittsburgh. Carnegie's right-hand man, Henry Clay Frick, enlisted 300 strikebreakers from the Pinkerton Detective Agency, already famous for its role in providing agents to infiltrate unions to hamper union activities. A bitter gun battle broke out, killing strikers and Pinkerton agents. It was ended when the Pennsylvania governor sent the state militia. The plant reopened, with reduced wages. During the whole episode Carnegie was on "vacation" in Scotland, trying to distance himself from criticism. "It was Frick, not me." The steel industry never unionized until the 1930s.

Andrew Carnegie gained widespread fame in the late nineteenth century for more than his successful steel enterprise. He wrote an influential essay, "The Gospel of Wealth," for the *North American Review*, June, 1889. Among its famous quotes were the following:

"The man who dies rich dies disgraced."

"Upon the sacredness of property civilization itself depends."

Wealth should not go to one's children; it often does not benefit them, but does the opposite. Wealth should not be left only at death. "Men who leave vast sums in this way may fairly be thought men who would not have left it at all had they been able to take it with them."

The highest life is not lived by imitating Christ, but "by recognizing the changed conditions of this age, and adopting modes . . . suitable to this age."

Almsgiving improves neither the individual nor the race. "Of every $1000 spent on charity, probably $950 is wasted."

The main consideration should be to help those who will help themselves. The best use of wealth is to "place within reach the ladders upon which the aspiring can climb – free libraries, parks, means of recreation, works of art" – all to improve public taste.

Among his business maxims:

"Capitalism is about turning luxuries into necessities."

"Find out the truth from experts."

"Pioneering don't pay." Which meant, do not be the first, the innovator; instead be the one who produces at the lowest cost.

When Carnegie retired and sold his steel company in 1901, it became the basis for the United States Steel Corporation, U.S. Steel. It was the world's first billion-dollar company, capitalized at $1.4 billion, two to three times larger than the federal government's annual budget. It was worth more than the value of all the land west of the Mississippi River combined. In 1901 U.S. Steel had over 100,000 employees, by 1929, 440,000. Because of Carnegie's vertical integration, the U.S. Steel company owned 41 coal and iron ore mines, over one thousand miles of railroad tracks, and 112 ore ships operating on the Great Lakes. U.S. Steel had 60% of the nation's steel-making capacity.

John D. Rockefeller

John D. Rockefeller also stressed reducing costs in his oil refining company. In one well-known example, Rockefeller watched a worker solder a barrel used for shipping oil. He asked how many drops of solder it took to seal the barrel. Perplexed, the worker confessed he did not know the exact number. The two of them counted and tested the hold. Discovering that 39 did the task, Rockefeller told him to use only 39 for each. Imagine constantly counting drops of solder! However, if the worker saved one or two drops each time, that meant reduced costs and the money transferred to Rockefeller's pocket.

He extracted rebates from shippers, getting a kickback on oil shipped on their railroads, even on shipments made by competitors. Why would a railroad agree to this? Why were shippers willing to pay rebates? The answer is that using a railroad's equipment, which had already been purchased, brought in some revenue in the face of unavoidable fixed costs. For example, today a family's automobile costs money even when it is not used – depreciation, insurance, wear and tear on the paint, battery wear, etc. Using it actually lowers the cost per mile driven in an accounting or bookkeeping sense. Shipping Rockefeller's oil, even at a reduced profit, brought in some money to offset a railroad's unavoidable costs. Rockefeller understood this major weakness for the railroads. He gained control of 84% to 95% of the nation's oil refining. Historians are unsure of the percentage; John D. probably knew exactly! His Standard Oil Company became the modern companies of Exxon, Mobil, Amoco, Chevron, Arco, Conoco, and Sohio added together.

When prices leveled off in the early twentieth century, a state regulatory commission, the Texas Railroad Commission, which actually regulated many industries, virtually set the world price for oil through its control of Texas oil wells and pipelines. OPEC, an international cartel, the Organization of Petroleum Exporting Countries, took over in the 1970s, before falling apart in the early twentieth-first century and then reviving. Cartels are agreements among companies or countries to maintain high prices by restricting competition or production. They are difficult to maintain. The production levels shift, and some company or country begins to feel cheated by the old formula dividing up the market.

John D. Rockefeller is easily the richest man in American history. In his lifetime he owned one sixty-fourth of the nation's total wealth. Today's richest individuals own a mere one-four-hundredth, just one-seventh of Rockefeller's wealth. His children received a 20¢ per week allowance, a nickel of which had to go into the Sunday School collection plate. A reporter once asked his grandson, Nelson Rockefeller, the vice president under Gerald Ford and a four-time governor of New York, a question about his grandfather. "Did your grandfather ever do anything illegal?" After thinking for a while the response was, "No, but he caused a lot of laws to be written." When he did it, it was not yet illegal, but everyone immediately said, "There ought to be a law against that."

Carnegie and Rockefeller were not alone in cutting costs. The Nabisco Company, started in 1898, first made an effort to buy out all their competitors. However, the company announced a new policy in its annual report to the stockholders in 1901.

> "In the past, the managers of large merchandizing corporations have found it necessary, for success, to control or limit competition. So when this company started, it was thought that we must control competition, and that to do this we must either fight competition or buy it. The first meant a ruinous war of prices, and a great loss of profit; the second, a constantly increasing capitalization. Experience soon proved that either course must bring disaster. We soon satisfied ourselves that within the Company itself we must look for success."

In other words – cut costs. The new policies were:

1. To improve the internal management of our business.
2. To purchase raw materials in large quantities.
3. To economize on the expenses of manufacturing.
4. To systematize and render more effective our sales department.
5. To improve the quality of our goods and the condition in which they reach the customer.
6. To buy out no competition.

Not all large businesses were successful. The Distillers and Cattle Feed Trust, a huge whiskey monopoly begun in 1887, consolidated approximately 80 plants to just 21 to limit production and to reduce competition. (A "trust" is a legal device by which stockholders in the same industry entrust control of their stock to a group of trustees, who then control production and prices to benefit all the formerly competing companies.) However, it was too easy for a new business to go into the liquor industry. It still is, note the number of small microbreweries constantly springing up. Eight years later, 1895, the Distillers and Cattle Feed Trust went out of business.

Management innovations in successful corporations led to the CEO dominated corporation, the bureaucratic firm, run by the Chief Executive Officer. The CEO oversaw the various departments of the corporation – manufacturing, sales, purchasing, finance, accounting, and legal – making decisions based on a constant flow of statistical information. As historian Alfred D. Chandler described it, in some industries the "visible hand" of management made decisions to allocate raw materials and to set prices, replacing the "invisible hand" of the market's supply and demand. Not much has changed in business structure in one hundred plus years. An era's business mentality influences much of the rest of society, spreading its ideas throughout the society. Watch for it as you live your life.

Robber Barons, Industrial Statesmen, or Philanthropists?

Finally, what have historians said about these late nineteenth century businessmen, 40,000 of whom were millionaires by 1900? When they were building up their industrial empires the public generally thought of them as *The Robber Barons*, the title of Matthew Josephson's 1934 book, published during the Great Depression, when such a description would have been popular. Rockefeller justified his monopoly. He saw himself as an agent of the future, of progress. "The day of combination is here to stay. Individualism is gone, never to return." Other critics pointed out that millionaire businessmen rarely gave away large sums of money until they were older, after about 1910, when they were, perhaps, concerned about the biblical dictum about rich men having difficulty getting into heaven.

One significant factor giving the United States victory in the Second World War was our overwhelming ability to outproduce our enemies. Now the question was reworded. To whom did the nation owe its incredible industrial might? The answer – those nineteenth century industrialists – now seen as "industrial statesmen" who created order and rationality in their chaotic industries and laid the foundation for America's great modern economy. They deserve praise, not condemnation. Historian Allan Nevins summarized the traits of a "Captain of Industry" in his biography of John D. Rockefeller. "Innovator, thinker, planner, bold entrepreneur, he was above all an organizer – one of the master organizers of the era. Taking the most confused, muddled, and anarchic of American industries, he organized it with completeness, efficiency, and constructive talent that amazed beholders and affected all business activities . . . . By virtue of this organizing power, backed by keenness of mind, tenacity of purposes, and firmness of character, he looms up as one of the most impressive figures of the century which his lifetime spanned." Nevins' two volume biography of Rockefeller's life is entitled, *Study in Power, John D. Rockefeller.* Those who exercise power always leave casualties. Focus on the accomplishments.

Both Rockefeller and Carnegie became prominent philanthropists. Together, John D. Rockefeller and Andrew Carnegie gave away about $950 million for various causes. For example, Carnegie provided funds for 2,800 libraries and 7,689 church organs, and to promote world peace. Rockefeller funded medical research, the building of colonial Williamsburg in Virginia, public health initiatives, and the University of Chicago. Other industrialists left similar legacies. However, their acts of philanthropy need to be weighed against their wage cuts for their workers. Overall, it is a mixed legacy.

30

URBANIZATION

Urban America changed dramatically between 1850 and 1900. The 1900 population of just New York City, 3.4 million, almost matched the nation's total urban population in 1850. Waves of immigrants flooded into the cities, mass transit systems sorted out the population, and industrialization created new and different types of employment. The modern city emerged from this interaction between mass man and mass technology. One word of caution, urbanization and industrialization occurred at the same time in the United States, but they are two different, yet parallel, historical developments. The fact they both occurred at the same time had momentous consequences for the nature of our cities. American cities differ drastically from European cities because urbanization preceded industrialization in Europe.

The Old City

The American city in 1850 had not really changed much from the colonial city. Among its chief characteristics were the following:

1. Until after the 1850s it was a compact city, one often centered around the waterfront, either of an ocean or a river.
2. It was a walking city; a person could easily walk to any destination.
3. Land use was mixed; commercial, residential, and industrial usage intermingled.
4. People were relatively integrated. There was little segregation by class, occupation, or immigrant status. Ben Franklin's closest neighbors were a merchant, a plumber, and a cooper, who made and repaired barrels.
5. Some suburbs already existed for the larger cities, such as Northern Liberties for Philadelphia.

The Lure of the City: What Draws People to a City?

Cities had, and still have, many advantages, such as being a place of openness to novel ideas; a place that permits conspicuous consumption; a place where a person could easily lose his or her past; a place where others tend to look the other way when ambition or greed takes a dishonest turn; and a place with a disproportionate number of a young people. Even today the average farmer is in his or her fifties. The greatest export for many farms and small towns is young people.

Changing the Old City – Transportation

Three forces changed the city during the late nineteenth century. The first was new forms of mass transportation. The omnibus, a wagon for carrying passengers, appeared first. It is the origin of the word "bus." By 1833 there were 80 in New York City, each following a regular route. They had two horses and carried twelve passengers, with a rope down the center of the wagon tied to the driver's ankle; a tug on the rope meant to stop at the next intersection. By 1853 there were 683 – over 120,000 people rode daily in New York City. One out of thirty Philadelphians used an omnibus daily in 1850.

Next, the commuter railroads, still the best way to get to any downtown, such as Chicago, Philadelphia, or New York City. For example, in 1859 forty trains daily ran between Philadelphia and the suburb of Germantown. However, such trips cost 15¢ to 25¢ each way, too much for laborers, who earned only $1-2 per day. Laborers walked to work, and research indicates that if the commute was longer than one-half hour they moved to be closer to their worksite. Modern research for Los Angeles gives the same length of time for what many apparently consider the limit for a satisfactory automobile commute, one-half hour.

Streetcars were an improvement over the omnibus. Rails permitted horse-drawn streetcars to travel at twice the speed of the omnibus, getting all the way up to 6-8 miles per hour. The horse-drawn car worked well, except for the horse droppings and the horses slipping on the ice or smooth paving stones from constantly walking on the same pathway. The next technological advance was the cable car. Chicago had over 1400 miles of continuous cable wire powered by machines. San Francisco's system is more famous, but it was not as extensive. In a cable system the cable constantly moves and the conductor must grasp the moving cable in such a way as to slowly build up speed. If you ever get to San Francisco, see the Cable Car Museum, which still operates the city's cable system. A break in the line sent workers scurrying to locate it, because the whole system run by that particular cable would shut down. The electric streetcar, invented by Frank Sprague in Richmond, Virginia, powered by overhead electric wires, replaced both horse-drawn and cable streetcars. Trolley cars got their name because of the "troller" that connected the car to the overhead electric wires. In 1890 there were

5,700 horse-powered, 500 cable, and 1,260 electric streetcars. Twelve years later, in 1902, the numbers were 250 horse, minimal cable, and 22,000 electric streetcars.

The streets became crowded and dangerous. One solution was the elevated railroad, or "el," because, as an example, Philadelphia had a railroad track or a streetcar track on every street. Only Broad Street, the pride of Philadelphia, lacked a railroad track. In just one year in Philadelphia 600 people died in accidents at one of the 8,000 places where a railroad crossed a street. That was over ten a week! Another solution was to go underground, the subway. Boston built the first American subway in 1897; New York City followed in 1904. One difficulty with the American built subway systems was their location, usually just under the street, unlike the European systems that were built far underground. Our subway trains rattled the streets and buildings. Still do.

Streets were rarely paved; city streets were dirty, wet, and filled with animal waste. In the central business district of Philadelphia the streets were washed six times a day to wash away the animal waste. In 1880 New York City, Boston, and Philadelphia combined did not have 10 miles of paved streets. Cobblestones, previously used for some streets, came from the rock piles maintained as ballast for ships. Ships are designed to sit low in the water. Ballast stabilizes a ship when the cargo is so light as to make sailing the ship dangerous. By 1900 all three cities – New York City, Boston, and Philadelphia – had extensive paved streets, thanks to the invention of the asphalt seamless paver. Smooth streets set off a bicycle craze in the 1890s.

Charges of political corruption tinged the building of subway systems, the elevated railroads, the trolley car systems, and the awarding of street-paving contracts. Corruption accusations and other cries for reform were part of the impetus behind the urban Progressive Movement. Those out of political power or favor often made corruption accusations. Some were justified and some unjustified.

Consequences of the Building of Transportation Systems

How did the new forms of transportation change the city? **First**, they expanded the city. In 1850 the borders of Boston were two miles from the central business district, CBD; in 1900 they stretched ten miles away. Today, London is 50 miles wide. On some occasions, it may take two days to cross from one side of Mexico City to the other. The growing city decentralized its economic functions. Downtown was no longer the only place to shop or to conduct business. Modern Los Angeles has six "downtowns," there is really no downtown central business district for Los Angeles. Instead, there are strip shopping areas. In the twentieth century many shopping areas moved off the streets, becoming the mall.

Second, the growing city sorted out its population, creating many new neighborhoods, each with fine social and economic distinctions. Many of these have pastoral sounding names – Woodside, Shipley Farms, Lakeview Estates – all without woods or farms or lakes. Suburbanites now possessed the serenity of the farm and woods AND the advantages of the city. These neighborhoods differed in price and desirability, although the reason why was often only price-based. What became the ideal was the detached, single-family dwelling with the manicured lawn. By 2016 over 60% of Americans owned their homes, a percentage unmatched by any other country. Widespread home ownership helps to explain our incredibly deep conservatism. Property ownership makes people both conservative and capitalistic. Possessions possess.

Third, the transportation systems created specialized land usages. Now rings surrounded the city and the CBD, the central business district. The poor lived in older housing adjacent to the CBD, with the middle class neighborhoods and the wealthy suburbs radiating outward. In the early twentieth century, urban sociologists, such as Park Burgess, called this the "concentric zone theory." An urban historian, Michael H. Ebner, labeled the resulting urban core and suburban periphery "dual metropolises" that differed greatly in race and wealth. Only New York City, centered on an island, does not conform to this model. As new sources of energy arrived, the older downtown industrial buildings were abandoned. Electricity negated the need for proximity to water power or the necessity for tall buildings, where belts coming off center shafts powered all the machinery. Now a business or factory could be a relatively flat building anywhere, especially along highways. Look at the abandoned buildings beside the CBD in any older city. New York City is an exception, although a fashionable loft apartment there exists only because it is a former factory building. European cities differ from American cities. Their industrial ring is on the outside, in the suburbs, while the area beside the CBD is a high-income residential neighborhood. Why? Because when industrialization hit Europe the best place to put factories was in the cheaper suburbs. Therefore, the working class lives in the suburbs.

Finally, speed and punctuality now became urban habits. One takes the 8:07 train rather than the next one or the one that comes around 8 o'clock. Mobility made the ideal of the stable neighborhood community impossible. The typical American still moves every seven years.

Changing the Old City – Industrialization

American cities now became, even more than before, centers of economic activity – places of mass production, mass consumption, and mass distribution of goods. The Internet may change that in the future. The major food distribution center for the Philadelphia metropolitan area is in South Philadelphia. It is the source of every area supermarket's perishables. The large downtown department store appeared in this era. New York City's Macy's, Chicago's Marshall Field's, and Philadelphia's John Wanamaker's revolutionized shopping with their innovations:

1. A large variety of goods under one roof.
2. Low competitive prices, made possible by dealing directly with suppliers and selling in volume.
3. One price for all customers, with guaranteed money back if dissatisfied.
4. Large-scale advertising.

Competition between cities increased as each city reached out for economic markets, pushing into their hinterland and competing with other cities. Northern New Jersey became part of New York City's markets and Southern New Jersey belonged to Philadelphia. This is still true. New Jersey is the most urbanized state in the country, but it does not have a single large market commercial television station in the state. New Jersey is, in essence, an extension of New York City and Philadelphia. The rivalry between St. Louis and Chicago fooled St. Louis. St. Louis made little effort to grow, secure in the knowledge that its position on the Mississippi River would in the future make St. Louis the premier American city. Meanwhile Chicago worked to expand. Chicago reversed the Chicago River to send its sewage waste away from its water supply, Lake Michigan. Chicago also vigorously pursued railroad connections. In the contest between New York City, Philadelphia, and Baltimore, New York City clearly won. In 1860 it was the number one port of entry for 991 out of the top 1000 goods imported into the United States. However, today New York City is losing its lead. Northeastern containerized shipping is moving more to New Jersey and Baltimore. Blessed with a perfect harbor, San Diego saw little to improve. Meanwhile upstart Los Angeles enticed railroads, built an artificial harbor, and won the race for urban supremacy in Southern California.

Industrialization stimulated city growth. In 1922 a Mexican finance minister observed that in the United States "capital is native, while labor is largely foreign," with the result that "labor is weakened." The large pool of unskilled immigrants provided the labor force for mass production industries, such as the shoe, textile, and carpet industries in Philadelphia. Immigrants and their American born children became the backbone of the labor force for many urban industries, such as 97% of New York City's garment industry and 92% of Chicago's meatpacking industry. New York City ruled supreme as an urban industrial site; at one time New York City had 10% of the entire nation's manufacturing.

Some cities grew by exploiting nearby resources, such as Milwaukee, beer from hops; Minneapolis, flour from wheat; Dallas, oil; Denver, minerals; and Cleveland, as a meeting point for iron ore and coal. Other cities became identified with a specific industry, and therefore, became vulnerable to downturns in that industry. For example, Akron, Ohio, tires; Grand Rapids, Michigan, furniture; Detroit, cars; Dayton, Ohio, cash registers; Troy, New York, cast-iron stoves; and Wilmington, Delaware, first chemicals and now credit cards.

Changing the Old City – Immigration

From 1860 to 1920 the urban population of the United States grew from 6.2 to 54.3 million, an increase of 48 million. America's internal immigrants, refugees from rural farms, were nicknamed "buckwheats." They were escaping the isolation and loneliness of the farm and small town America. But most of those moving into the cities came from overseas. Earlier some cities and states passed laws to restrict or to control immigration. However, in the Passenger Cases of 1849, *Smith v. Turner* and *Norris v. The City of Boston*, the Supreme Court ruled that immigration was "foreign commerce," which fell under Congress's powers. No major federal law restricted immigration in any manner until 1885, when the Foran Act, the Alien Contract Labor Law, prohibited the entry of workers already under contract for a job. It was also the last federal immigration act motivated solely by economic motives.

First Wave

The first wave of European immigrants ranged from the 1840s to 1880. This first wave came from:

> The British Isles – 47%
> Germany – 18%
> Italy – 10%
> Russia – 7%
> Sweden, Norway, Finland, Denmark – 7%
> Spain – 5%
> Portugal – 2%
> Austria – 2%
> France, Belgium, Netherlands, Switzerland – 2%

Who left Europe and where did they go? Note that not all immigrants came to the United States.

> United States – 63%   Australia – 5%
> Argentina – 10%   New Zealand – 2%
> Brazil – 6%   Uruguay – 2%
> Asiatic Russia – 6%   British West Indies – 1%
> Canada – 5%

Up to 1840 the United States rarely received more than 20,000 immigrants a year, mostly immigrants from the British Isles or smuggled slaves from Africa, in spite of the provision in the Constitution that outlawed the importation of slaves after 1808. Thanks to the Irish potato famine that began in 1845, and political upheavals elsewhere in Europe, a flood began. From 1850-1900 thirty million arrived. Irish Catholics came to escape the potato famine, while German Catholics and Protestants, who were disappointed by the failure of the liberal revolutions of 1848, also flowed in, and some English, Scandinavians, and Scots arrived. Andrew Carnegie's family was one. This wave of immigrants gave us some new drinking habits, including an affinity for beer and wine. The traditional American drinks up to that period had been rum and whisky.

Immigration also raised the nativist issue of religion. In the 1850s the short-lived American Party, or Know-Nothing Party, rode to political victories on the issue of nativism. Between 1840 and 1890, 5½ million Catholics entered the United States. By 1870, 40% of all churchgoers were Catholics, a major change for American society. There were few Catholics in colonial America, with only 56 Catholic churches out of 3142 congregations in 1775. In 1789 there were only 35,000 Catholics in America. By 1860 Catholics had become one of the largest denominations. This set off a reaction. The anti-Catholic American Protective Association, an organization formed to fight Catholic immigration, peaked in numbers in 1896 and then declined. An increase in anti-Catholicism appeared in many places, as shown by squabbles in the public schools over which version of the Bible to use for daily devotional reading. A few states even passed compulsory public school attendance laws, with no parochial schools allowed; court suits ended such laws. These issues led eventually to the creation of extensive urban Catholic school systems, which generally do not exist in other countries. In many Catholic countries, priests and nuns teach in the public schools. Not here.

Second Wave – the "New Immigrants"

The second wave, nicknamed the "new immigrants," arrived between 1880 and 1920. This group differed from the earlier one. Coming mainly from Southern and Eastern Europe, this wave of mostly rural, poor peasants arrived in great numbers – in the 1880s 5.2 million, in the 1900-1910 decade 8.8 million. To give some idea of the number of immigrants entering the country, New York City had more German-speaking people than any other city in the world except Vienna and Berlin, more Irish than anywhere but Dublin, more Russians than in Kiev, and more Italians than in Milan or Naples. Look at the following percentages from the 1910 census. The first column gives the percentage of foreign born, the second the percentage of native born with at least one foreign born parent. In other words, in the popular opinion of that era, they were not "real" Americans. One leading educator, Francis Walker, labeled them "beaten men from beaten races."

	Foreign Born	**One Parent Foreign Born**	**"Foreigners" (To "Real Americans")**
New York City	40.4%	38.2%	Total of 78.6%
Chicago	35.7%	41.8%	Total of 77.5%

Boston	35.9%	38.3%	Total of 74.2%
Detroit	33.6%	40.4%	Total of 74.0%
Milwaukee	29.8%	38.8%	Total of 68.6%

This wave was composed mainly of Catholics from Italy and Poland and Russians and Jews from Russia. At the end of the musical *"Fiddler on the Roof,"* one Jewish Russian immigrant is going to Chicago and another to Buffalo. Knowing nothing about American geography, the Buffalo man proudly says, "We'll be neighbors!" Before 1948 American immigration officials did not list "Jewish" or any religion as a separate classification. Therefore, historians can only guess the percentage of Jewish immigrants. Russian Jews had many reasons to leave Russia. The government officially sponsored pogroms against Jews, forcing them into smaller and smaller parcels of land. All these "new immigrants" had a double adjustment, from rural to urban and from foreign to American. The pressure was always on the immigrant to adjust. The difficulties of that adjustment are beautifully illustrated in the poetry of Professor Judith Ortiz Cofer, a former professor at the University of Georgia. Writing in the late twentieth century, her Latino women pray "in Spanish to an Anglo God / with a Jewish heritage," while "fervently hoping / that if not omnipotent, / at least He be bilingual."

Historians have gained insight into immigration from research by Jacob Vigdor, a professor of public policy at the University of Washington. Primarily researching present-day immigration, his writing warns us that assimilation is not a simple process. Assimilation has three facets, each of which follows a different timeline. One is *economic assimilation* – how easily, differently, and extensively do various immigrant groups merge into the economy and rise in economic status? Where and to what extent do they make a productive contribution to the economy? Second is *cultural assimilation* – to what extent do various groups of immigrants learn English, marry outside their group, and adopt the customs and practices of the native-born? Third is *civic assimilation* – to what extent do various immigrant groups participate in American society through naturalization, political activity, voting, and military service? These three assimilations – *economic, cultural, and civic* – differed for each immigrant group, in degree, extent, and timing, and still do.

Immigrants were drawn to America by what historians label "chain migration." Relatives and friends in the old European village kept receiving letters praising life in America. Soon they packed their bags and left. In the twenty-five years prior to the beginning of the First World War in 1914, one-half of all Italian immigrants to Cleveland came from only ten different villages in Southern Italy. Between 1850 and 1930, 45% of all the Italians who came to San Francisco came from nine communities in only four different Italian provinces. Between 1890 and 1930, 50% of all the marriages in Boston's North End Italian parishes were couples with roots from the same village in Italy.

In the old country these people had been part of a "network," and it continued here through community-centered ethnic activities. Ethnicity was strengthened by parochial schools, foreign language newspapers, the ethnic parish, fraternal and cultural groups, and entertainment, especially the new film industry. There were 800 German newspapers in the United States by 1890. In Baltimore four public elementary schools taught lessons in only German. The second generation of these "new immigrants" tended to become nationalistic towards the idealized old country, leading to nationalistic celebrations such as Columbus Day for Italians, which began around 1915, to organizations such as the Sons of Italy, and to an increase in Irish supporters of the IRA, the Irish Republican Army. For many immigrants, migration did not break down their traditional family patterns, just as it did not later for blacks coming from the South. Instead, migration appears to have actually strengthened traditional family patterns.

A large amount of ethnic conflict characterized the Catholic immigrant community. The previously arrived ethnic group often controlled the church hierarchy. For example, Italian immigrants confronted Irish priests. The Church resolved its ethnic conflict by creating American Catholic churches unlike those elsewhere, the ethnic parish. Look at the names to see if you are welcome – St. Anthony's, Italian; St. Patrick's, Irish; or St. Hedwig's, Polish. Within the Jewish community conflict surfaced between German, Polish, and Russian Jews, and between Orthodox, Conservative, Liberal, and Reform Jews.

In the Western United States lived tens of thousands of Chinese, as much as 20% of the population of Idaho at one point, 50,000 in just San Francisco. In a referendum in 1879 California residents voted their opposition to Chinese immigration, 154,638 to 883, or 99.4% favoring exclusion. The state constitution of 1879 forbade their employment by public bodies and called upon the legislature to protect the state from the burdens and evils arising from their presence. Such agitation led Congress to enact the national Chinese Exclusion Act in 1882. Chinese were the first immigrant ethnic group specifically excluded. Provisions in the 1882 Chinese Exclusion Act called for renewal every ten years. During the debate over the 1892 renewal, a House of Representatives committee report asserted that "American citizens will not and can not afford to stand idly by and see this undesirable race carry away the fruits of labor which justly belongs to them." In 1902 the exclusion was made permanent. The restriction was repealed during the Second World War when it understandably became a source of embarrassment in our relationship with one of our allies, China. The sectional nature of the 1902 vote in the House of Representatives is revealing. The East and Midwest voted for it 112-37, the West and South, 89-0. The 1882 law contradicted the Burlingame Treaty of 1868, in which China and the United States agreed to the free movement of residents between the two countries. A later treaty in 1890 gave the United States the right to restrict Chinese immigrants. French Canadians in New England, numbering 800,000 first and second generation by 1900, were nicknamed the "Chinese of the Eastern states" and were equally unwelcomed.

Germans arrived with more money because they left Germany more for political reasons than for economic reasons. The political failure of the revolutions of 1848 drove liberals out, since they were certain that democracy in Germany's future was a hopeless dream. German immigrants tended to settle in the "German Triangle" – Cincinnati, Milwaukee, and St. Louis. They thrived in the beer industry in Milwaukee. The first kindergartens (note the German spelling) began in St. Louis.

Notice what group has not been mentioned, blacks. In 1890, 90% still lived in the rural South. By 1900, 32 cities had a black population over 10,000. However, in the North they were a small percentage of each city's population. Look at the following percentages of blacks in various cities in 1910 – New York City, 1.9%; Chicago, 2%; Cleveland, 1.5%; Milwaukee, .3%; Newark, 2.7%. The "great migration" to the urban North had not really begun. The presence of a cheap black labor supply in the South meant that few immigrants went into the South, which led to far greater differences between the Northern and Southern populations than existed before the Civil War.

Characteristics of the Immigrants – The American Identity

Historians and other academics use four models to explain how the **American Identity** was created out of immigrant diversity. **First**, the **"melting pot."** This term comes from a play written by a British Jewish immigrant playwright, Israel Zangwill, *The Melting Pot*, 1908. Melted and fused together, "Here shall they all unite to build the Republic of Man and the Kingdom of God." One difficulty with this term is that many were "un-melted," due to race and nationality. The "melting pot" of American myth and legend is overdone. It was more like a stew or salad bowl, with each ethnic group still easily identified. It was the second and third generations that easily fit in, as shown by the names on any college or school class roll.

Second is the **"Anglo-conformity model,"** which sees all immigrants adjusting to the dominant English-based model of society and culture and values, proving their worth by becoming just like us. A modern example is the push in some states to make English our official language.

Third is the **"structural pluralism model,"** which sees and welcomes a diverse American society whose groups can be differentiated by religion, race, nationality, occupation, class, and culture. Horace Kellan, a Jewish immigrant who became a highly respected philosophy professor, argued this view of immigration in a 1915 essay, "Democracy Versus the Melting Pot." Pluralism was, and is, our strength, not our weakness. Americans celebrate our differences together through parades, foods, festivals, and holidays. For example, on St. Patrick's Day many Americans consume green beer to celebrate what they are not, being Irish. The grocery stores push Mexican food for Cinco de Mayo, a relatively minor Mexican holiday. Independence Day in Mexico is September 16, ignored here.

Many nineteenth century immigrants came only to make money, intending and hoping to return home. An estimated 30-40% did go home, still a characteristic of some of today's immigrants. Immigrants also sent tons of money home to help relatives. Still do. Today millions of dollars in Social Security checks are sent overseas every month to Americans who retired to the "home country," especially Ireland, Italy, and Poland.

Two-thirds of all the immigrants lived in cities, often in concentrated areas. The Lower East Side in New York City had more people per square mile than anywhere else in the world. Educators worried over what to do with the immigrants. In New York City the school population jumped 60% from 1900 to 1914. The Superintendent, William H. Maxwell, decided to teach immigrants only in the English language. Today our schools try ESL, English as a Second Language. He devised a curriculum emphasizing practical science, physical education, manual training, and industrial arts for boys; and domestic arts and home economics for girls. However, few immigrants graduated; their families needed their income. The dream of rising by getting educated usually applied to the second or third generation. The one exception was Jews, who came from a religious tradition that emphasized education and from a group consciousness that led them to pool the neighborhood's money to send the brightest kids off to college. When they achieved success, they aided other Jewish kids. Jews also differed in another respect – they had no homeland in Europe that would welcome their return.

There was social, generational, and geographic mobility for immigrants in America, but there was not as much as mythmakers would have us believe. Based on computerized studies of the manuscript census returns, city directories, tax records, and newspapers in an effort to research history "from the bottom up," historians find a different story. The cities experienced great population turnover. Between 1870 and 1880, 56% of Atlanta's population left. Between 1910 and 1920, 57% of Boston's population moved out of Boston, and in that decade 138,000 families moved in. Research on Philadelphia in the late nineteenth century found a report on the city's school population that gave the student population as increasing from 90,000 to 93,000 in one year. How many students were new to the city's schools? Watch how you phrase your questions when you do research. The same report stated that 58,000 of these students were new to the Philadelphia school system. So much for education being the path to upward mobility. This fluidity of the population weakened the development of a sense of neighborliness, at least as an ideal. Neighborliness is still weak in America. Since the average family moves once every seven years, where is today's sense of stable neighborliness?

There is a theory among politicians and the public that over time today's new immigrants will replicate the earlier immigrant experience. These groups will rise as generations pass and will be absorbed into the melting pot of America. This concept of assimilation, the **Fourth**, is called the **"bootstraps theory,"** the idea that each group pulls itself up by its own efforts. There is no need to provide any government help. However, the changing nature of the economy and the constant turnover in a city's population means that there is no such thing as a similar experience for immigrants. The city of 1850 was not equal to the city of 1880 nor of 1910 nor of 1930 nor of 1970 nor of 2010. These are different cities, with different opportunity structures of skilled and unskilled jobs, adequate housing, and public education. Blacks, who migrated from the American South, Latinos, Hispanics, Asians, Africans, and Middle Easterners face a different city today, just as did each wave of immigrants in the past.

Building the Physical City

New York City had a momentous impact on city housing by setting the standard lot size in 1811 at 25 feet wide by 100 feet deep. This meant that there would be little open space between houses, leaving no green space for the city block. The discovery of "balloon" construction, apparently first started in Chicago in 1833, with wooden studs every sixteen inches rather than solid stone or brick walls, led to more rapid construction.

In the 1860s and 1870s tenements first appeared, defined in 1870 as any building housing three or more families. They were 4-6 stories high, with 16 to 24 families, amounting to as many as 150 people per building. The number of tenement buildings in New York City shows the overcrowding: 1879, 21,000; 1888, 32,000; 1900, 43,000. Visit the Tenement Museum in New York City on Orchard Street, near the Manhattan side of the Brooklyn Bridge. Reformers pushed for the adoption of the "dumbbell tenement" as a reform. By 1900 it was considered anything but a reform. A dumbbell tenement is easy to imagine. Picture a row of hand-held dumbbell weights lined up on a shelf, side-by side, stacked up, with the fronts and backs pressed together. As a six story tenement it had very little cross ventilation, and, no toilets, just outhouses. Two inventions that dramatically changed the physical city were the elevator and steel-frame construction, first used in Chicago in 1884. Now height was no longer a drawback.

Fires were always a threat, with the Chicago fire of 1871 being a good example. It destroyed 18,000 buildings, one-third of the city, and made 150,000 people homeless. The fire was so destructive it put 51 insurance companies out of business. The next year 800 buildings burned down in Boston. Boston, Portland, and Philadelphia all mandated slate roofs as a safety measure. However, the additional weight created structural problems for property owners, businesses, and homeowners.

The state of public health in the last half of the nineteenth century is comical to us today. In 1877 Philadelphia had 82,000 cesspools (outhouses) and Washington, D.C., had 56,000. They filled up and needed to be emptied occasionally. Imagine leaky wagons filled with human waste moving down the streets carrying waste to the outskirts of the city. Debates raged in many cities over the question of combined or separate sewers for rainwater runoff and sanitary sewers. If combined, they occasionally backed up in a severe rainstorm, flooding streets and basements with sewage. Horse manure was a problem. In the 1830s horse manure lost its place as the farmers' number-one fertilizer. Guano, dried bird droppings from islands off the west coast of South America, increased crop yields by 300 percent. In 1900 New York City had 200,000 horses, each of which deposited an average 10 to 20 pounds of manure per day, adding up to between two and four million pounds daily, and farmers no longer wanted it. It lined the streets in banks pushed to the side. In some vacant lots manure was piled as high as 60 feet. In addition, the horses that lived in the city died in the city, as did 15,000 in New York City in 1880. Getting rid of them was a problem.

Reformers originally pushed the park movement to bring the benefits of the countryside into the city. Central Park in New York City, designed by Frederick Law Olmsted, is the best known park from this era. Parks did not really catch on until the late nineteenth century. There was a dearth of open space in cities, especially the older cities.

The City "Boss"

Many urbanites and later historians condemned the late nineteenth century's municipal governments. Every city government seemed to have a "boss." Was the boss someone who brought order out of chaos? Was the boss someone who solved problems by cutting through the red tape? On the other hand, did the boss function as a corrupt ally for his ethnic group and businesses, like Boss Tweed in New York City? James Bryce, a British diplomat who later became an American citizen, and also Theodore Roosevelt's good friend, called city governments "the one conspicuous failure of the United States." Andrew White, president of Cornell University, called city governments "the worst in Christendom – the most expensive, the most inefficient, and the most corrupt."

So, was the city by 1900 a success or a failure? Problems may have persisted by 1900, but the truth is that in America's cities the supply of water was the most abundant, the street lights were the most brilliant, the parks the grandest, the libraries the largest, and the public transportation systems the fastest of any city in the world. In *The Unheralded Triumph: City Government in America, 1870-1900*, urban historian Jon Teaford finds many reasons to applaud late nineteenth century city governments. They met the "challenges of diversity, growth, and financing with remarkable success." The city politicians "also achieved an uneasy balance of the conflicting forces within the city, accommodating each through a distribution of authority." The real problem, as far as many reformers and upper class critics were concerned, was the ethnic and class background of the municipal politicians.

An American Tradition – Anti-Urbanism

Americans were not sure about the nineteenth century city. Even today many Americans often hold curiously anti-urban attitudes, and this in an increasingly urban nation. A popular book written in 1885 by Rev. Josiah Strong, *Our Country: Its Possible Future and Its Present Crisis*, succinctly summarized the nineteenth century attitude of our cities' critics. He opposed immigrants, Catholics, Mormons, saloons, tobacco, large cities, socialists, political machines, and concentrated wealth. In other words, everything non-American! He did not miss any urban topic in his criticism. He later echoed these sentiments in his 1907 book, *The Challenge of the City*. Among his indictments of American cities were the following:

"The first city was built by the first murderer, and crime and vice and wretchedness have festered in it ever since."

"The city is the nerve center of our civilization. It is also the storm center. The fact, therefore, that it is growing much more rapidly than the whole population is full of significance."

"The city has become a serious menace to our civilization. It has a peculiar attraction for the immigrant." (Our policies toward immigrants and immigration are still controversial. It was not until 1947, in the early Cold War period, that the federal government moved the bronze tablet containing Emma Lazarus' poem, "*The New Colossus*," from an obscure location to beside the main entrance to the Statue of Liberty, whose actual name was *Liberty Enlightening the World*. Sixty-four years after it was written, Americans finally welcomed "your tired, your poor, your huddled masses yearning to breathe free." Do today's Americans still welcome those "yearning to breathe free"?)

"Because our cities are so largely foreign, Romanism (the Catholic Church) finds in them its chief strength."

"Not only does the proportion of the poor increase with the growth of the city, but their condition becomes more wretched. The poor of a city of 8,000 inhabitants are well off compared with many in New York; and there are no such depths of woe, such utter and heart-wringing wretchedness in New York as in London."

"For the same reason a saloon, together with the intemperance and the liquor power which it represents, is multiplied in the city."

"Socialism not only centers in the city, but is almost confined to it, and the materials of its growth are multiplied with the growth of the city. Here is heaped the social dynamite, here inequality is the greatest." What is silly about this comment is that Karl Marx, the intellectual father of communism, held a dim view of American socialists. He dismissed his American followers as "middle class humbugs and worn-out Yankee swindlers in the Reform business." For example, they crazily pushed for women's rights ahead of empowering workers.

In Europe, Oswald Spengler, the German social commentator, echoed Josiah Strong's sentiments in *The Decline of the West*, 1926. He lamented that the city had replaced the country. "In place of a type-true people, born of and grown in the soil, there is a new sort of nomad, cohering unstably in fluid masses, the parasitical city-dweller, tradition-less, utterly matter-of-fact, religionless, clever, unfruitful, deeply contemptuous of the countryman and especially that highest form of countryman, the country gentleman." Cities simply have too many lower class people.

Economic changes in the late nineteenth century produced the modern metropolis and a sense of anti-urbanism. A Harvard philosopher and his wife, Morton and Lucia White, succinctly captured the wide range of American anti-urbanism in *The Intellectual Versus the City*, p. 222. The city "is too big, too noisy, too dusky, too dirty, too smelly, too commercial, too crowded, too full of immigrants, too full of Jews, too full of Irishmen, Italians, Poles, too artificial, destructive of conversation, destructive of communication, too greedy, too capitalistic, too full of automobiles, too full of smog, too full of dust, too heartless, too intellectual, too scientific, insufficiently poetic, too lacking in manners, too mechanical, destructive of family life, tribal and patriotic feeling." Other than that, cities are a great place to live!

31

POLITICS IN THE LATE NINETEENTH CENTURY

Historiography of Political History
Historians look at many different factors when studying political history. Politics is a complex subject. One must consider competing economic interests, the complex interplay of motivations, ethnic loyalties and prejudices, cultural heritage, religious convictions, and ideology. The energies that shape public life are emotional as well as rational, cultural as well as economic, ideological as well as practical. There are two ways to present an overview of American political activity. One is the "Party Systems." A second way historians look at politics is from the viewpoint of the average voter.

Politics From the Viewpoint of the Average Voter
The **"politics of assent"** characterized politics stretching from the colonial period to the 1820s. Essentially, it was plebiscitarian, meaning, "This is what we did, do you approve?" Rather than asking or seeking the public's opinion and direction, politicians did what they knew the public needed, and watched the results of the next election to see if the voters understood what was really in their best interests. Sometimes the public did; sometimes the public did not.

The political party of the masses arrived in the 1820-1900 period, characterized by the **"politics of partisanship"** with party loyalty, parades, and carnivals. Voting was more an act of party affiliation rather than a judgment rendered after a thoughtful consideration of the issues. Voter loyalty was linked to comradeship more than to policy. It resembled the loyalty one has to a college sports team. Think about it. How many players on the team does any fan know personally? One always voted for his party, no matter what the current issues.

From the Progressive Era to the end of the Second World War in 1945 the voter thoughtfully studied and debated issues like civil service reform, which awarded government jobs based on examinations, the secret ballot, also known as the Australian ballot, prohibition, and suffrage for women. In the **"politics of the informed citizen"** the voter was supposedly independent, rational, and educated on the issues. The ideal voter was the nonpartisan voter. Voting became more logical, and thus, less exciting or enjoyable to the voter. Voter turnout dropped, from about 80% in the 1890s to 49% by 1924.

After 1945 the arena for political activity shifted. Now it was the **"politics of rights"** – for blacks, women, gays, handicapped, etc. The courtroom was added to the voting booth as a place for political contests. Individuals and organizations, such as the NAACP or the Sierra Club, filed lawsuits. In addition, the battles over rights were also fought out in everyday life – in the streets, in the schools, in the workplace, in the home, and even in the marriage. Americans accepted a more privatized ideal of citizenship, more cerebral and less fun, like spinach, unappealing, but good for you. Voter turnout continued to be low; the ballot box was often not the primary scene for political fights over the politics of rights, as it had been earlier for other issues. Now it is the street demonstration or the courtroom. A county clerk in Kentucky could object to issuing a marriage license for a gay couple. Politicians quickly jumped on the controversy, but the courts decided the issue, as the politicians knew they would.

Politics from the Viewpoint of Party Systems

Some historians and political scientists use the concept of party systems to study American political history. Simply stated, it means grouping the presidential elections into different systems and seeing similarities between the politics and elections within the period of that party system. The dates for the party systems vary from historian to historian, but generally, they are as follows:

> First Party System – 1790 to 1824
> Second Party System – 1824 to 1860
> Third Party System – 1860 to 1896
> Fourth Party System – 1896 to 1932
> Fifth Party System – 1932 to 1968
> Sixth Party System – 1968 to ????
> (Has the Seventh Party System begun?)

The previous party system dissolves due to some crisis or major change in the characteristics of popular support or the arrival of new issues. The elections that usher in a new system are termed "defining elections" or "turning point elections." The First Party System ended with the death of the Federalist Party on the national scene, the ending of many foreign policy issues, and the expansion of suffrage to all white males.

The Second ended with the outbreak of the Civil War. The depression of 1893 and the resulting economic chaos ended the Third. The Fourth ended because of another depression, the Great Depression. The Fifth was a casualty of the turbulent decade of the 1960s. If someone wants to win the presidency, he or she should be ready with the right issues when the Sixth ends, unless it has already and we are not yet aware of it.

Years from now it is possible that the economic downturn that began in 2007 may be seen as ushering in the Seventh Party System with the 2008 election. Fundraising, media coverage, and the use of the Internet have become more significant parts of politics. One feature since 2008 has been the extensive and widespread bitterness in both the public and in elected leaders, as shown by the Tea Party emergence and Republican Senate leader Mitch McConnell's obstinate stand in 2008 to do everything to oppose anything President Obama proposed. It was matched by the widespread women's march the day after Donald Trump's inauguration. The depth of this anger and opposition was not present in the early years of the Sixth Party System. Perhaps, it is just a hardening of the ideological gap between the two parties. Or, a deepening of the gap that will characterize the Seventh Party System. We shall see. Historians will decide. Remember, historians assign names and arbitrary dates to eras, referred to as periodization.

Each party system has unique characteristics that differ from those that precede or follow. There is a dramatic difference between the presidents of the First and Second Party Systems. Almost all of the first six presidents would have been remembered in history books if they had not served as president. George Washington, John Adams, Thomas Jefferson, James Madison, James Monroe, and John Quincy Adams are giants among the Founding Fathers and early leaders. In contrast to the First, no president during the Second Party System would have been remembered, except for Andrew Jackson and his escapades against the British and the Indians and in taking Florida. James K. Polk often appears on historians' lists of outstanding presidents, making him a second exception to the run of mediocre men in the White House. When you think of great or even above average presidents, the names Martin Van Buren, John Tyler, Zachary Taylor, Millard Fillmore, Franklin Pierce, and James Buchanan do not roll off your tongue. They were military heroes or professional politicians who headed a state political machine. The national convention selected the candidates, unlike the First's dependence upon a caucus of Congressional party leaders. Politics was now a business, a way for the ambitious to rise. For the First, politics was a call to serve the nation, one often reluctantly answered. The leaders of the First came from the wealthy elite; the Second from anywhere, even humble origins. In the First, the leaders ruled FOR the people, who were not fully capable of understanding what was in their best interests. In the Second, the leaders governed in the NAME of the people. It was not yet government of the people, by the people, and for the people, but it was a lot closer to it than in the First Party System.

Property requirements restricted suffrage in the First. By 1828 only six states still had property requirements for voting. The basis for determining the right to vote changed greatly from the First to the Second. Reserved campaigns characterized the First. Presidential candidates did not campaign. Voters already knew enough about them to make up their minds. In the Second, campaigns were mass hoopla with slogans, parades, and bonfire rallies. The quintessential Second Party election took place in 1840 when the Whigs ran on slogans and no platform. The 1840 Whig candidate, William Henry Harrison, was the first presidential candidate to give speeches. About what?

The issues that dominated the politics of the First Party System were missing in the Second. After the Monroe Doctrine in 1823, foreign affairs took a back seat in national politics. Beginning in the 1790s, politics revolved around the two visions and colorful personalities of Alexander Hamilton and Thomas Jefferson, leaders of their respective parties, Federalists and Republicans. In the Second the Whigs suffered from a leadership split personality – Henry Clay, Daniel Webster, and John Calhoun. The Republican Party of Jefferson became the Democratic Party of Jackson, giving the entire era a nickname, Jacksonian Democracy, or the Rise of the Common Man. Jackson's personality dominated the period. The new issues in the Jacksonian era were the tariff, Indian removal, internal improvements, land policy, and the abolition or expansion of slavery. The Civil War and Reconstruction ended the Second Party System.

You should know the characteristics of each party system and be able to differentiate between the system that precedes it and the one that follows. Especially, know the "defining elections" that usher in the change. Use similar criteria – the characteristics of the leaders, the nominating procedures and the conventions, changes in the suffrage base, which group of voters lean toward which party, the role of money in campaigns, the advent of the media, and the foreign and domestic issues of that period.

American politics today is still in the Sixth Party System. Corporate campaign contributions are a significant part of the Sixth. The campaign financing law, written by politicians for politicians, limits an individual to contributing only $1,000 to a candidate. However, contributions to a PAC, a **P**olitical **A**ction **C**ommittee, are without limits. The committee, because it is not a person, is free to funnel the funds to any candidate, as much as desired. By 1988, 1800 conservative corporate PACs raised millions of dollars for Republicans. Only 355 labor union PACs raised money for Democrats. Note how much the primaries of the Sixth Party System have negated the role of the convention. All the party convention does is ratify the primary results from long, long campaigns. As the Sixth Party System matured, ideology became more and more important, substituting for thoughtful discourse and compromise. As late as the 1980s members of the Senate and the House of Representatives frequently voted for proposals advocated by the opposite party. Beginning in the mid-1990s, however, voting in Congress began, 90%

of the time, to follow the party line, that party's announced position. President Ronald Reagan, described as a pragmatic ideologue, would probably have been rejected as the Republican Party's nominee by the late Sixth Party System – too flexible. Ideological rigidity means that little seems to be accomplished, according to each voter's individual list of what is important. Worse yet, the lists vary widely from one person to another and from one time to another within the Sixth Party System. This makes all voters, and many elected politicians, frustrated with politics, politicians, and the political system.

The media role changed during the Sixth Party System. A novel from the 1960s, *The 480*, by Eugene Burdick, presented a presidential campaign run by computer experts, who split the voting population into distinct groups, sending different campaign literature to each group. Their candidate won. After initially celebrating their victory, the euphoria ended when one raised a question. "What does our candidate really believe?" Political advertising slices the electorate into segments. As one advertising executive admitted, "It is really the voter who is packaged by media, not the candidate." Many voters vote for a candidate because they *think* the candidate *thinks* the way they do. Maybe. Maybe not.

Keep these two organizational schemes – politics as viewed by the average voter or party systems – in mind as you study the politics of any era. It will help make sense of the political activity.

Politics in the Late Nineteenth Century: The Conventional View

A book by James Bryce, *The American Commonwealth*, published in 1888, heavily shaped the conventional view of late nineteenth century politics. A British citizen, Bryce was an astute observer of American politics, a good friend of Theodore Roosevelt, and, from 1907-1913, the British ambassador to the United States. His book greatly influenced the views of later historians. One chapter was entitled "Why Great Men Are Not Chosen President." His conclusion – both parties were more interested in winning elections to gain patronage jobs for their followers. Neither was interested in putting the best man up for election. Instead they wanted the candidate who would appeal to the voters. Bryce claimed parties were in danger of losing their functional usefulness because they failed to offer the voters an opportunity to vote on issues and because they primarily used public office to reward party workers. "Neither party has any clean-cut principles, any distinctive tenets. Both have traditions. Both claim to have tendencies. Both have certainly war cries, organizations, and interests enlisted in their support. But those interests are in the main the interests of getting or keeping the patronage of government. Distinctive tenets and policies, points of political doctrine and points of political practice, have all but vanished . . . . All has been lost except office or the hope of it." In another chapter he explained the differences between the two major political parties. The two major parties in this period "were like two bottles. Each bore a label denoting the kind of liquor it contained, but each was empty."

He had no kind words for the caliber of our presidential candidates. "Since the heroes of the Revolution died with Jefferson and Adams and Madison, no person except General Grant has reached the (presidential) chair whose name would have been remembered had he not been President, and no President except Abraham Lincoln has displayed rare or striking qualities in the chair." His book was among the best sellers of that era.

A second contemporary critic, Henry Adams, the grandson of John Quincy Adams, was a highly respected historian. He still is. He left some damaging quotes. "One might search the whole list of Congress, Judiciary, and Executive during the twenty-five years, 1870-1895 and find little but damaged reputations." "The period was poor in purpose and barren in results." "No period so thoroughly ordinary had been known in American politics since Christopher Columbus first disturbed the balance of American society."

A future president, Woodrow Wilson, argued in *Congressional Government*, 1885, that Congress lacked leaders. He was particularly harsh on the Senate. "No one exercises the special trust of acknowledged leadership. The Senate is merely a body of critics." (quoted in David J. Rothman, *Politics and Power, The United States Senate, 1869-1901.*)

A later historian, Charles A. Beard, dismissed the era as simply an "age of negation." There was nothing positive to say about it. Two Pulitzer Prize winning historians, Samuel Eliot Morison and Henry Steele Commager, labeled the late nineteenth century "the dreariest chapter in American politics, in which the titular leaders contributed nothing of lasting importance to American politics or American life." It was not all dreary. A New York state boss, Senator Roscoe Conkling, provided some juicy quotes. "Parties are not built by deportment or by ladies magazines or by gush." "Politics is a rotten business." "Nothing counts except to win."

The nickname for this period came from a novel by Mark Twain and Charles Dudley Warner, *The Gilded Age*. The novel is pure satire. The main character, Colonel Beriah Sellers, is a corrupt politician always involved in some slippery get-rich-quick scheme in this incredibly materialistic age. The president of the Southern Pacific Railroad, Collis P. Huntington, divided all politicians into three categories: the "communists," wild-eyed radicals; the "commercial," those who were purchasable; and the "clean," those who sought to do what was right, no money involved. He found few in the last category.

The Grant administration set the tone for politics. Scandals rocked it; there was the Whiskey Ring, which involved the Secretary of the Treasury, and the Crédit Mobilier scandal, involving the building of the transcontinental railroad. The central institution at every level of government seemed to be, as critics said, the hog trough. What is in it for me?

To What Extent is This Criticism Deserved?

Some historians argue that the primary feature of American politics is our widespread agreement on fundamentals, meaning that in every era our political disagreements are really better characterized as "surface agitation." The function of political parties in our system is to compromise within the party before there is compromise between the parties. This is why most legislation offends few people, and seems to change little. The witty observations of intellectuals such as Bryce and the juicy quotes left their impact. Some historians have charged other historians with paying too much attention to commentators' biting criticisms rather than to the sincerity and accomplishments of the late nineteenth century's politicians. Historian David J. Rothman, in *Politics and Power, The United States Senate, 1869-1901*, defended the politics of the Third Party System. "The post-Civil War years did not represent the acme of corruption. Rather, it witnessed the start of the modern system by which pressure groups vied for government support." (pp. 220.) Something new had entered the political arena, what was referred to then as the "Third House of Congress," organized lobbyists. Still, the Gilded Age was not without its memorable moments.

Election of 1876

The election of 1876 led to threats by governors to march on Washington with their state militia. Remember, the Civil War had ended just eleven years earlier. Some veterans would have been excited to fight again! This election gave Republican Rutherford B. Hayes the victory, narrowly. The electoral vote was Hayes, 185, Samuel J. Tilden, 184. At the first count early on election eve, Hayes had 165 electoral votes and Tilden 184, with 20 votes in dispute. Nineteen of the disputed votes came from Florida, South Carolina, and Louisiana. In addition, because an elector in Oregon was a postmaster, which is a federal office, his vote was disallowed because the Constitution stipulates that no federal officeholder may be an elector. It added up to 20 disputed votes. How did this happen? On election eve, as crafty Republican leaders in Washington saw the election slipping away, they prevailed upon their colleagues to use whatever method possible (use your imagination!) to have the three Southern states – Florida, South Carolina, and Louisiana – send two different results to Congress, one saying the Republican Hayes won and one saying the Democrat Tilden won (which he had done).

Since the Constitution offered no guidance when states sent confusing results, Congress created a commission of fifteen members to resolve the dilemma of the disputed Electoral College votes. From the House of Representatives, controlled by Democrats, came three Democrats and two Republicans. From the Senate, controlled by Republicans, came two Democrats and three Republicans. The bill creating the commission appointed five Supreme Court judges, four specifically named in the bill, two Republicans and two Democrats, with an understanding that the fifth judge would be Justice David Davis, a true independent. However, Justice Davis had always dreamed of being a senator. Suddenly the senator from his home state resigned and the governor offered Justice Davis an appointment as a U.S. Senator. He took it. Since only Republican judges remained on the Supreme Court, a Republican, Justice Joseph Bradley, became the fifteenth member of the commission, making it eight Republicans and seven Democrats. By a vote of 8-7, the commission awarded all 20 disputed votes to Hayes in the so-called Compromise of 1877 or Bargain of 1877, which ended Reconstruction in the South in return for Hayes becoming president. Afterwards Hayes was nicknamed "Old 8 to 7," "His Fraudulence," and the "de facto president." He had a rough four years; he had no interest in running for reelection in 1880.

Election of 1884

The election of 1884 is famous as an election that gave voters a clear choice. Do you as a voter want a president who is privately immoral or a president who is publicly immoral? The Republican Party dumped a sitting president, Chester A. Arthur, who was in ill health, to nominate James G. Blaine from Maine, Speaker of the House of Representatives and the leader of a faction of the Republican Party nicknamed the Half-Breeds. The Half-Breeds opposed the continuation of Radical Republican policies toward the South and were open to the possibility of some reform on civil service and the tariff. The opposing Republican faction, the Stalwarts, led by Senator Roscoe Conkling from New York, supported Grant and Radical Republican policies in the South, favored continuing high tariffs, and opposed all civil service reform.

Blaine regularly attended church and taught adult Sunday School classes. A devoted family man, he was a model private citizen. He was a consummate politician who never forgot a face or name. However, in his autobiography, *Twenty Years in Congress*, he could not name a single piece of legislation for which he was responsible. The ultimate "wheeler and dealer," he signed many letters with a caution to "Burn this letter" to prevent news of a shady deal from becoming public. Opponents attacked him during the campaign with "Blaine, Blaine, the continental liar from the state of Maine." Overcome by such unjust (?) criticism, he collapsed, conveniently, at the front entrance while leaving a church service. Reform oriented Republicans deserted him. They were nicknamed Mugwumps, or "goo-goos," which stood for "good government." The term Mugwumps has many tales about its origins. The best one is that they had their mug on one side of the fence and their wump on the other. Another was that a Mugwump was "a person educated beyond his intellect." In an age of party loyalty, they were shunned for having principles, which Blaine lacked. One rival in the Stalwart faction of the Republican Party was asked to campaign for Blaine. A lawyer, he responded, "I don't engage in criminal practice."

Democrats countered with a reform candidate, (Stephen) Grover Cleveland, who had been elected mayor of Buffalo in 1881 and governor of New York in 1882. His supporters said, "We love him for the enemies he has made." Newspaper mogul Joseph Pulitzer gave four reasons for endorsing him, "One, he's an honest man; two, he's an honest man: three, he's an honest man; four, he's an honest man." The election pitted honesty against corruption; however, during the campaign interesting and unexpected developments surfaced.

A minister in Buffalo, Rev. George Ball, wrote a letter to the *Buffalo Evening Telegraph* revealing that ten years earlier a widow named Maria Halpin, who was described as "very popular" with the barroom crowd, had given birth to an illegitimate child that she named Oscar Folsom Cleveland. She claimed Cleveland was the father. Oscar Folsom was Cleveland's law partner and best friend; he was married, with a family. Cleveland was a bachelor. The speculation in Buffalo was that Oscar Folsom was the baby's father and that Cleveland accepted responsibility to save him the embarrassment. Another story was that Maria wanted Cleveland to marry her, and so she claimed it was his child to force him to marry her. The truth is many men could have been the father of that child! During the campaign Republican kids sang a ditty, "Ma, Ma, where's my pa, he's gone to the White House, ha, ha, ha!"

Years before this campaign, Oscar Folsom, Cleveland's law partner, died in a carriage accident. Cleveland became the executor of his estate and the ward of Frances Folsom, Oscar's daughter. He bought Frances her first baby carriage. While he was in the White House, he married her. She had just graduated from college at 21 years old; he was 49. Historians compare her impact in Washington to that of Jackie Kennedy. They had five children, including a girl, Ruth, immortalized by the candy bar named in her honor, *Baby Ruth*.

Blaine made two crucial mistakes during the campaign. First, he attended a fund-raising feast for millionaire Robber Barons at Delmonico's Restaurant in New York City. Cartoonists had a ball with it. Second, Blaine was present at another dinner when a Protestant minister referred to the Democratic Party as the party of "Rum, Romanism, and Rebellion," in other words, drunks, Catholics, and Southerners. Irish Catholics were furious. Their criticism directed against Blaine was unfair and unjustified; Blaine's mother was a Catholic and he was no bigot. The Irish vote swung to the Democrats, which swung the state of New York to the Democrats by 600 votes, giving Cleveland New York's 36 electoral votes and a narrow victory.

In the 1888 election, in which Republican Benjamin Harrison defeated Cleveland, Harrison observed on election night how Providence (God) had made him president. One of his advisors could not let it pass without correction. He quipped that the president would never know how many men had approached the gates of the penitentiary to get him elected. Corruption at the ballot box won it. During this campaign a wily politician, Charles F. Murchison, claiming to be a recent British immigrant, sent a letter to the British ambassador. The Murchison letter, sent in September, asked the British ambassador which candidate would be best for England. On October 24, ambassador Sir Lionel Sackville-West's foolish reply was published in newspapers. He urged a vote for Cleveland. This time the Irish voters switched to voting Republican, winning New York, and Cleveland lost.

Stalemate – The Chief Characteristic of the Era
The Republican Party's Assets

The North won the Civil War, giving the Republican Party a claim to being the savior of the Union. The Republican Party enjoyed a vast voting bloc, the GAR, the Grand Army of the Republic, a fraternal organization of Union veterans. Some wags said that GAR really stood for "Generally All Republicans." Voters were urged to "Vote as you shot," and politicians frequently practiced "Waving the bloody shirt," evoking memories of wartime sacrifices. Republicans reminded voters that during the Civil War, while "not every Democrat was a traitor; every traitor was a Democrat." Many political candidates for state and national offices were former Civil War generals or officers, such as Ulysses S. Grant, Rutherford B. Hayes, and James A. Garfield. In death, Abraham Lincoln, the Great Emancipator, gave the Republicans an image as the great humanitarian political party.

The Republican Party's Liabilities

Among the Republican Party's liabilities was the simple fact that this was not a period of Republican domination. If one just looks at the presidency, it seems so. However, look carefully at the national vote totals and the composition of the Senate and the House of Representatives. It was really an era of political stalemate and equilibrium, in which the bitter fight for control of the federal government occupied all the energy of the two parties. Only in the 1880 election did Republicans gain a majority of the popular vote, but their plurality was less than 1/10 of one percent.

Look carefully at the results for the presidential elections during the Third Party System. Especially note the closeness of the popular vote in the five elections from 1876 to 1892.

		Popular Vote	Electoral College
1864	Abraham Lincoln, R	2,213,665	212
	George B. McClellan, D	1,802,237	21
1868	Ulysses S. Grant, R	3,012,833	214
	Horatio Seymour, D	2,703,249	80
1872	Ulysses S. Grant, R	3,597,132	286
	Horace Greeley, D	2,834,125	66
1876	Rutherford B. Hayes, R	4,036,298	185
	Samuel J. Tilden, D	4,300,590	184

(Tilden 264,292 majority, lost in the Electoral College)

1880	James A. Garfield, R	4,454,416	214

(Garfield won by only 9,464 out of 8,899,368 total)

	Winfield S. Hancock, D	4,444,952	155

Garfield was assassinated, and Chester A. Arthur became president

1884	Grover Cleveland, D	4,874,986	219

(Cleveland won by 23,005 out of 8,726,967 total)

	James G. Blaine, R	4,851,981	182

1888	Benjamin Harrison, R	5,439,853	233
	Grover Cleveland, D	5,540,309	168

(Cleveland's had a 100,456 popular majority, but lost in the Electoral College)

1892	Grover Cleveland, D	5,556,918	277

(Cleveland won by 380,810)

	Benjamin Harrison, R	5,176,108	145
	James B. Weaver, Populist	1,041,028	22

1896	William McKinley, R	7,104,779	271
	William J. Bryan, D	6,502,925	176

(Note the larger popular vote difference for 1896; the electorate was changing as it moved into the Fourth Party System.)

Looking at all the states in the union between 1876 and 1892, all but four consistently voted for the same party in every presidential election. The Democratic Party "Solid South" was not the only "solid" part of the country. Of the four, California and Nevada did not count much, since both had a small number of Electoral College votes. Victory turned on winning one of two key states, Indiana or New York. These two states were rewarded by each party's selection of candidates. Out of the 20 presidential and vice-presidential candidates between 1876 and 1892, New York had eight and Indiana five. Only in 1889-1891 did the White House, Senate, and House belong to the Republicans. This was the infamous "Billion Dollar Congress," when Republicans spent wildly to negate the argument that the tariff was too high, as shown by the money piling up in the treasury. (It was 48% on incoming goods.) That Congress enacted 531 laws, guided by "Czar" Thomas B. Reed in the House, far more than the 317 average for any Congress between 1875 and 1889. This level of legislative activity was not matched until Theodore Roosevelt's second term.

Voters reacted by kicking out the Republicans. In the 1890 Congressional elections, Democrats won 235 seats in the House to 88 for the Republicans. However, in 1894 the reverse happened. In the largest transfer of power in the history of the United States to that date, the Republicans picked up 117 seats and the Democrats lost 113. A third party, the Populists, won the rest. In 24 states no Democrat won election to a national office. The onset of the depression in 1893 caused the Democratic loses. One characteristic of the Third Party System was the variety of third parties that won Congressional and Electoral College votes – the Greenback Party, many local labor parties, and the Populist Party. (The rise of the Populist Party is explained in the following chapter.) For four years, following the elections of 1894 and 1896, Populists held the balance of power in the Senate.

The Democratic Party's Assets

The major asset for the Democratic Party was their firm hold on the South. Just as the North voted Republican, the South remembered the legacy of the Civil War and Reconstruction and voted Democratic. This gave the Democrats a dependable 11 Southern states, with 112 electoral votes, 22 senators, and 90 Representatives in the House.

The Democratic Party's Liabilities

However, the Southern domination of the Democratic Party was their chief liability. This backbone of the Democratic Party had enough influence to tarnish any pretense of touting the Democrats as a party in the national interest. The South could never deliver enough electoral votes to win the presidency for the Democrats. In the 1830s the Democratic Party had adopted a two-thirds rule, meaning that any nominee at the party's national convention had to win the support of at least two-thirds of the delegates, which essentially gave the South a veto over any potential nominee, practically ensuring defeat for any Democrat running for the presidency. At various times the presence of and the subterranean influence of the KKK, the Ku Klux Klan, among Southern Democrats further reduced the Democratic Party's national appeal.

The first two Southerners elected president on their own after the Civil War were Jimmy Carter from Georgia in 1976 and Bill Clinton from Arkansas in 1992. Texan Lyndon Johnson became president by succeeding from the vice-presidency. Woodrow Wilson, raised in the South, lived in New Jersey when he ran for president, serving as governor, and previously, as the president of Princeton University. Split along North-South lines, this lack of cohesiveness among Democrats during the Third Party System meant that the party was more inclined to oppose what the Republicans did than to advocate ideas of its own. When Grover Cleveland won the presidency and the Democrats won both houses of Congress in 1892, it was the first time since 1856 that the Democratic Party controlled all three. Then the depression of 1893 hit, killing the Democrats in the elections of 1894. Except for two brief periods, neither party was able to control the Senate, the House, and the presidency at the same time during the Third Party System.

Democrats in this era held a negative theory of government. A popular saying said that a Republican does not want you to drink beer on Sunday, but a Democrat thinks government should not be deciding such matters. The Republican Party was the party of reform and activism, especially on economic development issues. Unlike during the Second Party System, most voters wanted the government to aid the economy, which made the Republicans more appealing.

The Political Climate, the Zeitgeist of the Era

The ideal president in this period did very little; Congress dominated. One politician declared that when a Congressman visited the White House it was to give advice, not to receive it. Cleveland vetoed many fraudulent veterans' pensions and also fought for a lower tariff. His strong stands on these issues divided his Democratic Party and united the Republicans, leading to his defeat in 1888. It was widely believed that Lincoln bore part of the responsibility for starting the Civil War because of his action in sending supplies to Fort Sumter, without consulting Congress. In addition, early in this era, Congress impeached President Andrew Johnson. Be careful using the word "impeach." Impeach means to bring charges, it is the beginning of a procedure. It does not mean removing from office. According to the Constitution a simple majority of the House of Representatives votes to approve an article of impeachment. Then the Senate acts as the judge and jury. A two-thirds Senate vote is necessary to remove a federal official.

Congressmen firmly believed that the Constitution listed the powers of Congress first, in Article I, because Congress is the most important branch of the national government. Congress formulates policy; all the president does is execute Congress's decisions. Not until the "turning point election" of 1896 did this image of the president begin to change. William McKinley, as the first "modern" president, was much closer to being the Chief Legislator, a president who initiates major legislation, as Americans are accustomed to seeing today.

The ideal Third Party System presidential candidate had an affable personality and a willingness to cooperate with the party bosses. He had to appeal to various factions within the party with no views that would alienate a powerful voting bloc. It helped to reside in a pivotal state, usually Ohio, the "mother of presidents," or New York or Indiana. Ideally, he had a good Civil War record. It was also necessary that he had few political enemies, always difficult for any politician, anywhere, anytime. Vice-presidential candidates balanced the ticket geographically or as a representative of another party faction. Note that none of the vice presidents in the Third Party System ever later became a presidential candidate. Other than the two vice presidents who succeeded to the presidency on the death of the president, Andrew Johnson for Abraham Lincoln and Chester A. Arthur for James A. Garfield, few people today would be able to name any of the era's vice presidents.

Historical analysis of the voting in Congress in this period shows that the primary determinant of a Congressman's vote was not his political party but his section of the country. Bear that in mind when looking at support for various laws passed in this period. With Congress divided politically by party and by section, and the president ignored, not much was accomplished in facing national issues such as the tariff, currency, monopolies, etc. However, many historians have pointed out that state and locally oriented issues dominated politics – Jim Crow laws, immigration, Granger laws, etc. Be sure to differentiate between the two types of laws – national or state – when you look at the legislative achievements and failures of the Third Party System.

The Third Party System

Know the characteristics of each party system and be able to differentiate between the system that precedes it and the one that follows. Especially know the defining elections that usher in the change. Use similar criteria – characteristics of the leaders, the nominating procedures and the conventions, changes in the suffrage base, which group of voters lean toward which party, the role of money in campaigns, the role of the media, and the foreign and domestic issues of that period. In describing a party system, note that specific issues dominate; the leaders are similar in background; the two major parties hold a consistent ideological position throughout the period; and, specific groups of voters loyally support their party. Turning point elections give new definitions to important issues and usher in a new party system. Now the electorate expects something different from politics and politicians.

In the Third Party System, 1860-1896, after the Civil War and Reconstruction, parties tended to follow the politics of evasion, not confronting major issues at the federal level – tariff, antitrust, currency, inflation and deflation, and civil service. In many respects, all these national issues are similar to our current concerns over revising Social Security. It arouses no passion, is extremely complicated, and offers no clear easy solution. Any solution brings no political dividend. Thus, neither voters nor politicians want to tackle the issue. It is a no-win issue. So were the tariff, antitrust, currency, inflation and deflation, and civil service. The editor of the *Atlantic Monthly*, Walter Hines Page, referred to these issues as "difficult and important tasks, indeed, but they have not been exciting." This led to inertia, doing nothing to avoid alienating any group of voters. How then does one explain the high voter turnout in the Third Party System, which rose to 70-80%? The reason was the state and local issues. The electorate was keenly interested in issues involving race, immigrants, temperance, railroad rates, and parochial schools, all primarily state and local issues.

The Republican Party, a new political party, born just before the Civil War, was centered in the North and Midwest, the area of the rise of industry. The Democratic Party existed mainly in the South. Republicans were the party of social reform, inclined toward the politics of morality, as shown by Republican leadership for the following examples. In

1889 Wisconsin passed a law that a school could only be accredited if lessons were taught in English. In 1887 the American Protective Association urged restrictions on immigration, to hasten assimilation of those here, and limits to parochial schools. Two icons of nationalism appeared within two years – the *Pledge of Allegiance* in 1892 and the song, *"America the Beautiful,"* in 1893. Americans needed to protect the country from immigrant influence.

The Democratic Party was the party of limited and negative government. President Cleveland in 1887 vetoed the Texas Seed Bill, which appropriated federal funds for drought-stricken farmers. He lectured the bill's supporters, "The people support the government. The government does not support the people." This is certainly a different stand for the Democrats from that taken in the New Deal in the Fifth Party System, 1932-1968. Cleveland sounded more like Republican Herbert Hoover in the 1930s. The Democrats included Roman Catholics and Southerners, both of whom endorsed cultural and economic laissez faire. Leave us alone. Was drinking beer on Sunday an issue of control or of freedom? To the Democrats it was an issue of freedom. To the Republicans it was a nuisance that needed to be controlled.

The bitter class warfare of the 1890s and the fallout from the depression that began in 1893 disrupted and terminated the Third Party System. Most turning point elections owe their changes to economic disruptions. To those who lived in the 1890s, it seemed as if class warfare had broken out. Two bitter strikes resulted in great property damage and many deaths – the Homestead strike and the Pullman strike. In 1892 workers went on strike at Carnegie's Homestead Plant, southeast of Pittsburgh. Carnegie's right-hand man, Henry Clay Frick, enlisted 300 strikebreakers from the Pinkerton Detective Agency, already famous for its role in providing agents to infiltrate unions to hamper union activities. A gun battle broke out, killing strikers and Pinkerton agents. It ended when the Pennsylvania governor sent the state militia. In the Pullman strike the American Railway Union, newly created by Eugene V. Debs, led a nation-wide boycott of all trains with a Pullman sleeping car. George Pullman had created a "company town," Pullman, Illinois. He controlled the town and everything in it. In 1894 Pullman cut wages while maintaining the high rent on workers' houses. The strike that followed spread to 27 states, accompanied by widespread destruction of railroad property. President Cleveland ended it by calling out the U.S. Army. Stung by widespread unemployment from the depression of 1893, Jacob Coxey, an Ohio businessman, led a march on Washington, D.C., to publicize the need for government created jobs building public works – bridges, roads, etc. These three events frightened many in the middle and upper classes. Finally, throw in the rise of the farmers, the Populist Party (explained in the following chapter), and "everything nailed down seemed to be becoming loose."

The Election of 1896
The Democratic Party candidate, William Jennings Bryan, presented himself as a prophet calling for a moral political revival, as shown in the language of his Cross of

Gold speech at the 1896 Democratic convention. He challenged those who believed money had to be backed by only gold, the gold standard. "If they dare to come out in the open field and defend the gold standard as a good thing, we will fight them to the uttermost . . . . You shall not press down upon the brow of labor this crown of thorns, you shall not crucify mankind upon a cross of gold." The class warfare of workers versus big business was now joined by the uprising of farmers against the cities. "You come to us and tell us that the great cities are in favor of the gold standard; we reply that the great cities rest upon our broad and fertile prairies. Burn down your cities and leave our farms, and your cities will spring up again as if by magic; but destroy our farms and the grass will grow in the streets of every city in the country." The two national parties exchanged cultural identities in 1896, ushering in the Fourth Party System. The Republicans became the party of pragmatism and professional organization. Lyman Trumbull, one of the founders of the Republican Party in 1856 and a co-author of the Thirteenth Amendment, blasted the new Republican Party focus for ignoring reform. Bryan's Democrats now became the party of reform.

The main issue in the election in 1896 was control of federal government policies for the benefit of industry or for the benefit of agriculture. Industry won. The main issues in the Fourth Party System, ushered in by the 1896 election, were regulating or not regulating big business, foreign expansion, the First World War, and the question of our leadership in world affairs. Republicans became the more conservative party. In the Third the Democrats had been.

Briefly, the Fifth and Sixth Party Systems
Briefly, to continue, in the Fifth Party System, 1932-1968, the dominating issues and characteristics were the Great Depression; the expansion of the federal government; the creation of the welfare state; the threat presented by the rise of totalitarianism, fascism and communism; and our leadership in world affairs. The dominant Democratic Party was home to the South, labor unions, minorities, Catholics, Jews, intellectuals, and big city machines.

In the Sixth Party System, 1968-????, the electorate became increasingly conservative; the push for civil rights undermined the Democratic Party coalition from the Fifth; Republicans captured the South; the welfare state waned; racial and gender justice concerns appeared; and presidential leadership over Congress declined. Some historians labeled the Sixth Party System the Second Gilded Age. Not a compliment. Congress asserted itself repeatedly, in the War Powers Act, in the 1994 Republican program with Speaker Newt Gingrich, and in the House of Representatives stonewalling against President Obama. Congress impeached (brought charges) against one president, Bill Clinton, and was in the process of doing so when another president resigned, Richard Nixon.

Our position of world leadership and our foreign policies became more complicated with the end of the American and Russian superpower domination of the free and communist worlds; the rise of the Third World or LDCs, <u>L</u>ess <u>D</u>eveloped <u>C</u>ountries; and the economic revival of the defeated and exhausted nations of the Second World War – Japan, China, England, France, Italy, and Germany. In the Sixth Party System there seemed to be no clear consensus on many issues facing the country. No political agendas seemed viable. If Americans were asked to make a list of the five most important issues facing the country, not only would each list have different items on it, each list would be in a different order. The Washington, D.C., political confusion over what issues to face and how to resolve them reflected the voters' confusion, frustrating everyone.

32

THE POPULIST REVOLT

The Myth of the Wild West

The cowboy and the "Wild West" both represent an over-romanticized era in American history. Contrary to old Hollywood movies and television shows, 25-40% of the cowboys were black or Hispanic. It was not a glamorous job. Sitting on a horse for a whole day riding in the dust stirred up by a herd of cattle was not great fun. The "Wild West" lasted only 15 to 20 years, from 1865 to 1880 or 1885. The old television show, "Gunsmoke" lasted longer, 21 years, 645 episodes. Celebrated outlaws such as Jesse James or Billy the Kid rode harder and shot straighter in the dime novels and movies than they ever did in real life. Billy the Kid's IQ has been estimated to have been in the 70s. The six-shooters cowboys carried were designed for rapid shooting from a horse, not for accuracy. That took a rifle. Few Westerners were marksmen. It was the number of shots that eventually hit your target, rarely the first few. Buffalo Bill's Wild West Show, featuring the sharpshooter Anne Oakley, helped to perpetuate this myth of how the West was conquered. All around the world the cowboy still remains a symbol of American rugged individualism.

Recently a group of historians emerged writing about the "New" Western History, an example of how social history and new viewpoints can enrich a subfield of history. It presents a more balanced view of the West, less of a paradigm of the cavalry wars and cowboys versus Indians. In short, it does not reflect nor rival what Hollywood has emphasized over the years. It recognizes the ethnic diversity of the West, especially the Asian, Hispanic, and Indian cultures and their interactions and contributions. Unlike previous Western histories, such as Frederick Jackson Turner, "The Significance of the Frontier in American History," and Walter Prescott Webb, *The Great Plains*, the advance of the frontier and the environment do not of necessity lead to a distinct culture, economy, people, attitudes, etc. The New Western History emphasizes the extent to which the federal government gave the West as a region historical themes not relevant to other parts of the country, such as its military conquests and modern defense facilities, the different governmental bureaucracies that function primarily in the West, and the large amount of government-owned land, land never originally sold. Other themes are the history of women in all their varied roles; Indian history other than as combatants; Asian immigration and popular responses; Hispanic response to, and adaptation to, increasing Anglo domination; the rise, significance, and role of cities; and the region prior to the coming of whites in large numbers in the late nineteenth century. See Patricia Nelson Limerick, *The Legacy of Conquest: The Unbroken Past of the American West*.

The history of the late nineteenth century West was the history of the conquest of the soil by farmers, but it was not without difficulties. American culture in the nineteenth century still embraced the myth of the farmer as the backbone of the republic, as symbolized by Thomas Jefferson's characterization of farmers as "the chosen people of God." But farmers faced a myriad collection of problems as they hit the Great Plains.

The Farmers' Physical Problems

Historian Walter Prescott Webb said there were three distinguishing geographic characteristics of the Great Plains – it is flat, treeless, and "a region where rainfall is insufficient for ordinary intensive agriculture common to lands of humid climate." All three caused problems for farmers.

rainfall – The first American explorers to cross the Great Plains, Lewis and Clark in 1804-1806, and Major Stephen Long's expedition the next decade, called it the Great American Desert, because there were no trees. Explorer John Wesley Powell's 1869 report to Congress said, "To a great extent, the redemption of all these lands will require extensive and comprehensive plans, for the execution of which aggregated capital or cooperative labor will be necessary. Here, individual farmers, being poor men, cannot undertake the task." The insufficient amount of, and inconsistency of, rainfall made their Eastern farming methods and equipment inadequate. Their plows had difficulty busting through the intertwined roots of the prairie grass. When industry finally developed steel plows that removed the stubborn grass cover, the limited rainfall led to occasional dust storms, the best known being the infamous Dust Bowl in the 1930s. Eventually farmers learned to practice extensive rather than intensive farming to reap the same yield they got in the Midwest. One hundred sixty acres, the size of the 1862 Homestead Land Grant, proved to be too small. Huge corporate-financed "bonanza farms" expanded all over the Great Plains.

weather – The pioneers were not prepared for the range of weather extremes, the intense summer heat and the bitter winds sweeping down from Canada and the blowing snow. The absence of natural barriers meant that nothing stopped the hot winds blowing northward in the summer or the cold winds blowing southward in the winter.

flash floods – Too frequently, when it did rain in the summer, virtual cloudbursts poured down. Walls of water swept down almost dry river beds, flowing too swiftly to soak in to benefit the soil. Cities and towns on the Great Plains still suffer from occasional flooding, in spite of many modern dams.

housing – With low rainfall few trees grew on the Great Plains, meaning lumber for building houses was almost nonexistent. Hence, a farmer had to use what was available. Early houses were built out of chucks of sod, sod-houses, with occasional rattlesnakes coming out of the walls.

fencing – With few trees farmers also lacked wood for fencing, which was necessary to keep out roaming cattle and buffalo herds. They experimented. By 1881, out of 1229 patents for fences registered in the U.S. Patent Office, 696 came from states on or near the Great Plains. The ultimate solution was barbed wire. If you ever go near either one, stop to see the Barbed Wire Museums in La Crosse, Kansas, or McLean, Texas.

insects – Sometimes dark clouds on the horizon brought not rain, but insects, hungry insects, especially grasshoppers. Read Rose Wilder Lane's *Young Pioneers*. Try to picture grasshoppers, 4 to 6 inches deep, eating the wooden handle off the shovel. For four years, 1873 to 1877, Rocky Mountain locusts, a species that vanished twenty-five years later, swept over the Great Plains each summer, eating everything in their path. It took some swarms five days to pass. Nothing edible survived.

water – Back east all you had to do to get a well was dig, maybe 6 to 15 feet. Not so on the Great Plains, where the water table might be 150-180 feet down. Digging a well required using professional well drillers, who traveled the Plains. Windmills, to pull the water up to the surface, were purchased from mail order catalogs. The water table in the states on the Great Plains, the Ogallala Aquifer, is currently dropping. A future water crisis is coming.

Social Problems Plagued the Farmers

Social problems plagued farm families on the Great Plains. Since farms were widely separated due to extensive farming, farmers suffered from the social isolation of few neighbors, inadequate educational opportunities, and a lack of medical, religious, and recreational facilities. The number one social problem in farm families was alcohol. All these difficulties led to a growing awareness of narrow opportunities and declining prestige. Their self-image dropped. It is one thing to be degraded; it is another thing to think those degrading you might be right. One wag in western Kansas summed it up perfectly:

> "250 miles to the nearest Post Office
> 100 miles to wood
> 20 miles to water
> 6 inches to Hell"

Farmers began to think of themselves as hillbillies, hicks, and hayseeds. This self-reflection was helped along by the Montgomery Ward catalog and the Sears catalog, nicknamed the Wish Book. One could even purchase an entire house, arriving in a huge kit. Richard Nixon grew up in one. Browsing the catalog pages made a person realize what you did not have and what you could not afford. Read Willa Cather's *My Antonia*, a story about Bohemian immigrants in Nebraska and their difficulties as seen through a young girl's life and experiences. Or, Ole Rolvaag, *Giants in the Earth*, the hardships of a Norwegian immigrant family farming in South Dakota; or, Rose Wilder Lane, *Young Pioneers*, former title, *Let the Hurricane Roar*, the life of a young couple homesteading in the Dakotas in the 1870s. Rose Wilder Lane was the daughter of Laura Ingalls Wilder, together they wrote the *Little House* series about life on the Great Plains.

The Farmers' Economic Problems

The most crucial problems farmers faced were economic in nature. Their most basic problem was that farming had become a business rather than a way of life.

overexpansion and overproduction – In the two decades after 1850 the population on the Great Plains increased five times. Between 1870 and 1900 the total number of acres of farmland in America doubled and the number of farmers tripled. A quick thought about these numbers reveals that there were simply too many amateur farmers, too many new to farming as an occupation. Food is what an economist calls an inelastic and undifferentiated product. A tomato is a tomato. A consumer does not differentiate between two tomatoes, one simply selects the cheaper one. A consumer has many choices of different foods and one can consume only so much. If the price drops, one does not consume more. For this reason, increased production drives prices down. Because food sells in a competitive market, each individual farmer produced more in reaction to falling prices, which drove prices down even farther. Look at the changes in these two commodity prices:

corn	1867–78¢ a bushel	1873–31¢	1889–23¢
wheat	1867–$2.00 a bushel	1889–70¢	

Between 1872 and 1902, American wheat production increased seven times, 700 percent. All farmers in the late nineteenth century suffered from the worldwide expansion of farming. New competition came from Australia, Argentina, Russia, and Canada. Improved farming methods reduced the time to produce twenty-seven different crops by 48%, flooding the markets. As a group farmers got better and better at producing more and more. However, for many farmers this meant that despite their hard effort, their incomes declined. The old adage, "work hard and get ahead" seemed upside down.

equipment – Farmers faced high prices for the equipment necessary to increase productivity, and they purchased farm equipment in what was an increasingly monopolistic or oligopolistic market with a small number of sellers. McCormick reapers, necessary for wheat farmers, reached annual sales of 15,000 by the 1870s. At a time when many farmers netted only several hundred dollars each year, the cost of all the farm equipment for a typical farm was approximately $700 to $1,000. To be successful on the Great Plains a farmer needed to irrigate, to employ heavy machinery, and to enrich the soil with fertilizers. Only large agri-business "bonanza" farms could easily afford that.

mortgages – On the Great Plains the average mortgage was for only $4\frac{1}{2}$ years; thus one bad year finished a farmer. Your debt became too much to make up. Our modern long term 25 or 30-year mortgage did not arrive until the 1930s. Mortgage interest rates went as high as 15%. In the decade of the 1880s mortgage debt grew two and one-half times faster than farm productivity. By 1890 Kansas, Minnesota, Nebraska, and the Dakotas had more farm mortgages than farm families. Some farm families had a second mortgage.

transportation costs – The prices charged by railroads to ship farm produce seemed to be too unfair and too high. Railroads charged more per mile for short hauls than for long hauls. The difference in prices seemed arbitrary to farmers. In Frank Norris' 1901 novel, *The Octopus*, a farmer asks the railroad agent how the railroad determines its pricing policy. The reply from the cynical agent was "all-the-traffic-will-bear." In defense of the railroad's prices, compare the prices today for air travel. Often the New York City to Los Angeles ticket is less than a much shorter flight from New York City to Springfield, Missouri. Why? No competition on one leg of the shorter flight. The modern airline situation existed for the railroads back then. Frequently only one railroad line served small towns in farming areas. In defense of the railroads, during the 1890s a quarter of all railroads went bankrupt, just as airlines occasionally struggle financially today. Railroad shipping rates actually fell faster than other prices in this period. Even so, farmers found any defense of railroad pricing unfathomable.

currency – This was a period of deflation, falling prices, which may be good or bad. Deflation or inflation, rising prices, is always relative in terms of its impact on different individuals. Deflation is especially hard on people in debt. They paid back their debts in dearer money, money worth more than what they borrowed. Look at the impact of deflation in terms of a farmer's production. In 1888 it took 174 bushels of wheat to pay just the interest on a $2,000 mortgage at 8%. By 1895 it took 320 bushels, because competition and deflation drove down the price of wheat. The "American Dream" is to work hard and get ahead. It was becoming more like the "American Nightmare" to farmers.

Many farmers came to believe that all their economic problems had to have an origin in a financial or banking conspiracy. For those of you who think this is silly thinking, look at statistics about what the public believed, and still does, about November 22,

1963, the day of the assassination of President John F. Kennedy. Conspiracy thinking is a way to explain the unimaginable or the incomprehensible. Among farmers, a new theory of economic history developed to explain who was responsible for the farmers' economic problems. Obviously, it was Eastern bankers and their allies, the Jewish European bankers, particularly those English bankers, the Rothschild family. They had some logical reasons to believe this. Almost everyone, and certainly all bankers, believed that paper currency had to be backed by a precious metal, referred to as the bullion theory of money. Great Britain adopted the gold standard for their currency in 1816. Other countries had either a silver standard or a bimetallic standard, gold and silver backing their paper currency. As the world's economy became more intertwined in the late nineteenth century, British investors pushed for a uniform international monetary standard, gold, their standard. By the 1870s virtually every major nation involved in the world's trading economy had followed their lead.

A period of intense anti-Semitism in Europe in the late nineteenth century fueled the farmers' conspiratorial logic against Jewish bankers. Watch the musical or movie, "*Fiddler on the Roof.*" The Russian government repeatedly forced Jews to move to within a constantly shrinking pale, a boundary. This is the origin of the phrase "beyond the pale." A pale is a stick. Many were stuck into the ground to mark a boundary; being beyond the boundary is being "beyond the pale." In many countries throughout Europe anti-Semitism was used to promote nationalism. A German history professor, Heinrich von Treitschke, credited Jews with earlier playing "a necessary role in German history, because of their ability in the management of money." But, now, since Aryans had mastered the intricacies of international finance, "the Jews are no longer necessary." They are "of no further use to the world." These attitudes laid the groundwork for the Holocaust. One trick in promoting nationalism was, and still is, to emphasize the differences between "them" and "us." It continues to be a factor in both the politics of the Middle East and the politics of some Americans opposed to both illegal and legal immigrants.

Political Solutions to Economic Problems

In 1860 farmers were 60% of the labor force; by 1900, only 37% of the labor force. This meant that farmers were a declining percentage of the work force and, therefore, a declining political factor as voters. In addition, farm production represented a declining percentage of the nation's wealth. It slid from one-third to one-quarter. Overall, agriculture was a declining industry relative to other industries, in both political influence and in financial promise.

Farm groups had great difficulty wrestling remedial legislation from state legislatures and from Congress. Legislative bodies were increasingly partial to, if not seemingly owned by, big business interests. State and national legislators received free passes to ride the railroads. The legislative needs and demands of industry, railroads, and banking always seemed to be ahead of the farmers' problems.

However, the farmers' basic problem was their pursuit of political solutions to economic problems, as best illustrated by their efforts at currency reform, such as getting the federal government to print more greenbacks, paper currency. The federal government would not do it. Next, farmers urged the government to return to the earlier bimetallic basis of currency, which had been a ratio of 16-1 for silver and gold. What is the origin of 16 to 1? It is the approximate ratio of silver to gold that exists in nature; for every 16 ounces of silver there is 1 ounce of gold. Realizing this, the federal government set 16 to 1 as the legal ratio in 1834. Beginning with the California gold strike of 1849, there were seven gold rushes, which led to too much gold in relation to silver. There is a principle in economics, Gresham's law, which says that when there are two forms of currency, people use the cheap one and save the more valuable one. All of us do this. When you reach into your wallet, you tend to use the crappy looking dollar bills before the crisp ones. Why? The new crisp ones are more valuable. No, they are not! In the nineteenth century, people stopped using silver-backed money and used the crappy, less valuable gold-backed money. Therefore, the federal government recognized reality and went off the bimetallic system. After 1873 the United States had only gold-backed currency.

Later, when massive amounts of silver were discovered, there was no market for it. Just the Comstock Lode in Nevada produced over $900,000,000 worth of silver. The market price of silver dropped to about one-half what it would have been at 16 to 1, meaning that it was now about 32-34 to 1. The silver movement, a loose coalition of silver mine owners and politicians, grew in influence from the admission of six new Western states in 1889-1890, all with a strong interest in silver mines – North Dakota, South Dakota, Montana, Washington, Idaho, and Wyoming. A strange alliance slowly grew between the silver mine owners, looking toward the federal government as the primary purchaser of their silver, and the debt-ridden farmers, who wanted inflation to climb out of debt by raising the price of their farm products, which they assumed would rise faster than the price of the goods they purchased. Increasing the money supply would cause the inflation the farmers desired. The demonetization of silver in 1873, which had virtually no opposition, now became to farmers and silver mine owners, the "Crime of '73."

One historian referred to "free silver," this push to convert all the silver that was being mined into currency, as the "cowbird" of the farmers' movement. A cowbird, for you city folks, does not build a nest. Instead, it lays its eggs in another bird's nest and lets those birds raise their offspring. Since cowbirds are big birds, the huge cowbird baby pushes all the smaller babies out of the nest. In other words, free silver became THE reform among farmers, pushing all their other reforms to secondary importance.

At any time in the economy, prices are a function of the relationship between the money supply and the economy's GDP, the Gross Domestic Product, a measurement of the value of all the goods and services produced in that year in that country. The following explanation, greatly simplified, is what one sees in an economic textbook.

P = prices of goods and services
M = money supply
V = the velocity of money, how quickly it moves through the economy
GDP, the Gross Domestic Product = the value of a nation's total goods and services produced in one year.

The relationship between them is expressed by M x V = P x GDP, money supply times the velocity of it equals prices times the GDP. If you remember your simple math, if the economy grows the GDP increases, forcing the right side of the equation to increase. Now something on the left side must also increase, such as the amount of money in circulation, the money supply. If it does not, then the other part of the right side, prices, must decrease to maintain the equation in equilibrium. If productivity increases the GDP faster than the money supply, it causes deflation, falling prices. If the total amount of money in circulation increases faster than the GDP, it causes inflation, rising prices.

In an attempt to introduce economic stability, the National Banking Acts of 1863 and 1864 created minimal federal control over the nation's currency and banking system. These acts proved to be inadequate. From the end of the Civil War to 1890, the nation's GDP tripled while the supply of money in circulation increased by less than 50%, causing deflation. The prevailing government policy now is to maintain a slight inflation rate in order to encourage businesses and individuals to borrow to stimulate economic growth. Today, as a very simplistic explanation, the federal government controls the money supply by printing more or less currency and by increasing or lowering the interest rate that banks must pay to borrow currency from the Federal Reserve. However, the Federal Reserve Banking system was not established until 1913.

An economist defines money as

1. a standard of value
2. a medium of exchange
3. a store of wealth

Money is money because the federal government, by law, has established it as "legal tender" for all debts, "public or private." Read both sides of a dollar bill. Thus, from a farmer's viewpoint, all the government needed to do was just print more currency, causing inflation and easing their debt burden. However, in the late nineteenth century Eastern bankers seemed to believe that what would have been God's Eleventh Commandment was "Thou shall have gold-backed currency." The federal government listened to Eastern bankers rather than to hayseed farmers. Historical research indicates that many protesting farmers were marginal farmers, who were normally not involved in the political system. In short, they were amateurs in farming AND in politics. Amateurs usually do not perform well against professionals; in this case, against professional bankers and professional politicians.

Munn and *Wabash*

Farmers also tried to solve other economic problems by political means by first gaining control of state and local governments. The pro-farmer state legislators passed the so-called Granger Laws, named for the Grange, an organization of farmers, to regulate rates for railroads and grain elevators, where grain was stored at the stations prior to shipment. Challenged in court by grain elevator owners, the farmers won in *Munn v. Illinois* in 1877, a 7-2 Supreme Court decision that stated, "private property clothed in the public interest can be regulated for the public good." The common good authorizes "the establishment of laws requiring each citizen to so conduct himself, and to so use his property, as not unnecessarily to injure another . . . ."

However, farmers lost in 1886 in the Wabash case, *Wabash v. Illinois.* Five Supreme Court justices had been replaced since the *Munn* decision in 1877. Four of the new justices voted with the majority, 6-3. The Supreme Court ruled that Illinois could not prohibit "long haul and short haul rate differences" on railroads that crossed a state border, because they were involved in *interstate* commerce, a responsibility of the federal government. States could regulate only *intrastate* commerce, that which is entirely within a state's borders. This led Congress to create the Interstate Commerce Act, for which Eastern merchants had also lobbied. Supported by a majority of both parties in Congress, it required all railroad rates to be reasonable and just, which was not defined in the legislation. The ICC, or Interstate Commerce Commission, created by the Interstate Commerce Act, proved to be ineffective. The definition of "illegal" was too fuzzy. Railroads challenged every ICC decision in court, tying up cases for years. The ICC was the first permanent regulatory agency in the federal government. Now there are over 1800 of them. Not even one is mentioned in the Constitution. In the late twentieth century Congress abolished the ICC. Supreme Court decisions continued to weaken the *Munn* decision. Finally, in 1906, the Hepburn Act added teeth to efforts to regulate railroad rates. Within the next five years the ICC reduced railroad rates by one-half. For most farmers on the Great Plains, it was too late.

The Election of 1896

The crowning political effort by protesting farmers was the creation of a new national political party. The Populist Party uprising in 1892 was the political expression of the farmers' economic discontent. Earlier the Farmers Alliance and the Grange unsuccessfully tried to halt the farmers' decline. A strong showing by the Populist Party at the polls in 1892 convinced some Democrats that there was much to be gained by stealing the Populist Party's appeal. The party leaders ignored the incumbent Democratic president, Grover Cleveland. In 1896 Democrats hijacked the Populist Party platform. This is why third parties never break through into the political mainstream. One of the dominant parties, Democratic or Republican, steals their ideas and their followers. The Populists tried to preserve their party by also nominating the Democratic candidate, William Jennings Bryan, for president and a different candidate, Tom Watson of Georgia for vice president, a rabid racist. They hoped Bryan would find Watson so objectionable that Bryan would withdraw as the Democratic candidate. He remained silent about Watson.

Williams Jennings Bryan, a 36-year-old Congressman from Nebraska, won the Democratic Party's nomination on the fifth ballot. His "Cross of Gold" speech created an uproar, stampeding the convention to endorse an expansion of the currency, nicknamed "free silver." The Republican candidate was William McKinley from Ohio. This election was a turning point election, one that ended the Third Party System and inaugurated the Fourth Party System. The major issue facing voters in 1896 was control of the federal government for control of federal policy to benefit either agriculture or industry. McKinley, the Republicans, and industry won. In many respects William Jennings Bryan was more of a celebrity in the 1896 election than a candidate. People came out to see him. He visited more states, gave more speeches, and travelled more than any previous candidate.

The farmers' political efforts failed; as a third party the Populist Party lost in 1892, the Democratic Party, supported by many Populists, lost in 1896. The national policy makers in future Congresses would permanently be more pro-industry than pro-agriculture. Farmers were unsuccessful in solving their problems politically and continued to decline in income and in prestige. In many respects, they represented a passing era. As historian Lawrence Goodwyn wrote, Populism was less than a political platform or a political campaign; it was more of "a spirit of egalitarian hope expressed . . . in a self-generated culture of collective dignity and individual longing." The world had changed; their dreams had not adjusted. In the emerging consumption-oriented urban society, making money to purchase material goods counted. Farmers still thought of farming as a way of life; it no longer was. It had become a business.

33

INTELLECTUAL CURRENTS IN THE LATE NINETEENTH CENTURY

The End of Transcendentalism

The antebellum philosophical literary theme of Transcendentalism evaporated under the harsh realities of the Civil War, urbanization, industrialization, and the widening impact of one of the nineteenth century's most influential books – Charles Darwin's *Origin of Species*, published in 1859. The full title was *On the Origin of Species by Means of Natural Selection, or the Preservation of Favoured Races in the Struggle for Life*. Darwin's theory of evolution undermined the basic tenets of Transcendentalism. Transcendentalism was a paradise of absolutes; all moral values were absolute. Right and wrong were clear-cut and the universe was fixed in place and unchanging. There was no place for such thinking after Darwin. The philosophical basis of Transcendentalism rested on assumptions that were not susceptible to proof, such as intuition, subjectivity, and deduction from thinking, similar to that expressed in the Declaration of Independence as "self-evident truths." The scientific thinking of Darwin rested on proof; nothing was, nor is, self-evident in science. Darwin's theory of evolution is still referred to as a theory because in scientific methodology all theories must be subjected to repetition in scientific tests to confirm the theory. The evidence for evolution is overwhelming, according to scientists, but given the incredible long time spans involved in evolution, as a practical matter, the theory is not capable of being extensively tested. Hence, it remains the "theory" of evolution. Gravity is also a scientific "theory." Do not test it!

The Impact of Darwinism

Darwinism led to the development of new thinking in science and in popular thought. Intellectuals and average citizens always borrow ideas, methodologies, and vocabulary from fields outside their chief area of interest. Later, this happened to the theories and writings of Sigmund Freud and Albert Einstein. At the popular level, Freud's ideas justified what many considered odd behavior and Einstein gave everyone the perfect ending to any argument – all things are relative! The phrase "quantum leap" refers to a huge jump in the popular mind today. However, any scientist will tell you that a quantum leap is so small you could not see it, no one ever has. People borrow constantly from other fields, but they do not always borrow intelligently.

In 1860 almost everyone believed in the story of creation found in Genesis in the Bible. By 1870 one heard many jokes about the "missing link" in evolution. Thirty years later one-half of Americans believed that man evolved from an organism that evolved from slime. In short, the last half of the nineteenth century was an era of intellectual turmoil caused by the harshness of the Civil War, the problems and promises of urbanization and industrialization, and the rise of scientific thinking. The implications of evolution were incorporated into every field of thought – science, law, history, economics, sociology, philosophy, art, and religion. This impact remains. Today's religious fundamentalism is, in essence, still, mainly a reaction against Darwinism.

Social Darwinism

Initially Darwinism seemed useful to justify established conservative thinking about economics and society. The British intellectual, Herbert Spencer, coined the phrase "survival of the fittest," applying it to social classes and to individuals. Darwin never did use that phrase; he referred to evolutionary change as "descent with modification," a less brutal concept. Darwinian thinking applied to society by others, Herbert Spencer the most influential, seemed to justify the prevailing conservative outlook of "survival of the fittest" in two ways.

First, when survival of the fittest and the struggle for existence were applied to the life of man in society, it suggested that nature proved that the best competitors in a competitive situation would win, and this would lead to continuing improvement. This was not really a new idea, but now it had a new justification, a scientifically based justification. The word "scientist" was coined in 1834. Scientists and scientific investigation were very popular by the middle of the nineteenth century. In addition, the public began to eagerly follow explorations of prehistoric sites and ancient ruins, such as the newly discovered city of Pompeii, which had been buried by volcanic ash. Traveling lecturers in this period were common, moving from town to town. Called the Lyceum Movement before the Civil War and the Chautauqua, for where it originated in upstate New York, in the late nineteenth century, it brought entertainment to small towns. Think of these lecturers as the PBS TV stations of their time. As an example of the new thinking, here is a minister's lecture entitled "The Relation of Wealth to Morals," given on the lecture circuit. Especially note his explanation (placed in italics) for why some people become wealthy.

"Two principles lead us through life. First, that man conquers nature and draws to himself material wealth as naturally as the oak tree draws the nutrients from the earth.

The other principle is that, in the long run, *it is only to the man of morality that wealth comes.* Since God's universe is one of harmony, we know that it is only by working along His laws, natural and spiritual, that we can work with efficiency. Only by working along the lines of right thinking and right living can the secrets and wealth of Nature be revealed."

Second, the improvement and development of a society must be slow and unhurried. Evolution advances at its own pace. Therefore, attempts to reform society are out of place and self-defeating. Reform always fails. Darwinism applied to thinking about society came to be called Social Darwinism. It was applied to business and economic activity and society as a whole as the only means to guarantee true social progress. The following observations, which became widely accepted everyday truths, exemplified this thinking:

> "The poor deserve to be poor; they are poor because they have defective characters and values."
>
> "There is not a poor person in the United States who was not made poor by his own shortcomings."
> (The English Elizabethan Poor Law of 1601 had differentiated between the "deserving poor," those worthwhile individuals who had fallen on hard times and deserved charity, and the "idle poor," who deserved nothing. Social Darwinism made no such distinction.)
>
> "The only real job of government is to preserve order, maintain courts, and enforce contracts."
>
> "The natural aristocracy should rule; they can be recognized by their wealth."
>
> "Never give a sucker an even break."
>
> "All life is a struggle."

William Graham Sumner

The world's leading advocate and defender of Social Darwinism was Herbert Spencer, an Englishman, a good friend of industrialist Andrew Carnegie. By 1903 Spencer had sold 368,755 books about Darwinian principles applied to society. In one of the humorous ironies of history, Herbert Spencer and the socialist Karl Marx are buried in the same cemetery, London's Highgate Cemetery, where their tombstones face one another. One wonders what they talk about after dusk.

The most influential advocate of Social Darwinism in America was William Graham Sumner. Sumner graduated from Yale; then traveled to Europe to study theology. He returned to serve as a pastor for two years before his reputation led to a position teaching political and social science at Yale. Among his widely read works were *What Social Classes Owe to Each Other*, 1883; and two essays, "The Forgotten Man," 1883; and "The

Absurd Effort to Make the World Over," 1894. In all his writings and lectures he upheld the business ethic, laissez faire capitalism and the free enterprise system. In this period the test of being designated as an "economist" was that you espoused only the classical laissez faire thinking of Adam Smith in *The Wealth of Nations*. All others who claimed to be economists were considered quacks!

Sumner believed natural laws determined man's social and economic behavior. Any attempts to change or to ameliorate these forces were doomed to fail. Legislation would only do "a great deal of mischief." "Man is in a stream and is swept along with it. All his sciences and philosophy come to him out of it. Therefore the tide will not be changed by us." "The stage of the industrial organization existing at any time, and the rate of its development, are the absolutely controlling social facts. It controls us all because we are in it. It creates the conditions of our existence, sets the limits of our social activity, regulates the bonds of our social relations, determines our conceptions of good and evil, suggests our life-philosophy, molds our inherited political institutions, and reforms the oldest and toughest customs, like marriage and property."

"The captains of industry made their great fortunes because of their own efforts. The great mistake made by the critical public is to assume that if wealth was not in the hands of the big businessmen, it would be spread among the people and workers. This is not true. Without the captains of industry the wealth would never have been created."

"Let every man be sober, industrious, prudent and wise, and bring up his children to be so likewise, and poverty will be abolished in a few generations. Human progress is at bottom moral progress; and moral progress comes only from acquiring the proper economic virtues." In other words, man is primarily an economic being. As for people in the slums and tenement houses – "the evidence is that they like that life, and are indifferent to what others consider its evils and discomforts – they consider it part of the excitement and entertainment of city life."

"Society has to care for the true paupers and the physically incapacitated, but whatever money you divert to the support of shiftless and good-for-nothing people is diverted from some other use, which means that it comes from a productive person and goes to a non-productive person. Sentiment is irrelevant to the situation. We can find no sentiment whatsoever in nature; that all comes from man. Poverty belongs to the struggle for existence, and we are all born into that struggle. Poverty is something you can not eradicate. Focusing on the indigent and the seemingly unfortunate is a terrible mistake because reformers overlook "The Forgotten Man" – the simple, honest laborer, ready to earn his living by productive work. The Forgotten Man should not be forced to share his hard-earned income with the lazy poor. As for charity, it is a silly notion that beggars live at the expense of the rich. The truth is that those who eat and produce not, live at the expense of those who labor and produce. The next time that you are tempted to give to charity, I ask you to stop and remember the Forgotten Man and understand that if you put your dollar in the savings bank it will go to swell the capital of the country which is available for division among those who, while they earn it, will reproduce it with increase."

"As for criminals, a man who has committed a crime is a burden on society and an injury to it. He is a destructive and not a productive force and everybody is worse off for his existence than if he did not exist. Whence, then, does he obtain the right to be taught or reformed at the public's expense? Don't waste money trying to rehabilitate criminals."

Sumner opposed ALL government interference – including high tariffs and government subsidies of the railroads, both of which business leaders endorsed. Government interference was not only futile; it was harmful as well, because it eroded personal liberty. "At bottom there are two chief things with which government has to deal. They are the property of men and the honor of women. These it has to defend against crime." He opposed the Spanish-American War because he considered all war and preparation for war to be a waste of valuable resources. Industrialists and business leaders tried to get him fired from Yale for saying this.

Andrew Carnegie – *The Gospel of Wealth*

How was one supposed to endure the swings of the business cycle and the accompanying periodic stretches of unemployment? Andrew Carnegie had an answer in his essay, "The Gospel of Wealth," written in 1889. The wealthy man is the trustee of society's wealth, the one who is responsible for reallocating his wealth to benefit society, especially the industrious, ambitious lower class. Carnegie built thousands of libraries, where anyone could learn and then apply his acquired learning to rise. Why was the wealthy man justified in his wealth? The wealthy man knows better than the poor worker how to best use money. If profits went to increased wages, it would be dissipated in typical lower class vices, like alcohol. Notice how a constant theme among the rich was the idea that the poor put themselves into their poverty and thoughtlessly pursued behaviors that cemented them in poverty. It is better to provide avenues for only the ambitious poor, such as a library, where a poor person could acquire an education on his own in order to rise. Forget about the rest.

Reform Darwinism – Lester Frank Ward

Social Darwinism was one way of applying Darwin's principles to social thought. However, there was another application of Darwinian theories, called Reform Darwinism, a reaction against the heartlessness of Social Darwinism. The leading proponent of Reform Darwinism was Lester Frank Ward, a geologist and paleontologist. He became one of the leaders in the newly emerging field of sociology, which advocated using the scientific method to solve social problems. Ward spent most of his career as a scientist working for the federal government's U.S. Geological Survey. Towards the end of his life he held a chair in Sociology at Brown University.

Ward argued that ideas such as survival of the fittest no longer applied to humans. Man's intelligence had moved him up to the top of the evolutionary scale. Because of his intelligence, man can plan and order his world as he sees fit. Government itself is also a product of evolution. Society is not caught in the grip of natural laws playing a deadly game of survival of the fittest. To interfere, to regulate, to plan, and to deliberately change were simply intelligent things to do. The means to bring about a better world is the scientific method; let both men and governments apply it. Ward argued in *Dynamic Sociology*, 1883, for "the improvement of society by cold calculation," by socially organized and guided reform. Society must create a meritocracy to equalize opportunity for all, thereby removing the advantages possessed by those with undeserved power, accidental position or wealth, or antisocial cunning.

Wealth is not an absolute possession, but a trust for the benefit of society. The accumulation of wealth without a sense of social responsibility is dangerous. Most revolutions in the past had been political; those of the future would be social, directed against a wealthy class too blind to sense a changing spirit in society, a rising anger over a non-producing idle leisure class. As an interesting side observation, think of the logic of this question, raised in opposition to Social Darwinism. If, according to Darwinian thinking, the creator of wealth deserves it because he produced it, why do his wife or children deserve any of it by inheritance?

Richard T. Ely

Another advocate of Reform Darwinism was Richard T. Ely, an economics professor at Johns Hopkins University and, for most of his later career, at the University of Wisconsin. Ely rejected Adam Smith's classical laissez faire thinking. (A "quack" rather than an economist to Herbert Spencer and William Graham Sumner.) "We hold that the doctrine of laissez faire is unsafe in politics and unsound in morals, and that it suggests an inadequate explanation of the relations between the government and the citizens. In other words we believe in the existence of a system of social ethics; we do not believe that any man lives for himself alone, nor yet do we believe social classes are devoid of mutual obligations corresponding to their infinitely varied inter-relations."

Social Gospel

A third response to Darwinism was the Social Gospel movement. In Europe and in the United States many religious leaders became concerned that among workers, especially in the cities, disinterest in, if not the rejection of, Christianity seemed to be closely connected with the daily misery in which workers lived. In *Sin and Society*, 1907, Edward A. Ross identified a "confusion of ethics which resulted from the attempt to apply the moral code of an individualistic, agrarian society to the practices of a corporate and industrial society."

Walter Rauschenbusch

The leading advocate of the Social Gospel movement was a professor of church history at Rochester Theological Seminary, Walter Rauschenbusch. His book titles show the basic thinking of the Social Gospel: *Christianity and the Social Crisis*, 1907; *Christianizing the Social Order*, 1912; *Dare We Be Christians?*, 1914; *The Social Principles of Jesus*, 1916; and *A Theology for the Social Gospel*, 1917. He believed that "Christianity is in its nature revolutionary."

"Men must be made to realize that they are not serving God in their scramble for money. If a man sacrifices his human dignity and self-respect to increase his income, or stunts his intellectual growth and his human affections to swell his bank account, he is to that extent serving mammon and denying God. Likewise if he uses up and injures the life of his fellow men to make money for himself, he serves mammon and denies God. Our industrial order does both. It makes property the end, and man the means to produce it. A society that treats men as machines to produce will eventually be visited by violent class conflict. It is the task and responsibility of the minister to act as buffers and interpreters between the rich and the poor, capital and labor." He wanted to use Christianity to Christianize the industrial society. In 1850 the only role of the church was individual conversion. Now Rauschenbusch urged church leaders to lead the effort to reform society. The National Council of Churches, formed in 1908, was an outgrowth of this movement.

The Catholic Church

In Europe, the Vatican, traditionally a very conservative voice on public matters, joined in the criticism of Social Darwinism, adding a voice to the Social Gospel and enlisting many Catholic priests into laboring to improve the lot of the lower classes. Pope Leo XIII issued an encyclical, *Rerum Novarum*, in 1891. It castigated capitalism for its impersonal financial and heartless exploitation of workers. It endorsed the formation of Christian trade unions and the right of the government to interfere in the economy to initiate social legislation to protect workers against exploitation and to ameliorate their economic misery.

Later, in 1931, Pope Pius XI in *Quadragesimo Anno*, the fortieth anniversary of the 1891 encyclical, said that property is legitimate and "man is born to labor as the bird to fly." However, capitalists had grasped excessive advantages, leaving the workers a bare minimum. Worse still, competition produced immense power and despotic domination concentrated in the hands of a few. Capital and labor alike must be subordinated to the good of the whole community. Free competition must be limited, workers must receive a just wage sufficient to overcome their proletarian condition, and the owners of factories should receive only a just share of the fruits of production. Pope John XXIII continued this theme, 1958-1963. In his two major encyclicals, *Mater et Magistra*, 1961, and *Pacem in Terris*, 1963, he emphasized social justice and worker participation in the decisions that affected them, while also calling for an end to international conflict.

Literature and Darwinism

Criticism of the prevailing industrial methods and the everyday burdens on the working class appeared as a theme in two books that masqueraded as deep economic thought: Edward Bellamy's novel, *Looking Backward, 2000-1887,* and Henry George's *Progress and Poverty.* Bellamy, the son of a Massachusetts Baptist minister, wrote a novel about a future utopia, which would arrive by the year 2000. The novel's hero wakes up from a deep sleep in 2000 to discover that all the conflicts in society are gone. The national government directs all the economic activities of production and distribution and guarantees the security of all individuals. Competition was no longer necessary; through cooperation everyone had all they needed or wanted. Obviously, the ideas and concepts of socialism influenced Bellamy, although he was careful not to use that word, he called his program "nationalism." His novel sparked the creation of thousands of Bellamy Clubs, where excited people gathered to dream and to discuss how to make the novel's society into a real achievement.

Henry George's *Progress and Poverty* sold over three million copies. He was born into a poor family in Philadelphia and later moved to California in 1857. He addressed the dilemma of the widening extremes of wealth produced by the new industrial society – the paradox of the simultaneous growth of our nation's wealth accompanied by an increase in the number of people living in poverty.

"The association of poverty with progress is the great enigma of our times. It is the central fact from which spring industrial, social, and political difficulties that perplex the world, and with which statesmanship and philanthropy and education grapple in vain. From it come the clouds that overhang the future of the most progressive and self-reliant nations. So long as all increased wealth which modern progress brings goes but to build up great fortunes, to increase luxury and make sharper the contrast between the House of Have and the House of Want, progress is not real and cannot be permanent." The increase in the number of poor people endangered our future. "It is not from top to bottom that societies die; it is from bottom to top."

He advocated a new means of taxation, "the single tax." His rationale was that much of the wealth held by a few individuals resulted not from production, but from higher land values. The profit on the increased value of a piece of land, the difference between the purchase price and selling price of that land, resulted from speculation or good fortune rather than from productive labor or wisely managed investment. All of you are aware of a piece of property that has risen in value because of changes *around* that property, not because of changes done *to* that property by the owner. So, the owner benefits by doing nothing. Unfair! Henry George proposed a 100% tax on the profit on the sale of land, "on which and from which all must live." Using this source of tax revenue, created by society and returning to society, there would be no need for any other tax; this would be "the single tax." Changes in society created the increased value of that property; society should reap all the benefit. "The effect of putting all taxation upon the value of the land would be to relieve the harder working farmers of all taxation." Farmers bought this rationale.

He did identify a modern problem. The current practice of raising taxes on those who improve their property can lead a person to not improve their property. Thus, property taxes, widely used by local governments, promote the non-improvement of land and property.

Henry George believed government-administered technology would alleviate social ills. His book was one of the three best-sellers of the entire nineteenth century. He capitalized on his popularity to run for mayor of New York City in 1886. He came in second, beating a future president, Theodore Roosevelt, who came in third.

One of George's devotees created the first version of a game widely loved today – *Monopoly*. The version created by Elizabeth Phillips in 1903, *The Landlord's Game*, sought to show the plight of the masses gouged by high rents. The game went through many changes before emerging as the Atlantic City-based game in 1935, when Parker Brothers bought the rights.

Other literary works also hammered away at Social Darwinism. In *A Living Wage*, 1906, Rev. John A. Ryan, among others, urged "a living wage" for workers that offered an "American standard of living." You still see efforts to define both, especially in the traditionally low paid service occupations. Stephen Crane, a young novelist noted for his realism, argued that their environment molds people. Change the environment and governments can change the people. His criticisms of the worst features of Social Darwinism are themes in *Maggie, A Girl of the Streets*, and a short story, "The Open Boat." In "*The Open Boat*" four survivors from a shipwreck are slowly sinking, discussing how to survive by working together, survival of the group, not just the fittest. Maggie tries to make something of her life in the slum, but eventually her limited opportunities leave no choice except prostitution. Jack London's short story "*To Build a Fire*" showed the extreme consequences of competition as advocated by those who praised "survival of the fittest." In "*To Build a Fire*" a man and his dog fight to stay alive in the freezing cold. When the dog realizes the man is losing his battle, the dog turns and calmly abandons his master, concerned only about his own survival and his next meal. A Kansas minister, Charles M. Sheldon, wrote *In His Steps* in 1896, the story of a small-town congregation that began to base their daily conduct on the teachings of Jesus. The "good" people of the fictional town of Raymond, actually Topeka, Kansas, were united by their slogan, "What Would Jesus Do?" It sold over 23 million copies by 1925.

If you read all the novels and books written by critics in the late nineteenth century, one pattern jumps out at you. The corrupt city politicians and unscrupulous business-men all have immigrant-sounding names. The "good" people and reformers all have WASP names, White Anglo-Saxon Protestant names. It was clear who, at bottom, was ruining American society.

The New Philosophy, Pragmatism

Darwinism had an impact on all facets of society and on all thought. In the scientific world of Darwin, "truth" was a hypothesis that could stand laboratory-type testing. Testing, experimentation, and the scientific method could be applied to all aspects of everyday life. This attitude led to a new philosophy called pragmatism, better known politically now as liberalism. Pragmatism claimed that moral standards were the prod-uct of social evolution and the environment and therefore were not absolute. Attitudes evolve to become more correct, closer to "truth," at least "truth" as it is now defined. Laws came from the social needs of the moment, not from any eternal wisdom. Fixed ideas were out of place in politics and economics as well as in science and religion. In pragmatism the truth was not fixed or absolute; the "truth" was what worked. The only true test of any idea or policy was the conduct it dictates or inspires. Was an act right or wrong? Check its consequences.

The impact of this thinking on other disciplines was revolutionary. In education the new remedy was to make education functional. It is the job of the education system to prepare good workers and well-adjusted citizens. At Columbia University John Dewey created Progressive Education, which advocated practical education. Participation in a student government helped students learn citizenship, while business courses for those going into business and shop courses for noncollege students would prepare them for their place in the work force. In higher education graduate training leading to the PhD was imported from Europe. The United States had only one PhD in 1870, and 382 by 1900. Johns Hopkins University Graduate School adopted the German system of lehr-freiheit, freedom to teach, and lern-freiheit, freedom to learn, in service to a "pure science," the research ideal, which would lead our society to "truths" in every academic field.

New thinking developed in other fields also. For the legal profession, laws were no longer absolute; they needed to be reinterpreted in light of current thinking, conditions, and consequences. For example, a question that is still asked – should state legislatures abolish capital punishment? That discussion now revolved around the question of what are the consequences of having it or not having it. Notice that research solves such a question. Many economists now claimed that it was possible to manage our economic system; society is not at the mercy of unseen large forces like the business cycle. In religion there was less emphasis on the Ten Commandments and more emphasis on the

Sermon on the Mount, and how to apply Christian teachings rather than merely study-ing them. Among the organizations that grew in response to this new thinking were the Salvation Army, the YMCA, and the YWCA, which stood for the Young Men's or Women's Christian Association.

Scholarly thinking even changed for historians. Now all historical truth became relative; coming out of the values and perspectives of that historian writing at that time period. Therefore, history must be constantly rewritten to reflect the present "truth," which previous generations overlooked, blinded by their values. As an example, reflect upon how much more is now in history textbooks about the history of women, com-pared to years ago – such as the Sheppard-Towner Act, a federal welfare program for pregnant women adopted in the 1920s; the Cable Act, which granted married women U.S. citizenship independent of their husband's status, if they otherwise qualified; and *Minor v. Happersett,* in which the Supreme Court ruled that suffrage for women was not a right of citizenship. The field of history is closer to the "truth," at least for now.

34

PROGRESSIVISM

Historians and the Origins of Progressivism

The origins of Progressivism present a dilemma for historians. Why did it happen? What ideas undergirded it? What did it try to do?

The Progressive Reform Movement is ill-defined in origins, focus, and accomplishments. The only description historians can agree upon, most of them, is that it was a widespread effort to resolve the worst features of urbanization and industrialization, with moral overtones. There seemed to be a moral dimension to every problem. Their morally based intentions undergird both the Mann Act, aimed at suppressing the "white-slavery" traffic in prostitution, and the push for the Eighteenth Amendment to outlaw alcohol. The brothel and the saloon were the two "bastions of urban vice." Progressivism's leading figures shared an image of society as a collective whole rather than a mere collection of isolated, individual atoms. Therefore, reformers should forge a new social order, one capable of continuously adjusting to changes in industrialization and urbanization. More than previous reformers, the Progressives relied upon statistics and detailed investigations to set their priorities. By creating and then staffing government bureaucratic agencies with experts, reformers could monitor and alleviate social problems through "intelligent social engineering." The defense of society, it was asserted, needed to be turned over to professionals, the expert bureaucrats. As Woodrow Wilson explained, "The old political formulas do not fit the present problems; they read now like documents taken out of a forgotten age." Some reformers favored forcing people to become better citizens; other reformers wanted to alleviate the harshness of the factory and the city and to create a physical environment that would subsequently produce better citizens. Same goals, different methods. Woodrow Wilson's 1912 inaugural address declared that the Progressive Reform spirit intended "to cleanse, to reconsider, to restore, to correct the evil without impairing the good, to purify and humanize every process of our common life." That sure clears it up!

Historians have suggested that Progressivism:

Grew out of the public's indignation and anger over the **abuses of big business**, or what historian David Thelen labeled "corporate arrogance." It was anti-big business, an attempt to punish and to control big business. Historian Arthur Schlesinger, Jr., argued that swings between periods of business domination and periods of reform to restrain business characterize all American history. It was time for reform efforts because there is a rhythm to our **cycles of reform**. A student of American history should be prepared to compare and contrast these "cycles of reform."

Grew out of **publicity** about the bad conditions and increasing inequality in American life. The term "Muckrakers" was a disparaging nickname created by Theodore Roosevelt criticizing journalists who looked for "bad" things, muck, to write about. The name stuck, without the connotation. Muckrakers created the groundswell of public opinion that led to the Progressive Movement. Among them were the following:

> Henry Demarest Lloyd, whose *Wealth Against Commonwealth* highlighted the illegal, or at least unfair, methods of the Standard Oil Company, especially rebates. "Believing wealth to be good, the people believed the wealthy to be good." Not John D. Rockefeller, according to Lloyd. Ida Tarbell's *The History of the Standard Oil Company* also blasted Rockefeller.
>
> Thorstein Veblen, in *The Theory of the Leisure Class*, introduced the phrase "conspicuous consumption" to describe the luxurious lifestyle of the super-rich.
>
> Jacob Riis, in *How the Other Half Lives* and *The Battle with the Slum*, gave a human dimension to urban slum conditions and street youth, the city's "throwaways."
>
> Frank Norris, in *The Octopus*, showed how railroads conspired in setting rates, summarized in the memorable phrase, "all-the-traffic-will-bear."
>
> Lincoln Steffens, in *The Shame of the Cities*, probed political corruption and revealed how big businesses worked closely with corrupt politicians to get what each wanted, at the expense of the taxpaying public. Who cared? Not Philadelphia, it was "corrupt and contented." In the early 1960s a similar type book, Michael Harrington, *The Other America*, was a catalyst to the Great Society reforms of Lyndon Johnson's administration.

Grew out of the impetus of the **Populist Movement**, as argued by historian John D. Hicks in *The Populist Revolt*. Look at the 1892 platform of the Populist Party and you will find many of the accomplishments of Progressivism listed as objectives of the Populists. The hero of the Populists was the three-time Democratic Party candidate, William Jennings Bryan, who lost in 1896, 1900, and 1908. In a biography of Bryan written by his wife and daughter, they pointed in the last chapter to all the ideas and proposals he advocated that became laws during the Progressive Era. The list is impressive, and long. However, as the Kansas editor William Allen White observed, Progressivism caught Populism at the swimming hole, and stole all their clothes "except for the frayed underdrawers of free silver." In short, there are similarities, but parentage is hard to prove because not all Populist ideas made it into Progressivism, especially the major reform of free silver.

Grew out of the **"status anxieties"** of the middle class. Historian Richard Hofstadter, in *The Age of Reform*, saw reform as the middle class upset at the breakdown of their "island communities." The term "island communities" comes from historian Robert Wiebe, *The Search for Order, 1877-1920*. It refers to how the isolated, stable small town, local elites found themselves becoming less important with the rise of increased connections to the larger world. Reflect for a moment on how exposure to superb professional athletes on national television minimizes the achievements of small town high school athletes. For Hofstadter and Wiebe, reformers attempted to reassert middle class values against big business. Progressives grew concerned over the fierce class-based labor strife, the ethnic-oriented anti-immigration push, and the small number of state victories for woman's suffrage. Everyone seemed to place their personal, class, and ethnic concerns above the public interest. Enlarging the position and power of a homogeneous middle class would solve these problems. The difference between this argument and the first one above is the focus on the psychological needs of the people originating the reform rather than the abuses of those businesses targeted for reform.

Grew out of an anti-business impulse; however, big business became involved and moved into the so-called "reform" movement to control and to influence the outcome of "reform" legislation. Progressives created regulatory commissions, but big business put its own people on them. Historian Gabriel Kolko, in *The Triumph of Conservatism*, called this **"political capitalism"** and showed how big business used the umbrella of political reform to drive smaller competitors out of business. The Meat Inspection Act did not come solely out of public revulsion from Upton Sinclair's *The Jungle*. There was already widespread concern over the quality and reputation of American meat products, which hurt the sale of canned meat here and abroad. A new labeling system helped. After all, what is better than "U.S. Grade A inspected"? It gives the impression that the grades go all the way down the alphabet. They do not! The larger meat companies made certain that the new law helped the big meat packers and hurt their smaller competitors. The law provided that the meat inspectors, employees of the federal government, were to be paid by the meat companies, which added new employees with no increase in productivity. Smaller companies saw their costs increase, giving an advantage to the larger companies, who more easily absorbed the non-productive new inspectors in their larger facilities. So, where was the "reform"? Non-existent – instead, it was **"political capitalism."**

Similar things still happen. President Barack Obama's health care reform actually ended up with Congress solidifying the profits and positions of the health insurance companies. The lobbyists working for the health care industry outnumbered members of Congress by seven to one. There are 535 members of Congress. Do the math. When a proposed piece of legislation is directed against an industry, it gets involved and controls the impact. That is what lobbyists are for. Instead of being "reformed," business uses the political system to its advantage by shaping and controlling the outcome of reform efforts, what Kolko labeled "political capitalism."

The Significant Component: Upper, Middle, or Working Class?

After all this confusion comes yet another angle. When looking at a reform movement, what does a historian focus on? Who backed the attempts at reform? Or, the leadership? Some historians call Progressivism a middle class movement based on the leaders and what they said and did. Another group of historians argues that the upper class led, reasserting its influence and control that had been lost to labor unions, city bosses, and crude businessmen. There is a principle of political science that the larger the size of the electorate, the higher the social class of the winner. Upper class reformers lobbied at the state level for such reforms as city-wide school boards and park commissions, which the governor often appointed, bypassing local municipal control. They also backed state legislation that led to smaller city councils. Throughout much of the nineteenth century Philadelphia's city council, with over 400 members, had a reputation, deserved or not, as "the largest legislative body in Christianity." A city council of 7 to 11 was easier to influence and to get "decent" people elected to it.

Whatever started Progressivism, historian Joseph Huthmacher identified the essence of Progressivism as the voting support that came from the working class. Workers urged reforms against business and supported labor unions, based on their everyday experiences. The disaster at the Triangle Shirtwaist Company in New York City's garment district is an example. A fire on March 25, 1911, caused the death of 146 women. It led to safety regulations in the workplace, fought for by politicians from working class legislative districts. The resulting safety laws and regulations owe their creation more to working class political support than to shocked and concerned middle class do-gooders.

New Ideas and Outlooks: New Political Thinking

Whatever it was and whatever caused it, the motley collection of reforms called Progressivism clearly had new ideas and new outlooks. Two ideas surfaced repeatedly in Progressivism – **efficiency** and **democracy**. There was a determined effort to make all aspects of modern life more efficient, including even the design of kitchens, how to arrange the triangle for efficiency – the refrigerator, the stove, and the sink. Where should each be located? It saw the birth of the industrial engineer, the efficiency expert, pioneered by Frederick W. Taylor. Taylor invented "scientific management," the practice of eliminating wasted time in a worker's movements. Workers, especially those on assembly lines, grew to despise "Taylorism" for leaving them so little control over their workplace. Some historians see the emphasis on efficiency as part of an "organizational synthesis" that evolved during the late nineteenth century and stretched into the 1920s and beyond. It meant the creation of efficient bureaucracies run by "experts," to modernize all levels of government, business, and industry. Our national greatness demanded it. Gifford Pinchot, the conservationist, said that, "In the great commercial struggle between nations which is eventually to determine the welfare of all, national efficiency will be the deciding factor."

The book and movie, "*Cheaper By the Dozen*," is a perfect example of Progressivism as a collection of reforms rather than a coherent philosophy. In the story the married couple are devotees of Taylor's "scientific management," efficiency experts, which represented a new emphasis in the work world and in government bureaucracies. Another reformer comes to visit the family home to enlist their support for her reform – birth control and family planning. However, the couple's children keep coming in and being introduced. All twelve of them! Finally the disgusted birth control reformer gets up and leaves.

Ideas were very important in Progressivism. The goal was to make actions and institutions reasonable. In a 1918 lecture German scholar Max Weber urged politicians to be passionate "in the sense of matter-of-factness." All parts of society needed clear thinking, correct thinking, which should be passionately applied, calmly, by those with expertise. What was new in this era was the arrival of this competing political philosophy, Progressivism, that challenged the two older political philosophies of Conservatism and Socialism.

Radical – Liberal – Moderate – Conservative – Reactionary – Neo – Ultra

First, a word of caution about politically vague words. **Radical** refers to drastic, sweeping, even violent changes, or advocating revolutionary and widespread changes in the government or at the roots of society. **Conservative** refers to conserving, preserving the existing order of things, or opposition to changing, especially sudden change. A conservative objects to reliance upon abstract reasoning to solve a problem. Stay with the previous models and solutions that respect the continuity of experiences, traditions, and history. A **moderate** favors ends and means that are neither excessive nor extreme. **Reactionary** refers to a desire to move society backwards to a previous order, often idealized beyond reality. Young people are well acquainted with older people telling them how much better things were in the old days. None of the quaint homes of the sturdy pioneers had modern indoor plumbing. All of us prefer the decadence of indoor toilets to the good old days. **Liberal** refers to advocating changes in laws and institutions to keep up with changing conditions; a liberal is tolerant and broad-minded. The extreme liberal, according to an old quip, is so tolerant he cannot enjoy a good argument with himself. President Franklin Roosevelt, an avowed liberal by the ending of the New Deal, gave us a set of humorous definitions for these terms in 1939. "A conservative is a man with two perfectly good legs who, however, has never learned to walk forwards. . . . A reactionary is a somnambulist walking backwards. . . . A radical is a man with both feet firmly planted in the air. . . . A liberal is a man who uses his legs and his arms at the behest – at the command – of his head."

The prefix **neo**, as for example, a neoleftist, means the person described is either a recent convert, presumably from the opposing position, or he or she espouses ideas that are further to the left of what most people traditionally associate with the left ideological position. The prefix **ultra**, as in ultraconservative, means the person takes the extreme ideological position, in this case far to the right of even those who consider themselves on the right.

All these terms confuse students because they refer to both ends and means and because they can be used as both adjectives and nouns. One can pursue conservative goals by radical means. The revolutionary Founding Fathers were, after all, guilty of treason against the British government. From the British point of view the American actions were quite radical. Their ends were conservative; their means were not. Around 1900 a group of American radicals created a new political party, the Socialist Party, trying to use the existing political structure to introduce their Socialist program to change that political structure. Picture someone running for office who says, "When elected I will abolish the office to which I have been elected." Their ends were radical; their means were not. In your personal life avoid quickly labeling people, ideas, and political movements. A person may be liberal on race relations and conservative on religion, morals, and family values. Do not use facile labels as substitutes for analytical thinking. Probe your subject more deeply.

Left – Right – Center
Everyone has an ideology (the word ideology is from the Greek for the science of ideas), knowingly or unknowingly, that they share with others in their daily interactions. A shared ideology consists of how a group of individuals view their surrounding world, their thoughts about various aspects of it, and their reactions to whatever forces impinge upon them, all of which add up to a common understanding and perception of their small part of the world. It may contain fuzzy thinking, myths, stupid analysis, and misunderstanding; but, it is their own, and they act upon it.

Left, right, and center as identifications for ideological positions have too many definitions. It is best to return to their origins. The terms left-right-center came from the French Revolution. The revolutionary legislature met in a building with a visitors' balcony on one end. From the viewpoint of the speaker addressing the seated legislature, those on the left, the mob's friends, sat beneath the visitors' balcony; those on the right sat as far away from the visitors' balcony as possible because the mob threw garbage and offal at its enemies during debates. The left thought in terms of the masses, proposing laws for the benefit of the masses. The right thought in terms of the individual, proposing laws to permit individual and class differences and emphasizing order and traditional attitudes. The center, similar to a wheat field in the wind, followed shifting public opinion.

Notice that these are not ideological definitions; each of us individually places ourselves on the continuum between the two points of extreme left and extreme right. In American politics a liberal is to the left of the center and a conservative is to the right of the center. But, in all honesty, few American politicians stray too far from the center. The mythical average voter is a 49-year-old woman who lives in a suburb in the Midwest. She hardly qualifies for either extreme position and our successful liberal and conservative politicians understand that.

Remember some quirks about ideology. First, people are not poured into concrete. Their ideas may change over the years. Second, ideology rarely overcomes all other factors. One leftist may mistrust another. Occasionally in history, the masses have not sympathized with their leftist rulers and force became necessary to "improve" the masses. When Joseph Stalin collectivized the farms in Russia in the 1930s, he forced millions of peasants off their privately owned farms. As many as ten million peasants who resisted were killed. Those peasants failed to realize collectivization was in their best interests; therefore, they had to be forced to do what was best for them, but "best" existed only in the opinion of their leftist government. Also, there is no direct link between the amount of one's personal property and his or her distance from the ideological center. Any government policy or program affects two people differently. A belief in reduced taxation always benefits wealthier individuals more. The extreme left position implies government of the masses, by the masses, and for the masses. The extreme right champions the near absence of government to permit each individual to govern only himself.

History textbooks often overemphasize ideological positions because they produce juicy quotes. One United States senator opposed the Progressive Era Meat Inspection Act because it took away an individual's God-given right to poison himself by eating tainted canned meat. If the government guaranteed the safety of each can of meat, it ended the mystery of eating canned meat, your individual right to play can-opener roulette. Two derogatory quotes from two hundred years ago perfectly described the masses from the upper class viewpoint. The first came from a British aristocrat, "the dirty people of no name," emphasizing their lack of aristocratic breeding. The British jurist, William Blackstone, described the lower class as "in so mean a situation as to be esteemed to have no will of their own." Be leery of summarizing the totality of an individual's existence and responsibility to others in one word or phrase such as liberal or conservative. Because people live in a community, we must do some things in common. The real question is what and to what extent.

First, a look at the two prevailing political philosophies around 1900 – conservatism and socialism.

The Conservative Creed and the Nature of Man

Man is a flawed creature, prone to do evil things. People are frail creatures unable to withstand the evil impulses within themselves. Life is a "succession of pitiful compromises with fate." The present is uncertain and the future is unknowable; therefore, the only way to prevent anarchy, chaos, and disaster is to cling to the time-tested methods of the past. "God Almighty made men and certain laws which are essential to their progress in civilization and Congressmen cannot break these natural laws without causing suffering." Note the emphasis on "natural" laws.

A future president, Calvin Coolidge, explained the conservative creed in *"Have Faith in Massachusetts,"* a speech to his fellow members of the Massachusetts State Legislature on January 7, 1914.

> "The people cannot look to legislation generally for success. Industry, thrift, character, are not conferred by act or resolve. Government cannot relieve from toil. It can provide no substitute for the rewards of service. It can, of course, care for the defective and recognize distinguished merit. The normal must care for themselves. Self-government means self-support."

Any attempt by the government to achieve greater equality is always accompanied by an enlargement of governmental authority, and therefore, a corresponding reduction in liberty. Inequality, rather than equality, is natural because the average person contributes little to progress. Conservatives wanted to protect the rights of the outstanding contributors to society. The graduated income tax makes no sense; people who earn a lot of money create jobs for the "others." The masses were "political junk." Democratic systems of government lead to demagogues or bad policies. The mob's collective IQ is one example where the whole is less than the sum of its parts. Elihu Root, who served as Theodore Roosevelt's Secretary of War and as a senator from New York, added that legislatures should "reject every proposal which involves the idea that the people can rule merely by voting." The voice of the people is not the voice of God; it is instead the voice of stupidity.

The Conservative Creed and the Nature of Progress

The application of natural laws, God's laws, is the key to progress. Man cannot cause progress, because progress is far beyond the capacity of humankind to guide or to invent. Do not change things – you will screw it up! Reason cannot solve political problems because a person never gets all the premises into their thinking. Your thinking will be inadequate. The only regulation of the economy should be by supply and demand, which God created.

Men can only discover God's laws; they cannot change them. Progress is God's progress, which takes generations, not years or days. People cannot understand God's plans, the only real definition of progress. As the Roman Empire deteriorated, St. Augustine, the leading theologian of his time, and maybe of all time, wrestled with the question of how God could permit his only Christian empire on earth to fall apart. His conclusion – *The City of God* – which said that there is no steady movement upward and onward towards progress, but there is movement toward the City of God on earth, God's establishment of His earthly kingdom. Human beings do not, and cannot, understand God's timetable or plans. If things seem to be getting worse, they are getting worse. However, it is all in God's plan. Individuals may just happen to be unlucky enough to live during a period of long societal decline. As Coolidge said, "Men do not make laws. They do but discover them. Laws must be justified by something more than the will of the majority. They must rest on the eternal foundation of righteousness." In the words of the German philosopher, Hölderlin, what has always made the government "a hell on earth has been precisely that man has tried to make it his heaven."

Man measures progress by the acquisition of property, material wealth. Coolidge said, "Man is born into the universe with a personality that is his own. Man has a right that is founded upon the constitution of the universe to have property that is his own. Ultimately, property rights and personal rights are the same thing. The one cannot be preserved if the other be violated. (This is why Conservatives believe one is justified in using a gun to protect one's property. It is the same as protecting yourself from attack.) Each man is entitled to his rights and the rewards of his service, be they never so large or never so small." Theodore Roosevelt, a Progressive, once said that the rights of human beings were superior to property rights, a statement many Conservatives would disagree with.

Conservatives feared national disunity, social conflict, and cultural decadence. They generally opposed new ideas, which gave them a reputation for anti-intellectualism. What they valued was tradition. They endorsed G. K. Chesterton's observation: "Tradition means giving votes to the most obscure of all classes – our ancestors. It is the democracy of the dead. Tradition refuses to submit to the small and arrogant oligarchy of those who merely happen to be walking around." In the words of Edmund Burke, the conservative English critic of the violence of the French Revolution, "All change must be gradual and must respect national and historical traditions." Elihu Root added, "it is not merely useless but injurious for government to attempt too much."

Modern **Libertarians** are often politically grouped with Conservatives. They, however, tend to support only a bare minimum of government activity and are closer to classical economists, trusting the market to guide the economy. Libertarians criticize modern Conservatives for being willing to use the power of government to defend established privilege. Libertarians believe that government should never confer any right, privilege, power, or advantage on any group; and, treat each group equally by doing next to nothing for all groups.

The Radical Rationale, Socialism, and the Nature of Man

There is nothing evil in human nature. Society teaches and defines each individual. Man is born with tabula rasa, a "blank slate" as a mind. Man is a mirror that reflects his environment, chiefly his materialistic environment. No ideas exist as absolutes outside of the environment. Ideas come from one's interaction with the environment, which defines all abstract words – love, beauty, truth, God – to him or her. This is why definitions of abstractions are different for everyone.

Two authors from this era illustrate the Socialist-leaning criticism of conservatism and Social Darwinism – Stephen Crane in *"The Open Boat"* and *Maggie, A Girl of the Streets*, and Jack London in *"To Build a Fire."* All three of these show the worst consequences of conservative thinking. In the short story *"The Open Boat"* four survivors from a shipwreck are slowly sinking, discussing how to survive by working together. When they decide to individually swim for the shore, only three make it. The strongest swimmer does not. In *Maggie, A Girl of the Streets*, Maggie tries to make something of her life in the slum, but eventually her limited opportunities leave no choice except prostitution. In London's short story, *"To Build a Fire,"* a man and his dog fight to stay alive in the freezing Yukon cold. When the dog realizes the man is losing his battle, the dog turns and calmly abandons his master, concerned only about his own survival, trotting back to where he knew there were "other food-providers and fire-providers."

The Radical Rationale, Socialism, and the Nature of Progress

Progress to a Socialist was scientific. The nineteenth century was a great age for searching for overarching laws and sweeping explanations in many fields, such as chemistry (the Periodic Table) and evolution (Darwinism). Karl Marx was both a product of this viewpoint and a participant in the nineteenth century's epistemology, which is the study of the nature of and limits of a field of knowledge. He researched history and discovered, but did not invent, the laws of economics that determined the workings of society. This permitted him to be able to know, not just predict, the future in its broad outlines – hence his Theory of History. There are five stages or societies in history: primitive, slavery, feudalism, capitalism, and socialism, Marx asserted. Man is a creation of and a creature of his economic class. Marx discovered the role of classes within each of these economic systems – the exploited class; the ruling class, the owners of the means of production; and the rising class, which will take over in the next stage. A brief, violent revolution ushers in each new stage. All this was inevitable; it was only a matter of time before progress, defined as the march of history forward, would institute the classless society – socialism, the final stage. The 1904 platform of the U.S. Socialist Party explained it: "The Socialist program is not a theory imposed upon society for its acceptance or rejection, it is but the interpretation of what is sooner or later inevitable."

As a student of history, you must realize that this is prior to the Bolshevik Russian revolution. Do not read history backwards. Do not take today's knowledge and understanding back into a previous period of history. Try to understand their thinking at that time. Progressive era socialism pre-dates the 1917 Russian Bolshevik Revolution. After the Bolshevik Revolution it was virtually impossible to advocate socialism in the United States as a viable political and economic philosophy. No matter what an American Socialist advocated, his opponent replied, "You claim that . . . , but in Russia . . . ." And, of course, it pre-dates the 1991 collapse of Russian communism, which also makes it difficult to advocate socialism as a workable system. Even China, officially still communist, has greatly modified their socialist economy.

Why did socialism not catch on in America? Dozens of scholars and even Karl Marx have kicked around that question. Probably the best short answer came from historian Alan Dawley, "the ballot box was the coffin of class consciousness." Nineteenth century America, to paraphrase Lincoln, became a political society characterized by government "of the masses, by the masses, and for the masses." Cynics may argue with that, and they have a point, but generally it remains true. Surprises occasionally spring out of the ballot box on election day. The masses vote. Mass democracy was soon joined by two economic functions – mass production and mass consumption. Class distinctions and differences never had a chance to develop deep roots. Economic opportunity, or, more correctly, the dream of economic opportunity and achievement, limited the appeal of socialism.

During the Progressive era, millions of Americans were attracted to socialism. Not later, and not now. But, socialism was a viable alternative political program in the early 1900s. Woodrow Wilson even predicted in 1906 that automobiles would bring socialism to America by promoting envy of the rich. Henry Ford's cheap Model T stopped that. Socialists were elected to many offices across the country. The mayors of Reading, Pennsylvania, Bridgeport, Connecticut, and Milwaukee, Wisconsin, were socialists, for many years, into the 1940s. In the party's strongest showing, 1912, they elected 34 socialist mayors, and socialist councilmen or school board members in 169 cities. The party's presidential candidate, Eugene V. Debs, garnered one million votes, topping double digits in seven states. The party appeared to have a bright future.

Socialism was never a coherent political and economic philosophy. Socialists fought among themselves. There were quarrels between the "pure Socialists," who advocated doing nothing and, therefore, the socialist revolution will arrive faster, according to Marx's theories, and the "sewer Socialists," who wanted to make the lives of workers easier and healthier, now. However, this could possibly put off the coming socialist revolution by defusing worker anger.

Now a new way of thinking entered onto the political scene, Progressivism. Progressivism had two key words associated with it – democracy and efficiency.

The Progressive Profile and the Nature of Man

The Conservative was pessimistic; the Progressive was optimistic. Progressives had a deep faith in man and in his collective ability to better his station on earth. They used phrases like "the beautiful people," and "the essential nobility of man." "In the end the people are bound to do the right thing, no matter how much they fail at times." They saw not the mob, but the people, with incredible potential, putty that could be shaped to create a better world in the future. How was this to be accomplished? The individual must be free to develop to his fullest capacity in order to bring benefits to society. Note that the Progressive "individual" was not self-centered or selfish. Good individuals, working together through cooperation, could solve society's problems. Progressives tended to oppose all organizations hampering the free individual – political machines, unions, monopolies, trusts.

Democracy was not just a belief for Progressives. It was more like a faith; "it is primarily a mode of associated living" composed of individuals who each consider their actions in reference to their impact on others. The right to choose was more important than the ability to choose wisely. "Democracy is a soul-satisfying thing." The solution to most problems was to apply more effective democratic methods. They preached Christian ethics, applying them to politics. In reforming individuals, such as juvenile delinquents, the solution was to preach Christian ethics and morals. Children were "putty," capable of being reshaped to compensate for their dismal surroundings. The movement had a righteous and evangelical character, "a political carnival of purity." A character in William T. Snead's *If Christ Came to Chicago*, 1894, explained that Christian-based reform must be accomplished through politics, for "it is by politics, through politics and in politics that the work of redemption must be wrought."

With a dual focus that was political *and* moral, Progressives divided over economic policy. Should big businesses be broken up by antitrust laws to restore competition and thus regulate businesses through the workings of the free market? Or, should the bigness of big business be accepted and then monitored and regulated by the federal government to punish wrongdoing? There were good trusts and bad trusts. Good trusts would be left alone. In the 1912 election Democrat Woodrow Wilson advocated breaking up all the trusts, part of his approach called the New Freedom. In contrast, his opponent, Progressive Party candidate Theodore Roosevelt, urged accepting the reality of modern American industry and giving the federal government the power to regulate big business, an approach he termed the New Nationalism. Even though Wilson won in 1912, the trend of subsequent federal government policy toward monopolies and trusts more closely followed Roosevelt's New Nationalism.

The Progressive Profile and the Nature of Progress

Inequality caused both injustice and evil in the world. If inequality could be wiped out, the result would be a more honest, neighborly, helpful, and capable individual. Two organizations founded in this era for young people, the Boy Scouts and the Girl Scouts, embraced these values. The earlier nineteenth century viewed poverty as a problem solved by giving charity to deserving individuals. The Progressives viewed poverty as the result of structural impediments in society.

Man is malleable. Central to Progressive thinking was the idea that man, more good than evil, had the power through his moral good sense and intellect to change his environment and himself. By working together, people could make the world better. Man is neither chained to his past, as the Conservatives believed, nor riding automatically into a predetermined future, as the Socialists believed. Man is a free agent who controls his own destiny. The way to improve society is to improve each building block of society, each individual. Improve the individual and society as a whole will progress. If someone fails the first time, try again, and again, and again. The little children's book, "*The Little Engine That Could*," perfectly illustrates this approach to education. Everyone can learn; and everyone must learn. Our progress depends upon it. This led to a new approach in education. Columbia University Professor John Dewey's "Progressive Education" advocated "learning by doing." The basic progressive means to a better future was the public school, which explained the middle class's drive for universal, secular, and free public education.

There is no such thing as absolute truth. The test of any idea or policy is in its consequences. The test of a truth is the conduct it inspires. Is something right or wrong? Check the consequences. "Should states have a death penalty?" The Conservative quotes the Bible, selected verses, and replies "eye for an eye and tooth for a tooth." The Socialist says, no. Every criminal is himself also a victim, a product of his or her environment, a prisoner in a society that causes crime by permitting the horrible attitudes and poverty of the capitalist economic system. The Progressive says, let's gather statistics and study the impact of the death penalty. Does it reduce murders? If so, keep it; if not, abolish it. But, first, let's gather statistics upon which to base our decision.

Statistics do not sway Conservatives. As Ronald Reagan said once, "Facts are stupid things."

Progressives believed that moral standards evolved; they are not absolute truths. Fixed ideas are out of place in politics, economics, science, religion, and judicial decisions. Laws come from the society's needs of that moment, not from any eternal wisdom. One of the founders of the Boston University School of Law wrote that "the notion of abstract, eternal principles as a governing power, with their author the external sovereign, must go." The "external sovereign" was a reference to God. In his 1912 campaign to regain the White House, Theodore Roosevelt said that, "every judge is bound to consider two separate elements in his decision of a case, one the terms of the law; the other the conditions of actual life to which the law is to be applied."

The world is fully knowable. The universe is an orderly system operating according to laws, whose detailed workings are being uncovered bit by bit by scientists and rational thinking. Human beings are fully capable of understanding this orderly universe through the innate human quality called "reason," which liberates humanity from the bondage of superstition and permits all men and women to recognize and to agree upon objective truths.

In the twentieth century Progressivism came to be called by another name – Liberalism. One of the difficulties Liberals always faced and will face is this lack of a cohesive body of ideas that holds the faithful followers together. Progressivism, or Liberalism, is more an approach to political challenges than it is a ready, prescribed program or agenda. (The source for much of the explanation of the political thinking in this era is the chapter on "The Progressive Profile" in George E. Mowry, *The Era of Theodore Roosevelt and the Birth of Modern America, 1900-1912.*)

What Were Progressives Trying to Do? – Change the Structure of Government

Progressives believed that many political problems could be alleviated by making government more democratic, both in ends and in means – what is being done and how one goes about doing it. Progressives sought to change the structure or machinery of government, although in actual practice it was more like tinkering than change. Reformers felt governments were too much controlled by the few. They must be modified to make it harder for the few to control and easier for the many to control. More democracy was the answer.

Reforms appeared in the state and the local governments, several originating in Oregon or Wisconsin. The best known Progressive governor was Robert M. La Follette of Wisconsin, whose innovations earned Wisconsin the nickname of "laboratory for democracy." After serving in Congress as a Republican Party loyalist, Wisconsin's party "bosses" stymied his attempts to win the nomination as a candidate for governor. When he finally reached the governor's office in 1901, La Follette was determined to implement a program of reform, which became known as the "Wisconsin Idea." Among his ideas was the **direct primary**, which allowed the party's voters to select the candidates, negating the bosses' control. Control of the nominating process had meant control of the candidates. In 1906 La Follette began a long career in the Senate, carrying his Progressive fight to Washington.

Two ideas emerged in Oregon, the **initiative** and the **referendum**, trying to bring "pure" democracy to the legislative process. One of the tricks politicians play in legislatures is for each house in a two-house legislature to pass bills on the same topic, but with slight variations, a word or two. Then each house fails to pass the other house's bill. Because a bill must be passed by both houses in the same exact wording in order to become a law, it never becomes a law. The perplexed voter cannot understand why a widely supported bill was never passed. Through a petition to the legislature, the **initiative** forced a question to be put on the ballot at an election. "Should the state legislature vote on this proposed bill, as written. Yes or no." Playing games was over. The **referendum,** also placed on the ballot, allowed the voters, rather than the legislators to vote on a proposed bill, without changes or amendments. Legislators grew to like this. They did not have to face controversial bills, especially those on moral issues. Another reform was the **recall**, which enabled voters to vote an elected official out of office in a special election before the term ended. By 1912 seven Western states had adopted the recall. Earlier the **secret ballot** had begun in the 1880s in the Pacific Northwest, apparently influenced by nearby British Columbia. This idea came originally from Australia, where it was adopted in the 1850s, and then spread to England and Canada. The English Ballot Act of 1872 introduced the secret ballot into British voting. In American elections before the secret ballot voting procedures varied. In some places a voter deposited a colored card into a ballot box, such as red one for Republican or blue one for Democratic. Or, a voter put the card into the Republican box or the Democratic box. Anyone watching could see how a person voted. And, they did watch. Sometimes the factory owner marched his workers down to the polls, passing out the already marked ballots on the way.

Progressives pushed four constitutional amendments through Congress and the state legislatures. The **Sixteenth Amendment** ended the haggling over the constitutionality of the **income tax** by specifically permitting it. A major stumbling block had been the provision in the Constitution requiring all federal taxes to be levied based on population. This meant, for example, that if Iowa had 2.6% of the nation's population, Iowans paid no more than 2.6% of federal taxes. The large states put this provision in the original Constitution to prevent the small states from joining forces to lay a disproportionate tax burden on the outvoted bigger states. The income tax was intended to replace dependence on the tariff. The first income tax ranged from only one percent on incomes above $3,000 to seven percent on incomes above $500,000. The average worker earned far less than $3,000 a year. It was closer to $500-$700. England first levied an income tax to help pay for the Napoleonic Wars in the early nineteenth century. Sweden was the first country to introduce a permanent income tax, in 1860. The income tax was widely adopted throughout Europe in the late 1880s and early 1890s. By 1910 only France, the United States, Belgium, and Hungary did not levy taxes on incomes. The First World War brought the income tax to all modern nations.

The **Seventeenth Amendment** provided for the **direct election of senators** by voters rather than by state legislatures, as stipulated by the original Constitution. Similar to the direct primary at the state level, this amendment sought to curtail the power of the party bosses.

At the local level there were two new forms of city government. The **city manager plan**, originated in Dayton, Ohio, employed a professional manager to run the city on a day-by-day basis, theoretically removing petty politics from minute decision-making. The **commission plan** was adopted by Galveston, Texas, after a devastating hurricane. It fixed clear responsibility within the various city departments. Voters elected the head of each department – police, parks, sanitation, fire, streets, etc. Some cities opted for **municipal ownership of utilities** to counter utility companies, such as electric companies, gas companies, and streetcar systems. Progressive mayors worked to alleviate the worst features of urban America by programs like establishing parks, creating evening schools for workers to better themselves, and supporting the rights of labor unions. The best examples were Hazen Pingree in Detroit from 1889 to 1897 and Samuel "Golden Rule" Jones in Toledo from 1889 to 1905.

What Were Progressives Trying to Do? – Regulation of Big Business

At every level of government Progressives wanted to regulate big business to protect the public interest and the consumer. But how? To what purpose? The uncertainty over approach and goal is best illustrated by the 1912 election between Theodore Roosevelt and Democrat Woodrow Wilson. Both candidates were regarded as Progressives. Historians consider President William Howard Taft, 1908-1912, to also be a Progressive president. His rift with Theodore Roosevelt was personal as well as political. Roosevelt had broken away from the Republicans when he was unable to secure the party's nomination. He created a new party, the Progressive Party. Incumbent William Howard Taft, running as a Republican, came in third. The disagreements between the two Progressives, Wilson and Roosevelt, are subtle. Wilson favored breaking up the trusts through antitrust laws and federal lawsuits, thus letting the marketplace become competitive. Trusts had unfairly used bigness to squelch small businesses. Roosevelt argued that bigness in business was here to stay. Look at any major industrial country. The better approach was to accept trusts and regulate them, differentiating between "good" trusts and "bad" trusts.

At the turn of the century three financial giants, all regarded as notorious Robber Barons – J. P. Morgan, James J. Hill, and E. H. Harriman – fought for control of all the railroads running west from Chicago to the Pacific coast. Frustrated in their separate efforts, they joined forces to create the Northern Securities Company, which owned a majority of the stock in both the Northern Pacific and the Great Northern railroads, which together owned enough stock to control the Burlington Railroad. A trust now controlled the entire railroad transportation network for one quarter of the nation. President Theodore Roosevelt, who had assumed the presidency upon the assassination of McKinley, ordered his Attorney General to file a lawsuit in 1902 under the morbid Sherman Antitrust Law of 1890. All previous attempts to break up trusts had failed. Not now. The Supreme Court ruled 5-4 in 1904 that the Northern Securities Company violated the Sherman Antitrust Act. To Roosevelt it was a "bad" trust.

Later the Supreme Court created a "rule of reason" in three cases involving the American Tobacco Company, Standard Oil, and U.S. Steel. While Wilson won the 1912 election, the Supreme Court endorsed and applied Theodore Roosevelt's New Nationalism position, differentiating between good and bad trusts. The Supreme Court assumed the responsibility for determining if a specific trust was good or bad, what it termed the "rule of reason." Standard Oil of New Jersey was dissolved under the Court's "rule of reason." The American Tobacco Company was bad, but not too bad, and so it was forced to reorganize to stimulate competition. The United States Steel Corporation did not have to be dissolved; it was a "good" trust. The antitrust laws applied only to "bad" trusts. After winning the election of 1912, Woodrow Wilson added the Clayton Antitrust Act to the nation's antitrust approach, specifying what constituted "bad" practices, such as interlocking directorates. J. P. Morgan was famous for putting members of his banking interests on the board of directors for supposedly competing companies. Sharing information through these interlocking directorates, the competing companies all followed similar policies, such as raising their prices at the same time. So much for competition. Not after the Clayton Act. Regulated monopoly accurately describes the federal government's policy since the Progressive era, however that policy was applied inconsistently and infrequently. One historian, Richard Hofstadter, asked in an article in a book in 1965, *"What Ever Happened to the Antitrust Movement?"* It seemed to have been shelved somewhere under, "no longer applicable."

During Roosevelt's and Wilson's administrations, 1901-1908 and 1912-1920, several laws were passed by Congress to regulate big business. The Hepburn Act empowered the ICC, the Interstate Commerce Commission, to fix reasonable railroad rates, the Federal Reserve Act regulated banking, and the Elkins Act declared railroad rebates illegal. States and local governments enacted similar laws. Many states created regulatory commissions to try to control railroads and utilities.

The most celebrated Progressive laws were the Meat Inspection Act and the Pure Food and Drug Act, passed the same day, June 30, 1906. These two acts are often linked together in American history textbooks as premier examples of Progressive Movement reform. The colorful stories about the meatpacking industry from Upton Sinclair's *The Jungle*, and Theodore Roosevelt's disgust over his breakfast sausage, give the Meat Inspection Act more attention. However, the drug part of the Pure Food and Drug Act deserves equal emphasis. During the Progressive era many organizations, such as the American Medical Association, established standards in their fields to elevate their professional image in the public's eye. The Pure Food and Drug Act required the content labeling of medicines, specifically targeting morphine, opium, and cocaine. There will be more about this law in the later chapter on "The War on Drugs." Another example of a law to protect consumers was Wilson's push for the Federal Trade Commission, which was empowered to issue "cease and desist" orders to businesses ordering them to stop doing something. Prior to this law any new government regulation was countered by lawsuits that tied up the regulation in the courts for years. Now businesses had to immediately stop what they were doing, such as making a bogus claim in an advertisement. "This little pill in your gas tank will double your mileage, if you drive twice as far." (Consumers might read it as double your miles-per-gallon. Read the advertisement again. It means?) Businesses could still sue, but the practice deemed illegal had to pause.

What Were Progressives Trying to Do? – Expand the Powers of Government
Progressives urged the American people to give more powers to the national government, as advocated by Herbert Croly in his book, *The Promise of American Life*, 1909. They sought to expand the powers of government to relieve social and economic distress. These powers are known as the "police powers," traditionally reserved to the state governments to ensure the health, safety, and morals of their people. However, in the Progressive era the federal government began to move into this area.

Much celebrated, and difficult to understand today with the weakening of state laws against marijuana, the **Eighteenth Amendment** prohibited the "**manufacture, sale, or transportation of intoxicating liquors**." Why? Prohibition was a middle-class led moral crusade, an anti-urban, anti-immigrant, anti-labor, and anti-party boss movement that swept across the nation from the West and South. It also had elements of anti-big business, anti-trust. Liquor was the nation's fifth largest industry. Some historians consider it primarily an anti-saloon campaign, led by the Anti-Saloon League. Strikes originated in saloons, where workers plotted against employers. And reformers asserted that immigrants wasted their money in saloons when they should be taking care of their families and seeking to better themselves. In many ways it was linked to woman's suffrage. As women got the vote in Western states they fought to eradicate alcohol, seen as a threat to the family home. Even alcoholics celebrated in bars the night before Prohibition went into effect. "My children will be free of the demon rum." If one has ever observed an alcoholic, it is easy to understand this moralistic crusade to "improve" society. However, it contributed to an urban crime wave in the 1920s.

The last Progressive amendment was **woman's suffrage**, achieved by the **Nineteenth Amendment**. The struggle had been long, dating from the Seneca Falls

Convention in 1848. Women were bitterly disappointed by the passage of the Fifteenth Amendment, granting black males the right to vote. Politicians urged women to backtrack, because this was "the Negroes' Hour." The women's hour arrived a half century later, after long, long campaigns and much agitation. The American Equal Rights Association, founded in 1866 to gain the right to vote for blacks AND women, splintered over the question of supporting "the Negroes' hour." It fell apart in 1869 as members divided, some supporting just suffrage for blacks and others holding out for both. Many men opposed suffrage because they believed women would vote as a bloc. However, not until 1964 did a gender gap appear, a significant difference between the way men and women voted. In the early twentieth century granting women the vote was an idea whose time had come, all around the world. In 1917 communist Russia became the first major country to grant the vote to all men and women, universal suffrage, regardless of property. Look at this list of the march of woman's suffrage.

1906 – Finland	1921 – Poland
1913 – Norway	1925 – Hungary
1915 – Denmark, Ireland	1945 – Italy, France
1917 – Russia, Netherlands	1971 – Switzerland
1918 – Czechoslovakia, Great Britain (on a limited basis)	
1919 – Germany	
1920 – Austria, United States	

Few Latin American countries granted women the vote until after the Second World War.

Prior to the Progressive era workplace safety was an issue between the employer and the individual employee. If you were injured on the job, you were often fired. "Handicapped" was not in the nineteenth century's vocabulary. And, business accommodation of handicapped workers was limited to a few sympathetic employers. Two disasters in this era galvanized public opinion, alerting the public to urge their state and local governments to become involved in creating and enforcing safety rules and regulations in the workplace. The best known was the Triangle Shirtwaist Factory fire on March 25, 1911. The factory, a lower Manhattan sweatshop, was located on the 8th, 9th, and 10th floors of a building. To stop workers from taking breaks on the fire escape, the owners locked some of the doors. A fire broke out. The narrow stairway and the single (of four) operating elevator carried a few to safety. Many of the rest were trapped. Some escaped by going up and jumping to a roof next door. Those trapped with flames at their backs jumped, horrifying spectators. The total dead was 146. Guilty of only a single violation, the owners were fired $25. This fire led to the enactment of thousands of **safety regulations**, all over the country. Many state legislators still get ideas by paying close attention to what is going on in other state legislatures. An earlier New York City disaster, the fire aboard a local cruise ship, the *General Slocum* in 1904, killing 1,021 people, also led to new safety regulations. Until September 11, 2001, the attack on the World Trade Center, these two disasters were remembered as New York City's most tragic.

However, the courts put limits on the power of governments to protect workers. The Supreme Court in 1905 declared unconstitutional a state law limiting the hours of employees in a bakery, *Lochner v. New York*. Workers had the right to sign a contract. If a worker agreed to work 14 hours a day for six days, it was his "right" to sign that contract for an 84-hour week. However, in 1908 the Supreme Court did uphold a law limiting working hours for women in *Muller v. Oregon*. Part of the defense of the Oregon law before the Supreme Court was the "Brandeis brief," named for the defense attorney, Louis Brandeis, a future Supreme Court justice. He presented a collection of statistics showing the impact of long working hours on the health of women, and therefore, on their ability to give birth to healthy children, jeopardizing the nation's future. The Court agreed, state legislatures could **protect women in the work place**. There is honest concern among women labor leaders today. If true legal equality for women arrives, such as an Equal Rights Amendment, what will happen to the existing legislation that protects women in hazardous jobs? Would it remain legal to have legislation that applies to just women?

The attack on alcohol was not the only attempt to protect the nation's morals. The Mann Act made it illegal to transport a female across a state line for immoral purposes; it tried to limit prostitution, the "**social evil**," a major concern to many Progressives. Prostitution threatened the middle class family because venereal diseases limited the ability to reproduce, and thus contributed to a larger problem, class suicide. This was the concept that the better classes were not reproducing enough children to maintain their class dominance and to preserve civilization's best attributes. The average number of children born to women surviving to menopause dropped steadily during the nineteenth century: 1800, 7.04; 1840, 6.14; 1880, 4.24; 1900, 3.56. The poor had too many children; the middle class needed to produce more, to save the country. Class suicide was also sometimes called "race suicide." In the 1900 popular mind, nationality and race were virtually interchangeable terms. In addition, the poor were mainly immigrants, and, therefore, not really considered to be in the same class, race, or nationality as most middle class Americans.

One woman, Margaret Sanger, a nurse, is forever identified with the issue of **birth control**, a term she coined in 1915. Her motive was to protect the health of mothers. Birth control information had become increasingly available in Europe by the 1880s, when a German gynecologist invented the diaphragm. Not here. The Comstock Law of 1873 defined contraceptive devices as obscene and prohibited sending information about them through the mail. The Supreme Court ruling in *United States v. One Package*, 1936, virtually ended this part of the Comstock Law. The "package" was an imported package of contraceptive devices. By the time Margaret Sanger died in 1966, the birth control pill had been invented and the Supreme Court had established a right to privacy, a legal right to use birth control, in *Griswold v. Connecticut*, 1965. In 1921 she established the Birth Control Federation of America, which later became Planned Parenthood. By the early 1940s there were over eight hundred birth control clinics in America.

Settlement houses, called "spearheads for reform" by a historian, gave college-educated women a mission and a purpose in life – to improve the lot of the urban poor, which often was really a desire to lift the poor up to middle class standards. The best known were Jane Addams, Hull House in Chicago, which was modeled on Toynbee Hall in London; Janie Porter Barrett, Locust Street Settlement House in Hampton, Virginia; and Lillian Wald, Henry Street Settlement House, New York City. While their numbers were small, 75% of all women who earned doctoral degrees in the Gilded Age remained single, an indication of self-sufficiency. Many professions were closed to women, including becoming a lawyer. The Illinois Supreme Court turned down Myra Bradwell, the first woman to seek admittance to the bar, in 1869. On appeal, the U.S. Supreme Court turned her down on technical grounds, but the Illinois state legislature allowed her to practice. The first woman admitted to practice before the U.S. Supreme Court was Belva Lockwood in 1879.

The Progressive Movement and the New Deal?

One popular question among historians is asking whether or not the New Deal was a continuation of the Progressive Movement. There is a thread of governmental institutions and programs – national, state, local – that runs from the Progressive movement to the governmental agencies created to fight the First World War and, contradictory to most textbooks, through the Twenties. One example is the efforts to enforce Prohibition and the new immigration laws, also a Progressive concern. This thread continues into the alphabet agencies of the New Deal and even into the domestic wartime agencies created to fight the Second World War. However, in *A Nation Among Nations*, historian Thomas Bender argues that while Progressivism did protect women, the home, and traditional family moral values, it led to some unforeseen consequences. Preoccupation with women, the home, and the family obscured the ability to see the need for protection and security for everyone, for all workers. It was the impact of the Great Depression that forced "a wider consideration of workers' rights, the value of state intervention in the workplace, and the importance of social (security) insurance." Note that Bender's comparison implies a *wider* "state intervention" during the New Deal, not a completely new and different departure. Historians argue over how consistent that "thread" of "state intervention" was. Be prepared to assess and to analyze this "thread of governmental intervention" in the Progressive Movement, the New Deal, and even in President Lyndon Johnson's Great Society of the 1960s.

35

AMERICAN FOREIGN POLICIES, 1890-1914

During the years from 1890 to 1914, the United States established many foreign policies that remained patterns for the twentieth century and beyond. The ultimate result would be the creation of **PAX AMERICANA**, an American peace, a role that would swell the country with pride and yet be an unending source of frustration.

When looking at foreign policy, anytime, now, in the past, or in the future, be aware that prior assumptions always color the way a person looks at foreign policy. There are three schools of historiography, the study of the writing of history, for diplomatic history. The following summaries will help you know the assumptions behind anything you read about American foreign policy.

Radical School of American Foreign Policy Historiography

The two best-known Radical School historians are William Appleman Williams, for his characterization of American foreign policy as "non-colonial imperialism," and Howard Zinn, for his textbook, *A People's History of the United States*. Radical diplomatic historians believe our industrial and economic elite control American foreign policy in order to gain access to economic markets and resources. In the process the public is manipulated, misled, lied to, or propagandized into believing that foreign policy objectives are matters of national concern, rather than primarily corporate or elite concern. The rallying cry of democratic ideals, national honor, and national security masks their real purpose. The masses fight; the elite gains. The victims of another nation's imperialism agreed with Max Weber's famous characterization of the nation-state as possessing "a monopoly on the legitimate use of violence in the enforcement of order," as that nation-state defined order. Following the Spanish-American War, in the Philippines the native population resisted our take-over, fighting for independence. The United States won, after our brutal tactics killed an estimated 13% of their population and the U.S. lost over 4,000 American soldiers. Among the reasons President McKinley cited for annexing the Philippines was "that we could not turn them over to France or Germany, our commercial rivals in the Orient – that would be bad business and discreditable." There were other reasons given by McKinley; however, Radical historians would move this economic justification to the top of their list to explain why the U.S. annexed the Philippines.

In the nineteenth century imperialism, the grabbing of colonies, enlarged national territories. European powers established great empires. By 1914 Britain had an empire 140 times its size; Belgium, 80 times its size, The Netherlands, 60 times; France, 20. It just so happened that most of the territory the United States grabbed in our Manifest Destiny push was contiguous rather than distant. As the twentieth century dawned, the United States continued to be imperialistic, now grabbing distant colonies. Between 1889 and 1904 the U.S. acquired the Philippines, Puerto Rico, and Guam from Spain, divided Samoa with Germany, and took the Canal Zone from Colombia, all while establishing an economic hegemony over the Caribbean and northern Latin America. The ABC powers – Argentina, Brazil, and Chile – limited our penetration into southern South America.

The United States later expanded this approach all over the world, aggressively seeking new markets and new sources of raw materials. In the process, to safeguard our economic interests, the nation became the opposite of what it had been at its birth in 1776. The country sold its birthright for economic gain via trade. Today the United States is the most anti-progressive and anti-revolutionary nation in the world. The Declaration of Independence has been put on a shelf. The Declaration of Independence sounds good, but the elite assert that the United States cannot profitably run its foreign policy by those principles.

Radical historians do not view our foreign policy as something separated from American domestic priorities. Foreign policies grow out of domestic policies and domestic needs, never the reverse. Radical historians feel that our aggressive foreign policy is used to distract attention away from the nation adopting a better approach to our domestic needs. What they prefer is domestic policies that seek solutions to the plight of the poor and disadvantaged classes. If Congress would redistribute income within the United States through domestic policies, such as higher income taxes and programs to raise the income of the poor, the domestic economy could absorb the goods now produced for foreign markets and make the American imperialistic search for overseas markets unnecessary.

Radical historians encounter difficulties proving their case. There is an old statement among historians, "No documents, no proof, no history." Radical historians rarely find specific documents that prove their thesis. However, they really do not need them. They approach the study of history with a sense that the upper classes and business elite set the overall tone and orientation in American society and American foreign policy through their domination of corporations, churches, governments, universities, foundations, and so on.

They are somewhat influenced by Vladimir Lenin's adaptation of Karl Marx's thinking, the argument that a nation's imperialist thrust is the last attempt by the capitalist classes to protect themselves by diverting attention away from domestic inequities. In short, foreign policy is a flag-waving sideshow while domestic economic oppression continues.

Realist School of American Foreign Policy Historiography

The Realist School of historiography emerged as a criticism of what it saw as wide swings in American twentieth century foreign policy. America sought to "make the world safe for democracy" in the First World War and ended up making it safe, as Winston Churchill later said, for dictatorship. When the world did not follow America's leadership, the United States withdrew into a cocoon and failed to prevent the beginning of the Second World War. These wide swings in policy are not in our best interest. America regards itself as a special nation, not bound by the same rules and consequences as everyone else. Americans see themselves as "special," known also as "American Exceptionalism."

In the nineteenth century the United States avoided involvement in major European wars only because none happened. From 1815 to 1914 there were only several short wars. Americans mistakenly came to believe the United States avoided involvement because we willed it. Believing that peace is the normal and natural condition of humankind, Americans go off on crusades periodically to cleanse the world of evil and withdraw from involvement when things do not go our way.

Realists want a foreign policy determined by experts, not by mislead, misinformed public opinion. The nation needs to keep long-range goals and national interests in mind and pursue consistent policies that are in America's best interests and stop branding other countries as evil. Evil exists in the world; it is not the job of the United States to fix every problem by applying moral principles. Too often Americans pursue total victory, which creates a worse mess. Americans tend to see war as similar to a sports event. Who is number one? American foreign policy leaders need to recognize when the enemy's tenacity and commitment are stronger than our own. In December, 1966, in the middle of the Vietnam War, the *New York Times* correspondent Harrison Salisbury interviewed Pham Van Dong, the North Vietnamese Prime Minister. "How long do you Americans want to fight? . . . One year? Two years? Five years? Ten years? Twenty years? We will be glad to accommodate you." They were and they did. At the end of the Second World War, the United States pressed total surrender upon the evil Japanese Empire, thereby creating a power vacuum in East Asia. Ever since 1945 the United States has been the policeman of East Asia, while Japan rebuilt its economy. The United States would have been better off with a chastised Japan than a defeated Japan – no Korean War, no Vietnam War, no costly attention to Communist China. Japan would have been the first line of defense against communism in that part of the world. The danger in the Middle East today is that American policies might create another power vacuum. In every Middle Eastern country, including Israel, hard liners and extremists are growing. Extremists love the opportunities that come from power vacuums.

In *Politics Among Nations: The Struggle for Power and Peace*, Hans J. Morgenthau succinctly summarized the different approaches. "The moralist asks: 'Is this policy in accord with moral principles?' And the political realist asks: 'How does this policy affect the power of the nation?'"

Nationalist School of American Foreign Policy Historiography (the one in almost every school textbook)

Return to an earlier statement, foreign policy is an offshoot of domestic policy. Nationalists say that American foreign policy combines a realistic concept of self-interest with a generous support of other nations' goals of democracy, self-determination, and economic prosperity. Our commitment to high ideals underlies a foreign policy record that should be a source of great pride. Our Declaration of Independence, which begins "When in the course of *human* events," and our Constitution, have inspired people all around the world, and they should, because these documents epitomize the aspirations of humanity, not just Americans. People all over the world want to be just like Americans or want to live here. American foreign policy is a record of unselfish idealism unequaled in the history of the world, according to the Nationalist School. When Woodrow Wilson was touring the country promoting his Versailles Treaty with the League of Nations, he told an audience in South Dakota, "Sometimes people call me an idealist. Well, that is the way I know I am an American. America is the only idealistic nation in the world." To Wilson that was part of our **American Identity**, our American Exceptionalism.

The United States has made some mistakes in the past, such as joining in the imperialism of the late nineteenth century, but we corrected those mistakes. Yes, the U.S. was an imperialist power, but we were a *good* imperialist power, prepared from the beginning to eventually end our control. Diplomatic historian Samuel Flagg Bemis called Americans "benevolent imperialists." For example, the United States built many roads, bridges, schools, etc., to improve the Philippines. The delegate from the Philippines, addressing the United Nations on October 5, 1960, summed up our approach. "The Americans are no saints, but this you can say of them; as "imperialists" they proved to be more inept than their rivals in the game; they allowed us too many liberties; and now that we are independent, (since 1946) they know better than to disregard our opinions or to ignore our rights. Here is one little interesting detail: You can discuss, argue and talk back to the Americans, as we have discussed, argued, and talked back to them during all the years of our subjection, and since then – without being slapped down or getting shot at dawn."

Two other examples are the Marshall Plan after the Second World War, which helped to rebuild Western Europe, and an editorial that appeared in the *Manchester Guardian*, a leftist British newspaper usually critical of the United States, on our bicentennial on July 4, 1976. "We have often been critical of the United States, but the truth of the matter is that what the world needs is more countries like the United States rather than fewer."

As you read comments about U.S. foreign policy – try to figure out what assumptions the writer has – radical, realist, or nationalist, or a weird combination.

Why the Interest in Foreign Affairs Around 1890?
The Economic Reasons

By 1900 the United States was the world's greatest industrial power, interested in markets and raw materials for industrial growth, just as it is vitally interested in oil today. A British prime minister, Lloyd George, once said that "one trades even with cannibals." All trade is good; it makes money for the country. Senator Albert Beveridge of Indiana bragged in 1898 that "American factories are making more than the American people can use: American soil is producing more than they can consume. Fate has written our policy for us, the trade of the world must and shall be ours."

For any business enterprise, the easiest way to expand production is to increase the company's foreign trade. A large corporation often has a static share of the domestic market. For a modern example, even a strong, costly advertising campaign to lure Coca Cola or Pepsi drinkers into switching brands often has negligible results. The easier growth area is the foreign markets. In addition, manufacturers feared that our industrial productive capacity exceeded what our domestic market could absorb. Our total exports between 1865 and 1898 jumped from $281 million to $1.2 billion; our imports from $239 million to $616 million. The 1870s began a hundred year period during which our exports exceeded our imports every year except for three. In spite of this jump, at no time did our exports constitute more than 7.2% of our Gross Domestic Product, our GDP, the total value of all the goods and services produced in one year. By 1900 the U.S. exported 15% of our iron and steel products; 25% of our sewing machines; 57% of our illuminating oil; 70-80 % of our cotton crop; and 25% of our wheat. The United States was only 5% of the world's population, but the U.S. provided 32% of the entire world's food supply, exporting much of our surplus agricultural production.

Some historians would later call this expansion of American trade the "Open Door" policy, borrowing the term used to describe the approach by the United States that no nation should have any special advantage in any particular market, such as "spheres of influence" in China. Our assumption was, of course, that since the United States and U.S. products were superior, an open and fair field would find the Americans the winner.

National Pride, American Greatness

The decade of the 1890s witnessed new public expressions of national pride. In 1892 Francis Bellamy wrote the *Pledge of Allegiance*, which quickly caught on among the public, especially in schools. The next year *"America the Beautiful"* was written and first sung. During these years observances of Flag Day slowly spread annually on June 14 and everyone began standing for *The Star-Spangled Banner* for public gatherings. Up until this period the United States was isolated to a great extent, although isolation was a policy more than a reality, and not much of a policy. Capt. Alfred Thayer Mahan, in *The Influence of Sea Power Upon History*, advocated the idea that greatness came from naval power and control of the seas to control the paths of trade and raw materials flowing to the industrial nations. Mahan's ideas clicked with people like Theodore Roosevelt and Senator Henry Cabot Lodge of Massachusetts. But, they felt that while economic interests were important in asserting a larger role for the United States, the prime factor was "national honor." This sense of emerging national greatness for the United States was illustrated by one of Theodore Roosevelt's friends, Brooks Adams, who was the grandson of John Quincy Adams. "We shall, likely enough, be greater later, but it is the dawn which is always golden. The first taste of power is always the greatest." (quoted in *Inevitable Revolutions: The United States in Central America*, by Walter LaFeber.) It was as if the Darwinian emphasis on struggle and competition was an end in itself. In a speech in 1897 Theodore Roosevelt used the word "war" 62 times, "no triumph of peace is quite so great as the supreme triumphs of war."

Racism

Racism found a comfortable home in Darwinian thinking. A British author, Rudyard Kipling, wrote a poem, *"The White Man's Burden,"* to urge Americans to join the task of civilizing the lower races. Duty calls! Read it on the Internet. Earlier he dashed off a poem after a rare victory in 1896 by African warriors in the Sudan against Italian troops. That poem included the line, "ere's to you, Fuzzy-Wuzzy." In this period of history "imperialism" had no bad connotations; it was a positive word to those practicing it. Americans enjoy Tarzan movies, interesting shots of cute animals and lightly clad men and women. However, go back and read the original 1914 *Tarzan of the Apes*, or any of the 22 sequels, as many people did. While Tarzan has some harsh words for civilized society, he had much more condemnation for the stupidity of the "savage and cruel" African natives.

"Christian Racism" was an important component of racism. Rev. Josiah Strong wrote in *Our Country*, 1885, sales of which topped 175,000, that the United States was divinely commissioned to spread political liberty, Protestant Christianity, commerce, and civilized values all over the earth. Note his assumptions – "God, with infinite wisdom and skill is training the Anglo-Saxon race for the final competition of races." "This powerful race will move down upon Mexico, down upon Central and South America, out upon the islands of the sea, over upon Africa and beyond." In a cruder version, Senator Albert Beveridge said in 1899 that God had prepared English-speaking Anglo-Saxons to become "the master organizers of the world to establish and administer governments among savages and senile peoples." His reference to the English-speaking peoples was shared. The U.S. Commissioner of Indian Affairs, J. D. C. Atkins, stated in 1886 that all school instruction for Indians must be in English because it was "the language of the greatest, most powerful, and most enterprising nationalities beneath the sun." The British imperialist, Cecil Rhodes, said, "I contend that we are the finest race in the world and that the more of the world we inhabit the better it is." Both Theodore Roosevelt and Woodrow Wilson agreed. From his viewpoint Roosevelt put the people of Asia, Latin America, and Africa in "the childhood state of race development." Wilson put them "in the childhood of their political growth." Foreign missionaries were a significant source for educating the public in this period. The number of Protestant missionaries in China rose from 436 in 1874 to 5,462 in 1914. They claimed 100,000 converts by 1900.

Citizenship Rights

These attitudes found their fullest racial expression in several court cases, the *Insular Cases*, among which were *Downes v. Bidwell*, 1900, and *De Lima v. Bidwell*, 1901. In these cases the Supreme Court held that while certain **fundamental rights** were common to all people and therefore rights that colonial subjects were entitled to, other rights were **formal rights**, rights that could be extended to colonial people only by an act of Congress, such as the historic Anglo-Saxon rights: trial by jury, right to elect legislative representatives, and no taxation without representation. Secretary of War Elihu Root explained the court's thinking, "As near as I can make out the Constitution follows the flag – but doesn't quite catch up with it." In essence, a second rank of citizenship existed; colonials were not citizens until Congress specifically conferred citizenship upon them. Prior to this era, the residents in all the territories acquired by the United States automatically became U.S. citizens, except for Indians. All Indians finally became citizens in 1924. They apparently had lived here long enough to qualify. It should be noted, however, that some tribes and individuals had been granted citizenship before this.

It is interesting that the same Supreme Court judge, Justice Henry B. Brown, wrote the *Downes* opinion and the *Plessy* "separate but equal" opinion. The rationale and the wording are similar. The ultimate racist insult in this era came when Japan asked for the inclusion of a simple statement in the Versailles Peace Treaty that ended the First World War, "The races of mankind are equal." President Woodrow Wilson said, NO! In many respects this attitude continued into the Second World War. During the war Americans demonized Hitler more than they demonized the German people; however, in the Pacific theater they demonized the Japanese people more than their leaders. Our racist examples promoted similar policies elsewhere – Australia's "white Australia policy" and South Africa's 1911 adoption of segregation, which evolved into apartheid.

A growing insensitivity toward the nationalism of other peoples and a sense of racism accompanied our expansion and economic growth. Remember the development of segregation in the South at this time; the two parallel developments were not isolated events. Foreign policies grow out of domestic needs and perceptions, out of domestic policies, not the reverse. This is why specific foreign policy matters are rarely important enough to be even a major factor in a national election.

The "Psychic Crisis" of the 1890s
Changes in our foreign policies seemed to fit right in with all the other crazy changes going on. The decade of the 1890s had one crisis after another – economic depression, strikes such as the Pullman and Homestead strikes, the Populist Party revolt, increased racist fears and Jim Crow laws in the South, and Coxey's march on Washington. Just add overseas adventures to this list.

Our Isolation Up to the 1890s
There were good reasons for American isolation up to this point. Distance physically isolated the U.S. The record by ship from New York City to London was seven and a half days, from New York City to Hong Kong, 120 days. Think how much communications and missiles have shrunk the modern world. Americans were proud of their isolation. It was easier to advance American interests if the United States stayed away from the contamination of European nations, as stated in the Monroe Doctrine. In addition, isolation shielded America from decadent European institutions and customs. The size of the American armed forces reflected this sense of security and safe distance. In 1895 the U.S. Army had 25,000 men, 15% of whom deserted each year. It was smaller than that of Bulgaria, and the navy ranked tenth in the world. And, this was after the United States started to modernize the navy in 1883 with the construction of our "ABC" cruisers, the *Atlanta, Boston,* and *Chicago*. By 1900 the U.S. navy ranked sixth. The United States may have thought of itself as isolated, but it has never been completely isolated.

Our Relationships With Other World Powers

During these years the United States established two fundamental foreign policies toward Europe that defined the U.S. role throughout the twentieth century and into the twentieth-first.

First, friendship with **Great Britain** would be the cornerstone of our foreign policies. The great German statesman in the late nineteenth century, Otto von Bismarck, stated that one of the most significant factors that would influence the twentieth century would be the fact that the Americans and the English spoke the same language. He was right. **Second**, it was the critical role of the United States as a neutral power to prevent a general war in Europe.

Russia – American and **Russian** interests started to collide in this period, challenging the myth of a "natural friendship" between the two nations, as imagined by naïve Americans. This misconception had grown from Russia's abandonment of her Oregon territory claims and from Russian naval fleet visits during the Civil War to Northern ports, which was seen as a show of support for the Union. Actually, the real reason for the latter was that Russia expected a European war to break out and did not want their fleet trapped by ice. Third, the sale of Alaska was regarded as a favor to the United States. This picture changed when Russia became an Asian power in the late nineteenth century by building the Trans-Siberian Railroad, which led to a clash with another emerging Asian power, Japan. During the Russo-Japanese War, 1904-1905, the United States at one point threatened to enter the war to force both sides to the bargaining table for peace negotiations. The United States wanted neither Russia nor Japan to dominate Manchuria. Theodore Roosevelt did get the Nobel Peace Prize and the United States did get the prestige of playing the role of peacemaker. However, the U.S. earned the disdain of Russia and Russians. Russian officials complained publicly about the United States supporting non-Christian "monkeys." Japan was also not pleased at being stopped short of victory by being forced to the peace table. The Japanese people, and many other Asians, believed Japan had won, the first non-white nation to beat the Europeans.

Germany – Our relations with **Germany** steadily worsened over several issues. There was friction over the Pacific island of Samoa in 1872 when a U.S. naval officer negotiated a treaty to give the United States Pago Pago, an excellent harbor there. In this time period coal-fueled ships needed coal stations to refuel. Germany had designs on Samoa and for a while it looked as if a war would break out. When Admiral George Dewey attacked the Spanish at Manila Bay during the Spanish-American War, a German fleet was nearby. To do what? It was seen as a threat, as was the heavy German immigration into Latin America. In addition, from the American viewpoint, German ships were too energetic in collecting debts owed by Venezuela, violating the spirit of the Monroe Doctrine. The United States was beginning to see the Caribbean Sea as the sole possession of the United States. American interests and goals far outweighed those of other nations.

Great Britain – Our relationship with **Great Britain** improved. There were occasional misunderstandings, but overall this was a period of improving relations. Potential for conflict existed. Great Britain controlled as much of North America as the United States did, Canada, had possessions in Central America, and dominated trade with Latin America. Rhodes Scholarships began at this time, funded by the British imperialist, Cecil Rhodes. They still provide annual scholarships for approximately thirty Americans to study at Oxford University in England for two to three years, a prestigious award. The Rhodes Scholarships create life-long links between American and British intellectuals and politicians. Great Britain felt isolated in a Europe dominated by alliances, the Triple Alliance of Germany, Austria-Hungary, and Italy, and the Franco-Russian Alliance. At one point, in 1902, Great Britain signed an alliance with Japan. England benefited from the support of many Anglophiles in this era on this side of the Atlantic. Woodrow Wilson had written his doctoral thesis on the advantages of the British parliamentary system. In the American system the president is not connected to Congress and has to depend on party leaders in the House and Senate to pass legislation. And sometimes his party does not have a majority in one or both houses. The British prime minister is the leader of the majority party in Parliament, making it easier to achieve his or her goals. Influential Americans also held favorable images of Great Britain because of their social connections. Many wealthy Americans, such as Andrew Carnegie, lived part of the year in Scotland and England. In addition, many daughters of wealthy American industrialists married British nobles with impressive titles, long pedigrees, and empty wallets.

A major turning point in British-U.S. relations grew out of a boundary dispute between Venezuela and British Guiana in 1895. Gold had been discovered in the disputed area and Britain had ambitions to secure the territory up to the mouth of the Orinoco River. At President Cleveland's request, Secretary of State Richard Olney sent a strong note, stronger than Cleveland intended, to Great Britain stating that the United States was "practically sovereign on this continent," demanding international arbitration to settle the issue. Congress also unanimously passed a resolution calling on Great Britain to submit the dispute to arbitration. After ignoring the United States for months, a second belligerent note forced Great Britain to respond. Britain realized the United States was deadly serious about this, because the U.S. began to mobilize the American navy. Joseph Chamberlain, the British Colonial Secretary, stated in a speech in January, 1896, that war between the United States and Great Britain "would be an absurdity as well as a crime." He hoped that the United States and Great Britain would act together "in defense of a common cause sanctioned by humanity and justice."

Great Britain, feeling isolated, was more concerned about events in Africa, Asia, and Europe. The other European powers had reacted harshly to Britain's activities in the Boer War in Southern Africa. It shocked the British, leading them to conclude that they should abandon their tradition of "splendid isolation" and seek cooperation with other nations, such as the United States, Japan, France, and Russia. For the whole twentieth century Great Britain supported our Pax Americana, which in reality trumpeted Anglo-Saxon peace and principles.

France – Our relations with **France** greatly improved and became very cordial, especially after the gift of the Statue of Liberty in 1886 (which was originally called Liberty Enlightening the World). A French educator came up with the idea as a response to Lincoln's tragic assassination in 1865. President Theodore Roosevelt and the French ambassador became such good friends that Teddy jokingly referred to Jean-Jules Jusserand as having "taken the Oath as Secretary of State." In 1917, during the First World War, Jusserand won the Pulitzer Prize in history for *With Americans Past and Present Days*, a collection of stories featuring French contributions to winning the War for Independence, the American Revolution. The best example of our cordial relationship was Col. Charles Stanton's comment on July 4, 1917, when American troops arrived in Paris joining the British and French in the First World War. Colonel Stanton was an aide to General John J. Pershing, the head of the American Expeditionary Forces, the first U.S. troops to enter the war. During a ceremony at Lafayette's tomb, Stanton said, "America has joined forces with the Allied Powers, and what we have of blood and treasure are yours. Therefore it is that with loving pride we drape the colors in tribute of respect to this citizen of your great republic. And here and now, in the presence of the illustrious dead, we pledge our hearts and our honor in carrying this war to a successful issue. Lafayette, we are here." Many Americans felt a sincere affection for France for her aid during the American Revolution.

Major Areas of American Interest and Activity – Caribbean Sea

The Caribbean Sea became an American lake. During the Venezuelan boundary affair in 1895, the U.S. transformed the Monroe Doctrine into a new entity, into a sacred principle for all time, "this is our hemisphere!" Previously the United States had actually depended on British support and acquiescence for enforcement of the precepts of the Monroe Doctrine. This time it was asserted against Great Britain. The U.S. brought it up again during a second Venezuelan affair in 1902 over debts owed to British and German investors. Later President Theodore Roosevelt added a corollary to the Monroe Doctrine, the Roosevelt Corollary, which switched the Monroe Doctrine from a negative policy – Europe, this is what you *cannot do* in our hemisphere – into a positive policy, this is what the United States *will do* in our hemisphere. President Theodore Roosevelt announced his Roosevelt Corollary on Dec. 6, 1904. Because of "chronic wrongdoing" by Caribbean nations, "the United States was to take on a role as an international police power" in order to prevent another nation from doing it.

This new policy opposed the Drago Doctrine, issued by Luis M. Drago, the Argentine foreign minister in 1903, during the Venezuelan finances dispute. The Drago Doctrine declared that armed intervention in, or territorial occupation of, a Latin

American nation should not result from matters related to the public finances of that nation. Our Latin American neighbors were not pleased at American actions, to put it mildly. That did not stop American intervention. Twenty times between 1898 and 1920 American troops landed in various Caribbean countries without an invitation. U.S. troops occupied Santo Domingo, now the Dominican Republic, from 1905 to 1941, collecting their tariffs, giving 45% to the Dominican government, and using 55% to pay off their national debt. Our troops were stationed there from 1916 to 1924. Responding to charges that he intended to seize territory, Theodore Roosevelt replied colorfully, "The United States had no more desire for Dominican territory than a gorged boa constrictor would for swallowing a porcupine wrong-end-to." The U.S. also sent troops to Haiti, 1915-1934, and supervised their finances, 1916-1941; to Nicaragua for financial supervision, 1911-1924, and three times, 1909-1910, 1912-1925, and 1926-1933, the U.S. sent troops. The Platt Amendment to the Cuban Constitution gave the United States the right to intervene in Cuban affairs, which happened, sending troops in 1906-1909, 1912, and 1917-1922. The U.S. did this in spite of our own prewar Teller Amendment, which had stated in 1898 that the United States had no designs on Cuba.

As a result of the Spanish-American War, 1898, the U.S. gained new acquisitions and new responsibilities. Guantanamo Bay became an American naval base, which encompassed 47 square miles in Cuba. The United States intervened in Cuba in 1904-1906; took the Panama Canal Zone from Colombia in 1903, and bought the Virgin Islands in 1917 from Denmark. After declaring ourselves the financial overseer in the Caribbean, the U.S. intervened in Guatemala from 1904-1906, and also intervened in the Mexican Revolution from 1914 to 1917, and, so on, and so on, and so on.

President Taft's administration, 1908-1912, supported "dollar diplomacy" in the Caribbean, the idea that U.S. soldiers would defend American investors and investments in the Caribbean against interference by local governments. The idea that a government possessed the right to intervene in a foreign country to protect its citizens OR corporations had been inherited from Roman law. It was reasserted by Lord Palmerston for the British government in his famous "Don Pacifico" speech to the House of Commons in 1850. Other nations quickly jumped on the bandwagon. The next president, Woodrow Wilson, continued Taft's policy. Latin Americans considered "dollar diplomacy" to be U.S. sanctioned imperialistic robbery of their resources.

Major Areas of American Interest and Activity – Panama
The United States signed the Clayton-Bulwer Treaty with Great Britain in 1850. California gold rush fever excited talk of the United States taking Panama and building a canal. The treaty stipulated that any canal across Panama would be under joint Anglo-American control. Each country feared the other's gaining access to a canal that was toll free for only one country, a great trade advantage. The Suez Canal

opened in Egypt in 1869 and spurred interest in a Panama Canal. A French company organized by Ferdinard de Lesseps, a French diplomat who had been the guiding promotor behind the construction of the Suez Canal, began work in Panama in 1881-1887. After getting only one-third of the way, the company went bankrupt. Meanwhile, American interest leaned more towards Nicaragua, (where a canal is currently being dug) because the French company demanded payment for what it had done so far. In the 1890s interest grew again because of the tale of the *U.S.S. Oregon*, which rushed from Oregon to Cuba to join the Spanish-American War. It arrived after 68 days, after the war ended, and had traveled 14,000 miles, three times the distance if a canal existed. First, the U.S. negotiated the Hay-Pauncefote Treaty with Britain in 1901, which replaced the Clayton-Bulwer Treaty. It granted the United States the right to build, control, and fortify a canal, if all nations paid the same tolls. The U.S. next negotiated the Hay-Herran Treaty in 1903 with Colombia, the country that owned Panama. It provided for a six-mile wide strip, a $10,000,000 payment and a $250,000 yearly rent. The Colombian Senate unanimously rejected the proposed treaty. Colombian politicians were angry because the bankrupt French Company was to get $40 million for the rights to what they had dug so far.

On November 3, 1903, a revolution broke out in Panama, shortly after the *U.S.S. Nashville* arrived. Three other American cruisers were in the area. The United States quickly recognized the new country of Panama and on November 18 signed the Hay-Bunau-Varilla Treaty between the United States and Panama. One small incongruity was that Philippe Bunau-Varilla was an official of the French canal company who had declared himself the new foreign minister of Panama. He had never even lived in Panama! He was in Washington during the revolution. When the new Panamanian government protested that no Panamanian had signed the treaty, the United States threatened to withdraw our protection from Colombian troops. The only change from the earlier failed treaty with Colombia was the expansion of the zone to ten miles. It was ratified 66-14 by the U.S. Senate. The "Colossus of the North," our nickname throughout Latin America, "made the dirt fly," as Theodore Roosevelt proclaimed. When Theodore Roosevelt explained what he had done and asked the cabinet if he had satisfactorily defended himself, Secretary of War Elihu Root, replied, "You certainly have. You have shown that you were accused of seduction and you have conclusively proved that you were guilty of rape." John Stevens, the chief engineer up to 1907, solved the great engineering problems, including the building of a lock canal rather than a sea level canal. The sea levels on the two sides differ due to currents and tides. A sea level canal would have had a current, not a good idea for a canal. Then George Washington Goethals took over to finish the engineering challenge. William Gorgas, who had cleaned up Havana, finally turned the Canal Zone into a healthy place to live, controlling the mosquito population to end malaria and yellow fever. Earlier the French effort had led to 20,000 deaths; the American effort cost only 5,000. By 1914 the Panama Canal Zone death rate was 6/1000; it was 14.1/1000 in the United States. In 1922 the United States paid $25 million to Colombia, conscience money or "canalimony," said some.

In 1979 the United States completed negotiations begun under President Ford to return the Canal Zone on Dec 31, 1999. This Panama Canal Treaty revoked the Hay-Bunau-Varilla Treaty, which would have expired on Dec. 31, 1999. The Treaty Concerning the Permanent Neutrality and Operation of the Panama Canal guaranteed neutrality, non-discrimination in tolls, and preferential treatment for U.S. naval vessels in emergencies. A 68-32 Senate vote ratified both treaties. The negative votes really did not need to be concerned. American officials were blunt. When asked by reporters what the American response would be if Panama shut down the canal, officials replied, "We will move in and close down the Panamanian government . . . ."

Major Areas of American Interest and Activity – East Asia

In East Asia the United States increasingly expanded her territory and role, seemingly becoming the protector of China and China's interests. However, by so doing, the U.S. antagonized Japan, which was looking to expand its territory and markets in East Asia. The main attraction was the China market, or what one historian called "the myth of the China market." One major reason justifying taking the Philippines was that they would be "a stepping-stone to China." Riches would flow if only the U.S. could gain exclusive trade rights in the Pacific. It was not true then and it is not true now. American trade with Latin America far exceeded our China trade. Cuba alone imported goods worth $165 million in 1916, a year when China imported just $32 million worth of goods. Subtract out oil imports and look at our current international trade patterns. Most of our trade still goes where it went then, to Canada, Mexico, and Europe. In 1875 it was 86%, by 1900, 81.4%, with 44% to just Great Britain and France. Just 12.5% in 1875 went to Asia; by 1900 it rose to 14.3%, with only 3% going to Japan and China.

The great powers at the end of the nineteenth century feared China would go the way of Africa, recently partitioned by the European powers at the Berlin Congress of 1884-1885. This fear intensified after the Sino-Japanese War of 1895 between Japan and China revealed how weak and defenseless China was. China's major weakness was its inability to see the threat posed by modern war technology. As a superior civilization, China saw nothing in Western technology or culture worth adopting. Chinese leaders succinctly expressed their nineteenth century attitude toward Westerners, "an inferior race, the Hairy Ones, without manners or music, unversed in the Six Fine Arts and the Five Classics." In 1898 and 1899 Great Britain, Russia, Germany, Japan, and France obtained exclusive 99 year leases for different Chinese ports. The United States arrived on the scene too late.

Major Areas of American Interest and Activity – The Open Door Notes

China – Our response to the carving up of China was the Open Door policy. Secretary of State John Hay sent a circular letter, September, 1899, asking all the major powers to keep all Chinese ports open on equal terms, to levy equal taxes on imports, and to charge equal railroad rates within their spheres of influence. Hay boldly announced that the European powers all "guaranteed" the Open Door. None had! However, no country wanted to publicly admit a desire to discriminate against the Chinese or to dismember China. This popularized an image among the American public of the United States as China's protector and special friend, which continued until the communists took over the Chinese government in 1949. The United States established itself as the major obstacle to Japan's interests and expansionist designs. In short, it made us Japan's enemy, as the Second World War showed. Now an admiral, Alfred Thayer Mahan had closely advised Hay on his Open Door Notes.

In 1900 some Chinese staged the Boxer Rebellion, killing 242 missionaries and foreigners. Chinese mobs attacked diplomatic compounds in Peking (now Beijing), which were rescued by an international joint military expedition of 19,000 troops, including 3,000 Americans. China was forced to pay an indemnity of $333 million, the U.S. share being $25 million. In 1907 the U.S. returned $11 million, in 1924, $6 million, both of which funded scholarships to educate Chinese students in the United States. (Ironically, the Chinese scientist who guided the creation of China's first atomic bomb had been the recipient of one of these scholarships.) Hay, fearful of a war of partition, sent a second note, July, 1900, urging all the major powers to preserve China's territorial integrity. He again boldly announced that all had agreed.

Japan – Our relations with **Japan** steadily worsened. After being forcibly opened in 1854 by America's Commodore Matthew Perry, Japan's reformers realized they needed to westernize. In 1867 they overthrew the old government and in 1868 began the Meiji Restoration, aimed at establishing Japan as a technologically powerful, modern country free from Western domination, Wakon, Yūsei, "Japanese spirit, Western technique." They succeeded. Japan's power grew, as shown by its victory in the Sino-Japanese War in 1895 against China and the stalemated draw in the Russo-Japanese War, 1904-05. Theodore Roosevelt won the Nobel Prize for his role in forcing an end to the war with the Treaty of Portsmouth, New Hampshire, but no Japanese person would have voted for him. Many in Japan felt they would have won the war and the peace without American interference.

During this era, there was a "yellow peril" concern in California and throughout the West, a fear that Orientals were taking over the West coast states. Immigrants from Japan increased from 25,000 in the 1890s to 125,000 between 1901 and 1908. On October 11, 1906, after a major earthquake in San Francisco, the San Francisco School Board, in the spirit of racism, opened a single Oriental Public School, throwing all Chinese, Japanese, and Korean children together. Japan officially objected both to the segregation and to being grouped with other Asians. Many Asian nationalities discriminated against other Asians, and still do. Western nations were not the only people practicing racism. President Theodore Roosevelt brought the San Francisco School Board all the way to the White House for lunch, but could not get them to change their policy.

The president's policies toward Japan were a curious mixture of soothing Japanese anger, satisfying Japanese ambition, saving the Philippines from Japanese aggression, and showing the Japanese he was not afraid of them. Under the Gentleman's Agreement, 1907, Japan restricted emigration to the United States to only "gentlemen." Japan had an official policy at this time of encouraging emigration. Japan was too crowded. Now Japanese emigrants went in large numbers to Brazil, Argentina, and Peru. Theodore Roosevelt sent the Great White Fleet to visit Japan in 1908. The Japanese were not impressed at our naval power. Be careful about "teaching lessons" in your foreign policy. The lesson learned may not be the one you think you are teaching. Under the Root-Takahira Agreement, 1908, each country, the United States and Japan, agreed to respect the other's possessions in the Far East, chiefly aimed at the Philippines and Korea, which Japan officially annexed in 1910.

A New Departure for U.S. Foreign Policy?

To many Americans the acquisition of an American Empire seemed contrary to what the nation had stood for since 1776. The Anti-Imperialist League led the 1899 fight against the ratification of the Treaty of Paris, which ended the Spanish-American War. Opponents of the treaty included such prominent figures as Mark Twain, Samuel Gompers, Andrew Carnegie, Jane Addams, William Jennings Bryan, William Graham Sumner, and two former presidents, Grover Cleveland and Benjamin Harrison. The treaty passed 57-27, just one vote more than the two-thirds needed. Was imperialism something new in U.S. History? Does the ratification of the 1899 Treaty of Paris mark a new departure in American foreign policy?

Many historians have argued that the United States had always been an imperialist nation; but our "empire" up to this point had been areas contiguous to the United States. Americans marched across the North American continent, subduing native peoples and wrestling territory from Mexico, Spain, France, Great Britain, and Russia. The U.S. acquired Alaska in 1867, and then moved into the Pacific Ocean, grabbing the Samoan Islands and then Hawaii during the Spanish-American War. President William McKinley said, "We need Hawaii just as much and good deal more than we did California, it is manifest destiny." In 1875 Hawaiians had signed a treaty with the United States forbidding them from giving any of their territory to another foreign power. An 1893 coup led by local Americans established a republic, which lasted until annexation in 1898. In essence, the American-owned Dole Pineapple Company ran Hawaii after the coup. Only 2,800 were qualified to vote in the new Hawaiian Republic and very few were natives. Earlier, in the 1840s, the U.S. warned other nations not to try to annex the

Hawaiian Islands. In 1881 Secretary of State James G. Blaine had declared that Hawaii and Cuba were within the "American system." Even President Cleveland, who opposed annexation, had declared Hawaii off limits to Great Britain, Japan, and Russia.

The United States had been interested in Puerto Rico for a long time. As early as 1891, Secretary of State James G. Blaine had included Puerto Rico on a list of "places of sufficient value to be taken." The United States acquired Puerto Rico in the treaty that ended the Spanish-American War. Later the Foraker Act designated Puerto Rico as an unincorporated territory, an "insular territory," a new legal status. Congress granted the natives citizenship in 1917, but used property requirements and literacy tests to limit voting to only 30% of the potential voters. Puerto Ricans had more democratic rights under Spanish rule than they did after American "liberation." Today many Puerto Ricans refer to themselves as the world's oldest colony, a Spanish colony after 1492 and then an American colony since 1898. Puerto Rico's status as a colony now stretches over five centuries.

American success fed a feeling of American uniqueness, what has come to be called "American Exceptionalism," that special something that makes the United States not only more powerful than, BUT also better than, all the other nations of the world. There is a degree of arrogance that goes with believing that the United States is better than other countries. Many students are familiar with this attitude in athletic contests. Its place in foreign policy is questionable. This sense of mission, our image of ourselves as a special nation, would be tested – severely after 1914 by the First World War and the Versailles Treaty and repeatedly throughout the twentieth century. It still is being tested in the twenty-first century.

The American "empire" would prove to be more than just territorial, as an astute English editor observed. In *The Americanization of the World; or, the Trend of the Twentieth Century*, written in 1902, William T. Snead saw America's influence abroad as increasingly economic, intellectual, and cultural, to the dismay of many people who lived in other countries. In many respects his observation was very accurate. The twentieth century was the "American Century," in very many ways.

36

THE FIRST WORLD WAR

Long Range Causes

Historians give many reasons for the long-range causes of the First World War. Imperialism is often the first one mentioned. There were rivalries between the great powers in Africa, in Asia, and even in the Pacific Islands, Samoa, for example. However, for all the major powers of Europe the greatest prize, for economic and strategic reasons, was the Turkish Ottoman Empire, the "sick man of Europe," so nicknamed in 1721 by an Austrian official. Politically weak, it seemed unable to put up much resistance to military or economic penetration and control by any foreign power.

Yet, it remains true that the outbreak of a European war is difficult to explain. Europeans enjoyed a robust economy in the prewar years, an annual growth rate of 5%. Passports did not yet exist; no governmental official questioned visitors. A person traveling from one country to another across Europe in 1914 would find similar class, religious, economic, political, and aristocratic societies and institutions everywhere. Many of the ruling monarchs were related. The king of England, the Russian czar's wife, and the German emperor were all cousins. Many financial and commercial establishments in the European economy were interlinked. For example, Lloyd's of London, the huge insurance company, insured most of Germany's merchant marine fleet on the eve of the First World War. Almost all the governments were limited monarchies, with varying degrees of democracy. All the countries were politically stable, with the single exception of France. It suffered through 43 governments and 26 prime ministers between 1890 and 1914.

However, tension filled the air in 1914. There were leftover ill feelings from the Franco-Prussian War, 1870-1871. Otto von Bismarck, prime minister of Prussia and then Germany, used that war to create a united Germany. Bismarck provoked a war with

France to force the Catholic south German states – Bavaria, Württ-Emberg, and Baden – who all looked to Catholic France for leadership and protection, to join the Protestant, Prussian-dominated German Confederation. German nationalism generated by the war allowed Bismarck to establish the new country of modern Germany, which was actually created in a ceremony held at the palace of Versailles in France. Germany seized two pieces of territory along France's eastern border, Alsace and Lorraine. After this humiliation, France sought revenge, and her territory returned. The Place de la Concorde is a street in Paris where every French city is represented by a statue. The statue for Strasbourg, in German-held Alsace, was continually veiled in black after 1871. France's national anthem had been written in Strasbourg, now located in a foreign country.

Triple Alliance to Central Powers

After the Franco-Prussian War, France's main foreign policy objective was revenge against Germany. France spent years searching for potential allies. Perhaps this was a factor in giving the United States the Statue of Liberty? Maybe! Bismarck, a master diplomat, isolated France after the Franco-Prussian War. He negotiated a treaty with Russia, already indebted to Bismarck for helping to put down a revolt in Russian-owned Poland in 1863, and established an understanding with Great Britain. Germany tacitly agreed, unofficially, not to build up her navy, which Great Britain would have seen as potentially threatening. Naval strength is crucial to an island nation. Also aiding Germany was the fact that in their long history France and Great Britain were rarely allies. Moreover, Bismarck linked Germany, Austria-Hungary, and Russia in the Three Emperors' League, an informal arrangement and understanding. In 1879 Bismarck enlisted Austria-Hungary in a Dual Alliance, which Austria thought protected her from Russia. The addition of Italy in 1882 augmented the alliance, making it the Triple Alliance. Earlier, in 1877, Bismarck signed a Reinsurance Treaty with Russia, supposedly protecting Russia against Austria-Hungary. Both Austria-Hungary and Russia wanted to believe Bismarck was on their side, and so each did. What Bismarck really wanted was to prevent any country from being available to form an alliance with France, and he succeeded.

This secure German position began to evaporate when Kaiser Wilhelm I died in 1888. His ill son, Frederick III, died just three months later. The new German emperor, young Wilhelm II, 1888-1918, Kaiser Wilhelm, resented the old prime minister, who seemed to think he was the emperor. Within a short time the new emperor dismissed Bismarck. Then Kaiser Wilhelm, who loved ships, proceeded to build up the navy, arousing fear in Great Britain. Feeling a need to protect their island, the British government adopted a policy of building two ships for every one Germany built, which was expensive, but deemed vital. In 1898 Great Britain funded the building of 11 new battleships, to be ready by 1905. Two years later the British laid plans to build 38 battle-ships over the next 38 years. The soaring costs incurred to increase the navy damaged the British public's image of Germans and of Germany, giving Germany an incredibly bad image in Great Britain.

The expansion of German influence into the Middle East also aroused British concern. Germany's newly built Berlin to Baghdad railroad, nicknamed "the Orient Express" (featured in many spy novels and movies because it passes through so many capitals), threatened what the British considered their "lifeline" to India, the Suez Canal. This railroad could potentially quickly carry German soldiers into the Middle East to seize the Suez Canal, isolating and weakening India, which the British considered to be their most important colony. The British navy would then have to sail around Africa to defend India against the Germans, a difficult task. At this time, and later under Adolf Hitler, the concept of *Mitteleuropa* attracted and intrigued Germans, the idea of a central and eastern Europe dominated by Germany, similar to the American concept of a west-ward moving Manifest Destiny.

The new German emperor also ignored Russia, letting the Reinsurance Treaty from 1877 lapse, and therefore giving France an opportunity to gain an ally. European diplo-mats had long believed that France and Russia could never be allies. They had little in common. Bismarck and other European diplomats were also convinced that the axiom was true that "the bear and the whale could never come together," meaning Russia and Great Britain. These axioms proved to be incorrect. Money won a friend. By 1914 French banks and French people held 40% of Russia's government bonds, 80% of the amount owned by foreigners.

Triple Entente to Allies

After a sustained effort, France enticed Russia into an alliance and resolved her differ-ences with Great Britain, drawing Great Britain into France's embrace. After this long diplomatic effort, stretching over several decades, France, Russia, and Great Britain fi-nally entered into the Triple Entente, or in the French definition of entente, a triple "un-derstanding," which was less binding than an alliance. Then France wooed Italy away from strongly supporting Germany's Triple Alliance, by promising to support Italy's acquisition of part of Austria-Hungry, at some point in the future. It is not difficult to give away another country's territory. When the First World War began Italy declared neutrality, and a year later joined France, Great Britain, and Russia against Germany and Austria-Hungary. After the fighting began, this group became known as the Allies. Germany and her allies became the Central Powers.

Austria-Hungary, Germany's chief partner, proved to be a weak ally. Austria-Hungry had become almost ungovernable due to ethnic differences. When the First

World War began the empire's army expanded. Here were the languages spoken by every 100 soldiers in the Austrian-Hungarian army:

German – 25   Ukrainian – 8
Magyar – 23 (Hungarian)   Romanian – 7
Czech – 13   Slovak – 5
Serbian-Croatian – 9   Slovene – 3
Polish – 8   Italian – 1

Imagine the difficulty involved for an officer in simply giving an order.

The Beginning of the First World War: Russia Versus Austria-Hungary

The alliance system poured the relationships between the nations of Europe into concrete, leaving little flexibility for diplomatic solutions for differences. Later the Cold War between Russia and the United States, lasting from 1945 to 1991, replicated this scenario due to the fear of nuclear weapons. All that was needed to set off a European war was an incident. The incident occurred on June 28, 1914. It was the assassination of Archduke Francis Ferdinand, the heir to the throne of Austria-Hungary and his wife, Sophie, by Gavrilo Princip, a young Serbian anarchist. Anarchists believed that government was the source of all evil; therefore, the way to improve the world was to kill government leaders. In the years preceding the First World War, anarchists killed the Spanish premier in 1897, the Empress of Austria-Hungary in 1898, the King of Italy in 1900, and President William McKinley in 1901. It is easy to understand why government officials saw both nationalism and anarchism as ideas that had to be snuffed out.

Intrigue marked the days between June 28 and July 28 following the assassination, when Austria-Hungary forced Serbia into an impossible position. The Austrians insisted that Serbia dismiss all government officials and army officers that Austria designated, and that Austrian officials participate in Serbia's investigation of a possible conspiracy that led up to the assassination. Unconditional acceptance was demanded within 48 hours. The Austrian ambassador who delivered the ultimatum was already packing to leave. He expected Serbia to reject it. Indeed, the ultimatum was designed to be so insulting that Serbia had to reject it. Serbia did accept almost all the provisions, except the major one requiring Austrian participation in the investigation inside Serbia.

Germany backed her ally, Austria-Hungary. Germany was concerned that the death of the heir to the throne foreshadowed the collapse of the Austro-Hungarian Empire, leaving Germany without a major ally. Germany and Austria-Hungary wanted a localized Austro-Serbian war, another war limited to only the Balkan peninsula. There had been a war in the Balkans from October 1912 to May 1913, and another one from June to August 1913. In the first Montenegro, Bulgaria, Serbia, and Greece defeated Turkey. Following a dispute over the spoils, Serbia, Greece, Rumania, and Turkey defeated Bulgaria. A great power like Austria-Hungary knew not to start a major war in early August. That is too late. A country began a major war in the spring, maximizing conquests before winter weather slowed down the army. Little Serbia had no chance against Austria-Hungary. Early in the First World War Serbia lost 1/6 of her population to war, famine, and epidemics.

Serbs are ethnically Slavic, as are Russians. Serbia, called "Russia's little Slav brother," expected Russian protection against Austria-Hungary. In an earlier incident, the Russians had failed to stop Austria-Hungary from annexing nearby Bosnia. In 1908 Russia and Austria-Hungary had issued a joint call for an international conference. The two powers secretly already agreed to give Bosnia to Austria-Hungary in return for Russia gaining control of the Turkish Straits, giving Russia an outlet into the Mediterranean Sea. The conference was never held. France and Great Britain were cool to the idea of Russia gaining the Turkish Straits. While Russia felt it received a humiliating setback, Austria-Hungary took Bosnia and laughed. Russia vowed not to back down the next time. Sometimes it is good to back down. It depends on the issue. Do not always stand up to every challenge; the cost might exceed any imagined benefit.

The crisis in 1914 was the next time. This time Russia mobilized her army, intending only to threaten Austria-Hungry. However, Russia had no plan to mobilize only half her army on one front, and so when the entire Russian army mobilized, it threatened Germany, which bordered Russia. Germany had a plan to win the expected European war, by acting quickly. Because Russia and France were allies, Germany needed a strategy to attack France and Russia at the same time, and therefore accomplish something no country had ever done up to that point – win a two-front war.

Schlieffen Plan

Germany's Schlieffen Plan intended to defeat France in just six weeks. The plan, worked out by General Alfred von Schlieffen, the army's Chief of Staff from 1891 to 1905, used 1/8 of Germany's army to hold off Russia until France was quickly defeated. Then the railroads, with 500 trains running daily, would carry the soldiers from France to the Eastern Front. If Russia, expected to be slow, was allowed to fully mobilize her army, Germany's plan became unworkable. Thus, to have any chance of victory Germany had to invade Belgium to attack France, going around France's defensive barriers. Germany first asked permission to march her army through neutral Belgium. The Belgians unexpectedly refused and fought, causing further delays for German troops.

If a war came, everyone expected a short, brief war. Long wars, like long sieges, were supposed to have disappeared along with medieval military technology. The Hundred Years' War of the fourteenth century had been followed by the Thirty Years' War of the seventeenth century. The 23-year long French Revolution and Napoleonic wars of 1792 to 1815 were followed by short, decisive campaigns that made maximum use of rapid railroad movement. The Prussian wars against Denmark in 1864, Austria in 1866, and France, 1870-1871, reinforced the notion that science and technology made quick knockout blows possible and long wars impossible to sustain. Everyone seemed to overlook the American Civil War. The kind of war that many Europeans expected bore little resemblance to the horrors of the war they finally got from 1914 to 1918.

Mobilization, War

By August 3rd everyone had declared war, including Great Britain, after Germany executed its Schlieffen Plan to invade France through Belgium. Great Britain had an 1839 treaty with Belgium that guaranteed Belgium's neutrality and a foreign policy principle that only weak powers should control the European coastline opposite the Thames River. Hence, the invasion of Belgium threatened Great Britain. This was not a foolish idea. During the Second World War Germans launched V-2 rockets on London from France, the Netherlands, and Belgium. The Schlieffen Plan proved to not be feasible. First, the Belgians decided to resist the Germans. It took a month to defeat Belgium, permitting France to mobilize her army adequately. Second, the planned distances covered by swift marches were too ambitious for the infantry, negating the speed and precision required for success.

The British, just as every other country did, announced that they were dragged into the war, but their aims were high and noble, unlike everyone else's, according to the British government. Prime Minister Herbert H. Asquith announced on August 5, 1914, "No nation has ever entered into a great struggle – and this is one of the greatest in history – with a clearer conscience and a stronger conviction that it is fighting not for aggression or the advancement of its own interests, but for principles whose maintenance is vital to the civilized world." When the communists took over Russia in 1917, they released copies of all the secret treaties between the Allies – Great Britain, France, Russia, Italy, and Japan – designating the territorial gains to be awarded after the war. Noble indeed! The duplicity was there for the entire world to see. Normally secret governmental records remain sealed until 70-75 years have passed. After the war ended each government issued an official history of the outbreak of the war, vindicating its conduct during the six weeks leading up to the beginning of hostilities. They were nicknamed for the color of their covers – white, blue, yellow, etc., all self-serving and defensive. Apparently, no country caused the war.

And, the German Schlieffen Plan was not unique, because all countries had, and still have, plans for wars. France's plan to attack Germany was Plan 17; Russia's Plan 19. In the First Persian Gulf War in 1991, American planes and satellites took pictures of the Iraqi defensive troop formations. Those formations were copied out of the Soviet Union's desert war manual. The United States military had already extensively made plans for fighting Russia; the only change was that now it was Iraq.

Initial American Reaction to the "Great War," 1914-1917

There they go again, the same old Europeans, the same old Europe, the same old wars – the American people want nothing to do with it. After all, the United States had stayed out of all European wars since 1815. The real reason the United States stayed out was that Europe did not really have any, just brief ones, no major wars. Americans believed that the United States had stayed out of Europe's messy affairs because we willed it. However, the American public were mistaken in this thinking; the United States had been involved in every major European war since 1492. And, in all likelihood, it will be in the future. The United States has too many ties to Europe, such as ethnic, trade, financial, religious, and similar foreign policies. The official U.S. reaction was neutrality. Unofficially, Americans were not at all neutral. The new Secretary of State, Robert Lansing, referred to Germany in 1915 as "the great menace to democracy." President Woodrow Wilson called for neutrality in word and deed, asking Americans to be "impartial in thought as well as in action." However, this was impossible, because the government could not speak for all Americans.

The differing ethnic backgrounds of Americans stirred up feelings. In 1914 Wilson said, "We have to be neutral, since otherwise our mixed populations would wage war on each other." More than one-third of Americans were either foreign-born or had at least one foreign-born parent. America's heterogeneous population invites emotional debate, and always will. Just listen to those who call in to talk radio shows today. Ultimately, many German-Americans changed the spelling or pronunciation of their family's name to something that sounded more English, for example, Schumacher became Shoemaker. Except for the Irish and the Germans, most Americans were pro-Allies; nearly 60% had some British ancestry, and many remembered the French contributions to winning our Revolutionary War. But, it got complicated. Britain's brutal suppression of the Irish Easter Rebellion in 1916 angered many Americans, and not just Irish-Americans. Hatred for Russia among Jews and Scandinavians led many of them to favor Germany. Italian-Americans became pro-Allies after 1915, when Italy joined the Allies.

The Submarine, Complicating our Neutrality
The submarine, a new weapon, was seen as unethical. Under the rules of international warfare a warship could only sink an unarmed merchant ship if it first stopped the ship, informed the ship that it was going to sink it, gave the ship time to radio its position, and gave the crew time to get into lifeboats. Soon British merchant ships began carrying large wooden boxes on the main deck. As a German submarine approached to warn them, one side of the box fell down, revealing a grinning crew of gunners with a heavy artillery gun. Sometimes merchant ships rammed the submarines. The line between civilian and military became unclear. German submarines started sinking without notice, often operating in wolf packs, *wolfsrude*. Great Britain mined the North Sea and Germany declared the waters around Great Britain a war zone. A crucial incident on May 7, 1915, illustrated the dilemma facing America and Americans. On that date the British passenger ship, the *Lusitania*, was sunk off the southern coast of Ireland by a

German submarine, U-20. The "U" is for *Unterseeboot*, German for "undersea boat." It killed 1198 people, including 94 children and 35 babies, and 128 of the 197 Americans on the ship. Bodies washed up on the Irish coast for weeks. The British made certain pictures of the bodies appeared in American newspapers.

Should those 197 Americans have been on that ship? In theory, the protection of the entire American military goes everywhere with every American traveler. Still true. Thus, in theory any American can go anywhere if the United States is not at war with the nation he or she visits. In theory. Historians know the *Lusitania* was carrying crates of small arms, thus, according to international law, the Germans were justified in sinking the ship. However, it looked barbaric, and the British had a field day painting the Germans as horrible Huns. Today the site is still a restricted zone, off limits to any divers. The British still do not want to publicize the existence of the small arms on the *Lusitania*.

The United States diplomatically protested to the Germans. Four months later, in August, German subs sank the *Arabic*, another passenger liner, in the Irish Channel on August 19, 1915, taking 44 lives, including 2 Americans. Wilson did nothing after the German government disavowed the attack and issued a statement on September 1st promising warnings and more caution toward unarmed vessels. This was an early test of Wilson's commitment to neutrality. He passed it.

Later German subs sank the *Sussex*, a British channel steamer, in March 1916, with 80 injured, including 4 Americans. President Woodrow Wilson threatened to sever diplomatic relations with Germany. Germany responded with the "Sussex Pledge," in which they promised not to sink unarmed ships in or out of the war zone without warning and without attempting to save lives. It cooled the situation. Later the Gore-McLemore Resolution was proposed in Congress, declaring that no U.S. citizen had the right to travel on armed merchant ships or ships carrying contraband. It did not pass.

By January, 1917, the German military realized the stalemated war was lost, unless they could win in one quick push. They decided to resume their policy of unrestricted submarine warfare on February 1, using their 100 remaining submarines. The German people were not told that defeat was a possibility. This helps to explain why Hitler's later comments that Germany lost the war because of betrayal struck a responsive chord. Right before the United States declared war on Germany, German submarines were attacking any ship that neared Great Britain or France. This was the major reason that the United States entered the war. There were additional reasons.

Propaganda

Propaganda became a part of modern warfare as it emerged during the First World War. Simply put, the French and British were better at it. Allied propaganda clearly gave the Germans an image problem. In 1915 the British issued the Bryce Report, written by James Bryce, a former ambassador to the United States. Bryce was a good friend of Theodore Roosevelt and the author of a well-received book on American politics, *The*

American Commonwealth. The Bryce Report castigated the Germans for their treatment of civilians in German-occupied regions of France and Belgium, citing massacres, looting, burning, and wanton destruction of property.

The Germans did a poor job controlling their public image. They put a warning in newspapers beside the notices of a ship departing from an American port. Beside the notice of the departure of the *Lusitania* from New York City had been the following newspaper notice: "Travelers intending to embark on the Atlantic voyage are reminded that a state of war exists between Germany . . . and Great Britain; that the zone of war includes the waters adjacent to the British Isles . . . and that travelers sailing in the war zone on ships of Great Britain or her allies do so at their own risk." Signed, Imperial German Embassy. To Germans this official notice issued by the German government absolved them of any consequences. This sterile warning to the American public could not compete with the British newspaper pictures of bloated bodies washing up on the Irish coast.

Two Belgian atrocities added to Germany's poor image in America. In October, 1915, a German firing squad publicly executed Edith Cavell, a British nurse, for spying in Belgium. She was guilty of spying, and execution by firing squad was the traditional punishment. But, the British press castigated the Germans for shooting a woman, and a nurse. How barbaric! A woman! A nurse! Another blow to the German image was that in 1914 they deported 10,000 Belgian workers to work in German factories. President Wilson called it, "One of the most unjustifiable incidents of the present war."

Loans

There had been an economic recession in the U.S. prior to the war, which had stretched from 1912 to 1914. The industrial production boost from the outbreak of the European war ended it. By April 1917, American trade to the Allies had increased from $800,000,000 in 1914 to $3 billion. Trade to the Central Powers fell from $169,000,000 to $1 million. In 1914 our Allies to Central Powers trade imbalance was 5:1; in 1917 it was 3,000:1. Was the United States neutral? Then loans became necessary to continue sales to the Allies, who had run out of money. Wilson's first Secretary of State, William Jennings Bryan, resigned in protest against America's lopsided trade imbalance and loans going only to the Allies, saying, "Money is the greatest contraband of all." Later, in an attempt to avoid becoming involved in the possibility of the Second World War, Congress in the 1930s passed Neutrality Acts to avoid a repeat of this situation, asking for "cash and carry." The United States will sell to anyone, for cash, come and get the goods, we do not deliver.

According to the rules of international warfare at that time, neutral nations could continue trading in time of war, but their ships could be stopped, searched, and contraband seized without compensation. Every time the Germans did something to upset the United States the British quietly expanded their list of what constituted contraband.

Eventually even food and medical supplies were on their list. Wilson acquiesced in British violations of our neutral rights, for a good reason; by 1916 the British were purchasing $83 million worth of American goods each week.

Zimmermann Note

On January 17, 1917, the German foreign minister, Arthur Zimmermann, sent a telegram to the German ambassador to Mexico, ordering him to offer Mexico the American states of New Mexico, Arizona, and Texas if Mexico would join Germany in an alliance against the United States. Mexico was expected to invade the United States and to occupy American soldiers, who would then not be available to fight in Europe. The British intercepted the telegram, decoded it, and sent a copy to the U.S. government and to American newspapers. It was published on March 1. The public was outraged. Anyone who follows professional sports knows that there are constant rumors of proposed "deals" and "trades" that never happen. This is also normal in diplomatic relations. Part of the telegram informed the German ambassador that Germany's use of "ruthless submarine warfare now promises to compel England to make peace in a few months." Germany planned, in early 1917, to ignore the American concerns about interfering with neutral shipping. Germany would win the war before the U.S. troops arrived in large enough numbers to make an impact, especially if Mexico became involved.

Opportunity: The Two Russian Revolutions in 1917

Russia was hardly a democratic government before the First World War. Only 9,500 voters in Moscow, with a population of 1,500,000, could vote for the city council. Russia made it difficult for the Allies to portray the war as a noble cause of democracy against the Huns.

On March 8, 1917, a revolution convulsed Russia, a democratic revolution. By July Alexander Kerensky became the new prime minister. Russia now had a democratic government; the absolute rule of the czar ended and he became a mere figurehead. However, the new democratic government made a fateful decision to continue the war, a war greatly disliked by the average Russian. In just 1915 two million Russians had died. By 1918, the First World War had killed 6 to 8 million Russians. The country had been incredibly unprepared for war in 1914, especially modern warfare as it emerged during the First World War. Three-quarters of the ill-prepared soldiers heading to the battlefront lines did not even have rifles. They were instructed to pick up the rifles of dead soldiers. Watch the movie *Dr. Zhivago*, the early part takes place during the First World War. The chaotic Russian army defies description. There are simply no words to adequately describe how bad it was.

From the American viewpoint the Kerensky revolution had been a blessing. The United States could now claim that the war in Europe was democracy fighting against the "Huns," a noble effort "to save the world for democracy," in Wilson's dramatic phrase. However, later, on November 9, 1917, (October 24 on the outdated Russian calendar then in use) the Bolshevik Revolution took control. The first priority for the Bolsheviks, or Communists, was to consolidate their control within Russia. Thus, in March 1918, the Bolsheviks took Russia out of the war, signing a peace treaty with Germany, the Treaty of Brest-Litovsk. The Germans then shifted their soldiers from the Eastern Front and launched a massive offensive on the Western Front, aiming for victory before the Americans could arrive in large numbers. Previously, many in the United States, including the American leaders, believed fresh American troops would swing the balance and prevent a German victory. However, the German troops freed up by the peace treaty with Russia counterbalanced the American troops.

By this time, after three long years, President Woodrow Wilson and others began to see the war as an opportunity. To do what? To create a new world order. To prevent another "Great War," or, as it was also called then, the "War of the Nations." War would be an instrument to prevent future wars. In his April 1917 war message to Congress, Wilson said, "We have no selfish ends to serve, we desire no conquest, no dominion." However, he also stirred up a desire to crush Germany. "Force, Force to the utmost, Force without stint or limit, the righteous and triumphant Force which shall make Right the law of the world, and cast every selfish dominion down in the dust." His own words came back to haunt him when he said, privately, "Once lead this people into war they will forget there ever was such a thing as tolerance." Passion raised is difficult to soothe.

Fourteen Points

In January, 1918, Wilson had announced his Fourteen Points, his outline for the postwar world. It was a rebuttal to the leader of the Bolsheviks, Vladimir Lenin, for publicizing the Allies' secret treaties, which revealed their imperialistic plans. Historians refer to Wilson's program as "liberal internationalism." It rested on the conviction that economic and political progress went hand-in-hand. Greater democratic freedom for the whole world would follow from America's increased worldwide investment and trade. The difficulty with creating a new world order was that the old one had to first be dismantled. The challenge was the concept of national sovereignty, which recognized no authority higher than the nation. Today national sovereignty appears to be being undermined by the United Nations, by the regrouping of some nations such as the European Union, by the movement of peoples all around the world, and by trade. The French and Germans adopted dual citizenship after the Second World War. Currently, a European Parliament meets in Strasburg, France. Most of Europe has a single currency, the Euro. One does not need a passport to drive from one European Union country to another, which was also the situation prior to the First World War.

Is the nation-state, an entity really in existence only since 1648, disappearing? It is at its strongest when national boundaries perfectly coincide with ethnic boundaries. However, this is rare around the world, and it assumes there will be no future population shifts. The two greatest ingredients causing change for any society at any time are shifts in the demographic profile of the nation's population and advances in technology – neither of which are predictable or controllable.

The Versailles Peace Conference, January to June, 1919

After American participation and German exhaustion combined to end the war, the victors faced the difficult task of agreeing upon the peace terms. President Woodrow Wilson had already announced his terms, the Fourteen Points. In many respects, the Fourteen Points represented the imposition of Anglo-Saxon principles of democracy and capitalism upon the whole world, a Pax Americana. After the Bolshevik Revolution of November, 1917, the new Communist Russian government concluded an armistice with Germany on December 5 and published their archival copies of the Allies' secret agreements, which showed the war was being fought for the same old reasons – to gain territory, to gain colonies, etc. No idealism was apparent, just old-fashioned, rotten, typical European diplomacy. To counter this impression Wilson issued his Fourteen Points in January, 1918, asserting that the Allies were really fighting for high ideals. Now Wilson was pressured to deliver on these high ideals and grand statements is-sued during the war. However, the other leaders of the Big Four – the United States, Great Britain, France, and Italy – had other reasons, namely the usual ones, for being at the Peace Conference. Their desires were closer to the treaties the Bolsheviks had published. A spirit of revenge prevailed among the Allied leaders, especially for Great Britain's Lloyd George and France's Georges Clemenceau. France lost two million men in the war and most of the fighting on the Western Front took place on French soil, leaving behind a devastated countryside.

President Wilson sailed to Europe on the *U.S.S. George Washington*. Some of his crit-ics said he walked over on the water, a snide reference to Wilson thinking he was like Christ, saving the world. In France, and elsewhere, the public gave him a hero's welcome. Children threw flowers in his path. One of Wilson's reasons for going to war was to cre-ate a different world following the war. However, as the historian J. C. Levenson wrote in *Pastmasters*, "The great beliefs that carry nations through wars do not lead quickly and clearly to practical programs for reorganizing society in the aftermath of wars."

The Big Four hammered out a peace treaty, the Versailles Treaty, formally present-ing it on June 28, 1919. It was a dictated peace. The Allies did not permit Germany to participate in the discussions. Among the major provisions were the following:

> Article 10 (often written as Article X) – An internationally enforced collective security. All the nations of the world, minus those evil na-tions which started the war – Germany and Austria-Hungary – would join together in an international association to prevent wars. How was this to be accomplished? Any attack on a member nation of the League of Nations would be met by a military response by all the other

members. Wilson considered this provision to be the heart of the League of Nations. It had been the culminating point, Point Fourteen, in his Fourteen Points speech in January, 1918, outlining the American plans for the post-war world. Point Fourteen stated that "A general association of nations must be formed under specific covenants for the purpose of affording mutual guarantees of political independence and territorial integrity to great and small states alike."

Article 231 – Germany received total blame for starting the war, the war-guilt clause, drafted by the future American Secretary of State, John Foster Dulles.

Mandate system – The colonies of the defeated powers were given to the Allies, under League of Nations supervision, which caused the leader of the nascent Chinese Communist Party, Mao Zedong, then a young library assistant in China, to remark, "So much for national self-determination, I think it is really shameless!" The Mandate system also bitterly disappointed a young Vietnamese seeking independence for his country, Ho Chi Minh, who became the Communist leader of North Vietnam.

Germany lost 1/8 of her prewar territory.

Austria-Hungary was broken up and numerous new countries created in Central and Eastern Europe – small countries that together constituted a power vacuum, inviting invasion by larger countries.

The Republican Senate Rejects the Versailles Treaty

The U.S. Senate must ratify all treaties, but Wilson made too many mistakes to ensure a chance for ratification. Wilson did not include any Republicans in the peace conference delegation. And, no senators. There was a non-presidential midterm election in November, 1918. Wars carry a sense of sacrifice. After a war ends, the political party in power during the war is usually voted out. The war is over, the usual reaction is – out with those who forced the public to sacrifice. Republicans gained control of the Senate, where a 2/3 vote was needed to approve a treaty, 64 votes at that time. In March, 1919, 39 of the 96 senators signed a Round Robin Declaration stating that they could not vote for the treaty as written. That was more than enough to defeat the treaty. Just 33 votes would prevent approval. Wilson refused to modify the terms of the treaty.

The chairman of the Senate Foreign Relations Committee, and also Senate Majority Leader, Senator Henry Cabot Lodge of Massachusetts, was a bitter foe of Wilson. Their differences ranged from petty and personal to political and philosophical. When Lodge later led a Senate delegation to visit the ill president, he told Wilson that they were praying for him. Wilson replied, "Which way?" Lodge graduated from Harvard; Wilson had been president of Princeton. They both sent one another copies of the other one's

speeches, after correcting the grammar. Lodge, claiming that the treaty was too complex for his committee members to understand, took six weeks to personally read the
treaty to the Senate Foreign Relations Committee. There is a principle of legislative
management that the longer you stall a piece of pending legislation, the less likely it is to
pass eventually. People start to nit-pick.

Meanwhile, Wilson toured the country to drum up public support. He suffered a stroke
in Colorado. Rushed back to the White House, he became bedridden, with only his wife,
Edith, and his doctor permitted to see him. Some historians claim Edith was our first
woman president, that she really made the decisions rather than relaying questions to her
husband. When the political procedure demanded it, Wilson was unable to provide the
necessary leadership to push the treaty through the Senate. Senator Henry Cabot Lodge
proposed reservations, including that the United States had no obligation under Article X
to supply troops unless Congress gave its approval. Remember, under our Constitution,
Congress declares war. The Democratic Minority Leader, Senator Gilbert Hitchcock, created his own list of reservations, after consulting with Wilson after he recovered slightly from
his stroke. His reservations stated that the request for troops under Article X was only an
advisory request because only Congress has the power to declare war. Neither of these positions pleased the "Irreconcilables," the 13 senators who said that under no conditions would
they accept joining the League of Nations. Wilson refused to change the treaty. Look carefully at the different votes taken on approving the treaty – Democrats plus Irreconcilables
voted against the treaty with the Lodge reservations; Republicans plus Irreconcilables voted
against the treaty without the Lodge reservations and with the Hitchcock reservations. The
"for" votes were always a long way from the 64 needed.

There were five separate Senate votes taken on the Versailles Treaty:

November, 1919	For	Against
With the Lodge reservations	39	55
With the Hitchcock reservations	41	50
With the Lodge reservations	41	51
Without reservations	38	53
March, 1919		
With the Lodge reservations	49	35

Who is more to blame for the defeat of the Versailles Treaty? Lodge? Wilson? Their
deep personal animosity made compromise unthinkable, for either. Is half a loaf better than none? Wilson said that without approval there would be another war. Is it
better to be a prophet? What is an effective leader? A compromiser? A prophet? A
stick-to-the-correct-idea person? A leader must be able to distinguish between what is
essential, what is desirable, and what is possible. Woodrow Wilson, as a political science
professor, once presented an academic definition of leadership in a democracy. He said,

"Leadership is interpretation.... A leader must read the common thought and test and calculate the preparation of the nation for the next step in the progress of politics." He seemed to have forgotten his own observation. (Quoted in Jean H. Baker, "The South Has Been Wronged: James Buchanan and the Secession Crisis" in *James Buchanan and the Coming of the Civil War*, ed. By John W. Quist and Michael J. Birkner.) In truth, the Second World War was unavoidable; it was really the First World War continued.

In his Fourteen Points speech Wilson set goals that no president or nation could achieve. Look carefully at the verbs used for the Fourteen Points. Most of them use "should," meaning they are open to negotiation. The one establishing the League of Nations uses "must." Wilson would not budge on the League. Early in his presidency he had said that it would be an "irony of fate" if he had to focus on foreign policy as president. He was inexperienced in diplomacy, had not traveled much outside the United States, and knew little of other countries or cultures, with the exception of Great Britain. He understood his weaknesses; but he did not remember them. He was uncompromising once he made up his mind, and he had difficulty working with those he considered less intelligent, which meant everyone.

In 1919 America had no tradition of a bipartisan foreign policy. That would come with and after the Second World War. Wilson had also stretched the powers of the executive branch, just as Lincoln had during the Civil War. Congress wanted to regain its power and prestige. The American people had enough things to do here; forget about being policeman of an ungrateful world. Finally, 1920 was a presidential election year, which colored every political act preceding it.

A Benign Peace or a Carthaginian Peace?

There are two kinds of effective peace treaties, the Benign Peace Treaty or the Carthaginian Peace Treaty. In a Benign Peace Treaty the defeated enemy is treated so kindly that they become your ally or friend. At the very least, they are no longer your potential enemy. The treaty at the end of the Austro-Prussian War of 1866 was a benign treaty. Germany and Austria-Hungary later became allies. A Carthaginian Peace obliterates your foe. Be careful. If this sounds attractive, be aware that this creates a power vacuum, one into which other countries may venture, leading to future difficulties or wars. A Carthaginian Peace is named for what Rome did to Carthage after the Third Punic War, the third war between Rome and Carthage, a city-state in North Africa. Rome tore down all the city's buildings and plowed salt into their soil. Carthage never recovered. There was no Fourth Punic War. The Versailles Treaty was neither Benign nor Carthaginian. One of the "lessons" of history seems to be that you should do one or the other, never halfway between. Instead of achieving a lasting peace, the Versailles Treaty created the situations and feed the emotions that led to the Second World War.

37

THE TWENTIES

Cultural Conflict

The Twenties was a decade of cultural conflict between the emerging new urban values and the retreating old Victorian and rural values of small town America, with overtones of concern over the issues of race and religion. As an illustration of how strict things had been – why was chicken referred to as "white" or "dark" meat? So that family dinners were not embarrassed by speaking of "legs" or "breasts". The revivalist preacher, Billy Sunday, captured the essence of the conflict in a single sentence in 1925. "Our country is filled with a socialistic, IWW, communistic, radical, lawless, anti-American, anti-Church, anti-God, anti-marriage gang and they are laying the eggs of rebellion and unrest in labour and capital and home; and we have some of them in the universities."

Many believed that a previous "consensus of shared values" had broken down. How to return to it? This concern surfaced in many areas of American life. In art it appeared in the starkness of the paintings and the city subjects in the "Ashcan School" of art, introduced to the public by the 1913 Armory Show exhibit in New York City. As a comment on the disappearing agricultural foundation of American society, the family farmer, look at *American Gothic*, Grant Wood's portrait of his sister and his dentist, interpreted by many as a satirical parody on rural America. Compare Wood's *American Gothic* with his *Daughters of Revolution*, a satirical portrayal of the smug, old, bedrock elite members of the patriotic organization, The Daughters of the American Revolution. In an era of change, some aspects of society remained. Or, did they? Look up several Ashcan School paintings, and *American Gothic* and *Daughters of Revolution* on the Internet. In the Twenties this concern and conflict was often referred to as modernism versus traditionalism. It was similar to the late twentieth century and early twentieth-first century, when America divided between Red States and Blue States, again mainly over cultural values.

In 1924 Horace Kallen coined the term "cultural pluralism," arguing that America's ethnic and racial diversity was a strength, not a concern. Kallen, a philosopher who taught for decades at the New School in New York City, viewed advocates of the Melting Pot assimilation theory as demanding what America must become to save itself from immigrant contamination. He also used the phrase "symphony of civilizations" to describe our **American Identity**. His point of view was not new in American history. For example, in the mid-nineteenth century the poet Walt Whitman opened his *Leaves of Grass* with, *"Here is not merely a nation but a teeming nation of nations."* However, not until the 1960s would a sizeable number of Americans even begin to embrace the concept of "cultural pluralism" as something positive.

Changing Standards of Morality

Changing standards of morality caused widespread concern. Evidence of a new hedonistic lifestyle and immoral behavior was everywhere – thinner clothes, sleeveless dresses, the Charleston dance craze, and sensuous jazz music. Other evidence included the following:

Women enjoyed more independence in the Twenties because employment opportunities during the First World War led to greater financial security, and the Nineteenth Amendment gave women the vote, leading to further feelings of independence.

Contraceptives and knowledge of birth control became more widespread.

The automobile, nicknamed "the bedroom on wheels," led to less parental supervision for dating. The term "dating," widely used by youngsters in the Twenties, shocked older people because the word previously referred to a meeting with a prostitute. The accepted older term had been "courting."

The automobile both changed and frightened America. Earlier Woodrow Wilson had predicted that the automobile would bring socialism by promoting envy of the rich. Automobile registrations hit one million in 1913 and ten million by 1923. The price of a Model T Ford in 1910 was $950, but in 1924 only $290, or three month's income, thus putting it within reach of the average American. At the end of the 1920s college students were asked to rank the greatest people of all time. Their list: Jesus Christ, Napoleon, and, third, Henry Ford. It is strange to see Jesus and Henry Ford on the same list; Ford was an extremely bigoted anti-Semite.

There was an attack on the double standard. Previously there were different standards of expected behavior concerning sex for males and females. In the Twenties women began to assert their right to imitate male standards, arguing that only affection was necessary for sex. In the 1890s there had been an attempt to raise male standards; in the 1920s female standards declined; in the 1960s all standards were thrown out.

Throughout history, standards, rather than behavior, have periodically gone up and down. Depend on it doing so again in your lifetime.

The population had begun to shift to urban areas. The 1920 census was the first that recorded that a majority of Americans lived in cities. The impersonality of the city, and the tendency in urbanites to look the other way over moral issues, disturbed rural America.

Freudian psychology became popular and filtered down to the level of the supermarket tabloid, which still simplifies complex scientific theories into one or two paragraphs for the average person. The message was that repressed desires caused mental illness. Throwing values out the window will protect your mental health. This was not exactly what Sigmund Freud wrote, not even close. Freud's two central theories – the force of the unconscious mental life and the importance of childhood sexuality to personality development – arose from his attempts to understand and to treat mental illness. The widespread feeling that the First World War revealed the depth of irrational human behavior popularized his work in the Twenties. Freud's research and writing weakened the previous prevailing belief that reason controlled the behavior of the educated portion of humanity, and that humans are fully aware of what they do and why they do it.

Here are several comical examples of small town America fighting back. A legislator introduced a bill in the Oregon state legislature creating a fine and imprisonment for any woman who wore a skirt three inches above her knee. A small town in North Carolina passed an ordinance outlawing sex, except between married couples, if used moderately, after dark, with the shades drawn.

Why Did Moral Values Change?

The answer to that question is the First World War. Wilfred Owen was an English poet killed during the war. He left behind several poems written in the trenches during the war, "*Disabled*," and "*Dulce et Decorum Est*," a satirical poem that ends with:

> "The old lie: Dulce et decorum est
> Pro patria mori."

Latin for "It is sweet and right to die for your country." Also, read two poems written in the aftermath of the war by T. S. Eliot, "*The Wasteland*," and "*The Hollow Men*," which ends with:

> "This is the way the world ends,
> this is the way the world ends,
> this is the way the world ends,
> not with a bang but a whimper."

Shirley Millard was a nurse at a hospital in France near the front lines. She saw the effects of poisoned gas and the 1918 flu epidemic. Here is her diary entry for Armistice Day, November 11, 1918, the day the First World War ended.

"Charley, a paralyzed American sergeant, died this morning. I held his hand as he went and could not keep back the tears. Near the end he saw me crying and patted my hand with his two living fingers to comfort me. I cannot describe that boy's sweetness. He took part of my heart with him. Everybody around the place was in tears."

"Just after he went, someone came into the ward and said: 'Armistice! The staff cars have just passed by the gate on their way to Senlis to sign an armistice!'"

"There is no armistice for Charley or for any of the others in that ward. One of the boys began to sob. I went and talked soothingly to him, but what could I say, knowing he would die before night?"

"Well, it's over. I have to keep telling myself. It's over, it's over, it's over."

"But there is still that letter to write to Charley's mother. I can hear commotion and shouting through the hospital as I write this. The chapel bell is ringing wildly."

"I am glad it is over, but my heart is heavy as lead. Must write that letter."

"One of the girls came looking for me. They have opened champagne for the staff in the dining hall. I told her to get out."

"Can't seem to pull myself together."

I Saw Them Die: The Diary and Recollections of Shirley Millard

David Guterson's novel *Snow Falling on Cedars* is set in the aftermath of the Second World War. It contains an excellent description of the impact of war upon a soldier, any war upon any soldier. In this passage, a man is reflecting on how he feels sitting in a college classroom after returning home from the Second World War, now minus an arm.

"He didn't like very many people anymore or very many things, either. He preferred not to be this way, but there it was, he was like that. His cynicism – a veteran's cynicism – was a thing that disturbed him all the time. It seemed to him after the war that the world was thoroughly altered. It was not even a thing you could explain to anybody, why it was that everything was folly. People appeared enormously foolish to him. He understood that they were only animated cavities full of jelly and strings and liquids. He had seen the insides of jaggedly ripped-open dead people. He knew, for instance, what brains looked like spilling out of somebody's head. In the context of all this, much of what went on in normal life seemed wholly and disturbingly ridiculous. He found that he was irritated with complete strangers. If someone in one of his classes spoke to him he answered stiffly, tersely. He could never tell if they were relaxed enough about his arm to say what they were really thinking. He sensed their need to extend sympathy to him, and this irritated him even more. The arm was a grim enough thing without that, and he felt sure it was entirely disgusting. He could repel people if he chose by wearing to class a short-sleeved shirt that revealed the scar tissue on his stump. He never did this, however, he didn't exactly want to *repel* people. Anyway, he had this view of things – that most human activity was utterly folly, his own included, and that his existence in the world made others nervous. He could not help but possess this unhappy perspective, no matter how much he might not want it. It was his and he suffered from it numbly." (p. 26)

Vietnam veteran and author Tim O'Brien, who wrote *The Things They Carried* and *If I Die in a Combat Zone*, added a retrospective look at the Vietnam War in 2015, which could be said of all wars. "There's this mistaken notion that wars end, but they don't end. What about the women that married the veterans and had to sit through silent dinner after silent dinner? Somewhere in this country there's a 95-year-old woman who will wake up at night and say, 'Where's my baby?' The answer is, her baby has been dead for 45 years. But the war's not over for that Gold Star mother. It'll never be over, and you can't expect it to be over."

Or, consider the observation of Lieutenant Lewis B. Fuller, injured in Vietnam. A land mine ripped off both his legs; he survived. One of his first thoughts was that he had "been forever set apart from the rest of humanity." Years later, after struggling with alcoholism, he took his own life. This "apartness" from the rest of society characterizes all veterans of all wars. They either talk about their wartime experiences incessantly or not at all. Mostly the latter. Why bother, no one would understand.

One company of American soldiers stormed up a hill during the First World War against a German machine gun. Five out of 320 survived. Read what many historians consider the greatest personal story of combat, written by E. B. Sledge, a longtime professor of biology at the University of Montevallo in Alabama. His book, *With The Old Breed at Peleliu and Okinawa*, is a searing account of an enlisted man's experiences in the Pacific theater during the Second World War and his struggles to make sense out of the emotions of hate and love, kill or be killed. It haunted him for the rest of his life. Another superb portrayal of the emotional stress and strain of war is *All Quiet on the Western Front*, by Erich Maria Remarque, a German author's novel set in the First World War. War is not good for human beings. In many respects, war strips away the veneer of civilization and values. One of the lessons of war is that there seems to be no reason to uphold moral standards. The years following the First World War marked the first time in history that many former soldiers began to write about their personal experiences, providing intimate details of the horrors of war.

The Rise of the Ku Klux Klan

The Ku Klux Klan boasted it had five million members in the Twenties. The KKK was politically strong in over twenty states, including the South and states as diverse as Delaware, Indiana, Rhode Island, Kansas, Pennsylvania and Oregon. (Oregon's 1857 constitution excluded free blacks from the state. It ratified the Fifteenth Amendment in 1959.) Only 16% of its members were Southerners. The largest state Klan was in Indiana. The Klan sponsored social events – square dances, rodeos, and carnivals. In Montgomery County, just outside Philadelphia, the Klan held a rally on July 4, 1923, that attracted 30,000 people. The Klan in the Twenties was a small town movement primarily, although recent migrants to the cities from small towns and rural areas supported a vibrant KKK in the cities. Chicago's Klan had 40,000 members. The KKK was more of a fraternal movement, a patriotic defense of the old order rather than just an anti-black organization, as characterized the previous Klan following the Civil War. The Twenties Klan disliked Jews, Catholics, blacks, immigrants, unions, socialists, and communists; in other words, anyone who was not truly American! Fortunately for the KKK its rebirth came just as *"The Birth of A Nation"* came out, one of the first full-length feature films. It portrayed Reconstruction from the Southern viewpoint and depicted blacks as incompetent, foolish legislators. The first KKK supposedly rescued the South from oppressive black rule during Reconstruction. This new KKK even had their own vocabulary and secret nomenclature, cementing a feeling of fraternalism that excluded outsiders. Among their terms and meanings were:

> AYAK – Are you a Klansman?
> AKIA – A Klansman I am
> CYGNAB – Can you give number and board, meaning what local Klan Klavern?
> KIGY – Klansman, I greet you

These are not intellectually challenging to decipher! Or, to remember, which says a lot about the IQ of those who joined.

One Klan leader, Hiram Evans, explained the Klan's perspective in a widely read magazine article in 1926, "The Klan's Fight for Americanism," *North American Review*. He asserted that the Klan stood for three great racial instincts – Patriotism, meaning "a racial understanding of Americanism," White, and Protestantism. Note that Patriotism and Protestantism are *racial*. Several excerpts follow:

> "The Klan, therefore, has now come to speak for the great mass of Americans of the old pioneer stock . . . . as distinguished from the intellectually mongrelized "Liberals.""

"These are, in the first place, a blend of various peoples of the so-called Nordic race, the race which, with all its faults, has given the world almost the whole of modern civilization. The Klan does not try to represent any people but these."

"These Nordic Americans for the last generation have found themselves increasingly uncomfortable, and finally deeply distressed."

"Presently we began to find that we were dealing with strange ideas; policies that always sounded well, but somehow always made us still more uncomfortable."

"Finally came the moral breakdown that has been going on for two decades. One by one all our traditional moral standards went by the boards, or were so disregarded that they ceased to be binding. The sacredness of our Sabbath, of our homes, of chastity, and finally even of our right to teach our children in our own schools fundamental facts and truths were torn away from us."

"One more point about the present attitude of the old-stock American: he has revived and increased his long-standing distrust of the Roman Catholic Church. It is for this that the native Americans, and the Klan as their leader, are most often denounced as intolerant and prejudiced . . . ."

"The Ku Klux Klan, in short, is an organization which gives expression, direction and purpose to the most vital instincts, hopes, and resentments of the old-stock Americans, provides them with leadership, and is enlisting and preparing them for militant, constructive action toward fulfilling their racial and national destiny . . . . The Klan literally is once more the embattled American farmer and artisan, coördinated into a disciplined and growing army, and launched upon a definite crusade for Americanism!"

"Thus the Klan goes back to the American racial instincts, and to the common sense which is their first product, as the basis of its beliefs and methods . . . ."

"There are three of these great racial instincts, vital elements in both the historic and the present attempts to build an America which shall fulfill the aspirations and justify the heroism of the men who made the nation. These are the instincts of loyalty to the white race, to the traditions of America, and to the spirit of Protestantism, which has been an essential part of Americanism ever since the days of Roanoke and Plymouth Rock. They are condensed into the Klan slogan: 'Native, white, Protestant supremacy.'"

The predominantly lower-class appeal of the Klan echoed the Populist movement pronouncements. Note the quote above, "The Klan literally is once more the embattled American farmer and artisan . . . ." The 1892 Omaha Populist Party platform said, "We seek to restore the government of the Republic to the hands of the "plain people," with which class it originated." Just as the Populists, the Klan felt that control of the country had slipped away from them, somehow. As examples of the KKK's influence in the Twenties:

1. The Oregon legislature passed a law requiring all children to attend public schools, essentially outlawing Catholic parochial schools. The Supreme Court overturned the law in *Pierce v. Society of Sisters*, 1925.
2. Throughout the decade, there was a rising chorus of calls to censor movies, mainly because they showed too much sex.
3. The Democratic Party convention in 1924 split between two men, backed, without their blessing, by anti-Klan and pro-Klan supporters, Al Smith of New York and William McAdoo of North Carolina. It took 103 ballots to select a compromise candidate, John W. Davis, and his running mate, Charles Bryan, William Jennings Bryan's brother. The Democratic Party's two-thirds rule, which required the nominee to have two-thirds of the convention vote, gave the South extraordinary power and influence over the selection of the final candidate. During this convention, there was a floor fight over a platform plank condemning the Klan. It passed by less than five votes.

Intellectuals fed these attitudes with their "scientific" books and research about the problem of "race suicide," the fear that upper class and middle class whites were not reproducing in sufficient numbers to maintain their dominance over the "undesirables." Theodore Roosevelt had earlier called it the "warfare of the cradle," the fear that the better people would be "overwhelmed by the lower races." The new science of eugenics, Greek for "good" and "inheritance," supposedly proved that preserving the best of the white race was compelling for the survival of civilization. Madison Grant's *The Passing of the Great Race* sold 1,500,000 copies. A New York City lawyer from an old wealth family, Grant argued that the "Nordic Race," those from Northern Europe, were responsible for all of Europe's advances. The danger facing America was the recent increase in non-Nordics surging into the U.S. See Nell Painter's incredible book, *The History of White People*, for the pseudoscientific history of "white" as an idea. (She is a black Princeton professor.) The book will make you laugh and cry at the same time. How in the world could people think . . .? But, they did.

The Urban Black Population

For the first time, there was a substantial black population in major Northern cities, where life seemed to go in several different directions. In the first six months of 1919 there were 25 race riots; the most infamous one was in Chicago, where there were 38 dead and 537 injured. The most destructive and deadly riot occurred in 1921 in Tulsa, Oklahoma, which killed 75 and made over a thousand blacks homeless. These riots were all partially caused by a brief recession after the war, which led to concern over jobs for white veterans, because hundreds of thousands of blacks had come north for factory jobs during the war. Now returning white veterans saw these blacks as competitors for jobs. There was also concern over how returning black soldiers would readjust to a subordinate, second-class status.

As the racial riots immediately following the war ended, continued migration into Northern cities created large neighborhoods that were almost completely populated by blacks, such as Harlem in New York City. This sizeable population nursed a black urban culture featuring both racial pride and protest against continued discrimination. Nicknamed the "Harlem Renaissance," an outpouring of literary work in New York City appealed to the growing black middle class. Three literary works show the range and appeal – poems by Claude McKay, *"If We Must Die,"* and Langston Hughes, *"Harlem"* (also referred to as *"Dream Deferred"*) and Claude McKay's novel, *Home to Harlem*.

Racial pride and protest were also part of Marcus Garvey's Universal Negro Improvement Association, the UNIA. Garvey, born in Jamaica, became involved in union activities as a young printer. Later he traveled throughout Central America and lived in England for a few years. By 1912 these varied experiences made him a firm advocate of Pan-Africanism and Black Nationalism. He moved the UNIA headquarters to New York City in 1916. In Harlem, Garvey founded *Negro World*, a weekly newspaper. The UNIA was the first organization that struck a responsive chord among lower class Northern urban blacks and Africans overseas. Over 25,000 delegates from 25 different countries attended the first UNIA international convention in 1920 in Harlem. Garvey's speech to the convention advocated a black deity, extolled African beauty, what would later be called "black is beautiful," celebrated the achievements of blacks throughout history, and urged a back-to-Africa movement. In addition, he created several black-owned businesses, the Black Star Steamship Company and the Negro Factories Corporation. He said black-owned, black-operated businesses were the key to economic independence. Note that in this respect, he was in the Booker T. Washington tradition that argued for dependence on economic self-help. He organized massive parades through Harlem and many low class blacks joined his organization. At that time neither the Urban League of Booker T. Washington nor the NAACP of W.E.B. Du Bois were mass organizations for lower class blacks; each was a specialty organization, with a single focus – jobs for Washington and court suits for Du Bois. After continuous attempts, in 1925 the federal government finally convicted Garvey of fraud for his handling of the funds of the Black Star Steamship Line. It was really closer to incompetence than fraud; he was not a businessman. He was sentenced to five years in prison. President Calvin Coolidge commuted his sentence two years later; he was immediately deported back to Jamaica. He died in London, alone, forgotten, and poor, on the eve of the Second World War.

Many whites, and also middle class blacks, considered Garvey a threat. Garvey's place in the history of American blacks is questioned. Rev. Martin Luther King, Jr., called Garvey "the first man on a mass scale and level to give Negroes a sense of dignity and destiny." However, W.E.B. Du Bois labeled Garvey "the most dangerous enemy of the Negro race," and "a lunatic or a traitor." Garvey's responding remarks about W.E.B. Du Bois border on the unprintable.

Religious Fundamentalism

The Scopes Trial in Dayton, Tennessee, raised the issue of teaching the theory of evolution in public schools. Scientific terminology refers to evolution as a theory only because it cannot be replicated completely in a laboratory, as the scientific method requires. Gravity is also a theory to scientists. Do not try to float off a tall building. Under pressure from religious Fundamentalists, the Tennessee legislature passed the Butler Act in March, 1925, making it a crime to teach in any state-supported school "any theory that denies the story of the Divine Creation of man as taught in the Bible, and to teach instead that man has descended from a lower order of animals." Local businessmen in Dayton saw the law as a good chance to bring some business and publicity for the town and to put Dayton on the map. What happened far exceeded their dreams and became a media circus. Today the town annually reenacts the event, hosting the Scopes Trial Festival, with a new trial, *Front Page News*, that concludes that evolution is incorrect, a belief currently supported by 42% of all Americans.

It was clear from the start what the ruling would be. Judge John Ralston began the trial with a prayer. On the wall behind him was a large banner that said, "Read Your Bible Daily." The three-time Democratic Party presidential candidate, William Jennings Bryan, unofficially aided the prosecution. The famed Chicago lawyer, Clarence Darrow, led the defense. Darrow wanted to call scientists to the stand as witnesses. The judge refused, ruling that scientific evidence was not admissible. Since Bryan was not an official member of the prosecution team, Darrow surprised everyone by calling Bryan to the witness stand as an expert on the Bible. The judge temporarily dismissed the jury, which was not present for Bryan's testimony. Bryan expected questions on evolution. Instead, he got questions on the credibility of the Bible. Bryan testified under oath that God created the world in 4004 B.C., the day before Sunday, October 23, as calculated centuries ago by an Irish clergyman, Bishop Ussher, and that the great flood came in

2348 B.C. Bryan fudged a little with regard to the stories of how a whale could swallow Jonah and how Adam and Eve's sons, Cain and Abel, found their wives. Concerned over Bryan's apparent contradictions of the exactness of the Bible, the judge abruptly stopped Darrow's cross-examination of Bryan. Fundamentalists were stunned at Bryan's fudging on the exactness of the Bible.

Darrow refused to give a closing argument after the jury returned, leaving Bryan's shocking testimony as the last word. Under Tennessee law, the prosecution could therefore not give its position in a closing argument. After deliberating nine minutes the jury reported its verdict, finding John Scopes guilty; the judge fined him $100. The *Baltimore Sun* paid it. Scopes went to graduate school at the University of Chicago, earned a Master's Degree, and became an outstanding geologist. William Jennings Bryan died five days after the trial ended. The Tennessee Supreme Court later overturned the decision on a technicality, ruling that the jury, rather than the judge, was supposed to determine the amount of the fine. Two later court cases raised similar issues for public schools. *Edwards v. Aguillard,* 1987, voided a Louisiana law requiring the teaching of "creationism" if the theory of evolution was being taught; and *Kitzmiller v. Dover,* 2005, a Pennsylvania case, ended an attempt to make "intelligent design" part of the curriculum.

However, in one way the Fundamentalists won. The publishers modified the textbook involved in the trial, George Hunter's *Civic Biology.* They removed the word *evolution* from the textbook and the index, while keeping most of the text that presented evolution as a topic, thus angering Hunter. Even today over twenty states have textbook approval committees with citizen watchdogs, no particular level of education required, who must "approve" a textbook for use in that state. Smart publishers knuckle under to their not so subtle "suggestions" for presenting controversial topics. For example, if a student or teacher compares any of Shakespeare's plays in a high school textbook with another source, he or she will find that the "naughty" parts are missing in the textbook.

Nativism – Fear or Hatred of Foreigners

Congress passed three laws in the Twenties to control immigration – in 1921, 1924, and 1927. There was a huge surge in immigrants after the First World War. In 1919 only 100,000 came in, due to the chaotic aftermath of the war; in 1920, 430,000; in 1921, 805,000. The term "nativism" had been coined around 1840, during another era of concern over immigrants.

In the Red Scare atmosphere of the early Twenties there was a widespread fear of radicals, especially among businesspersons after the 1917 Bolshevik communist revolution. Normally business is not anti-immigrant because immigrants are a source of cheap labor. But, what radical ideas they brought. In Seattle, a general strike paralyzed the city, clearly an imported socialist European labor tactic. In Boston the police went on strike, horribly unheard of, and even un-American. Wartime inflation had completely undermined wages by the end of the war, which led to over four million workers going on strike, making it the greatest wave of labor unrest in American history. The hardest hit was the steel industry. Several prominent political leaders had bombs mailed to them. This rarely accomplishes its objective, because staff people open the mail. Unions also supported curtailing immigration because of a perceived competition for jobs.

Attorney General A. Mitchell Palmer overreacted or underreacted, depending on one's point of view. He ordered raids and deportations, overlooking any need to respect constitutional rights. The governor of Massachusetts, Calvin Coolidge, wrote an article for the *Saturday Evening Post*, a weekly magazine, *"Are the Reds Stalking Our College Women?"* He feared the spread of communist influence among female college students, because he thought they were too softhearted to be logical about economic dogma.

The patriotism stirred up to fight the First World War made Americans extremely anti-foreign. The Espionage Act of 1917 and an amendment to it, the 1918 Sedition Act, led to several sensational court cases. One judge, who sentenced 83 members of the radical union, the Industrial Workers of the World, to long prison terms, characterized German-Americans as a grave threat. "Their hearts are reeking with disloyalty." (John Nicholas, *The "S" Word: A Short History of an American Tradition . . . Socialism*, p. 159.) The socialist labor leader, Eugene V. Debs, was sentenced to ten years in the Atlanta Federal Penitentiary for a speech against the war, for saying that America's youth were "fit for something better than slavery and cannon fodder." As prisoner #9653, he received almost a million votes for president on the Socialist Party ticket in 1920. *Schenck v. U.S.* concerned defendants arrested for sending out 15,000 leaflets to draftees urging them to oppose the draft. It contained a copy of the Thirteenth Amendment, which outlawed slavery and "involuntary servitude," or the draft, according to them. In the case of *Abrams v. U.S.*, five Russian immigrants were arrested for writing anti-war propaganda. In Indiana, after the war ended, a jury deliberated two minutes before acquitting a man for murder for shooting a man in public who yelled, "To hell with the United States!" Oklahoma banned speaking German on the telephone, which probably made it harder to catch German spies. Leadership in the White House endorsed nativism. President Woodrow Wilson said of hyphenated Americans, "Any man who carries a hyphen about with him carries a dagger that he is ready to plunge into the vitals of this Republic whenever he gets ready." Theodore Roosevelt added, "There is no room in this country for hyphenated Americans."

A film producer spent ten years in prison for a Revolutionary War film that depicted the British, our current allies, in a poor light. Obviously, Americans fought against the British during the Revolutionary War. Later in the decade, in 1927, the Supreme Court ruled in *Rice v. Gong Lum* that Chinese students could be barred from white schools. There were limits, however. In 1919 Nebraska mandated that all teaching instruction must be in English. Imagine trying to teach a foreign language only in English. A teacher of German was arrested. The Supreme Court overturned the Nebraska law in *Meyer v. Nebraska* and upheld the right of a student to learn a foreign language. Probably no decade in American history matches some of this foolishness. None of it made the United States safer.

The huge influx of immigrants in 1921 scared many Americans, especially since there now existed convincing scientific proof of immigrant inferiority. During the First World War the army administered IQ tests to 1,750,000 draftees. The IQ test was part of new thinking about the mind and an embracing of the new science of statistics. The APA, the American Psychological Association, had been founded in 1895. In 1905 Alfred Binet and Theodore Simon devised an intelligence scale, tested children of all ages, and created "normal" definitions and ranges. A psychologist later introduced the term intelligence quotient, IQ, mental age divided by chronological age. First World War draftees took either the written Alpha test or the Beta test, which had pantomime instructions for illiterates. Begun in January 1918, eventually 1.7 million were tested. The testing was justified by the need to expand the army's officers from 9,000 to 200,000. Most recruits left school between the 5th and 7th grades, weighed 141 lbs., and averaged 5' 8½." The test "proved" that 47% of whites and 89% of blacks were feebleminded, meaning they had a mental age under 12 years old. One question was on Edgar Allen Poe's poem, "*The Raven*," which begins:

> "Once upon a midnight dreary, while I pondered, weak and weary,
> Over many a quaint and curious volume of forgotten lore—
> While I nodded, nearly napping, suddenly there came a tapping,
> As of some one gently rapping, rapping at my chamber door.
> Tis some visitor," I muttered, "tapping at my chamber door—
> Only this and nothing more."

Are you familiar with rest of the poem, or in the category of the feebleminded? !!!

In 1912 a psychologist administered IQ tests to a very small sample of immigrants. Modern statisticians laugh at the unscientific size of his sample. You need at least 400 plus to be accurate within 2-3%. He used less than 40 to conclude that feeblemindedness was typical of our immigrants, so labelling 83% of Jews, 80% of Hungarians, 79% of Italians, and 87% of Russians. Politicians jumped on this "scientific" research to justify closing the gates to protect America.

All this IQ testing proved what everyone already believed. Yet, it did not. Originally, the army Beta test showed no difference between the scores for blacks and whites. The test questions were changed until a difference appeared. The United States is once more in an age when testing "accurately" describes every single student. Surely students wonder who makes up these questions and what their assumptions are. As another example of how completely this era embraced testing, many colleges began to use the College Entrance Examination, the SAT, seen originally as a "pure" intelligence test, which accurately predicted academic performance for the first year of college.

The Immigration Acts

On thirty-two different occasions one house of Congress had passed a literacy test for immigrants. The House of Representatives had recently passed a literacy test five times – 1895, 1897, 1913, 1915, and 1917. The Senate passed all but the first. The president vetoed each one; however, Congress passed the 1917 act over Wilson's veto. Some Americans argued that immigrants benefited American culture. In his 1916 essay, "*Trans-National America*," philosopher Randolph Bourne characterized American society as a "federation of cultures" enriched by immigrant music, customs, food, and other expressions, representing one definition of our **American Identity**. Randolph Bourne was a leftist social critic who argued against what many commentators claimed was the failure of the "melting pot" to blend all immigrants into a seamless American society. The Twenties brought a challenge to Bourne's defense of a "federation of cultures."

Francis A. Walker, a professor of political economy at Yale, feared what was then called "race suicide," the failure of the "decent" middle and upper classes to reproduce sufficiently to maintain their numbers, and thus, their control. Our country faced a new threat.

> "The entrance into our political, social, and industrial life of such vast masses of peasantry, degraded below our utmost conceptions, is a matter of which no intelligent patriot can look upon without the gravest apprehension and alarm. These people have no history behind them which is of a nature to give encouragement. They have none of the inherited instincts and tendencies which made it comparatively easy to deal with the immigration of olden times. They are beaten men from beaten races; representing the worst failures in the struggle for existence."

Another scholar called immigrants "hirsute, low-browed, big-faced persons of obviously low mentality. . . . (who) clearly belong in skins, in wattled huts at the close of the Great Ice Age. These oxlike men are descendants of those who always stayed behind."

The new immigration laws hit Southern and Eastern Europeans hard. The 1924 law, the Johnson-Reed Act or National Origins Act, established a method for determining the number permitted from each nation by basing it upon that nation's percentage of the population here in the 1910 census. Total European immigration was limited to 150,000 per year. When everyone realized that it still let in too many inferior "beaten men from beaten races," Southern and Eastern Europeans, Congress changed the base year in 1927 to the 1890 census. For several examples of the impact of the revised law:

The 1910 Base:	The 1890 Base:
42,000 Italians	6,000 Italians
3,000 Greeks	100 Greeks
30,000 Poles	6,000 Poles

Each nation was guaranteed 100. The tiny European nation of Andorra was permitted 100, as was Greece. Asians were barred. The new laws also created a new category, the "illegal alien," leading to the creation of the federal government's Border Patrol. A new category was added to the census for 1930 – Mexican. They had been "white" in 1920.

Prohibition

The first effective single-issue lobby organizations in American history, the Anti-Saloon League and the Woman's Christian Temperance Union, or the WCTU, were the powers behind the passage of the Eighteenth Amendment and the Volstead Act, which implemented prohibition after the Eighteenth Amendment became part of the Constitution. The campaign focused on the urban saloon, seen as a place that promoted poverty and where unions recruited members and planned strikes. It was widely believed that immigrant drinking was the cause of poverty. The old question was answered, "Do people drink because they are poor or are they poor because they drink?" They are poor because they drink; every reformer knew that. Wiping out alcohol would wipe out poverty. Liquor was a threat to the family unit, destroying the happy home. In addition, without alcohol, safety in the work force would improve.

Overall, it was a "noble experiment," an attempt to make people and the world better. Many celebrated in saloons the night before prohibition went into effect. A new world was dawning; people were happy that their children would be free from the demon rum. Almost every family had someone who drank too much. It did not work out as foreseen. There were less than 3,000 federal agents in the Prohibition Bureau for the whole country, an insufficient number to enforce prohibition. That number reveals the lack of commitment on the part of Congress to fund Prohibition. Enforcement was also very low on the priority list for most local police departments.

Attention-Getting Court Cases

The Twenties had several sensational court cases in addition to the Scopes trial. In Massachusetts the Sacco and Vanzetti case spanned the whole decade and became a polarizing issue. Two immigrants were convicted of a murder committed during a robbery. Did they do it? On the other hand, were they primarily guilty of being foreigners?

Or, radicals? Debate still rages among scholars. The truth is unclear. However, does it really matter? What many Americans believed was that the country had gotten rid of two radical immigrants who had no good reason to be here. The whole episode shocked many intellectuals, sparking protests here at home and in Europe. Nicola Sacco and Bartolomeo Vanzetti were pardoned in 1977, long after they were executed. In another case in Illinois two young men, Nathan Leopold and Richard Loeb, were convicted of killing a young boy in a murder for the thrill of it. One dropped his glasses at the murder scene, which had a rare prescription, eventually leading the police to him. Watch Alfred Hitchcock's riveting film, "*Rope*," based on this case. Many Americans asked, "What is wrong with our youth?" Years later, shootings at Sandy Hook Elementary School in Connecticut, Columbine High School in Colorado, and Emanuel African Methodist Episcopal Church in Charleston, South Carolina, evoked a similar question. In every case it probably only meant that there were one or two nuts loose.

Concerns over moral values tend to surface during periods of relative prosperity. During the Twenties rural, small town America fought against the sins of urban America over loose sexual standards, alcohol, and the role of the Bible in public education. The urbanites seemed to win those battles. In addition, conflicts arose over our **American Identity**. Was there a place for immigrants and blacks within American society? Americans focused on these questions and issues during the decade. Little did they realize what desperate economic concerns were on the horizon. Concerns over moral values were shortly to evaporate.

38

THE CRASH AND THE GREAT DEPRESSION

Definitions – Depression, Recession

There is an old joke that a recession is when you lose your job and a depression is when I lose mine. This is not far from the truth. A depression is a severe downturn in the economy, generally defined as at least a 10% drop in the Gross Domestic Product. A recession is a less severe decline in the economy that lasts for at least two consecutive quarters, six months.

The Initial Crash

One must differentiate between the 1929 stock market crash and the depression. The stock market crash refers only to the drop in stock prices. It does not necessarily have to lead to a depression. The stock market crashed for many reasons. One was the too rapid rise in stock prices that preceded the crash. General Electric went up in 18 months from $128 to $396, RCA, Radio Corporation of America, from $94 to $505. A buying frenzy developed prior to the crash, with many speculators and brokers buying stocks on margin with borrowed money, meaning they put a small percentage down, such as 10%, toward their purchase and promised to pay the rest in a short time, such as 30 days. They believed that with the rising price of stocks they could sell in 30 days and gain enough to pay off the loan and still have a large profit left over. It worked, until falling stock prices left a debt that exceeded any price they could get for their stock purchased on margin, on which they owed money. This set off a selling panic, which only drove stock prices down faster, causing the crash.

A total of $32 billion evaporated during October 1929. By 1932 the losses hit $74 billion, three times the total cost of the First World War. Stocks dropped to 11% of their highest value. Try to imagine a person buying a car for $40,000 and realizing a month later that he or she had to sell it, and the best offer was $4,400.

Stock owners and brokers did not actually lose that much money because unless you sell the stock, you do not have the money that you would have made as a profit. All you have is the feeling that "I could have been rich." If you did not sell the stock, you never really had the money. What disappeared were paper profits. Joseph Kennedy, future president John F. Kennedy's father, a notorious stock manipulator, pulled out of the stock market in September when his shoeshine boy started giving him stock tips. Kennedy realized the stock market was malfunctioning.

It is curious that the crash happened at the end of the 1920s. That decade saw the "cult of the businessman." In the Twenties the covers of *Time* magazine featured more businessmen than during any other decade in our history, before or since. The business class mistakenly thought their corporate interest coincided with the national interest. The best example of that attitude is a misquote from the 1950s, "What is good for General Motors is good for the country." (Charles Wilson, the president of GM, actually replied to a Senate Committee asking him to sell his GM stock before becoming Secretary of Defense with, "because for years I thought what was good for our country was good for General Motors, and vice versa.") Misquote or not, the attitude was there in the Twenties – the national interest and the corporate interest were synonymous.

Innovators like Pierre S. du Pont and Alfred Sloan at General Motors fine-tuned corporate management practices, stimulating expansion. This "managerial revolution," the rise of the professional manager, and the creation of the Federal Reserve System in 1913, led businessmen to believe that as professional managers they could, through data gathering and economic intelligence, head off any depression. The public agreed. In 1929 $6 billion worth of IPOs, initial public offerings of stock for new companies, were issued, $1 billion in September – one month before the crash. They did not see it coming.

Incomes initially dropped 4%; but purchasing dropped 20%. Recessions and depressions frighten people into curtailing spending, which pushes the decline even deeper. President Herbert Hoover tried to cheerlead the way out:

> "Prosperity is just around the corner."
> "Nobody is actually starving."
> "The hobos, for example, are better fed than they have ever been."
> "The fundamental business of the country is on a sound and prosperous basis."

He made the last statement the day after Black Thursday, October 24, 1929, the first severe drop in stock prices. Black Tuesday, an even greater drop, followed five days later. His Secretary of the Treasury, Andrew Mellon, said, "I see nothing in the present situation that is either menacing or warrants pessimism." This raises a significant question that still applies – do statements by politicians have a major impact on the economy to any great degree?

Hoover earlier stated in the 1928 campaign that he envisioned the president's role in the economy as that of an "umpire instead of a player in the economic game." The job of the government was to give advice and to gather useful information, useful to various segments of the economy. The president should not take action. As an example of the federal government's limited economic responsibilities, the first year the federal government ever gathered reliable unemployment statistics was 1930.

Hoover actually did more to fight the depression than any previous president had ever done. However, it was grossly inadequate. For example, he got Congress to pass the RFC, the Reconstruction Finance Corporation, which loaned $3 billion to businesses in an attempt to stabilize the economy, a tactic repeated later by President Barack Obama. Hoover also supported a bill to increase the availability of mortgages, which became the Federal Home Loan Bank Act, in many ways the basis for the New Deal's Federal Housing Administration. In addition, he pushed for the Glass-Steagall Banking Act of 1932, to increase the number of loans to individuals and businesses. None of it seemed to substantially affect the economy.

Why From a Crash to a Depression?
Once again, differentiate between the 1929 stock market crash and the depression. The stock market crash refers only to the drop in stock prices. Because it immediately hurts only those who own stocks, it does not necessarily have to lead to a depression. The years 1987 and 2008 saw similar steep drops in the stock market. Why was there a depression after 1929, a recession in 2008, and nothing in 1987? For 1929 these reasons have been offered by economists and historians:

A Bad Distribution of Income
The bad distribution of income throughout the economy had consequences following the crash in 1929. The top 5% of the population received one-third of all personal income, equal to that of the bottom 42%. If those at the top reduced their spending, it significantly impacted the economy. Since many of them owned stock and lost potential gains in the crash, they were frightened into curtailing spending, an attitude they carried to work as corporate executives. Much of the Twenties economic boom rested on consumer credit purchases. Buying on credit by the lower two-thirds of the population stimulated the economy, but it meant that their future dollars were now unavailable for purchasing, because those dollars were committed to paying their personal debt. Look at these economic statistics:

> productivity in the 1920s went up 42%
> output per worker went up 43% (the difference between productivity
>   and output is due to the use of labor saving devices and machinery)
> profits went up 62%

dividends went up 65%

workers' wages went up only 12%

pay for factory workers went up only 20%

In other words, corporations made money, lots of money, but most of the increased profit went to stockholders and corporation mangers, not to the workers, who collectively constituted the backbone of the purchasing public. The popular image of the Twenties is that it was one long party, with liberated young women, the Charleston dance craze, and lots of moonshine liquor, *The Great Gatsby* writ large. You got a different tale if you interviewed the entire working class, especially farmers and factory workers. In addition, capital investment did not keep up with profits; the rich got greedy and did not reinvest their profits back into the businesses. The great industrialist Andrew Carnegie frequently said that the road to wealth was to plow the profits back into the business. Not in the Twenties; it did not happen.

Too Much Bad Corporate Restructuring

"A flood tide of corporate larceny" hit when companies purchased other companies. The Twenties saw a great increase in the number of holding companies and investment trusts, which did not increase production and added nothing to productivity, while increasing the purchasing corporation's debt. For those corporations, too much corporate income was earmarked for debt repayment. Dividends from operating companies, those producing a product or service, paid for the stocks and bonds of holding companies, a sort of reverse leverage. Think of the situation when Company A buys Company B and then fires part of the workforce of Company B to help pay for the takeover of Company B. Where is there an increase in productivity in this scenario? Nowhere. Company A gets larger and acquires more debt. Structural weaknesses lay under what seemed to be a solid corporate structure. In 1930, 26,355 business firms went bankrupt.

For a later example, at one time Seagram's, the Canadian whiskey company, tried to gain control of the DuPont Company by slowly and silently buying DuPont stock. They got about 35%, enough to obtain a few positions on the DuPont Company Board of Directors. What did the money used to purchase the DuPont stock do for the Seagram's Company? Nothing at all. That money could have been used to reinvest in Seagram's to increase productivity. Instead it simply bought stock in another company, neither increasing productivity nor output nor quality nor sales in either company.

Bad Banking Structure

The weak banks not only destroyed the other weak banks; they also weakened the strong banks. From just January to June 1929, before the October stock market crash, 346 banks failed. Any savings account a person had in one of these banks was gone, forever.

This led lots of people to distrust banks. Consequently, many people saved their money by stuffing it "under their mattress," which meant that less money was available in banks for someone to borrow to invest in their company or to build a house. This lead to fewer jobs being created.

Foreign Trade Problems

High tariffs compounded international trade problems. Both the Fordney-McCumber Tariff, 1922, and the Hawley-Smoot Tariff, 1930, created barriers to trade. The first introduced the "American selling price," which stipulated that the tariff on imported goods was based on the selling price of that item in the U.S. domestic market. It raised the price of all imported items above the price of American products. Twenty-three other nations retaliated by raising their tariffs on American exports. Over a thousand economists urged President Hoover to not sign the Hawley-Smoot Tariff, passed by Congress in 1930. He did anyway. It was politically difficult not to sign a bill ostensibly protecting American businesses. Once any company felt that it could no longer increase its sales in the American domestic market, the best move for that company was to expand their exports, increasing sales in foreign markets. However, high tariffs in foreign countries hindered the selling of American products. If one country raised its tariffs, other countries raised their tariffs in retaliation. The net impact of every country raising tariffs to "protect" their own businesses was to hurt all businesses, everywhere. It was self-defeating. Between 1929 and 1932, world trade dropped 60 percent.

A high tariff sounds good politically. "I am the candidate for office who will protect American jobs." That statement needs a disclaimer – "but not necessarily your job." As any economist will explain, because countries specialize in the products they can produce more cheaply, called "comparative advantage," increased trade benefits both American companies, who are able to gain new markets, and American consumers, who enjoy lower prices on imported goods. Workers and consumers in both countries benefit. In the subsequent reorientation of segments of each country's economy, some American industries will gain jobs. However, because some American workers will lose their jobs, lowering tariffs is politically dangerous. This is why President Lyndon Johnson, LBJ, once said, "Be a free trader and don't tell anyone."

The war debts imbroglio presented an additional impediment to international trade and finances after the First World War. The war left Great Britain, and especially France, in dismal economic shape. Both our wartime allies encountered difficulties paying back their debts owed to the United States for loans during the war to purchase supplies. They argued that since many more British and France soldiers had been killed during the war, their nations' sacrifices more than matched the money the U.S. had loaned to them. Unequal sacrifices meant that there was no need to pay back the loans. Americans did not view this issue in the same light. Throughout the 1920s and 1930s the American public increasingly believed that our entry into the First World War had been a mistake, peaking at 64% by 1937. The war debts issue ranked as the number one reason. A debt is a debt, pay up. The Versailles Treaty forced Germany to pay the costs, called reparations, for all damages caused by the First World War. Germany paid reparations to France and Great Britain – Great Britain and France paid back their loans to the United States. When Germany could no longer pay, the U.S. banks issued new loans to Germany. The money traveled in a circle. All that was needed to disrupt the cycle was one country sliding into economic trouble. Germany hit the bottom first, by the mid-1920s. The worldwide depression put every country into economic trouble, leading to an international economic imbroglio. Who would or could purchase our products? Or anyone's products?

The Sorry State of Economic Intelligence

Around the world national economies struggled to recover from the dislocating and disrupting impact of the First World War. The years prior to the war marked the first real era of globalization, especially in finance. In many countries, financial wizards (?) blamed financial globalization for *causing* the war. Retreating toward the goal of self-sufficiency, called autarky, politicians in every country sought legislation to restrict trade, migration, and the flow of investment. Their vision of their economy stopped at the nation's borders. Thank goodness that shortsightedness did not happen after the Second World War.

The decade of the Twenties was "a triumph of dogma over thought." Mistakes were made in many respects. First, two definitions:

> Monetary policy is the controlling of the nation's money supply.
> Fiscal policy is the government's taxing and spending policies.

In the late 1920s the Federal Reserve, fearing inflation, tightened credit, which was the opposite monetary policy it should have followed after the crash. Many economists say tight credit is the most important factor in turning a recession into a depression. This policy made individuals and businesses unwilling to borrow, and therefore unwilling to spend. The price of money, the interest rate charged by banks, was too high.

In 1930 the federal government had a budget surplus, which was the opposite fiscal policy it should have followed. Instead of removing money from the national economy, the government should have spent money by running a deficit in order to stimulate economic growth. Early in the crash and initial downturn, both fiscal policy and monetary policy were misused or rejected. However, both are in truth sometimes politically difficult to sell to the public right before an election. No voter likes a tax increase, even if it will prevent inflation in the future.

A Fundamental Change in Consumer Thinking

In the Twenties consumers, influenced by increased advertising, accepted the idea of consumer debt and shook off the old-fashioned ideas of thrift and self-denial. They purchased cars, radios, and household electrical appliances in order to enjoy an increased standard of living. However, once a purchase was made by credit, those dollars were no longer available to stimulate the economy in the future.

Europe's Non-Recovery

Europe's inability to rebound from the First World War put a drag on the world's economy. The British historian, Eric Hobsbawm, called the years from 1914 to 1948 "The Age of Catastrophe." Hyperinflation in Germany reached incredible heights, dropping the value of a German mark, the equivalent of the American dollar. In 1914 one dollar equaled 4.2 marks, but by November, 1923, a dollar was worth 4,200,000,000,000 marks (4.2 trillion). Thus, marks became worthless, except if burned as fuel. Unemployment in Europe rose after the war, averaging 10-18 percent, and never returned to normal prewar numbers. Only the economy of the United States recovered to full employment in the Twenties. At the depth of the Great Depression's unemployment crisis, every European nation suffered higher unemployment than did the United States. The term was not used then, but the "global economy" was already here, and it was not working very well.

An Inventory Recession

An inventory recession preceded the October crash, weakening the economy. Factory and store inventories were too large; thus, some workers were laid off. This further reduced consumption, because the laid-off workers could not spend money they no longer received. Then came the stock market crash. A fear of the unknown paralyzed everyone. Initially, following the crash, wages dipped only 4%, but consumer spending went down 20% because people were afraid that their future income would decline. By not spending money, this led to more workers being laid off, thus creating a further decline.

So, Why a Depression?

Stock prices dropped 75%, a huge decline, but they had been too high. In addition, only about 2-3% of the population even owned stocks, 4 million people out of 120 million. The price-earnings ratio, the P-E ratio, is the relationship between the price of the stock and the dividend paid by the company. If the P-E ratio is 20-1, or 5%, it means that a stock worth one dollar will earn five cents a year in dividends. If the P-E ratio is 33-1, or 3%, it means that a stock worth one dollar will earn three cents a year. P-E ratios in the Twenties dropped below one percent for many stocks, soaring to over 100-1. Clearly, the stock prices were too high. However, optimism still prevailed. Many felt that they could always make more money by selling the stock at a higher price within a short time. Too many speculators (they were not investors!) thought that P-E ratios were an old-fashioned indicator of the value of a stock. The market was going to keep going up, up, up, up, and, everybody would get rich! Black Thursday popped that bubble.

Statistics – What the Depression Meant Between 1929 and 1933

The average weekly wage dropped from $25.03 to $16.73.

Annual per capita income dropped from $857 to $446.

The average number of hours worked per week dropped from 44.2 to 38.1. This means that very few workers logged overtime and the average worker who kept his or her job still faced reduced income.

Unemployment rose from 3.2% to 25%. If the modern definition of unemployment is used, the overall national rate was actually closer to 33%. It was up to 50% in some cities. Where do urban unemployed people get food? The rural poor often had gardens. In addition, there was the concept of *underemployment*, those who still worked but now worked far fewer hours than previously. Technically they were employed, and therefore not among the unemployment statistics. However, their reduced hours meant their pocketbooks had less money.

GDP, the Gross Domestic Product, the value of all the nation's goods and services produced in one year, dropped from $104 billion to $56 billion.

Corporate income fell from $161,158,206,000 to $84,234,006,000.

Dividends declined from $9,808,455,000 to $3,229,502,000.

The wholesale price index fell from 61.9 to 42.8, meaning wholesale prices dropped by one-third.

The index of farm prices fell from 58.6 to 28.7, meaning farm prices dropped by more than 50%. A bushel of wheat in Chicago sold for $2.98 in 1920, $1 in 1929, and 30 cents in 1930. Why bother planting it? Meanwhile people were starving in the cities.

Land prices dropped by 50%.

Construction bottomed out, with non-residential construction dropping from $2,694,000,000 to $406,000,000, down 85%; residential construction fell from $3,625,000,000 to $470,000,000, down 87%. Residential building had already been weak before the downturn, a harbinger of things to come. After hitting a peak in 1925, home building permits fell 30% by 1929 and collapsed in the early depression years. By 1939 home building permits had not returned to even the rock-bottom 1930 level. Farm construction was no better, falling from $307,000,000 to $49,000,000, down 84%.

By 1933 seven million families had NO income. Unemployment in Rhode Island was 36%, in Michigan, 45%, and even higher in the major cities.

From 1929 to 1933 the Depression Worsened

The U.S. Steel Company in 1928 had 225,000 workers. In April, 1933, the company employed zero workers; the mangers had even fired themselves. Overall, steel production was down to one-fifth of capacity.

Agricultural prices dropped 86% between 1929 and 1933. American grain prices dropped to match those during the reign of England's Elizabeth I, 1558-1603.

In April, 1932, 4,000 immigrant workers sailed back to Europe.

In 1933 one-half of all mortgages were technically in default; actual foreclosures averaged one thousand per day.

Two million young people roamed the country. It was not spring break. They were looking for work.

An estimated 27% of Pennsylvania schoolchildren suffered from malnutrition.

In the worst years Chicago teachers received empty pay envelopes for five out of thirteen months. Many survived by eating supper with a different student's family each night.

An African village in Cameroon heard of the plight of New York City's poor and mailed the village's total cash, $3.77, for the relief of the poor in New York City.

Shanty-towns sprang up everywhere, nicknamed Hoovervilles. One was 38 blocks long beside the Hudson River in New York City. "Hoover blankets," as newspapers were called, kept many warm. "Hoover cars" provided transportation in the rural South, cars stripped of their engine and most heavy parts and then hooked up to a mule.

On the Hit Parade in 1932 two of the number one songs that year were "Can I Sleep in Your Barn Tonight, Mister?" and "Brother, Can You Spare a Dime?"

The Election of 1932 – FDR

In spite of depression, or war, or anything, the United States still holds a presidential election every four years. The Republicans reluctantly re-nominated Herbert Hoover. It would be an admission of failure to not re-nominate a sitting president. The Democrat candidate, Franklin D. Roosevelt, won in a landslide, 472-59 in the electoral vote. The inauguration was not until March 4. The Twentieth-second Amendment, passed in 1933, would change the inauguration date to our present January 20. Between the election in November and the inauguration on March 4, the economy sank deeper and deeper. FDR had no power yet, and Hoover, for all practical purposes, was no longer president.

On Inauguration Day the army placed machine guns on the rooftops along the route from the Capitol back to the White House, ready for whatever uprising might be coming and whatever revolution might break out. It was one of the darkest days in our history. Then FDR gave his inaugural speech, with that memorable line, "The only thing we have to fear is fear itself." His upbeat speech, his big smile, and his campaign song, "Happy Days are Here Again," offered hope. Everyone wondered, "Now what?" So did the new president. At this stage his New Deal was more of a slogan than a concrete plan to fight the depression.

But what could the federal government possibly do? It was not a presence in the lives of many Americans. Historian William Leuchtenburg described it perfectly.

> "If you had walked into any American town in 1932, you would have had a hard time detecting any sign of a federal presence, save perhaps for the post office and even many of today's post offices date from the 1930s. Washington rarely affected people's lives directly. There was no national old-age pension system, no federal unemployment compensation, no aid to dependent children, no federal housing, no regulation of the stock market, no withholding tax, no federal school lunch, no farm subsidy, no national minimum wage law, no welfare state."

(William Leuchtenburg, "The Achievement of the New Deal," Harvard Sitkoff, ed., *Fifty Years Later: The New Deal Evaluated*, Knopf, 1985)

By the time the Second World War began to draw most of the nation's attention, much had changed because of the New Deal in those American towns, and in the cities, and on the farms.

39

FDR AND THE NEW DEAL

What Was "New" about the New Deal?

First Innovation: The federal government has **the duty to intervene in all aspects of economic life**. Washington, D.C., assumed a responsibility for planning and managing the economy, fulfilling the promise in the Preamble to the Constitution to "promote the general welfare." The federal government assumed the obligation to maintain the nation's prosperity. So did other governments around the world. In 1935 the prime minister, R. B. Bennett, a staunch conservative, shocked the Canadian public by stating "that free competition and the open market place, as they were known in the old days, have lost their place in the system, and that the only substitute for them, in modern times, is government regulation and control." Why? While earlier depressions were maladjustments in the economy, "this depression is a catastrophe, and therefore demands the intervention of the Government . . . ."

Washington, D.C., assumed a duty to promote a reasonably fair distribution not only of wealth, but also of power and status, what Franklin D. Roosevelt called "the good things of life." This equitable sharing of prosperity would include those previously excluded. This also shows up in FDR's pre-Second World War "Four Freedoms" speech, which included freedom from fear and freedom from want.

How was this to be accomplished? It would have to be done by using two federal government economic tools, monetary policy and fiscal policy, to manipulate and fine-tune the economy. John Maynard Keynes, a British economist, originated these ideas; hence, the approach is called Keynesian economics.

Monetary policy means using the powers of the federal government to control the price and volume of money. The price of money is the interest rate; the volume of money is the amount of money in the economy. Both these factors – interest rates and the amount of money in circulation – influence and control the rate of inflation in the economy. In theory, having high interest rates and high inflation at the same time is impossible, but it happened in the 1970s. The injustice of raising interest rates is that it affects some segments of the population immediately and hurts some segments more than others, such as builders of homes, real estate salespeople, automobile salespeople, and students beginning college.

Fiscal policy means using the powers of the federal government to control the taxing and spending policies of the federal government. By raising taxes the government takes money out of circulation, by lowering taxes the government puts money into circulation. The question is how much and which set of consumers benefit – poor, middle, or rich. If the government decides to lower spending or to not spend, it fails to stimulate the economy. This puts the brakes on an economy experiencing inflation. The injustice of the manipulation of fiscal policy is that it affects some segments of the population immediately or hurts others more. Changes in our incredibly complex tax code, through cuts or new taxes, benefit some and hurt others. For example, today's policy of no tax on the capital gains on the sale of a home (a concept that was part of the income tax code as originally implemented in 1913) up to $500,000 per couple or $250,000 per individual, stimulates the real estate industry, but it also disproportionately benefits those who own more valuable homes.

Through the multiplier effect the government stimulates the economy by spending money. The impact can be multiples as high as seven. Why? How? For each federal dollar spent, the business or person who receives it saves a small percentage and then spends the remainder, as does every other business or person who subsequently receives what is left of the original dollar. Eventually, that one dollar may be spent as much as seven times, which means the economy is stimulated by seven dollars, not just by the original one dollar. Conversely, when the government takes a dollar out of the economy by increasing a tax, the net impact is equivalent to taking more than one dollar out of the economy. Why? Because the average person saves a certain percentage of each dollar he or she earns, which becomes available for banks to lend to others. If a new tax takes a dollar out of circulation, part of it will not be available for investment, and the economy will not be stimulated by spending the remainder. If the savings rate changes, the number seven in this example would go up or down.

The major difficulty with the Keynesian approach is that either tactic – monetary policy or fiscal policy – hurts some segment of the economy, which is not a wise thing to do politically. Voters remember tax increases. Political considerations also adversely affect the timing of policy changes or implementation. This means that the correct policy is often not followed when it should be, worsening the economic situation. When did voters ever hear of a politician winning election to office on a promise to raise taxes? If there is a period of inflation, money needs to be taken out of circulation to reduce the inflation. The voter says, "Take somebody else's money." In a society that holds equality in high esteem, any governmental act seen as unfairly impacting one segment of the population will get a politician in deep trouble. The political difficulties involved in applying Keynesian economics explain why it has never been consistently applied over an extended period of time.

Second Innovation: The second innovation of the New Deal gave birth to the **welfare state**, the idea that there should be a floor below which individuals should not be permitted to fall financially, and a ceiling above which individuals should not be permitted to rise, enforced by high taxes. Conservative critics misunderstood the welfare state. In many ways it preserved capitalism by giving those at the bottom the hope of upward movement, the dream of opportunity, without guaranteeing that individual's desired outcome. "You are not cemented in your place; work hard, rise." It preserved the class nature of society while dangling before an individual the hope of rising. The welfare state did not intend to threaten or to replace capitalism. It was superimposed on the capitalist system and left the profit motive in place. Over time, holes appeared in both the floor and the ceiling. At one time as much as $5\frac{1}{2}\%$ of the federal budget went for welfare, now it is $1\frac{1}{2}\%$. President Bill Clinton's 1996 Personal Responsibility and Work Opportunity Act virtually ended the federal government's welfare role, limiting the time one could receive welfare and shifting almost all governmental administrative responsibility to the states.

Third Innovation: The third innovation was to provide **a sense of security** – to the economy, to individuals, and to society – for example, with mortgages and Social Security. Many New Deal social policies – such as the insuring of savings accounts, mortgage insurance, Social Security, and unemployment insurance – were efforts to insure individuals against the risks of modern society. Americans did not have to look far to see these ideas in action. They had been in place elsewhere for decades in Europe, New Zealand, and Australia. Germany pioneered in beginning social security under Bismarck in the late nineteenth century.

Efforts in three areas accomplished these goals. New Deal policies focused on relief, recovery, and reform. In truth, there are elements of each in almost every piece of New Deal legislation. They are arbitrarily categorized below.

Recovery

The crisis atmosphere of 1929 to 1933 frightened everyone. FDR won election in November, but he did not take office until March 4, 1933, as the Constitution originally stipulated. During these four months the economy continued its plunge, uncertain about the future. Some said that 1929 would one day be in the history books alongside 476 AD, the fall of the Roman Empire and the beginning of the first Dark Ages. The year 1929 would begin the second Dark Ages. A dying former president, Calvin

Coolidge, was asked by a reporter on January 1, 1933, what he foresaw for the future of the country. His reply, "I see no hope for mankind." This, coming from an insider, gave people pause. He died four days later. Many individuals believe that dying people, worried about their soul, always tell the truth. Hence, they thought that this must be the end of Western civilization. For the first time in the history of capitalism, dating from Adam Smith's *The Wealth of Nations*, 1776, the very existence of capitalism seemed endangered.

FDR said little during the campaign about his plans. Assured of victory, he did not want to alienate any potential group of voters. This led one popular political commentator, Walter Lippmann, to describe FDR in 1932 as "a pleasant man, who, without any important qualifications for office, would very much like to be President." Witty, but inaccurate. As the governor of New York since 1929, FDR had begun many initiatives to fight the effects of the depression within the state of New York. On Monday, March 4, 1933, FDR took the oath of office. He went immediately to the White House to begin working with his advisors, nicknamed the "brain trust," (also called the "brains trust") mostly academics with pet proposals. There were no inaugural balls, no celebrations. Essentially, FDR adopted a "do anything" approach to fight the Depression.

Thus began the most productive burst of Congressional output in our history, the "Hundred Days," which produced 15 major pieces of legislation. Congress presented almost no opposition to White House proposals, partly because the Democratic Party controlled both houses and partly because Congress was ready to try anything to help the desperate situation. In the Senate it was 60-35, Democrats to Republicans. Democrats would gain nine senators in the 1934 elections. In the House of Representatives, it was 310-117, Democrats to Republicans. Democrats would gain nine Representatives in the 1934 elections. It is rare for the party in power in the White House to increase its representation in the Senate or House during an off year election. The Democratic Party gains in the 1934 mid-term, non-presidential election year show how desperate the situation remained.

Banks – The immediate crisis was the lack of cash in the economy. *Fortune* magazine estimated that 27.5 million Americans had no regular income. By March 4, 1933, all the banks were closed in 38 of the 48 states. The entire banking system was bankrupt. Overall bank reserves were down to $6 billion, against liabilities of $41 billion. During the week before the inauguration, frightened wealthy people withdrew $250,000,000 in gold from banks. There is a theory among some investors that gold will keep its value because it is a precious and prized commodity, like diamonds. The problem with gold is that it may go down in value, be stolen, or fail to appreciate, and of course, it cannot generate interest or investment income. In the past forty to fifty years, gold has dropped in value. However, if a person no longer trusts the currency, the government, or the future, he or she will grab anything they believe is durable.

Out of the advisors huddled around the president emerged a proposed bill. On Saturday, March 9, the **Emergency Banking Relief Act**, actually written by Hoover's Treasury officials, was introduced into the House of Representatives at 1 o'clock, passed by a voice vote after 38 minutes of debate (only one copy of the bill was available), passed by the Senate 73-7 at 7:30 pm, and signed by the president at 8:36 pm. It holds the record for the fastest piece of legislation ever adopted. Sunday night, before the banks reopened on Monday, the president gave the first of his "fireside chats" over the radio, telling the public the banks were now safe. On Monday morning people lined up to put their money back into banks. They trusted their new president. Raymond Moley, an advisor who later broke with Roosevelt and became a bitter critic, always believed that Roosevelt "saved capitalism in eight days." The newly created **FDIC, Federal Deposit Insurance Corporation**, insured individual bank accounts up to $5,000 per account and stopped panic runs on banks. The American Bankers Association, beginning the attack on the New Deal by the rich and well-born, pronounced it "unsound, unscientific, unjust and dangerous." They had nothing to suggest in place of it.

SEC – The Securities Exchange Act created the **Securities and Exchange Commission** to stop dishonest stock manipulation. Corporate officers had to disclose every important element about their stock, including insider trading and ownership, to prevent fraud. FDR appointed Joseph Kennedy, future president John F. Kennedy's father, as the first head. When FDR was criticized for appointing him, he replied, "Who else do you put in charge of the hen house?" The answer, of course, is the fox; he knows all the tricks. Joseph Kennedy had a reputation as a notorious stock manipulator; he knew all the tricks.

AAA – the **Agricultural Adjustment Act.** This idea came from Milburn Wilson, a Montana State College professor. Because overproduction caused the farming crisis, something needed to be done to reduce production to stabilize prices. Because this bill was passed in May, after crops had been planted, farmers were paid $6-$20 per acre to plow their crops under and to kill farm animals. Federal government volunteers, 23,000, enforced the law by visiting farms. In short, farmers were paid to NOT produce. The Secretary of Agriculture defended it as not the ideal of "any sane society," but necessary due to the "almost insane lack of world statesmanship in stabilizing world prices." In the South, where many farmers still used mules for plowing, farmers had difficulty getting them to walk over the crops, which they had been trained not to do. Critics said the mules were smarter than Washington. In the West, farmers drove sheep and cows over cliffs. Baby pigs had their throats slit. Meanwhile many in the cities were hungry. Why not give the farm crops to the hungry? Because it would not raise the price of farm goods, the problem the AAA was trying to solve, since prices were too low.

NRA – the **National Recovery Act**. In industry the problem was seen as too much competition. The solution, therefore, was to establish codes regulating each industry whereby government, labor, and industry would work together to bring rational stability to production and pricing, and then to divide up the market. Over 500 industries developed codes, written primarily by the largest firms in that industry. Who benefited? In order – big business, smaller business firms, labor unions, and at the bottom, consumers. However, the codes had no enforcement provisions; compliance was voluntary. Each code recognized the right of unions to exist in that industry, as provided in section 7a of the National Recovery Act, a great victory for organized labor. The minimum wage, then $12 a week, was introduced, and maximum work hours were set at 40 hours per week. The average wage for those who still had a job was $50-$60 per week; thus the minimum wage was low, as it remains today, especially if one were to ask workers. Stores displayed Blue Eagle stickers to show compliance with the NRA, just as today stores display symbols indicating what credit cards they accept.

Both the AAA and the NRA made mistakes. There were no precedents for such new and tricky approaches as official price fixing, subsidies, and production controls. President Coolidge once said that government programs, once begun, have alike no end and no justice. This may be true, but it can also be said of many programs and policies adopted by any business, bureaucracy, or institution. The Supreme Court later declared both the AAA and the NRA unconstitutional; otherwise, it is difficult to see how politicians would have ended them.

The *Schechter Poultry* case in 1935 declared the NRA unconstitutional. Four Schechter brothers were charged with delivering sick chickens, violating the code. The Supreme Court found the NRA unconstitutional because it granted legislative powers to the executive branch. It was a bad day for the president. Two other cases decided that day ended the moratorium on mortgages as well as the president's power to remove members from independent regulatory commissions. The *U.S. v. Butler* case in 1936 declared the AAA unconstitutional for the same reason as the NRA. These experiences show why the president later tried his ill-fated court-packing scheme.

With large Democratic majorities in both the Senate and the House of Representatives, FDR tried to get around the conservative Supreme Court, which he viewed as a roadblock to his New Deal legislation. In February, 1937, FDR sent a bill to Congress proposing to enlarge the Supreme Court, appointing a new justice for every Supreme Court member over seventy. The rationale was that it would reduce the workload for the older justices. The president, under the Constitution, holds the power to appoint new Supreme Court justices. Thus, FDR would "pack" the Court with six liberal justices. Public opinion exploded against the idea. Public anger against one of the three major branches of the federal government is one thing. Permanently altering the Constitutional balance of power is unacceptable. FDR lost. The bill went down to an inglorious defeat. However, the Supreme Court began to reverse its conservative, ideological-driven decisions and to approve New Deal laws. FDR claimed he lost the battle but won the war. Perhaps, but it tarnished his reputation and began an unofficial alliance in Congress between conservative Southern Democrats and conservative Republicans. After 1937, liberal proposals faced a more formidable barrier in Congress.

Relief

CCC – the **Civilian Conservation Corps**, put young men to work, 300,000 by July 1, 1933, in 1,300 camps planting trees and doing conservation work. Some textbooks overemphasize the conservation and environmental aspects of the CCC. One New Deal scholar realistically defined the CCC as 90% jobs and 10% conservation. They were paid $30 a month, $25 of which was sent home to their families. What did they get – three square meals, honest work, a good night's sleep, and positive feelings from working again. Critics compared the CCC young men to Hitler's Nazi Youth. Critics always say where an initiative will ultimately lead, thus employing a scare tactic. They had nothing to offer to increase employment, just criticism.

    CWA – the **Civil Works Administration**, paid 40 cents per hour for unskilled workers and $1 per hour for skilled workers. The CWA put four million people to work in two months, building roads, providing free plays by actors, cataloging archives, etc. A high percentage, 86%, of the money appropriated for the CWA was used for wages.

    WPA – the **Works Progress Administration**, later replaced the CWA. Within a short time, it became the nation's largest employer, hiring eight million people in five years. Among the WPA's projects were La Guardia Airport in New York City, the St. Louis riverfront, the San Antonio River Walk, the American Guide book series for tourists for each state, 500,000 miles of highways, and 40,000 school buildings. It even hired 100 workers to walk around Washington, D.C., with high balloons to scare birds away. Critics had a ball, calling WPA "we poke along."

    PWA – the **Public Works Administration**, spent $6 billion in six years building mostly large projects, such as the Grand Coulee Dam on the Columbia River in Washington, the New York City Triborough Bridge, and the Chicago city sewer system. It also spent $824 million for military needs – two aircraft carriers, the *Yorktown* and the *Enterprise*, four cruisers, one hundred airplanes, and fifty airports.

    NYA – the **National Youth Administration**, put college students to work part-time so they could stay in college. Among those who benefited was a later critic, Richard Nixon, who was able to stay at Duke Law School. Lyndon Baines Johnson, after serving as a Congressional aide, began his Texas political career as the NYA director for Texas.

Reform

TVA – the **Tennessee Valley Authority**, benefited seven states by controlling floods and providing electricity in an area where private electric companies refused to go, because the prospects for profits were so poor. During the First World War the federal government built a large hydroelectric power plant and two munitions plants at Muscle Shoals, Alabama, on the Tennessee River. After the war, the government tried to sell them to private power companies, but found no buyers. An idea grew among some politicians that it should be expanded. It bore fruit in the TVA. When finished, the TVA system was touted as a model for building eight similar hydroelectric systems across the country. Private electric companies politically stopped the plans for the others. Run as a separate corporation, the government-owned TVA (socialism!) still provides the nation's cheapest electricity; and, it makes a profit every year.

REA – the **Rural Electrification Administration**, provided loans to farm co-ops to build electric power systems to provide farms with electricity. The percentage of farms with electricity increased from 11% to 89% by 1940.

FHA – the **Federal Housing Administration**, guaranteed mortgage loans granted by banks; thus, there was no risk to a bank or to a mortgage company. This stimulated the construction industry, its main purpose. It also benefited a lot of first-time buyers, who no longer had to save the traditional 20% down payment to purchase a house.

Social Security provided money for two different groups of people. One portion of the Social Security taxes goes to the states to fund their unemployment insurance, a program completely controlled by the states. The second beneficiary is retirees, who initially received $15 to $85 per month, and children under 18 who had one deceased parent, who also received a monthly check. If that child went to college, he or she received Social Security up to age 22. The Reagan administration ended payments to college students. The purpose of Social Security was, and is, to pump spending money into the economy, money for the unemployed and the elderly, and to keep two groups out of the work force, old folks and kids. It is what an economist calls a "transfer payment." It transfers money from one group to another, from taxpayers to retirees and the unemployed. Today 9% of seniors live below the poverty level. Without Social Security, 54% would. The recipients spend money, which provides jobs for other workers in the economy.

Some people today criticize Social Security by claiming that an individual could save more by investing in a private personal investment account. This may be true in some cases. However, Social Security was, and is, intended to aid society, not individuals. The small amounts in the Social Security checks guarantee that the recipients will spend that money, thus keeping other workers employed. This cushions the impact of a downward spiraling economy. In addition, a personal retirement account is at the mercy of the economy, especially the stock market. What about the individual who would have retired in 2007 using only a private stock fund compared to one who retired in December, 2008, after a stock market crash? Also, for either individual, what if their bank or investment company failed, as many did early in the Great Depression? A person could do everything the financial experts tell them to do to prepare for a solid retirement and not get it, through no fault of their own. Read the fine print in investing literature. The first recipient of a Social Security check was Ida Fuller of Ludlow, Vermont. Her first monthly check for $22.54 was issued in 1940. She had paid $20 into the system. She died in 1974 at 99. She beat the system by about $9,000. The secret to winning as an individual with Social Security is simple – live.

Assessment of the New Deal's Impact

Which New Deal? Some historians divide the New Deal into a First and Second New Deal, lumping together in the Second New Deal the Works Progress Administration, Social Security, the National Labor Relations Act, the National Housing Act, the Fair Labor Standards Act, and the REA, the Rural Electrification Administration. In some respects the Second New Deal was a reaction to Roosevelt's most vocal critics. Father Charles Coughlin, the Catholic radio priest, railed against the New Deal, claiming it was a communist conspiracy. His national weekly radio broadcasts promoted fascism and anti-Semitism. A California doctor, Dr. Francis E. Townsend, proposed granting monthly $200 pensions to the elderly, an idea that foreshadowed Social Security. A Louisiana senator, often labeled by historians as our first national demagogue, Huey Long, urged confiscating the fortunes of the wealthy, a popular stand during the Great Depression. His "Share the Wealth" Clubs called for a redistribution of that confiscated wealth through an immediate cash grant to every family of $5,000 and an annual guaranteed income for every worker of $2,500. Neither Townsend nor Long provided details as to how the money for their programs would be raised. Long proudly shouted, "All you have to do is believe!" Another Californian, the author of *The Jungle*, published during the Progressive Movement, Upton Sinclair, created EPIC, "End Poverty in California," during his 1934 campaign for governor of California. Again, details were lacking. Popular enthusiasm rallied behind all four critics, but they all faded from the political scene. The poet, Wallace Stevens, caught the atmosphere generated by these four with his observation that "at the moment, all the madmen are politicians." The Second New Deal stressed security and aiding the poor more than the First New Deal. However, by 1937 both New Deals were winding down and would soon be over.

The New Deal is difficult for a historian to digest or to research. In the National Archives the New Deal material extends for 2,076 linear feet, the length of almost seven football fields. The National Archives estimates that there are about 2000 pages per foot, thus there are over four million pieces of paper records to look at if you want to completely research the entire New Deal, in all its aspects. And, this is just the records at the National Archives. Reading all the New Deal pages would take, at 300 days per year, 173 years. Still, historians are able to draw some conclusions.

Labor – In 1933 there were 2.8 million union members, and in 1941, 8.4 million. Feeding the increase was the rise of the CIO, the Congress of Industrial Organizations, whose members were unskilled workers in big industries — steel, auto, rubber. The newly formed UAW, United Automobile Workers, invented the effective sit-down strike. New Deal legislation gave workers minimum wage and maximum hour laws, with a rate of time and one-half for hours over forty hours and double time for over sixty hours. Thanks to the Wagner Act, the NLRB, the National Labor Relations Board, conducted the balloting for initial union recognition voting. Most bitter strikes have been over initial recognition. The question a company faced was simple. Do a majority of workers support this union? Now a vote by the workers replaced a strike as the test. Otherwise, a company had to challenge the union organizers and leaders by forcing a strike to see if a majority of the workers really did support the union.

Income — FDR declared in 1937, "I see one-third of a nation ill-housed, ill-clad, ill-nourished." What was the impact of the New Deal on income? The various New Deal taxes did reduce the income of the wealthy, but only by giving the second top fifth a larger tax burden. Today the American economy is back to an income distribution similar to what existed prior to 1929. President Ronald Reagan's Tax Act of 1986 ended the heavier taxes the New Deal put on the wealthy.

The George W. Bush administration in the early twenty-first century pushed taxes on the wealthy down even further. Economists claim, given all the exclusions, that under the current federal tax code the wealthy now actually pay a smaller percentage of their income in taxes than the middle class. If anyone suffers from insomnia, get comfortable in bed and start reading the tax code. Economists also point out that when you include all types of state, local, and federal taxes, that everyone — poor, middle, rich — now pays about one-third of their income in taxes. A federal flat tax on incomes, which the wealthy argue would be fair, would actually result in a lower overall tax percentage for the wealthy; all others would pay more.

Minorities — Before FDR's arrival, white Anglo-Saxon Protestant males, WASPs, controlled the national government. As historian William Leuchtenburg explained in *Franklin D. Roosevelt and the New Deal*, "When Roosevelt took office, the country, to a very large extent, responded to the will of a single element: the white, Anglo-Saxon, Protestant property-holding class. Under the New Deal, new groups took their place in the sun." Blacks and Jews came to feel they had a friend in the White House. Several top inner circle advisors were Jewish. Blacks never made it into the inner circle, but Mary McLeod Bethune served as a special adviser on minority affairs, conveying the views of her colleagues, which came to be called the "black cabinet." An educator, she had established a private secondary school for blacks in Daytona Beach, Florida. Over the years it grew to become a junior college, then a college, and now a university, Bethune-Cookman University. Pro-black legislation faced a formidable barrier; nobody wanted to ruffle the feathers of powerful Southern senators and congressmen. Southerners were a crucial component of the Democratic Party's political coalition.

Because Southerners controlled the committees in Congress (as the chairmen) due to their longevity and seniority, blacks gained little in terms of concrete accomplishments. The NYA and CCC in the North included blacks, but not in the South. The TVA was segregated. Local authorities distributed relief money according to their formulas. In Jacksonville, Florida, for example, blacks made up 75% of those on relief, but the city government distributed the funds according to the percentage of the city's population, with the result that blacks, 75% of the city's population on relief, received 45% of the relief money. Whites, who made up 25% of those on relief, got 55% of the relief funds.

Still, many blacks and Jews felt that, "On a very wide front and in the truest public sense, Franklin Roosevelt included the excluded." By 1941, 150,000 blacks were federal government employees, three times the number in the Hoover administration. At a public meeting in Alabama the president's wife, Eleanor Roosevelt, realized that the races were segregated, blacks on one side, whites on the other. She picked up her chair and moved it to the middle of the center aisle. Eleanor Roosevelt was also responsible for getting approval for singer Marian Anderson to perform on federal land at the Lincoln Memorial after the Daughters of the American Revolution denied her use of their Constitution Hall because of her race. The "black cabinet," an unofficial group of black advisors, also provided a voice within the Roosevelt administration. These symbolic gestures made blacks feel that they had a friend in the White House. They switched to voting Democratic in large numbers. However, for the average black man a remark quoted in *Hard Times*, by Studs Terkel, (a Pulitzer Prize winning author well-known for his oral histories), said it best. "If you can tell me the difference between the depression today and the depression of 1932 for a black man, I'd like to know it."

Behind the dreary statistics for blacks lurks a potential long-range impact. The Farm Security Administration enabled 50,000 black tenant farmers and sharecroppers to purchase farms in the South. While farming was often not a financially rewarding occupation, owning one's own farm apparently had an impact in other ways. As one historian explained, "There is a high correlation between the location of extensive FSA (Farm Security Administration) operations in the 1930s and the rapidity of political modernization in black communities in the South in the 1960s." Economic gains in the 1930s apparently laid the groundwork for political efforts at the local level in the later civil rights movement. Mexicans also suffered during the Depression. Throughout the Southwest trains and buses shipped many Mexicans "back" to Mexico, both voluntarily and involuntarily, including many who were American citizens. There was no demand for their labor.

Housing – The FHA, the **Federal Housing Administration**, stimulated the housing industry by making it easier to meet the down payment, which had formerly been 20% to 30%. The National Housing Act that created the FHA passed June 27, 1934. Housing starts in 1933 were 93,000; in 1941, 619,000. New houses meant jobs.

Economists assert that each new house built is equivalent to adding 2.97 jobs to the economy for a full year. The percentage of owner-occupied dwellings increased from 44% in 1934 to 63% in 1972. However, FHA policies also speeded up urban blight by adopting a uniform system of real estate appraisal that tended to undervalue urban property, thus encouraging the building of suburbia. The HOLC, the federal Home Owners Loan Corporation, began "redlining" and using credit maps to prevent the undesirable infiltration of Jews and blacks. Redlining referred to a bank drawing a line on a city map to indicate an area in which they would not grant loans for mortgages to purchase a house. Banks deny they still do this, but the Bronx in New York City is the county at the absolute bottom nation-wide in total FHA guaranteed mortgages received.

Women – The New Deal programs favored giving jobs to men before women. The argument prevailed that a man needed a job before a family needed the second income, which assumed that all women existed securely under the financially adequate loving care of a male – husband, father, son, etc. The federal government, and many state and local governments also, permitted only one member of a married couple to hold a government job.

Solving Unemployment – Here the New Deal failed; the Second World War solved the nation's unemployment problem.

Attacking Poverty – Again, the New Deal failed overall.

Financial Institutions – In providing a more modern system of financial institutions, the New Deal was successful, as shown by Social Security, the regulation of the Stock Market, and the insurance of bank deposits through the FDIC, the Federal Deposit Insurance Corporation.

"the good things of life" – The New Deal sought to finish the task of promoting a reasonable distribution, not only of wealth, but also of power and status, or what FDR vaguely called "the good things of life." This equitable sharing of prosperity was supposed to include those previously excluded. The New Deal was not altogether successful. Most of the significant social and economic changes in American society came during, and because of, the Second World War. The creation of the welfare state helped the very poor. In 1950 a British sociologist, T. H. Marshall, analyzed what the establishment of the welfare state had accomplished. He wrote, "There is a general enrichment of the concrete substance of civilized life, a general reduction of risk and insecurity, an equalization between the more or less fortunate at all levels—between the healthy and the sick, the employed and the unemployed, the old and the active, the bachelor and the father of a large family." (quoted in Alan Wolfe, *The Future of Liberalism*, p. 80.)

The early New Deal was clearly neither anti-business nor opposed to the wealthy class. However, FDR's reforms were seen as such by big business, as the New Deal unfolded. By 1936, after the Supreme Court ended the NRA and AAA, a different FDR campaigned for reelection. The 1936 FDR could be labeled as anti-wealthy class (the Revenue Tax Act of 1936 raised rates on corporations and wealthy individuals) and anti-business (FDR was frustrated by the constant criticism and opposition of businessmen.) In one of his typically folksy stories, FDR compared businessmen to an ungrateful person rescued (by the New Deal) from drowning, who now complained that his rescuer failed to retrieve his hat.

But, the New Deal was no revolution; in the long run it strengthened corporate capitalism. FDR was a fiscal moderate preoccupied with balancing the budget. The British economist John Maynard Keynes tried to explain fiscal policy and monetary policy to the president during an interview in the Oval Office. FDR's questions frustrated Keynes, who said Roosevelt just did not get it! FDR always worried about deficit spending. Once he tried to balance the budget and ended up contributing to a slide into a recession in 1937-38. He once even proposed that the federal government buy bankrupt banks and turn them into post offices. This would mean no public works expenditures to stimulate the economy, the opposite of the theory of Keynesian economics.

So, What Was the Impact of the New Deal?

Was there a philosophy to the New Deal? Was it consistent? Once a reporter asked FDR about his political philosophy. He responded that he was "a Christian and a Democrat." Not much of a political philosophy there. Another time FDR referred to himself as a practical idealist. His close advisors found it difficult "to read his mind with any precision." Critics said he did not have one. Many historians label the New Deal as just a "try anything" approach without any consistent political philosophy. FDR once explained his basic philosophy as, "Try something. If it works, keep doing it. Of it doesn't, try something else. But above all, try something." For Roosevelt, approach and intention meant more than consistency. He often referred to a quotation by the poet Dante to explain his efforts.

> "Governments can err, Presidents do make mistakes, but the immortal Dante tells us that Divine Justice weights the sins of the cold-blooded and the sins of the warm-hearted on a different scale. Better the occasional faults of a government living in the spirit of charity, than the consistent omissions of a government frozen in the ice of its own indifference."

In his 1941 "Four Freedoms" speech, FDR commented on what was necessary for a healthy and strong democracy. It was an excellent description of the New Deal effort.

"The basic things expected by our people of their political and economic systems are simple. They are:

> Equality of opportunity for youth and for others.
> Jobs for those who can work.
> Security for those who need it.

The ending of special privilege for the few.

The preservation of civil liberties for all.

The enjoyment of the fruits of scientific progress in a wider and constantly rising standard of living."

One leftist historian, Barton Bernstein, in *Towards A New Past*, bluntly declared the New
Deal a failure. "The New Deal failed to solve the problem of depression, it failed to
raise the impoverished, it failed to redistribute income, it failed to extend equality and
generally countenanced racial discrimination and segregation."

Whatever it was, it was different from Progressive Reform. A student of American
history should be able to compare the three reform eras in the twentieth century –
Progressivism, the New Deal, and the Great Society in the 1960s. The historian Otis
Graham, in *An Encore for Reform*, researched what Progressives still alive in the 1930s
thought of the New Deal. Surviving Progressives overwhelmingly opposed the New
Deal. They saw it as something different. The historian Richard Hofstadter said
the New Deal was different, because its central problem was unlike the problems of
Progressivism. It was different in spirit, ideas, and techniques. The New Deal lacked
the strong moral overtones of the Progressive Movement. The concern in the New Deal
was the economy; the Progressive Movement took place in a period of prosperity.

Political scientist Alan Wolfe saw a similarity between the New Deal and the Great
Society. In *The Future of Liberalism*, p. 236, he asserted, "The unifying element behind so
many of the reforms passed during the period of the Great Society was the same liberal
impetus that had characterized the New Deal: individuals, through government, could
gain some degree of mastery over their lives."

The emergence and demands of a large and powerful labor movement, coupled
with the interests of the unemployed, gave reform, by the end of the New Deal, a
more democratic tinge than had been previously present in most American reform
movements. In addition, there were new issues. Now reform embraced topics like
Social Security, unemployment insurance, wages and hours, and housing. Two topics that occupied much of the energy of the Progressives were ignored – the big city
political machines and antitrust or antimonopoly. The New Deal had no clear or
consistent policy on business consolidation, the trusts, or monopolies. Bigness was
subordinated to recovery. For Progressives such as Theodore Roosevelt, Woodrow
Wilson, Louis Brandeis, and Robert La Follette, economic life was an expression of
character. For New Deal liberals economic life was no longer a field for correcting
defective moral behavior. The New Deal was a response to an economic nightmare,
and an inadequate response at that. The Second World War rescued Americans from
the worst of the Great Depression.

40

FROM THE FIRST WORLD WAR TO THE SECOND WORLD WAR

From the League of Nations to the United Nations

The ghost of Woodrow Wilson haunted Franklin Roosevelt. He served as Wilson's Assistant Secretary of the Navy during the First World War and was the vice-presidential candidate for the Democratic Party in 1920, the year of the so-called solemn referendum on the League of Nations. FDR had known Wilson well, and he wanted to avoid Wilson's mistakes. An international organization was clearly needed. That lesson was learned too late. Would it have prevented the Second World War? There is lots of room here for counterfactual history, "what if" such and such had happened? "What if" is great for speculation and discussion, but "what if" did not happen.

FDR said in 1941 on December 9, two days after Pearl Harbor – "We are going to win the war, and we are going to win the peace that follows." He wanted different long-term results from this war. In a speech he planned to deliver on April 13, 1945, the day after he died, President Franklin Roosevelt had written, "More than an end to war, we want an end to the beginnings of all wars." Vice President Henry Wallace said in 1942. "We failed our job after World War I …. But by our errors we learned and after this war we shall be in a position to utilize our knowledge in building a world which is economically, politically, and I hope, spiritually sound." Secretary of State Cordell Hall, near the end of the Second World War, said, "A world in economic chaos would be a breeding ground for trouble and war." The Italian fascist dictator Benito Mussolini had announced shortly after taking power in 1922, "We have buried the putrid corpse of liberty." The United States could not let this happen again. During the war the U.S. had a strong commitment to creating a viable, workable United Nations, which affected many different decisions – military, political, economic, and diplomatic.

Preventing the First World War, Too Late

American foreign policy after turning down membership in the League of Nations was not consistent. The United States was NOT an isolationist nation in our foreign policy during the 1920s and 1930s. The title of the chapter on the 1920s in George C. Herring's *From Colony to Superpower: U.S. Foreign Relations since 1776*, explains our position as "Involvement Without Commitment." From 1914 to 1924 thousands of Americans, through the Red Cross, funneled millions of dollars into humanitarian relief efforts in Europe and the Middle East. Indeed, in the 1920s the United States was an important nation in the international economy. The U.S. produced 85% of the world's cars, 70% of its oil, 40% of its coal, and 46% of its total industrial goods. Americans consumed 70% of the world's rubber supply and 60% of the world's output of eight other raw materials. However, the nation was reluctant to involve itself deeply in the same old policies and international politics of other nations. A later Secretary of State, Dean Rusk, once observed to a British Foreign Secretary that one could "Scratch any American and underneath you'll find an isolationist." The mistakes of the First World War were seared into everyone's mind. Historian Barbara Tuchman aptly summarized the effect of the First World War; it was "a burnt path across history." An unforgettable lesson, but an unclear lesson.

Five Power – Naval Disarmament

During President Warren G. Harding's administration the United States hosted a naval disarmament conference in Washington. While the delegates were still finding their seats, the United States Secretary of State Charles Evans Hughes proposed a freeze on large ships. Eventually the Five Power Treaty, February 6, 1922, did that, setting up a 5-5-3-1.67-1.67 ratio for the United States-Great Britain-Japan-Italy-France, freezing battleship, cruiser, and aircraft carrier construction for ten years. Japan was not pleased at the ratio, calling it "Rolls Royce, Rolls Royce, Ford." A provision in the treaty to freeze the status quo in the Pacific Ocean placated Japan, but this left the U.S. owned Philippines vulnerable and defenseless. Like most disarmament treaties, it tried to maintain the status quo in a constantly changing world. Few large ships were built; other ships were. In the next seven years the British built 74 ships; the Japanese 125; the Italians 82; the French 119; and, the Americans 11. Not a wise policy on our part.

The most significant part of the conference was not the naval limits; it was the shift in power in the Pacific Ocean from Great Britain to the United States. In essence, Great Britain handed the Pacific over to United States for peacekeeping. The Washington Naval Disarmament Conference generated two other treaties. In the Four Power Treaty Japan and Great Britain ended their mutual defense pact from 1902 and the United States, Great Britain, Japan, and France agreed to talk concerning matters of mutual regard, December 13, 1921. The Nine Power Treaty, also February 6, 1922, continued the earlier thread of America's Open Door policy towards China, in which the United States presented itself as the protector of China. It pledged the signers – United States, Great Britain, Japan, France, Italy, China, Belgium, Portugal, and the Netherlands – to respect the sovereignty and territorial integrity of China. Violations of this treaty would later be the primary basis for American protests against the Japanese invasion of China in the 1930s.

Kellogg-Briand Pact

After the First World War France sought an alliance with Great Britain and/or the United States. Neither one was interested. Building on the goodwill generated by Charles Lindbergh's trans-Atlantic flight, French discussions with the American secretary of state produced the Kellogg-Briand Treaty. Originally involving only France and the United States, it outlawed offensive war. Negotiated in 1927 and ratified in 1928, eventually 62 countries signed it. It had no enforcement provisions.

Germany and the War Guilt Clause

Meanwhile, Germans, from their viewpoint, suffered one insult after another. Article 231 of the Versailles Treaty placed the entire blame for starting the First World War on Germany. It said Germans must accept the "responsibility of Germany and her allies for causing all the loss and damage to which the Allied and Associated Governments and their nationals have been subjected as a consequence of the war imposed upon them by the aggression of Germany and her allies." Article 232 made Germany responsible for paying *all* the costs that *all* the Allied countries suffered for the First World War. Until 1926 Germany was not allowed in the League of Nations. As one example of many minor social insults, Germans were not allowed on the golf course at the League of Nations headquarters until 1929.

Scholars in all countries were starting to question assigning sole guilt to Germany for the beginning of the First World War. Historians still debate who was responsible and to what degree. The consensus is generally Serbia, Austria-Hungary, Russia, France, Germany, and then Great Britain, in that order. You will read a different listing in each country's history textbooks. In the Twenties and Thirties uncertainty over the blame for the First World War made Allied political leaders hesitant about enforcing the harsh provisions of the Versailles Treaty. However, the blame and the shame remained for Germans.

Versailles Treaty

Other provisions in the Versailles Treaty forced Germany to hand over most of its merchant marine, a quarter of its fishing boats, and a large percentage of its locomotives and railroad cars. It had to build 200,000 tons of shipping each year for five years, all of which went to the Allies. It had to make yearly deliveries of coal to France, Italy, and Belgium. The German army was limited to 100,000 men, with 12-year enlistments to prevent building up a reserve corps. The German navy was limited to only 6 battleships, 6 cruisers, 12 destroyers, and no new submarines. The military was forbidden to manufacture military aircraft, heavy artillery, tanks, or poisoned gas. The political unification of Austria and Germany was prohibited.

Even the procedure used to sign the Versailles Treaty insulted Germans. Germany did not take part in the treaty discussions, negotiations, or decisions. When the German delegation arrived in Paris to sign the treaty, they were kept behind barbed wire for weeks. At the signing ceremony, when the French delegation entered the room, the Germans remained seated, a ceremonial insult of disrespect. It was obvious to everyone that a war of revenge was a strong probability.

The Versailles Treaty failed to resolve the ethnic identity dilemma in Eastern Europe. It was simply impossible to draw boundary lines that created new countries that constituted homogeneous homelands for each ethnic group. Minorities were always present, and it was impossible to satisfy all of the different ethnic groups. By creating a cluster of small, weak new nations, the Versailles Treaty, in essence, created a power vacuum in Eastern Europe in an attempt to satisfy each ethnic group's desire for their own country. Power vacuums attract larger predatory countries.

The Versailles Treaty contained the principle of collective security to prevent another war. However, two major powers, the United States and Russia, did not sign the treaty.

The Test for the League of Nations and the United States – Manchuria
In many respects the Second World War began on September 18, 1931, when Japan marched into Manchuria, which was part of northern China. Japan had invested heavily in Manchuria, which became an important source of Japan's food and raw materials; 40% of her foreign trade involved just that part of China. Secretary of State Henry Stimson urged President Herbert Hoover to respond strongly with sanctions. Instead, Hoover said he would not "allow under any circumstances anyone to deposit that baby in our lap." To Hoover sanctions were "like sticking pins in tigers." The best Stimson could get was the Stimson Doctrine, which expressed American nonrecognition of de facto changes brought about in violation of the Open Door or the Kellogg-Briand Treaty. In others words, Japan may be in control of Manchuria, but as far as the United States was concerned, Japan was not legally in control. Not much of a policy. Stimson himself called it "spears of straw and swords of ice." Japan was incensed. When the League also criticized the takeover, Japan walked out of the League of Nations, comparing Japan's treatment to Christ's crucifixion, a curious statement by a non-Christian country. Later Germany and Italy also pulled out of the League after receiving criticism.

In August, 1937, Japan attacked Shanghai and invaded China. During the invasion, in December, the *USS Panay*, an American gunboat, and a nearby British ship, were "accidently" attacked by Japanese airplanes – for hours. Two Americans were killed and several injured. Japan apologized and the U.S. accepted the apology. Japan learned something about American willingness to get involved in East Asian affairs. This incident certainly differed from American reaction to the *USS Maine* incident in 1898 in Havana harbor. Three months after the invasion FDR tried to rally public opinion with his "Quarantine the Aggressors speech." The American public was not interested.

American Isolationism

At home, isolationists grew in numbers. Charles Lindbergh, the famous aviator, visited Germany and came home convinced Germany would win a future war against France and Great Britain. Various organizations promoted noninvolvement, such as the America First Committee, which said – concentrate on defending America. It ballooned to 850,000 members in 450 local chapters. The Veterans of Future Wars was a tongue-in-cheek movement of college students who asked for their postwar bonus now, so they could spend it before dying in the next war. Political cartoonists drew "Hello Sucker" posters of maimed soldiers. Read the book or see the movie, *"All Quiet on the Western Front,"* which came out in 1929 and 1930. In all countries many were eager to avoid a repeat of the senseless slaughter of the First World War.

Scholars revised their ideas about which countries started the First World War and why and how the United States got dragged into it. In Congress the Ludlow Amendment to the Constitution was proposed, which would have required a national majority referendum vote to declare war, instead of having Congress declare war. A vote in the House of Representatives to force the bill out of committee failed, 188-209. If 11 representatives had switched their vote it would have passed and been voted on by the House. Earlier in the 1930s, the Senate's Nye Committee popularized the "Merchants of Death" theory that somehow American capitalists seeking profits dragged the United States into the First World War. Such a conclusion would have been widely believed during an economic downturn like the Great Depression. In 1937, 70% of Americans polled said our involvement in the First World War had been a mistake. These attitudes lead to the Neutrality Acts of the 1930s, all designed to avoid involvement in another perceived fiasco like the First World War. They were one war too late. The Second World War began for different reasons.

In Europe – Reparations

The First World War and the peace left many economic problems. Germany owed $33 billion in reparations; Great Britain and France owed $10 billion for loans from the United States. The British debt was one-half of the country's national income, the

French, two-thirds. Repaying it was virtually impossible for these two nations struggling to recover from the impact of the war. The whole war debts issue left every nation dissatisfied and frustrated. More than any other issue, it poisoned our relationship with our former allies. The British and the French argued that they suffered irreplaceable human losses while the United States suffered only financial losses. Call it even; the United States refused. The Johnson Debt Default Act, 1934, was very popular because it prohibited further loans to nations in default on war debt payments. Decades later older Americans still complained bitterly that the only nation that ever paid us back was Finland.

President Warren G. Harding was keenly aware of the problems foreign policy issues created for Wilson. He minimized foreign policy. Calvin Coolidge's autobiography, written after he left the presidency, did not even mention foreign policy. Herbert Hoover, on the other hand, had been a world famous international engineer, the head of the U.S. Food Relief program for Belgium after the end of the First World War, the United States reparations advisor at Versailles, and the Secretary of Commerce under Harding and Coolidge. Coolidge always complained that Hoover thought HE was president. The British economist, John Maynard Keynes, called Hoover the most knowledgeable person at the Versailles Conference. Of the three presidents in the Twenties, Hoover best understood the foreign policy dilemmas, but the Great Depression almost completely occupied Hoover's presidency, and he paid little attention to foreign policy issues.

Fascism and other ISMs
Modern political terminology uses "isms" as a shorthand description for complex economic and political systems. To simplify greatly, every society has two political possibilities, democracy and totalitarianism, and two economic possibilities, capitalism and socialism. In a totalitarian political system the government has total control, at least in theory. The major difference between capitalism and socialism is the ownership of the means used to produce and to distribute goods and services, either private or public. All societies mix the two methods. The difference is the percentage and the particular industries. Many modern European democratic governments use more public economic production than the United States, but these societies are far from socialistic. Avoid making bold, absolutist statements, such as "the New Deal introduced socialism and ended capitalism and laissez faire." Not true! If eighty percent of the goods and services are privately produced, a country is still capitalistic, even if segments of the economy are owned and operated by the government.

The combination of totalitarianism and socialism is called communism. Totalitarianism and capitalism is fascism. A third, which has no short name, exists in the United States, democracy and capitalism. The overwhelming majority of Americans believe in both democracy and capitalism. It is important for students to recognize the broad consensus within which disagreements arise between Americans. One historian characterized our political squabbles as "surface agitation." The fourth combination, democracy and socialism, exists more in theory, although some people in the countries of the former Soviet Union and Eastern European bloc originally saw it as an alternative to the older-style communism.

Think of these four distinctions as existing on a continuum.

totalitarianism	democracy	democracy	totalitarianism
a--------------------b----------------------c----------------------d------------------------e
socialism	socialism	capitalism	capitalism

Be aware that isms can confuse because they oversimplify. There are fine distinctions within each broad category. One communist nation can feel alienated from another communist nation due to disputes over ideological interpretations. An American, looking at the two communist nations from a long way away, may have trouble seeing the fine points separating the two different communist societies. In actuality communist nations existed all along the segment of the continuum line for totalitarianism-socialism, along the line above from a to b. It was difficult for Americans to understand, but there were "conservative" and "radical" communist nations.

Fascism belongs on the right, d to e above, but it really is part of a new left-right continuum. The terms left-right-center evolved in nineteenth century debates over property, individual liberties, and popular government. Fascism developed in the early twentieth century when two fundamental foundations of society began to erode: a faith in progress and in the capacity of reason to maintain a democratic and liberal society. Fascism focused on national power and domestic order. A mass movement, hostile to churches and individual rights, glorifying violence, somewhat anti-capitalist yet cozy with big business, it appealed to small businessmen and to a middle class who saw themselves as precariously perched just above poverty. Nineteenth century political debates assumed class-consciousness; fascism appealed across class lines in the name of national greatness. Look at the intellectual stirrings in the 1890-1920 era in art, painting, psychoanalysis, theology, social criticism, political debate, etc. The old paradigm was being attacked from many fronts. Fascism and communism defined the expanded, enlarged, new twentieth century left-right paradigm.

The Rise of Hitler, Nazi Party membership card #555
In the 1920s Germany was still being punished by the provisions of the Versailles Treaty. The Allied powers wanted revenge, not a revitalized Germany. Wild inflation undermined any opportunity for stable government. By 1923 the German mark, equivalent to our dollar, had virtually no value. German unemployment reached 44 percent in 1933

and led to the rise of Adolf Hitler that year. The fascist dictator Benito Mussolini had risen to power in Italy in 1922 for similar reasons and frustrations. The German political and military leaders all thought they could manipulate Hitler, a good soldier who had been awarded the Iron Cross during the First World War. The reverse happened. Hitler was very successful fighting the depression. His economic program of rebuilding the military and various big public works projects such as the Autobahn succeeded in eliminating unemployment in Germany, the only Western nation to accomplish that feat in the 1930s.

Hitler's rise to power lay in his understanding of the art of directing the minds of the masses, for whom he personally had contempt. In *Mein Kampf, My Battle* or *My Struggle*, written in 1924, he wrote, "The receptivity of the great masses is very limited, their intelligence is small. In consequence of these facts, all effective propaganda must be limited to a very few points and must harp on those in slogans until the last member of the public understands what you want him to understand." Hitler understood that to gain the support of the gullible it was only necessary to drum a ready-made system of values into their ears. Passion and emotion would override reason. He targeted those with low education and low intelligence, believing their views were less complex than those held by educated, intelligent people. "The driving force of the most important changes in this world has been found less in the scientific knowledge animating the masses but rather in a fanaticism dominating them and in a hysteria which drives them forward." "Therefore, keep the intellectual content of political propaganda simple, and repeat it often. Everything ought to be painted in black or white. Because the masses are not thinking a political leader need not fear to speak a lie, but the lie must be a big lie. Small lies people recognize, for they themselves tell them. Thus the effectiveness of a message depends not on its truth, but only on the fanaticism and passion with which it is conveyed; to a properly presented appeal the masses will respond by accepting what they are told." "The art of leadership . . . consists in consolidating the attention of the people against a single adversary and taking care that nothing will split up that attention."

It is easier for a skilled demagogue to get people to agree on what they hate or dislike than it is to recruit them to support a positive program. This is one of the secrets of the success of today's political talk radio. Adolf Hitler was the most skilled demagogue in European history. He fit into the twentieth century. As the theologian Reinhold Niebuhr pointed out in *Moral Man and Immoral Society*, one trait of the twentieth century was the ease with which nations and groups engaged in practices an individual would have found repugnant.

Among his big lies was Hitler's accusation that leftists burned the German parliament building in the Reichstag fire of February 27, 1933. To protect Germany, Hitler asked for the power to rule by emergency decree. This "temporary power" lasted until 1945, the end of the war. Another big lie was that communism was Jewish in origin. While Karl Marx's family background was Jewish, Marx's father joined the Presbyterian Church and had all his children baptized and confirmed. As an adult, Karl Marx became an extreme anti-Semite. His writings are sprinkled with anti-Jewish statements. See the chapter on Marx in Paul Johnson's *Intellectuals*, pp.52-81. Telling lies never bothered Hitler's conscience. He said, "Conscience is a Jewish invention. It is a blemish like circumcision."

Hitler's extreme hatred of Jews baffles scholars. He himself was 25% Jewish. He may have been that strange person in society, a self-hater. He may have blamed Jews because he was a "mommy's boy" and the death of his mother devastated him. In her last hours a Jewish physician, who Hitler may have somehow blamed for her death, attended her. As an Austrian youth he was an aspiring artist, but he could not break into the artistic circle in Vienna, which was disproportionately Jewish. He may have simply found a convenient political scapegoat. However, his policies seem to indicate his hatred ran much deeper.

Both Poland and Romania experienced virulent anti-Semitism after the First World War. Anti-Semitism grew all over Europe in the late nineteenth century, pushed by conservatives as a political movement rather than as an individual attitude. It was a way to stimulate nationalism, very much of an "us versus them" attitude. Nationalism would limit the attraction and appeal of socialism and communism, which emphasized the unity of all working class people everywhere. Among many national leaders, the declining birth rate (a rate of 2.1 children per family is needed to maintain a stable population) fed fears that the future would see a decrease in the middle class. This led those concerned to promote fears that the future would see an increase in "undesirables," defined as Jews, Slavs, and Gypsies. Between 1894 and 1899 in France the Dreyfus affair polarized the public, the arrest of a Jewish army officer for spying (based on flimsy evidence) and his conviction in two military trials. All the evidence clearly pointed to another officer. However, Captain Alfred Dreyfus, a Jew, was targeted.

Nazi Germany was the world's first major government to follow anti-Semitism as a policy leading to extermination. Anti-Judaism had always been part of Christianity because of the belief, disputed by some biblical scholars, that Jews killed Christ. Some scholars put the blame more on the Roman authorities. In addition, for those of you who are Christians, think how Christianity would have been different without Maundy Thursday, Good Friday, and Easter. You have to have Good Friday, the death of Christ, in order to get Easter, the most important day in Christian history. Hitler added anti-Semitism and racial doctrines to anti-Judaism and created a nightmare policy of extermination. Religion was something he used rather than something he followed. (Anti-Judaism refers to the disliking of Jews by Christians or Moslems based on the belief that their religious beliefs are correct and Jews are incorrect. Anti-Semitism is the belief that Jews are so much of a threat that they must be forced to emigrate or be exterminated.)

In 1938 came Kristallnacht, the Night of Broken Glass, when Nazi supporters smashed windows in Jewish stores, hospitals, and orphanages, and burned down synagogues. Nobody in authority attempted to stop them. The climax of the prewar anti-Semitism was the Nuremberg Laws of September 15, 1939. They deprived Jews and people of Jewish blood of German citizenship, prohibited marriage and sexual intercourse between people with Jewish blood and non-Jews, and denied Jews the right to employ non-Jewish servants. Whenever they left their house, Jews had to wear a bright yellow Star of David on their clothing. Germany, and many other countries, still have citizenship laws that differ from American laws. You must be ethnically German to qualify for German citizenship. Immigrants cannot become citizens by moving to Germany. The German-born children of immigrants are not eligible either.

In the late 1930s Hitler also began the T4 Project, using carbon monoxide poisoning to kill the mentally or physically handicapped and the elderly, those deemed useless and not capable of making a positive contribution to the Aryan gene pool. The master race must be protected.

The intellectual forefather of Nazism was Friedrich Nietzsche, 1844-1900. He believed Christian morality, with its praise of humility, frustrated the development of man's powers and suffocated human creativity. Only recognition of his natural instincts and drives could constitute the basis of a true ethical code and of a new society of equality. In the popular mind, this boiled down to a race of supermen. Originally, young people were the main adherents of the Nazis, but other than the lower middle class, no particular group or class backed Hitler. He appealed to many Germans, from all classes.

Hitler's image of America and Americans came from watching Hollywood silent films. He believed all American men were gay and that America was a "Jewish rubbish heap." The United States was "half-Judaized, half-Negrified." This attitude had deep roots in the German psyche. The head of the German military in the First World War, General Erich Ludendorff, said of Americans, "They can't fight. It's a race of mongrels." Hitler was bitterly disappointed during the 1936 Olympics in Berlin when an American black man, Jesse Owens, beat a German billed as the world's fastest human being. The German did not even finish second in the 100-meter dash. That honor fell to Mark Robinson, whose brother, Jackie, would later break major league baseball's color barrier. By the 1930s Germans had no respect for American military power or potential. Hitler said, "The inferiority and decadence of this allegedly new world is evident in its military inefficiency." In addition, the Nazis had a low image of American military technology. Herman Goring, the head of the Luftwaffe, the German air force, said, "The Americans can't build planes, only electric ice boxes and razor blades." Many American bombs dropped on Germany during the Second World War had refrigerators painted on them!

In 1938 Hitler took part of Czechoslovakia, the Sudetenland, violating the Versailles Treaty and testing the Allied response. The Allied powers' declaration at the Versailles Treaty Conference favoring homelands for ethnically identifiable populations undermined the resolve of the British and French leaders. Three million Germans lived in the Sudetenland section of Czechoslovakia, and only 700,000 Czechs. A mountainous area, it had been given to Czechoslovakia for defense against possible German attack. This region also contained most of Czechoslovakia's iron, steel, coal, and electricity production. Allied acquiescence in a German takeover would leave Czechoslovakia weak and defenseless. A hastily called international conference met at Munich to resolve the crisis. Germany's Adolf Hitler, his ally, Italy's Benito Mussolini, and British Prime Minister Neville Chamberlain and French Premier Edouard Daladier finally agreed to formally transfer the Sudetenland to German control in the Munich Pact. Chamberlain returned home to England, announcing that the agreement had secured "peace in our time." In reality, neither France nor England were prepared, either in terms of military strength or public opinion, to confront Hitler. Within a year the Second World War broke out.

Discussions at Munich led to appeasement, giving in to Hitler's demands, making this term one that would too easily be applied, often incorrectly, to future twentieth century situations. There are situations when one should walk away; you should not respond to every provocation. That puts the provoker in charge of your actions, not you. You are always responding to someone else. Later Hitler took Austria and all of Czechoslovakia. Meanwhile Hitler's ally, Italian Benito Mussolini, took Ethiopia, one of the last independent nations in Africa.

War came in 1939, in September, when both Germany and Russia agreed to divide Poland, which had existed as a modern country for only twenty years. In retrospect it appears a general war was not intended, just a division of Poland. A country should never start a major war in September; it should start in the spring, giving your army time to conquer territory before winter sets in. Finally, France and Great Britain declared war on Germany. But, for months nothing happened on the French-German border. Some of the public in France and England were lulled into believing there would be no war. However, in the spring of 1940 Germany invaded France and several other countries. France fell. Within a short time, Great Britain stood alone.

England's Prime Minister, Winston Churchill, described England's perilous situation graphically on June 18, 1940. "The Battle of Britain is about to begin. Upon this battle depends the survival of Christian civilization. Upon it depends our own British life, and the long continuity of our institutions. The whole fury and might of the enemy must very soon be turned on us. Hitler knows that he will have to break us in this island or lose the war. If we stand up to him, all Europe may be free and the life of the world may move forward into broad, sunlit uplands. But if we fail, then the whole world, including the United States, including all that we have known and cared for, will sink into the abyss of a new Dark Age."

Churchill inserted that phrase — "including the United States" — into his speech as an appeal for American involvement. Almost everyone in America knew the U.S. would eventually be drawn in. But, a vote on extending the draft two months later, August 12, 1940, barely passed the House of Representatives, 203-202, and only after a provision was added prohibiting military service outside the Western Hemisphere. We would defend America, but we would not fight in Europe. It was just as well, since our army ranked twentieth among the world's military powers, just behind the Dutch. Churchill kept up the pressure, courting Roosevelt. In September came the destroyers for bases deal — fifty old American destroyers given to England in exchange for ninety-nine year leases for American bases on British possessions in the Western Hemisphere. Between May 1940 and April 1945, Churchill sent, on average, a message to FDR every thirty-six hours. Britain, and Western Europe, needed the United States. FDR knew Congress was not ready. Neither were many Americans. Two days after the destroyer deal was announced the America First Committee began to organize as a lobby organization. The America First Committee opposed American involvement in what it termed "a European war." Within a short time, it had over 800,000 members.

Next came Lend-Lease in March, 1941, helped along by FDR's folksy garden hose story.

> "Suppose my neighbor's home catches fire, and I have a length of garden hose four or five hundred feet away. If he can take my garden hose and connect it up with his hydrant, I may help him to put out his fire. Now, what do I do? I don't say to him before that operation, 'Neighbor, my garden hose cost me $15; you have to pay me $15 for it.' What is the transaction that goes on? I don't want $15—I want my garden hose back after the fire is over. All right. If it goes through the fire all right, intact, without any damage to it, he gives it back to me and thanks me very much for the use of it. But suppose it gets smashed up—holes in it—during the fire; we don't have to have too much formality about it, but I say to him, 'I was glad to lend you that hose; I see I can't use it any more, it's all smashed up.' He says, 'How many feet of it were there?' I tell him. 'There were 150 feet of it.' He says, 'All right, I will replace it.' Now, if I get a nice garden hose back, I am in pretty good shape."

Critics said there is a lot of difference between lending a hose and lending weapons. Republican Senator Robert Taft of Ohio said it was more like lending chewing gum, one does not want it back. If our allies had not paid back their First World War debts, what were the odds they would replace military equipment?

Japan's Position

Eventually, as war engulfed Europe, Japan realized it had only one potential enemy to stop her expansion, the United States, hence the attack on Pearl Harbor. From the Japanese point of view Pearl Harbor was a preemptive strike, designed to end the war immediately, before the United States started one. From the American point of view, it was a sneak attack against an innocent country. In truth, both countries had been preparing for a Pacific war for decades. Naval planning on both sides assumed there would be a war between Japan and the United States. For ten years prior to 1941 the final exam question at the Japanese equivalent to our Naval Academy was, "How would you organize a sneak attack on Pearl Harbor?" Superior officers combed the student essays for ideas. Our Naval War College held many exercises planning a war against Japan. Japan and America were almost destined to collide, given their long history of acrimony. The United States forced Japan to open its ports in 1854; Theodore Roosevelt forced the Portsmouth Treaty on both sides ending the Russo-Japanese War, a war the Japanese thought they would eventually have won; the Open Door Notes in regard to China offended Japan, as did the Gentleman's Agreement; the lack of parity in the Five Power Naval Treaty showed disrespect for Japan as an emerging world power; and, the racial overtones in our 1920s immigration acts and President Wilson's insult at the Versailles Conference angered the Japanese. The Japanese had asked that a simple statement be put into the Versailles Treaty – "The races of mankind are equal." Wilson said, no.

Finally, our ownership of the Philippines, the Stimson Doctrine, the overall American protective relationship with China, and our generally pro-Chinese attitude put the United States into the position of blocking any move Japan might wish to make in East Asia. In the summer of 1940 Japan announced her plans for the Greater East Asia Co-Prosperity Sphere, declaring her political and economic hegemony in East Asia, somewhat similar to the American policies of Manifest Destiny and the Monroe Doctrine. By late 1941, because of the war in Europe, the United States was the only power standing in the way of fulfilling Japan's dreams of dominance in the Western Pacific. During what the U.S. referred to as the Second World War, the Japanese referred to it as the Great East Asian War. Japanese propaganda painted the war as Asia fighting against Western dominance, but, of course, now Japan would dominate. The people of East Asia understood that. On December 7, 1941, Japan attacked Pearl Harbor. Germany and Italy quickly declared war on the United States. The United States was now involved in the Second World War, fighting on two fronts. Up to this point, no nation had ever fought a war on two fronts and won. The president decided the European theater was more important. The U.S. put 85% of our military effort in

Europe and only 15% against Japan, essentially a holding operation until Hitler was defeated.

Despite our efforts, or, maybe, partly because of our efforts, war came. The U.S. Navy had already extended its convoys and patrols in the North Atlantic to protect shipping against German submarines. American ships had been attacked and American lives lost. It was just a matter of time. Most historians say that American involvement in the Second World War would have come regardless of any American policy; both Germany and Japan wanted it.

41

THE IMPACT OF THE SECOND WORLD WAR

In Worldwide Perspective: Eight to Two

In 1939 eight nations were considered relatively equal in military power: the United States, Great Britain, France, Germany, Japan, China, Russia, and Italy. By 1945, three were defeated – Germany, Japan, and Italy – and three were exhausted – Great Britain, France, and China. That left only the United States and Russia as major powers. Within a short time, these two became superpowers, something brand new in world diplomacy. Having just two superpowers made it easy for each to view issues as "us versus them," or "good people versus bad people." Each superpower had trouble understanding why their so-called allies did not always see issues the way the superpower did. While both superpowers led their alliances, originally nicknamed by journalists the First World (later the Free World) for the West and the Second World for the Soviet Union's group, their policies toward their European allies differed. Historian John Lewis Gaddis differentiated the two approaches as a Soviet "empire by imposition" and an American "empire by invitation."

Superpowers

In order to achieve the status of a superpower, a term coined in 1947, it was necessary to possess four characteristics:

1. the atomic bomb
2. the power to deliver it
3. a large enough population and geographic area to absorb a nuclear attack
4. the capacity to maintain a scientific and technological standard of living

Every nation without these four qualities was, at best, a second-rate power. However, one difficulty with being a superpower was the reluctance to use atomic bombs. China's Mao Zedong labeled the United States a "paper tiger." Mao said, unused power is not power. Threatening another country only works when they believe you might carry out your threat.

Balance of Terror
International diplomacy and politics changed from balance of power to a balance of terror. Atomic weapons undermined the old concept of a balance of power where two groupings balanced one another, as happened prior to the First World War, or, one nation remained aloof from alliances and preserved the balance. Historically, Great Britain played the role of the balancer in European diplomacy.

The End of Europe
From 1500 to 1945, European nations and European values dominated the world. By 1945 that was no longer true. The world changed from a European-centered world to a world stage. Now two non-European countries dominated – the United States and the Soviet Union. Forget geography, Europeans do not consider Russia part of Europe. As colonial empires crumbled following the war, new independent nations rose in Africa and Asia, called the Third World, challenging Western values and playing a role in world politics. European values no longer necessarily ruled. Many Europeans saw both the United States and the Soviet Union as countries filled with, at worst, barbarians, or, at best, uncultured people. Both had missed many of the experiences that molded and shaped Europe, such as the Renaissance, the Reformation, the Enlightenment, the age of the democratic revolutions, etc.

Europe, especially Eastern Europe, sustained incredible losses in the Second World War. Over 10% of the population of the Soviet Union, Estonia, Latvia, Lithuania, Poland, and Yugoslavia died during the war. The numbers are staggering:

Soviet Union – 21,500,000	Romania – 984,822
Yugoslavia – 1,700,000	Hungary – 750,000
Germany – 5,150,000	Poland – 6,797,822
Austria – 525,000	China's losses – beyond calculation

The totals for the Second World War worldwide were approximately 100,000,000 dead and 50,000,000 refugees. Historians will never know for certain. The U.S. losses were light, comparatively speaking, only 2% of the soldiers killed were Americans. The major fighting in Europe took place between Russia and Germany, as shown by the fact that 94% of the German army's casualties came on the Russian front. For every

American soldier killed in the Second World War the Russians lost 75 killed. Memories of horrific losses from two German invasions in twenty-seven years played a major role in Russia's Cold War fears of the revival of German military power, while Americans saw a rearmed Germany as a bulwark against communism. Russia kept some German prisoners of war for ten years after the war ended, using them to rebuild their devastated country. The Allies did the same, for a shorter number of years.

Domestic Impact: The Military Legacy

As historian Otto Friedrich said, the Second World War thrust the United States into becoming "a nation that would often have to bear the burdens of rescuing" the world. The Gross Domestic Product, GDP, is an economic measurement of the total value of all the goods and services produced in a country in one year. After 1945 the percentage of our annual Gross Domestic Product devoted to military defense averaged between 8% and 20%. Throughout most of American history, our military spending had been so small it had no impact on our economy. Not now.

A large military establishment became a permanent fixture in American life. This is not necessarily good or bad, just different. Opinions vary as to its impact on jobs, its impact as a stimulus to the economy, its impact and role on domestic politics, etc. One of President Eisenhower's last speeches before he left office warned about the "military-industrial complex" and its influence on budgets, expenditures, decision-making, politics, and policies. It referred to something entirely new in our history, the cozy relationship between those who supplied our military with weapons and services and those in Congress and the Pentagon who spent billions of tax dollars. British historian Anthony Badger labeled the relationship "a business–warfare–welfare state." Protecting defense contractors or civilian jobs at military bases became an important part of Congressional politics. Every politician wanted a military establishment in their state or Congressional district and fought against closing any facilities, even if the Pentagon no longer needed the base. Congress eventually created an independent commission to close unneeded bases. However, that did not happen for decades. There was also deep concern about a possible return of the Great Depression when the war ended. Would true world peace and reduced military expenditures lead to another 1929 type depression?

Another major change in American politics was the entry of the military hero into politics. In the past Americans voters elected generals to the presidency – George Washington, Andrew Jackson, Zachary Taylor, Ulysses S. Grant, to name a few, and Theodore Roosevelt climbed to political power stressing his exploits in the Spanish-American War. However, what was new was the *constant* presence of career military men as advisors or candidates. For example, there was Dwight Eisenhower, who cast his first vote just four years before being elected president in 1952; Douglas MacArthur, who was touted as a Republican presidential candidate; Curtis LeMay, who was third party candidate George Wallace's vice-presidential candidate in 1968; Oliver North, a major White House advisor for Nixon and Reagan; and Colin Powell and Arnold Schwarzkopf from the Iraq wars.

Again, Mark Twain quipped that there are two things you do not want to watch being made. One is sausage and the other is legislation. An FDR aide told reporters once that it was safe to ignore the president three times. The first time the president raised a question you replied, that is a great idea and I will get right on it. The second time the topic comes up you say a committee or task force is looking into it; the third time you respond that the recommendation is due to come out shortly. When asked by reporters, the aide replied that presidents are so busy with new things they rarely ever bring a topic up twice. Presidents also accept the fact that they rarely get all they want without changes. The increased political presence of career military men as critics and players introduced a new element into Washington politics. Military men are unaccustomed to working with legislatures; they are more accustomed to delegating responsibility. Washington politics does not work that way. Some career officers also proved to be more willing to circumvent procedures or laws, such as Col. Oliver North and the Iran-Contra affair.

The Iran-Contra Affair was a complicated scandal that surfaced during President Ronald Reagan's second term that involved two seemingly unrelated foreign policies. To greatly simplify, an Iranian revolution in 1979 overthrew a pro-American government and brought to power Ayatollah Khomeini, who threatened to export his radical Islamic revolution throughout the entire Middle East. After a mob overran the American embassy in Tehran in November, 1979, President Jimmy Carter imposed an arms embargo on Iran. Prior to this date, the United States had been the chief supplier of military weapons to Iran. In 1980 a war broke out between Iraq and Iran, lasting until 1988. The Iranian military needed spare parts and supplies, which were only available from the United States. In direct contradiction to America's arms embargo, Reagan administration officials began selling weapons to Iran in 1985. Why?

Col. Oliver North was a top White House aide who organized and ran the plan to circumvent the arms embargo. In Nicaragua a socialist-leaning rebel force, the Sandinistas, had emerged victorious in a civil war against the right-wing Somoza government. Many in the Reagan administration wanted the Sandinistas replaced. Thus, Reagan officials sought funding from Congress to support the Contras, another rebel group that opposed the Sandinistas, who were increasingly linked to communist Cuba and the Soviet Union. Instead of funding, Congress passed three Boland Amendments between 1982 and 1984, expressly prohibiting U.S. aid to the Contras. To evade Congress, Col. North sold weapons to Iran to obtain funds to support the Contras. Congress, and many Americans, were irate when the scheme became public. Col. North felt that because he knew better than Congress what American foreign policy should be, there was no need to listen to the nation's legislature.

Two New Players in the National Power Circle

The Second World War brought increased coordination between the three big players traditionally running the country – big business, the federal government, and organized labor. The war admitted two new institutions into the inner power circle – higher education and the scientific community. Universities received huge contracts for war-related scientific research. Massachusetts Institute of Technology got $117 million and Cal Tech $83 million. Other major beneficiaries were Harvard, Columbia, the University of California at Berkeley, Johns Hopkins, and the University of Chicago. Higher education joined what Eisenhower later termed the "military-industrial complex." Check any college catalog. Every major university has faculty members who do not teach classes. Why? They have a "grant" from a corporation or the Pentagon to do full-time research. At one time during the Cold War 25% of the world's scientists daily worked on weapons systems.

The worldwide nature of the Second World War created new dilemmas. For example, Japan captured the Dutch East Indies, modern Indonesia, the source for 98% of America's supply of natural rubber. During the war the federal government spent $700 million to develop a synthetic rubber industry. Since a government is not profit-driven, it can afford to do something a corporation cannot – "waste" research money "hoping" to discover something, like artificial rubber or a cure for a disease. In 1940 the United States was the world's largest importer of natural rubber; after the war the United States was the world's largest exporter of synthetic rubber. The government gave corporations the patents for a small fee. In short, the war flipped our capitalist economic philosophy upside down. The government was not supposed to be that deeply involved in the economy, but it was, because it had to be, and big business benefited. Government grants to universities removed major scientific and military obstacles, and they still do. Universities and the scientific community are still part of the inner circle of institutions that run our nation. What is wrong with that? Nothing, it was just new, different, and a little more complicated.

The Economy

The war dramatically affected the economy, especially by stimulating big business. The federal government awarded many war contracts on a cost-plus, fixed-fee basis, as was also done during the First World War. Instead of bidding on a contract, it was – you do it and tell us what it cost, and the government will add a profit. In defense of this approach, it was necessary because the military needs were so overwhelming that even major corporations were unsure about their expenses fulfilling a contract. However, the effect of this approach guaranteed big business a profit for war contracts. The war also introduced the concept of tax write-offs for businesses. Two-thirds of all the war contracts, a total of $117 billion, went to corporations in the top 100. General Motors got 8% of the $117 billion. In 1940 the top 100 corporations produced 30% of the nation's manufacturing; by 1943, it was 70%. Over 500,000 small businesses disappeared during the war. Big business came out of the Second World War much bigger and much stronger. Labor also benefited. Labor union membership grew from 8.5 million in 1940 to 15 million in 1945. It had been only 2.8 million in 1929, before the depression began. Agriculture benefited from the war, especially large corporate farms. Many small farms disappeared. Our total agricultural output increased 50% during the war.

Washington economic advisors wanted to avoid the mistakes made after the First World War, which many believed caused or contributed to the onset of the Great Depression. A brief depression had followed the First World War. In addition, memories of the Great Depression lingered. To prevent economic troubles the Office of War Mobilization and Reconversion advocated limited cutbacks in war production at the end of the war and a slow release of soldiers back into civilian life to facilitate the economic shift from war to peace. It did not happen. The soldiers wanted to come home. Their families wanted them to come home. Kids formed "Bring my daddy home" clubs. Elected politicians, senators and representatives, responded accordingly. Surprisingly, the economy did not slide into a depression, although there were numerous strikes in 1946 due to inflation.

The Expansion of the Federal Government
During the war, the executive branch gained power at the expense of the legislative branch, and it retained that power in the postwar period. By the end of the war, three million more employees worked in the federal bureaucracy, increasing from one million in 1940 to four million by 1945. In addition, many new executive agencies were either created during the war or their predecessors began during the war, such as the Council of Economic Advisors; the Central Intelligence Agency, the CIA; the Nuclear Regulatory Commission, the NRC; the Department of Defense, and the Joint Chiefs of Staff.

Finances
Financing the Second World War was much more complicated than financing the First World War. About one-fourth of the nation's annual production during the First World War went to fund the war, while it was twice that during the Second World War. The government imposed taxes and borrowed the rest. In 1945 the annual budget topped $100 billion, more than ten times prewar annual expenditures. Three tax bills were passed during the war.

One budget innovation appeared on October 12, 1942, when Beardsley Ruml, Chairman of the Federal Reserve Board of New York, proposed a new idea. All income taxes for the entire year were due the next 15th of April. This meant that any increased taxes due for tax year 1942 would not be collected until April, 1943. The government needed money now to fight the war. Ruml suggested forgetting about paying the 1942 taxes and placing everyone on a pay-as-you-go basis, withholding taxes from each pay-check. Eventually Congress passed a bill eliminating one-quarter of the 1942 income tax and putting all Americans on the withholding system. Check your paystub. Tax legislation during the war raised individual and corporate income taxes (not the rates) to 70% of the federal government's total tax income, up from 30% in the First World War and 40% during the New Deal. Meanwhile, the national debt rose from $43 billion in June 1940 to $269 billion in June 1946. The per capita debt of $2,000 contrasted sharply with that of $240 in 1919 or $75 in 1865. This massive borrowing by the federal government tripled the money supply and decentralized the banking industry, as banks throughout the nation grew.

The government tried to fight inflation. During the War of 1812 the rate of inflation was 40%; for the Civil War, 120%; for the First World War, 170%. During the Second World War wholesale prices rose 115% and the cost-of-living went up 76%. FDR asked Congress for the authority to impose price ceilings. In January 1942, Congress created the OPA, the Office of Price Administration. Later came the Office of Economic Stabilization. Overall, given the huge expenditures, the federal government did an excellent job controlling inflation during the war.

Draft and CO Status

The Selective Service Act of 1940 provided for a draft. The largest number of conscientious objectors, COs, imprisoned for refusing the draft were Jehovah's Witnesses, who requested exemption not as conscientious objectors but as ministers, claiming they were all ministers. Draft boards refused their request because they also had other jobs. Overall, three times as many conscientious objectors were imprisoned during the Second World War compared to the First World War. Conscientious objectors were only one-third of one percent of the 34 million registered under Selective Service. Among the other COs were Mennonites, Church of the Brethren, and Quakers. Many Mennonites and Quakers worked in war relief. After the war Quakers, who served as ambulance drivers during the Second World War, started the student exchange program, the AFS, which at that time stood for American Field Service (the official name now is AFS Intercultural Programs), to create a more peaceful world. The federal courts never established a clear definition of "religious training and belief," the criteria specified in the law for conscientious objector status. This issue would resurface during the Vietnam War.

In 1942 Congress included 18-year-olds under the Selective Service Act. Considerable public pressure opposed putting 18-year-olds into combat. After the Battle of the Bulge (which lasted from December, 1944, into January, 1945) resulted in the death of many young soldiers, Congress imposed a rule that such recruits needed a year's training. The army ignored the rule. Still, the average soldier in the Second World War was much older than in Vietnam, 26 versus 19.

The GI Bill

The American Legion's National Convention in 1943 issued a call for a GI Bill. Written by Harry W. Colmery, one of its members, the American Legion waged a public relations campaign for the bill. The influential publisher, William Randolph Hearst, threw his support behind the effort; all his newspapers hammered away at the idea. Strangely, the Veterans of Foreign Wars, the VFW, the Disabled American Veterans, the Military Order of the Purple Heart, and the Regular Veterans Organization all opposed it, claiming that it provided too little for veterans with physical and mental disabilities. This led to the inclusion of a provision funding veterans' hospitals. Opposition also came from Southerners, who labeled the idea "the most serious threat to the existing State and local control of education that has yet appeared in this country." They feared it would clash with segregation laws.

Many politicians feared the adverse impact of conversion back to a peacetime economy. In 1944, 8 million served in the military and 22 million worked in war production industries. To help ease the transition to a peacetime economy, Congress included economic provisions in the Rankin-Barden Bill, the Servicemen's Readjustment Act of 1944, popularly called the GI Bill. It provided unemployment insurance for veterans for 52 weeks at $20 per week. Many worried about the laziness encouraged by the "52-20 club." Actually very few veterans used the unemployment provision, and the average stay on unemployment was 17.2 weeks, and only 1 of 19 veterans used all 52 weeks. The GI Bill guaranteed 50% of a bank's loan to a veteran for a home or business, not to exceed $2,000.

The GI Bill also included a provision giving veterans attending college $500 annually for books and tuition and a monthly allowance for living expenses: $50 if single, $75 if married, and up to $90 with children. Annual tuition at even Ivy League colleges was much less than $500. By 1951, 2,350,000 had received college training, 3,430,000 had attended other schools, and 2,390,000 had taken on-the-job training. The GI Bill produced 450,000 engineers; 238,000 teachers; 91,000 scientists; 67,000 doctors; and 22,000 dentists. The bill's supporters initially thought that only a handful of veterans would take advantage of the offer to go to college or trade school, perhaps 8-12%. Nearly 50% did. By 1947 there were 2,328,000 students in American colleges. Four times as many students earned degrees in 1947 compared to 1940, when only 160,000 had.

The GI Bill caused a social revolution; the veterans revolutionized college life. As one civilian said at Lehigh University, "All they care about is their school work. They're grinds, every one of them. It's books, books, books all the time. They study so hard, we have to slave to keep up with them …. And when we have exams, the vets sit up all night studying. It makes us civilians too nervous to sleep!" Previously unofficial quotas limited the number of Jews and Catholics at most prestigious colleges. Note that blacks were not even mentioned in the previous sentence. Their unofficial quota was zero. Ivy

League schools traditionally reserved 50% of their openings for the children of alumni, coming from feeder prep schools. These restrictions disappeared under the veteran onslaught. Blacks also benefited, although segregation and the social atmosphere of postwar America limited the impact. Still, as historian Hilary Herbold wrote, "Clearly, the G.I. Bill was a crack in the wall of racism that had surrounded the American university system. It forced predominantly white colleges to allow a larger number of blacks to enroll, contributed to a more diverse curriculum at many HBCUs (Historically Black Colleges and Universities), and helped provide a foundation for the gradual growth of the black middle class." Over 64,000 recipients were female veterans. Many vets were first-generation college students or victims of the onset of the Great Depression, who either never intended to go to college nor had the opportunity. Before these years, college was almost exclusively a privilege for upper and middle class whites. The GI Bill eventually cost the government $5.5 billion, but the U.S. Treasury received more than $20 in taxes for each $1 spent. The lifetime taxes these educated veterans paid more than made up for the cost to educate them. It makes one wonder if paying students to go to college makes more sense than the current practice of charging them.

Think about the life of someone born around 1910-1915. Graduation from high school coincided with the Crash, then came the Great Depression, the draft, and the Second World War. Finally, the GI Bill dangled the prospect of the "good life" in front of many veterans. You would have studied! In addition, you would have enthusiastically embraced the flood of postwar consumer goods. Your children, growing up in the prosperous 1950s, became the anti-materialistic, protesting youth of the 1960s. These two generations did not understand one another, because they grew up in different worlds.

Why was it done? Why was the GI Bill passed? Remember the veterans march on Washington in 1932, the Bonus Army. FDR thought that the government had not done enough for returning veterans after the First World War. Another factor was everyone's fear that another depression would hit following the war. The Department of Labor predicted there would be 12 to 15 million unemployed after the war. It was cheaper to keep a man in college for a year than it was to keep him in the military. In addition, there was concern over the potential political impact of fascism, which in other countries had appealed to disgruntled veterans.

Social Impact of the War

Blacks served in large numbers in the military, although in segregated units. The Tuskegee Airmen, a selected segregated group of African-Americans pilots, earned praise following the war, much more so than during the war. The war pulled about 2,500,000 Southerners out of the South to serve in the military or to work in Northern factories. Many left their small town rural South for the first time and saw the possibility of something different, both personally and for the black community in general, promoted by black newspapers as the Double–V Campaign, victory abroad and at home, ending segregation. The war stimulated the great black migration out of the South that took place in the late 1940s and 1950s. Before the Second World War, the nation's black population was primarily rural and Southern. Within two decades after the Second World War, a new factor emerged in national politics, a Northern and Western black urban population that voted.

The war also had an impact on other minorities. One challenge all participants face in a war is cracking the enemy's codes to eavesdrop on their communications. Members of the Navajo tribe played a major role in the Pacific campaign communicating sensitive messages in their native language, completely befuddling the Japanese. After the war the Japanese kept asking what that language was. In 1969 the U.S. finally declassified this secret.

One blot was the treatment of Japanese-American citizens. Several months after the attack on Pearl Harbor, FDR's Executive Order 9066 moved all people of Japanese ancestry from the West Coast into relocation centers, kept under armed guard. From there they were moved to guarded camps throughout the West. Hawaii, which, unlike the West Coast, was attacked by Japanese armed forces, never followed the same policy, in spite of the much larger percentage of Japanese in the Hawaiian population. Future Hawaiian Senator Daniel Inouye remembered feverishly working on December 7th as a high school junior first-aid volunteer while speculating about the impact the war would have on his fellow Japanese-Americans. In 1977 Chief Justice of the Supreme Court Earl Warren described the relocation policy as "not in keeping with our American concept of freedom and the rights of citizens." "It demonstrates the cruelty of war when fear, get-tough military psychology, propaganda, and racial antagonism combine with one's responsibility for public security to produce such acts." In 1942 Earl Warren had been the attorney general of California and played a major part in creating the policy for which he later apologized. In 1988 Congress finally compensated those who were incarcerated with $20,000 and a letter of apology. Late in the war American military leaders permitted Japanese-Americans to enlist in the army, sending them to fight in Europe. The famed 442nd Regiment became the mostly highly decorated unit of the war, including 18 Medals of Honor. Daniel Inouye served in the 442nd, losing an arm. On his way home to Hawaii after the end of the war he stopped in San Francisco to get a haircut, wearing his uniform. He was told, "We don't serve Japs here."

The *Korematsu v. U.S.* court case grew out of the relocation policy. Fred Korematsu was arrested and convicted of noncompliance with the military order. The Supreme Court upheld the action in 1944 in a 6-3 decision based upon a broad interpretation of the nation's war powers. In his dissent Justice Robert Jackson explained Korematsu's dilemma. He "was convicted of an act not commonly a crime . . . being present in the state whereof he is a citizen, near the place where he was born, and where he lived all his life. Even more unusual is the series of military orders that make this conduct a crime. They forbid such a one to remain, and they also forbid him to leave. They were so drawn that the only way Korematsu could avoid violation was to give himself up to the military authority." Fred Korematsu had tried to enlist in the army, but was rejected because of ulcers. He then spent his life savings of $150 to learn welding to help the war effort. Instead, he was arrested and sent to a relocation camp.

Women served in the armed forces, about 350,000. Women also served in the domestic economy in large numbers during the war. In 1940 twelve million women worked outside the home. By 1945 nineteen million did. Many worked in factories and decided they liked the extra income. By 1950 as many women were back working in the labor force as had been when the war ended in 1945. Working women needed childcare facilities. The term "latch-key kid" was first used during the war, referring to kids who came home from school with the front door key around their neck, to an empty house, because mom worked and dad was in the military. The government responded by creating many government-run daycare and childcare centers during the Second World War. Perhaps that should be replicated.

Many Americans, for the first time in their lives, traveled around the country, seeing places like warm Southern California right before shipping out to the war in the Pacific. Upon returning, some just stayed in Southern California. Many moved to find jobs in the war-related industries. California alone grew by two million. There was a lot of disruption in the personal lives of Americans. The absentee fathers created many single parent families, contributing, according to sociologists, to high rates of juvenile delinquency in the 1950s.

Pollution

Finally, during the Second World War pollutants showed up for the first time as major problems. The word "smog" first came into use in 1943 in Los Angeles to describe a combination of smoke and fog. The insecticide DDT and plastics also became major parts of our war effort. All three – smog, DDT, and plastics – become factors in the future environmental movement.

American involvement in the Second World War profoundly changed American society. Americans who lived through the deprivation of the Great Depression and the stress of the Second World War found themselves in a different world after 1945. The GI Bill would bring "the good life" for many, fulfilling FDR's promise, at least for some Americans. The nation's economy expanded, easing fears of a return to the dismal Thirties. However, the war left a contradictory legacy. The domestic "good life" was overshadowed by the Cold War and the threat of nuclear weapons. What would the future hold?

42

THE LEGACY OF THE NEW DEAL AND THE BEGINNING OF THE COLD WAR

When a major war ends in any country where people vote for their leaders, the political party associated with the war is frequently voted out of office in the next election. The public mind associates the party in power during the war with sacrifices. The situation has changed, there is no longer a need for sacrifices; it is time for a change of government. England's Winston Churchill was voted out immediately. In the United States the Republicans gained control of the Senate and the House in the 1946 Congressional elections.

Two Questions
Two questions dominated the period following the Second World War.

> **First** – What about the New Deal programs? Were they a collection of Roosevelt policies, or a collection of Democratic Party policies, or a permanent, completely new direction for America? What should Republicans repeal? What could be repealed or modified?
>
> **Second** – What was America's international role as the strongest nation to emerge from the Second World War? Was the United States ready to embark on creating "The American Century," Pax Americana, when American values, power, and wealth would dominate the world with its democratic principles and free enterprise system to inaugurate a new age of world prosperity? Would "The American Way" become "The World's Way?"

On April 12, 1945, Franklin Roosevelt died in Warm Springs, Georgia. Harry S. Truman became president, the only non-college graduate president in the twentieth century, and in all probability, the last ever. Truman, told while dinning with friends at his home in Washington, went immediately to the White House to console Eleanor Roosevelt. He asked her, "What can I do for you?" Her response was, "What can I do for you?" Suddenly, Truman realized he was president of the United States. He wrote in his memoirs, "I felt as if the sun, the moon, and the stars fell on me." He had been the vice president only since January 20, 1945, less than three months. (Truman's middle initial is just an initial; he had no middle name. However, it still takes a period. He put the period in, so we should defer to his usage of his own name.)

A student of American history should be aware that a president, any president, does not enter the presidency unencumbered. A president inherits treaties, situations, policies, and commitments. A president is not free to suddenly and unexpectedly go off in a new direction. The most pressing immediate concerns Truman faced were dealing with Russia, deciding the status of post-war Europe, getting the United Nations off to a good start, and concluding the war against Japan. One major inheritance Truman acquired was the series of decisions made at Yalta in February by FDR, Churchill, and Stalin, the Russian leader.

Yalta – February, 1945

The president and his advisors expected the war against the fanatical Japanese to last two to three more years, into 1947 or 1948, with hundreds of thousands of casualties. Based on the Kamikaze suicide attacks and the high casualties invading Iwo Jima and Okinawa, American officials believed every inch of the Japanese home islands would have to be captured in horrendous house-to-house fighting. The weapon that might shorten that timetable, the atomic bomb, would not even be tested until July 16, 1945. In February it was only a hope; in July it became a reality; in August it became a weapon. The B-29 bomber, *Enola Gay*, dropped the first atomic bomb on Hiroshima on August 6, and *Bockscar* dropped the second on Nagasaki three days later. These were the only two in existence, but twelve more were in the plans, the next ones ready within two weeks. As an interesting historical sidelight, one victim of Hiroshima left the next day to seek safety with relatives in Nagasaki. He survived two atomic blasts, the only individual ever to do so.

The U.S. military needed Russian help to shorten the expected two to three years remaining in the Pacific war. While Russia was a major ally against Germany, Russia had not yet declared war against Japan. At Yalta, Russia agreed to enter the war in the Pacific ninety days after Germany surrendered. It was also agreed that Poland was to have a "democratic" government. However, as Americans would later learn, that word has different meanings. Communist Russia used the word primarily in an economic sense, emphasizing the economic equality of socialism; the West used the word primarily as a political word, emphasizing political rights such as those found in our Bill of Rights.

In February, another of FDR's goals was to get the new United Nations off on the right footing, primarily to avoid a Third World War. Many postwar problems were purposefully left for the United Nations to work out after the war, in order to force the major powers to continue to work together. There was to be no Versailles type postwar treaty. The United States was not repeating the mistakes of 1919. The foundation of the United Nations was the Security Council, composed of the five major powers – the United States, Great Britain, the Soviet Union, France, and China. Each had a veto over all Security Council decisions. Thus, no major power had a reason to leave the United Nations, as Japan, Italy, and Germany had left the League in the 1930s.

It was also decided that Germany, and especially the capital, Berlin, would be occupied by Allied soldiers. This time Germans would know they lost. There would be no myth of the "stab in the back by traitors" that fueled the rise of Hitler.

Should the Atomic Bomb Have Been Used?

No student of history can be neutral evaluating a historical event. Even professional historians bring values and moral judgments to their investigation of a topic. Students need to be alert to pre-existing factors that mold and shape the writing of history. Sometimes bias is obvious in the questions posed. Consider these statements and questions:

a. Why did the United States drop the atomic bomb on innocent, unsuspecting civilians at Hiroshima on August 6, 1945?
b. Japan was negotiating surrender terms, using the atomic bomb was unnecessary. Why did the United States choose to drop the atomic bomb?
c. Would the United States have used the atomic bomb on a white nation like Germany if it had been developed earlier?

Question "a" implies that the atomic bomb should have been used only on a purely military target. Behind the wording of this question is an assumption that using the atomic bomb was a mistake. The historian guided by this research question focuses on the target decision-making process. How and why did Hiroshima come to be the first atomic victim? Could the United States have merely demonstrated the bomb for Japanese observers?

Question "b" suggests there were alternatives, other than the atomic bomb, which could have been selected. It raises a question by inference. What were those alternatives and why were they rejected, if they were even considered at all? Historians writing during the Cold War lived with the daily threat of nuclear annihilation; the atomic bomb ushered in a dangerous new era in the world's history. Some regretted its initial use. Some historians assumed it was unnecessary to drop the atomic bomb, because Japan was about to surrender. How much longer could the war have gone on? What did American decision-makers know and when did they know it? Historians call the "what if" judgments "counterfactual history." It is great fun to rewrite history for a different ending, but can one be sure?

The passage of time adds new documents and perspectives. Normally, governments keep their archives closed for at least 75 years. In the early twentieth-first century, both Japan and the United States released documents revealing new details about the events surrounding the ending of the war. Japan was NOT negotiating surrender terms through Russian diplomats; it was negotiating an end to the fighting, a truce, permitting those in power to remain, a position unacceptable to the United States. It would in all probability lead to another war as soon as Japan rearmed. In addition, the atomic bomb far exceeded expectations in two ways. "Experts," the scientists who developed it, believed that dropping the bomb would kill 20,000 people. It killed 100,000. Second, even scientists did not yet completely understand radiation. It continued to kill after August. In the 1950s American shoe stores proudly featured small x-ray machines to check the position of your toes in your new shoes. One wonders what that repeated exposure did to employees and kids. Los Alamos, the site of the first atomic bomb testing, was so isolated that it appealed to movie companies as a site to film Wild West movies. Those associated with the early postwar films suffered horrendous cancer rates later; however, not until a 1984 court suit was a clear link established between cancer rates and nuclear testing. An awareness of radiation was not present in August, 1945. Others factors were.

One evening decades after the war, a group of about fifteen historians sat around causally discussing the dropping of the bomb. One said nothing. Finally, he blurted out, "Damn it, it was my seventh amphibious assault. How many do you think I could have survived!" Six times he invaded a Japanese held island, wading through water to get to a beach, while Japanese machine guns picked off the unprotected attackers. He was on the ships waiting to attack the Japanese home islands, amphibious assault number seven for him. When those soldiers heard about Hiroshima, they cheered. Try to understand the thinking of that time when you evaluate any event in history. Neither "innocent, unsuspecting civilians" nor "people" died at Hiroshima. The "enemy" died.

Question "c" approaches history from what is sometimes called "a grand theory." The historian asking this question apparently believes that race so dominates history that behind every decision must be a racial basis. In the Second World War, the United States acted out of racial motives, as it always does, according to this perspective. Never read a historical narrative without asking, what did this observer bring to his or her writing – what attitudes, what judgments, what background, what values? All these factors contribute to differing interpretations of historical events. Should the atomic bomb have been used? Think about it, from all perspectives, then decide.

Domestic Issues – Legacy of the New Deal

Coming out of the legacy of the New Deal, the business community perceived the federal government as strongly pro-union. Wages did not keep up with wartime inflation and big business renewed its fight against unions by denying pay increases in the months following the end of the Second World War. Workers responded by going on strike. In 1946 there were almost five thousand strikes involving 4.6 million workers. Republicans, who gained control of Congress in the 1946 elections, responded with the Taft-Hartley Act in 1947, passed over Truman's veto. This law turned the federal government away from being an advocate on the side of organized labor and made it more of a neutral umpire in business-labor clashes. This act created an eighty-day cooling off period for strikes in certain industries, extending the time for negotiations; permitted states to write right-to-work laws, which meant that a worker did not have to join a union in order to keep a job; outlawed the closed shop, which meant that a worker had to be a union member in order to get the job; and required union officers to swear an oath that they were not members of the Communist Party. (The concept of right-to-work laws originated in the 1930s in the South to give white workers an opportunity to avoid joining unions with black workers. The individual "liberty" right-to-work laws preserved was not a person's right to refuse to join a union, it was that person's right to not associate with blacks. Right-to-work laws acquired an additional meaning later, that a worker, any worker, had the "freedom" to not be forced to join a union. By the late 1940s the purpose of a right-to-work law was primarily to prevent unions from gaining a foothold within that state.)

Next on the Republican agenda was the Twenty-second Amendment, limiting a president to two terms. There would be no more four-term Democrats like FDR. This should be repealed. It also means there cannot be any three or four-term Republican presidents. Any president elected to a second term accomplishes little. Congress ignores him, knowing that the president's time is limited. Many Senators and Representatives will be in office long after the president is gone. They know it, and act accordingly. Domestic legislative victories or even initiatives rarely happen during a second term; most second term accomplishments are in foreign policy.

In the election of 1948, Truman surprised everyone by winning. Pollsters had stopped taking polls in September, because Truman was so far behind. The Republican candidate, Thomas Dewey, the governor of New York, was so certain of victory that he began announcing his cabinet. Truman, bolstered by re-election, tried to continue the legacy of the New Deal with his Fair Deal. He wanted eight more TVA type projects; national medical insurance; federal aid to schools; and low-income housing for the poor.

His only achievement was attaining some low-income housing projects. Meanwhile, the issue of loyalty oaths and the internal communist threat, fueled by irrational fears and political posturing, absorbed everyone's attention. Almost all of Truman's goals became unattainable.

The Cold War Develops – Asia, 1945 – 1953

Only the United States occupied Japan after the Second World War ended. There was no Russian help or participation. Our European allies were happy to hand this expense over to us. General Douglas MacArthur, a virtual dictator, forced democracy on the Japanese. It sounds like a contradiction, but it worked. One legacy of this experience was the belief that the United States could replicate this foreign policy achievement elsewhere. Maybe, maybe not. MacArthur at one point talked about preparing the Japanese for "formal conversion to the Christian faith" and using Japan "as a natural base from which in time to advance the Cross throughout all of Asia." Mixed motives, pushing both democracy and Christianity, are what make many countries today leery of our "real" intentions in helping them. The U.S. is better off sticking with only democracy. That is difficult enough to establish.

Korea, owned by prewar Japan, was divided between the North and the South. In many respects this simply recognized what was practical. When the war ended, Russian soldiers occupied the North. As promised, Russia entered the war ninety days, August 8, after Germany surrendered, advancing through Manchuria halfway down the Korean peninsula, in three days. When the United States asked the Russians to stop, they did. American military intelligence had determined that a large number of Japanese soldiers were in Manchuria and Korea. Instead, there were virtually no Japanese soldiers in either. The Russians had encountered no resistance. How does this fit into the Cold War idea that communist Russia was planning to conquer the world? Why stop if that is your policy? Maybe it was not their policy. When Russian and American soldiers withdrew several years later from North Korea and South Korea, the two powers left behind a divided country and two different governments, the communist North and the pro-American South. Note how the "divided" countries caused so much tension and problems in this era – North and South Korea, East and West Germany, North and South Vietnam, and China and Taiwan.

After the Second World War ended, the Chinese Civil War, dating from the 1920s, resumed with the communists winning control of all China in 1949 and the communist leader, Mao Zedong, replacing Jiang Jieshi. It was not surprising that Chiang Kai-shek, the former spelling of Jiang Jieshi, lost the civil war. Corruption was widespread in Chiang's government and peasants paid 147 different taxes, some collected 70 years in advance. The defeat of Chiang, or the victory of Mao, led the United States to adopt a two-China policy, recognizing Chiang's Nationalist Chinese government on the island of Taiwan as the legitimate government of China and not recognizing Mao's government as the legitimate government of mainland or Red China. No matter how much Americans disliked it, the communist Mao was in charge of China. In the long run, this worked to our benefit. The two superpowers, the United States and the Soviet Union, would eventually have to make room for a new, rising superpower, China. It presented the United States with the opportunity to play one communist country against another.

The Cold War Develops – Europe, 1945 – 1953

The initial crisis that stimulated the Cold War was the postwar instability in the Eastern Mediterranean. In Greece communist factions led one side in a civil war. In Turkey, Russia exerted pressure on the Turkish Straits, Russia's naval outlet into the Mediterranean Sea. President Truman responded to this crisis with a speech asking Congress for funds to back a new **Truman Doctrine**, a pledge of aid to any country fighting to prevent a communist takeover, although his speech announcing it never mentioned the word "communism." In order to get this passed, as one senator said, it was necessary to "scare the hell out of the country," all of which fed growing Cold War fears. An influential State Department official, George F. Kennan, sent a "long telegram" to President Truman from Moscow advocating the policy that would become **Containment**. He argued that communism suffered from many internal contradictions, weaknesses, and inconsistencies as a system. If the United States prevented communism from expanding, it would eventually fail internally, which is precisely what happened in 1991 – just not fast enough to suit many Americans.

Several other ideas floated in the air in this period. The **domino theory** stated that if one country succumbed to communism it endangered the countries around it, similar to a virus spreading. Therefore, the United States had to stop communism from an initial conquest, such as South Korea or South Vietnam, to save the neighboring countries from becoming communist. Another idea was the **credibility thesis**, the concept that in order to make our allies trust that the U.S. would come to their defense in places like Europe, it was necessary that the United States honor and live up to our treaty obligations everywhere. Thus, one reason the U.S. became involved in Vietnam was to prove the U.S. would defend Berlin. The only problem with this policy was that the U.S. had defense treaties with over fifty countries.

The newly created National Security Council adopted **NSC Resolution #68**, which endorsed a policy of spending billions for the defense of the free world and for fighting communism. The United States was the world's "last best hope of earth" (Lincoln's phrase) to maintain the idea of freedom against communist slavery. The **Marshall Plan**, proposed by Secretary of State George C. Marshall, aided European economic recovery. Communism and fascism thrive in economic chaos, and so the U.S. literally gave $17 billion to Western European countries, which they spent purchasing American goods, which helped to stimulate our economy. Russia forced the Eastern European countries to not participate. What made the Marshall Plan distinctive was that it offered aid to Europe as a whole, rather than to individual nations. This forced Europeans to work together. Truman called the Marshall Plan and the Truman Doctrine "two halves of the same walnut," meaning that they perfectly complemented one another, one giving economic aid and the other military aid.

The positions of the occupying armies at the end of the Second World War in Europe and the Yalta-adopted policy of occupying the defeated Axis powers made major territorial changes, such as those that followed the First World War, unnecessary. Instead, millions of people in different ethnic groups in Eastern Europe were "relocated" after the war. With Russian troops in Poland, Eastern Germany, Czechoslovakia, Hungary, Bulgaria, and Romania, an "**Iron Curtain**," Winston Churchill's phrase, divided the East and West. Both Germany and the capital city of Berlin, which was entirely inside the Russian occupied zone, were divided into four zones, occupied by Russian, American, British, and French soldiers. As the Cold War developed these divisions solidified into two new countries, East Germany and West Germany. West Berlin, created by joining the French, British, and American zones, became a constant thorn in the side of the Russians and a symbol of freedom to the West. Both sides focused on Berlin. Russia put up the Berlin Wall in 1961 to keep its people in and two American presidents, John F. Kennedy and Ronald Reagan, gave speeches at the Berlin Wall, attacking the Wall as a symbol of oppression.

Historians remain divided over the question of who started the Cold War and which event was pivotal. If Russia intended to take a hostile stand toward the West following the Second World War, it would have been foolish to permit the other three allies – the United States, Great Britain, and France – to also occupy Berlin, which was in the middle of Russian-occupied East Germany. Some historians claim this shows that Russia probably did not intend to start the Cold War. Scholars also debate the basis of Russian policies. Was Russia motivated primarily by the ideology of communism or by traditional Russian security and defense needs? In short, was the Soviet Union a communist country bent on world domination or just following policies that any government of Russia would have to follow due to geographic realities? Remember, Germany had previously invaded Russia twice in a twenty-seven-year span, causing huge casualties. Occupying Eastern Europe defended Mother Russia. In retrospect, it appears that the best argument is that **ideology** played the primary role in the genesis of the Cold War. Events kept it going. Berlin was the focal point for the first confrontation.

A crisis involving Berlin erupted in 1948 when Russia closed all the access roads and railroads leading into Berlin from the West, ostensibly for "repairs." The **Berlin blockade** lasted from July 1948 to May 1949. By airlifting supplies, the West provided all the necessities for the two million people living in West Berlin, thereby proving to Russia American resolve to stay in Berlin. American planes delivered over 2,500 planeloads;

sometimes on such a tight schedule that a plane landed every 45 seconds. Russia wanted the West out. Others also wanted out, of East Berlin. Berlin was a perpetual pain to the Russian and East German communist governments. Before the Berlin Wall went up in 1961, three million people fled through Berlin to the West. All one had to do was to walk from East Berlin to West Berlin and fly out to freedom. After 1961 it was no longer possible because the Berlin Wall divided the city.

In 1949 the U.S. joined **NATO**, the **North Atlantic Treaty Organization**, our first peacetime alliance. NATO included Belgium, the Netherlands, Luxembourg, France, the United Kingdom, Canada, Portugal, Denmark, Norway, and the United States. When a rearmed West Germany joined NATO in 1955, Russia responded by creating the **Warsaw Pact**. The Warsaw Pact included Bulgaria, Czechoslovakia, East Germany, Hungary, Poland, Romania, Albania (which later withdrew), and the Soviet Union. Now two alliances faced one another in Europe. While the concept of collective security theoretically lessened the danger to any one country, the two alliance systems essentially recreated the inflexible, rigid situation that existed prior to the First World War. An attack on one country was an attack on all countries in that alliance. While theoretically providing security, this system left no room for flexibility. In addition, as both Russia and the United States would learn, dealing with your so-called allies could be frustrating, principally France for the U.S. and Yugoslavia for Russia.

After the Second World War, some European leaders were determined to avoid the problems that led to two world wars. Europeans began to come together economically. The European Coal and Steel Community was created in 1951. Conceived by Robert Shuman, the French Foreign Minister from 1948 to 1953, it joined together the coal and steel resources of France, Germany, Italy, Belgium, Luxemburg, and the Netherlands. It operated as if there were no national boundaries. Incredibly successful in rebuilding Europe's economy, in 1957 it grew into the European Common Market, created to "prevent the race of nationalism, which is the true curse of the modern world." This later became the European Union, created by the Maastricht Treaty in 1992. By 1965, the Common Market replaced the United States as the world's number one leader in international trade; by 1973, it was three times ours. This economic status led European countries to feel comfortable challenging aspects of American foreign policy, much to the shock and displeasure of many Americans, who seemed to expect eternal subservient gratitude for the United States winning the Second World War. The world does not work that way. By the 1960s cracks were developing in the solid alliances of both sides; the Soviet Union as the head of the communist world and the United States as the head of the West. By the early 1970s the American dollar was no longer the primary basis for international currencies.

Korea, 1950 – 1953

A historian once referred to the Korean War as "the hardening of the arteries" for the Cold War. It introduced to the American people the concept of a limited war – limited in weapons, in area, and in goals. Limited war was not, and is not, a satisfying experience, as Americans would be reminded in Korea, Vietnam, Iraq, Afghanistan, and Syria. The UN officially classified the Korean War as a police action. President Bill Clinton officially renamed it a war in 1998. The Koran War included the dramatic confrontation between the popular Second World War hero and commander of UN forces in Korea, General Douglas MacArthur, and President Truman over American policy. Truman removed MacArthur of his command in Korea, and sent him home to an adoring public reception. MacArthur wanted to expand the Korean War to China. Truman and the Joint Chiefs of Staff did not. General Omar Bradley, Chairman of the Joint Chiefs of Staff, said expanding the war would involve us in "the wrong war, at the wrong place, at the wrong time, and with the wrong enemy." Limited war frustrated MacArthur. "War's very object is victory, not prolonged indecision. In war there can be no substitute for victory." Incorrect! A war is not in the same category as an athletic contest. Victory is not the purpose of war. War, by an old definition, is diplomacy carried out by other means. In other words, a country has diplomatic objectives it seeks to achieve – by any means. One possible means is war, which is always subordinate to the objective. The means is never more important than the objective.

Historians would learn later that both Russia and China tried to prevent North Korea from invading South Korea in 1950. However, in the 1950s the United States based its policies on the concept that Moscow orchestrated all communist activity anywhere in the world. It was not true. Communism was hardly the coordinated, monolithic force the U.S. perceived it to be. The Korean War ended in a stalemate in 1953, satisfying no one.

One little tidbit from the Korea War. Two months after the armistice ended the fighting, a North Korean pilot defected to South Korea in a state-of-the-art Russian jet fighter, a MIG-15. U.S. Intelligence was thrilled, and the pilot became wealthy, receiving the $100,000 reward offered for a Russian jet plane. However, No Kum-sok did not know about the reward; he just wanted his freedom. In his first few months in America he frequently traveled by train between Washington and New York City for debriefings. He liked the attractiveness of Newark, Delaware. Aware that the University of Delaware was a good engineering school, he enrolled as a student, graduating with a bachelor's degree in mechanical and electrical engineering. He went on to a career as an aeronautical engineer. The MIG-15 is now in the National Museum of the Air Force at Wright-Patterson Air Force Base in Dayton, Ohio.

43

IKE AND JFK, 1953 TO 1963

Eisenhower in the White House

To the disappointment of many conservatives, not much changed during the Eisenhower Republican administration. Eisenhower, nicknamed "Ike," faced many domestic policy questions when he became president in January of 1953. Should the New Deal continue? Was it a Democratic Party policy? Or a Franklin Roosevelt policy? Or maybe even a socialist policy? Ike did not encourage dismantling the New Deal; indeed, he even extended parts of it, such as Social Security coverage. His conservative critics nicknamed his administration the "Dime Store New Deal," a cheap version of the New Deal. Other issues grabbed everyone's attention.

McCarthyism

The Red Scare of McCarthyism was inspired by Republican Senator Joseph McCarthy from Wisconsin. McCarthy was a controversial, powerful senator who played a leading role in a crusade to ferret out communists within our state and national governments. Republican control of the Senate after the 1952 elections gave McCarthy the position of Chairman of the Senate Committee on Government Operations. He conducted numerous hearings, searching for "leftist" subversives in the national government. His accusations, which were accompanied by many violations of civil liberties, searched high and low for communists who had infiltrated our national and state governments. One courageous senator, a fellow Republican, Margaret Chase Smith of Maine, characterized McCarthyism as "the Four Horsemen of Calumny — Fear, Ignorance, Bigotry, and Smear." He gained a wide following. New York even required applicants for fishing licenses to renounce communism! Accusations tarred and feathered many people, but few communists were found after years of years of searching for "Reds" working to undermine American governments. Anyone who ever entertained any leftist idea was suspect, if it was to the left of the accuser. One individual listed as a potential subversive by the FBI was an eighth-grader who wrote his term paper on the American Socialist Party.

Sensitive, thinking intellectuals living in the Great Depression of the 1930s were certain that capitalism, and maybe democracy, had failed. What would replace them in the future? Only two choices presented themselves, communism and fascism. Of the two, communism, if one overlooked its many faults, seemed to be the more humanitarian choice, at least in its theories. This necessitated ignoring the worst aspects of communism as practiced in Russia. Fascism, in both theory and practice in Germany and Italy, held less appeal. Thus, many thoughtful, concerned intellectuals leaned leftward during the Thirties. That came back to haunt them during the early Cold War. A kind word or written comment in the Thirties branded you as a traitor, or at least a "fellow traveler," in the 1940s and 1950s. By then the United States faced the need to preserve our nation while locked in a deadly Cold War with an alien ideology diametrically opposed to everything America stood for. That struggle raised many questions, some of which remain today. Does our nation have to extend civil liberties to those individuals who are determined to destroy them? Or, is that not the point of civil liberties? Is the "free marketplace of ideas" sufficient to guard our liberties and guarantee our survival?

In 1947 United States Attorney General Thomas Clark published a list of organizations designated as subversive. Over time the list grew. Before President Nixon abolished it in 1974, the list contained hundreds of organizations. The Better Business Bureau and the Chamber of Commerce frequently reprinted the list, mailing it out to all businesses. Some organizations were obvious, such as the Ku Klux Klan and the Communist Party of the USA; but, the American Peace Crusade or the Massachusetts Committee for the Bill of Rights? A person could contribute a small check or say something vaguely supporting an apparently innocuous cause or organization and discover years later that he or she was on a list of suspected subversive persons because some leftist or socialist or communist either belonged to or spoke well of that organization. To put the nature of such accusations into perspective, Martin Luther King's drive for civil rights was suspect. Why? Because American communists supported it! How can a member of an organization be responsible for everything and anything any other member or supporter has ever done or said? One famous Herblock political cartoon showed a fan calling a baseball player a "communist" because he made an error. (Herbert Block was a political cartoonist for the *Washington Post*.) Such was the Zeitgeist of the era.

The Civil Rights Movement

Eisenhower was president when the momentous *Brown* decision desegregating public schools was announced in 1954. In many respects, the *Brown* decision and events such as the 1957 confrontation at Little Rock's Central High School were part of the Cold War. At Central High School in Little Rock, Arkansas, Governor Orval Faubus refused to permit the integration of the high school by nine black students. President Eisenhower responded by sending troops to uphold the Supreme Court decision. African and Asian newspapers closely followed such events. The U.S. government always trumpeted positive advances on media outlets in the Third World and on Radio Free Europe, which broadcast into the Eastern European Soviet satellites. More on the civil rights movement later; it deserves a full chapter.

Transportation and Education

Two of Ike's greatest accomplishments involved transportation. During his presidency Congress created the Interstate Highway system, consisting of more than 40,000 miles of four lane, limited access, divided highway, and the St. Lawrence Seaway with Canada, both of which boosted the economy and built up our military preparedness. In time of war the military has the authority to restrict the Interstate Highway system to exclusive military use. Some straight stretches of the Interstate Highways are emergency airfields. That is one reason why there are no billboards right beside the Interstate Highways.

Sputnik and the Space Race

Concerned over Russia's launching of the world's first satellite, Sputnik, Congress created the National Defense Education Act, pumping money into schools and teacher training, especially math and science. A college student receiving NDEA loans had 10% of the loan forgiven each of the first five years they taught in a public school. If the teacher paid back 10% each of those five years, there was no interest. In the end, the teacher paid back only 50%, with no interest. Sounds better than our current student loan policies. If one thinks of highly educated people as a national resource, American society needs to reward their desire to learn, not punish them with heavy student debt. Remember the long-term financial benefits to the U.S. Treasury from the GI Bill.

The Affluent Society

The economy grew in the late 1940s and the 1950s. Many Americans were very pleased by the rise in their standard of living. Think about the life of someone born around 1910. That person graduated from high school just in time for the Great Depression to get started. Then came the Second World War. Finally, after being discharged from military service at the age of 35, life began to get better.

Suburbia

As the suburbs grew, Americans could not decide whether the suburbs were good or bad. What did this new style of living mean? The urban historian Lewis Mumford knew – it was not good! Levittowns, mass-produced with assembly line methods, building as many as thirty houses per day, symbolized the post-Second World War suburban boom. The company built four towns. Three retain the name, Levittown, in New York, Pennsylvania, and Puerto Rico. At less than $8,000, these houses were cheaper than rented apartments. To Mumford the suburbs represented "a new kind of community . . . of unidentifiable houses lined up inflexibly, at uniform distances, on uniform roads, in a treeless communal waste, inhabited by people of the same class, the same income, the same age group, witnessing the same television performances, eating the same tasteless pre-fabricated foods (TV dinners were invented in the 1950s), from the same freezers, conforming in every outward and inward respect to a common mold . . . ." One of the builders, William Levitt, admitted that he once got lost in a Levittown. All the streets looked the same. Mumford lamented the absence of what he considered the ideal urban setting, the daily interaction found in mixed neighborhoods, mixed in class, age, income, and occasionally race, or at least nationality. "The cost of this detachment in space from other men is out of all proportion to its supposed benefits. The end product is an encapsulated life, spent more and more either in a motor car or within the cabin of darkness before a television set."

The suburban community lacked teenagers, senior citizens, and blacks. Each Levittown excluded blacks through restrictive covenant deeds. The New York Levittown originally had 82,000 whites, only whites; it is still less than one percent African-American. In August 1957, the first black family, Bill and Daisy Myers, moved in. Other critics added their voice, literally. Look up Malvina Reynolds' song on the Internet, "Little Boxes," recorded by Pete Seeger in 1963, which criticized the "ticky tacky houses" that produced conformity, consumerism, and political indifference, especially to the plight of the poor and blacks.

Sociologist Herbert Gans disagreed with Mumford. Gans moved his family into Levittown to study his neighbors. He found many positive features, such as a decline in xenophobia against Jews and Catholics, widespread participation in civic and social activities, keen interest in the schools, and an acceptance of those outside one's ethnic background. Family activities dominated. There were playgrounds everywhere and bars nowhere. Neither cultural nor political conformity characterized the town. Neither did a desire to "keep up with the Joneses" through what an earlier economist and sociologist, Thorstein Veblen, had labeled "conspicuous consumption." Their lives were far "superior to what prevailed among the working and lower middle classes of past generations."

Critics

However, the decade of the 1950s had other critics. The economist John Kenneth Galbraith, in *The Affluent Society*, decried the emphasis on personal goods to the detriment of public needs – schools, transportation, bridges, infrastructure, etc. Most

Americans just joyfully and thankfully adopted the book's title to describe what was finally due to them. Between 1950 and 1980 the population increased by 50%, but the number of cars quadrupled. Life was good, even if the roads were crowded and parking places were hard to find. But, in 1962 Rachel Carson, a biologist, published *Silent Spring*, a warning that Americans were destroying their environment in the mad pursuit of the good life and even endangering their survival.

Foreign Policies

Eisenhower's foreign policies did not really change much from Truman's foreign policies. Ike and his Secretary of State, John Foster Dulles, continued the Truman policies and added some emphasis. John Foster Dulles had an apocalyptic view of the world's struggle between the Free World and communism. Both his father and his grandfather were Presbyterian ministers. Dulles could not say the word communism without adding the adjective atheistic, "atheistic communism." He saw communism as a godless monolithic force directed from Moscow. He was certain that all communists around the world danced on Moscow's puppet strings.

The policy of **collective security** continued, eventually committing the United States to defend 54 nations. Some of these so-called new allies brought trouble. Supplying arms to Pakistan to fight communism unnerved India, because of old grievances against her neighboring country, Pakistan. American policymakers saw the world in black and white, freedom versus communism; every problem was a Cold War issue. Are you on our side or Russia's? Most of the rest of the world did not see it that way. Local disputes were more important to them.

Dulles also announced a policy of **massive retaliation**, which threatened to use all our atomic bombs, everything in our arsenal, to respond to any provocation. Joined to this approach was the **preemptive strike**, meaning the U.S. might attack another country to prevent that country from striking the U.S. first. Is that not what Japan did to America in 1941? Four times during Eisenhower's presidency, John Foster Dulles, Vice President Richard Nixon, and the Joint Chiefs of Staff urged a nuclear attack on Russia, a preemptive strike before their nuclear arsenal rivaled ours. Eisenhower said, "NO!"

Finally, the United States adopted a policy of having **a high ranking officer in a plane in the air** at all times so that if the United States was attacked and destroyed, there would still be someone who could give the official orders to send all the remaining missiles and drop all the atomic bombs. In addition, the U.S. periodically sent waves of bombers toward Russia and ordered them to turn back at the last minute. This policy was called **brinkmanship**. Critics called it a game of "chicken" to make the enemy wonder if the U.S. was nuts. The theory was that the Russians would not be nuts if they thought the U.S. was. Some superpower had to be sensible. Read the novel *Failsafe*; or, watch the movie with the same title. It is frightening.

JFK's Foreign Policy

During the campaign for the election of 1960 Democrat John F. Kennedy accused the Eisenhower administration and the Republican candidate, Richard M. Nixon, who had been Eisenhower's vice president, of permitting the development of a "missile gap," meaning that the Soviet Union had more missiles than the U.S. had, thus endangering our defense. It was not true. However, after winning the election partially on the premise of a missile gap, JFK had to embark on a buildup of our missile capability. It led Russia to respond by building more, thereby fueling the arms race. The arms race was the fear on both sides that one's potential enemy would achieve either a technological breakthrough or such a massive missile potential that one side would clearly become a second-rate power. Some called it MAD, for Mutually Armed Destruction. Few would survive, and those who did might wish they had not; therefore, no one would start a nuclear war. Critics labeled MAD an insane approach to national security.

A planned Central Intelligence Agency, CIA, project inherited from the Eisenhower administration proved to be an embarrassing failure for President John F. Kennedy. The Bay of Pigs invasion by Cuban exiles trying to overthrow Fidel Castro in Cuba failed miserably. In 1962 came the greatest crisis of the Cold War, the Cuban missile crisis. Russia began setting up missiles in Cuba, where Castro boldly announced that he was a communist. Earlier he encouraged leftist guerrilla warfare throughout Latin America. JFK responded to the missile threat with a naval blockade and threatened invasion, a strong reaction, but one that fortunately left a way out for Nikita Khrushchev, who removed the Cuban missiles provided the U.S. agreed to remove its missiles from Turkey. JFK had previously ordered the outdated missiles in Turkey removed. The Pentagon, which opposed the removal and was unsure if the young president had a backbone, did not carry out that order. Kennedy was irate when told the missiles were still in Turkey. However, it gave him a negotiating chip. Thank goodness.

With the end of the Cold War, historians have been able to see Russian documents and interview Russian officers stationed in Cuba at that time. They had nuclear warheads, they had missiles ready to fire, and they had authorization to fire those missiles if the United States invaded Cuba. In addition, Kennedy insiders by the end of the twentieth century began telling their story of the crisis and administration documents were declassified. They reveal that JFK purposely overreacted to reassure our allies and the American public that the U.S. would strongly react to any Russian provocation. In retrospect, it was too strong and too unnecessary; the Cuban missiles did not change the nuclear or missile balance of power. The United States still held an overwhelming advantage over the Russians. And, both sides knew it. Our European allies did not see as much at stake as the U.S. did. As France's Charles De Gaulle warned, alliance with the U.S. amounted to "annihilation without representation." Cooler heads in the Kremlin and the White House negotiated and signed the Test Ban Treaty in 1963, a small successful international beginning to limiting nuclear weapons. JFK's Peace Corps program tried to give Third World peoples a different image of America and Americans, one that sincerely tried to improve the everyday life of ordinary people.

The Free World Colossus

One leftist author during the 1960s said that the United States had an entirely different reputation overseas. In his book, *The Free World Colossus*, David Horowitz noted that the United States had over 400 military bases around the world. All the overseas military bases added together for all the other countries in the world could not match that number. The United States really was a free world colossus. It still is. But, was the United States a force for good or ill? The prime minister of Canada was once asked by an American reporter one of those questions that seem to fall into the category of, "I am asking this because I don't know what to ask." He said, "What is it like being beside the United States?" After thinking a few minutes, the prime minister replied that it was a lot like sleeping with an elephant. Every twitch makes you nervous because all the beast has to do is roll over in its sleep and we are gone. America's sheer size – economically, militarily, politically, culturally – has an impact all over the world, every day. It is not appreciated in many parts of the world.

Kennedy's legacy included an increased U.S. involvement in the imbroglio that became the Vietnam War, another limited war, as Korea had been, but this time a guerrilla war that frustrated the military, the government, and the public for years. Historians use it as a dividing line between distinct eras in American history. No one will ever know what JFK's long-range goal in Vietnam was. Kennedy's presidency ended on November 22, 1963, when he was assassinated in Dallas, Texas. Vice President Lyndon Johnson succeeded him.

44

THE ZEITGEIST OF THE 1960S:

Turmoil in Public Space

"Public Space" refers to the area of public interaction between people. The 1960s was a decade of incredible change, especially in public activism against the nation's perceived failings – racial discrimination, the war in Vietnam, gender discrimination, and strict sexual codes, all of which led to the civil rights movement, the antiwar movement, the women's movement, and the sexual revolution. In the words of an old saying, "Everything nailed down seemed to be coming loose."

Effects of the Civil Rights Movement

The civil rights movement used nonviolent resistance as a tactic. Nonviolent resistance asked participants to call attention, peacefully and lovingly, to the inequities of the political and social systems. Nonviolent resistance has four stages:

> Investigation of a problem
> Efforts to negotiate a solution
> Self-purification to get ready for public protest
> Direct action followed by further negotiation

Inspiration for nonviolent resistance came from several sources – Henry David Thoreau's "Civil Disobedience" essay, Gandhi's example of gaining independence for India and, most importantly, the Gospel's injunction to love one's enemies. The Christian message of hope and redemption deeply influenced all the early leaders of SCLC, the Southern Christian Leadership Conference, SNCC, the Student Nonviolent Coordinating Committee, and CORE, the Congress of Racial Equality. SNCC was founded in May, 1960, with a statement of purpose that included a call to the "Judaic-Christian traditions" that seek "a social order permeated by love." In Christian theology, if you only love those who love you, you have risked nothing. There is no risk in loving those who return love. The Gospel tells you to love those who do not love you. That is tough to do.

The forms of protest used by the civil rights movement – the boycott, the sit-in, the freedom ride, the mass march – were all efforts to keep the illegal protests civil. The authorities did not see them that way. Neither did the average Southerner. The protests were not only violations of the law; they were also violations of long-standing customs in the South. An elaborate etiquette reinforced the Southern caste system. Read John Howard Griffin's electrifying *Black Like Me*, which stunned white America when published in 1960. A white journalist, Griffin medically treated his skin to appear black. A white man inside an apparent black body, he traveled throughout the South and experienced what it meant to be black in the land of Jim Crow. Blacks stepped aside on the sidewalk or the street, blacks avoided looking directly into a white person's eyes, and even adult blacks were called by a diminutive name; males were "boy," women were "Missy," etc. To the overwhelming majority of white Southerners the civil rights protests were, first, an attack against segregation laws, and, second, a break in decorum, a threat to and an attack on standards of public behavior. It raised the question, even in the minds of whites who disliked segregation, "Where will it all end?"

Social equality, as a new standard of public interaction and behavior, is very confusing. The demand for social equality spills over into the realm of public politeness, raising significant questions about public interaction. It is not clear who should be showing what respect or politeness to whom. To your elders? To women? Should a man hold a door open for a woman, the rule for the previous generation? Or, is that demeaning to the woman? Should anyone hold a door for a disabled person, or for a parent pushing a stroller, or for someone carrying packages, or does equality trump politeness and mean that everyone negotiates the door for himself or herself?

Historian Kenneth Cmiel has explained the historic role and function of politeness. Politeness is a way of **being nice**. The introduction of civil etiquette into public behavior originated because one of the functions of politeness is:

> First, to reduce the amount of interpersonal violence. At some point or other we are all polite to people we do not like simply because we do not want to live in a contentious world. An example is how you behave when a police officer stops you, without what you feel is a good reason. Teenagers, the poor, and blacks are more familiar with this experience. "Yes, officer, no, officer" works better to defuse the interaction. "What the hell is this all about?" increases the tension, for both.

A second function of politeness is to reaffirm established social boundaries. When huge inequities exist in the social order, polite everyday custom reinforces them. For example, it reinforces social inequities when a man holds a door for a woman, or when a man is expected, by a waiter or waitress, to be the one to whom the bill is presented. Another situation arises when a man and a woman enter a car dealership to buy a new car. Invariably the salesperson speaks to the male, in spite of the fact that women now purchase more cars than do men.

In essence, in the civil rights movement, the first function of politeness, being nice, was used to attack the second function of politeness, maintaining the segregation system. The movement brought on violence against the protesters; indeed, Martin Luther King expected this, and welcomed it. The purpose of the movement was to force "the oppressor to commit his brutality openly – in the light of day – with the whole world looking on."

Until the middle of the 1950s the civil rights movement was primarily one of legal challenges inside courtrooms. However, after becoming a public process in the 1950s, by early 1964 the civil rights movement was restive; gains were not easy to point to. Protestors became willing to be more assertive, to be less polite, and to defend themselves. A combination of growing black nationalism, Malcolm X, grass roots activism, a sense of frustration, and growing antiestablishment sentiment in the culture at large all fed the new feelings. It was just a few steps to "Black Power," to the Black Panther movement, and to calls for violence by people like Stokely Carmichael and H. Rap Brown. "Whitey" now became the enemy. Two civil rights organizations, CORE and SNCC, expelled all their white members.

Real violence was rare, but what appeared in volume was *the talk* of violence. For radicals the angry words were part of their sense that polite society had it backwards – the true obscenities were the Vietnam War and racial hatred. Indeed, the very idea of obscenity had to be rethought. Here is a quote from H. Rap Brown, a black radical. "The dirtiest word in the English language is not "f-ck" or "sh-t," but the word "N(n-word)" coming from the mouth of Bull Conner, the sheriff of Birmingham, Alabama." You are today offended more by the N-word. But in the 1960s people were offended by all three. Until the 1960s profanity was much more private than public. It was rarely present on television or in films or in songs. The popular television comedy, "All in the Family," 1971-1979, is famous among trivia buffs as the first time in history that someone flushed a toilet on television or in a film. Shocking! Southerners and others who favored segregation, and who neither meant nor saw an intended offense in the N-word, were deeply offended by the first two. Meanwhile, many Northerners and blacks who opposed segregation were more offended by the last word, the N-word. In short, everyone was offended, which was the purpose of H. Rap Brown's remark. There was a disturbance in the public space, where everyone interacted with others. Everyone pondered, "Where will it all end?" More about the civil rights movement in the next chapter.

Concurrent Effects of the Counterculture Movement

The free speech movement at the Berkeley campus of the University of California in the fall of 1964 shocked the country. The University of California has multiple campuses, such as the University of California at Los Angeles, UCLA, the University of California at Riverside, at San Bernardino, etc. The Berkeley campus is the elite one in the California public university system, the hardest for a student to get accepted to. Many of the leaders of the free speech movement had worked in Mississippi and Alabama for SNCC during the Freedom Summer of 1964 and used Freedom Summer tactics at Berkeley – mass civil disobedience and sit-ins. One sit-in led to the arrest of 773 student protesters, dragged to the police vans by 367 officers. It took twelve hours to arrest them all.

In 1965 a new twist arrived at Berkeley. The campus had a tradition that on one particular street any person was allowed to speak about any topic, any time. In short, it was for soapbox orators, just like Hyde Park in London. A nonstudent on March 3 stood on that campus street corner at Berkeley and held up a sign that just said, "F-ck." When the authorities asked him to clarify his meaning, he added an exclamation point. He was arrested, which threw the campus into turmoil over the issue of "dirty speech" versus free speech. Dirty speech is offensive. Indeed, that is its purpose. It is meant to shock. Try to imagine someone using profanity during a church service.

Berkeley was the first campus forced to confront "dirty speech," news of which quickly spread through the media. Soon many other campuses faced increasingly vile and insulting language. College administrators were concerned – for two reasons. First, at that time the tradition of "in loco parentis" gave them the responsibility to do what any reasonable parent would do in this situation. Punish the kid. Put an end to this nonsense. Second, public colleges get their funding from the state legislature, and the public and the legislators were angry. "These kids are attending the most prestigious public university in the California system, the one we support with our tax money!" The Berkeley "dirty speech" issue was the number one reason why voters supported Ronald Reagan's successful campaign for governor of California in 1966. See Matthew Dallek, *The Right Moment: Ronald Reagan's First Victory and the Decisive Turning Point in American Politics*. Reagan's wit aptly stated what many without access to the media wanted to say. He once said, "A hippie is someone who looks like Tarzan, walks like Jane, and smells like Cheetah." (Cheetah was the monkey.)

The gap between the generations seemed huge. In 1968, during the height of the Vietnam War, radical students at Columbia University used a sit-in to take over the main administration building. They were protesting against the faculty's acceptance of a grant to evaluate weapons for the Pentagon and plans to build a gym that would force blacks out of an adjacent neighborhood. Remember, as stated earlier, during the Second World War higher education had joined the inner circle of institutions that run our country. The president of Columbia University, Grayson Kirk, captured the viewpoint of many critical older Americans. "Our young people, in disturbing numbers, appear to reject all forms of authority, from whatever source derived, and they have taken refuge in a turbulent and inchoate nihilism whose sole objectives are destruction. I know of no time in our history when the gap between the generations has been wider or more potentially dangerous." The New York City police soon gleefully dragged the protesters out, often by their feet. One must be careful, however, in making a blanket condemnation of all young people, as Grayson Kirk had done. A public opinion poll in 1969 asked, "Do you favor immediate withdrawal of all U.S. troops from Vietnam?" Those under 29 said no, 59%; those over 50 said no, 51%. Protesting students were very much in the public eye, thanks to the media, but they were never a majority of "Our young people."

Authenticity

Opponents of the prevailing values of society, the advocates of a counterculture from Rousseau through to the 1960s, always valued authenticity over civility. The requirement to be polite, being nice, does not encourage personal expression. In the 1960s people, mostly young, started wearing T-shirts with shocking messages, piercing their tongues and noses, males began wearing earrings, and drug use spread beyond the lower classes into the middle class. Their message to the rest of society was clear and offensive. That message was – "This is the real me. It offends people, but, hey, it's the real me. If it offends you, that's your problem." Today the tattoo and facial jewelry play this role of shocking many older people. Everyone gets tattoos so they can be individualistic, which makes no sense.

The counterculture movement challenged the traditional social standard to suppress impulsive behavior, arguing for the liberation of self in the name of personal freedom. It introduced the phrase, "doing my own thing." This translated into a colorful way of life – long hair, painted bodies, elaborate slang, and open sexuality. Hippies looked different, acted different, and were different. Drugs became part of this liberating experience, and were defended as such. Publicly shocking behavior was justified because it was publicly shocking behavior. That was part of the purpose of it. Many "normal" people do not believe that public space is an appropriate place in which to make personal expressions. The counterculture did, and does.

As an example, long hair became an issue in 1963 when the Beatles first became popular in the United States. However, look closely at those pictures from 1963 and 1964. Their hair is not long in the back or sides, but in the front. It was controversial because critics said it made it hard to tell the difference between boys and girls. It was not until 1966 that long hair for males appeared and became associated with a wholesale attack on the "American way of life." You can now see the connection in some people's minds between music and "everything is falling apart." The years 1967 and 1968 marked the high years of the counterculture. It lost its specialness and uniqueness when mainstream America began adopting some of its outward appearances. In 1967 the *New York Times* reported that even doctors and stockbrokers, "traditional squares," were starting to let their hair grow longer.

Effects of the Revolution in Sex Mores

The so-called revolution in sexual customs and mores actually had roots in the 1950s, just as the hippie movement did growing out of the Beat Generation. *Playboy* magazine first appeared in 1953. Helen Gurley Brown published *Sex and the Single Girl* in 1962, before the decade of the Sixties really began. It was not until 1971 that *Penthouse* first contained pictures of female genitalia; *Playboy* followed five months later. You can trace the changing decade through *Cosmopolitan* magazine articles between 1964 and 1970. In 1964 it ran such staid articles as "Catholics and Birth Control," and "Young Americans Facing Life with Dignity and Purpose." By 1969, however, one sees "The Ostentatious Orgasm," and "Pleasures of a Temporary Affair." Picture older people waiting in line at the grocery store to check out, glancing over the covers of the magazines on display. "My, how things have changed." For better, or for worse? The average voter was a 49-year-old woman; she was hardly a person who approved of such things.

Effects of Supreme Court Rulings

In the 1942 case *Chaplinsky v. New Hampshire* a defendant was convicted for calling someone a "damned racketeer" and a "damned fascist." The court said some utterances were of "such slight social value" that the First Amendment did not protect them. However, in the following years the Supreme Court slowly chipped away at its own ruling. The Court consistently set limits. It never accepted the legitimacy of violence, holding fast to the notion that the government has a monopoly on the legitimate use of force. Earlier American society had limited free speech on the grounds that *some* free speech *led* to violent behavior. After this case, the Court rewrote, case by case, the boundaries to enlarge the space for insulting speech and uncivil public behavior.

There were always significant qualifications for the workplace, schools, and courtrooms. There the boundaries differ. The Bill of Rights is limited inside a school. For example, a teacher or principal can search a locker or backpack, something a police officer cannot do without a search warrant. However, in the 1960s it turned out that kids did not lose all their rights when they walked into a school. When the courts upheld protests inside a school, it now rested on the grounds that it was not disruptive. The most important case in this regard was *Tinker v. Des Moines*, 1969. A handful of students were suspended in 1965 for wearing black armbands in protest against the Vietnam War, an action specifically prohibited by their school board. The Supreme Court vindicated the students, precisely because their action was civil. The Court noted that the students' actions did not involve "regulation of the length of skirts or type of clothing, hair style, or deportment." Nor did it concern "aggressive, disruptive action." Note that length of hair or skirt was considered disruptive behavior at that time.

Another Area of Change – Informalization

Informalization is a term invented by sociologists to describe periodic efforts to relax social etiquette. In the 1960s it appeared in the long hair in the workplace, the "casual Friday" dress code, calling your boss by his or her first name, decorating your office desk as "my space," wearing colorful patches on your clothes, and painting psychedelic colors and designs on your car, as if the car had just taken the drug LSD. Another manifestation was the practice of older patients being called by their first name in doctor's offices. All this shocked and disturbed older Americans and many young Americans, feeding the groundswell that burst on the political scene as the emergence of conservative politics with the election of Ronald Reagan.

Earlier, American society stressed the continuity between private everyday life, public actions, and the avoidance of violence. To keep violence from erupting, the first two had to remain "polite." The new 1960s thinking undercut that relationship. If you define civil behavior as the control of and the hiding of emotions, some of the new behavior norms were not civil. Freedom of expression became a higher value than civility, rationality, and politeness, all of which confused and angered many Americans.

Cultural Icons in the Public Memory

Be careful remembering the 1960s as a period of drugs, strife, and protest. When the U.S. Postal Service asked Americans in 1998 to vote for "the subjects that best commemorate the 1960s," the three winners as cultural icons were the Beatles, *Star Trek*, and Woodstock, the last curiously misnamed because that "happening" was actually miles away. Who would have guessed these three in 1960?

45

THE CIVIL RIGHTS MOVEMENT, OR, THE BLACK FREEDOM STRUGGLE

Why two different titles for this chapter? The Civil Rights Movement is the traditional name. The second, the Black Freedom Struggle, is a newer focus used by some black historians to emphasize that blacks were the principal participants who struggled and won civil rights. Benevolent whites did not bestow civil rights upon the black community. The victories were extracted from a reluctant white society. And, the struggle is not over.

The Cold War and the Courts

Racism appeared for the first time in Webster's Third International Dictionary, published in 1961. A similar word, racialism, had been around for several decades, but it was not widely used. In 1901, when the first Webster's International Dictionary came out, English had no single word embodying the idea of prejudice and discrimination based upon race. That does not mean it was not present. Hitler's genocide during the Second World War gave racism a bad image. Was that the logical conclusion to a nation's tacit endorsement of racism? Later, during the Cold War, racism became a factor in our image and in our relationship with Third World nations in Africa and Asia.

In 1944 a Swedish sociologist, Gunnar Myrdal, published *An American Dilemma*, a look at "the Negro problem," as it was called at that time. His contribution to the debate emphasized the great degree to which segregation and discrimination contradicted the principles that Americans claimed they stood for and believed in.

In this period black migration out of the South accelerated, three million leaving in the 1940s and 1950s. Never underestimate the degree to which changes in demography emerge as a factor causing other changes. As president, Truman desegregated the armed forces in 1948 by Executive Order 9981. In actuality, the Korean War really did it, creating an integrated army. The 1948 Democratic Party platform adopted a strong civil rights plank, due in part to the report of Truman's 1947 Commission on Civil Rights, *To Secure These Rights*. In an attempt to deny Truman's reelection and to punish the party, Southern Democrats formed the Dixiecrat Party led by Strom Thurmond, a rabid segregationist senator from South Carolina. The tactic failed; Truman won. The black vote in Northern cities helped Truman. In almost all states the Electoral College system gives the state's entire electoral vote to whomever wins that state's popular vote. If the two parties are relatively equal, a slight increase in a party's traditional voters means that party wins the whole state. The black vote in several states produced that result for the Democrats.

Meanwhile the NAACP chipped away at the legal foundation for segregation, established by the U.S. Supreme Court in *Plessy v. Ferguson*, 1896, the "separate but equal" decision. *Buchanan v. Warley*, 1917, had an unusual twist. A white man, Buchanan, sold a city lot to a black man, Warley. In an action unrelated to this particular sale, the city council for Louisville, Kentucky, passed an ordinance using zoning laws to create segregated residential neighborhoods. Citing the ordinance, Warley refused to complete the sale; Buchanan sued to get his money. Ignoring the minor financial issue involved, the U.S. Supreme Court ruled that Louisville's zoning laws were unconstitutional. In a later case, *Shelley v. Kraemer*, 1948, the Supreme Court ended a practice widely used to segregate neighborhoods. Builders placed a provision in a deed, called a restricted covenant, which stated that a house could not be sold to blacks (and often, also to Asians or Jews). It clearly violated the equal protection of the laws.

Three education cases undermined *Plessy*. Missouri had no law school for blacks. But the state did offer scholarships for black students to attend a law school outside the state. In *Missouri ex rel. Gaines v. Canada*, 1938, the U.S. Supreme Court declared that this practice violated the Fourteenth Amendment's equal protection of the laws. *Sweatt v. Painter*, 1950, was a law suit brought by a black man who was denied entrance to the all-white University of Texas law school. There was no Texas law school for blacks. The state legislature quickly put together a black law school, Texas Southern University. Not good enough, said the Supreme Court, the two schools were clearly not equal. Texas must integrate the all-white law school. *McLaurin v. Oklahoma Board of Regents*, 1950, involved segregated facilities at a graduate school for an admitted black student. For one example, he was not permitted to browse through the books in the library. He had to sit at an assigned table and wait for the library staff to bring books to him. The U.S. Supreme Court ruled that the University of Oklahoma must fully integrate an admitted graduate student.

A logical next step was the 1954 case, *Brown v. Board of Education, Topeka, Kansas*. Kansas permitted elementary school segregation by local option. Seventeen Southern and border states maintained segregated schools. (A few years earlier this was also true for some Northern starts, such as Pennsylvania and New York. It was still the situation in some Northern small towns. See *Sweet Land of Liberty: The Forgotten Struggle for Civil Rights in the North*, by Thomas J. Sugrue.) The unanimous decision was geographically balanced. On the Supreme Court were Chief Justice Earl Warren from California, Justice Hugo Black of Alabama, Justice Tom C. Clark of Texas, Justice William O. Douglas of Connecticut, Justice Felix Frankfurter of Massachusetts, Justice Robert H. Jackson of New York, Justice Sherman Minton of Indiana, Justice Harold H. Burton of Ohio, and Justice Stanley F. Reed of Kentucky – a mixture of Democrats and Republicans, liberals and conservatives, Northerners and Southerners. In 1955 came the Supreme Court's order on the implementation of the *Brown* decision, called *Brown II*, desegregate with "all deliberate speed" – vague wording. After efforts to negate *Brown* by the state legislature and board of education in Arkansas, the Supreme Court's ruling in a 1958 case, *Cooper v. Aaron*, explicitly stated that states could not disobey or ignore a Supreme Court decision they opposed, driving one more nail into the coffin and thus burying John Calhoun's antebellum theory of state nullification.

The first national crisis over desegregation hit in 1957 at Central High School in Little Rock, Arkansas, when Governor Orval Faubus refused to permit the integration of the high school. President Eisenhower responded by sending troops to uphold the Supreme Court decision, which he personally did not favor, privately arguing that you cannot force "matters of the heart."

Southern school boards dragged their feet for ten years after *Brown*. Only one percent of black children in the South attended desegregated schools by 1965. At that rate the nation's schools would be finally integrated in the year 2954. There was foot dragging elsewhere also. The federal Civil War Centennial Commission, created by Congress as the official organization to oversee observing the centennial of the Civil War, published a brochure, "Facts About the Civil War." Nowhere in the brochure did the words "Negro," the preferred term at that time, or "slavery" appear. Apparently neither one had anything to do with either causing the Civil War or with the Union victory! When a court ordered the city of Montgomery, Alabama, the first capital of the Confederacy, to allow blacks to enjoy the city zoo, the city closed the zoo and sold all the animals.

What role did the *Brown* decision play in the civil rights movement? One would think that it was an immediate and significant stimulus. Clayborne Carson, an African-American historian, presented an ambivalent legacy. "The Court did not offer an effective means to correct the problem it had identified." (p. 28) "The Court's ruling against school segregation encouraged African Americans to believe that the entire structure of white supremacy was illegitimate and legally vulnerable. But the civil rights struggles *Brown* inspired sought broader goals than the decision could deliver, and that gap fostered frustration and resentment among many black Americans. In short, the decision's virtues and limitations reflect both the achievements and the failures of the efforts made in the last half century (since 1954) to solve America's racial dilemma and to realize the nation's egalitarian ideals." (p. 26) (Clayborne Carson, "Two Cheers for *Brown v. Board of Education*," Journal of American History, June, 2004, pp. 26-31).

The Event, the Catalyst

Into this court-centered, legalistic attack on different parts of segregation arrived a diminutive 42-year-old woman, Rosa Parks. Bus drivers in Montgomery, Alabama, carried guns. Rosa Parks and a bus driver had had a confrontation in 1943. Black riders were required to board the bus at the front, pay their fare, get off the bus, and then re-board through the back door. Thinking it was funny, the driver pulled away before she could re-board. For twelve years she carefully avoided that particular driver, taking other routes or walking, if necessary. Startled by his unexpected presence on this bus route, she simply resolved to see any confrontation through to arrest, if it came to that. It did. She refused to get out of her seat and move to the back of the bus to stand. She understood the consequences; her arrest photo identified her as number 7053. Rosa Parks was not a nobody. She was a respected voice in the local and state black community, active in the Alabama NAACP, secretary for the local chapter since 1943. Meekness was not part of her family's tradition. Grandpa, once a slave and a strong supporter of Marcus Garvey, often sat on his porch holding his shotgun, ready for the KKK. She became the catalyst for the Montgomery bus boycott, 1956-1957. Instead of remaining just another victim of Jim Crow laws, her arrest stirred the local black Women's Political Council to print 50,000 leaflets calling for a bus boycott. The boycott was effective; the bus company lost approximately 65% of its regular income. The women forced a new, young minister, Rev. Martin Luther King, Jr., to lead the nonviolence campaign boycotting the bus system. As he revealed in his autobiographical writings, Martin Luther King, Jr., grew incredibly as a person, as a Christian, and as a leader during the campaign. His stirring speeches thrust him into prominence.

His personal background had not prepared him for the initial challenge. Dr. King grew up in a wealthy, privileged family in Atlanta, Georgia, the son of the leader of Atlanta's largest black church. In 1956 *Fortune* magazine called Auburn Street, the street on which he was born and raised, "The Richest Negro Street in the World." His family had a swimming pool in their backyard, quite unusual in the 1940s or 1950s. Under Martin Luther King's leadership public opinion in Montgomery's black community came together. The arrest of Rosa Parks took place on December 1. By December 5 the boycott was on. Almost a year later, in mid-November, the Supreme Court ruled segregation of the bus system unconstitutional.

The key to the new tactic was that it switched the drive for civil rights from a courtroom, legalistic movement to a street level, participatory movement. Now the average person could take part. Nothing deepens an individual's commitment as much as active participation. On February 1, 1960, four students from a black college, North Carolina A&T, did just that. They sat down at a local department store's lunch counter in Greensboro, and after being told they would not be served, refused to leave, a sit-in. For an understanding of how grassroots activism energized the movement, see the twenty-nine oral histories in Horace Huntley and John W. McKerley, *Foot Soldiers for Democracy: The Men, Women, and Children of the Birmingham Civil Rights Movement.* One day in Birmingham over 900 students, of all ages, marched; 2,500 demonstrated the next day, all greeted with powerful fire hoses. Participation was contagious.

Here are the primary methods used by the various civil rights organizations up to this time.

> NAACP, National Association for the Advancement of Colored People (The term preferred by W.E.B. Du Bois in 1910, to emphasize that the problem was not just in America, but one for all the world's colored people.) – sue in court
> Urban League – calm lobbying to corporate executives for jobs
> CORE, Congress of Racial Equality – mildly confrontational through nonviolent direct action
> SCLC, Southern Christian Leadership Conference – organized protests that the average person could participate in, making them more committed to the goals
> SNCC, Student Nonviolent Coordinating Committee – a student group, college and high school, similar to SCLC. HBCUs, historically black colleges and universities, already had a long tradition of student civil rights activism

Note that for the federal government, Congress and the president were not yet involved. Until the Montgomery bus boycott the civil rights movement was an NAACP court-led movement; after Montgomery, it became a widespread participatory movement. The highlight of the movement came in the 1963 March on Washington, when Martin Luther King Jr. gave his "I Have a Dream" speech before a crowd estimated at 250,000.

Some Victories, Some Gains, But

The 1964 Civil Rights Act, with the public accommodations section, was a significant victory. In a major change from previous laws and court decisions, Congress clearly made it illegal for individuals to discriminate. Corporations such as restaurants or businesses are legally considered individuals before the law and the courts. Up to this time the equal protection clause of the Fourteenth Amendment had generally been interpreted to apply only to actions taken by the state governments. That meant that an individual, meaning also a corporation or business, could legally discriminate. Not any longer.

President Lyndon Johnson purposefully signed the 1965 Voting Rights Act in the same room at the Capitol in which Lincoln signed the Emancipation Proclamation. The Voting Rights Act sent federal registrars into the South if a certain percentage, more than fifty percent, of potential voters in a region were not registered to vote. Historian Gary May, in *Bending Towards Justice: The Voting Rights Act and The Transformation of American Democracy*, called it "probably the most important piece of legislation passed in the Twentieth Century." The vote on the bill was Senate, 77-19, House, 333-85. By the spring of 1966 blacks were running for political office, not just voting, in Democratic Party primaries in every county in Alabama. Southern whites ran also, but to the Republican Party. In 1964 the Republican presidential candidate, Barry Goldwater, won 87% of the vote in Mississippi. Blacks were 36% of the population in Mississippi, but only 6.7% could vote. By 1981 the number of blacks who could vote rose to 70%. In 1964 there were only 103 elected black officials in the entire country. By 1979 that number rose to 4,607. However, the gains seemed to arrive too slowly.

Radicals Began to Appear – Divisions Among Blacks

Seething anger grew as civil rights demonstrators and workers were beaten, jailed, and killed. The world heavyweight-boxing champion, Muhammad Ali, refused to accept his draft notice for Vietnam and was stripped of his title. His explanation: "No Viet Cong ever called me 'nigger.'" During the Mississippi Summer Freedom Project in 1964 three young men – two white Northerners and one local black, Andrew Goodman, Mickey Schwerner, and James Chaney – were killed and buried in an earthen dam near Philadelphia, Mississippi. The three were registering people to vote. A local deputy sheriff was included in those convicted, decades later. Another vicious act was the bombing of a black church in Birmingham, Alabama, on a Sunday morning, killing four young girls. Read Dudley Randall's poignant poem, "Ballad of Birmingham," on the Internet. The local newspaper, the *Birmingham News*, deemed the story too insignificant for the front page. On Monday it appeared on page nine. During all the local civil rights protests the *Birmingham News* never published pictures showing the local black ministers leading the protests. This fed rumors throughout the white community that all the trouble was due to "outside agitators." "Our blacks are happy," was an oft-heard refrain. Really? Maybe not.

Just as blacks won major national legislative accomplishments, divisions appeared within the black community. Malcolm X called Martin Luther King a "professional beggar." "All you do is ask, ask, ask." "I demand!" He favored separation and community self-defense. He broke away from his original group, the Black Muslims, an indigenous American movement not recognized at that time as an Islamic sect, to convert to Islam. Malcolm X put an emphasis on African-American culture and history. In addition, he urged a revolution to "unbrainwash an entire people." Some blacks claim Black History begins with Malcolm X.

It really began with the efforts of two academic historians, Carter Goodwin Woodson and John Hope Franklin. Woodson started *The Journal of Negro History* in 1916 and founded Negro History Week in 1926, which later expanded to Black History Month. Why February? Lincoln's birthday. Woodson was born on December 19, 1875, in Virginia, and died April 4, 1950, in Washington, D.C. He earned his B.A. from the University of Chicago in 1907. He was the second African-American to receive a Ph.D. from Harvard, in 1912. In 1947 another well-known black scholar, John Hope Franklin, published *From Slavery to Freedom: A History of Negro Americans*, a superb, widely read, influential history.

Another radical voice was the Black Panther movement, located chiefly in Oakland, California, and Chicago. While the Black Panthers fed thousands of poor children free breakfasts and did other charitable activities, they became linked in the public eye with crime and drugs in the black community, used to raise funds for their political activities. Were they helpers or radicals or revolutionaries or criminals? It did not matter; the police and FBI crushed them.

A new term was heard in 1966, "Black Power." Which meant? The phrase seemed to mean all things to all people. Originally, Black Power was primarily a rural-based SNCC concept, used to rally the rural black poor to register to vote. The phrase frightened some whites. In 1966 SNCC began rejecting white members or white assistance. Until this point whites had been a significant portion of the membership of many black organizations. In the 1950s 90% of the NAACP members were white, mostly lawyers who offered their services without charging a fee.

Even Martin Luther King was becoming frustrated by 1968. The day he was assassinated he called his church to give the secretary the title of his sermon for the next Sunday. It was, "Why America May Go to Hell." When rioting broke out after King's murder in April, 1968, Stokely Carmichael, who later changed his name to Kwame Ture, said, "Now that they've taken Dr. King off, it's time to end this non-violence bullshit." King's death removed the only leader of national prominence that all blacks would listen to and follow. Now the movement lost its focus.

Meanwhile, the ghettos exploded in numerous American cities. In many cases a minor police incident provoked the violence. A riot broke out in Watts, a section of Los Angeles, on August 11, 1965, just five days after President Lyndon Johnson signed the Voting Rights Act. It ended with 34 dead, 4,000 in jail, property damage more than $40 million, and over 250 buildings burned down. In 1967 there were riots in 128 cities. Were they race riots or anger riots or commodity riots, which meant they were opportunities to grab stuff in the turmoil? Political protest or frustration? It depended on whom you asked. The 1968 National Advisory Commission on Civil Disorders, called the Kerner Commission Report, named for its head, Otto Kerner, a former governor of Illinois, investigated the causes of the riots. Here are the self-reported responses of blacks involved and uninvolved in the urban riots. Compare them. In many respects, the rioters and non-rioters represented two distinct groups within the black neighborhoods.

Blacks *INVOLVED* in the 1960s Urban Riots

Grew up in the neighborhood	74%
Education, beyond 8th grade	93%
Present job sufficient in salary	29%
Strong sense of racial pride	49%
Agree with statement, "Sometimes I hate white people."	72%
Hostile towards middle class blacks	71%
Agree, "Blacks who make a lot of money as just as bad as white people."	51%
Frequently discuss the need for black civil rights with friends	54%
Anger against politicians caused riots	43%
Anger against the police caused riots	71%

Blacks *UNINVOLVED* in the 1960s Urban Riots

Did not grow up in the neighborhood	47%
Education, less than 8th grade	72%
Present job sufficient in salary	45%
Strong sense of racial pride	22%
Agree with statement, "Sometimes I hate white people."	50%
Hostile towards middle class blacks	60%
Agree, "Blacks who make a lot of money as just as bad as white people."	35%
Frequently discuss the need for black civil rights with friends	35%
Anger against politicians caused riots	20%
Anger against police caused riots	49%

The Kerner Commission Report issued two contradictory recommendations, which addressed two popular responses to the urban riots. It called for

1. increasing social welfare expenditures
2. more effective use of force to suppress disturbances

That same year Congress passed the 1968 Fair Housing Act, which prohibited discrimination in housing.

Gains Appear, But

If you, just you, were Congress for a day, what legislation would you pass that is within the possibilities of our legal system to improve the historically disadvantaged position of blacks as shown in many statistical rankings – income, inherited wealth, educational achievement, school dropouts, teenage pregnancies, financial assets, etc.? Net worth for black households, defined as income minus debt, plus assets, averaged $2,000 in 2013. For white households, it was $117,000. By 1968 the civil rights movement had succeeded in gaining all the laws that seemed possible. Many believed that no additional legislation was possible.

When looking at the civil rights movement in this period, do not confuse these five terms:

> segregation – means to legally separate
> desegregation – means to legally end segregation; be careful, you can desegregate without integrating; desegregation is not the opposite of segregation
> integration – means to mix blacks and whites together, which may include forced mixing, as with court-ordered busing begun in *Swan v. Charlotte-Mecklenburg Board of Education*, 1971
> toleration – means not objecting to something or to someone; you can tolerate someone's presence and pay no attention to them
> acceptance – means accepting another person into your circle of friends and acquaintances

Which can be stopped by legally enforcing laws? You can legislate against segregation and discrimination, but toleration and acceptance are attitudes, impossible to legislate. In addition, can you force integration in all aspects of society? Many high school lunchrooms indicate otherwise.

Nixon Administration

When the Republicans won the election in 1968, would the Republican Party repeal the civil rights advances? The answer turned out to be "no." The Republican Party accepted the civil rights laws while they pursued additional policies and approaches in regard to blacks. The idea of "benign neglect" referred to a scaling down of promises to blacks to reduce the level of frustration. This approach was popular among whites.

In 1964, 68% of Northern whites supported President Lyndon Johnson's civil rights policies. By 1966 52% believed the government was pushing integration too much and too quickly. This switch in thinking was mainly caused by the urban riots. A poll in 1970 placed "Reducing Racial Discrimination" at number six on a list of issues that the public wanted the government to devote its attention to in the next two years. Only 25% supported it.

Republicans also began a "Southern metropolitan strategy," also referred to as a "Southern strategy," designed to attract Southern suburbanites into the Republican Party. Since the Civil War the South had been a Democratic Party stronghold. The new strategy worked for the GOP, and for more than just the Southern suburbs. Most Southerners climbed aboard. A majority of Southern whites began to vote Republican. Lyndon Johnson understood that this would happen. The evening after the day he signed the Civil Rights Act of 1964, Johnson told an aide, Bill Moyers, "I think we just delivered the South to the Republican Party for my lifetime and yours."

The "Philadelphia Plan," named for where it was first implemented in 1969, stated that union members and apprentices on federally contracted buildings and projects had to reflect the local community's racial percentages, to open up opportunities. For example, in 1970 blacks were only 1.7% of tool and die makers and 3.3% of sheet metal workers. If blacks were 35% of the local population, the sheet metal workers union had to have 35% black apprentices or union members while working on a federally funded project. Now the unions had to recruit blacks. Since unions traditionally supported Democrats, critics wondered if Nixon was motivated by a desire to aid blacks or to punish unions.

Originally begun in the Kennedy administration, LBJ defined affirmative action to require color-blind hiring, as stated in the 1964 Civil Rights Act. The Nixon administration redefined it to mean that a certain number of job openings *must* be set aside for *only* minorities.

This policy eventually led to the *Bakke* case, *Bakke v. Board of Regents*, 1978. This reverse discrimination case involved a claim by a white man, Allan Bakke, that he was the victim of racial discrimination. The Civil Rights Act of 1964 prohibited discrimination based upon race, but in order to compensate for the collective results of previous discriminatory practices, the University of California at Davis reserved sixteen of its one hundred annual openings for medical school specifically for non-whites. As LBJ had explained in 1965, "You do not take a person who, for years, has been hobbled by chains and liberate him, bring him up to the starting line of a race and then say, you are free to compete with all the others, and still justly believe that you have been completely fair." Many universities followed preferential practices as compensation for the past.

Objective test scores on the medical school entrance exam and judgments of his potential put Bakke outside the 84 slots for the highest 84 white applicants, but within the 16 positions reserved for non-whites. He sued on grounds of reverse discrimination, claiming violation of the 1964 Civil Rights Act. In a 5-4 decision, the Supreme Court upheld Bakke's admission but permitted the university's use of race to ensure a diverse student body. As Justice Harry Blackmun wrote in the decision, "In order to get beyond racism, we must first take account of race." This divided decision would lead to future court tests of the degree to which universities could use race in admitting students while still being non-discriminatory.

The Internalists Versus the Externalists

In the late twentieth century, a debate emerged within the black community over these two questions. What is the primary cause of the generally disadvantaged position of blacks in American society? How much of it is due to discrimination and how much of it is due to black behavior? Many statistics point to continued disadvantages for blacks. For example, the average black person leaves an estate of approximately $11,000 at death; the average white person leaves $150,000. Which children benefit more?

Henry Lewis Gates, Jr., a black Harvard professor, found that current census data indicates poverty could be wiped out within the black community if blacks did three things, which are also true of any other group:

1. graduate from high school, employers do not value a GED as equivalent to a high school diploma
2. wait until 21 to get married
3. wait until after marriage to have children

This advice is not moral; it is economic, based on the census data. Almost no individual who did these three things lives in poverty. In 1970 the poverty rate among blacks was 30%, due primarily to racism. Now the poverty rate is 21%, due primarily to family structure. Eighty-five percent of black children who live in poverty live with a mother and no father present, thus, only one income. If the mother has little education, that means a low income.

Earlier, both Booker T. Washington and W.E.B. Du Bois agreed on this point. In addition to protesting against white racial discrimination, Du Bois insisted that the bulk of the work for raising the black population must be done by blacks themselves, just as Booker T. Washington argued. Du Bois made this point in an 1897 essay, "The Conservation of Races." "We are diseased. We are developing criminal tendencies, and an alarmingly large percentage of our men and women are sexually impure . . . ." "Unless we conquer our present vices they will conquer us." Du Bois emphasized the need for a professionally trained, conventionally moral black elite, the Talented Tenth. Upon this elite rested the task of "lifting the rabble." He feared that if the elite dispersed into predominantly white neighborhoods the black masses would be left without proper leadership. When Du Bois later reread "The Conservation of Races" in 1934, he was "pleased to find myself so much in sympathy with myself." Du Bois always believed that, in his words, there were two "Negro problems" – the whites' Negro Problem, discrimination and oppression, and the blacks' Negro Problem, low behavioral standards. This question, the Internalists versus the Externalists, is still a topic of debate within the black community – "How much of it is them and how much of it is us?"

Difficulty in Gaining Legislative Representation and Political Power

Another lingering dilemma is how do you increase black political representation to be proportionate to the black population? Politically, the number of black representatives in state legislatures and Congress is not proportionate to the black percentage in the population.

Many traditional black institutions are declining, for example black colleges. Whites have discovered the low tuition at many historically black schools, such as Lincoln in Missouri; Delaware State; Bluefield State in West Virginia; and West Virginia State, all of which now have a significant white student body, and in some cases a daytime majority.

Has There Been Any Progress? Yes, In Many Areas, But

Some institutional racism and residual racism remains in society – and disputes continue over its existence and its impact and its reasons. One is police profiling, where the police investigating a crime target statistically likely suspects, young black males ages 16-35. Many black community leaders object to this practice as unfairly subjecting all young blacks to police questioning at a rate disproportionate to their percentage in the population. Police justify it as reflecting reality; even many black chiefs of police and police officers support it, such as a Los Angeles chief of police. It sometimes leads to tragedies, such as the 2014 shooting in Ferguson, Missouri. This practice continues to be a source of tension for the black community.

"Red-lining" of black neighborhoods has long been practiced. It means that banks draw, or imagine, lines on a city map designating an area within which they refuse to approve mortgages, believing that loans in "bad" neighborhoods are risky. The lowest number of FHA approved mortgage loans since the 1930s for any county in the United States belongs to the Bronx in New York City.

DWB, "driving while black," is the tendency, linked to police profiling, for the police to stop black drivers at numbers higher than their percentage within the local population.

Add to this list mistakes, insults, and thoughtless actions by American businesses and advertisers. The classic example is the goof by the toy company in 1997. They created an African-American Barbie doll, which they named "Oreo Barbie," completely unaware that in the black community "Oreo" is a disparaging slang term for someone who is black on the outside but white on the inside, someone who thinks and acts as a white person does. Whatever that is! Oreo Barbie was quickly yanked off the shelves.

Misinformation can easily and quickly be spread by the Internet and social media. The best example was a black comedian's joke that whites picked February as Black History Month because it is the shortest month. Not true. A black historian selected February to honor Lincoln.

Finally, the lack of overall economic improvement for blacks. During a 2016 commencement address at Stanford University, Vernon Jordan, a black activist who has been called "the Rosa Parks of Wall Street," stated that "It's much easier to integrate a lunch counter than it is to guarantee a livable income and a good solid job." The black Harvard historian, Henry Lewis Gates, Jr., described Vernon Jordan's lifetime efforts. "He realized that the first phase of the modern civil rights movement was fighting legal segregation, but the roots of racism were fundamentally economic." (*Louisville Defender*, June 2, 2016, p. 6A)

The achievements of the civil rights movement gave birth to a phenomenon unanticipated by black leaders. They should not have been surprised. Every accomplishment or achievement by one group in our society always generates a backlash of some sort from other groups. It may be as gentle as humor or snide remarks, or as vicious as the rebirth of organizations such as the KKK. Kwame Ture, formerly known as Stokely Carmichael, said in the 1980s that black leaders now faced a more subtle, sophisticated racism from politicians, one "cloaked in the garb of anti-racism." "Having succeeded in driving racism underground, we became comfortable and complacent, falsely believing this hidden creature was dead or dying." The civil rights movement morphed into more talk and less action. The nation's blacks saw the results of the election of 2016 as a significant slide backwards, a "whitelash" against a black president and blacks in general.

On the Positive Side

Cultural nationalism has grown, as shown by Kwanza, created by a Los Angeles activist, Maulana Ron Karenga, in 1966.

The first black Miss America contestant appeared in 1970. Previously, contestants had to be "of the white race."

Both a Hispanic Barbie and a Black Barbie appeared for the first time.

Education – In 1950 there were 83,000 blacks in college; now, there are over one million. More blacks are graduating from high school, 85.8%, but more also attend segregated schools, especially in cities.

Political Office – In 2016 over 10,500 blacks held an elected office.

Attitudes had improved by the 1990s, as shown by public opinion polls:

Do you approve of interracial marriages?
>   1968 – 17%
>   1997 – 61%
>   among those under 35 – 83% approved

Do you approve of interracial dating?
>   1987 – 45%
>   2003 – 78%

Would you move if a black family moved next door?
>   1958 – 44%
>   1998 – 1%

Friendship
>   1964 – 18% of all whites had a black friend, 1998, 86%
>   1964 – 18% of all blacks had a white friend, 1998, 87%

Friendship across racial boundaries breaks down stereotypes.

When black married couples, it does not matter if one or two incomes are present, are compared to white married couples, blacks earn 87% of white income. However, since 50% of all blacks live in the South, a historically low-income region, the real comparison should be much closer.

Is the civil rights movement over? Some historians are now using a different phrase to describe it, "The Long Civil Rights Movement." It is not over. How can it be? The election of a black president in 2008 and 2012 seemed to inaugurate a new era. However, during the long, bitter 2016 presidential campaign racism resurfaced, subtly. Many blacks were sincerely frightened by Trump's victory in 2016; less by the victor himself, but more by the verbal attacks on immigrants and minorities by his supporters. Adult blacks had been in this situation before. Many young blacks had not. The questions they raised asking what all this meant were met by insufficient assurances from older blacks. All the previous gains seemed less significant, less concrete, less permanent.

46

THE WOMEN'S MOVEMENT

Why a Women's Liberation Movement?

The first Webster's International Dictionary, published in 1901, had no term for prejudice or discrimination based on sex. Women active in civil rights organizations and the 1960s Student Left, who objected to the demeaning roles to which males relegated them – typing, making copies, taking notes, and sex – first used "male chauvinism" in the 1960s. Sexism, probably coined on the analogy of racism, entered our language only in the late 1960s.

American women were the most liberated in the world. So why was there a women's liberation movement? The major reason was discrimination and limited opportunities encountered in the workplace. "American society channels the opportunities for personal development into remunerated work, and correspondingly, it sets a high value upon this sort of achievement." Women had few opportunities to achieve. The average woman earned 59¢ for every dollar a man earned. In addition, women historically were denied access to the more rewarding forms of paid employment and denied socially applauded alternative activities outside of and inside the home. A frequently heard description of a woman's existence was, "I'm just a housewife."

Your personal identity as an adult in this society comes chiefly from your job, not from your family background and not from your leisure activities. When you enter the world of work you will also find that many of your social friends will be work-related, either colleagues or people in the same occupation. Ask any adult, "What do you do?" No person will answer, "I play tennis," except a professional tennis player. It is always what they do for a living. That primarily defines who you are.

Advice for Wives and Mothers

In the 1940s and 1950s the primary advice given to women was to play the role of mother and wife, and to play it well. Practically every mother closely followed the advice given in Dr. Benjamin Spock's book, *Baby and Child Care.* In the chapter on the "The Working Mother," one section answered the question, "To work or not to work?" If you decided to work, the price was steep.

"Some mothers **have** to work to make a living. Usually their children turn out all right, because some reasonably good arrangement is made for their care. But others grow up neglected and maladjusted. It would save money in the end if the government paid a comfortable allowance to all mothers of young children who would otherwise be compelled to work. You can think of it this way: useful, well-adjusted citizens are the most valuable possessions a country has, and good mother care during early childhood is the surest way to produce them. It doesn't make sense to let mothers go to work making dresses in a factory or tapping typewriters in an office, and have them pay other people to do a poorer job of bringing up their children."

"The important thing for a mother to realize is that the younger the child the more necessary it is for him to have a steady, loving person taking care of him. In most cases, the mother is the best one to give him this feeling of "belonging," safely and surely. She doesn't quit on the job, she doesn't turn against him, she isn't indifferent to him, she takes care of him always in the same familiar house. If a mother realizes clearly how vital this kind of care is to a small child, it may make it easier for her to decide that the extra money she might earn, or the satisfaction she might receive from an outside job, is not so important, after all."

Note the jobs Dr. Spock listed as typical for women – "making dresses in a factory or tapping typewriters in an office." He later apologized for so characterizing women's work.

The 1950s Home Economics Textbook

Kids got the same message at school. All the boys took a Wood Shop class to make a small piece of furniture, usually a telephone stand, and to learn small engine repair, so they could understand the car engine and the lawn mower, both much more simple back then. Girls took a Home Economics class so they could learn how to sew and how to cook. What follows is a list circulating since the 1970s, supposedly from a 1950s Home Economics textbook giving advice for wives, taken from a magazine that never existed, *Housekeeping Monthly.* It is a spoof. Still, the attitudes reflect those of the 1950s.

"Have dinner ready: Plan ahead, even the night before, to have a delicious meal – on time. This is a way of letting him know that you have been thinking about him and are concerned about his needs. Most men are hungry when they come home and the prospects of a good meal are part of the warm welcome needed.

Prepare yourself. Take 15 minutes to rest so you will be refreshed when he arrives. Touch up your makeup, put a ribbon in your hair to be fresh looking.

Some don'ts: Don't greet him with problems or complaints. Don't complain if he's late for dinner. Count this as minor compared with what he might have gone through that day.

Make him comfortable: Have him lean back in a comfortable chair or suggest he lie down in the bedroom. Have a cool or warm drink ready for him. Arrange his pillow and offer to take off his shoes. Speak in a low, soft soothing and pleasant voice. Allow him to relax-unwind.

Listen to him: You may have a dozen things to tell him, but the moment of his arrival is not the time. Let him talk first.

Make the evening his: Never complain if he does not take you out to dinner or to other places of entertainment. Instead, try to understand his world of strain and pressure, his need to be home and relax.

The goal: Try to make your home a place of peace and order where your husband can renew himself in body and spirit."

Women's Magazines

Women's magazines in those years emphasized domesticity. The articles on the cover featured mostly childcare and cooking. "How to Prepare a Great Meal in 15 Minutes." "How to Accomplish all Your Housework, Manage the Children, Do Volunteer Work, Help at Your Children's School, Be Popular in the Neighborhood, Remain Popular with your High School Friends, and Keep Up With Fashion."

There was also another area of emphasis – looking good – how to lose weight to look good for your husband, rather than for your own health. Sadly, this emphasis is still there. Look at the magazines and tabloids as you put your groceries on the checkout belt at the supermarket. "How to Lose 17 Pounds in Just Four Days." "Go Down Six Dress Sizes in Six Hours." "I Lost 72 Pounds Eating Everything, Seven Times a Day." Perhaps this is a little facetious. Today eating disorders affect one-third of all college women. Young men are now joining them. A study by Johns Hopkins University in 2000 showed that the BMI, Body Mass Index, of Miss Americas has declined gradually since the 1920s. If this trend continues, she will be invisible by 2320. "There she goes . . . ." Where? Fourteen of the winning Miss Americas in a twenty-five period would be classified as undernourished according to United Nations health standards. Maybe the prizes given to the winner should include restaurant coupons.

In addition to domesticity and weight loss, a third factor featured women as sex objects. *Playboy* magazine began in 1953, bringing what had been considered smut into mainstream America's living rooms. Now women felt they must be sexually appealing and great lovers, in addition to being good cooks, perfect mothers, volunteers for charities, school moms, thrifty shoppers, etc., and all the while being happy, and, quiet.

College

Women did go to college to get a degree, their MRS. Degree; 60% of college females dropped out to get married. You sent your daughter to college mainly to catch a college-educated man, not to get a degree.

The Catalyst

Into this placid, happy world came an immensely popular book. It put into print what many women were thinking – Betty Friedan's *The Feminine Mystique*, published in 1963. Friedan, a 1942 graduate of Smith College, an academic, upper class women's college, attended her fifteenth college reunion in 1957, using the occasion to survey her graduating class about their accomplishments. Over 90% described themselves as dissatisfied housewives with deep feelings of failure. It led to further research and to writing *The Feminine Mystique*, which struck a responsive chord, selling over one million copies. More than twenty publishing houses initially turned her down. The male editors saw no potential market for a book that talked about a problem that certainly did not exist. She finally found a publisher.

She addressed "The Problem That Has No Name," the title of the first chapter, the yearning for an identity beyond the nursery, the kitchen, the supermarket, and the bedroom; a desire to escape being trapped in the world of just marriage and motherhood, a life of playing a role rather than being a person.

> "The problem lay buried, unspoken, for many years in the minds of American women. It was a strange stirring, a sense of dissatisfaction, a yearning that women suffered in the middle of the twentieth century in the United States. Each suburban wife struggled with it alone. As she made the beds, shopped for groceries, matched slipcover material, ate peanut butter sandwiches with her children, chauffeured Cub Scouts and Brownies, lay beside her husband at night – she was afraid to ask even of herself the silent question – 'Is this all?'"

Friedan was already a successful writer and editor. However, she felt that something was wrong with her for not enjoying waxing the kitchen floor! Why am I not enjoying this? Why is this so unfulfilling? Her book advocated "a new life plan," a purposeful life for women in the public sphere, a life not defined by just the traditional roles of mother, wife, and housekeeper.

Another influential book, probably the most important work published in the twentieth century on women, had been published earlier in Europe in 1949. It became available in an English translation in 1953, Simone de Beauvoir's *The Second Sex*. Beauvoir argued that women lived lives of biological necessity, devoting their lives to raising children. They failed to achieve an authentic self through action and accomplishment, becoming mere objects, as seen and as defined, primarily, by men.

Gains

The catalyst for the women's movement, *The Feminine Mystique*, produced results. In 1966 Friedan and 27 professional women created NOW, the National Organization for

Women, in a crowded New York City hotel room. NOW was not interested in challenging the whole range of gender issues, such as an equal sharing of housework and parenting; virtually their only issues were equal pay and access to better jobs. In the 1940s and 1950s many women entered the workforce, although in 1960 only 250,000 women with small children worked outside their home. By 1950 there were as many women working as there had been in 1945, during the war effort. Many working class and middle class families needed the second income to maintain their family's standard of living.

Women also worked for another reason. The two most important factors influencing any society at any time are changes in technology and in demography, the population profile of a society. By 1950 significant demographic changes appeared concerning women. In 1900 the average woman married at 22, had her last child at 32, and died at 51, when her youngest child was 19. She spent her entire adult life as a wife and mother. In 1950 the average woman married at 20, had her last child at 26, and died at 65, long after her youngest child left the house. If that child left at 19, she lived 20 more years after her role as a household mother ended. What to do? Many decided to go to work – out of boredom. There were jobs for them in this pre-computer age. The number of clerical jobs in the workforce increased 20 times from 1900 to 1960, and 96% of the workers doing such jobs were women. Paradoxically, between 1940 and 1960, as the number of women in professions relative to men dropped, the absolute number of women in professional occupations rose 41%. In professions and in the workplace generally, women soon discovered that they had neither the pay that men enjoyed nor the same opportunities for advancement. In addition, there were hazards. Sexual harassment was not a workplace issue until the 1970s. If you were being hit on at work, the advice from everyone was to change jobs.

The Civil Rights Act of 1964

A 1971 court case involving Ida Phillips illustrates one of the themes of the women's movement after 1960. Martin Marietta Corporation denied Ida Phillips a new job within the company, only because she had small children, under the age of six. But, the company employed men with small children at this job. She sued under the Civil Rights Act of 1964, Section 7, which said that:

> "It shall be an unlawful employment practice for an employer to fail or refuse to hire or to discharge any individual or otherwise to discriminate against any individual with respect to his compensation, terms, conditions, or privileges or employment, because of such individual's race, color, religion, sex or national origin."

The Supreme Court ruled in favor of Ida Phillips, but held out the possibility that a company could discriminate if not having small children was a reasonable occupational qualification.

What makes this court decision interesting is how the word "sex" came to be part of the 1964 Civil Rights Act. During debate over the Civil Rights Act in the House of Representatives, Representative Howard "Judge" Smith, a conservative Democrat from Virginia, added the word "sex" by amendment. He was upset about the impending passage of a crazy law that prohibited racial discrimination. First elected to Congress in 1930, his thinking never evolved concerning civil rights for blacks. As a tactic to defeat that insane civil rights bill, he stuck in the foolish word "sex," knowing that the inclusion of the "women's rights part" would make this section of the law so ridiculous that the civil rights bill would not pass. It did! This is an old legislative tactic, amend a pending bill to death. Each small addition is sure to irritate a few potential supporters. Eventually it will no longer have majority support. His attempt backfired. Note, this gain for women did not come about because of efforts by the women's movement; in many respects it preceded the movement. This was also true of the Federal Equal Pay Act of 1963.

Court Cases

The greatest legal breakthrough for women since the Nineteenth Amendment came in another 1971 court case. Sally Reed, who lived in Idaho, was separated from her husband, Cecil, but not yet divorced. Their young son lived with Sally and had no contact with his father. The boy died, leaving no will and a small estate less than $1,000. According to Idaho law, males received preference over females as the administrator of an estate; the Probate Court appointed her husband as the administrator of their son's estate. Sally was furious. Her husband had not been part of their son's life. She sued under the equal protection clause of the Fourteenth Amendment, which states that no state may "deny to any person within its jurisdiction the equal protection of the laws." Idaho claimed their law was written this way to prevent disputes among relatives. The Supreme Court ruled in *Reed v. Reed* that the Idaho law made an arbitrary distinction not "rationally related" to efficient management of the estate. Sally Reed won. This is the first case in American history in which the Supreme Court declared that treating women and men differently might violate the Constitution. However, just when it seemed the Constitution was clearly nonsexist, two other cases clouded the legal basis for nondiscrimination.

In *Frontiero v. Richardson* in 1973, the Supreme Court struck down a federal law that allowed married males in the military to automatically claim extra housing and medical benefits, but required a married female in the military to prove her husband depended on her for over 50% of his support, before she could qualify for the same benefits. Out of the majority of the judges striking down the law, only four agreed the law was unconstitutional because it perpetuated the old-fashioned view that women were dependents rather than breadwinners, and therefore violated the Constitution's requirement of fairness and equity. Obviously, four is not a majority of the nine members on the Supreme Court.

In a 1975 case, *Schlesinger v. Ballard*, the Supreme Court upheld a U.S. Navy rule giving women four more years than men to achieve a promotion. The military has an "Up or Out Rule," meaning you are promoted within a certain time or you must resign. This prevents the military from becoming top-heavy with too many officers.

All of this meant that the question of whether or not the Constitution permitted distinctions based on sex was still up in the air. The courts seemed unwilling to strike down all laws that treated men and women differently. Clearly, what was needed was an Equal Rights Amendment, the ERA, which would settle the issue. In 1974, 74% of the public favored such an amendment to the Constitution. In the years that followed, those in favor never fell below 58% and those opposed never rose above 31%.

Although, to some, the ERA seemed a trivial matter. The headline in the *New York Times* when the House of Representatives passed the ERA was, "The Henpecked House." The whole women's movement seemed trivial to many men. Previously, the Washington administrative official in charge of enforcing the Civil Rights Act of 1964 had joked about the ban on sex discrimination. "It will give men equal opportunity to be *Playboy* bunnies." The first university women's studies program did not appear until 1968, at Cornell University; it was called The Feminist, Gender, and Sexuality Studies Program.

The Equal Rights Amendment Fails

An ERA was first proposed in 1923. It passed the House of Representatives in 1972, 354-23 and the Senate 84-8. In 1971 and 1972, nine states added Equal Rights Amendments to their state constitutions. Clearly, this was an idea whose time had come. So, why did it fail? Lots of reasons.

The illusion spread that the ERA was unnecessary; women had already achieved equality. Courts ordered the military academies to admit women. Title IX of the Education Amendments of 1972 guaranteed equal access to athletic programs for women. These opportunities had to be comparable to men's sports, and offered during the same sports season – for example, men's football and women's field hockey, traditional fall sports.

Unions and the leaders of the women's labor movement began to get edgy. What would happen to court decisions that specifically protected females in the workplace if the ERA passed? In *Muller v. Oregon*, 1908, the Supreme Court found that "in order to preserve the strength and vigor of the race [a] woman's physical structure, and the functions she performs in consequence thereof, justify special legislation restricting or qualifying the conditions under which she should be permitted to toil." Sickly mothers would produce unhealthy children. Thus, the government has a role to play in protecting women, and, therefore, preserving the future of our society. Would the ERA permit "special legislation" to protect the health of women in the workplace? For an in-depth look at this complex topic, see Nancy Woloch, *A Class by Herself: Protective Laws for Women Workers, 1890s-1990s*.

Radicals

In the 1970s militants radicalized the women's movement and left it divided internally. This phenomenon is not unusual. The British historian, Lord Acton, said it best. "At all times sincere friends of freedom have been rare, and its triumphs have been due to minorities, that have prevailed by associating themselves with auxiliaries whose object often differed from their own; and this association, which is always dangerous, has sometimes been disastrous." In any movement, cause, or organization, those who attend every meeting, often the most committed or the most fanatical, will eventually end up in leadership positions and, therefore, speak for the organization. If their ideas are too radical, it drives the less committed members out of the organization, further cementing the radicals' control and influence. This happened in the women's movement in the 1970s and 1980s.

One early radical group that emerged was the Redstockings, who issued a manifesto on July 7, 1969. They knew the source of all their problems. "Men have controlled all political, economic, and cultural institutions and backed up this control with physical force. They have used their power to keep women in an inferior position. *All men* receive economic, sexual, and psychological benefits from male supremacy. *All men* have oppressed women." (Italics in the original.)

The New York Radical Women took as a legal name, "The Feminists," which meant that their activities were reported in the newspapers as, "The Feminists said today that . . ." implying that the whole movement believed in their statements. The constitution of The Feminists restricted their membership; at least two-thirds of their members could not live with men, which implied to the public that they were minimally anti-male and, in all likelihood, mostly lesbians. And this is the voice of the entire feminist movement? It seemed so.

The New York Radical Women first appeared on the national scene in 1968 when they organized a protest at the Miss America Pageant in Atlantic City, New Jersey. They crowned a sheep as the winner, spoke only to female reporters, and tossed female paraphernalia – bras, girdles, wigs – into a trashcan. A newspaper article appeared claiming the women burned their bras in protest. Years later a historian interviewed those who took part. None of the participants remembered burning bras. The historian tracked down the newspaper article's author. It was false; he made it up. The average person from that generation still remembers the bra burning, an event that was not. That image remains. Thank goodness that all the information on the Internet today is 100% true.

Other radical organizations were WITCH, the Women's International Terrorist Conspiracy from Hell; and COYOTE, Cut Out Your Old Tired Ethics, an organization of prostitutes. New magazines and newspapers appeared directed toward women. These titles tell it all – *MS, Alpha, Off Our Backs, Up From Under.*

The women's movement began to be perceived by the public as a radical movement, one composed of lesbians, Marxists, socialists, and utopians. Betty Friedan referred to the entry of lesbians into the women's movement as "the lavender menace." What did gay issues have to do with the original purpose of NOW – jobs and professional opportunities? The radicals made the women's movement look as if it belonged more to the history of radicalism than to the history of feminism. Colorful individuals and their quotes added to the image. Shulamith Firestone said that women must end the childbearing function by replacing the nine month task of carrying a baby to birth by using either laboratory tubes or cows. No one interviewed cows to ask their opinion. Gloria Steinem called marriage a form of prostitution. She later got married. Kate Millet, in her book, *Sexual Politics*, said that society must free women from the traditional bonds of marriage and family by replacing these institutions with communal living. Roxanne Dunbar advocated destroying the three pillars of class and caste society – the family, private property, and the government. As if any of these can easily be destroyed in American society. These kinds of statements promoted the idea of women not as equals, but as superior to men.

The Broad-Based Counterreaction

They provoked a reaction. One was HOTDOG, Humanitarians Opposed To the Degradation of Our Girls, an anti-women's movement group that grew out of the Utah chapter of the super conservative John Birch Society. In California HOW, Happiness of Womanhood, baked bread for the California state legislators with a little sign on each loaf: "To the breadwinners from the breadbakers." Phyllis Schlafly, a lawyer who began her political activism campaigning for the 1964 conservative Republican candidate, Barry Goldwater, created STOP-ERA, Stop Taking Our Privileges. She said, "Women are happiest at home. They need protection at work. Chivalry promotes the position of women in society. The true American experience happens when a man's first significant purchase is a diamond for his bride and the largest financial investment of his life is a home for her to live in."

If one word could claim to have killed the ERA, it is the word abortion, especially in the case of *Roe v. Wade*, 1973, which challenged a Texas law. *Roe v. Wade* was one of a number of abortion cases making their way through the federal courts. In this complex decision, the Supreme Court held that a woman had the right to obtain an abortion during the first two trimesters of pregnancy. It invalidated laws that prohibited abortions, under some circumstances, in almost every state. A 1965 case preceded this Supreme Court decision, one that held significant ramifications that were not apparent at the time, but which clearly laid the groundwork for *Roe*. In *Griswold v. Connecticut* the Supreme Court struck down a Connecticut law that prohibited the dissemination of information about birth control to married couples. One judge called it an "uncommonly silly law." A later case, *Eisenstadt v. Baird*, in 1972 extended that right to unmarried individuals. Among the reasons given by Supreme Court justices for declaring the Connecticut law unconstitutional was a new concept, the "right to privacy," a right "implied" by the Constitution, but not stated specifically. If sexual intercourse was a "private" matter, then apparently a pregnancy that could result from it was also a "private" matter. A government had no right to interfere in an individual's private decision.

The appearance of the birth control pill had also made the Connecticut law outdated. The birth control pill resulted from long efforts by Margaret Sanger, the Progressive era reformer (who lived until 1966), and her wealthy friend, Katharine McCormick, who funded the research. A Catholic doctor from Massachusetts, John Rock, was instrumental in its initial testing and acceptance. He argued that it did not violate the teachings of the Catholic Church. The pill, he claimed, did not artificially impede natural intercourse in the way a diaphragm, a condom, or chemicals would. However, the papal encyclical issued by Pope Paul VI in 1968, *Humane Vitae* (*Of Human Life*), included birth control pills while reaffirming the Vatican's ban on all forms of artificial birth control. See the history and the impact of the birth control pill in *America and the Pill* by Elaine Tyler May.

Privacy was the basis of Roe's argument. Her attorney, Sarah Weddington, stated before the Supreme Court that, "We are not here to advocate abortion. We do not ask this Court to rule that abortion is good or desirable in any particular situation. We are here to advocate that the decision as to whether or not a particular woman will continue to carry or will terminate a pregnancy is a decision that should be made by that individual. That in fact she has a constitutional right to make that decision for herself, and that the state has shown no interest (meaning cause or reason) in interfering with that decision."

The *Roe v. Wade* decision enabled Phyllis Schlafly's STOP-ERA group to merge with the Catholic Church based Right-to-Life movement, sharing their computerized mailing and telephone lists. The Right-to-Life Movement had a much larger membership, so this really benefited STOP-ERA more.

Like so many other victories in the women's movement, this achievement, *Roe v. Wade*, did not result from the women's movement. Remember, the original issues of NOW – equal pay and equal job promotion opportunities. What is curious about the case and the Supreme Court decision is the position the women's movement had taken on abortion up to that moment – none. However, as an organization that said women should take control of their lives, they had to endorse the decision, but they did so reluctantly. This caused some members to quietly drop out and others to rearrange their priorities. If *Roe* was a victory for women, it was not a victory for NOW.

Misgivings began to arise over the full implications of a future ERA. In 1979 Russia invaded Afghanistan. At least, the United States called it an invasion. It was actually much more complicated. To greatly simplify, Russia replaced one ineffective pro-Russian government with another pro-Russian government, which also proven to be ineffective. President Jimmy Carter asked Congress to resume draft registration. In the interest of equality, he asked that the law also include women. NOW endorsed it, again, reluctantly. Congress failed to pass the draft registration law. Was this a defeat for the women's movement? It seemed that way.

Other questions arose. One senator opposed to the ERA cited public opinion polls. "Fully 77 percent of American women opposed equal treatment with respect to military service; 83 percent opposed the idea that a wife should be the breadwinner if she were a better wage earner than her husband; and 69 percent opposed the idea that a woman should pay alimony if she has money and her husband does not." As with all polls, the key is how the questions are worded and who is asked. Polls can be scientifically constructed or bogus. What about laws against rape? Would they now be void because of an ERA? Would the ERA require unisex bathrooms? "Would you want your daughter to have to share a public bathroom with a pervert?" Opponents asserted these extreme positions as likely in the future. These arguments unnerved many ERA supporters in the state legislatures. This tactic is known in debating as carrying a point of view ad nauseam, to an irrational conclusion, a sickening conclusion. Parents often do this arguing with their kids. "Mom, everyone else is allowed to do this." Mom, "If everyone else was allowed to jump off the (fill in the blank) bridge, would you?"

Some women began to shift their primary attention to health issues that affected women. A group, the Boston Women's Health Book Collective, BWHBC, published *Our Bodies, Ourselves*, in 1973. It sold four million copies and was translated into twelve languages. One famous cartoon from that era showed a mother nervously entering her young daughter's bedroom to begin "the discussion of the birds and the bees" by presenting her with a copy of *Our Bodies, Ourselves*. The daughter quickly hides the copy she is already reading.

Finally, women themselves began to have misgivings over their own goals. In the 1980s the feminist editor of a radical magazine, *Mother Jones*, wrote this in an editorial.

> "If a woman gets pregnant, 20 years ago the man married her, the honorable thing to do. Now he considers himself gallant if he agrees to split the abortion fee. Something was gained in 20 years, but something was lost."

Another feminist told a story about herself. On a hot summer day, she and her husband and young son were riding in their car when they passed a lady with large breasts. Her husband and son both commented, favorably. She wanted to yell at them both for seeing women as sex objects. However, she was pleased and relieved that her pre-teenage son liked girls. She sat there and said nothing, and was furious at herself. The personal had trumped the movement.

Unity?

The initial euphoria of the women's movement obscured many differences that existed among women. Sisterhood is nice, as is brotherhood for blacks. However, in 80% of the crimes committed by blacks the victim is also black. So much for brotherhood. Sisterhood is similar. It is an unreal slogan. The notion of "women" as a classification fell apart due to ethnic, class, racial, religious, regional, political, and sexual differences among women.

Old divisive questions resurfaced. What is the movement's position towards the traditional family, to strengthen it or to destroy it? Are women morally superior to men, or are they equals? Are women equal but different? Is the difference only biological? Or, are the biological differences unimportant and meaningless? Are the goals of the women's movement to be supportive of one another or to change society? Do women seek justice and equality for all women or to better society by expanding the influence of women?

Gains, But

Overall, the professions have opened up. By 2000 women were 55% of college undergraduates and over 50% of the entering class for medical schools and law schools. However, women still earned less than men. According to the National Women's Law Center, by 2015 a woman at the end of her professional career had earned 38% less than a male, a gap of $435,000.

Women are catching up to the paychecks of their male counterparts. Or, are they? From 1990 to 2000 the wages for female recent college graduates averaged 92% of that for males, an annual difference of $9,000. Add that differential up for a lifetime. Consider how much difference it makes trying to save for retirement – luxury versus sufficiency (maybe). Curiously, after 2000 the gap widened, to 84% in 2015 and then dropped to 79% in 2016. In only two occupations – special education teachers and postal carriers – do females equal males in wages.

The future for an ERA looks bleak. And, if one had been added to the Constitution, it may not have made much of a positive impact. Sweden is a very liberal society. Sweden has a law that a working mother can take off work up to 60 days per year per child for illness and be paid for the days missed. Women in Sweden average 62% of what men make for the same job. Employers refuse to raise the pay for women because of the ill children law. Brazil provides for 3-4 months paid maternity leave. Employers often do not hire young women unless they have a certificate of sterilization.

What does all this mean? In short, it may not be women that society devalues; it may be the one function that only women can do – produce children. Women who never left the workforce to have children are advancing up the corporate ladders, achieving salaries comparable to that of men, and becoming corporate CEOs. Women who periodically leave the workforce for bearing and raising children and later return to work are advancing at a much slower pace. It may be that it is not women our society does not appreciate – it might be children, other peoples' children. The United States is the only industrialized country on the globe that does NOT provide some form of paid maternity leave.

In many respects the women's movement moved into new issues and a new arena by the 1980s. The "personal became political" and the "political became personal." New issues crossed the boundaries between private and public. The emphasis now seemed to be less on the workplace and more on the personal – domestic violence, day care, abortion, and sexual harassment, all issues that do not play well in the public political arena. Legislatures wrestle with these issues, to the satisfaction of few women. Maybe, as with the Civil Rights Movement, the Women's Movement had gone as far as it was practical to go in terms of legislation. Now what?

47

VIETNAM AS AN EVENT IN THE COLD WAR

The Use of History

First, a brief word about the "use" of history. Does a knowledge of history aid those in positions of power who must make decisions? Two distinguished Harvard scholars suggested, hesitantly in 1986, in *Thinking in Time: The Uses of History for Decision-Makers*, that it does. The authors, Richard E. Neustadt and Ernest R. May, wrote "about how to *use* experience, whether remote or recent, in the process of deciding what to do today about the prospect for tomorrow." (p. xxii). They placed a premium on two points – "inventory" and "context." "'Inventory' simply means the stock of historical knowledge, the accumulated points of reference readily available within a given mind from which to pull analogies or time-lines as occasion warrants, or to test those drawn by others. 'Context' has a simple meaning too: The more history one knows, the better one understands the options." (pp. 244-245). Therefore, one can and does learn from history. Or, can we? Or, do we? Mark Twain also commented on the usefulness of history with a story about a cat. "A cat who jumps on a hot stove never jumps on a hot stove again. But, it also never jumps on a cold one." There are always "lessons." But what are they?

Even while the war in Vietnam raged, numerous books appeared that reflected confusion over the lessons this war held for the American people. Look at this sample of titles:

> Ernest Gruening and Howard Beaser, *Vietnam Folly* (1968)
> Chester L. Cooper, *The Lost Crusade* (1970)
> Joseph Buttinger, *Vietnam: The Unforgettable Tragedy* (1977)
> Paul Kattenburg, *The Vietnam Trauma in American Foreign Policy* (1980)
> Brian VanDeMark, *Into the Quagmire: Lyndon Johnson and the Escalation of Vietnam* (1995)

Tragedy, lost crusade, folly, and trauma – events perceived as disasters always encourage studies of HOW something happened. Perhaps the most telling polling statistic of this period is the following question. Not all the causes for the change were due to the war.

"Do you trust your governmental leaders?" 1968 – 76% said yes. 1994 – 19% said yes. A huge credibility gap had developed between our nation's political leaders and the public.

Indochina to 1954

In the nineteenth century, the French decided to make Indochina, the region south of China, into a colony. They began to assert control over the native peoples in the 1850s, finally finishing the task in 1917. That length of time should have sufficiently cautioned any Western designs on Indochina. Eventually the region called Indochina would become modern-day Vietnam, Laos, and Cambodia.

From 1941 to 1945, during the Second World War, the Japanese took over. In order to frustrate Japanese control the United States made vague promises for the future to Vietnamese guerrilla fighters, who greatly harassed their Japanese overlords during the Second World War. The United States knew so very little about Vietnam that at one point during the war President Franklin Roosevelt offered it to our ally, China. Chiang Kai-shek (in pinyin, Jiang Jieshi) quickly declined the offer. In a private comment to his aides, he compared the suggestion to offering someone a gift of a hornets' nest. What he did not tell FDR was that China had earlier controlled Vietnam for almost 1000 years – 1000 years of almost constant efforts to subdue them. France fared no better, facing constant attacks from nationalist rebels. The United States asked the leader of the anti-colonial rebels, who had been fighting the French since the 1920s, to fight the Japanese by guerrilla tactics. He agreed. He was Ho Chi Minh. Ho said many times that he loved the United States. He was born in 1890 and worked as a ship's cabin boy from the age of 12, visiting England, France, and Africa. For a year he lived in the United States in Brooklyn. He attended the Versailles Peace Conference in 1919, urging the colonial powers to end colonialism. Woodrow Wilson refused. In 1920 Ho was one of the founding members of the French Communist Party. Then he returned to Vietnam to organize resistance against the French.

When the Second World War ended, Ho and his troops celebrated on September 2, 1945, by reading a Declaration of Independence to a crowd in Hanoi estimated at 400,000 people. It began, "All men are created equal. They are endowed by their Creator with certain inalienable Rights; among these are Life, Liberty, and the pursuit of Happiness." It continued, and lifted whole phrases verbatim from our Declaration of Independence and the French Revolution's Declaration of the Rights of Man and the Citizen, 1791. "All men are born free and with equal rights, and must always remain free and have equal rights." Ho Chi Minh admired and loved the very best of the United States. At this point the U.S. faced the question of whether this was an anti-colonial rebellion or a communist led rebellion. Was Ho Chi Minh first and foremost a nationalist or first and foremost a communist?

France's attitude complicated the situation. France was one of the keys to our European foreign policy designed to keep Russian communism out of Western Europe after the Second World War. The Cold War had begun. France saw itself as still a colonial power, and still a major power. France did not want to lose her colonies, of which French Indochina was one. Hence, France vowed to subdue the Vietnamese rebels and the United States agreed to provide the military supplies. By 1954 the U.S. was furnishing 80% of the cost of the French effort to reconquer Indochina. In addition, the United States by this time believed in the domino theory, the idea that if one nation went communist its neighbors would be subjected to communist invasion or subversion, and they would consequently go communist, like a row of dominos being knocked down. The end for the French came in 1954 at Dien Bien Phu, an impregnable fortress the French built and then dared the Vietnamese guerrillas to attack. They did. Dien Bien Phu fell in May, 1954. The French were good at building impregnable fortresses. Remember the Maginot Line built before the Second World War?

Geneva Accords to JFK

At this point France and her American ally tried diplomacy to rescue a bad situation by calling for an international peace conference to discuss Indochina and Korea. Remember, the Korean War ended in 1953 with a truce, not a resolution of a divided Korea's future. North Korea refused to participate, and so only Indochina was on the agenda. The West hoped to win at the peace table what they had lost on the battlefield.

The Geneva Accords divided Indochina into three new countries – Cambodia, Laos, and Vietnam – with Vietnam temporarily divided at the 17th parallel into two "regrouping zones," North Vietnam and South Vietnam, with populations of 15 million and 13 million. Elections the next year, 1954, were to select a single leader and government for the united country of Vietnam. The United States refused to permit the elections to take place. After all, the nationalist (communist) Ho Chi Minh would have won. The U.S. then proceeded to begin creating something out of nothing – a new nation called South Vietnam, under the leadership of Ngo Dinh Diem, an American handpicked leader. Diem's regime was inefficient, unpopular, corrupt, and dictatorial, but, it was anti-communist, the only criterion that mattered.

JFK – The Early Cold War 1960s as a Period of Testing

The early 1960s was a period of Cold War thrusts and parries by both sides and by their allies, similar to a fencing dual. Shortly after taking office, President John F. Kennedy suffered through the ill-advised Bay of Pigs fiasco, in which a CIA makeshift army of Cuban exiles tried to invade Cuba to overthrow Castro. It was a disaster. In

August, 1961, the Berlin Wall went up. A year later, in October, 1962, the world held its breath during the Cuban Missile crisis, as close to nuclear war as there had ever been. Was Vietnam also a test of American resolve? Many American policy makers saw it as such. The Russians, or the Chinese, were probing to find our weaknesses, our lack of resolve. When JFK took over as president an estimated 15,000 Viet Cong guerrillas faced 250,000 South Vietnamese soldiers and 3,000 U.S. military "advisors," who often fought, unofficially. Officially, Laos was neutral, but in reality it was divided, half controlled by communists and half by a Western-backed government.

Guerrilla wars are difficult to win. In the places where guerrillas had been defeated after the Second World War, such as in Malaysia by the British, it appeared that the guerrillas had to be outnumbered by a 10-1 ratio. The guerrillas know where they plan to strike, it is necessary to guard every place. Long after the Vietnam War ended, Americans learned that every time the U.S. increased troop numbers, North Vietnam increased hers. Thus, the U.S. could never achieve the high ratio necessary. The U.S. was not facing a tiny, puny enemy. The North Vietnamese army was estimated to be the world's fifth or sixth largest.

In South Vietnam policymakers faced a question. Was the situation one of external aggression, an invasion, infiltration by the North Vietnamese into South Vietnam, OR, was the situation a peasant uprising against its own government? American officials saw it as an invasion, probably incorrectly, because early in the war most of the enemy weapons American soldiers captured from the Viet Cong were our weapons that had fallen into their hands.

By 1963 policymakers were very dissatisfied with the progress of the war. The U.S. government blamed the lack of progress on the leader, Diem. Buddhist monks protested against the South Vietnamese government by burning themselves alive in front of the capitol and the president's mansion. The American evening television news broadcast seven of these immolations. With U.S. backing, a group of generals overthrew President Diem and killed him, shocking the American leaders, especially Henry Cabot Lodge, the U.S. ambassador to South Vietnam, and President Kennedy. Diem was supposed to have been flown out of the country into exile. The generals took charge.

When President Kennedy was assassinated in November, 1963, he left behind a confused situation in Vietnam. Some of his closest advisors later said Kennedy intended to take our soldiers out of Vietnam after the 1964 election. If JFK did intend to withdraw, he never said so publicly, nor did he write it down. He did say once that sending more troops was like taking a drink of alcohol. After a while the effect wears off and you have to take another one. By the time of his assassination, JFK had raised the number of American troops in Vietnam to 16,732. By the end of 1963, 73 American soldiers had been killed.

Kennedy's successor, Lyndon Baines Johnson, faced three policy choices: he could admit defeat, continue the war at the current level, or enlarge American participation.

Johnson enlarged American participation, after promising during the 1964 presidential campaign that "American boys would not be sent to do the job of Asian boys." He ordered a new effort, code-named "A-34," a series of hit-and-run secret raids against North Vietnam. Throughout his presidency, Johnson could never understand why the American military could not pound the North Vietnamese into submission. As a Texas Hill Country product, he frequently exhorted our troops to "Hang that coonskin from the wall," a reference to displaying a trophy from raccoon hunting.

Escalation

The public endorsement of LBJ's stepped-up efforts arrived in the Gulf of Tonkin Resolution, passed by Congress in August, 1964, after an attack on American ships by North Vietnamese PT-boats. Subsequent investigation revealed that of the two incidents reported, one never happened. Historians now know that plans for escalation had already been made; the Gulf of Tonkin incident simply provided the excuse for seeking the public's approval. In February 1965, guerrillas attacked an American base at Pleiku. This led to Rolling Thunder, a bombing campaign against North Vietnam. In April 1965, American ground troops first went into action. By December the U.S. had 185,000 in Vietnam. However, since 113,000 South Vietnamese soldiers deserted that year, our involvement had little impact.

Why? Why the bombing of the southern half of North Vietnam? The military's goal was to stop the movement of supplies coming down the Ho Chi Minh Trail, a series of narrow footpaths. American superior technology would win the war. However, it took hundreds of tons of bombs and luck to kill just one enemy soldier with a backpack carrying supplies down the trail. Eventually the U.S. Army began issuing weekly statistics, which included the number of bridges destroyed in North Vietnam and along the Ho Chi Minh Trail. However, those "bridges" were unlike those in America. They were rope bridges with wooden boards as the walkway. The Vietnamese kept replacement parts in holes in the ground beside the bridges. Their record for rebuilding a bridge after an American plane destroyed one was 18 minutes. Many bridges were replaced before U.S. jet planes returned to their base. American superior technology would win this war?

Part of the basis for our commitment to the defense of South Vietnam was the "credibility thesis," the belief that the United States had to preserve our reputation as a nation that would abide by its agreements. In 1965 the Assistant Secretary of Defense, John McNaughton, outlined the "U.S. aims" in Vietnam:

> 70% to avoid a humiliating defeat, thus maintaining our image and
> credibility as a superpower, prepared to defend others
> 20% to keep South Vietnam out of Chinese hands
> 10% to permit the people of South Vietnam to enjoy a better life

The American death toll began to rise. The number of American soldiers killed by the end of each year was as follows:

1965	1,369
1966	5,008
1967	9,378
1968	14,592

The average American soldier in Vietnam was 19, compared to the average age of 26 for a soldier during the Second World War. It was a young man's war. This sparked protests from the young, especially college students.

Hawks and Doves

The division of the American public into hawks and doves (few Americans were neutral) began as the war dragged on and on. For some, it was not worth it. The estimated cost to kill one enemy soldier was $400,000, which required, on average, 75 bombs and 150 artillery shells. Not much of a return on the investment in arms.

The Army relied upon the draft to fill the ranks. Hence, young people were concerned about how the war affected their generation. Initially only non-college young men were drafted. However, remember, the 1960s was a decade of egalitarianism with the free speech movement, the civil rights movement, and the women's movement. Then the draft shifted to including drafting college students in reverse order of their GPA, their grade point average. Send only the dumb ones. After a while the draft changed to a nationally televised lottery, during which officials drew from two containers. One held a birthday date for that draft year, the second a number. April 10th could be number 256; October 15th could be 17. It was all in the luck of the draw, or rather, in two draws, pure chance. The Army usually drafted up to about number 195; above that, you were safe, below that, you were certain to go. It seemed fair enough, except to some who had low numbers. Two freshman college roommates went out drinking after one drew number 365 and the other number 1, lucky and unlucky. But, it is too simplistic to brand all the young as opponents of the war. A poll in 1969 asked, "Do you favor immediate withdrawal of all U.S. troops from Vietnam?" The national response was 36% yes, 57% no. For those under twenty-nine, all of whom knew someone serving in Vietnam, the response was 35% yes and 59% no.

Meanwhile, opponents of the war expanded their protests. Some draft evaders left for Canada or Europe, voting against the war with their feet. Families split when older veterans of the Second World War or the Korean War debated their sons over the merits of serving. College campuses organized "teach-ins," to discuss and debate American involvement. Proponents of the war soon discovered they were outnumbered and not welcome. National groups on both sides urged their followers to drive slowly with their headlights on for a particular day, to show your support or opposition to the war. Headlights back then did not come on automatically. Sometimes cars drove five abreast on interstate highways at 35 miles an hour, snarling traffic. Try to imagine the "road rage" this encouraged. In some secondary schools, the other side roughed up students wearing armbands for or against the war. In many instances the principal's feelings about the war often determined who received what punishment.

The young were not the only opponents. Some well-known public figures questioned American policy. The "father" of the policy of containment, former diplomat George F. Kennan, author of the famous "long telegram" and the Mister X *Foreign Policy* article advocating containment, publicly stated that containment was not an appropriate policy for Asia. It was designed as a European policy, not an Asian policy. The list of other opponents contained some impressive names – Senator J. William Fulbright, Chairman of the Senate Foreign Relations Committee, and therefore privy to all the secret information a president has access to; JFK's brother, Senator Robert Kennedy; Martin Luther King, Jr.; and, the author of the famous book on baby and child care, Dr. Benjamin Spock. The first woman elected to Congress, Jeannette Rankin, now in her eighties, a Republican from Montana, also demonstrated against the war. She is famous in American history as a sincere pacifist who voted against American participation in both the First and the Second World War, the only member of Congress to oppose the Second World War and one of fifty who opposed the First. She lost her next election both times. Over 200,000 demonstrators participated in the 1967 march on the Pentagon. After he privately told President Johnson that the U.S. could not win, LBJ shipped Secretary of Defense Robert McNamara off to the presidency of the World Bank.

In January, 1968, came the pivotal Tet Offensive. The Viet Cong and North Vietnamese captured 74 towns and cities in South Vietnam, holding most for a week. They held the ancient capital of Hue for a month. The fierce attack was a military failure; the VC, Viet Cong, lost 40,000 men and lost control of everything they captured. However, in many respects it was a political and psychological victory. Many in the American public began to think that the VC could do whatever, whenever. It was just a matter of time, their time. As one historian said, Tet "became the U.S. obituary in Vietnam."

1968 was a pivotal year in the American public's thinking. In his book, *Vietnam: The War at Home,* Thomas Powers explains, "The violence in Vietnam seemed to elicit a similar air of violence in the United States, an appetite for extremes: people felt that history was accelerating, time was running out, great issues were reaching a point of final decision."

The election of 1968 was unlike anything Americans had ever seen.   In the New Hampshire Democratic primary the president, LBJ, won with only 49.5% of the vote. His primary opponent, anti-war critic Senator Eugene McCarthy, (not related to the earlier anti-communist fanatic, Senator Joseph McCarthy) got 42.4% in spite of a lackluster effort.   LBJ shocked the nation on March 31, 1968, during a nationally televised speech at Johns Hopkins University, when he declared that he would neither seek nor accept his party's nomination.   In April Martin Luther King, Jr., was assassinated in Memphis, Tennessee.   Across the country black neighborhoods exploded.   In June Senator Robert Kennedy was assassinated, immediately after winning the California Democratic primary.   In August the Democratic National Convention featured shaking fists and name-calling, while outside, demonstrators battled with the Chicago police in what was later officially termed "a police riot."   To further complicate a chaotic election year, former Alabama Governor George Wallace joined the fray with a third party.   In many states, it was a tight three-way race between George Wallace, Democratic Vice President Hubert Humphrey, and Republican Richard Nixon.   Nixon won the national election.   However, what he now faced was a deeply divided nation.

Nixon – Vietnamization

Nixon's new war policy, called Vietnamization, sought to reduce the number of U.S. troops while widening the war to include more air attacks on neighboring Cambodia, in violation of explicit directives passed by Congress.   Too many Viet Cong supplies and quick attacks were coming from so-called neutral Cambodia.   There were 3,000 air strikes in 14 months.   When news leaked out, seven hundred college campuses exploded in protest, causing some governors to send in their national guard.   This led to tragic student deaths at Kent State University in Ohio and Jackson State University in Mississippi.   Many of the nation's colleges closed early that spring, close to one-third of them.   The college administrators announced, "As of today the semester has ended.   All students must leave the campus by tomorrow evening.   Professors, turn in your semester grades as of this point."   In New York City a group of hardhats, taking a lunch break at a construction site, watched an impromptu peace parade.   They put down their sandwiches and attacked the "peaceniks."   Such was the public's mood.

Congress responded by passing the War Powers Act of 1973, which limits the power of the president to commit American armed forces after sixty days.   In truth, this is meaningless in the short run.   All those men, women, ships, planes, and bombs are the president's, and the president can do whatever with them.   By the time the War Powers Act kicks in, it could be all over, literally.

Further complicating the year 1968 was the news, made public in 1969, of the My Lai incident, when the officer in charge, Lt. William Calley, ordered the deaths of almost 500 women, children, and old men, all civilians, captured in a village mistaken for a Viet Cong hamlet. Two prominent national politicians defended Calley, who was from Georgia: Republican President Richard Nixon and Jimmy Carter, the Georgia Democratic governor. Try to find a thread of consistency there. Equally shocking, the VC and the NRV, North Vietnamese regulars, had tortured and killed over 3,000 civilians when they captured Hue in the Tet Offensive. This war was on the national television news for 15-20 minutes every evening, the most reported and filmed war in history. The public saw scenes that only soldiers had known previously. One family in Minnesota saw their son die while they watched the news. When the army officer knocked on their door the next day to give them the bad news, they responded, "We already know, we saw it on TV."

Finally, the four sides, the United States, South Vietnam, North Vietnam, and the Viet Cong signed the Paris Accords in January, 1973. American active ground participation ended; but the U.S. still supplied the South Vietnamese. From 1973 to 1975 the war continued, but not for American soldiers. Many South Vietnam soldiers died in 1974 fighting against the VC and NVR, more than in 1965, 1966, or 1967. The war continued to April, 30, 1975, when the capital of South Vietnam, Saigon, fell. South Vietnam lost.

What Were the "Lessons of the Vietnam War"?

1. Between 1945 and 1975 the war created 7.8 million refugees, many of them "boat people," who fled on makeshift rafts. There were 905,512 Indochinese in the 1990 U.S. census. Who would have guessed that in 1960?
2. In a curious way, the war created distrust of the military by civilians and distrust of civilians by the military. Some soldiers in Vietnam put "UUUU" on their helmets, which stood for "the unwilling, led by the unqualified, doing the unnecessary, for the ungrateful."
3. Drug use among the troops received high publicity, making it appear that the Army was degenerating. Of the soldiers in Vietnam, 51% used marijuana and 28.5% hard narcotics. However, in Europe the numbers were 40% and 13%, and inside the United States the numbers were 41% and 20%. Not much difference. Revelations of drugs being smuggled back into the United States hidden inside returning bodies shocked everyone.
4. There were 788 incidents of "fragging," when American soldiers retaliated against their superiors by rolling grenades under their beds, causing 86 deaths and wounding 714.
5. Desertion rates rose, from 1.59% to 7.13%. In addition, 200,000 draft evaders fled the country.

6. Returning veterans came home to no parades, no welcome home, and no ceremony, returning as individuals into a society that seemed, to them, to be non-appreciative and unaware of their sacrifices. Veterans tended to only discuss their wartime experiences with other veterans. The military corrected that mistake in the Gulf War, the Iraq War, and the Afghanistan War. Units returned as units, to parades and ceremonies, and an official big "thank you."

7. Over 15,000,000 land mines were planted during the war. When the war ended, they remained in the ground, creating hazards for children playing, walkers walking, and farmers farming. By the end of the twentieth century many people across the globe were calling for ending the manufacturing of land mines, everywhere.

8. The United States invented and used 11.2 million gallons of Agent Orange to defoliate the jungle so our planes and helicopters could see through the thick tree canopy. It turned out to be cancer causing to Vietnamese, to our soldiers handling it and to civilians. By 2012 the United States was helping Vietnam clean it up.

9. Opposition to the draft led the United States to adopt an all-volunteer army. However, does it meet our needs? Future engagements in Iraq and Afghanistan used National Guard units, which were not previously seen by the public as playing that role.

10. Our soldiers left a legacy behind in Vietnam – children. Vietnamese culture rejected the mixed racial offspring. Discrimination is not something invented by whites. These children were called "boi-doi," "dust of life," virtual outcasts in Vietnamese society.

All wars have mixed results and mixed legacies. The war in Vietnam seemed to have more than its fair share. Part of the reason was the length of the war. As historian Arthur M. Schlesinger, Jr., explained in *The Imperial Presidency*, "Few wars are unpopular in their first thirty days." Another reason was that it was a frustrating "limited war," limited in goals, weapons, and geographic area. The mightiest nation in the history of the world could not use all its might. The nation did not begin to heal until the Vietnam Veterans Memorial was built on the Washington Mall in 1982. It still is healing over that war. The Second World War generation was called our "greatest generation." The Korean War was called, in time, "the good war." Vietnam still awaits a positive nickname for those who sacrificed.

48

INDIANS, 1848 TO THE PRESENT

Terminology

The first two paragraphs repeat what was stated earlier, in order to accommodate those who are using only volume II of this book. I am not trying to make a statement for or against "political correctness." I usually use "Indian" rather than Native-American, Original Peoples, First Peoples, Natives, or Amerindians. Why? I do so because modern Indians overwhelmingly use that term to describe themselves, often after first using their tribal name. People have a right to self-description. In many respects, the original Indians encountered by Europeans had the correct approach. They had no name for all Indians as a distinct group. Europeans gave them one. The commonly used word "tribe" also presents difficulties. As one historian pointed out, the modern Navajo Tribe Reservation is larger than Switzerland. So, do the Swiss people live in a nation while the Navajos live in a tribe? Let's try the reverse, that the Swiss live in a tribe and the Navajos live in a nation. See how silly names can be? In some respects words like clan, grouping, or band may, at times, be more accurate at a particular moment in history when describing a specific group of Indians.

Periodization and Indian History

The history of Indians ended at 1848 in an earlier chapter. Why 1848? Most history books divide U.S. History at the end of the Civil War and Reconstruction, 1865 to 1877. Periodization is a tool used by historians to break a particular topic into recognizable parts, with significant dates used as turning points delineating a change or the arrival of new issues, events, laws, etc. As one example, if the twentieth century is defined as a century of hot and cold wars, it makes sense to label it as extending from 1914 to 1991, or from the outbreak of the First World War to the end of the Cold War. If a historian defined it as a century of great technological inventions, he or she might make the automobile, transistor, computer, and Internet as the major turning points.

From the Policy of Separation to the Policy of Concentration

By 1848-1849, with the Mexican Cession and the California gold rush, the Policy of Separation no longer worked. Most Indians had been moved to the "West." At least in the 1830s it was the West. Not now. Americans needed to go through Indian lands, and later, after improvements in agriculture, settlers needed Indians removed from the Great Plains. Demands appeared that Indians surrender their nomadic way of life and "be like us," the superior race. Otherwise, they would disappear within 40-50 years.

The United States government switched to a Policy of Concentration, moving Indians willingly or unwillingly to reservations, preferably in out-of-the-way places everyone thought were devoid of usefulness. Understandably, some did not want to go, hence the Plains Wars from 1865 to the last battle, or rather massacre, at Wounded Knee in 1890. Two factors sealed the fate of the Indians. Epidemics swept the West, killing tens of thousands. And, unlike the experience for Indians east of the Mississippi River, no European power could be a potential ally. They had only their own resources and resourcefulness. Finally, industrialization produced more deadly weapons. The outcome was never in doubt.

Another component of the Concentration Policy was the increased role played by the federal government, which used the army to remove recalcitrants and federally-appointed agents to manage the reservations. The national government in Washington controlled all aspects of Indian affairs. This exclusion of the state governments may have been necessary to prevent a hydra-headed approach, but it carried major consequences for the future. One peculiarity of the modern West is the power and influence of the BIA, the Bureau of Indian Affairs, which manages 3,379,037 acres of land and the BLM, the Bureau of Land Management, which manages all the unsold land, 480,450,433 acres, making it the largest landholder on the continent. Combine the totals. That is a lot of land. Policy clashes between federal agencies and local and state governments have been and remain a bone of contention. If one adds the geographic distance to the equation, it is easy to see why sometimes Westerners seem to be referring to the federal government as a foreign government.

Historian Don Russell estimated that only 1% of the Indian population died fighting the U.S. Army and militias between 1798 and 1898, but 30-40% died from diseases. One-half of the Cheyenne nation died during the summer of the 1849 gold rush from diseases carried by dreamy-eyed, would-be gold miners. Disease and the destruction of the buffalo herds were the primary weapons subduing the Indians. Further weakening Indian resistance was a phenomenon still the topic of sensitive debate, Indians and alcohol. Whites quickly learned very early that alcohol had an incredible attraction for

Indians. Scholars from all fields of medicine, psychology, and sociology, to name just a few, have searched for reasons. One that may answer the quandary better than others is the assertion that Indians *used* alcohol in a different way. They deliberately consumed vast amounts quickly to reach something resembling a religious experience. The research goes on. So do the questions and accusations.

The implementation of the Concentration Policy began at the Fort Laramie Council in 1851. Almost 10,000 Plains Indians gathered with federal officials to hear the government's proposal. In return for safe passage to Oregon for settlers and the establishment of exact boundary areas for each tribe in the Northern Plains, Indians agreed to cease intertribal warfare. In return, the federal government would provide a generous annual payment of food and goods to each tribe. This was the Fort Laramie Treaty, securing (?) the Northern Plains. Why the question mark – some tribes did not attend, such as the powerful Comanche, who extended all the way down into Texas. Various treaties with individual tribes over the next few years pushed many of the Northern signees into the Indian Territory, modern Oklahoma.

The Civil War and the Great Plains

The Civil War interrupted the Concentration Policy. Once again, as with the American Revolution and the War of 1812, many Indians leaned towards the wrong side, such as the Chickasaw and Choctaw supporting the Confederacy. Mistake! Other tribes were bitterly split. It was not a case of loyalty to the U.S. government, especially given the history of ill treatment; most tribes saw no advantage to supporting either the Union or the Confederacy. For example, the Cherokee decided to be neutral. It did not matter. In essence, the Southern Plains Indians were destined to lose the Civil War and their land in Kansas, no matter which position they took. Congress pushed them all into the Indian Territory.

Sensing an opportunity, the Santee Sioux rose up in Minnesota during the Civil War and slaughtered between four hundred and eight hundred white settlers. The Santee Sioux were finally defeated by the Union Army in 1862. The Union Army captured 1,500 Santee Sioux. The army and the Minnesotans wanted to execute them all. President Lincoln halted the more draconian court orders while permitting 38 executions at Fort Mankato in 1862. In Colorado trouble brewed between gold-hungry whites (the Pikes Peak gold rush) and Cheyenne living in various encampments, as promised to them by the Fort Laramie Treaty. Everyone knows which side won. The campaign featured the infamous Sand Creek Massacre, an attack on a Cheyenne village of approximately 500, mostly women, children and the elderly. Because the chiefs were mistakenly under the impression that conflict had ended and peace had been restored, the warriors had been sent out on a long hunting expedition. Commanded by Colonel John Chivington, a state militia wiped out the village in 1864. News reports of mutilated bodies shocked the nation. A Congressional report after several investigations blasted Col. Chivington, who "deliberately planned and executed a foul and dastardly massacre which would have disgraced the . . . savage among those who were the victims of his cruelty." Chivington is famous for justifying such actions by observing that "nits make lice." Nits are baby lice. If you kill the kids you will not have to kill them as adults. He was also a Methodist minister. One wonders what the topic was for the next sermon he preached.

The Plains Wars to the Battle of the Little Bighorn

The end of the Civil War brought trouble for the Plains Indians. There was a backlog of pent-up demand of settlers anxious to swarm onto the farmland opened up by the Homestead Act of 1862. Also, the war created an organized army with a huge supply of battle-hardened veterans ready to secure peace on the Plains. A drive began to push the Plains Indians onto reservations – either by treaties or by the army. From Sand Creek in 1864 to the Battle of the Little Bighorn in 1876, relentless cavalry campaigns killed or rounded up men, women, and children. In a curious way, this drive was part of the national government's playing a larger role in Western concerns, unlike the experience in states east of the Mississippi River. This impact lasted a long time in the West, and some of it remains to this day – ownership of all unsold land, regulation of scarce water resources, subsidies to build the railroads, control of Indian reservations, laws regulating mining and timber cutting, control of radical labor unions such as the IWW, the Industrial Workers of the World, vicious anti-Chinese immigration laws, and a strong military presence. In short, the history of the West was different.

In both Congress and the Washington bureaucracy, a heated debate continued over what was labeled the "Transfer Issue," where Indian policy should be located – in the War Department or the Department of the Interior. In 1849 it had been transferred to the new Department of the Interior. It really came down to how one viewed the "Indian Problem." Was it best solved by military action or treaties? Which approach worked? In the military atmosphere in the years immediately following the Civil War the military attitude, which was to kill Indians, dominated.

To undermine the Indian will to fight, the U.S. government deliberately encouraged the wanton destruction of the Indians' major food source, the vast buffalo herds. The herds were virtually extinct by 1883, after about 13 million had been killed. Shooting a near-sighted buffalo (they smell trouble better than they see it) is about as exciting as shooting a cow. There was no hunting thrill; the only danger was a possible stampede in your direction set off by gunfire.

On the Plains the army faced a nomadic foe that used guerrilla hit-and-run tactics and avoided large engagements. Familiar with the terrain, the water sources, and the vast size of the Plains, Indians possessed many advantages. In the mid-1870s some warriors left reservations and created a large fighting force of Lakota Sioux, Northern

Cheyenne, and Arapaho led by Crazy Horse and Sitting Bull. A life farming on a reservation was not for Sitting Bull. "If the Great Spirit desired me to be a white man he would have made me so in the first place." When General George Armstrong Custer stumbled into a large encampment of Indians, he impulsively attacked a much larger foe, a military disaster that shocked the nation in the midst of celebrating the 1876 Centennial. Other units of the Seventh Cavalry also engaged Indians nearby. A stalemate ensued, but the Indians had to split up because there was not enough grass for their horses or food for such a large group. It may have gone into the history books as "Custer's Last Stand," but in reality it was the "Indians' Last Stand." Within a year all remaining 1100 renegade Indians on the Northern Plains surrendered or returned to their reservations. The Southern Great Plains Wars ended earlier with the Red River War, 1874-1875. The Great Plains were secure. Only mop-up remained. Geronimo, a colorful Apache chief, was the last to resist, but he surrendered in 1886. The Plains Indian Wars lasted longer in Hollywood films than they did in history.

The absolute end came in 1890 when a small contingent of Lakota Sioux, inspired by the Ghost Dance, which supposedly would return the buffalo and make Indians invincible to the white man's weapons, left their reservation. The Seventh Cavalry went after them. The Lakota Sioux had formed the nucleus of the Indians who annihilated Custer's Seventh Cavalry unit in 1876. Revenge – 25 soldiers and hundreds of Sioux died in the battle (or massacre) at Wounded Knee in South Dakota. Days after the December 29th battle, searchers found three children and five adults alive among the twisted frozen corpses. No one realized it at the time, but the Indian wars were completely over.

Dawes Act to 1930 – The Policy of Americanization

The Concentration Policy was over, a great success, since all the Indians now lived on reservations. Now what? What followed was a sincere new policy to make (force) Indians to be "just like us," known as the Americanization Policy. Missionaries, who needed a permit from the Bureau of Indian Affairs, moved onto the reservations to convert Indians. However, with so many different churches in America, missionaries often spent a great deal of their time fighting with one another or seeking a favored position in the Bureau of Indian Affairs. The battles between Catholic and Protestant missionaries were especially bitter, but those between different Protestant churches were not far behind.

A second means to acculturate Indians was to rescue the young from their tribes by forcibly sending them to special schools to learn the "White Man's Ways." Thousands of young Indians were sent to boarding schools away from the reservation. The first and best known was the Carlisle Indian Industrial School, founded in 1879 by Richard Henry Pratt, a former army officer. Popular culture today links the Carlisle Indian School to Coach Pop Warner's fabulous football teams and his greatest star, Jim Thorpe, voted the most outstanding athlete of the first half of the twentieth century. However, for most of the kids, Carlisle and every other boarding school resembled a long prison sentence. New arrivals were stripped of their Indian clothes, had their hair cut, and were prohibited from using their native language. The school's motto was "Kill the Indian and save the man" (and woman, since girls also attended boarding schools). One historian referred to it as "cultural rather than physical genocide." Mark Twain once observed that, "Soap and education are not as sudden as a massacre, but they are more deadly in the long run; because a half-massacred Indian may recover, but if you educate him and wash him, it is bound to finish him some time or other." When the kids returned to their reservations, they found their industrial skills useless, as the older Indians also regarded them – totally useless.

In spite of occasional harsh criticism, such as the 1928 Meriam Report, the federally controlled boarding school system persisted. The Meriam Report stated that "provisions for the care of Indian children in boarding schools are grossly inadequate." Finally, in 1975, the Indian Self-Determination and Education Assistance Act began to turn boarding schools and other educational programs over to tribal control. Through an earlier new program, begun in 1947, over 40,00 Indian children were placed in Mormon homes, which continued until 2000. In 1990 another law specifically protected native languages. Today Indian culture, language, and history are once more, as they were centuries before, under tribal control.

In 1871 the Indian Appropriations Act ended the policy of treaties regulating the relationship between the U.S. government and individual Indian tribes and declared that now the government could manage tribal affairs without tribal consent. Indian tribes were no longer semi-independent powers within the United States. This approach was upheld by the U.S. Supreme Court in *Lone Wolf v. Hitchcock*, 1903. Kiowa Chief Lone Wolf sued the Secretary of the Interior, charging that Congressional actions defrauded Indians of their land, in violation of their treaties. The Supreme Court ruled that Congress possessed the political authority to unilaterally void treaties between the United States and Indian tribes. The ruling declared that

> "These Indian tribes are the wards of the nation. They are communities dependent on the United States. Dependent largely for their daily food. Dependent for their political rights."

Indians had no legal right to appeal the decisions of Congress to the federal courts. This decision reversed the statements made by Chief Justice John Marshall in *Cherokee Nation v. Georgia*, 1831, and *Worcester v. Georgia*, 1832. Charles Wilkinson, a law professor, explained in *American Indians, Time, and the Law*, that Marshall had reasoned "that Indian tribes were sovereign before contact with Europeans and that some, but not all, sovereign powers continued in existence after relations with Europeans and the United States were established." In *Lone Wolf* the Court declared that the federal government served as the protector of the Indian tribes, which always faced hostile interactions with state and local governments, and therefore, "the tribes should presume that Congress would act in good faith to protect tribal needs." Had Congress done so in the past? Some scholars refer to *Lone Wolf* as the Indians' *Dred Scott* decision, stripping them of all their rights.

The paragraph above begins with the 1871 Indian Appropriations Act stating that Indian tribes were no longer semi-independent powers within the United States. Yet, curiously, the Supreme Court seemingly contradicted this statement in *Elk v. Wilkins*, 1884. John Elk, a Winnebago Indian, moved off the tribal reservation to live among whites. He tried to register to vote. After being denied, he sued claiming citizenship under the Fourteenth Amendment. The Supreme Court ruled that an Indian was not a citizen by virtue of being born in the United States. Instead, an Indian owed his loyalty to his tribe, which were "alien nations" or "distinct political communities."

In the last quarter of the nineteenth century, especially centered in New England, a movement arose to preserve Indians and Indian culture. Two books by Helen Hunt Jackson painted a pattern of governmental mistreatment, increasing interest in the cause. *A Century of Dishonor*, 1881, detailed the long history of the government's policies. She sent a copy to every member of Congress. *Ramona*, a novel published three years later, described how Indians in Southern California suffered after the U.S. gained the Mexican Cession. All this mounting concern from "do-gooders" ended up having a negative impact on Indians, from their point of view. The Dawes Severalty Act, 1887, sponsored by Henry Dawes, a senator from Massachusetts, dissolved the tribes as legal entities and granted to each individual Indian the opportunity to obtain a farm, from the land reserved for that Indian tribe's reservation. The catch, intended to prevent the new farmer from falling prey to unscrupulous whites, was that he could not sell the land for 25 years. Large chunks of the remaining reservation land were sold to white settlers, under the theory that since Indians were now farmers, the tribe no longer needed so much land. Sounds good. It was not. Indians lost 62% of their reservation land under the Dawes Act. Prior to the Dawes Act, they owned 8% of the continental United States, 150 million acres.

As readers learned previously in the section on the Agricultural Revolution in the late nineteenth century in the chapter titled, *The Populist Revolt*, agriculture was a declining industry — too many farmers, too much expansion, world-wide competition, falling prices, expensive farm equipment, high railroad shipping rates, and on and on. In addition, because Indians were now individual landowners, states and local governments began assessing property taxes. Welcome to the white man's world. Most Indians wanted no part of the Dawes Act offer, and those who ventured into farming usually returned to the reservation after a few years, broke after their farms had been seized for back taxes. They could not hold on for the required 25 years, thus they gained nothing. Historians estimate that 90% of the Indians lost the farms they gained under the Dawes Act. In 1904 the Steenerson Act and the Clapp Act granted 80 acres of tribal land to "worthy" individual Indians. Read "worthy" in that sentence to mean Indians willing to sell their rights to logging companies, the real purpose of the two acts.

Accompanying this new respect, or rather curiosity, for Indian culture was the appearance of the Indian as a romanticized relic of a dying past – a feature in traveling vaudeville shows. The most famous was *Buffalo Bill's Wild West Show*, which toured America and Europe from 1883 to 1913. Two of the many Indians in the show for a short time were Sitting Bull and Geronimo. Sitting Bull always gave away almost all his wages to the startled poor he met on the streets. Makes one wonder who was more civilized. Ever the showman, Buffalo Bill Cody set up a very popular exhibit near the Chicago World's Fair, the World's Columbian Exposition, in 1893. The promoters of the World's Fair tried to stop him, and failed. Perhaps they were right. What did Indians have to celebrate about the arrival of Columbus?

The Ultimate American Identity – Citizenship

In 1924 Congress decided that Indians had lived in America long enough to qualify for citizenship. In 1924 all Indians became American citizens according to the Indian Citizenship Act, also known as the Snyder Act. Approximately one-half of the Indian population were already citizens. Citizenship had been granted to some Indians or tribes in piecemeal fashion through treaties or as a reward for military service. The granting of citizenship in the 1920s, a positive accomplishment, must be balanced against comments made by the Commissioner of Indian Affairs. He threatened to fine Indians who participated in Indian religious ceremonies. Christian missionaries had urged him to take action. When the New Deal arrived with President Franklin Roosevelt's response to the Great Depression, Indians wondered what to expect. Yet another change in policy arrived.

John Collier – the Indian Reorganization Act of 1934

John Collier earned a reputation as a reformer working in the 1920s in various positions around the country that are best described as lingering holdovers from the Progressive Movement. Eventually he arrived in New Mexico and became enthralled with the Taos Indian culture. He played a major role in drumming up support to defeat the Bursum Bill, introduced in Congress by Senator Holm Bursum of New Mexico. (It was also known as the Fall Indian Omnibus Bill, for the Secretary of the Interior, Albert Fall.) The Bursum Bill would have, in effect, facilitated the transfer of Pueblo Indian land in New Mexico to whites. Collier's writings and activism defending Indian culture led President Franklin Roosevelt to appoint him as Commissioner of Indian Affairs in 1933; he served until 1945. Collier defended Indian religious practices, language, and culture. No more assimilation and Americanization. This was a new approach. He spent much of his early time fighting his subordinate employees in the Bureau of Indian Affairs. Their attitudes did not match his. By far his greatest accomplishment was the Indian Reorganization Act of 1934, also known as the Wheeler-Howard Act. It granted Indians the right to self-government, pledged the federal government's aid in finding jobs and improving economic conditions on the reservations, emphasized the need to preserve Indian culture, ended the land allotment program begun under the Dawes Act, and provided some financial compensation for land lost. Congress added a provision that required tribes accepting this act (each tribe had to vote on it) to establish a written constitutional tribal government. Opposition arose in some tribes when traditionalists preferred their own governmental mechanism. The vast majority of tribes approved.

During the Second World War Navajo Indians in the Pacific campaign against Japan served as radio transmitters, sending messages in Navajo. After the war the Japanese kept asking – what in the world was that language? It was kept secret until 1969, when the radio Indians finally received the public recognition they so richly deserved. Overall, the Second World War brought to Indians changes similar to those that affected blacks, women, and Hispanics. Jobs were plentiful, individual perspectives were broadened, military service brought honor and a sense of equality, and, also, a vision of what a more just and equal society could be. In this atmosphere, Indians created a national organization in 1944 to address common concerns, the National Congress of American Indians, NCAI. In 1946 Congress established the Indian Claims Commission to settle land claims. By the early 1970s Indian tribes had won over $400 million in claims.

The 1950s – The Policy of Termination and Relocation

Just when progress seemed on the horizon, several backward steps appeared. In essence, Congress moved towards reviving an old policy dressed up with a new name. Established by Congressional resolution in 1953, Termination sought to end federal control of 109 tribes, to extend state control and jurisdiction over reservations, and to end favorable benefits coming from the federal government. Put all Indians out on their own, as individuals. The goal was to draw Indians off the economically distressed reservations through urban job-training programs. The Indian Relocation Act of 1956 partially subsidized Indians who left reservations to acquire vocational skills in cities. These Eisenhower administration policies changed in the 1960s. Along with everything else, everything seemed to change in the 1960s.

1960s – Impact of the Civil Rights Movement

The Termination Policy drew many young Indians off reservations. In the urban setting they began to realize that tribal differences meant very little to the outside, non-Indian world. They also witnessed the beginnings of the civil rights movement. Students today cannot imagine how deeply the nascent civil rights movement touched the young, especially high school and college students. In the atmosphere of debates over race conducted in families, homes, schools, and churches, the young proved to be less prejudiced than their elders. The national television news portrayed injustices each night, feeding feelings that ranged from a seething anger to a conviction that changes must come. Young urban Indians were part of that experience. The media attention bore fruit in the 1960s.

The roots of the various equal rights and protest movements – women, Indians, Hispanics, handicapped, gays, anti-Vietnam War – grew out of the vocabulary, events, achievements of, and participation in, the black freedom struggle, the civil rights movement. The American Indian Movement, AIM, founded in 1968, with roots extending back to 1948, absorbed the urban young Indians. And, similar to SNCC, the Student Nonviolent Coordinating Committee, AIM became increasingly more radical and confrontational. AIM seized Alcatraz Island in 1969, an abandoned federal prison in San Francisco Bay, occupying it for eighteen months. It also took over the Bureau of Indian Affairs in 1972, similar to the 1968 takeover of Columbia University by student radicals. In 1973 AIM took control of the village of Wounded Knee, the site of the 1890 massacre, in what was really a challenge to the older, staid Indian leadership, not to federal authorities. One historian found 70 Indian takeovers or confrontations with authorities in this period. Activism was in the air.

As with the civil rights movement, federal court decisions played a significant role for Indians. In 1974 a U.S. District Court ruled in *United States v. Washington* that outsiders, non-Indians, could take no more than half of the annual salmon run going through lands granted to Indians by treaties. The decision was nicknamed the "Boldt decision," for the judge, George Boldt; it really was so nicknamed because it hit the Northwestern fishing industry like a "bolt" of lightning. Indians entered the fishing industry in increasing numbers; within ten years they were harvesting 49% of the salmon run.

Numerous lawsuits filed by tribes succeeded in winning claims for seized land. The cases ranged all over the country, including the Wampanoag claims to Martha's Vineyard, Catawba claims in South Carolina, Chippewa in Wisconsin, and Sioux in South Dakota. Through court-ordered compensation for seized land, millions of dollars flowed into tribal treasuries.

By far the greatest financial impact came from the court case of *California v. Cabazon Band of Mission Indians*, 1987. California claimed that state law prohibited a small gambling operation run by Indians. On appeal, the U.S. Supreme Court ruled that while the state of California could *regulate* gambling on an Indian reservation, it could not *prohibit* gambling. Casinos mushroomed on reservations, leading Congress to pass the Indian Gaming Reservation Act in 1988, regulating reservation gambling. Gambling revenues pumped lots of money into reservation coffers, $110 million in 1988. However, despite the image, casinos have not proven to be the panacea envisioned for Indian reservations. Many states also opened up casinos, seeing them as a source for revenue. However, the gambling portion of the American population is limited. Too much competition for gambling dollars limited everyone's income from casinos.

Intellectual Awakening

Accompanying the modern Indian movement, and contributing to it in many ways, was an outburst of intellectual activity. Dee Brown's *Bury My Heart at Wounded Knee: An Indian History of the American West*, caught on with the public, selling over four million copies. Vine Deloria, Jr., a Standing Rock Sioux, wrote a scathing indictment of past relations between whites and Indians, *Custer Died For Your Sins*. Guess who was responsible for the Indians' problems? N. Scott Momaday won the Pulitzer Prize in 1968 for his novel, *House Made of Dawn*. What many consider the greatest contribution was by Vine Deloria, Jr., *We Talk, You Listen*. The title said it all. Deloria attacked stereotyping, especially that found in Hollywood films. Films reflected what people believed, but because Hollywood is primarily interested in making money, films perpetuated old myths and created new ones. For example, changes arrived in the 1950s with the "All-American" Second World War films. Every army platoon had one of each – a Mexican who spoke poor English, a Northern urban black, a Southern rural black, a prejudiced Southerner, a mid-Western farm boy, a New York City Jewish intellectual, an Appalachian hillbilly, an old-wealth college graduate from an elite university, an Italian linked to the Mafia, an Irishman who loved whiskey, and finally, a real live Indian. In the end they all get along, just like in real life. Harmless entertainment? Maybe. Maybe not.

Deloria pointed out that to correct stereotypes society sometimes goes too far by endorsing minute cultural pluralism, making certain to include each ethnic group in every event in American history. Deloria castigated the attempt to maintain the same "white" reference framework while plugging "a few feathers, woolly heads, and sombreros into the famous events of American history." As another example, the state of New York requires U.S. History teachers in New York public schools to teach that the Founding Fathers gained inspiration for the Articles of Confederation and the Constitution from the example they found in the structure of the Iroquois Confederation government, which was, and is, located in New York. No reputable scholar endorses that; no evidence of it has been found in any of the papers of any of the Founding Fathers. That is overcorrection, creating new myths. Everyone in American society may gain from learning the history and experiences for their group. But, keep it balanced with reality. As Deloria stated,

> "The problem of stereotyping is not so much a racial problem as it is a problem of limited knowledge and perspective. Even though minority

groups have suffered in the past by ridiculous characterizations of themselves by white society, they must not fall into the same trap by simply reversing the process that has stereotyped them . . . . This ultimately means the creation of a new history and not mere amendments to the historical interpretations of white America."

Looking at history is like looking at a mirror. One must be careful to see what is really there rather than what one wants to see.

Indian pride grew from several events in the past few decades. In 1990 South Dakota observed the first Native American Day on what the rest of America was celebrating as Columbus Day. Some other states and local governments followed. An Indian, Ben Nighthorse Campbell, from Colorado, was elected to the House of Representatives and then in 1992 to the U.S. Senate. In 2004 the National Museum of the American Indian opened on the National Mall in Washington, D.C., a great visit. Finally, in 2007 the United Nations issued the UN Declaration on the Rights of Indigenous Peoples. As many historians pointed out, this would not have been approved anywhere in the world one hundred years earlier. The Zeitgeist of 1900 differed, greatly. Maybe some progress is being made.

49

COLD WAR LESSONS LEARNED AND ILLUSTRATIONS PROVIDED BY VIETNAM

Containment

Containment, the policy of preventing the spread of communism, proved to have both strengths and weaknesses. It was designed for Europe, to be used against Russia. The diplomat who created the rationale for Containment, George F. Kennan, first explained Containment in the "long telegram" sent from Moscow to President Truman and also in his "Mr. X" article published in the journal *Foreign Policy*. Kennan signed his article explaining Containment in *Foreign Affairs* as Mr. X to camouflage the authorship. But, everyone knew the scholarly Kennan was the author. Containment proved to be inappropriate for Africa, Asia, or the Middle East. The new nations of Africa and Asia wanted independence and economic stability, not participation in the Cold War. Communism had no appeal in the Middle East. When the Russians built the Aswan Dam for Egypt, the United States worried that communists were gaining a foothold in Egypt and throughout the Middle East. In reality, according to Egyptian law, a person could be executed in Egypt in the 1950s for being a communist. Atheistic communism did not sit well with Islamic countries. Communism was an atheistic ideology, an anathema to Muslims. What Egypt did, as did many small nations during the Cold War, was play one superpower off against the other. After the United States refused to help Egypt build the Aswan Dam, Russia stepped in, hoping to increase its influence in the area.

Domino Theory

The Domino Theory was the concept that if one nation fell to communism, its neighbors would shortly also fall, like a row of dominos. Russia held similar fears, believing that democracy was contagious, as shown by her actions overthrowing the Czechoslovakian government in 1948, subduing the 1956 Hungarian revolution, and when Russian tanks ended the "Prague spring" in 1968, when Czechoslovakia attempted to follow a different path for communism, one with more freedoms. Note that contrary to the domino theory, the countries around Vietnam did not go communist after the Vietnam War ended – the Philippines, Indonesia, Malaysia, Burma (Myanmar), and Thailand did not fall.

Third World Countries

Vietnam showed America's limited ability to understand Third World countries. The term Third World came from the early Cold War journalistic division of the globe into the First World, the United States and its allies; the Second World, Russia and its allies; and the rest, the underdeveloped nations and the European colonies. Only Third World stuck. The preferred term now is LDCs, less developed countries, or, you may see South versus North, Southern Hemisphere versus the richer Northern Hemisphere. Some scholars are now using Fourth World, to differentiate between the poor countries and the very poor countries. Many poor countries have economies that feature extractive products or one-crop economies, putting them at risk for swings in the global economy.

Americans did not understand Third World nationalism or anti-colonialism. Were anti-imperialist uprisings, "wars of national liberation" fought as guerrilla wars, anti-colonial or communist-inspired? Could someone be both a nationalist and a communist? North Vietnam's Ho Chi Minh was. Americans too often saw any military activity in any Third World country or European colony as communist-inspired. Perhaps our failure to see Fidel Castro as a possible communist prior to his taking over Cuba cast a pall over all subsequent evaluations of similar Third World rebellions.

In the Caribbean, the United States frequently intervened, such as in Guatemala in 1954, replacing a leftist government. In El Salvador the U.S. supported a right wing government, seeking order and stability at any cost to our ideals, and later, again in Nicaragua and Chile. In Panama, where the 1979 Canal Zone treaties promised to return control of that area to the Panamanian government in 2000, the U.S. later intervened to remove a president who was involved in the drug trade. The U.S. government supported and paid for "drug wars" in Colombia, seeing our drug problem as a supply problem more than a demand problem. Colombian peasants could make three to four times their annual income from coca leaves, the source of cocaine, rather than harvesting coffee beans. Is our drug problem a supply problem or a demand problem? It makes a difference which our government decides; it determines which policy approach is used.

The United States has a long history of intervening in Latin America. During the 1920 presidential campaign Franklin Roosevelt was the Democratic vice-presidential candidate. When a reporter asked him about Haiti's constitution, adopted during an occupation by American troops while FDR was serving as the Assistant Secretary of the Navy during the Wilson administration, he blurted out that it was a great constitution,

"I wrote it." (This has been disputed in David Pietrusza's *1920: The Year of Six Presidents*.) True or not, that approach continued, as shown by the Dominican Republic in 1965 and Grenada in 1983. Once a newly elected president of Bolivia was being interviewed by an American reporter, live on television. The reporter congratulated the winner on his victory, the choice of the people of Bolivia. He responded laughingly with a comment that the American CIA had made him president, not the voters. Many Americans believe that our current Western Hemisphere trade policies, such as NAFTA, the North American Free Trade Agreement, benefit Canada and Mexico more. American tourists casually discussing NAFTA with Mexicans get a different answer. And, all Latin Americans assert that trade with the United States has always been lopsided, to America's benefit.

Our Military Strength
During the Cold War era our military strength was primarily nuclear power, air power, and naval power. None of these could be used effectively in Vietnam. By 1967 the chairman of the Joint Chiefs of Staff stated that our planes had "struck all [the] worthwhile targets except the ports" of North Vietnam. The total tonnage of bombs dropped during the war in Vietnam was two and one-half times the tonnage dropped in the entire Second World War, including the two atomic bombs. The United States is the world's strongest nation, but it is not the strongest nation everywhere in the world all the time. Moreover, unless the United States can, or will, use its greatest strength, it loses an advantage. Mao Zedong called us a "paper tiger" for our nonuse of the atomic bomb. Our superior technology was not always capable of being used. In his campaigns for the White House Ronald Reagan exemplified a "technology is king" approach. He said, in 1976, while campaigning for the Republican nomination against President Gerald Ford, that under Secretary of State Henry Kissinger and Ford this country had become number two in a world where it is dangerous, if not fatal, to be second best. And, four years later, when he was the Republican nominee, "Let us not be satisfied with a foreign policy whose principle accomplishment seems to be our acquisition of the right to sell Pepsi-Cola in Siberia." He wanted strength, and more strength. At one point in the Cold War, the United States had enough atomic bombs to blow up the entire world nine times. Russia had enough for only five times. Therefore, the United States would win, 9-5. Or, would it? Would anybody?

Bipartisan Consensus Ends
Foreign policy grows out of domestic needs and policies. From 1945 into the 1960s the United States had a bipartisan foreign policy that focused on communism. No matter which political party controlled Congress or the presidency, our foreign policy remained the same. The war in Vietnam ended bipartisanship. Now everyone and anyone could criticize any aspect of our foreign policy, and they did, for political domestic and campaigning purposes. By the 1970s disagreement developed among policy makers in Congress, in the executive branch, and across the country. A former consensus about

how to combat communism broke down. Two new schools of thought developed. The *conservative internationalists* were strongly anti-communist and favored building up the military to "negotiate from strength" by making the other side fearful. This sounded good to many Americans. The money appropriated by Congress was primarily spent inside the United States. Conservative internationalists differentiated between "authoritarian" and "totalitarian" foreign governments. Non-democratic "authoritarian" governments were acceptable; communist "totalitarian" governments were not.

The *liberal internationalists* supported more non-military foreign aid to spread democracy and to improve the quality of health and human rights around the world, as favored by President Jimmy Carter. The money appropriated by Congress was primarily spent outside the United States. Liberal internationalists argued that foreign policy should address local problems with the need for flexibility on our part and with peace and economic development as unifying themes. For example, increased trade ties nations together economically. In 1971 our trade with the Soviet Union was $220 million. Two Republicans, Nixon and Ford, and one Democrat, Carter, expanded our trade with Russia, which climbed to $2.8 billion in 1978.

By the 1970s both the Republican and the Democratic parties divided into two wings in regard to foreign policy. Each party had conservative internationalists and liberal internationalists. Bipartisan foreign policy ended. Now American foreign policy depended upon which wing captured that party's nomination, and which party won the election. In short, American foreign policy became inconsistent, frustrating many Americans and our allies around the world.

Newness to Power

Our relative newness to power on the world scene that began during the Second World War perplexed our allies and many Americans. Some policies and decisions were clearly shortsighted. As previously noted, during the Second World War President Franklin Roosevelt offered the French colony of Vietnam to China. He was apparently unaware that China had controlled Vietnam from 111 BC to 938 AD, a thousand years of constantly putting down revolts and rebellions. The ruler of China, Chiang Kai-shek quickly declined the offer. (In pinyin, which is the modern translation of Chinese into English to more closely reflect Chinese pronunciation, his name is Jiang Jieshi.) He said to his aides that the offer was like giving someone a gift of a hornets' nest. In the 1980s the U.S. poured weapons into Iraq to aid that nation's fight against Iran. Later Americans fought two wars against Iraq, which used previously supplied American weapons against us. The U.S. also supplied weapons to the Afghans fighting against Russian occupation. Although we were successful in driving the Russians out of Afghanistan, that unstable country was left armed to the teeth, to our subsequent consternation.

Americans did not fully understand the complications behind European diplomacy, especially the policies of our allies and disagreements between our allies, such as

France's ties to her former colonies; France's fears of a revived Germany; France's veto of Great Britain's entry into the Common Market; or, the dispute between Greece and Turkey over Cyprus. To us the primary threat in the world was communism. Our allies often did not see every local dispute as part of the international communist conspiracy.

Hanging over American decision-makers was the "lesson" of Munich, when France and Great Britain failed to stand up against Adolf Hitler in 1938, selling out Czechoslovakia and therefore missing an opportunity to prevent the Second World War. Or, so the "lesson" suggested. Vietnam changed that outlook. Norman Podhoretz explained the impact in *Why We Were in Vietnam*. "The legacy of Munich had been a disposition, even a great readiness, to resist, by force if necessary, the expansion of totalitarianism; the legacy of Vietnam would obversely be a reluctance, even a refusal, to resist, especially if resistance required the use of force." From being too ready to intervene before Vietnam, policymakers slid to being too ready to not intervene after Vietnam, a conflict of "lessons." It took the Persian Gulf War in 1991 to shake off that reluctance. However, it is still there to a degree.

Communism – A Monolithic Force

Americans viewed Communism as a monolithic force run from Moscow. Every communist in the world was a puppet dancing on a string rigidly controlled from Moscow. And every communist nation followed Russia's directions. However, our alliances were not monolithic. Neither were Russia's. When Mao's army won the Chinese Civil War in 1949, establishing a communist government in China, the U.S. believed that Moscow had greatly increased its power. However, China was, and is, simply too big to be anyone's junior partner. The communist partnership, never much of one, fell apart in the 1960s. But American policymakers remained uncertain over who was in control of world communism.

When presidents said the United States had to meet the communist challenge in Vietnam, was it Russian, Chinese, or Vietnamese communism? The U.S. government saw it as Russian and/or Chinese. In reality, it turned out that the U.S. faced Vietnamese nationalism more than world communism. If the U.S. had lost the same percentage of soldiers killed as did the Viet Cong and North Vietnam, the U.S. would have lost ten million soldiers in the Vietnam War. North Vietnam and their Viet Cong allies were committed to victory, no matter what the cost.

The United States refused to officially recognize the communist government as legitimate when Mao's forces won the Chinese Civil War in 1949. The U.S. forgot the two criteria for recognizing a new government originally laid down by our first Secretary of State, Thomas Jefferson. His criteria – is the new government actually in control and do they have the support of their people? Finally, President Richard Nixon and his Secretary of State, Henry Kissinger, saw that opening up a relationship with China and U.S. recognition of China would give both communist giants an incentive to maintain better relations with the United States. The two-sided contest between the two superpowers, the United States and the USSR, became a three-sided contest. Picture two players at a chess match with a new third player complicating the game by also adding pieces and making moves.

Credibility Thesis

A fundamental part of our Cold War policies was the Credibility Thesis, the premise that the United States had to live up to our agreements anywhere in the world in order to prove that the U.S. would live up to them elsewhere. If the United States did not defend Vietnam, would Western Europeans and Russians not question our fortitude to stand up to a communist challenge over Berlin? The United States harbored a nagging concern that it would not be believed by countries the U.S. was obligated by treaties to defend. By the early 1970s Europeans were asking, "Would the United States risk a nuclear attack on New York City to defend Berlin?" Four presidents – Truman, Ike, JFK, and LBJ – had all promised to defend Vietnam. Therefore, presidents felt that the U.S. had to live up to our obligation to prove that the U.S. would live up to all our other obligations. However, the Vietnam of 1945 was not the Vietnam of 1954, or of 1960, or of 1965, or of 1969, or of 1975. Situations change. Changed situations call for reevaluation. But, here was what President Nixon said on the topic of the potential ramifications if the United States failed in Vietnam. "We would destroy ourselves if we pulled out in a way that wasn't really honorable." He also added that we did not want to appear to be "a pitiful, helpless giant." His Secretary of State, Henry Kissinger, said, "What is involved now is confidence in American promises." One must wonder what Native-Americans would say about the U.S. government's promises? The United States leads the world in broken treaties, mainly because the U.S. broke over 2,500 treaties with Indians. The nineteenth century German statesman Otto von Bismarck called a treaty "a mere scrap of paper." You never know what will happen until a situation actually happens. Promises are promises. Reality is sometimes something else.

Our Self-Image

America sees itself as a benevolent power, one that does a great deal of good in the world. President Franklin Roosevelt's Four Freedoms Speech before the Second World War said it best. What the United States wants for the whole world, not just for ourselves, is four essential human freedoms:

> "The first is freedom of speech and expression – everywhere in the world.
> The second is freedom of every person to worship God in his own way – everywhere in the world.

The third is freedom from want – which, translated into world terms, means economic understandings which secure to every nation a healthy peace time life for its inhabitants – everywhere in the world.

The fourth is freedom from fear – which, translated into world terms, means a worldwide reduction of armaments to such a point and in such a thorough fashion that no nation will be in a position to commit an act of physical aggression against any neighbor – anywhere in the world."

In addition, the United States gave the world the Declaration of Independence, the Peace Corps, the Marshall Plan, the Atlantic Charter, the Fourteen Points, and a home for the United Nations. During the Vietnam War American policymakers talked about building TVA-type dams on the Mekong River to provide electricity. American soldiers also built thousands of school buildings in Vietnam. However, as the seven-foot basketball superstar Wilt Chamberlain said once, "Nobody loves Goliath."

One casualty from the Vietnam War was our self-image. Vietnam was the best filmed, photographed, and reported war in our history. Americans watched fifteen to twenty minutes of the war every evening on the national news. Two pictures were especially memorable: a little girl running naked down a village road, her burning clothes stripped off, the victim of an American napalm attack on her village; and the Saigon chief of police executing a Viet Cong prisoner by shooting him, the picture showing the bullet exiting his head. The girl, who was unharmed, is now a citizen of Canada. In defense of the police chief, the Viet Cong forces had just overrun the area where his home was located, killing his entire family.

One shocking legacy was the shameful massacre of hundreds of children, women, and old men at the small Vietnamese village of My Lai. The officer responsible, Lt. William Calley, was defended by the governor of his home state, Georgia, Democrat Jimmy Carter, and by the president of the United States, Republican Richard Nixon. He served three and one-half years of base arrest, meaning he was confined to his military base. After he left the military, Calley became a salesman in his father-in-law's jewelry store. Events like My Lai and violent antiwar protests and attacks on protesters deeply disturbed Americans. Our image of ourselves was shaken, and questioned, and not just by Americans, but also by others around the world.

50

NATIONAL POLITICS: JFK TO JIMMY CARTER

Kennedy as President

The public remembers John F. Kennedy as a strong president; he is often awarded a high ranking in public opinion polls. However, his main contribution as a president came more in his memorable quotes. While he expressed a strong idealism that resonated with the young, he lacked a relationship with Congress that transformed ideas into legislation. Early in his presidency, he did have one major achievement. American steel companies raised their prices after negotiating a new labor agreement, contrary to what steel company executives had personally promised the president. JFK forced them to roll back their prices; he feared inflation. Overall, Kennedy's liberalism was a style more than a substance. Congress passed only 7 of the 23 major pieces of legislation he sent to Capitol Hill.

JFK was a strong Cold War warrior, but he also declared that "there cannot be an American solution to every world problem." He inherited the plans for the Bay of Pigs invasion of Cuba. It turned out to be a fiasco, and like the earlier U-2 incident under Eisenhower, made the United States look amateurish in foreign policy. Two accomplishments were the creation of the Peace Corps and the Nuclear Test Ban Treaty. Not starting the a third World War during the Cuban Missile crisis in the fall of 1962 was his greatest accomplishment. That confrontation was the closest the United States and the Soviet Union came during the Cold War to an all-out missile exchange.

During the late 1950s and the early 1960s numerous intellectuals laid the foundation for liberal thinking in their criticism of the status quo. Among them were the following:

John Kenneth Galbraith, *The Affluent Society*, 1958
Jane Jacobs, *The Death and Life of Great American Cities*, 1961

Rachel Carson, *Silent Spring*, 1962
Michael Harrington, *The Other America*, 1962
Betty Friedan, *The Feminine Mystique*, 1963
James Baldwin, *The Fire Next Time*, 1963
Ralph Nader, *Unsafe at Any Speed*, 1965

The decade of the 1960s also saw a membership increase in liberal activist organizations. For example, the American Civil Liberties Union, the ACLU, jumped from 52,000 members in 1960 to 100,000 in 1970, with more than 40 state affiliates. The environmental-oriented Sierra Club grew from 16,000 members in 1960 to over 100,000 in 1970.

LBJ, Lyndon Baines Johnson

LBJ, JFK's successor following the latter's assassination, was a legislative genius. As Majority Leader of the Senate in the 1950s he gave other senators the "Johnson treatment," named for his style of getting into his opponent's face to such an extent that they bent over backwards to get away. His leadership style was "consensus management," always winning because he always counted his votes before a formal roll call. He forged a durable political Senate majority that shared his vision of American society. He remains famous in Texas political lore because he always remembered the most recent vote totals for every county in Texas, all 254 of them. Those poor counties that voted against him received no political favors. Do not even bother to ask. He carried grudges and he got even.

Vice President under JFK, following Kennedy's assassination Johnson seized the reins and won on his own in 1964 against Barry Goldwater, the conservative senator from Arizona, who had written a conservative bible, *The Conscience of a Conservative*. Goldwater won only six states in 1964, Arizona and five deep South states.

LBJ's Great Society

Richard Goodwin, an advisor and speechwriter for both John F. Kennedy and Lyndon Johnson, is credited with coining the phrase, "Great Society." In his 1988 book, *Remembering America: A Voice From the Sixties*, Goodwin caught the Zeitgeist of the 1960s – everyone thought "their world was malleable to their grasp." The United States could make the world over. In many respects, LBJ saw his program as a continuation of the New Deal. However, there was no economic crisis, as there had been in the 1930s. Johnson was fortunate to have overwhelming Democratic majorities in both the Senate and the House.

Lyndon Johnson's Great Society seemed to have something for everyone. Black activism led to three civil rights laws – the Civil Rights Act of 1965, the Voting Rights Act of 1966, and the Fair Housing Act of 1968. (More on these in Chapter 45.) In addition, Robert C. Weaver became the first black person appointed to a cabinet position, head of the new Department of Housing and Urban Affairs.

The heart of Johnson's Great Society was his War on Poverty. Numerous federal agencies attempted to pull the poor out of their plight, ending what was termed "cycles of poverty." One controversial effort, Community Action Programs, sought to teach the poor how to organize, incorporate, and work together to improve their community by applying for foundation grants, pressuring government agencies, or suing landlords. They were often aided and advised in these efforts by VISTA volunteers, a domestic Peace Corps type program, somewhat similar to today's AmeriCorps. The Job Corps trained unskilled urbanites, especially high school dropouts, fitting them for blue collar jobs. Even children were included in the War on Poverty. Head Start tried to equalize the advantage middle class suburban kids enjoyed by sending impoverished kids to school early, before kindergarten. Public television joined in, creating Sesame Street. Look closely at the setting for Sesame Street; it is a poor urban neighborhood. Notice the trashcans in front of the houses.

The old folks also profited, gaining Medicare, federally financed health coverage for those over 65. Social Security was lifted out of the arena of periodic political infighting in Congress when Social Security and COLA were linked in 1972. COLA stands for Cost of Living Adjustments, automatic annual increases for Social Security recipients.

All major accomplishments, a politicians' dream – something for everyone. Almost. One group of voters, the white working class, felt that they did not benefit from this burst of Great Society legislation. They were increasing drawn toward a conservative political viewpoint of society's problems and promises, emerging as an electoral bedrock for conservative candidates. Urban riots, opposition to the Vietnam War, and rising prices led to voter dissatisfaction by 1966. Eight new Republican governors were elected, including Ronald Reagan in California, 47 new Republicans in the House of Representatives, and 3 new Republican senators. LBJ choose not run for reelection in 1968.

The 1970s

The politics of the 1970s really began with the election of 1968, in many ways the culmination of the decade of the 1960s. The assassinations of Martin Luther King and Senator Robert Kennedy, brother of JFK, removed two "spiritual" leaders from the political scene. The leadership of the civil rights movement shifted toward mediocrity. The man who now stood at the center of that movement was Ralph Abernathy, who lacked Martin Luther King's charisma. Radicalism, "black power," and the Black Panthers all contributed to the loss of a sense of direction within the civil rights movement.

The most descriptive statistic from the 1970s appeared in February, 1979. In a poll of the public 84% of Americans said they were dissatisfied with the state of the nation and were expecting worse times ahead. Yet, 75% said they were satisfied with their personal lives. How can one be comfortable on a sinking ship?

The decade of the 1970s was a clear turning point in our self-image and in our history. In the previous thirty years, 1940-1970, Americans held a sense of confidence and power. Americans believed we could do anything – serve as guardians of freedom, send a man to the moon, conquer the problems hindering social justice, eliminate poverty, and develop impressive technology, in short – control the universe, nothing seemed impossible.

In the 1970s it all changed. Americans became disillusioned about politics and the ability of government and society to bring about positive change. The prevailing mood transformed people into an increased concern with taking care of "me," hence the nickname for the decade, "the Me Generation." The average person now concentrated more on himself and his family instead of trying to make the world better. As a nation many Americans now had a sense of our limitations. The United States lost our first war, as the Vietnam War was seen, the Middle East became muddled, President Nixon resigned in disgrace, OPEC revealed our vulnerability to foreign oil, and Iranian revolutionaries openly defied and embarrassed us by taking our embassy staff as hostages.

The Watergate scandal led Americans to seriously question the ethics of our major political figures, including the president. Many lost respect for the entire political process. An increasingly declining voter turnout was accompanied by an attitude of "throw the rascals out." Between 1974 and 1992, the number of new members elected to the House of Representatives was the highest rate since the 1940s.

Richard Nixon

Richard Nixon had a stormy past relationship with the media. He strongly supported Republican Senator Joseph McCarthy's accusations that communists had infiltrated our federal bureaucracy, particularly the State Department. Alger Hiss, a high-ranking State Department official, was accused of passing secrets to Russia. A member of the House Un-American Activities Committee, HUAC, Nixon effectively gained media attention for his pursuit of Hiss. It paid off when Eisenhower put him on the ticket in 1952. As Eisenhower's vice-presidential candidate in 1952, Nixon defended receiving illegal campaign contributions in his televised "Checkers" speech, stubbornly declaring that he was not returning the dog; his young daughters loved it too much. Defeated as the 1960 Republican candidate for president, he lost the 1962 election for governor of California and blasted the media. "You won't have Nixon to kick around anymore." His political career seemed over, permanently, but between 1962 and 1968 he slowly rebuilt his following within the Republican Party, winning the nomination and the presidency in 1968.

Many Republicans and conservatives believed the media was vehemently anti-Nixon. It was. The liberal Democratic candidate for the Democrats in 1972, Senator George McGovern, told his staff during the campaign that "the Eastern Establishment media finally has a candidate who almost totally shares their views, the real ideological bent of the *New York Times*, the *Washington Post*, *Time*, *Newsweek*, and the three networks is on the side of amnesty for draft-dodging, pot, abortion, confiscation of wealth, unless it is theirs, massive increases in welfare, unilateral disarmament, reduction in our defenses and surrender in Vietnam." "At last," he concluded, "the country will find out whether what the media has been standing for during these last five years really represents the majority thinking." He lost! Nixon won reelection in 1972 by 60.7% to 38%. He lost only Massachusetts, winning 49 of the 50 states. However, after his second victory, the Watergate scandal eroded his presidency.

Domestic Policies

Things went very well in Nixon's first administration. His 1969 tax cut gave the average family a 20% reduction, the Gross Domestic Product grew annually at 6.3%, and stocks passed the 1,000 Dow Jones mark for the first time. Among the features of his first administration:

1. The "Southern Strategy," also called the "Southern Metropolitan Strategy." It catered to the needs and interests of the South, to build up the Republican Party in the South, which had been a Democratic stronghold ever since Reconstruction. It subtly made a racist appeal to white voters.
2. Soft pedaling civil rights and desegregation, a policy called "benign neglect."
3. Appointing conservative judges to the Supreme Court and other federal courts.
4. Checking inflation, which for a short time led to wage and price controls.

Nixon's major difficulty was his relationship with Congress. Congress felt that recent presidents, LBJ the best example, had assumed too much of Congress's powers and prerogatives. In the fighting between Nixon and Congress, Nixon vetoed 15 bills. His successor, Ford, in just two years, would veto 49. Congress constantly overrode many vetoes, which included giving the vote to 18-year-olds, anti-pollution legislation, and funds for hospital and university construction projects. The strongest rebuke from Congress was the 1973 War Powers Act. It restricted a president's military options by setting a 60-day limit on the presidential power to commit troops to hostilities abroad or into situations where hostilities were imminent. After that the president had to obtain specific Congressional approval. We are not going to have another Vietnam quagmire, at least not one caused by a president. Congress declares wars, now even "unofficial" wars.

Congress also sued President Nixon in federal court and won. Nixon refused to spend some money Congress appropriated. The Supreme Court ruled that the president had to spend appropriations as Congress directed. Congress made certain that a future president would not try impounding funds again. The Congressional Budget and Impoundment Act of 1974 requires a president to spend the money Congress appropriates. Nixon's struggles against Congress earned his administration the nickname "the Imperial Presidency" for his wide use of the doctrine of executive privilege and his attempt at selective enforcement of federal laws.

His administration deserves credit for passing OSHA, which created the Occupational, Safety, and Health Administration; the EPA, the Environmental Protection Act; and for linking Social Security increases to the cost-of-living index. Nixon tried to shift much of the responsibility for social welfare to state governments and individuals by overhauling the welfare system and strengthening state and local government treasuries through revenue sharing, from the huge budget surplus expected with the end of the Vietnam War, the so-called "peace dividend." Congress refused, because it wanted to retain a role for the federal government in the area of social reform, and, also, the "peace dividend" surplus never materialized. Nixon proposed an innovative idea, the FAP, the Family Assistance Plan, a $1600 guaranteed annual income for every family, which included abolishing most welfare plans. His primary motive was to put most welfare workers, likely Democrats, out of work. The FAP required no social welfare agencies; it was supposed to work through the IRS and filing your income tax return.

Watergate – Nixon's Undoing

JFK and LBJ both recorded some phone calls in the Oval Office; JFK taped 325 White House conversations. Why? Phone calls, then, presented a problem. What was said? What was promised? What was said to whom? And, by whom?

Nixon installed a voice-activated taping system for two reasons. First, he was posterity conscious; his wanted to leave an accurate account of what actually happened in the Oval Office to prevent future liberal historians from misrepresenting his administration. Second, he suffered from paranoia over news leaks. In Nixon's first five months in office, there were 21 leaks of classified National Security Council documents to *The New York Times* and *The Washington Post*. On June 13, 1971, these two newspapers published the "Pentagon Papers," a 7,000-page survey of U.S. involvement in Vietnam, prepared as an in-house Pentagon document by the military for the military. Daniel Ellsberg, an employee of a think tank, the Rand Corporation, leaked it, a major security breach. The "Pentagon Papers" criticized U.S. policy and actions in Vietnam, obviously something the administration did not want the public to read.

National Security Advisor Henry Kissinger urged action to prevent us from looking weak diplomatically. Our lack of control over secrets was more than just embarrassing. At that time, the U.S. was secretly and separately negotiating with China, North Vietnam, and Russia.

This concern led CREEP, the Committee to Re-Elect the President for the 1972 campaign, to create the "Plumbers" to look for leaks. The nickname came from the grandmother of one of the group. Upon hearing that her grandson was running a unit to stop leaks, she said, "David (Young) is returning to the family trade." Grandpa had been a plumber. They began by breaking into the office of Daniel Ellsberg's psychiatrist to get information to use against him. Do not worry, psychiatrists do not keep written records that describe or incriminate.

The "Plumbers" next target was the Democratic National Party headquarters at the Watergate building in Washington, near the Mall, in late May, 1972, and on June 17, when five men, including several Cubans, were caught. The Cubans had been told that the national Democratic Party planned to recognize Castro's government, and thus it was easy to find willing participants in the Cuban refugee community with links to the CIA. No one has ever produced a plausible political justification for the break-in. Any national political party headquarters exists to disseminate information, not to hide secret information. Its job is publicity, publicity, publicity, not secrecy.

The White House quickly denied involvement. Initially, the burglary was considered an insignificant news event. *The Washington Post* assigned two young reporters – Bob Woodward and Carl Bernstein – to cover it. Woodward had just joined the newspaper; Bernstein was responsible for covering only local police and court issues. The next year, 1973, they won the Pulitzer Prize for Public Service for their investigation of Watergate. In July, John Mitchell, the former Attorney General, resigned as the head of CREEP. In August *The Washington Post* traced a money trail from CREEP to the Watergate burglars. During the summer and fall of 1972, while the election was going on between Nixon and McGovern, *The Washington Post*, very anti-Nixon, had 79 front-page articles about Watergate prior to election day. However, it was not an issue during the election. There was no strong link to the White House.

In January, 1973, the Watergate burglars went on trial. In March, during the sentencing after they were found guilty, Judge John Sirica gave them a tongue-lashing and threatened long jail terms unless the five original defendants provided evidence against other members of the administration. One, G. Gordon Liddy, who refused, was sentenced to 20 years in jail. Another, James McCord, handed the judge a note saying that perjury, lying under oath, had been committed during the trial. That led others to look for connections.

In February, Congress held a hearing to confirm a new head for the FBI. L. Patrick Gray, who had been serving as the acting head, was grilled about his actions concerning Watergate. He admitted that at the request of the White House the FBI did not pursue a rigorous investigation, and that documents had been destroyed. He did not become the new FBI head.

In April, Nixon announced the resignations of his top White House aides, H. R. Haldeman and John Ehrlichman, Attorney General Richard Kleindienst, and the dismissal of his personal attorney, John Dean. The implication seemed to be that Dean was responsible. In May a Senate Committee on Presidential Campaign Activities began to conduct hearings, which continued until November. In four days of testimony, June 25-29, Dean said Nixon was to blame, that Nixon may have known about the burglary before it happened, and that Nixon was involved in the cover-up. However, there was no way to prove anything. It was Dean's word against the president's. Then, during a committee session on July 16, 1973, a minor presidential aide, Alexander Butterfield, accidently revealed the existence of the Oval Office taping system. Nixon originally had LBJ's taping system taken out, but restored it to prevent liberal historians from misrepresenting his Vietnam policy.

Now the fight was on. The Senate Committee wanted the tapes. Nixon claimed "executive privilege" and national security issues. Congress did not buy the argument. They took it to the Supreme Court.

Meanwhile, Vice President Spiro Agnew was accused of taking kickbacks from contractors, which began while he was governor of Maryland. He faced 40 counts for taking bribes, criminal conspiracy, and tax fraud. Contractors testified that they delivered briefcases containing $50,000 personally to Agnew at the White House. Agnew resigned October 9, 1973, as part of a deal. The charges were to be dropped if he resigned, which he did. The fear was that Nixon would be impeached while the vice president's trial for corruption and bribery was still going on, making Agnew the new president.

On October 12 a federal appeals court ordered the tapes turned over to a Special Prosecutor in the Attorney General's Office. The Special Prosecutor position had been created at the insistence of the Senate Watergate Committee. After all, it is difficult to investigate yourself, for the Nixon administration to investigate the Nixon administration. On October 21 came the "Saturday Night Massacre," when Nixon ordered his Attorney General to fire the Special Prosecutor, to make Watergate go away. Why Saturday night? Nixon believed that by Monday morning it would be lost in the unreported weekend news. Instead, the Attorney General refused, and resigned in protest, as did the Assistant Attorney General. Finally, the next highest official fired the Special Prosecutor. That official was Robert Bork, who was later rejected by the Senate as a Supreme Court appointee. On Monday morning the newspapers exploded.

Under the Twenty-fifth Amendment, passed in the wake of JFK's assassination, the president appoints a new vice president when that office is vacant, with the approval of both houses of Congress. Nixon wanted John Connally of Texas to be the new vice president; the Democratic Senate refused, hence Gerald Ford, the Republican Minority Leader of the House, became vice president.

In March of 1974, a grand jury indicted seven top White House aides and named Nixon an unindicted co-conspirator. Finally, in April 1974, a new special prosecutor subpoenaed the tapes. Nixon responded by supplying edited transcripts, with expletives deleted. The public was sickened by the foul language and by the clear indication that Nixon was hiding something. One of the tapes, from two days after the break-in, had a strange 18½ minute gap. It had been erased, repeatedly.

On July 27, the House Judiciary Committee passed the first article of impeachment against Nixon, charging him with obstruction of justice in attempting to cover up the Watergate break-in. Two days later they passed two more. In practice, the concept of impeachment as inherited from the British meant simply that one group of politicians replaced someone from another group, high crimes and misdemeanors notwithstanding. The president kept saying, "I am not a crook." It did not matter. Impeachment is a removal procedure, not a criminal trial. Nixon thought he could win in the Senate and remain in office. On the thirteen previous occasions in our history when the House impeached a public official, the Senate convicted only four. Senator Barry Goldwater, a previous Republican presidential candidate, led a delegation of senators to tell the president that he could count on the vote of less than fifteen senators. On August 8, President Nixon announced he would resign the next day. He sent his letter of resignation to the Secretary of State, the keeper of the official seal of the United States. He left Washington on August 9, 1974, an ignoble end to the political career of the man who holds the record for most appearances on the cover of *Time* magazine in the twentieth century. He is also the only person ever elected twice to both the vice-presidency and the presidency.

On August 20, the House accepted the final report of the impeachment inquiry by a vote of 412-3. In the next year four top aides of the Nixon administration were convicted and sentenced, along with four cabinet members. In 1976 the state of New York disbarred Nixon, prohibiting him from practicing law in New York, his residence prior to the election of 1968. The last Watergate associate got out of prison in 1979. Twenty-five men served terms ranging from 25 days to $52\frac{1}{2}$ months.

Ford

Appointed vice president after Nixon's Vice President, Spiro Agnew, resigned, Gerald Ford was well qualified to be president. A graduate of the University of Michigan and Yale Law School, he had been a long-time Republican Minority Leader of the House of Representatives. He was our first president who was not elected. Neither was his vice president, Nelson Rockefeller, a former four term governor of New York. (And, the grandson of John D. Rockefeller, of Standard Oil fame.) These two represented the moderate, Eastern-dominated wing of the Republican Party, from which Southern and Western conservatives rescued the party with Reagan's nomination in 1980.

Ford had some critics. LBJ said Ford was "so dumb he couldn't fart and chew gum at the same time." (A good nickname for LBJ is "Texas crude.") Also, "The trouble with Gerry is that he used to play football without a helmet." Ford starred as a lineman for the University of Michigan, and was voted most valuable by his teammates. Two professional football teams wanted to draft him; he wanted to go to law school. Unassertive, sometimes inarticulate, he suffered from inner ear troubles, which caused him to fall often due to lack of balance. Your sense of balance is primarily determined by part of your inner ear mechanism. Photographers seemed to always be around to take his picture when he stumbled or fell. His wife, Betty, had a drinking problem. You may recognize the name of the rehab clinic many Hollywood celebrities are admitted to, the Betty Ford Clinic.

Ford immediately disarmed his critics in his first address to Congress and the nation. "The long nightmare is over." And, "I'm a Ford, not a Lincoln," suggesting that he realized he was in over his head, declaring that we all have to pull together to help. Then came his pardon of Nixon on September 8, "a full, free and absolute pardon" for any crimes Nixon may have committed during his presidency. There was a huge public outcry. Some politicians, such as Democratic Senator Joe Biden, a future vice president, courageously sided with the president. It was time to move on. Nixon's name on the listing of presidents will forever bear an asterisk. At the bottom of the page, it will say, *resigned. That is enough. For the rest of American history every elementary school class looking at the list of presidents will notice the asterisk. One student will ask what it means. The answer, "He did something bad and had to resign." Imagine the shocked little faces! That is sufficient punishment.

Ford's biggest problem was a recession in 1974 and 1975 that led to stagflation, rising unemployment and rising inflation. Theoretically, this was impossible according to Keynesian economic theory. It happened; and nobody had any answers.

1976 Election, Carter Wins

Jimmy Carter won in 1976 by capturing the Democratic primaries, a characteristic of the Sixth Party System. The party bosses now played a less significant role, no longer selecting their party's candidate at their convention in a "smoke-filled room." A former governor of Georgia, Carter campaigned as an outsider running against Washington, D.C., and against Richard Nixon, declaring, "I will never lie to you." His message spoke to the degree of distrust resulting from Nixon's lying about the bombing of Cambodia and the Watergate break-in. The basic trust of the American people in the political system was now being called into question.

Carter defeated Ford, 287-240 in the Electoral College; note how close the vote was. In the popular vote, Carter won 60% of the Catholics, and blacks voted 15-1 for him. However, 51% of whites voted Republican, a portending of the rising conservative vote among whites.

After taking the oath of office, Carter walked from the Capitol to the White House. A loner, an intellectual, knowledgeable about nuclear engineering from his early naval career, and an avowed anti-Washington candidate, he found himself in Washington after winning. Washington reciprocated; he was intensely disliked by the D.C. establishment. He saw Congress as a collection of special interests and himself as a "trustee of the public good," above politics. His idol was Harry Truman. He claimed he was not a politician, just a combination of a retired naval officer, a peanut farmer, an engineer, and a "born-again" Christian who also happened to be a public servant. In truth, he had sought or held public office since 1962. His criticism of Congress and his inability or unwillingness to get along with Congress led to what critics called "permanent deadlock." He sent over 200 proposals to Congress; 60% of them passed – a very good record, but he was seen as ineffective.

Accomplishments

In his first act as president, Carter pardoned draft evaders from the Vietnam War, which was not seen as a positive accomplishment by many Americans. Pardons had happened after every previous American war, and sooner after the war than when the Vietnam pardons occurred. He created two new cabinet departments, the Department of Education and the Department of Energy. The Department of Health and Human Services remained after Education split off. He set aside 100 million acres for conservation in Alaska, approximately the size of California. During his administration farm exports set records. Probably Carter's greatest achievement was the Camp David Accords, a peace treaty between Israel and Egypt, signed on March 27, 1979. Deregulation of the economy began under Carter. Many people think this was a conservative Republican idea under Reagan, but it was instead an idea whose time had come, as many from both parties endorsed it. A Democratic senator, Ted Kennedy, brother of JFK, pushed for deregulation of the trucking industry, while other areas deregulated were the airlines, long distance moving, and banking, which led to the savings and loan debacle in the late 1980s. These were solid accomplishments, but the public's overall judgment of Carter's administration labeled it a failure, as shown in the following areas.

Carter's Failures

1. The economy: The prime rate, the interest rate the Federal Reserve charges banks to borrow money, rose from 6.8% in 1976 to more than 20% in 1980. Inflation totaled 35% in just three years. Inflation hits three areas of the economy the hardest – car loans, the construction industry, and those on fixed incomes. Much of the increase came from the actions of OPEC, an oil embargo that lasted six months, 1973-1974, and raised oil prices 387%. The embargo happened because the United States resupplied Israel immediately after the Egyptians dealt Israel a punishing blow in the Yom Kippur War in October, 1973, wiping out 1/5 of Israel's air force and 1/3 of Israel's tanks in just four days.

2. The "Misery Index": Politicians invented the "Misery Index," combining the inflation rate and the unemployment rate. That number soared in the late 1970s.

3. The Iranian hostage situation, 1979: During a revolution a mob overran the U.S. embassy, holding over 50 Americans hostage. Carter helped to make the hostage crisis part of America's daily life; he wore two wristwatches, one Washington, D.C., time and the other Tehran time. During the crisis, the national news television broadcasts introduced each nightly segment with a statement like, "Day 206, America held hostage." America was not held hostage; some Americans were. A failed rescue attempt exacerbated the crisis when a desert sandstorm immobilized American helicopters outside the capital, Tehran. The hostages were supposed to be delivered to the Americans by the Iranian military, but they got cold feet and backed down from their promise. Why did the Iranian military want the hostages out of Iran? Because the U.S. had supplied almost all their weapons, purchased from U.S. weapons manufacturers. When the U.S. cut off trade with Iran they could not get spare parts for their military equipment. Iran was fighting a war against Iraq. One jet plane had 106,000 parts. You cannot substitute duct tape for a needed part. All this made Carter look bad, but he could not defend the failed mission publicly for fear of getting the Iranian military leaders in trouble. They seemed to be the only potential hope to get the hostages returned. The hostages were released the day Reagan took the oath of office as president, January 20, 1981. Why that day? Carter was finished and the Iranian revolutionaries wanted to spoil Reagan's spotlight.

4. Energy: President Carter was never able to create a viable energy policy. This left us still vulnerable to another OPEC embargo, but much less so by 2016. Congress opposed many of Carter's ideas on energy. Which energy source for the future – nuclear, solar, wind, tidal? In the end, little was done.

5. Afghanistan: The "invasion" of Afghanistan in 1979 by Soviet military forces led Carter to request Congress to reinstitute the draft. Was this a local problem or an aggressive communist expansion? Actually, the Soviet Union was merely replacing one ineffective pro-communist government with another ineffective pro-communist government. It quickly became, as Russian journalists labeled it, "Russia's Vietnam," a nightmare for the Soviet Union. Congress refused to revive the draft, a defeat for Carter, in the public's eye. To punish the Russians, Carter boycotted the 1980 Olympics in Moscow, believing that when the Russian people asked why the Americans had not come they would condemn their own government's "invasion" of Afghanistan. It did not happen. Instead, Russia boycotted the 1984 Los Angeles Olympics. This caused the International Olympic Committee to declare that any country that boycotted two straight Olympics was permanently out.

1980 Election

Carter's advisors badly misjudged the temperament of the American people in 1980. They wanted Reagan to win the Republican presidential nomination. Carter would defeat Reagan by an even bigger margin than LBJ's victory over Goldwater in 1964. It did not happen. Reagan won easily. Remember the public opinion poll given earlier – 84% were dissatisfied with the state of the nation and expecting worse times ahead. That spells defeat for incumbents.

The Sixth Party System

Begun in 1968, by 1980 the characteristics of the Sixth Party System had clearly begun to take shape. Neither party dominated the presidency. Congress seemed to be winning the war against presidential prerogative and power. No president in the Sixth Party System had matched the leadership of Congress shown by FDR or LBJ. Ideology replaced political discussion and compromise. The electorate was divided, leading to stalemate in Congress and even within the parties. Both fundraising and the media played a larger role in political campaigns. These characteristics of the Sixth Party System solidified after the election of 1980. Together, the South and suburbanites became the chief components of a more conservative electorate, crucial voting blocks for the Republican Party. Republicans under Ronald Reagan enjoyed what everyone considered a clear mandate in the 1980s. The nation had turned toward conservatism.

51

THE RISE OF CONSERVATISM

Polls tell revealing statistics. In a February, 1979, poll of Americans 84% said they were dissatisfied with the state of the nation and were expecting worse times ahead. Yet 75% said they were satisfied with their personal lives. That is like having a comfortable deck chair on the *Titanic*. Obviously, there was widespread dissatisfaction with politicians and the government. This perception helps to explain the rise of conservatism. As an example of how much things changed – in 1970 the most requested vanity license plate in California was "Peace." In 1984 it was "Go For It."

The Conservative Outlook
Conservatives and the conservative outlook can be described in many different ways. Their **Weltanschauung** (German for "world plus perception"), their view of the world, can be described as a difference in **goals**.

> One group focuses mainly on economic concerns, specifically on op-position to government action, or inaction, that impedes the vital-ity of the business community.
>
> A second group centers their attention mainly on cultural concerns, on the constantly changing issues of race, immigration, reli-gion, gender, family, sexuality, and patriotism. In 1960 about 250,000 unmarried couples lived together; now millions do. It means that?
>
> A third group is primarily interested in asserting America's role in in-ternational affairs.

Another difference is the **methods** used to accomplish their objectives. Traditionalists stress the virtues of order, local custom, and natural law. Libertarians promote limited government, laissez-faire economics, and individual autonomy. The militant internationalists endorsed a strong national defense to fight communism and totalitarianism, and now, terrorism.

Generally, conservatives endorse a "negative liberty," one defined not as society acquiring liberty, justice, equality, and democracy for the masses, but a liberty that protects the individual against encroachments by the government. Human society is viewed as complex, and thus any governmental attempt to improve things for the masses is seen as ignoring the limitations of politics. Their political opponents, liberals and leftists, endorse a different point of view. The philosopher George Santayana explained liberals positively and conservatives negatively in 1920. "He belonged to the left, which, as they say in Spain, is the side of the heart, as the right is that of the liver." Think bile.

The Legacy of the New Deal

In many respects, by the 1960s New Deal programs existed without the rhetoric, the reasons, and the emotions that accompanied the creation and original rationale of those programs. After the Second World War many conservatives resumed their prewar negative response to the New Deal and its programs. What conservatives sought was what they considered the opposite of the New Deal.

Ideologically, conservatives demanded a restoration of the individual's lost personal liberty. The New Deal bred an increasingly unhealthy dependence on government programs. Conservatives argued that dependence on the government sapped individual initiative and enterprise. The overall result was a hodgepodge of welfare programs that kept the idle poor in their poverty. Meanwhile, business enterprises were hindered by high taxes, excessive red tape, and government bureaucracy. Conservatives demanded a minimal government in scope, power, and responsibility, curiously endorsing a quotation attributed to a president not viewed in his time as a conservative, Thomas Jefferson, "That government is best which governs least."

The presidency had become too powerful and too liberal. It needed to be curtailed. This is the rationale behind the Twenty-second Amendment, which limits the president to two terms. In addition, this attitude explains why two presidents during the Sixth Party System, a Republican and a Democrat, Richard Nixon and Bill Clinton, faced impeachment. As one cartoonist quipped, "The president was whipped and sent to his room." Congress clearly understood the impact of impeaching Nixon. As a conservative Southern Congressman said, "one of the effects of our action here will be to reduce the influence and power of the Office of the President." It was not just Nixon that Congress was after, it was the powers of the presidency.

During the New Deal, political power had shifted more to the national government. This had to be reversed. More power and responsibility should rest in the state and local governments. The best government, it was argued, is the one closest to the people who are affected by governmental decisions and policies. The national government had grown faster than the state and local governments. (That trend has reversed. Since 1990, the number of federal employees has declined by 402,000, while state and local governments added 2.1 million workers, not including those in education.) While president, Nixon advocated his "New Federalism" policy, under which states would have more leeway on how they spent their federal dollars, rather than following Congressional dictates. Congress, wishing to remain powerful, instead continued to dictate how state and local governments spent federal dollars for specific programs.

America needed a strong foreign policy, especially against the threat of communism. Conservatives saw an ominous similarity in the expansion of government in Russia and the expansion of the national government here. What is humorous about this is that FDR's most vocal critic in the early New Deal was the American Communist Party. Communists did not see a similarity. If one thinks of the government as an evil entity, something that exists with a life and purpose of its own, you can see how someone like Timothy McVeigh ultimately reached the conclusion that the federal government was evil, and therefore he was justified in blowing up a federal building in Oklahoma City in 1995, killing 168 people. He was not, according to him, attacking defenseless civilian workers and children in a day care center. He was attacking a thing, the government.

Concern had grown over the impact of the welfare state and egalitarian government programs. The WASP (white, Anglo-Saxon Protestant) elite were increasingly forced to share positions in the government with Catholics, Jews, labor leaders, African-Americans, and intellectuals. Before the New Deal, elite universities maintained unpublicized, unstated small quotas for Jews and minorities and reserved most spots for the children of alumni, the children of the elite. A meritocracy, in which positions are awarded based on merit, only makes sense to those outside the positions of power. While many conservatives endorsed competition as an abstract principle, there were areas of life in which competition should not exist. A conservative says, my children, of course, should be privileged. As one critic of the Bush family politicians said, wealthy people are "born on third base and think they hit a triple." It is not far to home plate if you start on third base. Too many kids do a poor job of selecting their parents.

The issue of immigration raised concerns. In 1965 Congress enacted the Hart-Cellar Act, also called the Immigration and Nationality Act. It ended the philosophy behind the immigration acts of the 1920s – that national quotas would keep out undesirable races and nationalities. Now two numbers set annual limits – 120,000 could enter from the Western Hemisphere and 170,000 from the rest of the world. The law had many unforeseen consequences. Neither limit counted for occupations needed for U.S. businesses. The rise of the computer industry in Silicon Valley drew many technologically savvy immigrants from abroad. A "family friendly" provision was designed to make it easier to bring family members of immigrants already here, reuniting families. One immigrant arrived, became a citizen, and shortly afterwards his "family" members followed – wife, children, brothers, sisters, grandparents, uncles, cousins, etc. The law created a new category of immigrants, "illegal aliens." Because the 120,000 limit for those from Mexico and Latin America proved to be far below the labor pool demanded by American farms and industries, millions of "illegals" flooded into the U.S. The percentage of immigrants in the U.S. population rose, rapidly. The nation must be protected from this immigrant invasion! There were too many Asians in top colleges and universities in California and too many Hispanics in the Southwest, according to conservatives. A statewide referendum in California, Proposition 187, limited state funds to public schools with illegal aliens enrolled. (It was declared unconstitutional.) Immigration and immigration restriction were constant political issues after the Second World War. However, there was one big surprise. Religion, specifically Catholicism, was not an issue this time, as it had been earlier. Throughout the country, at various times, there were political pushes in state legislatures to make English our official language. The United States does not have an official language. There may not be a need for one. Current immigrants are learning English faster than any previous group of immigrants in any prior period of American history.

Business leaders worried about the future of the free enterprise system. The antiestablishment turmoil of the 1960s made many business leaders sincerely fearful for the future of capitalism and free enterprise. Two major business organizations, the National Association of Manufacturers and the U.S. Chamber of Commerce, responded and vigorously recruited new members by decrying government regulations and attacking consumer interest groups, such as Nader's Raiders. The nation's top CEOs organized the Business Roundtable to coordinate efforts to stop what they considered the anti-business momentum in Washington, D.C. In short, as the 1970s began, businesses became more involved in the business of politics because they felt politics was too involved in the business of business. Pro-Conservative PAC's, Political Action Committees, multiplied. (Benjamin Waterhouse, *The Politics of Business from Nixon to NAFTA*)

Some historians have pointed out that the success of the New Deal programs lifted many Americans into the middle class. Now secure, they grew to dislike government programs they perceived as threats to their new status and economic security. Instead of remaining liberal Democrats, helping the downtrodden, they switched to becoming conservative Republicans. Nothing makes a person become conservative as much as the acquisition of status and property. Another major group of new conservatives were those just above the poor, what sociologists refer to as "poor but honest working class." They feared falling below their precarious status and were angry at governmental programs designed to help those just below them. In their minds the hard-working, honest people got nothing from the government; the lazy poor got welfare, lots of it.

Intellectual Trends

Several intellectual trends in the 1940s and 1950s aided the acceptance of conservative thought. The leading historians and social scientists of the post-war era, influenced by the overwhelming American industrial productive capacity that won the Second World War, developed an outlook called "Consensus." Consensus thinking saw in the American past, and presumably the present, an absence of conflict, suggesting that America had always been a conservative country that valued the sanctity of private property and sought change through practical liberalism rather than European radicalism or socialism. Americans are a conservative people.

A second trend was an accompanying re-conceptualization of American politics. The older historical conceptualization, known as Progressive Historiography, saw politics as primarily a conflict in which the "people" fought against the "interests." Think of the Meat Inspection Act or the Pure Food and Drug Act, passed in 1906, both of which can be seen as the "people," Congress, successfully curtailing the "interests," big business. However, if historians now viewed past politics as consensus, then current politics needed a new definition. What emerged among scholars was a view of politics as a spectrum that ran from the left through the center to the right. Historians and political scientists argued that the primary feature of American politics is our widespread agreement on fundamentals. In every era, our political disagreements are really best described as "surface agitation." The American people and politicians occupied *The Vital Center*, the title of a book by historian Arthur M. Schlesinger, Jr. Our politicians were unlike politicians in other countries, where a strong Right or Left espoused policies that were shortsighted, naïve, and un-American. America was different. And, by implication, better.

The impact of this thinking put all political debate within the American tradition, far removed from foreign ideologies. Conservative criticism was, therefore, within the American tradition, and not a precursor to establishing fascism in America. Discrediting ideas by linking them to their worst proponents is an old debating tactic. For example, claiming that everyone opposed to abortion favors killing doctors who perform abortions. A very small number of extreme anti-abortionists may, and have done so, but that does not mean everyone opposed to abortion agrees with such a radical act.

One unifying intellectual conservative criticism was a 1944 book, *The Road to Serfdom*, by Frederick Hayek, an Austrian-born economist and political philosopher who taught at the prestigious London School of Economics and Political Science. He argued that there was a philosophical affinity between any collectivist political movement, like socialism or New Deal liberalism, and the forces of totalitarianism. Any attempt to use central planning to control the economic freedom of individuals would inevitably lead to stronger measures of control, to serfdom. "Economic control is not merely control of a sector of human life which can be separated from the rest. It is control of the means of all our ends. And whoever has sole control of the means must also determine which ends are to be served, which values are to be rated higher and which lower – in short, what men should believe and strive for." In a similar vein the economist Milton Friedman argued in 1962 that, "The great advances of civilization, whether in architecture or painting, in science or literature, in industry or agriculture, have never come from centralized government."

J. Edgar Hoover, the director of the FBI, published *Masters of Deceit: The Story of Communism in America and How to Fight It*, in 1958. He emphasized the communist threat. "In a country with over 170,000,000 inhabitants there are fewer than 6,200 agents of the FBI. Hence all of the agents are not available for the investigation of subversive activities. We need the help of *all* loyal Americans." "We, as a people, have not been sufficiently articulate and forceful in expressing pride in our traditions and ideas. In our homes and our schools we need to learn how to 'let freedom ring.' Most Americans believe that our light of freedom is a shining light. As Americans we should stand up, speak of it, and let the world see this light, rather than conceal it."

The leading popular intellectual conservative in the 1950s and 1960s was Barry Goldwater, a senator from Arizona. His book, *The Conscience of a Conservative*, published in 1960, called for dismantling federal government regulations over the economy and closing the various social service agencies. The book was actually ghostwritten by L. Brent Bozell, the brother-in-law of William F. Buckley, the founder and editor of the conservative *National Review* magazine. Clarence Manion, an official of the National Council of the John Birch Society, aided in the publication. The book was distributed free to bookstores, which received 100% of the sale as profit. Therefore, they displayed it prominently on the counter and sales leaped. In 1964 Goldwater captured the Republican nomination and concluded his acceptance speech at the GOP convention with, "Let me remind you, that extremism in defense of liberty is no vice and that moderation in pursuit of justice is no virtue." True to his word, he campaigned against Social Security in Florida, where many retirees lived.

In the 1964 election Goldwater, nicknamed AuH20, took six states – Arizona, Mississippi, Alabama, Georgia, Louisiana, and South Carolina, but not Florida, as the old folks wanted their Social Security checks. In a preview of things to come for the Republican Party, Goldwater won only 4 of the nation's 61 largest metropolitan areas, which were sliding into a fixed position in the Democratic column. One impact of this election was the transformation of what had been discussions of intellectual ideas by small groups into a grassroots effort to spread their conservative gospel. Door-to-door contact and campaign leaflets replaced books and editorials.

Three popular novels also gave readers a sense of unease about where our society might be heading – Aldous Huxley's *Brave New World*, 1932; and George Orwell's *Animal Farm*, 1945, and *1984: A Novel*, 1949. Was this America's future?

In a curious way, media technological advances fed the growth of political polarization. For example, the arrival of Fox News and MSNBC gave viewers the opportunity to watch ONLY those talk shows, commentators, and newscasts that reinforced their thinking. The essence of understanding a topic, any topic, is to learn from all perspectives. You should always expose yourself to a point of view you know you will not agree with. Why? First, it will clarify and sharpen your thinking. Second, it will arm you for future debates or discussions. Third, you may realize your thinking is fuzzy and needs to change. In today's world, it is relatively easy to never expose yourself to an opposing point of view, which cements individuals more deeply into the perspective they already hold, creates group polarization, and ends discussions before they have an opportunity to begin. Americans not only do not talk to one another politically, Americans do not WANT to talk to one another. When your mind is made up, the last thing you want is to have it confused by facts. Compromise, the heart of our legislative politics, needs communication and listening and thoughtful discussion. Intellectual polarization, on the part of liberals and conservatives, makes that impossible.

Development of Suburbia

Another building block for conservatism was the development of suburbia. The "suburban warrior" became an important part of the emerging conservative constituency. After they had achieved prosperity and the good life, many suburbanites fought against threats to their new status and prosperity. Some historians and political scientists have argued that the New Deal coalition was *too* successful, as shown by unions raising wages and the FHA helping more people obtain mortgages. Many of FDR's supporters in the 1930s Democratic Party coalition – intellectuals, Southerners, blacks, members of labor unions, and ethnic groups in the cities (Poles, Italians, Jews, and Irish) – improved their financial status, moved to the suburbs, and became more conservative. These new suburbanites opposed efforts to aid inner cities, attacked proponents of higher taxes for new social programs, and generally wanted to defend the status quo. They opposed the UN, especially UNICEF, the United Nations International Children's Emergency Fund. It was considered an organization that propagandized schoolchildren around the world with internationalist ideas and principles of "one-worldism," goals that were aligned with communist ideology, and, therefore, goals that had to be wrong. If communists endorsed it, it had to be bad. Little kids going trick-or-treating for UNICEF on Halloween sometimes received a profane berating from that otherwise kind lady down the street. "Suburban warriors" opposed sex education in public schools, fought for pro-American textbooks, urged censorship for movies, and hunted high and low for communists and leftists in their communities.

What was different about this activity was the presence of suburban homemakers, "kitchen table activists," as the leaders and the doers, holding meetings, gathering petitions, attending school board meetings, etc. The 1950s revival of domesticity and the defense of the domestic ideal had a politically radicalizing effect on women. A poll in 1954 indicated that women tended to be less tolerant of communists, socialists, and atheists than men were. In the late 1940s and the 1950s the **American Identity** was restructured to emphasize that the United States was not a socialist country and socialism was un-American. One way to fight for the American way was by opening Christian bookstores, which specialized in conservative anticommunist and religious literature. The store's weekends and evenings were devoted to discussion circles led by volunteers. By 1965 there were twenty such bookstores in just the greater Los Angeles area. There had been none in 1945. This grassroots activity went unnoticed by national media institutions like television networks and large newspapers. (Lisa McGirr, *Suburban Warriors: The Origins of the Rise of the American Right*)

The Great Society – LBJ

LBJ's Great Society programs, an extension of the New Deal, were too expensive. Welfare programs such as AFDC, Aid to Families with Dependent Children, fostered a "cycle of dependency" with successive generations of the poor learning to live off welfare, permanently. In addition, by many measurements, society seemed to be declining, not improving. Rising rates for social ills such as teenage pregnancies, illegitimate births, street crime, and drug use paralleled the increased spending to solve them. Increasingly one heard comments about the misguided approach of "throwing" money at social ills. The division between liberals and conservatives essentially came down to disagreement over the causes. Were "root causes" such as bad schools, ghetto conditions, unemployment, and discrimination the main reasons for poverty and crime? Or, were permissive parents, wrist-slapping courts, and hampering of police to blame?

A Republican Party strategist, Kevin Phillips, charged in 1969 in *The Emerging Republican Majority* that in FDR's New Deal the Democrats taxed the few, the rich, to benefit the many. In the Great Society the Democrats taxed the many to benefit the few, the poor, minorities, etc. True or not, many working class and middle class Americans were inclined to agree. In addition, the Great Society plunged the nation into the thicket of racial politics with the Civil Rights Act in 1964 and the Voting Rights Act in 1965. Initially this seemed to benefit the Democrats. Not one congressman who voted for the 1964 Civil Rights bill was defeated for re-election; half of those who voted against it went down to defeat. The public and the Johnson administration were all of a single mind. Or, were they?

The foundation for a white backlash had already been laid. All "revolutions" have backlashes. The migration of blacks out of the South that began in earnest after the Second World War had been accompanied by the white flight to suburbia. This fed perceptions that blacks were taking over the cities and taking jobs out of the hands of urban whites, all orchestrated by the Democratic Party in Washington, D.C. Some saw links between federal support of civil rights and communist inspired efforts to undermine America by promoting discord. It is easy to find what you are looking for if you know what you are looking for. It must be here, somewhere. All you need is a single piece of communist propaganda favoring civil rights to establish the link or the identification of a former communist background for any second or third tier civil rights advocate or participant. Many people can easily be tarred with an old statement or association, especially those who lead an active public life. You will hear more of this in the future because now nothing ever disappears from the Internet. The rise of black radicalism, "Black Power," and urban race riots fueled the perception that lawlessness was a more important issue than civil rights. In the public's mind, the Republican Party became identified with a less than enthusiastic approach to civil rights. The election of 1968 began a forty-year string of presidential elections in which a majority of black voters and a majority of white voters backed different candidates. Eight Republican senators had voted against the 1964 Civil Rights Act, including Barry Goldwater, the party's candidate for the presidency in 1964.

Associated with the white backlash was former Alabama Governor George Wallace's campaign for the Democratic nomination in 1968. After failing to gain the nomination as a Democrat, he organized a third party and ran as an independent. He captured many Southern votes. After the Republicans won in 1968, Nixon began a "Southern Strategy" to woo Southerners away from their historic loyalty to the Democratic Party, building a Republican constituency in the South, especially by opposing busing, which became a symbol for cooling it on racial issues. It worked. In 1960 there had been only seven Republican Congressmen from the South, and almost no local offices filled by Republicans. That started to change, rapidly.

Another factor complicating national politics was the altered perception of the Democratic Party's liberal leaders. In FDR's coalition, liberals clearly stood for the worker. However, by the 1960s they were increasingly seen as arrogant elitists, "limousine liberals," who advocated policies to solve social problems, such as by integration or busing, that never affected the elite upper crust. "They send their kids to private schools. They order ours bussed across town to achieve their vision of the great society, whatever that is." During the Great Depression in the 1930s the rich Republicans were seen as arrogant royalists, when occasional sympathetic remarks surfaced describing how the poor's suffering led them to reduce their consumption of caviar. A bad public image. By the 1960s working class Americans started to see liberal Democratic policies as being done *to* them, rather than *for* them. Increasingly, working class Democrats identified with the conservative Republicans who criticized Washington and liberals.

The Youth Revolt and the Counter Culture Movement

The decade from 1958 to 1968 was an era of unprecedented economic prosperity. People could afford to become concerned about non-bread-and-butter issues. Many young people did, but not all, not even a majority. Most college students in this decade were working class children of blue-collar workers and first generation college attendees who were trying to achieve the American Dream of material success. They were more interested in occupational mobility and generational mobility.

The Youth Revolt was a vocal minority that rejected middle class values. They rejected material progress as well as the work ethic. Their new issue was the "quality of life." They asserted the right to engage in instant gratification through drugs. Marijuana had been illegal since 1937 and LSD since 1965. They espoused sexual experimentation, as opposed to delayed gratification, which is typical of middle class values. Middle class kids constantly hear, "study hard, the rewards come later." The appearance of books that seemed to be "manuals" unnerved many in the older generation, for example, Helen Gurley Brown, *Sex and the Single Girl*, Masters and Johnson, *Human Sexual Response*, and Alex Comfort, *The Joy of Sex*.

Their vision of communal harmony ran counter to conventional lifestyles. By 1970 there were 30,000 communes with 750,000 people living in them. Unmarried couples lived together openly, a shock to older Americans. Think of all the different connotations in these words and phrases that were used at one time or another – shacking up, cohabitation, living-in-sin, wild wedlock (Martin Luther's term from the early 1500s), domestic partner, friend, significant other, live-in-girlfriend, live-in-boyfriend, and, my favorite description, current. Each shocked that era's conservatives.

What the so-called New Left of the youth revolt wanted politically was a "participatory democracy," and an immediate end to all forms of inequality and injustice. The civil rights movement had a profound impact and influence on those who grew to intellectual maturity in these years. The New Left had a commitment to morality over expediency, justice over compromise, and love over hatred. They called themselves the "new left," to differentiate themselves from the labor leaders and socialists of the "old left." The old left had a program; the new left had a vision. Hence the bumper sticker, "Make love, not war." However, our political system does not work that way. It is based on compromise, compromise, compromise, compromise. Deeply held ideas and visions are resistant to compromise. Successful legislation is the product of numerous compromises. Any visionary of any cause will be repulsed by the legislative process and by the resulting legislation, no matter what the law. Mark Twain once quipped that there are two things you do not want to watch being made – sausage and legislation.

The public's thinking combined the Youth Revolt with all the mass demonstrations of the era. There were anti-Vietnam war protests; demonstrations for Native-American rights, featuring "Red Power;" civil rights marches and "Black Power" confrontations; and woman's liberation protests. As one historian described it, all these public events were seen as part political revival meeting, part rock concert, and part psychedelic "happening." During an antiwar march on the Pentagon, hippie Abbie Hoffman espoused, "make revolution for the hell of it," and claimed he was going to levitate the Pentagon. During the Democratic national convention in Chicago in 1968 street protestors nominated a pig as their presidential candidate. The media, especially television, exhaustingly chronicled all these events. A four-day music festival on a farm in upstate New York, attended by 400,000 people and remembered in popular culture as Woodstock, marked the end of the era. The mass demonstrations and the urban riots all suggested the decline of public order. Disorder was ruling the day, reflecting a general social decay in America, as evidenced by rising crime rates, legalization of abortions, the increase in "out-of-wedlock" pregnancies, the rising divorce rate, and the proliferation of obscene books and films. Hollywood self-censorship had previously been so strict that it was not until the 1970s that someone actually flushed a toilet on live television.

New Left participants who later came to regret the tone and direction of the 1960s became critics of the left wing and the Democratic Party. These **neoconservatives**, new converts to conservatism, provided a crucial voice, the voice of insiders who now saw the error of their former ways. Criticism from a former insider is hard to refute. Presumably, they know. In the abolitionist movement before the Civil War, the Grimké sisters, Sarah and Angelina, former South Carolina slave owners turned abolitionists, were powerful advocates for the abolition of slavery. Older conservatives are sometimes called paleocons, as in Paleolithic, Stone Age. Conservative Irving Kristol, the "father of neo-conservatism," defined a neoconservative as "a liberal who has been mugged by reality." Traditional conservatives looked back nostalgically to a pastoral America of small towns. However, neoconservatives are at home in the modern economic and political world and are not hostile to government itself, endorsing government laws and actions to achieve their ends, something traditional conservatives would not sanction. Neither are they moralistic on social policy. Neoconservatives supported religious values and traditional morality on pragmatic grounds as necessary to hold society together. Their biggest impact may be in foreign policy. The nation has a responsibility to engage in an economic, political, and military campaign for world democracy and capitalism, if the U.S. is to succeed in the war against terrorism.

Homosexual Rights and Gay Liberation

Changes in sexual standards and customs always run into powerful constraints. Changes violate religious traditions, at least somebody's religious tradition. In religious disputes among Christians there is always the dilemma, what do you emphasize, the Old Testament or the Sermon on the Mount? Is a religious person one who studies the Bible or one who practices what the Bible says? And, which part of which Bible? Those who know for certain are not troubled by such questions.

Homosexuality exploded onto the public scene in the 1960s. The word had been first used in the 1890s. By the 1960s many homosexual sexual acts were illegal in most states, although, as victimless crimes, they were rarely enforced. However, as anyone who has received a traffic ticket or a parking ticket knows, laws always seem to be unevenly and unfairly enforced. All the issue of homosexuality needed was a crusading sheriff, an overzealous police officer, or a district attorney running for reelection on a moral cleanup platform, and the general "live and let live" philosophy toward victimless crimes evaporated. The consequences ranged from harassment to prison terms to personal disgrace. Popular medical lore and common sense denounced homosexuality as criminal, pathological, and ridiculous. Prior to the 1960s almost no one stood up for gay rights. Even the ACLU, the American Civil Liberties Union, had never accepted court cases involving allegations of discrimination against homosexuals in the workplace. In 1966 the ACLU reversed its earlier policy of refusing to consider homosexual practices as a subject for potential civil rights violations. In 1971 the American Psychological Association stopped calling homosexuality a "mental illness."

After the Second World War gay organizations started to emerge. One national organization grew out of a group of communists who had worked for the third party Progressive Party candidate in 1948, Henry Wallace, who had broken off from the Democrats. One consequence of this association with communism was the assertion that gayness was "foreign" and "un-American." That gay group, which called itself the Mattachine Society, organized in 1950. Two others were ONE, Inc., and the Daughters of Bilitis, the name coming from a fictional lesbian in a late nineteenth century poem by French poet Pierre Louÿs. The National Conference of Homophile Organizations held the first national convention of homosexuals in Kansas City in 1966.

The "incident," the spark that brought the issue of homosexuality into public view, was a June 1969 police raid on a popular gay bar frequented by men, the Stonewall Inn on Christopher Street in New York City. Unlike previous incidents, this time the patrons fought back, rioting for five days and nights. It sparked the birth of new activism. By the early 1970s there was a mass movement of homosexuals demanding nondiscrimination. Many Americans were genuinely dismayed by it. As a George W. Bush voter in Indiana said in 2004, "I'm not against homosexuals, but, this gay marriage thing is going too far."

Evangelical Christians
One continuous theme in conservative thought was the idea that many political problems are essentially, when you come right down to it, religious and moral problems. During the 1950s and 1960s Evangelical Christians began to be alarmed by what they

saw as an ominous drift toward secular liberalism, as shown by Supreme Court decisions that trivialized religion and promoted immorality. The first was the decision on school prayer in 1962 in *Engel v. Vitale*. The specific prayer found to be unconstitutional was, "Almighty God, we acknowledge our dependence upon Thee, and we beg thy blessings upon us, our parents, our teachers and our country." Many Christians, and others, were outraged. Many people assume there is a link between saying prayers and reading the Bible in public schools and better student behavior. They have no proof. No body of research either disputes or supports this position. However, when you know something for certain, you do not need proof. The second case in 1963 outlawed Bible reading, *Abington Township v. Schempp*. A third abandoned moral oversight of the arts, in *Redrup v. New York*, in 1966. Both the New York school prayer and the Pennsylvania Bible reading cases carefully stipulated that what was unconstitutional was neither prayer nor reading the Bible, but school authorities dictating which prayer and which Bible. However, in the public's mind, it was chasing God out of the public schools.

In 1955 sociologist Will Herberg argued in *Protestant-Catholic-Jew: An Essay in American Religious Sociology* that American patterns of assimilation now reflected a triple melting pot, where religious identity had gradually replaced ethnic identity, and where conformity had become our highest norm, the new "common religion" was the "American way of life," what you could think of as our **American Identity**. Both secular conformity and the increased significance of religious issues combined to worry fundamentalists.

Evangelical Christians felt confronted by a widespread modern philosophy they labeled "secular humanism." It has three components. First, the elevation of human reasoning above divine revelation. Second, a faith in the ability of humans to work out solutions to human problems. Third, a reliance on situational ethics and moral relativism rather than adherence to the moral precepts of the Bible. In short, where was God in all this?

The last building block politicizing Evangelical Christians fell into place during the Carter administration. The final straw was the Carter administration's 1975 demand that church affiliated schools, because they were tax-exempt, either adopt affirmative action programs or lose their tax exemption, as the Supreme Court had ruled in *Coit v. Green* in 1971. Bob Jones University, a conservative fundamentalist university, denied admission to single blacks, accepting only married blacks, and banned interracial dating. Outraged Conservative Christians responded by becoming Christian Conservatives. Note the switch in the adjectives and the nouns. They became more political. Televangelists like Pat Robertson and his Christian Crusade and Jerry Falwell and his Moral Majority were the best examples. Falwell vowed to get Americans "saved, baptized, and registered," (to vote). By 1980 radio and television evangelists reached 27 million people daily.

Jerry Falwell created Liberty College, (now Liberty University) touted as a Protestant rival to Catholic Notre Dame University. In 1979 it had 1,500 students; by 2016 Liberty

University had over 15,000, the online program has over 100,000. Falwell built the Thomas Road Baptist Church in Lynchburg, Virginia, from 34 members to over 18,000. In 1979 Falwell suddenly felt God calling him to enlist "the good people of America" in a crusade against permissiveness and moral decay. To Falwell some sins were public and societal; the entire nation had fallen into a cauldron of sinful behavior, not just some individuals. He formed the Moral Majority to fight the pornography, obscenity, vulgarity, and profanity that pervaded public school education under the guise of sex education and values clarification. It was a struggle between values clarification and situational ethics versus absolute values, God's values. Another area of activity was the Campus Crusade for Christ, begun in 1951, which expanded rapidly in the 1960s. By the middle of the 1970s the organization had a staff of 6,500 and an annual budget of $42 million, with a presence on almost every college campus.

Be careful discussing conservative Christians. Evangelicals are not a cohesive, solid group. They can be divided into fundamentalists, Pentecostals, charismatics, and neo-evangelicals. There has often been considerable hostility between them. Neo-evangelicals believe the Bible is the inerrant word of God, but it does need explained and applied. The popular preacher Billy Graham was a neo-evangelical. Pentecostals believe that many additional gifts of the Holy Spirit are important, especially "speaking in tongues." Charismatics also believe that such gifts are important. While they are found in many denominations, their chief effort is interdenominational worship or large nondenominational churches. Fundamentalists believe the Bible is literally true, word for word, but only the King James Version, and they reject the idea of gifts. Jerry Falwell once joked that people who spoke in tongues had eaten too much pizza the day before. A leading fundamentalist preacher in the early twentieth century called Pentecostals "the vomit of Satan." Anything Satan cannot stomach is bad, very bad.

The political Christian Right was never as strong as it looked to its opponents. The Moral Majority was composed almost exclusively of members of Falwell's denomination, the Baptist Bible Fellowship, and in many states it existed on paper rather than as a viable organization. The Moral Majority disbanded in 1989, frustrated. It later was revived in 2004. Pat Robertson urged members of the Christian Coalition to "mainstream the message" to broaden the appeal. They now couched their arguments in the "rights" language of liberalism: the right of the unborn in opposing abortion, the right of Christian children to exercise their religious beliefs in schools, the right of parents to home-school their children, and in Indiana in 2015, the right of a business not to serve those who violate the proprietor's religious beliefs. The rationale was different, and the agenda had not changed, but success was limited.

The televangelist scandals of 1987 and 1988 disgraced the message and the movement. Jim and Tammy Faye Baker of the PTL Club, "Praise The Lord Club," faced charges of sexual, drug, and financial misconduct. Jim Baker went to prison. Jimmy

Swaggart, famous for his exhortations calling Christians to live morally upright lives, was caught with a prostitute.

By the late 1990s some leaders and followers started to abandon religious-based politics. Some, like Paul Weyrich, announced that the "cultural wars" were lost. Many felt betrayed by Pat Robertson, who, in an effort to broaden his political appeal, moderated his stand on some issues, such as abortion, stating that he understood China's use of forced abortions and that efforts here in the United States should change to limiting abortions because an outright ban was not achievable. George W. Bush's 2000 campaign effort to reach out to homosexuals and Dick Cheney's nomination as the vice-presidential candidate disturbed fundamentalists. Cheney's daughter is gay. By this time there was an organization of gay Republicans within the party, the Log Cabin Republicans. Nevertheless, fundamentalists still voted. Eighty percent of those identifying themselves as part of the Religious Right voted for Bush in 2000 and even more in 2004. Their problem is that their electoral support has not earned them rewards. They were good at mobilizing support and helping to win elections, but not politically savvy enough in the legislative process to negotiate, to compromise, or to take half a loaf when that was all one could get. If you refuse to compromise moral values, you usually gain nothing from the legislative process. In addition, there were questions about the sincerity of their fellow conservatives. When conservative Christians visited the White House, George W. Bush administration staff members referred to them as "the nut cases."

Building an Organizational Base

Beginning in the 1970s there was an outburst of conservative organizations to save the nation. In 1973 Paul Weyrich created the Heritage Foundation, an information clearinghouse for right-wing causes. Joseph Coors and the Coors family pumped tons of money into conservative organizations and causes, joined later by the Koch brothers, Charles and David. In 1974 came the Committee for the Survival of a Free Congress and in 1975 the National Conservative Political Action Committee. In 1972 there were 113 Political Action Committees; by 1984, 4,009. Republican Congressional candidates outspent Democrats seven to three. Money talks in campaigns. Ronald Reagan added the crowning statement characterizing the Sixth Party System when he said that only a candidate who can attract financial support should seek office. Conservative organizations pioneered in using computerized lists for direct-mail solicitation to raise money for conservative candidates, recognizing that small contributions add up and that contributors became committed to those they supported financially. All this effort combined to defeat a dozen liberal senators and representatives in the congressional elections of 1978 and the 1980 presidential year election. (PAC figures from Edward Pessen, "The Beginnings, Evolution, and Morphology of American Major Parties," *Reviews in American History*, September, 1987, p. 392)

Conservatives captured the national Republican Party, as shown by the 1980 Republican Party platform, which promised a constitutional amendment to ban abortions. Traditionally, American political parties did not have principles. Party platforms were usually purposefully vague in order to not alienate any group of potential voters.

From the 1930s to the 1960s conservatives argued their ideas in the name of freedom, seeing opposing policies and ideas as dangerous to the spread of freedom. During the Second World War, business repeatedly added a "fifth freedom" to Roosevelt's Four Freedoms, "free enterprise." Beginning in the 1970s, they reframed arguments for their traditional policy goals by using the language and logic of the marketplace, such as smaller government and lower taxes, as the keys leading to prosperity. Now the emphasis became prosperity rather than freedom. Conversely, the Democrats, emphasizing the dangers of budget deficits, began to be perceived as the "dreary party of fiscal responsibility" by always talking about budget deficits. Conservatives had an agenda, an agenda of policies. Democrats seemed to be saying, "No, we cannot afford that." In politics, agendas work better. In the Sixth Party System voters in the political center were increasingly drawn toward the more positive conservative message. America still had the institutions of the New Deal, but it no longer had the rhetoric, the rationale, and the emotions that supported those New Deal innovations, hence support for them weakened.

Conservatives labeled the Democratic Party the party of the "outsider" groups. Rev. Jesse Jackson even adopted this approach in his run for the Democratic nomination in 1988 with his "Rainbow Coalition," which argued for including those traditionally outside the power elite – blacks, Hispanics, women, gays, peace protesters, young, etc. The problem with the Rainbow approach is that it places too much emphasis on victimization as a tactic. A policy of victimization requires your opponent to do something, to undergo a change of heart and to let you into the places where real power exists and where decisions are made, all of which assumes that your opponent has a heart and a conscience. It is a bankrupt tactic; there is no alternative to the failure to elicit a sympathetic response. In addition, do not forget that the "outsiders" really had nothing in common except their "outsider" status. One group may even despise another group. Gay women's groups and gay men's groups had to learn to work together. Think about it. If your group is anti-men, as far as you are concerned there is no difference between a gay man and a straight man. Neither LGBT thinking nor LGBT organizations had yet arrived on the political scene.

A Conservative Nation?

So, did conservatives win? It depends on whom you ask and what you ask. Politically, conservatives won in the political arena with a revived Republican Party, although Barack Obama's victories in 2008 and 2012 revealed a national weakness for the Republicans.

The 2016 campaign seemed to reflect a conservative temperament in the electorate. However, Hillary Clinton polled three million more popular votes than Donald Trump. Republican Party strategists admitted that if just four counties in Florida and one in Michigan had voted differently, the 2016 election would have put Hillary Clinton in the White House. All of this means? Culturally, to a certain extent, the counterculture won. Look at the television schedule for one week, especially the subjects discussed on the talk shows. Behavior once deemed abhorrent can now be seriously, but very superficially, publicly discussed as part of a viable lifestyle. These talk shows challenge older definitions of acceptable public and private conduct.

In spite of occupying the White House in the 1980s, three books published in that decade disturbed conservatives, who were concerned over the direction of America. The first was an excellent academic book by a historian, Paul Kennedy, *The Rise and Fall of the Great Powers*. It became a popular best seller. Paul Kennedy blamed the overextension of power and the consequential stress on national resources for ultimately undermining a great power's strength. Many conservatives, who never read the book, used this theme to indicate that the United States was in a similar position. Two other books decried the sorry state of American education, Allan Bloom, *The Closing of the American Mind*, and E. D. Hirsch, Jr., *Cultural Literacy: What Every American Needs to Know*. The first lashed out at the low quality of American intellectual life and the second complained about how the traditional core values of America were missing in the current public school curriculum. The message was clear. There is no need for multiculturalism in America. Follow the traditional culture. Researchers later found that by taking our inner city schools out of the numerous comparative international tests, our national testing results jumped impressively. American schools were not failing; it was more that Americans were permitting their inner city schools to fail.

One persistent theme in conservative books and talk shows is the perception that America is in decline. This surfaced in Donald Trump's 2016 campaign to "make America great again," implying that it had slipped. The term "Cultural Wars" refers to the ongoing debate between liberals and conservatives over different fundamental American values – historical, political, and moral. Both liberals and conservatives emphasize different facets of American History, using selected examples to support their political philosophy. As an example, the Smithsonian Museum's planned fiftieth year exhibit featuring the *Enola Gay*, the B-29 that dropped the first atomic bomb on Hiroshima in 1945, initially raised the same questions some historians have. Was it a good idea to drop the bomb? Was Japan close to surrendering, meaning the bomb was unnecessary? Would the United States have dropped it on a white nation like Germany? (Almost all historians believe so.) The conservative outcry scuttled the exhibit's interpretative commentary. The historian Carl Becker was right. The only history that counts is the history the average person carries around in his or her head. History is the only academic discipline in which amateurs challenge experts in that profession, especially super patriotic amateurs. The attempt in the mid-1990s by teachers and historians to create national standards for teaching history led to a Senate vote condemning them, 99-1.

A shift to the right in the 1980s and 1990s was evident in the failure of the Equal Rights Amendment for women, the gradual erosion of affirmative action, and the increasingly conservative decisions of the Supreme Court. Divisions among conservatives remained between the cultural conservatives and the economic conservatives. Cultural conservatives would use government to enforce their ideas; traditional conservatives believe any enlargement of government is bad. Conservatives have yet to offer a model that would protect the average citizen against impersonal economic forces in which one man's freedom leads to another's subjection. Opposing mandated health care or advocating the privatization of social security may lead to freedom and liberty for those who can afford it, but what does it do for those who cannot? If the past is any guide, the nation will continue to swing periodically between conservative and liberal policies, with a great deal of inconsistency. In the past Americans have not been ideologically minded, except for short periods.

52

NATIONAL POLITICS: RONALD REAGAN TO BILL CLINTON

Ronald Reagan

Ronald Reagan was born in a small town in the Midwest, Dixon, Illinois, and graduated, without an impressive transcript, from Eureka College, majoring in sociology and minoring in economics. His later critics would argue that he never read another economics book. His father worked in retail, selling shoes, and moved from job to job. When the Great Depression began, Reagan's father plunged into local politics as a strong supporter of the New Deal. So did his son. In the 1930s Reagan moved into radio, acquiring a regional reputation as a sports broadcaster. At that time sports broadcasters listened to football or baseball games on the telephone and imaginatively recreated the plays over the radio. It was too expensive to send broadcasters and equipment to the games. Along the way Reagan developed an itch for Hollywood and left a good broadcasting job to drive to Hollywood to become an actor.

His major asset, being an experienced horseman, made him a natural for grade "B" Western movies. His fellow actors liked him more than film critics and Hollywood producers and directors. In the 1940s he became the president of the Screen Actors Guild, the actors' union, and remained a strong Democrat. In the early 1950s, just as his film career was fading, he became the host for *General Electric Theater*, a weekly television show of original dramas. As a spokesman for GE, he traveled around the country giving speeches to managerial executives and various community business groups. In this capacity, reflecting upon the topics of his conversations with business leaders, Reagan became increasingly critical of governmental regulation of business, high taxes, and the stifling of private enterprise. He changed from a union leader New Deal Democrat into a spokesman FOR big business.

Ronald Reagan dramatically arrived on the national political scene at the 1964 Republican Party Convention. There he gave a nationally televised, prime time speech that has been often referred to by historians as "The Speech." It was a masterful, original statement of conservative principles, dramatically delivered by a trained public speaker. While Barry Goldwater, the Republican nominee that year, easily was defeated by Lyndon Johnson, the new rising star for the Republican Party was clearly Reagan.

Governor Ronald Reagan

A group of conservative California businessmen prevailed on Reagan to run for governor. He sheepishly admitted that he knew almost nothing about state issues. They promised to coach him; he agreed to run. His message resonated with California voters in the 1960s. The average voter is a suburban woman around 49 years old, hardly a typical 1960s radical or demonstrator. He won by focusing his campaign against obnoxious rebelling college students and their elite, liberal universities filled with left-wing professors. He urged respect for law and order and a return to simple basics in education. He opposed coddling welfare recipients and offered instead hard work and self-denial. In place of welfare, he argued for the traditional Yankee-WASP ethic of self-reliance and unrestrained freedom of enterprise. Getting ahead, he asserted, was the job of every individual. See Matthew Dallek, *The Right Moment: Ronald Reagan's First Victory and the Decisive Turning Point in American Politics*, which chronicles Reagan's rise to become the governor of California.

His record as governor belied his campaign promises. He raised taxes and the state debt and signed a law permitting some abortions. His record illustrated one of his qualities as a campaigner – say what appealed to conservatives and often actually do something else. In many respects, Reagan as a governor, and as a president, was more of a social conservative than a fiscal conservative in his policies, and he was not much of a social conservative. He was a former union leader, divorced (our first divorced president), and his second wife was already pregnant at their wedding ceremony. He hardly qualified as a poster child for conservative moral values. However, he became their hero, their symbol of conservative moral values. This scenario was repeated in the 2016 campaign with another candidate whose profile was similar to Reagan's, Donald Trump. In politics, symbols often carry more weight than reality.

On the national scene, he challenged President Gerald Ford for the Republican nomination in 1976 and almost won his party's endorsement, which would have sidelined a sitting president. It is very rare in American history for a party convention to repudiate its own president. In 1980 he did win the nomination and defeated President Jimmy Carter 489-49 in the Electoral College and 51% to 41% in the popular vote. John Anderson, a third party candidate, got the rest. However, victory was not as overwhelming as it appeared. Apathy reigned in the aftermath of Nixon's Watergate scandal. Only 27% of those eligible to vote voted for Reagan. Many potential voters did not vote. Republicans captured the Senate for the first time in 26 years and gained hundreds of state legislative seats. The election was a national shift to the right. Yet, it was really more of a personal victory for Reagan. Or, perhaps more correctly, it was a vote against Carter.

The Sixth Party System Arrives

The Fifth Party System coalition put together by FDR's New Deal was falling apart. In 1980 only 43% of Catholics, only 50% of Jews, and only 49% of union members voted Democratic. However, 92% of blacks remained Democratic voters, foreshadowing a trend in the emerging Sixth Party System that Southern whites would become Republicans and nationally blacks would faithfully remain Democrats. The Fifth Party System was truly dead – FDR's coalition of blacks, Catholics, ethnics, Jews, the South, big city machines, intellectuals, and unions.

The Sixth Party System seemed to indicate Carter was a Watergate blip on the trend toward conservatism, with elections now dominated by Republican supporters, especially the suburban electorate. For the first time in our history, the suburban population outnumbered the city population nationally. Some political observers said that after the election of John F. Kennedy in 1960, Catholics no longer felt a need to vote Democratic in protest against their exclusion from the power elite, since a Catholic now could be president. After Carter's election, the first Southerner elected since before the Civil War, many Southerners also stopped seeing the Democratic Party as their only possible home. Lyndon B. Johnson does not count as an elected Southerner because he was elected in 1964 while president, having taken over after Kennedy's assassination. WASP America, white Anglo-Saxon Protestant America, bastion of the power elite, seemed more inclusive than ever before.

Late in the 1960s the Democratic Party appeared to be becoming the party of "outsider groups," the advocate for the poor, blacks, Hispanics, women, protesting youth, gay liberation, anti-war protesters, and Vietnam War draft-dodgers. The party's old guard still controlled the 1968 Democratic National Convention; but by 1972, everything changed. Compared to 1968, the percentage of women, blacks, and delegates under thirty attending the 1972 Democratic National Convention rose from 12% to 38%, 5% to 15%, and 3% to 23%. Millions of Americans, offended by attacks on their core values and cultural traditions, shifted toward the Republican Party and conservatives because there was no longer a place for them in the Democratic Party. Or, so they thought.

Reagan as President

Reagan adopted a new economic policy, supply-side economics, to get out of the Carter doldrums. It advocated boosting the economy by slashing government spending and lowering taxes. This would free up money for investment, stimulating the economy. Before dismissing this thinking, you must understand that the economist who founded this school of economics was awarded the Nobel Prize in Economics in 1999, Robert Mundell. Reagan's tax cuts rewarded the wealthy. The top 1% had their taxes cut 25%, the bottom 40% not at all. The tax cut cost $280 billion in potential federal revenue; meanwhile, defense spending rose sharply. Later, economists all said that what brought an economic recovery was neither the tax cuts nor the budget cuts, but huge increased defense spending under Reagan. Another policy was to shift the welfare burden to the states because local supervision was a better way to end "welfare cheats." By the end of his second term, Reagan had slashed total federal spending for social programs from $42 billion to $18 billion. Conservatives realized that rather than trying to cut social programs by fighting to enact new legislation, it was easier to squeeze funding for social programs by reducing revenue through tax cuts. Reagan approved. This method was less dramatic, less confrontational, and less noticed, but effective in the long run. Social programs withered on the vine.

During his campaign, Reagan announced his opposition to many issues near and dear to liberals and, also, to many voters in the center. Reagan

1. opposed busing to integrate schools
2. favored an end to abortions
3. opposed the EPA, the Environmental Protection Agency
4. opposed the federal Department of Education, calling for abolishing it
5. opposed the Department of Energy

Some of these are state issues that do not fall under the federal government, such as abortion. In many respects they are "symbolic issues" that stir people up, but the federal government can do little about them, short of amending the Constitution, an unlikely event.

As president, Reagan stood up to the federally employed air traffic controllers when they went on strike, an illegal action according to their union agreement, and clearly unpopular with the public. Reagan fired all 15,000 of them. Other than his tax cuts, Reagan generally left Congress alone to pursue its own agenda. Critics called him a 9-5 president. He did tell his aides not to bother him in the evenings; if it was not an emergency it could wait until morning. He spent one-fourth of his working days, Monday to Friday, on vacation. It raises an interesting question. To what degree *should* a president engage in micro-managing. Some have, some have not. Reagan did not.

Reagan curtailed the federal government, trying to reduce what it could and should do. He cut the staff at FTC, the Federal Trade Commission; at OSHA, the Occupation, Safety, and Health Administration; at the Antitrust Department; and at the National

Highway Traffic Safety Administration. The new head of the Environmental Protection Agency, Anne Gorsuch (Anne Burford after 1983), startled employees on her first day with her announcement that her sole purpose was to impede the work of the agency. At the Interior Department, James Watt stated the same thing. Reagan tried to fire five of the six members of the Civil Rights Commission, but Congress created a new commission, with half the appointments made by Congress.

Evaluating the Reagan Presidency

Before evaluating the Reagan presidency one confronts the chore of assessing Reagan as a person. He reminds us of Winston Churchill's classic description of Russia, "a riddle wrapped in a mystery inside an enigma." At the end of his second term a national TV commentator asked Reagan if his Hollywood background helped him in politics. His reply, "There have been times in this office when I've wondered how you could do this job if you hadn't been an actor." (David Greenberg, *Republic of Spin: An Inside History of the American Presidency*). His own children said he often looked at them as if he did not recognize them. As the graduation speaker for his son's high school graduation, Reagan introduced himself to his own son. His strongest supporters and closest aides made some curious observations. These quotes are from Peggy Noonan, *What I Saw at the Revolution*. She was a strong Reagan supporter and one of his speechwriters. She knew him well. James Baker, "He is the kindest and most impersonal man I ever knew." Two others, "Behind those warm eyes is a lack of curiosity that is, somehow, disorienting." And, "Beneath the lava flow of warmth there is something as impervious as a glacier." White House staffers often joked about Reagan's cold aloofness, "Who was that masked man?" Yet, Mother Theresa caught something else during a visit. "In him, greatness and simplicity are one." He received and personally responded to more mail than any other president. The public loved him; he left the presidency with the same high public adoration that he had received for eight years. In the twentieth century, only FDR matched that.

In spite of his policies, or because of them, take your pick, Reagan won reelection in the 1984 over Walter Mondale, Carter's former vice president. During the campaign Reagan got a question from his staff. "What about the deficit?" It had dramatically increased during his first term. Reagan's answer, "Don't worry, the national debt is not a political problem." He was right; most voters do not understand a national debt. The increase in the national debt under Reagan and the George H. W. Bush administration that followed exceeded all the previous presidential administrations added together. So much for a traditional conservative fiscal approach. Obviously, late twentieth century conservatives in the Sixth Party System differed from anti-New Deal conservatives in the Fifth Party System. Be careful, the definitions of, and the traits of, liberals and conservatives may change from one party system to another, as they did from the Fifth to the Sixth.

Historians and Political Scientists wrestle with an assessment of the Reagan administration. It had the highest number of indicted officials for any presidential administration in American history. Yet, Reagan was nicknamed the "The Teflon President," because nothing stuck to him personally. The closest personal tarnish was the Iran-Contra affair. Twice Congress passed explicit directives, one by a vote of 411-0 in the House of Representatives, directing administration officials to avoid getting involved in a civil war in Nicaragua. However, ignoring Congress, White House officials used contributions from conservative millionaires and funds from the illegal sale of weapons to Iran to support Contra guerrillas fighting against the leftist government of Nicaragua. White House aide Col. Oliver North directed the scheme. When it became public, Congress was furious. Two questions arose. Did Reagan know? Or, was he not in control of his own administration? Reagan personally weathered the crisis because most felt that he was oblivious to it all. Either way was scary, that he knew and acted illegally, or that he was unaware of what his subordinates were doing. By the end of his administration many touted Ronald Reagan as a candidate to add to the faces on Mount Rushmore. His supporters praised the "Reagan Revolution." But, did it exist? Had there been a "Reagan Revolution"?

Reagan got credit for repealing welfare state liberalism, but it had been declining since the late 1960s; few social welfare programs enjoy deep support among the electorate. He also supposedly began checking harsh environmental legislation, but big business had already launched a fight against environmental and consumer legislation. A broad-based corporate counterattack was already underway. Strangely, in1984, 20% of those who voted for Reagan expressed serious doubts about his domestic policies and another 20% said they did not care much about any issues. Was he just personally popular? The Democratic Party had begun to splinter, mostly over the issue of race. Many working class blue-collar workers voted against the Democrats rather than for Republicans and conservatism. Finally, it is difficult to label Reagan a conservative. He was privately lukewarm on abortion, AIDS, and social issues. Indeed, the Southern conservative Senator, Jesse Helms, continually criticized Reagan's policies as insufficiently conservative, especially on abortion and school prayer, issues important to church-going fundamentalists. Reagan was one of our few presidents who never attended church while he was president. Not once in eight years. His college girlfriend blasted him, calling him a hypocrite.

The Reagan administration experienced one disaster, the Challenger. NASA, seeking to boost interest in space exploration among kids all over the world, originally planned to have Sesame Street's Big Bird accompany the crew on the Challenger, which exploded in 1986 shortly after takeoff, killing the crew and a teacher accompanying the trip, Christa McAuliffe. If Big Bird had been along, it would have added to the public relations disaster for the space program.

George H. W. Bush

Reagan's vice president, George H. W. Bush, grew up in a prominent New England family. His father, Prescott Bush, was a Wall Street executive and a senator from Connecticut, 1952-1963. These connections helped his son, who made the most of them. George H. W., nicknamed "Poppy" during his Yale years, joined the navy immediately after prep school and served as a naval aviator during the Second World War, the youngest ever up to that point. He served honorably, and was awarded the Distinguished Flying Cross and several other medals. Entering Yale University after the war, he graduated in just two and a half years. Then he plunged into the business world, where he eventually created his own oil company in Texas, earning a tidy fortune. Political ambition led to a seat in the House of Representatives from Houston, Texas, and an unsuccessful campaign for the senate. President Nixon appointed him the U.S. Ambassador to the United Nations for two years. Next, he served briefly as the chairman of the Republican National Committee, the chief U.S. representative in China (an unofficial post because the U.S. had not yet officially recognized China; that would come in 1979), and as Director of the CIA, the Central Intelligence Agency. His campaign for the Republican nomination in 1980 faltered, but Reagan selected him as his vice-presidential running mate.

George H. W. Bush served Reagan well and faithfully for eight years. With Reagan's strong endorsement, Bush secured the Republican nomination in the 1988 election, running against Democratic Governor Michael Dukakis of Massachusetts. Vice presidents are at a political disadvantage during a run for the presidency. They rarely speak out in support or opposition to a president's policies. Thus, being a vice president relegates one to the back stage of national politics. One political wag called it "four years of rest and a good income." Before Bush, the last sitting vice president to win the presidency was Martin Van Buren in 1836. However, Bush won, greatly helped by Reagan's popular coattails. His pledge of "no new taxes" came back to haunt him later during his 1992 reelection campaign. Reagan's deficits forced a Bush tax increase.

Bush as President

Bush had a difficult task. It would have been impossible for anyone to follow the very popular Reagan. One of Bush's major accomplishments was the Americans with Disabilities Act, which countered employment discrimination against the disabled and mandated easier access to public facilities. During Bush's administration, the national debt skyrocketed. Deregulation of the banking industry, passed under the Reagan administration in 1982, led to the savings and loan debacle. Thousands of savings and loan banks, previously restricted to just issuing home mortgages, were now allowed to make loans for any reason. Some ambitious bank managers took great risks, tossing many savings and loan banks into a financial sinkhole. Most of the bankruptcies were in Texas, a state which had no state governmental oversight of the banking industry.

However, due to the FDIC, the federal government had to bail all of them out to protect depositors. Amazingly, banking deregulation would lead to another crisis under his son's administration that contributed to a recession beginning in 2007. Maybe banks and bankers need regulation. The "free market" seems to be insufficient to protect the public against the banking industry's occasional innovations. Bush was more successful in foreign affairs. Operation Desert Storm successfully removed Iraq's Saddam Hussein from power. Two momentous changes occurred during Bush's presidency – the fall of the Berlin Wall in 1989 and the collapse of the Soviet Union in 1991.

Election of 1992

Few things haunt a politician as much as a previous absolute statement. During the 1988 campaign, Bush boldly stated, "Read my lips: No new taxes." When the reality of his predecessor's disastrous deficit legacy became unavoidable, Bush was forced to lead a fight to raise taxes. One newspaper headline said, "Read My Lips: I Lied." He paid for it in 1992, losing to Bill Clinton, the young Democratic governor of Arkansas.

Bush's Democratic Party opponent, Bill Clinton, had served as the attorney general of Arkansas and as the governor, 1979-1981 and 1983-1992. His political ambition was sparked by his selection in 1963 as one of the Arkansas Boys State representatives to Boys Nation, an annual event sponsored by the American Legion. (There is also a Girls Nation.) Two boys from each state go to Washington. One of Clinton's most prized personal possessions is a photograph of him shaking hands with President John F. Kennedy during the Boys Nation visit to the White House. After graduating from Georgetown University, he won a prestigious Rhodes Scholarship to Oxford in England. Next it was on to Yale Law School, where he met his wife, Hillary. Politically ambitious, he rose rapidly in Arkansas, gaining a reputation as an education reformer. His fellow governors elected him as the chair of the National Governors Association. When he took the oath of office in 1993, he was only 46 years old, one of our youngest presidents.

The two party conventions in 1992 emphasized their differences over women's issues. The Republicans featured something new in politics – the candidates' wives, Barbara Bush and Marilyn Quayle, spoke to the convention delegates, emphasizing traditional family values and their role as mothers and helpmates to their husbands. After their victory on election night, Bill Clinton and Al Gore used the word "gender" in describing one of the criteria by which they expected to be judged. Party positions on women's issues were hardening, one feature of the Sixth Party System.

President Bill Clinton

As president, Bill Clinton had both major accomplishments and disappointing failures. He failed to push a national health care plan through Congress. He did get the Family and Medical Leave Act, giving mothers or fathers up to twelve weeks leave to stay home to care for a new baby. Your job was guaranteed when you returned, but you received no pay while you missed work. The United States is the only industrial nation on the globe that does not provide some form of paid maternity or child care leave. Another accomplishment was NAFTA, (endorsed by Reagan in his 1980 campaign) the North American Free Trade Agreement between Canada, Mexico, and the United States, which removed all trade barriers between them, creating a huge free trade zone. Ever since the citizens in all three countries have argued over which country benefited the most. The debate continues; it is always an election issue. Donald Trump condemned it in his 2016 campaign. Economists argue that NAFTA has a positive economic impact on all three countries. Clinton achieved a minor miracle, something unheard of in recent American history – in two of his eight years, 1998 and 2000, the federal government had a budget surplus.

In 1996 Bill Clinton pushed through Congress a law "to end welfare as we know it." It ended AFDC, Aid to Families with Dependent Children, replacing it with the Personal Responsibility and Work Opportunity Act, setting up the program entitled, Temporary Assistance to Needy Families, TANF. Conservatives supported it. One liberal senator labeled it "the most brutal act of social policy since Reconstruction." It cut the number of people on welfare in half. The maximum lifetime benefit was five years. It required heads of households on welfare to find work within two years. Bill Clinton's eight year presidency was characterized as "triangularization," putting the president in the center in legislative battles between conservatives and liberals. It earned him two terms in the White House and the enmity of both liberals and conservatives, over different issues. But, the public loved Bill Clinton. His approval rating when he left the White House was the highest of any president since the Second World War.

The Elections of 1994 and 1996

The Congressional election of 1994 swept Republicans into control of the House of Representatives, for the first time in forty years. The Speaker of the House, Newt Gingrich, boldly proclaimed a "Contract with America," a conservative Republican agenda to reduce government, to hinder the EPA, to eliminate funding for Head Start, and to lower taxes. The Democratic controlled Senate was having none of it.

By 1996 it was clear that a lot had changed in one hundred years. Some historians were calling the Sixth Party System the Second Gilded Age, not a compliment. Geographic areas controlled by the Democrats in 1896 now voted Republican; Republican areas now voted Democratic. For example, Congressional Democrats in 1996 gained 19 seats in the Midwest, the Pacific Coast, and New England, including the entire Massachusetts delegation. Clinton's second campaign also captured four Southern states, with Florida as the most significant. Florida would continue to barely shift from one party to the other with each election, often by less than one percent of the vote.

Red States and Blue States

Party gains and losses in Congress now followed a North-South polarization. The Republican Party strategy, beginning in the 1960s, exploited the turmoil surrounding the ending of segregation to break up the "Solid South," the Democratic stranglehold on the South it had held since the Civil War. However, in so doing, the Republican Party undermined its support in the North. The outcome was that the Republican Party took positions that made it difficult to achieve a majority of the national popular vote. Hillary Clinton polled almost three million more popular votes than Donald Trump in 2016. But, only the Electoral College vote counts. This characteristic of the Sixth Party System, a status as a minority party in popular voting, led Republican conservatives to gerrymander Congressional and state legislative districts. (Something Democrats had also done in the past.) Conservatives also pushed for laws requiring stricter voter identification rules at the polling places. Out of the millions of votes cast over the previous twenty years, scholars were able to find less than a dozen cases of voter fraud. The real purpose seemed to be reducing the number of minority voters. The central core of the Republican Party, the right-wing South, opposed abortion, was hostile to the federal government, supported states' rights, endorsed nativism, opposed environmentalism, spurred multiculturalism, and supported school prayer. This set of issues had the effect of driving many women and Hispanics out of the Republican Party. In six of the seven elections between 1992 and 2016, the Republican Party failed to win a majority of the votes cast for president. In spite of victories, neither George W. Bush in 2000 or 2004 nor Donald Trump in 2016 won a majority of the popular vote. When the election of 2000 put a Republican into the White House, it was something political observers in both parties felt was increasingly becoming impossible. The 2004 and 2016 elections proved otherwise. In the politics of the Sixth Party System nothing seemed impossible, except Congress passing laws favorable to your issues.

53

THE WAR ON DRUGS

Europeans criticize Americans for declaring a "war" on everything – drugs, crime, poverty, communism, terrorism, etc. They have a point. The problem with a "war" is that unless there is a victory and a final surrender, you can feel as if you did not win. Sometimes reduction is a praiseworthy achievement, a reduction in the crime rate, in drug use, or in terrorist acts. Between 1905 and 1920, our first drug war fought opium-based products. The second, in the Johnson and Nixon administrations in the 1960s and 1970s, targeted LSD and marijuana. The third, starting in the 1980s, focused on cocaine, especially crack.

For an excellent history of the early period, see Anthony Marcus, "How America Fought Its First Drug War: The Harrison Act," in *Turning Points: Making Decisions in American History*, vol. II, and, the last chapter in Norman H. Clark, *Deliver Us from Evil: An Interpretation of American Prohibition*. These are the sources for some of what follows.

Before 1900

As early as the late eighteenth century concoctions using morphine, made from opium, and coca were widely prescribed in narcotic prescriptions such as "laudanum," a mixture of wine, spices, and opium, and "black drop." Both were used to treat "melancholy," what people today refer to as depression. Readers of mystery stories all know that the greatest fictional detective of all time – Sherlock Holmes – occasionally used drugs, an addiction that the main character wrestles with in the modern Holmes television series, *Elementary*. Opium imports grew from 24,000 pounds in 1840 to 400,000 pounds in 1872. Women, old folks, Civil War veterans, and the wealthy were common users. It was the drug of choice among the middle and upper classes; alcohol was for the lower and working classes. Other painkilling or mitigating drugs had not yet been discovered, and so narcotics served to stop pain and to stimulate the immune system. It did wonders for teething babies, for women suffering from menstrual cramps, or for whatever ailment one had. Because penicillin and antibiotics lay far into the future, the best many doctors could do for their patients to alleviate pain was to camouflage it. By 1900 drug company scientists had created all the paraphernalia and drugs associated with the modern drug culture, manufacturing cocaine, heroin, and hypodermic needles. You could even order needles and a small amount of cocaine through the Sears, Roebuck & Company catalog. An estimated one out of every 400 Americans used varying amounts of narcotics. The United States led the Western world in opium and morphine use; per capita use rose from 12 grams to 52 grams by 1900. It was cheap, about 75 cents a month for a daily habit, less than 3¢ a day.

Our First Drug War

Two laws often linked together in American history textbooks as premier examples of Progressive Movement reform – the Pure Food and Drug Act and the Meat Inspection Act – passed Congress on the same day in 1906. The colorful stories about the meat-packing industry from Upton Sinclair's *The Jungle* and Theodore Roosevelt's disgust over his breakfast sausage guarantee that the Meat Inspection Act gets more attention. However, the drug part of the Pure Food and Drug Act deserves more space in history textbooks. During the Progressive era many organizations, such as the American Medical Association, the AMA, established standards in their fields, both to elevate their image in the public's eye and to become more professional. The AMA pushed for the Pure Food and Drug Act, which required the content labeling of medicines, specifically targeting morphine, opium, heroin, cannabis indica, cocaine, and several other drugs. Shortly afterwards, in 1909, the importing of opium was banned. Its widespread use by Chinese immigrants was a factor. Earlier, in 1875, San Francisco had prohibited opium dens, and the federal government in 1887 prohibited Chinese, and only the Chinese, from importing opium. Any other American could import opium before it was banned in 1909. In 1914 New York became the first state to regulate drug abuse. New York's state law prohibited pharmacies from dispensing hypodermic syringes, opium, or any of its derivatives without a physician's prescription. Addicts could be arrested and committed to a hospital until "cured."

Harrison Act

One of the consistent, reoccurring themes in the history of drugs is the question of supply and demand. Are drugs a problem because the supply is available, or, are drugs a problem because of a demand for them? Which is the chicken and which is the egg? The answer makes a lot of difference. It determines where you put your effort to fight drug abuse and how you go about it.

The first federal drug act grew out of several international diplomatic conferences that attempted to get narcotics producing countries to curtail supply. (One American delegate to one of the conferences had been the driving force behind the first state law outlawing marijuana, California, 1913.) The drug supplying countries responded that it was the responsibility of the leading drug using countries to limit their demand. The supply countries raking in huge profits were Germany, Switzerland, and Turkey, along with many Latin American countries. To reassure other nations that the United States was trying to reduce drug use, Congress responded by adopting the Harrison Act in 1914, a revenue act requiring the registration and taxation of narcotics prescriptions, not really for the purpose of raising revenue, but rather to control prescriptions. It required the registration of and the taxation of all "who produce, import, manufacture, compound, deal in, dispense, sell, distribute or give away opium or coca leaves, their salts, derivatives or preparations."

In Congress the proposed law provoked neither extended debate nor militancy nor emotion, unlike the contemporary crusade against alcohol. It was as if the attitude of Congress was, "OK, if that's what The Hague International Narcotic Control Convention wants, that's what we'll pass." Think of it as a follow-up to a low-level diplomatic endeavor. Two court cases that grew out of the act, *U.S. v. Doremus* and *Webb v. U.S.*, upheld the federal government's power to criminalize opiates, even those prescribed as a maintenance drug for addicts. Nine years later, by 1923, 75% of all the women incarcerated in federal prisons were there for violating the Harrison Act. It is still true today that the vast majority of those in prisons are there for drug offenses.

This was the first encounter with a bedeviling question about drugs. How do you help people get off addiction? Are gradually prescribed smaller and smaller doses an effective potential treatment? Is this method a legal treatment? Not any longer. After the Harrison Act, now addiction, all addiction, became a crime. Why did (and still does) the public and the law consider alcoholism to be an illness and drug addiction to be a crime? Are drugs a medical problem or a police problem? However, at the very least, as one sociologist wrote in disgust in 1940, we had not yet reached the point where society's treatment of addicts rivaled that given to the Salem witches.

Reefer Madness

"*Reefer Madness*" was a curious film produced in 1936 to warn parents about the dangers of their children using marijuana, which had become popular in urban black neighborhoods. One consequence of the 1920s and 1930s white interest in jazz music was an accompanying exposure to marijuana, in songs like "Reefer Man," "When I Get Low, I Get High," and "Texas Tea Party." Usage spread out of the black neighborhoods. The setting for "*Reefer Madness*" is a high school PTA (Parent-Teacher Association) meeting, where the principal shows a film that portrays marijuana as a killer drug that leads to crime and insanity. The original title was *"Tell Your Children,"* and the last scene carries that stern warning to all the parents in bold print. It was a failure as a film, unprofitable; critics labeled it one of the worst films ever made. However, it became a cult film in the 1960s. Decriminalization advocates used it as an example of how the government lies about the dangers of marijuana. However, no government had produced it or used it in that manner. It was, in truth, simply a very bad grade B movie.

By 1937 possession of marijuana was a crime in some states. The Federal Bureau of Narcotics, created in 1930, pushed for a federal law criminalizing marijuana, which was enacted in 1937 in the Marihuana Tax Act. (The federal government consistently uses the spelling "marihuana," the Mexican spelling.) Using marijuana was already a crime in ten states, chiefly western states concerned over use by Mexican immigrants. Two pieces of legislation in the 1950s set mandatory sentences, two to ten years in prison — the 1952 Boggs Act and the 1956 Narcotics Control Act.

The 1960s Counterculture

In the 1960s young people between 15 and 24 years old constituted almost 18 percent of the population. The post-Second World War baby boom had grown up. This youth-dominated portion of the population was a huge market for Hollywood's entertainment endeavors — rock bands, films, and television — and a market for drugs. Half of all 18-year-olds were in college, the highest percentage of first-generation college students in our history. The later popular image of the 1960s is that everyone was strung out on drugs. A common observation heard later was that "if you remembered the 1960s, you weren't there." Too strung out to remember. Not true. Driven by a dream of upward mobility, most students studied, to rise financially above their parents. By definition, getting an education is a focus on the future, not the present. College meant a ticket to the good life. But, enough young people did experiment with drugs and protests and movements to change America — civil rights, anti-Vietnam War protests, women's rights, communes, and environmentalism — to create a "counterculture" (term coined by historian Theodore Roszak) that rejected hard work, sexual restraints, and self-denial of the moment.

Two other drugs became popular in the 1960s. LSD was developed by a pharmaceutical company in the 1930s as a treatment for schizophrenia. A Harvard psychologist, Dr. Timothy Leary, who extensively experimented with LSD, lysergic acid diethylamide, urged everyone to try hallucinogenic or psychedelic drugs — "turn on, tune in, and drop out." He followed his own advice, causing Harvard University to fire him. Mescaline, made from the peyote cactus and long used by Indians in Mexico and the Southwest, was added to the mix of popular drugs. How was this lifestyle financially possible? One overlooked factor in the history of this decade is the robust economy. Even college graduates with poor transcripts got jobs. Neither money woes nor a jobless future threatened. Two rock show extravaganzas, Woodstock and Altamont, closed the decade.

The counterculture movement challenged polite society's social requirement to suppress impulsive behavior. It argued for the liberation of self in the name of personal freedom. It introduced the phrase, "doing my own thing." Long hair, painted bodies, elaborate slang, and open sexuality translated into a colorful way of life. Drugs became part of this liberating experience and were defended as such. Publicly shocking behavior was justified because it was publicly shocking behavior. That was part of the purpose. Many "normal" people do not believe that public space is an appropriate place to make personal expressions. The counterculture did. In their multiple movements and non-traditional lifestyles, the counterculture naively believed it was creating a better world. Those in positions of authority felt otherwise.

The Second War on Drugs

The excesses of the 1960s led the Lyndon Johnson and Richard Nixon administrations to launch a Second War on Drugs. The unlicensed manufacture or sale of LSD became a federal crime in 1965. President Nixon created the Drug Enforcement Agency by executive order in 1973. Feeding this Second War on Drugs was a genuine concern about the future of America. Polls revealed that nearly half of all American youth believed they lived in a "sick society." They stated that neither marriage, nor having children, nor patriotism, nor religion, nor moral values seemed important. Propelling this criticism was anger at the war in Vietnam and at the slow pace of civil rights achievements for blacks, and an awakening movement of women and protesting Native-Americans. Some young people withdrew into isolated communes, considered by them to be "islands of decency," rejecting traditional American societal values. Were drugs the cause of youth alienation or the result of it? Older Americans, the average voter was 49 years old, believed that pervasive drug use was more a contributing factor than a result of the youth protests.

The Third War on Drugs

The 1970s and 1980s saw the increased use of cocaine and crack cocaine, particularly in the poorer areas of urban America, just as blue collar factory jobs there seemed to evaporate. One community activist characterized such neighborhoods as "deserts of hopelessness." Some turned to selling drugs, which gangs soon efficiently organized. However, it led to turf wars. The Rev. Jesse Jackson, the civil rights leader, said bluntly that drugs were doing more to harm the ghetto population than white racism ever did. The fastest growing segment of our prison population was drug offenders, just as it was in 1923 with the Harrison Act. By 1980 more than one third of young adults smoked marijuana. The president's wife, Nancy Reagan, advised the young to "just say no." That policy did not work.

Having our armed forces operate in the opium growing areas of Southeast Asia meant that some Vietnam War veterans returned as experienced drug users or even addicts. Drug use among our troops received media publicity, making it appear that the army was degenerating. Of our soldiers in Vietnam, 51% used marijuana and 28.5% hard narcotics. However, in Europe, the numbers were 40% and 13%, and inside the United States, the numbers were 41% and 20%. Serving in Vietnam was not the sole cause of the increased drug use. Revelations of drugs from Vietnam being smuggled into the United States inside bodies shipped home for burial shocked and sickened everyone.

When George H. W. Bush followed Ronald Reagan in the White House, the anti-drug campaign shifted. Fifty percent of Americans thought drugs were a major threat facing the country. Bush declared a "war on drugs" and created a new agency, the Office of National Drug Control Policy, with a Drug Czar, William Bennett, to throw the federal government's resources behind the fight. The federal drug-control budget tripled. Earlier, in the Reagan administration, new practices emerged out of the 1986 and 1988 Drug Abuse Acts. Businesses were now required to educate workers and to create a "drug-free workplace." Schools were encouraged to have anti-drug programs. Under these laws now both the seller and the user could receive criminal and/or civil penalties, designed primarily for the user caught with small amounts. The fines could go as high as $10,000, even for those not convicted of a crime. The 1986 law contained mandatory minimum sentences, which would later become a debated topic. It prevented a judge from being able to use his or her discretion and judgment in that particular case, leading to long mandatory sentences. By 1990 half of those in federal prisons were incarcerated for drug offenses. These draconian laws disproportionately hit minority urban neighborhoods.

Mandatory Sentencing

Mandatory sentencing did not hit just urban minority neighborhoods. In an article in *The Nation* in 2012, Judge Mark Bennett of the Northern Iowa District Federal Court spoke out on the topic of mandatory sentencing. Supreme Court justices and federal district judges rarely comment publicly on legal matters. Judge Bennett did. In his nineteen years as a federal district judge, he had sentenced 1,092 people to prison for mandatory terms from five years to life without parole, all for drug offenses. "Here in the heartland, I sentence more drug offenders in a single year than the average federal district judge in New York City, Washington, Chicago, Minneapolis, and San Francisco – combined."

Northern Iowa is a rural area. However, drugs are everywhere. In rural Iowa the drug of choice is meth, methamphetamine. The typical user is a low class white person. In urban minority areas, it is crack cocaine. The typical user is a low class black person. Both drugs fall under mandatory federal sentencing laws. Sixty-two percent of all the federal judges think that mandatory sentences for drug offenses are too harsh. The vast majority sentenced are addicts, not hardened criminals, drug lords, or drug kingpins. Those at the top of the illegal drug supply chain are rarely caught. The United States leads the world in terms of the percentage of our adult population behind bars. Almost 700 out of every 100,000 Americans are locked up. China and Russia follow on the list – China in total number, Russia in percentage.

Demand Problem or Supply Problem?

Billions of federal dollars also went to stop drugs from entering the country. Again, the question was raised – Is drug use a demand problem or a supply problem? In many states, such as Virginia and California, to name just two, the number one cash crop is illegally grown marijuana. Across the United States, federal and state park rangers warn visitors to be careful of booby traps in isolated areas of our national and state parks and forests. Marijuana growers protect their turf.

At one time authorities thought they had a new detection method when they discovered the ability to detect cocaine on paper money. However, traces of cocaine are on almost all dollar bills. Interdiction of supply does not seem to put a dent into the street price of illegal drugs, which suggests that so much enters the country that an occasional financial loss is meaningless in the overall picture.

A few states have already begun to decriminalize some drugs or to make fewer arrests. The police frequently ignore drug use in many communities, if it is not accompanied by violence, such as gang turf wars or shootings. Referendums in two states in 2012, Washington and Colorado, pointed to a new direction, essentially legalizing the use of marijuana. This caused the governments of several drug supplying countries, such as Mexico, to reevaluate their militant anti-drug campaigns. Although these "drug wars" were financed by the United States, it was Mexico's soldiers and police who were killed in battles against the drug cartels.

Business principles guide illegal businesses just as they do legal businesses. Drug cartels are businesses; they seek profits. When police practices or state laws essentially legalized the use or growing of marijuana, profits slipped because the price fell. Many drug cartels which specialized in the production of marijuana switched to producing heroin. Heroin is commonly "cut" by sellers. They take pure heroin and dilute it with various white substances, such as rat poison, detergents, baking powder, etc., resulting in a product that is frequently only 5-10% heroin. The former marijuana producing drug cartels, trying to muscle into the existing heroin trade, provided purer forms of heroin, often as much as 100%. Obviously, an addict taking a drug that is 10 to 20 times stronger sometimes led to fatalities.

Should drugs be legalized? This debate will be part of public discussion far into the future. On one side are those who champion the individual – what I do is my business, my business only. My individual rights protect me; it is a private matter that does not concern the public. There is always a dividing line between private morality and public morality. Does it matter where that line is? Yes. The right to use drugs involves more than an individual's rights. If our society accepts widespread drug use, even if such rights remain marginally illegal, or just minimally offensive, what message is being sent to young people who are growing up and struggling with decisions about what constitutes right or wrong, as defined by many sources – parents, friends, schools, churches, governments, etc.? Are the individual "rights" of drug users consistent with the "rights" philosophy espoused by the Founding Fathers, or a misuse of that philosophy? Wrestle with your answer.

54

THE ENVIRONMENTAL MOVEMENT

Origins, Progressive Era

Concern over the environment surfaced during the Progressive Reform Era, 1890 to 1920, when public awareness emerged that there were limits to our natural resources. For example, by 1897 lumber companies had stripped Michigan's forests of 97% of its white pine lumber. No one planted new seedlings. Two significant definitions emerged:

> *Conservation* called for the wise management of natural resources for continued efficient utilitarian purposes. Advocates were conservationists.
>
> *Preservation* called for the nonuse of nature's utopias, so they could help the human soul reconnect with nature. Advocates were preservationists. The nineteenth century urban park movement, such as building Central Park in New York City, was also driven by a desire to recreate "nature" in the city, giving to the beleaguered urbanite a soul-satisfying respite.

Against both approaches stood businesses who sought profitable exploitation now, let the future take care of itself. Two pivotal events illustrated the differences between these two approaches, the Hetch Hetchy controversy and the Ballinger-Pinchot controversy.

Hetch Hetchy

Hetch Hetchy is a valley inside Yosemite National Park. The city of San Francisco wanted to build a dam there on the Tuolumne River to obtain water and to provide hydroelectric power. John Muir and others fought it for years, to save the isolated, pristine valley. He called Hetch Hetchy "one of Nature's rarest and most precious mountain temples." Muir was a preservationist. One acquaintance said that Muir had "no social sense, with him, it is God and the rock where God put it and that is the end of the story." He even opposed killing scorpions. Muir viewed Yosemite as one of nature's cathedrals; his God was "the God of the mountains." But Muir was not as dogmatic as often depicted. He ultimately concluded that Yosemite should be open to tourists who could be respectful of nature's beauty. Come, look, be inspired, worship, pick up your trash, and leave. Muir would have supported the National Park Service's symbol to prevent wildfires, Smokey Bear. (No "the" in Smokey's official name.)

Initially denied access, the devastating 1906 earthquake and the accompanying fires increased sympathy for San Francisco's plight. In 1908 the Secretary of the Interior approved the flooding of Hetch Hetchy. Before final approval in 1913, the controversy educated the public in the subtle differences between conservation and preservation. Muir and his allies launched a five-year effort to stop the dam, the first major public lobbying effort over an environmental issue. One early supporter of Muir's position, Congressman William Kent of California, ended up favoring the dam. Why? Because he advocated municipal ownership of Hetch Hetchy, out of fear that the powerful Pacific Gas and Electric Corporation would gain ownership of it. This illustrates a trait of Progressive Era reforms. They sometimes contradicted one another, in this situation municipal ownership of municipal services versus conservation and preservation. San Francisco got the dam and the water, which today supplies 300 million gallons each day. Los Angeles did the same, secretly securing vast tracts of land east of the city and then building an aqueduct by 1913 that virtually emptied the Owens Valley of water. Local farmers were ruined, because not enough water remained to grow anything.

If an individual wants to become both rich and famous, figure out a way to cheaply distill sea water into drinking water. Engineers already know how, but the cost is too high. Invent a way to do it cheaply, then get in touch with me – we will be rich. Trust me, the demand will lead to lots of money.

The Ballinger-Pinchot Controversy

Gifford Pinchot, a very close friend of President Theodore Roosevelt, was our first scientifically trained forester, educated at the French National School of Forestry. In 1905 Roosevelt appointed Pinchot to be the head of the U.S. Forest Service, which was under the Department of Agriculture. Later, in the subsequent administration, serving under President William Howard Taft, Pinchot became involved in several bitter controversies with the Secretary of the Interior, Richard Ballinger, who, for one example, aided mining and lumber companies in gaining access to federal land in Alaska. Narrowly speaking, Ballinger had not committed any illegal acts, but Pinchot was outraged, and said so, repeatedly and publicly. (As a sidelight, to illustrate how difficult it is to shoehorn people into categories in history, Ballinger had opposed the construction of Hetch Hetchy Dam.) President Taft fired Pinchot, which contributed to the growing personal and political rift between Theodore Roosevelt and William Howard Taft, which would surface in the 1912 election, when they both ran for the presidency, splintering the Republican Party. The public simplified the complex issues in the controversy to the differences between Pinchot's managed use of natural resources, *conservation*, and Ballinger's endorsement of corporate *exploitation* of natural resources on federally owned land.

Progressive Era Conservation Legislation

In spite of these two controversies, the Progressive Era saw the enactment of many laws favorable to the environmental movement and to conservation. The federal government no longer simply dispensed federal lands cheaply and easily to private ownership. This represented a major change in the historic view of the purpose of federally owned land – to get settlers on it or to make it useful to business. Think of the rationale behind the Homestead Act of 1862 and the Transcontinental Railroad grants.

The Forest Reserve Act, 1891, actually Amendment 24 of the General Appropriations Act of 1891, authorized the president to set aside forest reserve lands and to establish a national system of forest administration. It also repealed the Timber Culture Act of 1873 and the Timber and Stone Act of 1878, both of which had helped to transfer land to logging corporations. Many state and municipal governments passed laws to clean up drinking water sources and to address sewage waste problems. Out West the Carey Act, 1894, authorized the president to grant each state up to one million acres for irrigation and reclamation. The 1902 Newlands Act, also called the National Reclamation Act, granted the proceeds from the sale of public land in 16 western states to fund irrigation projects. The Antiquities Act, 1906, authorized the president to create National Monuments and to set aside any land with historic or natural interest. The highlight of the Progressive era was President Theodore Roosevelt's White House Conservation Conference, 1908, chaired by Gifford Pinchot, to publicize conservation.

1920 to 1950

The thirty years following the First World War were quiet decades for environmentalism. The major environmental issue of the Twenties was the Teapot Dome scandal, involving the leasing of federal oil reserves at Teapot Dome, Wyoming, and Elk Hills, California, to private interests by Secretary of the Interior Albert Fall, who was later convicted of accepting bribes. While the New Deal had conservation overtones in many of its programs – Civilian Conservation Corps, Tennessee Valley Authority, Grand Coulee Dam, Dust Bowl challenge, Flood Control Act of 1936, etc., – the main focus of the New Deal legislation was always jobs.

Modern Environmentalism Emerges

As a set of ideas, the environmental movement that developed after 1960 added new features to conservation and preservation, such as

1.   an increased emphasis on the present
2.   an anti-materialism
3.   a decline in the belief that technology could solve all problems
4.   an awareness that in some ways technological improvements created new problems, such as the invention of disposable diapers

In the 1950s and 1960s environmentalism shifted from an elitist appreciation of the wilderness to a middle class concern over the "Quality of Life," one of several new concerns that became part of everyday life and politics. Environmentalism changed into a movement characterized by large organizations, whose members were mainly educated, middle class suburbanites. A growing number of people questioned our orgy of materialistic consumption, citing its high environmental costs. Included also was a fear of the consequences of technologically induced abundance, especially concerning the nuclear power industry. In 1958 the internationally recognized peace symbol first appeared in England at a rally against nuclear power and nuclear weapons. It combines the semaphore flag code for "N," two flags held at 45° downward, and for "D," two flags straight up and down, ND, "nuclear disarmament."

The Intellectual Stimulus

There were a few lonely voices speaking for the environment before 1900. In many respects, the European cultural and intellectual movement known as Romanticism found expression in the Hudson River School of art, which glorified the beauty of American landscapes. Henry David Thoreau's *Walden*, published in 1854, emphasized the serenity gained from communing with nature. Our ambassador to Italy, George Perkins Marsh, wrote *Man and Nature* in 1864, citing extensive deforestation as a primary factor weakening the Roman Empire. But by the 1950s progress, which included ignoring the consequences to the environment, had become almost a secular religion. American companies proclaimed, "Progress is our most important product," and "Better living through chemistry." Maybe. Maybe not.

By far the most significant intellectual stimulus to environmentalism was Rachel Carson's *Silent Spring*, 1962. She selected the title to describe a future spring when birds and their songs would no longer exist. Historian Stephen Fox called her book "The *Uncle Tom's Cabin* of modern environmentalism." Carson warned that "We are adding a new chapter and a new kind of havoc – the direct killing of birds, mammals, fishes, and indeed practically every form of wildlife by chemical insecticides indiscriminately sprayed on the land." (p. 85) She said insecticides should be relabeled "biocides." Americans faced the question of "whether any civilization can wage relentless war on life without destroying itself, and without losing the right to be called civilized." Over two hundred new pesticides were developed after the Second World War. Carson specifically targeted a widely-used pesticide, DDT, first created in 1943. DDT is so indestructible that fifty years later almost all older Americans still had traces of it in their bodies. *Silent Spring* spent 31 weeks on the *New York Times* best-seller list. A federal government career employee, Rachel Carson rose in the Department of Interior to become the editor-in-chief of its publications. She had previously written *Under the Sea-Wind* and *The Sea Around Us*, both well received by scholars and the public. The chemical industry spent $250,000 on a campaign to prove that she was a "hysterical fool" and to refute her charges. They failed. In bitter irony, she discovered a malignant lump in her breast; she died in 1964 at age 56.

Earlier, Vance Packard, in *The Waste Makers*, denounced our throwaway society and the planned obsolescence built into many products. Stewart Udall, *The Quiet Crisis*, 1963, addressed the belief that science and technology could solve all of our difficulties. He reintroduced the idea of scarcity and finite resources. He asserted that society faced a whole class of problems that technology could not solve. He suggested that it was necessary for modern man to give up some freedoms, many technology-based, to preserve our common areas, such as national parks. Individualism needed to be sacrificed, for every one could not "do their own thing" in a shared, increasingly crowded world. In *Small is Beautiful* economist E. F. Schumacher attacked uncontrolled material growth. Paul Ehrlich, in *The Population Bomb*, 1968, warned that population growth was dooming the planet.

Barry Commoner, in *The Closing Circle*, 1971, described many new environmental problems, such as how detergents continued to create suds as waste water tumbled down every stream in America, and how chemicals made you think your bed sheets hanging on the clothes line were whiter, when all they did was reflect sunlight better, due to a chemical coating. A biologist, he is credited with popularizing the term "ecology," the relationship between living organisms and their environment. Eco is Greek for "home," thus ecology is the study of our home, earth.

Several events in the West, due to water needs, surfaced in the 1950s and inundated Congress with tons of protest mail. The first was a proposal to partially flood the Grand Canyon, part of a plan to build a series of dams flooding 150 miles of the Colorado River. The mail was 80-1 against. The second was the Echo Dam project, a dam that would flood Dinosaur National Monument in northeast Utah and northwest Colorado. The public outcry stopped both efforts in Congress. The ruckus reintroduced to the public concepts that were part of John Muir's world – that there was "sacred space" and "profane space." Water shortages continue to plague the West. You will hear more about this issue in the future.

In 1965 the federal courts ruled that a conservation group, such as the Sierra Club, could legally bring a lawsuit to protect the public interest. Normally law suits must be started by an "injured" party. Now, the injured party could be the public. The issue in the law suit was the attempt by Con Ed, Consolidated Edison, the New York utility company, to build a power plant at Storm King Mountain in upstate New York on the scenic Hudson River.

Environmentalism moved to the forefront in national politics by 1970. All the traditional environmental organizations gained members during the 1960s, creating a reservoir of people and lobbyists ready to contact Congress over issues. Look at the following increases: National Wildlife Federation doubled to 540,000; Audubon Society doubled to 81,500; Wilderness Society doubled to 54,000; Sierra Club more than quintupled to 113,000. These newer members were more prone to activism, through contacting their Congressional representatives.

Pollution Headlines: 1960s to the 1980s

Isolated, unconnected events in the 1960s, 1970s, and 1980s constantly reminded everyone of environmental issues. These events dramatized the image of thoughtless insensitivity and a lack of concern on the part of government and business to an issue that was becoming increasingly important to a growing number of people. Each of the major environmental events showed the public one more new threat or new crisis. As examples:

1. New York City, a thermal air inversion in 1966, 80 people died. Earlier, in 1947 in Donora, Pennsylvania, a thermal inversion killed twenty and sickened six thousand. A thermal inversion happens when a layer of high cold air (which is heavy) traps warm air (lighter) underneath it, acting as a barrier, causing pollutants to build up within the warm air mass. Imagine chimney smoke and car exhaust fumes rising in the air about thirty feet, and staying there, and then slowly pushing downward because they could not rise.

2. Oil spills: In the English Channel in 1967 the tanker ship *Torrey Canyon* spilled 117,000 tons of crude oil. Off Santa Barbara millions of gallons hit the California coastline in 1969 when a platform oil well blew up.

3. New organizations spread the message that technology needed to be curtailed. Ralph Nader, in *Unsafe at Any Speed*, exposed the unsafe features of cars. His "Nader's Raiders" investigated and publicized other unsafe corporate products. Nader founded Public Citizen in 1971, an NGO, a **n**ongovernmental **o**rganization, that conducted research in the public interest, especially in regard to consumer safety and protection.

4. In Cleveland the Cuyahoga River caught fire, roaring five stories into the sky, burning several bridges and befuddling firefighters. Oil on the surface burned.

5. Lake Erie was declared to be dying in 1969 from a lack of oxygen, leading to speculation that in the future stinky green algae would cascade over Niagara Falls, ruining Niagara Falls as a honeymoon destination.

6. Controversies stewed over the impact on wildlife while oil companies built the Trans-Alaska pipeline, which finally opened in 1977.

7. A nuclear power plant meltdown at Three Mile Island in Pennsylvania happened after the release of a movie on the same theoretical event, *The China Syndrome*. The *China* in the title referred to a meltdown possibly going all the way through the earth to the other side. However, Three Mile Island was real, not a movie.

8. Lead-based paint, widely used until this time, was discovered to become poisonous as it grew old and deteriorated, especially presenting a danger to young children in poor neighborhoods, where landlords spent little on upkeep.

9. *Time* magazine skipped an individual for Man-of-the-Year in 1988 and instead called earth the "Planet of the Year."

10. In 1989 the tanker *Exxon Valdez* spilled approximately eleven million gallons of crude oil all over pristine Prince William Sound in Alaska.

11. Elsewhere, in Bhopal, India, toxic gas escaped from a pesticide factory, killing 2,500 and injuring over 200,000 in 1984. In Russia a leak from a nuclear power plant at Chernobyl exposed a large population to radioactivity in 1986, forcing 100,000 people to permanently move.

12. Problems continued to appear after the 1980s. The worst example was the water crisis in Flint, Michigan, in 2014-2016, which sickened those in Flint and, in a different way, television viewers across the country.

Is Government the Solution or Part of the Problem?

In the late 1970s public officials finally admitted what had been suspected for some time. A working class neighborhood near Niagara Falls, New York, had been built on top of a former canal, Love Canal, into which the Hooker Chemical Company dumped tons of chemical waste. This pollution led to birth defects and unusually high rates of cancer and deafness in the neighborhood's children. Several working-class women living in the area led the protest against Love Canal and emerged as knowledgeable opponents of the local, state, and federal governments. Their story exemplified the growing belief that governments were a major component of environmental problems. Here are excerpts from Lois Marie Gibbs' book, *Love Canal: My Story*.

"Almost everyone has heard about Love Canal, but not many people know what it is all about. The Love Canal story is about a thousand families who lived near the site of an abandoned toxic chemical waste dump. More important, it is a warning of what could happen in any American community. We have very little protection against the toxic chemical wastes that threaten to poison our water, our air, and our food. The federal and state governments have agreed to move away everyone who wants to move; but they didn't at first. We had to work to achieve that goal. Love Canal is the story of how government tends to solve a problem, and of how we, or-dinary citizens of the United States, can take control of our own lives by insisting that we be heard. . . .

Love Canal actually began for me in June 1978 with Mike Brown's articles in the *Niagara Falls Gazette*. . . . I decided I needed to do some investigating.

I went to my brother-in-law, Wayne Hadley, a biologist and, at the time, a professor at the State University of New York at Buffalo. I asked him to translate some of that jibberjabber in the articles into English. . . . I was really alarmed by his answer. Some of the chemicals, he said, can affect the nervous system.

The New York State Health Department held a public meeting in June 1978. It was the first one I attended. . . . (The) staff explained that they . . . wanted to take samples—of blood, air, and soil, as well as from sump pumps. They wanted to find out if there really was a problem. . . . No one would, or could, give us straight answers. . . . I was learning that you can't trust government to look out for your interests. If you insist to government officials strongly enough, they might do the right thing. The Niagara County Health Department and other government officials had known about . . . Love Canal for a long time but had ignored it. Maybe it was the state's fiscal deficits or the blizzard of 1977. Whatever the reason, it was ignored, and the public's health was thereby jeopardized."

(As a sidelight, a word of caution. Before you purchase a house at some point in the future, research the land-use history of the area. Your family's health depends upon it.)

Legislation and Accomplishments

What accomplishments could the environmentalists point to? There were many:

1. The major environmental organizations now had many lobbyists in Washington. They constantly kept the impact of environmental concerns before Congress.
2. Signed into law by President Nixon on January 1, 1970, the National Environmental Policy Act of 1969 established one of the largest federal gov-ernment agencies, the Environmental Protection Agency, the EPA. The law required Environmental Impact Statements, known as EIS, for all federally-funded construction projects.
3. Nixon's second major piece of legislation was the Endangered Species Act of 1973, protecting life, in a world that has seen many species disappear.

4. The third Nixon administration law was the Occupational Safety and Health Act, which created the Occupational Safety and Health Administration, OSHA, charged with protecting workers from a wide range of worksite hazards.

5. Our air and water is purer, thanks to the Clean Air Acts of 1963, 1965, 1970, and 1990; the Air Quality Control Act of 1967; the Clean Water Acts of 1960, 1972, and 1987; the Water Quality Acts of 1965 and 1970; the Solid Waste Act of 1965; the Water Pollution Control Act, 1972; the Wilderness Act, 1964; and the Coastal Zone Management Act, 1976.

6. In 1982 Congress passed what the *New York Times* referred to much later as "the most important environmental law that nobody has ever heard of" – the Coastal Barrier Resources Act of 1982, which has saved over 800 barrier areas from development. Briefly, it stated that if developers wanted to build at the seashore on storm prone barrier areas, they would do so without taxpayer expense – no federal funds for subsidized flood insurance and no federal funds to rebuild.

7. The federal government established the Superfund in 1980 to clean up toxic waste sites.

The Backlash Begins, In the 1970s

Great Accomplishments, but, there was a backlash. Why? As historian Joseph E. Taylor III stated, "Environmental battles are rarely just about saving nature – they are also about for whom it will be saved." Some Americans came to see the proponents of environmentalism as outside of or in conflict with traditional American values, such as the following:

> restraint rather than "go-getterism"
> a finite world rather than "the sky is the limit"
> shared property rather than individual property rights
> the community rather than the individual
> interconnectedness rather than self-reliance

Finally, the 1960s had been a great decade of economic growth and prosperity. The stalled economy between the 1970s and the 1990s undermined the argument that abundance had satiated all the American people and, therefore, "less was good."

The backlash appeared in different forms. The discovery of a tiny, hitherto unknown fish species, the "snail darter" held up construction of the much-needed Tellico Dam in Tennessee. Provisions of the Endangered Species Act delayed the project for two years. Congress finally resolved it by a specific law exempting the Tellico Dam from environmental laws. When Congress renewed the Endangered Species Act in 1978, it was weakened.

A "Sagebrush Rebellion" erupted in the western states, beginning in 1979 in Nevada, which is nicknamed the Sagebrush State. Westerners had always argued for more local control of federal lands. They echoed an earlier statement by Secretary of the Interior Richard Ballinger, part of the Progressive era's Ballinger-Pinchot controversy. *The New York Times* quoted him in 1910, "a greater obligation rests on the States than upon the General Government to inaugurate laws to prevent waste in the utilization of National resources." However, in 1976 Congress passed the Federal Land Policy and Management Act, stating that federally-owned land would *perpetually* remain under federal control. By the legal concept of eminent domain, the federal government owns all the land never sold. Since so much of the West is unproductive land, no individual or corporation ever purchased it, making the federal government the biggest landowner in many western states, over 90% of Alaska and 81% of Nevada. Other states range from Colorado's 36% to Utah's 66%. As the Bureau of Land Management and other federal agencies enforced more and more policies to protect the environment, Westerners felt as if they bore an unfair burden. After all, there was no federally-owned land in any of the original thirteen states, or in Texas, which had been an independent country. They demanded lifting all the restrictions on local control of natural resources. So, was the prime issue local control or exploitation? Depended upon whom you asked.

Many "Sagebrushers" were anti-Washington political conservatives who accompanied Ronald Reagan into Washington after the election of 1980. Reagan appointed James Watt as his Secretary of the Interior. Watt had founded the Mountain States Legal Foundation, an anti-environmental advocacy group. He frankly announced his plans to make federal resources accessible to private interests, environmental law or no law. Use, not preservation, was his motto. "We will mine more, drill more, cut more timber." The traditional environmental groups – Sierra Club, Wilderness Society, and the Audubon Society – exploded in anger. Eventually several public relations gaffes forced him to resign. The controversies over Watt also fueled the rise of radical environmentalists, such as those who chained themselves to trees to hinder logging operations. Earth First, Planet Drum, Clamshell Alliance, and U.S. Greens were some of the decentralized new radical environmental organizations.

Anne Burford (Anne Gorsuch when appointed), head of the EPA, the Environmental Protection Agency, announced to her startled employees upon assuming office that she intended to do all she could to negate the EPA's efforts and to abolish the EPA. She was eventually forced out of office, but her husband, Robert Burford, remained as the head of the BLM, the Bureau of Land Management. The BLM especially rankles Westerners; it manages 480,000,000 acres of federal land, almost all of it in the West. Rita Lavelle, who had served as a Consumer Affairs administrator under Reagan when he was governor of California, took the same negative approach as head of the Superfund. The Superfund, an agency in the EPA, is responsible for cleaning up toxic waste sites. Not much was cleaned up in these years. Conservation was not high on Reagan's priority list. As governor of California Reagan opposed expanding California's Redwood National Park, "A tree is a tree. How many more do you have to look at?" As for trees playing a positive role in maintaining the quality of the air we breathe, Reagan also said, "Trees cause more pollution than automobiles do."

The Delaney Clause, an amendment to the Pure Food and Drug Act, frustrates many who feel environmental laws go too far. Passed in 1958, it requires processed foods to show virtually no trace of carcinogenic pesticides. Back then researchers could identify the presence of pesticides in one part per million. Now it is one billion times better. For you weak mathematicians that number is one in a quintillion, one single drop of all the water in the five Great Lakes combined. Some standards seem impossibly high. (From John Steele Gordon, "The American Environment," *American Heritage*, 1993.)

International Efforts

Everywhere people face global changes caused by HIPPO – habitat destruction, invasive species, pollution, overpopulation, and overharvesting. Some scientists posit that half of all our plant and animal species could be gone by the end of the twenty-first century.

The Stockholm Conference in 1972 took the first step, creating the UN Environment Programme, staffed by nearly one thousand employees, and aimed at "the protection and improvement of the human environment." The United States took the lead in negotiating an international agreement to address ozone depletion in the 1987 Montreal *Protocol on Substances That Deplete the Ozone Layer*. However, the United States refused to endorse the treaties and declarations of the 1992 Rio de Janeiro "Earth Summit," which aimed at limiting carbon emissions globally, preserving forests, and protecting species. In the same vein, the United States also refused to sign the Kyoto Protocol of 1997, which generated worldwide plans for reducing global warming. It was signed by 178 nations.

The Challenge

One annual event reminds us all of our fragile earth, Earth Day. Earth Day originated in the minds of the staff of Senator Gaylord Nelson of Wisconsin. It enabled an anxious public to become involved. Now citizen activism characterized the environmental movement. In addition, the public came to view governmental agencies as driven more by private economic interests than by ecology concerns. Government was part of the problem rather than part of the solution.

Environmentalism had changed. It was more than just preserving the environment out of respect for Mother Nature or responsibly using natural resources. Now health issues to protect humans and the quality of life mattered more. Former Vice President Al Gore's film documentary, "*An Inconvenient Truth*," and his book, *An Inconvenient Truth:*

The Planetary Emergency of Global Warming and What We Can Do About It, published in 2006, pointed to the major worldwide challenge facing environmentalists. Worldwide, 97% of all scientists believe global warming is a problem, but political conservatives continue to doubt the reality of global warming. A Republican conservative from Oklahoma said in 2003, "With all of the hysteria, all of the fear, all of the phony science, could it be that man-made global warming is the greatest hoax ever perpetuated on the American people? It sure sounds like it."

Other concerns cloud environmental issues. Energy sources are necessary in our modern society. Which should we use? Also, what about our future ability to reproduce? Everywhere the average male's sperm count has declined by 50% in just fifty years. We daily produce tons of trash. Where do we put it? Pollution, health, and safety concerns lead many to say, NIMBY, "**n**ot **i**n **m**y **b**ack **y**ard." If not, where? What the world and the United States lack is an agreed-upon set of policies or philosophies toward the earth, energy use, and the environment. Maybe it will come in your lifetime.

55

THE SOCIAL BARGAIN: THE NEXT CHALLENGE

The Long View: War and Industrialization

It is easy to view the twentieth century as a century of war and of the full impact of industrialization. The years from 1914 to 1991, the real twentieth century, saw wars and a struggle with fascism and communism that made it easier – perhaps even possible – for the United States to cope with a wide array of domestic social problems. Mobilization for global conflict and reacting to the impact of industrialization led to a "social bargain" that effectively modernized and democratized traditional American institutions.

Taking the long view, the long term effects of industrialization brought capitalist cycles of boom and bust, which generated demands for governmental intervention and management of the economy. The emergence of a mass urban working class produced what was called "the social problem," the urban poor. The presence of the poor in large numbers, and the fear among low class workers of falling into the ranks of the unemployed, led to demands for social "safety nets" of labor laws, unemployment insurance, retirement income, health care, and welfare.

Any discussion of history encourages counterfactual history, plugging "What if" questions into analyzing past events. Some historians argue that if economic "safety nets" had not been created, there likely would have been widespread social turmoil or even political revolutions. Of course, this is only educated speculation. However, it is true that any individual always has two potential responses to a societal crisis, especially an economic downturn. You can blame yourself for where you are in the economic pecking order, or you can blame those above you, pick up a gun, and start shooting. Labor unrest, inspired by perceptions that the capitalist system was grossly unfair, such as the Great Railroad strike of 1877, the Homestead strike of 1892, the Pullman strike of 1894, the Bonus Army march in 1932, and the sit-down strikes of the 1930s – raised fears that a "revolution" was coming. Revolutions in other countries happened when those who maintained order in that society, the police and the military, shifted their loyalty away from the principles espoused by the upper class and government leaders and instead identified with the misery of their brothers and sisters in the lower classes. The United States never reached that point. But, sometimes social tension festered.

Industrial societies became much more occupationally and socially stratified with the arrival of factories and working class neighborhoods. In the early twentieth century urban sociologists developed the concentric zone theory to describe the clear zones of wealth and status that extended out from the city's downtown: the central business district shopping area, the poor low class neighborhoods, the working class neighborhoods, the middle class neighborhoods, and, finally, the wealthy homes far from the urban core. By the early twentieth century, there were fewer mixed-class, urban neighborhoods. Previously, mixed-class neighborhoods had been more typical. Describe yourself and your neighbors in five words – note the economic and social class similarities. This physical separation by class occurred while technology was integrating and linking everyone – by roads, by telephones, by television, by the Internet, by computers, by cell phones, and on and on. These two forces, one integrating and one separating, generated a need for new forms of **National Identity** and cohesion. The older forms of National Identity and cohesion were ethnicity, religion, and a shared heritage or history. However, these no longer provided sufficient cohesiveness and National Identity.

Changes in Four Areas – The Social Bargain

Seventy-five years of global engagement in wars and the adjustment to industrialization produced changes in four domestic areas – the strength of the national government; economic management; social equity and welfare; and National Identity. In short, industrialization and the threat or actuality of war forced a "social bargain," but it was an accidental one, one created without a national consensus on why or what was created. In the words from *Alice in Wonderland*, our modern society just "grewed and grewed."

The Strength of the National Government

The federal government's powers grew at the expense of the states. The Department of Homeland Security is just the latest example. Historically the safety of American citizens primarily resided in the hands of the states and the creations of the state government: sheriff's department, state police, county police, and city police. The number of FBI agents is actually very small, about 15,000, and their responsibilities were limited by law. All this changed during the twentieth century as the powers of the federal government grew.

Within the federal government greater power and influence accrued to the executive branch at the expense of the other two, Congress and the federal courts. The executive branch muscled its way into the state responsibility to maintain public safety for its citizens. Look at the law enforcement areas into which the federal government moved in the past one hundred years – airport security, Homeland Security, border patrol, immigration control, FBI, CIA, DEA, drugs, and anti-terrorism. Add to this list President Eisenhower's warning of the increased influence of the "military-industrial complex." All these efforts to adjust to war and the effects of industrialization collided with the traditional twin pillars of the American political system – individualism and limited government – that had, and have, always imposed considerable constraints on **National Identity** and cohesion. Think of the arguments by state governments against federal laws and judicial decisions ending segregation. After the ending of the Cold War, these two pillars, individualism and limited government, reemerged as powerful political factors.

Economic Management

The challenges of wars – First, Second, and Cold – and the Great Depression made it politically necessary for the federal government to manage labor and capital in pursuit of maximum economic output. Beginning with Progressivism and the New Deal, this became a permanent feature of the federal government. It was a managed peace to avoid class warfare, brokered by the federal government through maximum hour and minimum wage laws, the National Labor Relations Board, NLRB, the Federal Reserve, the Full Employment Act of 1946, safety laws for the workplace, the Occupational, Safety and Health Administration, OSHA, and Keynesian management of the economy. Government subsidizing of research in atomic energy, aeronautics, and space all dramatically spurred the growth of new industries. Even the building of the Interstate Highway System, the space race, and educational funding, such as the National Defense Education Act, were primarily justified as defense measures. The ability to justify local and federal governmental support for technological innovation and industrial development will likely face future opposition because the rationale for it will decline. While the impact of corporate business decisions is felt in the local economy, the thinking of corporate management tends to be wider, even international. As internationalization of the economy increases, the government's capability to intervene in or to manage the economy will likely weaken.

Modern capitalism no longer resembles the description found in older economic textbooks. In theory, investors purchased stock in a company, followed the activities of the company, and controlled the decisions of the company executives through voting as stockholders at the annual meeting. Not now. The present is not what it used to be. Now company executives frequently use retained earnings, not invested funds. Thus, they are not as responsible to investors for their actions. Errant managers can also easily escape punishment from stockholders. There are just too many stockholders to rally support for changes, and stocks are traded so frequently that the long-term shareholder is rare. The average share of stock is now held for only nine months. Pension or hedge fund management companies, primarily interested in either quick or dependable returns, now manage or own most stocks. This means that corporate managers rarely face discipline and, therefore, answer only to themselves, which frequently includes a well-paid, pliant board of directors. What this will mean for the future of capitalism is still to be determined.

As a further complication, international corporations are capable of avoiding national governmental regulations. International corporations have become too large to police themselves; some companies have 300,000 employees. Finally, to what nation's values, if any, would an international corporation adhere? Why should it? What this means for the future of capitalism is still to be determined.

Equity, Social Class, Income Differential, and Quality of Life

Numerous laws tried to make Americans more equal in terms of race, gender, and income. For example – the GI Bill, the integration of the armed forces, the Civil Rights Act of 1964, the Voting Rights Act of 1965, the Fair Housing Act of 1968, and the 1972 Title IX amendments were all changes toward equality. Note, toward equality, we are not there; we have not arrived. Barack Obama, in his book, *The Audacity of Hope*, 2006, urged Americans to view racial issues "on a split screen" to permit us "to maintain in our sights the kind of America that we want while looking squarely at America as it is."

American capitalists met the Cold War threat of the attraction of a communist "workers' paradise" by offering health benefits, sufficient wages for adequate housing, full employment, and pensions. Pensions are now disappearing. Only about 15% of the top corporations still have defined benefit pensions, meaning that you are guaranteed an income for retirement. That percentage will decrease in the future. Most companies are shifting their health benefit costs on to their employees. Few Americans are satisfied with the certainty of their future income. They are not happily looking forward to retirement.

Financial experts are advising everyone to save $14,000 to $28,000 each year, beginning with your first year of employment, to create a pool of almost one million dollars for retirement. How does one do that? Every financial advisor suggests putting some retirement investments into the stock market. Will the stock market behave the same way in the future as it has in the past, growing about 8% per year on average, with 50-60% of the American people in it, as compared to previous percentages under 5%? We shall see. You are betting your retirement income on it. It is an unknown, a big unknown.

What does scientific biological research teach us about many of the political and economic assumptions that underlie much of our political debate? Is man an economic animal, primarily motivated by self-interest? Does the pursuit of individual self-interest add up to what is best for society as a whole? In *The Social Conquest of Earth*, Harvard scientist Edward O. Wilson asserted that "groups of altruists in prehistoric times prevailed over groups of individuals in selfish disarray. Our species is not *Homo oeconomicus*. At the end of the day, it emerges as something more complicated and interesting."

"Nevertheless, an iron rule exists in genetic social evolution. It is that selfish individuals beat altruistic individuals, while groups of altruists beat groups of selfish individuals. The victory can never be complete; the balance of selection pressures cannot move to either extreme. If individual selection were to dominate, societies would dissolve. If group selection were to dominate, human groups would come to resemble ant colonies."

The most advanced modern societies "that do best for their citizens in quality of life, from education and medical care to crime control and collective self-esteem, also have the lowest income differential between the wealthiest and poorest citizens. Among twenty-three of the world's wealthiest countries and individual U.S. states, according to an analysis in 2009 by Richard Wilkinson and Kate Pickett, Japan, the Nordic countries, (Norway, Sweden, Denmark, and Finland) and the U.S. state of New Hampshire have both the narrowest wealth differential and the highest average quality of life. At the bottom are the United Kingdom, Portugal, and the remainder of the United States." (quotes from Edward O. Wilson, *The Social Conquest of Earth*, pp. 251, 243, 250.)

National Identity and Cohesion

In the early twentieth century, Americans overcame deep sectional and ethnic centrifugal tendencies in American society. In essence, the twentieth century integrated the West and the South into the national economy and society and integrated the previous outsider groups – Catholics, Jews, immigrants, and blacks. With the end of the Cold War, now what? Are the Blue State – Red State divisions semi-permanent? Ask any member of a minority group if they are satisfied with their piece of the American pie. Almost all laws passed by Congress have an expiration date. They must be renewed. The Voting Rights Act of 1965, labeled by historian Gary May as "probably the most important piece of legislation passed in the Twentieth Century," was renewed five times since 1965, most recently in 2006. However, the Supreme Court weakened it in 2013 in *Shelby County v. Holder*, leading many states to enact stricter voter identification laws, in spite of research that found less than a handful of these violations over several decades, in the entire country.

The Demise of Cohesiveness

What holds Americans together as a people? Is multiculturalism a threat to unity? Or, is it sometimes only a commercially-oriented promotion? The grocery stores make a fuss over Cinco de Mayo, May 5, pushing sales of Mexican food. Any Mexican will tell you that September 16, Independence Day, is far more significant.

President Woodrow Wilson opposed emphasizing our different identities. He believed the key to America was our shared *political* ideals. Addressing the debate over multiculturalism in the 1990s, historian Hans Vought summarized Wilson's position. "We can abandon all hope of cultural cohesiveness, and either Balkanize our society or water down our ideals to meaninglessness. Or we can try to follow the middle road that Wilson attempted to lay down: teaching immigrants what it means to be Americans, but at the same time learning and adopting from them what their cultures have to offer." (Hans Vought, "Division and Reunion: Woodrow Wilson, Immigration, and the Myth of American Unity," *Journal of American Ethnic History*, Spring, 1994, p. 45.)

Class division and class conflict are likely to re-emerge with the communist system no longer around as a yardstick against which to measure the position, possibilities, and promise available for our working class. In the early Cold War years every high school social studies textbook had charts comparing how long an American worker labored to afford a specific item – a car, a loaf of bread, a pound of butter, a television set – compared to their Russian communist counterpart. Americans were always much better off, needing much less working time. However, neither rent nor medical costs were ever compared. Russians outdid us in both areas, rents were frozen at 4% of your income and medical care was free, as was medical education. Both communism and the comparisons are gone. In 2015, 11.25 million American households spent over 50% of their monthly income on rent and other housing expenses, such as utilities. The current standard of comparison to judge the lot of our workers now has shifted to comparisons with workers in LDCs, Less Developed Countries, also called Third World countries. Recent immigrants boast how great the United States is, and send billions of dollars back to their families overseas, just as immigrants did in the nineteenth century. For Mexico, it is the largest component in their economy, exceeding the nation's income from any exported crop or product. Class conflict could very well lead to a weakening of our political commitment to social welfare in our society. How many times have you heard that poor immigrants are willing to take low-income jobs? Is that a justification for retaining low-income jobs? The average wage per hour is $14. Multiply $14 times 40 hours times 52 weeks – $29,120. Not much, really, as take-home pay after deductions. What has happened in the last twenty to thirty years to the gap between the income of the average worker and the average CEO? In 2015 it was 382 times larger. What was it in the middle of the Cold War? It was in the teens. What does the average American think about this?

Our economic system functions under the theories of capitalism. The father of capitalism was the Scottish philosopher Adam Smith, who set forth capitalism's basic premises in *The Wealth of Nations,* 1776. The principles are simple: take risks, work hard, save your money, invest it, enjoy the fruits of your labor. You as an individual are primarily responsible for yourself and your loved ones. Life under capitalism can range from very good to very harsh for individuals. In 2016 an estimated 45,000,000 Americans lived below the poverty line. There is no room for complaining; everyone knows the rules. You deserve to be where you find yourself. However, earlier Adam Smith had written another book, which he considered his finest work, *The Theory of Moral Sentiments*, 1759, in which he stated, "Society . . . cannot exist among those who are at all times ready to hurt and injure one another . . . . Justice is the main pillar that upholds the whole edifice. If it is removed, the great, the immense fabric of human society . . . must in a moment crumble into atoms." As long as the results of capitalism seem fair and just to *all* those under it, capitalism will remain secure. To survive *politically* our economic system of capitalism must continue to be seen as fair and just.

As democracy and capitalism spread throughout the world, our distinctiveness as a "free" people will diminish. A foreign ambassador once observed, "The United States is not a country. It is a container of individuals." (After pausing, he added, "Until you attack them.") As the United States moves on the world stage from an age of geopolitics to one of geoeconomics, Americans will lose their distinctiveness and possibly, therefore, see their common unique **American Identity** erode.

Our complex domestic problems no longer face the need for some, or any, clear policy in the face of the totalitarian threat or attraction of fascism or communism for American workers. Thus, American politicians have not faced many problems. Each election brings promises of a new policy. What follows is usually little or nothing.

> Look at our arguments over health care – Yet health care costs take 1/6 of our income. And, the average working couple retiring today will receive in Medicare benefits three times the total amount they paid into the system in payroll taxes during all the years they worked. Obviously, this cannot continue.
>
> Look at the absence of a policy towards paid national maternity leave for women following childbirth. Only eight countries in the world have no policy. The United States is the only industrialized nation on the list.
>
> Look at our drug policy – Is the "War on Drugs" a success? Hardly! Our society has not decided if addiction is a crime or an illness.
>
> Look at our underage drinking policy – Thirty percent of all alcohol sold goes to underage drinkers.
>
> Look at our energy policy – Does the United States have a comprehensive approach?

> Look at our transportation system – Our dependence upon cars will only worsen travel conditions.
>
> Look at our municipal services infrastructure and our transportation infrastructure – They all need to be updated.
>
> Look at our immigration policy – Both the present and the future are unclear.
>
> Look at the fears many people have as they look towards the financial aspects of retirement. Financial advisors receive payment while the client takes the risk. In essence, the financial advisor is only a salesperson, read the fine print. You could follow all the rules and advice and end up with very little for your retirement.

There is not much effective political or presidential or Congressional leadership on these issues. Moreover, underlying ideological, political, class, sectional, racial, ethnic, and gender perspectives seem to preclude agreement on any policy at all. If you ask any politician or average citizen what are the five most important issues facing this country, you will get different lists. In addition, the issues will be in different order, if they even have the same issues on any two lists. The problem is not just Washington, D.C.; it is all of us. As soon as any legislature, Congress or state, passes a law on any of these topics, one hears cries of "scrap it, change it, repeal it."

The market economy is creating an increasingly unfair society for most of us. Between 1959 and 2007 consumer debt jumped from 16% to 24% of disposable personal income; mortgage debt jumped from 54% to 140% of disposable personal income (what is left to spend after taxes). Between 1979 and 2007, before the recession of 2008 hit:

> the poorest 20% saw their incomes fall 12%
> the middle 60% saw almost no change in their income
> the top 10% saw their incomes rise by 45%
> the top 5% saw their incomes rise 68%
> the top 1% saw their incomes rise 135%
> the top 1/10 of one percent saw their incomes rise by 226%

As of 2017, few individuals in the bottom 80% had recovered to their 2007 level. The average income, adjusted for inflation, for 90% of the American people is the same as it was in 1966, based on data from the IRS, the Internal Revenue Service. In short, 90% do NOT FEEL as if they are getting ahead and believe they face an uncertain future. They have good reason to so believe. Data from the Federal Reserve Board indicates that the median household wealth headed by a 65-year-old is 20 times that of the 35-year-old headed household. Thirty years ago, the gap was less, 8 times. From 1941 to

2000 the average annual growth rate for the American economy was 3.5%. From 2000 to 2017 the American economy reached this "average" only one year.

By 2014 total student loan debt exceeded credit card debt. Because student loans come from the federal government, declaring bankruptcy does not erase them. That debt follows you forever. How will struggling college graduates, and those who do not graduate, pay it back while beginning their careers? This is a time bomb waiting to happen. And, heaven forbid that a college graduate dies before paying back the debt. His or her heirs receive forgiveness for the debt, BUT, the Internal Revenue Service, the IRS, considers that forgiven amount to be taxable income. Now, the heirs owe taxes on income they do not possess, and never did!

From media commentators Americans often hear complaints about how unfair graduated tax rates are. Why not convert to a federal flat tax? It resonates as a political issue; everyone pays the same rate, true democracy. But, look back at periods of sustained economic growth in our history. The tax rates were high for the upper end. The economy's growth rate was independent of the existence of high tax rates. High tax rates did not, do not, and will not prevent prosperity. However, attacking them has great political appeal. But, isn't a federal flat tax more fair? Not really. Any economist will tell you that when federal, state, and local taxes are added together, the average poor, middle, and upper class person pays, in taxes, about one-third of their income that they spend. Note, what they spend, not what is earned. Wealthier people spend a smaller percentage of their income than the middle class, which spends a smaller percentage than the poor.

The "Social Bargain" Falls Apart
What might be the long-range impact of these trends on our **National Identity**, our cohesiveness as a people? The jury is still out.

Some of the information and conceptual framework for this chapter is from an article by Daniel Deudney and G. John Ikenberry in *Current History*, "America After the Long War," November 1995, pp. 364-369.

56

AMERICA AS HYPERPOWER, 1992 TO 2016

The End of the Cold War

With the 1989 "velvet revolution" in Czechoslovakia (a non-violent revolution) and the collapse of the Soviet Union after 1991, democracy swept over the former Soviet Eastern European satellites. The United States gained a new status, what a French journalist nicknamed in 1999, "hyperpower," a level above superpower status. The emergence of democracies and market economies in the former Soviet satellites, Latin America, and even South Africa with Nelson Mandela, seemed to promise a new age of prosperity, peace, and global freedom. American conservative Francis Fukuyama advanced the argument in *The End of History and the Last Man*, published in 1992, that because history can be defined as the story of competing ideas, the collapse of the Soviet Union meant that authoritarian communism as a political system and socialism as an economic system were done, gone forever. Now all nations would become liberal democracies with capitalist economies. The First Gulf War, 1990-1991, seemed to fulfill Woodrow Wilson's Treaty of Versailles vision of how the concept of collective security would operate to maintain world peace through the League of Nations. The whole world would become more peaceful, more democratic, and more capitalistic. The United States won; our system triumphed. The world would become like us! The "American Century" would stretch into the future even further. Henry Luce, the founder of *Time*, *Life*, and *Fortune* magazines, created the phrase "American Century" in an editorial in *Life* magazine in February, 1941, before the U.S. entered the Second World War. He urged the American people and government to use their power to transform the world, remaking it to conform to American principles, to the benefit of mankind. With the end of the Cold War, that goal was achievable.

Why Did It Not Last?

In an odd way, the Cold War and the Cold War alliances had imposed order upon the world. Historian John Lewis Gaddis renamed the Cold War as "the Long Peace." It was, in many ways, especially in comparison to the first half of the twentieth century. Its end allowed submerged local disputes to reemerge and new forces to arrive, forces that divided people. In many areas societies fragmented. Nationalism, ethnic rivalries, tribal hatreds, secessionist movements, and "ethnic cleansing" ended up making the world more violent than during the Cold War. For the year 1993, the *New York Times* counted 48 such conflicts, such as the Serbs, Croats, and Muslims in the former Yugoslavia, Sunni and Shiite Muslims and Kurds in the Middle East, and, later, Coptic Christians in Egypt.

The world seemed to shrink. A communications revolution consisting of computers, the Internet, cell phones, and cable and satellite television brought the world together. Nothing was local. It was now impossible for governments to control the flow of information. Or, the spread of diseases like AIDS or Ebola. The globalization of trade led to the rise of transnational corporations that exploited cheap labor in developing countries for the international market. Corporations outsourced American jobs to cheaper labor markets, causing unemployment in some industries and reducing the number of workers in traditional labor unions. Having the 2012 U.S. Olympic Team's clothing made in China did not sit well with either the American people or American politicians. One major manufacturer of sneakers moved their operations to four different countries in four years, reducing labor costs each year. By the mid-1990s Coca-Cola sold four out of every five of their bottles or cans outside the United States. The typical household in the world consumes 1.4 bottles or cans of Coca-Cola each day. Coca-Cola is one of the two most widely recognized words or phrases in the world. OK is the other one.

Even a product labeled "Made in USA" may not be. The accepted definition of "Made in USA" is that either 75% of it was made here or it was finished here. Many women's shoes are imported from abroad, without the heels, which are added here, and then the shoe is stamped "Made in USA." Maybe. Maybe not. Clothing manufacturing is a notorious sweatshop industry; it always has been. American sports paraphernalia flooded the world. NBA, MLB, and NFL logos were everywhere, although the translation sometimes lost something. The NBA Chicago Bulls became the "Chicago Oxen" in China. Trade agreements had become a major component of diplomacy, for example, the Bill Clinton administration concluded more than 300 trade agreements with foreign countries. Donald Trump's campaign for the presidency in 2016 promised to renegotiate all of them.

Trade seemed to tie the world closer together. Or, did it? Not everyone was pleased by the global market. In Europe the flood of American products is termed

"Americanization" and provokes angry reactions. The Disneyland built outside Paris had many opponents. France's Cultural Minister called it a "cultural Chernobyl" for France, a reference to the Soviet Union's nuclear disaster. In many respects NAFTA, the North American Free Trade Agreement between Canada, Mexico, and the United States, benefited us the most, with North America becoming an enlargement of the American domestic market. Before NAFTA, young girls in Mexico could not purchase a Barbie doll; the Mexican doll market was protected against foreign competitors. Now many Mexican toy companies are out of business. The ultimate irony is that Taco Bell is successfully operating in Mexico City. The U.S. gained the most from NAFTA. During the first seven months of 2013 the U.S. sold $130.3 billion worth of exports to Mexico; by comparison, the U.S. sold $63.8 billion to China.

The ubiquity of American culture angered more than the French. In the Middle East Islamic fundamentalists railed against modernization and American popular culture, ironically using modern communications devices to plot against America through cell phones, computers, and the Internet. Islamic critics differentiate between "modernization," the incorporation of modern technology into their society, and "Westernization," the incorporation of Western culture, which conflicts with traditional Islamic teachings. Political Scientist Benjamin Barber summarized it in his book as *Jihad vs. McWorld.*

All of this means what for the future? Will the Cold War conflicts be replaced by economic conflicts between what is known in the United Nations as the South versus the North? These terms come from the fact that the Northern Hemisphere countries tend to be more prosperous. Will the future bring massive migration to the more prosperous countries? Look at the weekly Mediterranean Sea disasters for "boat people" fleeing Africa to get to Europe for a chance, just a chance, to live at a low standard of living. Would you risk your life in the hope that you could get a job driving a truck or sweeping a floor? They do. Will people in the "have-not" nations continue to quietly accept their "have-not" status? We shall see. The Third World nations, now often referred to as LDCs, Less Developed Countries, are constantly falling further and further behind the advanced nations. In 1850 the national income gap between the "haves" and the "have-nots" was a multiple of five, but by 1970, it was fourteen. At what point does their increasing relative poverty make them say, "Enough, we are coming after you as economic terrorists." Would it not be wiser, and safer, for the advanced countries to improve Third World economies?

America's Position

The Basketball Hall of Fame seven-foot superstar, Wilt Chamberlain, said once, "Nobody loves Goliath." Our economy is 40% larger than the next highest country. Our defense spending is more than the next six combined; our military is more powerful than the next twelve combined. In 2013 the figures for spending on weapons for the top five countries were as follows: United States, $640 billion; China, $188 billion; Russia, $88 billion; Saudi Arabia, $67 billion, and France $61 billion. The world's total was $1.8 trillion, one-third of it was ours. Our "soft power" is immense, because of the appeal everywhere of American products, lifestyle, culture, and values.

The U.S. Faces Two Choices
One possible policy focus would be to reshape the world forcefully by imposing our democracy and our market capitalism upon the rest of the world by hindering or preventing the rise of new rivals seeking to achieve regional power status – countries such as India, Pakistan, Iran, China, Brazil, Indonesia, South Africa, Nigeria, etc. In other words, go it alone. However, while the United States is the most powerful nation on the face of the globe, that does not mean that the United States is powerful everywhere on the globe at all times. It is a big world. Moreover, our own goals sometimes conflict. For example, while the United States supports the spread of human rights, our insistence on ending Chinese violations might lead to a reaction by China that interferes with our desire for low priced trade goods.

Another possible policy focus would be to accept that the world is still a dangerous place, and that many local conflicts will continue to pop up around the world. The United States should monitor them, but not get involved unless there are clear objectives and a definitive timetable to withdraw, unlike Vietnam. You may call this approach either of two names, either the Vietnam Syndrome, or the Powell Doctrine, from General Colin Powell when he was the Chairman of the Joint Chiefs of Staff. During his administration, President Bill Clinton dispatched military forces 84 times in eight years. Was this the new approach?

Which Approach Works – When and Where?
In the Middle East the U.S. verbally supported the "Arab Spring" movements, populist efforts to bring democracy, which may in the long run end up making life more difficult for us and for our ally, Israel. But, this is just one of a multitude of dilemmas the United States, and everyone else, faces in the Middle East. How will anyone ever resolve the Gordian Knot of areas such as the West Bank and the Gaza Strip? These areas have changed ownership, or rather control, frequently through warfare. Now Hamas, a political party, which is less of a political party and more of a militant movement, controls Gaza, challenging the government of Palestine. Gaza, part of Palestine, is no longer controlled by the Palestinian government. After winning the 1967 Six-Day War, Israeli settlers moved into the West Bank (of the Jordan River), an area east of Israel to the Dead Sea and the border of Jordan. The international community, including the United Nations and the International Court of Justice, consider the West Bank to be occupied territory, not legally part of Israel. To which country *should* Palestine and/or the West

Bank belong? Palestinian refugees, such as Fawaz Turki, writing over sixty-five years ago, still see Israel as their homeland, a land to which "a people (Jews) had come, a foreign community of colonizers, aided by a Western world in a hurry to rid itself of guilt and shame (for the Holocaust), demanding independence from history, from heaven, and from us." Once president of Egypt, Gamal Abdel Nasser asked why the United States and the European countries did not punish Germany by giving Jews a part of Germany to establish their own country after the Holocaust. From the Jewish side, the response was that Israel was holy ground, given to the Jews by God. Try to think of a solution to that dilemma that satisfies everyone. What about the growth of nuclear weapons in the Middle East? How does that change our policies? Was the incident in 2012 at Benghazi, Libya, when a mob attacked our embassy, a harbinger of things to come?

What, in Islamic countries, does the average person or even leader know about the United States? Many Americans believe that religiously inspired acts of humanitarian aid are a side of American society that should be a more visible part of our foreign policy, sometimes referred to as humanitarian efforts or the "softer" side of our foreign policy. In the Middle East one of our allies is the oil-rich nation of Saudi Arabia. Thus, it makes sense that the United States and our humanitarian aid efforts are well received. Read the following excerpts from a 10th grade Saudi history textbook that every student is required to use. This government written textbook warns students to be suspicious of Westerners. In a brief passage the textbook assesses the sorry state of Western Civilization.

"The Western civilization, which has lost the meaning of spirituality, finds itself in its turn on the verge of an abyss. It is a civilization on the way to dissolution and extinction."

"The real goal pursued by the orientalists (meaning Westerners) through their study of Islamic culture in its various stages is shaking Islam's highest values in the minds of its sons, on the one hand, and affirming the superiority and power of Western civilization, on the other hand. For this end they strive to present any call for holding Islam as a reactionary and backward one. They also strive to defeat the Muslims spiritually and intellectually, by eliminating the spirit of pride in Islam in the Muslim's heart and by dissolving his Islamic personality, so that he will become a stranger in his own society, secular in his way of thinking and a Westerner in his orientation."

"In the field of medical care, hospitals and clinics have been spread in the Muslim countries. They have been provided with doctors who use the medical profession as a guise behind which they hide their true intentions. One of the female Christianizers said, while giving advice to a doctor who was going on a Christianization mission: 'You must seize these opportunities to reach Muslims' ears and hearts and repeat the Gospels to them. Beware not to miss the opportunity of medical practice in the clinics and hospitals, for it is the most precious one ever of (all) these opportunities.'"

(These quotes are from *History Lessons, How Textbooks from Around the World Portray U.S. History*, by Dana Lindaman and Kyle Ward, pp. 371, 368, 369.)

Each year the entire Arab world translates only about 350 Western books into Arabic, hardly sufficient to grasp the nuances of Western society. But, the West translates about the same number of books from Arabic into English each year. How well can we understand one another? A poll in Jordan, a neighbor of Israel, revealed that 50% of the population believed that American Jews (only 3% of America's population) control American foreign policy. Misunderstandings abound on all sides.

The United States is not greatly loved throughout much of Latin America. In Haiti, the country's military overthrew a popularly elected government in 1991. Angry mobs on the docks forced an American warship to leave. So much for a show of American force there. Perhaps past events influenced our reception. One Venezuelan scholar added up all the occasions when the United States intervened militarily somewhere in Latin America – 150 times. That Venezuelan scholar, Fernando Báez, sees the United States as a country that "has been hijacked by a political class with a military vocation that long ago surrendered to corporate interests that destroy the environment and manipulate the politics of entire continents, having given in to the commercialization of freedom rather than the freedom of commerce." *How They See Us: Meditations on America*, edited by James Atlas, Atlas & Co., New York, 2010. He is not alone in holding this point of view.

The late communist leader of China, Mao Zedong, once called the United States a "paper tiger" because the U.S. did not use our atomic bombs. When should one be used? Having the ability to blow up the entire world nine times still does not enable us to impose our will everywhere in the world, in spite of the fact that the U.S. could completely destroy that part of the world. Frustrating!

One great issue in the decade of the 1990s was Serbia and "ethnic cleansing" in the former Balkan country of Yugoslavia. Finally, after three years of inaction, in 1995, the United States and NATO acted in the Balkans, forcing a peace, called by one journalist "an imperfect peace to a very imperfect part of the world after an unusually cruel war." The policy change was mainly due to the forceful personality of the new Secretary of State, Madeleine Albright, our first female Secretary of State. It flared up again in 1997 when Kosovo, with an overwhelming majority Muslim population, tried to win its independence from Serbia. Serbian military actions were cruel, extending to ethnic cleansing. Arab Muslim countries offered no aid to their fellow Muslims. Israel sent medical and humanitarian aid. Israel said, "We have seen this before. We Jews suffered from this under Hitler." Serbia limited their attacks on the theory that only "a village a day keeps NATO away." Albright forced the Bill Clinton administration to act, along with NATO. It was a new war, a high tech war. American B-2 Stealth bombers delivered pinpoint bombs on Serbian targets. Finally, the Serb leader, Slobodan Milosevic, conceded. He was later put on trial for war crimes at The Hague by an international United Nations tribunal. He died shortly afterwards, before the trial ended.

Two situations in Africa aroused the public in the 1990s, but not enough to endorse extensive or heavy involvement. The horrible events in Rwanda in Africa in 1994 brought no response from the United States or from Europe. The United States, and other countries, looked the other way when ethnic cleansing took place, what one writer called "the fastest, most efficient, killing spree of the twentieth century." The vengeful Hutu tribe murdered an estimated 800,000 rival Tutsis, usually in machete attacks, also cutting off the hands of children and letting them live. In the previous year, 1993, Somalia, in East Africa, was best described as a humanitarian disaster. UN and U.S. troops were unable to protect any one or any side in a country in which the government literally evaporated. When warlord soldiers dragged the dead bodies of American peacekeepers through the streets, the U.S. opted for immediate withdrawal.

Terrorist attacks hit New York City's World Trade Center in 1993, a U.S. base in Saudi Arabia in 1996, our embassies in Kenya and Tanzania in 1998, and the destroyer USS Cole in the Persian Gulf in 2000. No decade during the Cold War matched this one for isolated "incidents" around the world. Later, in 2015 a husband and wife team massacred fourteen in San Bernardino, California, shortly after the world witnessed another attack in Paris. The next year brought a mass killing at a nightclub in Orlando, Florida.

The Bush Administration

The George W. Bush administration, elected in 2000, adopted the first approach, go it alone. During the presidential campaign Bush said, "We don't need to have the 82nd Airborne escorting kids to kindergarten" in the Balkans. His National Security Adviser and later Secretary of State, Condoleezza Rice, said that the United States would no longer be the world's 911, referring to the emergency telephone number. Two forceful personalities, Secretary of Defense Donald Rumsfeld and Vice President Dick Cheney, pushed for an aggressive approach on foreign policy, to go it alone. The United States refused to sign the Kyoto Protocol to limit global environmental damage. The U.S. stopped talks with North Korea to limit their missile and nuclear bomb programs. Later, in 2012 and 2013, North Korea tested nuclear bombs. In 2015 they tested their first missile launching submarine.

September 11, 2001, had come as a shock, killing almost 3,000 people in three separate attacks. In addition to the World Trade Center, the Pentagon was attacked. In Pennsylvania rebelling passengers crashed a hijacked plane to thwart a second attack on Washington, D.C. Why the terrorist attacks? What was their rationale?

Their real objective, according to Bin Laden's al Qaeda, was the governments of Saudi Arabia, Egypt, Pakistan, and Jordan, all called the "near enemy," because they were backed by the "far enemy," the United States. By exposing America's vulnerability, they hoped to destroy the aura of American military power and protection. They also hoped to goad the United States into attacking a Muslim country, which would unify Muslims in a holy war against America. The attacks were a colossal failure for the U.S. intelligence community. Various government agencies failed to share bits of information that, if coordinated, would have been significant. For example, an intercepted communication during the summer stated that something "spectacular" was going to happen. In addition, terrorists attempted to enroll at several private pilot training facilities, requesting minimal training, saying that they did not need to learn how to land an airplane, just how to fly one. Several names of the terrorists who entered the United States were already in government data bases as potential terrorists.

Sunny Singh, from India, was one of twenty-one writers who responded to an American editor's request to answer this question, "How do you see us?" He pointed out that in an odd way the United States may have encouraged terrorists through our Hollywood approach to making films.

> "After all, it was America's film industry that taught us that individual desire, motivation, and judgment – culminating in violence – was an appropriate, even ideal, response to the corrupt, decadent, tyrannical authority. Whether through Clint Eastwood in *The Pale Rider* or Robert De Niro in *Godfather II* or Sylvester Stallone with the supportive *jihadis* in *Rambo III*, Hollywood taught us that the only way to react was to take up weapons against injustice."
>
> "And make no mistake; the Hollywood hero has long been a delinquent. Living by his own rules, which often pit him against the state and society, the American hero, in much of the world is still the lone cowboy – Henry Fonda on a horse, Sylvester Stallone in a jeep, or Will Smith in a spacecraft – who rides in to challenge and overthrow an oppressive, tyrannical authority."

How They See Us: Meditations on America, edited by James Atlas, Atlas & Co., New York, 2010.

Afghanistan

Our first response to the 9/11 attacks was to go into Afghanistan to hunt down al Qaeda and Bin Laden. Our efforts there, without sufficient ground troops, destabilized the country and led to the rise of the Taliban and warlords. It later came back to haunt us.

Iraq

Next the Bush administration shifted its attention to Iraq, mostly at Cheney's and Rumsfeld's urging. The administration claimed that Iraq had WMDs, Weapons of

Mass Destruction. Clearly, Cheney and Rumsfeld were also angry that the First Gulf War in 1991 had not deposed Saddam Hussein. In October, 2001, Congress passed a resolution to use U.S. military forces against Iraq, 77-23 in the Senate and 296-133 in the House. It was Vietnam all over again. The administration's haughty demeanor squandered much of the international goodwill from the 9/11 attacks. The French criticized our move. The House of Representatives, with a Republican majority, voted to rename the House cafeteria's French Fries as "Freedom Fries." Cute! Accomplished what? Despite much arm-twisting, neither our allies nor the UN went along with our planned invasion.

Operation Iraq Freedom proved to be a textbook operation, militarily. In three weeks U.S. forces were in Baghdad. However, because the U.S. did not have enough troops to act as a police force, an orgy of lawlessness broke out. Looting and killing increased as ethnic hatreds surfaced involving Kurds, Shiites, Sunnis, and other ethnic groups. There had been virtually no planning for the conclusion of hostilities. The Bush administration assumed American soldiers would be welcomed as liberators, just as they were when Americans liberated Western Europe in 1945, and that democracy and market-driven capitalism would quickly take root. It did not happen. The U.S. disbanded the Iraqi police and the Iraqi army, without taking their guns, all 350,000 of them! By 2003 the situation in Iraq was that of a classic guerrilla war.

Who won the war, Operation Iraq Freedom? Iran, a nation of mostly Shiites, no longer faced a rival local power of Sunnis on their border. Al Qaeda revived. The Iraqis quickly lost faith in the United States as an authority controlling the country. The only building our armed forces securely protected was the oil ministry, feeding critics who accused us of basing our foreign policy on oil.

After Iraq, the U.S. turned its attention to Afghanistan in a war that bogged down for years. We finally got Bin Laden, achieving one goal. However, overall our involvement in Afghanistan seemed to destabilize that country even more. Engaging in "nation-building" and playing the role of global policeman are not satisfying responsibilities. The future awaits.

What is clear is revealed in another quote from *How They See Us*, by Italian Gianni Riotta, quoting his father. "There is not a single problem in the world that can be solved without America, but America alone cannot solve any problem."

A Final Observation

Increasingly we see in the news that some group or organization calls for easing the "pain" of history by obliterating part of the past. Buildings must be renamed, monuments torn down, or individuals erased from the textbooks. Times change. Values change. When and why was a building named? Why was that particular monument erected? History, which has some warts and ugliness, continues to serve as a record of the heights and the depths to which humans can aspire and fall. But, let us HONOR that which WE find worthy. Two professional historical organizations – the American Historical Association and the Organization of American Historians – issued or endorsed statements like the following.

> "To remove a monument or to change the name of a school or street, is not to erase history, but rather to alter or call attention to a previous interpretation of history. To remove such monuments is neither to "change" history nor "erase" it. What changes with such removals is what American communities decide is worthy of civic honor."

While some individuals believe history does not change, what we think about it and how we think about it does change. Future generations will become upset at something being done today. Good! That means they will have achieved "progress," as defined by them. However, hold off on absolute judgments or condemnations. The best admonition I have encountered against judging the past too harshly comes, curiously, not from a historian, but from a physician, Dr. L. Lewis Wall. In a comment cautioning against attacking nineteenth century medical practices, Dr. L. Lewis Wall wrote the following:

> "It is difficult to make fair assessments of the . . . ethics of past practitioners . . . in a [modern] society that has moved in a different direction, developed different values, and has wrestled – often unsuccessfully – with ethical issues of sex, race, gender, and class that were not perceived as problematic by those who lived during an earlier period of history."

Times change. Values change. We can learn from and judge those we encounter in history. And, we should. That is the primary function of history. We cannot change it; nor can we erase it. But, we can, and must, *try* to arrive at a more *accurate* picture. That awareness and knowledge will help us see ourselves as we are, while trying to decide where we would like to go as a community. What did happen in the past and why? For example, what motivated those monument designers and committees? What values were they stressing? The "why" is the sticky part of history. It is also the cornerstone of endless discussions – have fun!

INDEX

96533836R10422

Made in the USA
Columbia, SC
02 June 2018